501

MUST-DRIVE CARS

501
MUST-DRIVE CARS

Fid Backhouse, Kieran Fogarty and Sal Oliver

ß Bounty
Books

Publisher: Polly Manguel

Project Editor: Emma Beare

Designer: Ron Callow/Design 23

Picture Library Manager: Jennifer Veall

Production Manager: Neil Randles

First published in Great Britain in 2009 by
Bounty Books, a division of Octopus Publishing Group Limited
2-4 Heron Quays, London E14 4JP
www.octopusbooks.co.uk

An Hachette UK Company
www.hachette.co.uk

A CIP catalogue record is available from the British Library

ISBN: 978-0-753718-73-5

Printed and bound in China

Contents

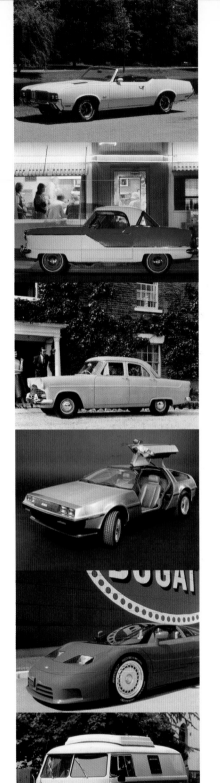

Introduction

Within these pages, you'll find cars from all over the world, of all sorts, shapes and sizes – from tiny microcars to gigantic behemoths, from stately sedans to death-defying racers, 1920s classics to post-modern concept prototypes, almost unobtainable rarities like the exotic Bugatti Royale to models manufactured in their millions like the Fiat 124, gallant failures like the Cord 810 to runaway successes like the Triumph TR6.

It is extraordinary to think that scarcely more than one hundred years ago Queen Victoria's long reign was drawing to a close, at the end of an era that saw the dramatic unfolding of a world-changing Industrial Revolution in Western Europe and the beginnings of serious industrialization in the USA, a superpower in waiting. History doesn't record what the elderly Queen thought of those new-fangled horseless carriages that started appearing on Britain's streets – but in 1896 the law that required road-going 'locomotives' to be led by a pedestrian carrying a red flag was repealed, allowing 'light locomotives' to proceed at a dizzying 14 mph (22 km/h). 'The Century of the Automobile' had dawned.

In due course, the building of cars would become the world's single most important manufacturing sector, both in its own right and – more significantly – by generating massive spin-off economic growth. Nowhere was this truer than in the USA. That vast young country acquired its first coast-to-coast motor route, the Lincoln Highway, in 1913 and the way in which economic activity and prosperity spread along its entire length like wildfire was a blueprint for things to come, as the automobile rapidly opened up a continent. Meanwhile, oil production to fuel those burgeoning internal combustion engines became a boom industry.

In those early years car manufacture attracted a host of clever engineers, eager entrepreneurs and downright chancers who started operating in almost every country of the developed world. The decade before World War I saw rapid technological advance, and by the dawn of the Roaring Twenties foundations for the modern automobile had been well and truly laid. This book tells the fascinating story of the motorcar's extraordinary evolution since then, by highlighting some of the most iconic

vehicles ever produced. These are the ones that we'd all love to drive if we were lucky enough to get the chance, for they encompass the most important, interesting, exciting or desirable cars ever built – often with all four qualities represented in one car.

The reason that the car is deeply entrenched in the affections of so many – and remains an unflagging object of desire – is that it represents the ultimate expression of personal freedom. Once that basic motivation is established, the car is capable of stirring all sorts of other emotions. Cars can be beautiful works of automotive art or thrilling driving machines, status symbols or vital workhorses . . . even a serious investment proposition. It is no accident that many of the cars featured in these pages come with price tags bearing lots of zeros, as competition to own these very special classics from the annals of motoring history drives prices to dizzy heights.

Of course the automobile's very success has created problems. With the people of emerging nations keen to share motoring freedoms long enjoyed in the industrialized world – China is now challenging the USA as the largest single automobile market – the problem of vehicle emissions contributing to the rapid advance of global warming can only become more severe. At the same time, the very things that make the car so desirable in the first place – fast, convenient and flexible personal transport coupled with the freedom of the open road – are slowly being smothered by the sheer volume of traffic.

Realistically, there's no way that drivers will be persuaded to give up cars en masse, nor any possibility that people around the world will abandon their dreams of joining the empowered motoring fraternity. It may seem like a recipe for ultimate disaster, but this book's closing chapter contains tantalizing hints that car-makers are close to perfecting the alternative technologies that may well make this 'The Century of the Green Machine'.

For now though, whether your fantasy is to roar off behind the wheel of a Lamborghini, be swept off in a chauffeur driven Mercedes-Benz, take to the highway in a Ford Pickup, go for a Sunday drive down country lanes in a Morris Minor or even just spend your days tinkering with your old MG, *501 Must-Drive Cars* is a book to linger over and to dream on.

1920s & 1930s

Alfa Romeo RL

ALFA was founded in 1910 and began operations by producing the open-topped 24 HP, designed by Giuseppe Merosi. This was made in various configurations and raced in the 1911 Targa Florio, Sicily's famous long-distance endurance test – a shrewd move that brought recognition and commercial success. But World War 1 ended car production as ALFA turned to the manufacture of military equipment.

In 1920, renamed Alfa Romeo, the company started building cars again, initially assembling parts left lying around the factory since 1915. But a new model was introduced in 1922, also designed by Merosi, that would establish Alfa's reputation for producing great sports cars. The RL series was an unqualified success, with over 2,600 vehicles produced in five years. Three versions were made – Normale, Turismo and Sport – underlining the common practice of putting different body shapes on the same chassis. It was also usual for outside coachbuilders to receive a rolling chassis and add their own distinctive bodywork.

This creative approach suited the Italian temperament perfectly, and one outfit that took full advantage was the design company founded by Ugo Zagato in 1923 that still operates in Milan. From the beginning Zagato was known for producing rakish, high-performance cars that were streamlined and aerodynamically efficient – a reputation first established by the stunning Alfa Romeo RL Supersport Zagato of 1926.

This attractive two-door drophead coupe extended the RL range significantly and was both expensive and exclusive (only 88 made). But Zagato didn't have the RL custom market all to themselves – coachbuilders Castagna had already produced the brushed-aluminium RL Supersport Castagna in 1925. It wasn't as fast as the Zagato, but was also a spectacular addition to Alfa's highly regarded RL series. Catch an RL if you win a lottery jackpot, then enjoy the drive of a lifetime.

This drophead coupe version featured in Alfa's RL series.

COUNTRY OF ORIGIN:
Italy
FIRST MANUFACTURED:
1922 (until 1927)
ENGINE:
2,944 cc Straight Six
PERFORMANCE:
The sporty Zagato achieved a top speed of 93 mph (150 km/h).
YOU SHOULD KNOW:
One of the drivers who formed the successful 1923 Alfa racing team – which used a modified version of the RL series, the RL TF (Targa Florio) – was a talented young fellow named Enzo Ferrari.

Alfa Romeo 8C 2300

The 8C (for eight-cylinder) engine was designed by Vittorio Jano and introduced by Alfa Romeo in 1931. In various forms this brilliant power plant with its finned aluminium casing was destined to propel the company's sought-after cars throughout the 1930s and become synonymous with triumph on the racetrack and prestige on the street.

The 8C's first incarnation was in the 8C 2300, which came in long (*lungo*) or short (*corto*) versions, plus a shorter-still Spider Corsa racing chassis. Road cars were mostly created by outside coachbuilders who added bodywork to a rolling chassis. However, Alfa did build their own bodies – occasionally even converting redundant race cars for road use.

This meant that – like many vehicles produced in the 1930s – the 8C 2300 Series road cars ended up with a plethora of body styles. Indeed, there were no two the same in the production run of 188 cars, with an assortment created by talented design-and-build companies such as Zagato, Farina, Figoni, Brianza, Carlton, Castagna and Touring. But they all had one thing in common – graceful lines that make these exclusive vehicles as sought after today as they were in the 1930s. The *lungo* chassis was used for elegant four-seater bodies and the *corto* chassis for more sporty open-top or coupe coachwork.

In fact, racing remained the name of the game and the three versions of the 8C 2300 are generally known by their competition designations – Le Mans for long-chassis versions (as the 24-hour race specified a four-seater), Mille Miglia for the short-chassis cars and Monza for the racing version. The reason behind the enduring success of the Alfa Romeo 8C 2300 was both simple and complex – it simply had the best build quality and was the most technically advanced, competitive car of its era.

COUNTRY OF ORIGIN:
Italy
FIRST MANUFACTURED:
1931 (until 1935)
ENGINE:
2,336 cc Straight Eight
PERFORMANCE:
The boat-tailed Monza racing version was capable of 140 mph (225 km/h)
YOU SHOULD KNOW:
If you can't find one to drive, at least try to listen to one – the throaty roar of Jano's 8C engine is unmistakable, having been described by one over-enthusiastic fan as 'a symphony in which each gear tooth and roll bearing plays a note'.

The same chassis was used for many body styles, including this mouthwatering roadster.

Alfa Romeo 8C 2900B

COUNTRY OF ORIGIN:
Italy
FIRST MANUFACTURED:
1935 (until 1939)
ENGINE:
2,905 cc DOHC Straight Eight
PERFORMANCE:
Top speed of around 120 mph
(175 km/h), depending on bodywork.
YOU SHOULD KNOW:
Finding an 8C 2900B Spider for that
thrilling 'must drive' moment won't
be easy – only 30 were ever made
(20 short wheelbase, 10 long
wheelbase) and anyone lucky (and
rich) enough to own one guards it
like the Crown Jewels.

*The beautiful 8C 2900B
convertible was a potent racer
turned road car.*

In the 1930s, Europe's dictators saw motor-racing success as
excellent publicity for their countries, and German-Italian rivalry
saw the production of some very seductive racing cars. Italy's
contributions were impressive. The Alfa Romeo P3 – the world's
first single-seater Grand Prix car – was one of the 8C Series. Its
successor was the 8C 2900A, powered by a bored-out version of
Vittorio Jano's 8C engine. This advanced flying machine was soon
winning races, and Alfa Romeo decided to cash in on its supercar
status by producing a road-going version.

Thus was the 8C 2900B conceived and born, a sibling of the
Grand Prix car with a road body and slightly detuned engine. There
were two versions – long and short chassis – and such was the cost
of these magnificent machines that only a few were ever made,
making them incredibly rare, with some two-thirds of the run being
open-topped Spiders and the rest being sports coupes. Although
one or two 8C 2900Bs had factory bodywork, most were supplied to
external coachbuilders in rolling chassis form for finishing.

The results were stunning – as all those enthusiasts who regard
the 8C 2900B as one of the very best pre-war passenger sports cars
will testify. They are true masterpieces of elegance with a beauty
and charm that make them
irresistible, always
gathering an admiring
crowd when they appear at
classic car shows. Most of
the bodies were made by
the Touring company, who
used an innovatory
lightweight metal
framework developed by
Zagato. Their long-
wheelbase convertibles are
the *crème de la crème*
visually, but every single
8C 2900B is a masterpiece,
including one or two
special racing versions. The
varying body styles are
invariably slender and
elegant, introducing the
ala spessa concept that
incorporated previously
separate elements like
mudguards and lights into
streamlined bodywork.

Alvis Speed 25

One car every dashing man about town coveted in the 1930s was the gorgeous Alvis Speed 25 – a sleek machine that would never fail to look super-stylish arriving outside a stately home ahead of that discreetly decadent country-house weekend. Opinions haven't changed. Many classic car aficionados consider the beautifully proportioned Speed 25 to be one of the finest vehicles produced in the 1930s – not only for its stunning appearance, but also for advanced technical features that characterized all Alvis cars and make them a pleasure to drive today.

The marque produced its first vehicles in 1920 and continued in business until the 1960s. Although Alvis built various saloons, the company's real forte was the sports tourer. The powerful Speed 25's immediate predecessor, the racy Speed 20 series, was introduced by Alvis after a brief foray into front-wheel drive with the pretty, innovative but not-very-successful 4/15s and 8/15s of the late 1920s.

Capitalizing on their sporty reputation, Alvis produced the popular Silver Eagle in 1928 with the option of a two-seater, coupe, drophead coupe or saloon body. The Speed 20 Series followed in 1932, ushering in the spectacular flowering that Alvis enjoyed in the 1930s. This came to a climax with the introduction of the Speed 25 in 1936, and who can say how far the company would have developed this superb model if World War II had not intervened.

Three types of Speed 25 were manufactured – a two-door sports tourer, a two-door drophead coupe and a two-door sports saloon. Today, these sought-after classics command top prices, and their quality build has ensured that over half the production run has survived. Anyone lucky enough to slip behind the wheel of a Speed 25 (over 200 are out there somewhere) will be effortlessly transported back to the Golden Era of Alvis.

This splendidly stylish Alvis sports Saloon is an enduring 1930s design classic.

COUNTRY OF ORIGIN:
UK
FIRST MANUFACTURED:
1936 (until 1940)
ENGINE:
3,571 cc OHV Straight Six
PERFORMANCE:
Top speed of around 90 mph
(145 km/h)
YOU SHOULD KNOW:
The end of the line for the Speed 25 came in late 1940, production ceasing abruptly when the Luftwaffe bombed the Alvis factory in Coventry – and when the company resumed car manufacture in 1946 it was with the solid but much-less-glamorous TA-14.

The Speedster – tremendous straight line speed but not quite so good around corners.

Auburn Speedster 851

Several thousand Auburn 851s in various body styles were sold by entrepreneur Errett Lobban Cord at the height of The Great Depression – no mean feat. The star was the Speedster 851 – developed from earlier Speedsters that had been produced since 1929 with enough fresh features to justify a new-model tag in fixed-head and convertible coupe form. Improvements designed by ex-Duesenberg maestro Gordon Buehrig included a raked radiator, sinuous front bumpers, teardrop headlamps and flowing lines ending in a characteristic boat tail.

After decades of unremarkable life in the automobile business, making an assortment of worthy cars without really capturing the public's imagination, Auburn finally earned a place in the motoring hall of fame with one of the few sports cars produced in America before World War II – a powerful, stylish machine that helped to establish the American trend towards size coupled with tremendous straight-line performance, with the added bonus of a reasonable price tag. This was because the Speedster 851 was offered as a loss-leader in the hope that admirers lured into the showroom by its delicious looks would actually buy a cheaper but more profitable model – a ploy that worked so well that only a few hundred Speedsters were manufactured.

Following a New Year's Day launch in 1935, the Speedster 851 was duly promoted on the grounds of . . . speed. A top-of-the-range supercharged SC model with its four external exhaust pipes and no additional modifications did an amazing 12-hour endurance run during which it averaged over 100 mph (160 km/h) in the hands of land-speed record holder Ab Jenkins, who went on to set many other records. Although there was little or no change, 1936 cars were given an 852 designation. When sales collapsed, production ended and the Auburn company folded in 1937.

COUNTRY OF ORIGIN:
USA.
FIRST MANUFACTURED:
1935
ENGINE:
4.6 l (280 cid) Flathead Straight Eight
PERFORMANCE:
Top speed of 103 mph (166 km/h);
0-60 mph (97km/h) in 15 secs
YOU SHOULD KNOW:
The Auburn company's art deco former headquarters building in Auburn, Indiana, is now a National Historic Landmark that houses the Auburn Cord Duesenberg Automobile Museum.

Austin 7

If there's one quintessential British pre-war car it must surely be the Austin 7, one of the most popular small cars ever produced. After a slow start in 1922 with barely two thousand 'Sevens' sold, progress was spectacular. Before the outbreak of World War II abruptly ended production in 1939, over 290,000 had rolled off the line in Britain. Overseas manufacture was licensed in France, Germany and the USA, whilst Japan's reputation for copying others' technology was partially established when Nissan used the Austin 7 as the template for its first cars.

This iconic 'people's car' owed its inception to Sir Herbert Austin, who bulldozed his board of directors into sanctioning a 'big saloon in miniature' and personally designed it in conjunction with Stanley Edge, who was responsible for the engine. The first production model was the AB Tourer. With a wheelbase of just 6 ft 3 in (1.9 m) and weighing in at a mere 794 lb (360 kg) it used a small, economical engine mounted on an A-frame chassis. This may be one of the easiest 'must-drive' cars to find, but double-declutching should be mastered before taking to the road.

There were six types produced over time – tourers, saloons, cabriolets, sports, coupes and vans – most with many variants as technical advances were regularly introduced. In addition, the distinctive two-tone Austin 7 Swallow was coachbuilt by William Lyons of the Swallow Sidecar Company. A Swallow open tourer was introduced in 1927 with a saloon following in 1928. Some 3500 Swallows were produced in various body styles before Lyons started making his own SS (later Jaguar) cars in 1932. He backed a good pony. By the end of the 1920s the runaway success of the Austin 7 had effectively wiped out most other small British cars and cyclecars.

The dinky little 'people's car' came in many shapes and sizes.

COUNTRY OF ORIGIN:
UK
FIRST MANUFACTURED:
1922 (until 1939)
ENGINE:
747 cc Straight Four
PERFORMANCE:
Most models had a top speed of 50 mph (80 km/h)
YOU SHOULD KNOW:
The Austin 7 name had such resonance that the company recycled it twice after World War II – firstly on A30 models of the early 1950s and then on the mould-breaking Mini in 1959.

Bentley 8L

COUNTRY OF ORIGIN:
UK
FIRST MANUFACTURED:
1930 (until 1931)
ENGINE:
7,983 cc Straight Six
PERFORMANCE:
Over 100 mph (161 km/h) with the
heaviest limousine coachwork.
YOU SHOULD KNOW:
With their exemplary build quality,
many of the Bentley 8Ls that were
manufactured are still around, but
such is their cachet that well-
restored examples sell at auction for
up to $1.5 million . . . and beyond.

It was the last of the line – and the most impressive. The 8 litre Bentley made its debut at the Olympia Motor Show in 1930 and caused a sensation. It was the largest car hitherto made in Britain and a serious competitor for the Rolls-Royce Phantom II. This was W O Bentley's shot at producing a headline-stealer that would catapult him to the top of the luxury car league, thus stealing Rolls-Royce's mantle and rescuing Bentley from financial difficulty.

The ploy was a gallant failure. Only one hundred 8Ls were produced and by mid-1931 Bentley Motors was bankrupt. W O Bentley thought the receiver's sale would see Napiers of Acton emerge with the assets and was already planning a Napier-Bentley with his new partner. But Rolls-Royce, slyly acting through an intermediary, outbid Napier and promptly killed off the 8L.

It was a clever move. The 8L was a formidable challenger for anything Rolls-Royce made. A state-of-the-art engine offered innovatory features like twin-spark ignition and four valves per cylinder, plus a sturdy chassis with servo-assisted brakes all round, making this an exclusive but expensive vehicle. Bentley Motors supplied a rolling chassis (in short or long wheelbase) and the customer was required to employ a coachbuilder to add bodywork.

Famous names like H J Mulliner, Gurney Nutting and Barker duly obliged, creating a variety of body styles. Most were built on the long chassis, with relatively few buyers choosing the short version. Although the idea was to compete with the luxury saloons of the era, around 20 8Ls were finished with stunning open-topped bodies and even the limousines tended to have racy lines. Whatever bodywork was chosen, the package offered incomparable smoothness and quietness of ride and these magnificent machines are a pleasure to drive, now as then.

The Bentley was sold in chassis form with the purchaser's choice of body added by an independent coachbuilder.

BMW 328

First buy the BMW company, then you may get to drive a 328 Mille Miglia – if you ask very nicely. This stupendous vehicle now lives in the company museum and was the culmination of the Bavarian Motor Works' effort to produce the finest sports car of the 1930s. Many believe they succeeded, with the 328 series achieving glory on the track and prestige on the road in that feverish world where successful sports and racing cars were often one and the same.

The technically advanced BMW 328 appeared in 1936, winning at the testing Nürburgring and proving virtually unbeatable in 2 litre class racing. With its elegantly cowled back wheels, long hood and distinctive dashboard the 328 was also a 'must drive' hit with lovers of fast, stylish cars. The compact two-seater roadster had a bonnet secured with leather straps that concealed the potent lightweight engine, and these examples were mostly assembled at the factory. However, there were cabriolet versions by outside coachbuilders, noted for their luxurious finish and elegant style.

Only six of the ultimate Mille Miglia model were ever assembled, three in Germany and three in Italy. This fabulous aluminium-bodied car was specifically designed to compete in the near-thousand-mile road race and won the 2 litre class in 1938, before Baron von Kanstein won the 1940 event outright in his gleaming silver 328 – though not before one navigator refused to race after experiencing the Count's manic driving. Just before the race ended, his replacement was surprised when the grateful von Kanstein changed places to allow his navigator the glory of driving over the winning line. Few can ever share those magical moments behind the wheel of a BMW 328 Mille Miglia, but there's always an outside chance of piloting a regular 328 – around 425 of these fabulous machines were made and over 200 survive.

BMW's 328 proved to be a real winner in every sense of the word, combining track and road success in one package.

COUNTRY OF ORIGIN:
Germany
FIRST YEAR OF MANUFACTURE:
1936 (until 1940)
ENGINE:
1,971 cc OHV Straight Six
PERFORMANCE:
The race-winning 328 Mille Miglia of 1940 achieved a top speed of 139 mph (224 km/h).
YOU SHOULD KNOW:
There is a British element to this German success story – BMW sold the 328 in rolling chassis form to the British Frazer Nash company who added bodywork and sold it as the Frazer Nash-BMW 328.

The Bugatti Type 35 was the archetypal 1920s racing car.

Bugatti Type 35

Conceived by a brilliant Italian and built in France, this is the ultimate vintage racing car. The two-seater Bugatti Type 35 was certainly the most successful racer of all time, various models winning over two thousand races and establishing the marque's mythical status. This blue bombshell with its superb handling and reliable engine was the first Bugatti to feature that iconic arched radiator and remains an all-time favourite with classic car aficionados. With nearly 350 Type 35s made, plenty survive to thrill weekend drivers.

The original Type 35 of 1924 had a new engine with five main bearings and a unique ball-bearing system that allowed this potent power plant to rev at an impressive 6000 rpm and produce 90 hp. This state-of-the-art machine was expensive and complicated, so the Type 35A of 1925 addressed the problem. The public swiftly nicknamed this simplified model 'The Tecla' after a maker of cheap jewellery, but it was nonetheless hugely successful.

Although Ettore Bugatti claimed to dislike forced induction, he allowed Type 36C cars to be fitted with a supercharger that boosted power output by a third and brought two French Grand Prix victories (1928 and 1930). Type 35T with a bored-out engine was created for Sicily's famous endurance race and swiftly christened the Bugatti Targa Florio – justifying the nickname with straight victories between 1925 and 1929. Its successor – the final Type 35 – was the 35B (originally 35TC) of 1927. It was the same as the 35T with the addition of a large supercharger. A 35B won the French Grand Prix of 1929. The Bugatti Type 37 was an extension of the 35 series. This sports car reused the chassis and body of the 35 but had a smaller 1,496 cc engine – supercharged in the Type 37A. Type 39 was visually identical to the Type 35, but with a smaller engine.

COUNTRY OF ORIGIN:
France
FIRST MANUFACTURED:
1924 (until 1931)
ENGINE:
1,991 cc or 2,262 cc Straight Eight
PERFORMANCE:
Varied according to model, with around 90 mph (145 km/h) being the norm.
YOU SHOULD KNOW:
When a customer had the temerity to complain that the brakes on his Type 35 left something to be desired it is said that Ettore Bugatti disdainfully replied 'I make my cars to go, not to stop'.

Bugatti Type 44

Can the word 'common' be applied to any Bugatti? It seems insulting to tar this prestigious marque with such a mundane description, but if a Bugatti can ever be thus described it must be the Type 44, because more of these popular vehicles were produced than any other type. So if there's one Bugatti the enthusiast can realistically aspire to drive, this is it . . . and the experience should be a real pleasure.

The wire-wheeled Type 44 was Bugatti's first true touring car. A new engine was created from two cast-iron four-cylinder blocks with a single overhead camshaft delivering its power through a four-speed manual gearbox to drive the rear wheels. Teamed with the proven chassis developed for the earlier Type 38, this offered the smoothest of rides with all the creature comforts. As a result, the Type 44 proved to be immensely popular and sold very well.

This highly-rated classic benefits from the fact that today's survivors come with a considerable assortment of attractive body styles fitted by top coachbuilders that included Kellner, James Young, Weymann, Gerber, Gangloff and Graber. Among the bodies they created were roadsters, coupes, two-door tourers and four-door saloons.

Common it may have been by Bugatti standards, but that is a relative term – just under 1,100 Type 44s were built out of the grand total of 7,900 cars that actually emerged from the factory at Molsheim between the company's foundation in 1909 and the effective end of car production with the death of Ettore Bugatti's son Jean whilst testing a Type 57 racing car in 1939, and the subsequent advent of World War II. Attempts were made to establish new model lines after 1945, but these proved unsuccessful and the company was finally sold to Hispano-Suiza in 1963.

COUNTRY OF ORIGIN:
France
FIRST MANUFACTURED:
1927 (until 1930)
ENGINE:
2,992 cc Straight Eight
PERFORMANCE:
Top speed around 85 mph (137 km/h) according to body type
YOU SHOULD KNOW:
The most unusual Type 44 was the wooden-bodied fire tender constructed on a Type 44 chassis used at Bugatti's Molsheim factory in the late 1920s and 1930s – whether or not it was ever put to the test is not recorded.

The Type 44 was the first Bugatti created exclusively for road rather than track use.

Bugatti Royale

COUNTRY OF ORIGIN:
France
FIRST MANUFACTURED:
1927 (until 1933)
ENGINE:
12,763 cc Straight Eight
PERFORMANCE:
Capable of 100 mph (161 km/h)
YOU SHOULD KNOW:
Economic disaster eventually turned to a modest triumph when Ettore Bugatti cannily recycled unused 'Royale' engines to power a new line of railcars.

The simple 'Bugatti Type 41' designation hardly hints at the grandeur it represents, for this is one of the most impressive automobiles ever created. No wonder the Type 41 was swiftly nicknamed 'The Royale', for it was intended as luxurious transport for monarchs and heads of state.

Measuring in at an impressive 6.4 m (21 ft) in length, each Royale was treated to a different body created by a leading coachbuilder. Sadly for the visionary Ettore Bugatti, his grand design was conceived in the extravagant 1920s, with the prototype completed in 1927. But it was launched as the world tumbled into recession and only half a dozen Royales were built, of which three were sold. One went to France, another to Germany and the third to England.

Ettore's plan to build 25 of these magnificent machines sank beneath the weight of economic adversity, and after failing to sell half the limited production run the dream was over. All six Royales still exist, though not all in original form – two have been rebodied more than once. In chassis number order there's the Coupe Napoleon (Ettore's own car that has had five different bodies), the Binder Coupe de Ville (two bodies), the Weinberger (original roadster body), the Park Ward (original limousine body), the racy Kelner coupe (original grand tourer body) and finally (though possibly the first made) the Double Berline de Voyage (original body).

Whilst driving one of these beauties is not a realistic ambition, seeing one most certainly is – the Coupe Napoleon is in France's Mulhouse National Automobile Museum, together with an authentic replica of No 2 with original roadster body. The Weinberger cabriolet now resides in The Henry Ford, that impressive museum in Dearborn, Michigan created by someone who operated at the diametrically opposite end of the automotive spectrum.

Ettore Bugatti's idea of the ultimate luxury car proved to be too expensive even for the wealthiest of customers.

Bugatti Type 55

These fabulous machines are rare as hen's teeth, so would-be pilots can only dream of taking to the road in one – but what a dream. Only 38 supercharged Bugatti Type 55s were ever made, over half of those in the launch year, 1932. These were true supercars intended for the very rich and the apparently limited production run stands up well beside Ettore Bugatti's contemporaneous attempt to produce the ultimate in motoring luxury – the glorious but ill-fated Type 41 Royale.

The Type 55 came into being after the famous Bugatti Type 35 racing car reached the end of its shelf life after sweeping all before it in the 1920s – track success that duly led to a road-going version, the Type 43 Grand Sport. But it became obvious to Ettore and his son Jean that the Type 35 had to be replaced, and the pleasing result was the Type 51, shown at the Paris Motor Show in 1930 and destined to continue Bugatti's winning ways on Europe's motor-racing circuits.

Although the four-seater Type 43 Grand Sport was well liked and still selling well, Jean persuaded his father to launch the Type 55 Super Sport – a spectacular derivative of the Type 51 racer. The new two-seater Super Sport had an engine carried over from the racing car, but fitted to a broader ladder chassis more suitable for stable roadwork – a combination that offered the sort of impressive top speed and first-class roadholding expected by those willing to pay a handsome premium price.

The factory offered a standard coupe body, but this was quickly eclipsed by a simply stunning two-seater roadster body designed by Jean Bugatti when he was just 22 years old, which unsurprisingly proved to be the popular choice of the well-heeled purchasers of this all-time great.

COUNTRY OF ORIGIN:
France
FIRST MANUFACTURED:
1932 (until 1935)
ENGINE:
2,262 cc DOHC Straight Eight
PERFORMANCE:
Top speed was 112 mph (180 km/h)
YOU SHOULD KNOW:
Jean Bugatti's sublime roadster body is recognised as one of the most elegant ever to grace an automobile – ensuring that the few surviving examples have taken their place right at the top of the classic car pricelist.

Jean Bugatti designed this raffish two-seater and persuaded his father that it should be put into production.

Bugatti Type 57

This superb series was the first (and last) fruit of Bugatti's decision to design a single chassis suitable for every body type, where previously there had been separate options for different styles of coachwork. As a result, the Type 57 was fitted with a variety of bodies, though the factory only offered four options, all with flowing lines, designed by Ettore Bugatti's son Jean. Three were named after Alpine peaks – the two-door, four-seater Ventoux, the four-door Galabier and the two-door Stelvio convertible, actually built by external supplier Gangloff. The fourth, an expensive two-seater, was dubbed the Atalante.

The 57 came in many body styles – but this Atlantic was the most exclusive of all.

Coachbuilders other than Bugatti and Gangloff were responsible for creating some of the finest prewar shapes ever designed and fitting them to Type 57s, making it one of the most handsome and interesting series produced by the Molsheim factory. Star cars include those by English builders Corsica and Vanden Plas, Vanvooren (a one-off for the future Shah of Persia) and Voll & Ruhrbeck. They mainly produced long, low coupes, dropheads and cabriolets.

Performance was boosted with the addition of a supercharger in 1936 to create the Type 57C, whilst a shorter and lower version was introduced as the Type 57S. When these were put together as the rare type SC the result was a great looker with awesome performance for its day. There were various short-run derivations like the exclusive Atlantic SC coupe developed from the 1935 Aérolithe concept car. This extraordinary machine had an aluminium body made in two halves and joined along the centerline, but only three were ever made.

What are the chances of getting a drive? Well, around 700 Type 57s (all versions) were made and plenty of these splendidly evocative machines have survived. But that doesn't mean persuading a besotted owner to hand over the keys will be easy!

COUNTRY OF ORIGIN:
France
FIRST MANUFACTURED:
1934 (until 1940)
ENGINE:
3,257 cc DOHC Straight Eight
PERFORMANCE:
Up to 125 mph (200 km/h)
YOU SHOULD KNOW:
The Type 57 was Jean Bugatti's triumph . . . not only was he the designer but he also took charge of production, as father Ettore was at the Paris office supervising the money-making contract to produce railcars for the French government.

Buick Roadmaster

This is a respected name in US automotive history, for when Buick revamped its model range in 1936 as America started to emerge from the Great Depression, 'Roadmaster' was the title chosen for newcomers designed to replace the company's former Series 80 model. The name lasted until 1958 and badged a number of evolution models that were quintessentially American, before being revived briefly in the 1990s.

From 1936 to 1948 General Motors' Roadmaster range consisted of a sedan, coupe, convertible phaeton and station wagon. These imposing long-wheelbase vehicles shared a basic structure with top-of-the-range Oldsmobile stablemates and remain a pleasure to drive today, giving a wonderful sense of stately progress on soft suspension. Innovative features included GM's all-steel 'turret top' body, bullet-shaped headlights and a raked windscreen. The Roadmaster also incorporated technical advances like independent front suspension and hydraulic brakes.

The very name conjured up an image of supremacy – exactly as GM intended – and these highway cruisers were an instant success, with a competitive price tag ensuring that 17,000 Roadmasters were snapped up in the first year of production. The sportiest option was the four-door soft-top phaeton, though the car-buying public much preferred the sturdy sedan.

As sales slowly declined, cosmetic modifications took place, including a slight reduction in size and fitting (in 1941) of the powerful Fireball Eight engine with twin carburettors. Changes were small, but visually enhanced these handsome vehicles. New styling was finally introduced for 1942, but production was suspended as a result of wartime stringency and the new models would serve as the basis of the first Buicks produced after World War II. From 1946 until they were superseded after 1958, the Roadmaster became Buick's top-of-the-range offering and variants included the last wood-bodied station wagon to be produced in the USA, the 1953 Model 79-R.

COUNTRY OF ORIGIN:
USA
FIRST MANUFACTURED:
1936 (until 1958)
ENGINE:
5.2 l (320 cid) OHV Straight Eight
PERFORMANCE:
Top speed of 90 mph (145 km/h)
YOU SHOULD KNOW:
In the GM 'family', carefully structured to appeal to all levels of buyer, Buick occupied the Number Three slot behind Cadillac and La Salle, but ahead of Oldsmobile, Pontiac and Chevrolet.

This Roadmaster convertible phaeton couldn't be more typical of 1930s American automobile design at its best.

Buick Century

COUNTRY OF ORIGIN:
USA
FIRST MANUFACTURED:
1936 (until 1942)
ENGINE:
5.2 l (320 cid) Straight Eight
PERFORMANCE:
Top speed around 98 mph (158 km/h)
YOU SHOULD KNOW:
The Century was the fastest Buick of its generation, and (in language that seems quaint today but was racy at the time) this speedy vehicle was nicknamed "The Banker's Hotrod".

1936 was a good year for Buick, with the entire model range being successfully redesigned by the brilliant Harley J Earl and relaunched with suggestive new names. One of the most imaginative creations in the new four-model range was the Buick Century, which replaced the old Series 60. The concept that ruled from 1936 to 1942 was simple but effective – the Century (hinting that it could reach the magic 'ton' when flat out) would be the company's speediest offering, created by mating the short-wheelbase Buick Special from the bottom of the range with a larger engine from the superior Roadmaster (powerful enough to propel 40-seater buses).

The combination of light bodywork and massive motor was not altogether successful, as those who still drive one of these nonetheless popular machines will testify. The Century certainly lives up to its name by delivering fantastic straight-line speed but handling isn't brilliant and high-speed cornering can be problematical. It came in various body styles, with the regular four-door sedan comfortably outselling the other options – nowadays deemed more desirable and including two-door sedans, a Victoria coupe, sleek fastback sedanets and rare open-top phaetons. Interestingly, the Century was supplied as a rolling chassis so various classic examples with custom coachwork may be found.

The 1936 Buicks effectively saved the company, which had nearly foundered during The Great Depression. But the four new models – The Special, Century, Roadmaster and Limited – sold well as the economy (and consumer confidence) revived and the coffers refilled again. Even so, although sales levels remained good the Century was discontinued for the abortive 1942 model year and didn't reappear immediately after World War II, though the Century badge was subsequently revived twice – from 1954 to 1958 and 1973 to 2005.

The Century range rescued the Buick company by selling well.

Cadillac Sixteen

During the 1930s the stately flagship of General Motors' extensive empire was the Cadillac Sixteen, a luxury car aimed at America's most status-conscious auto buyers. GM's cunning plan got off to a great start at the beginning of the decade, but ended in tears.

The 1930 Cadillac Sixteen had an all-new V16 engine, the first such power plant to reach a production car in the USA. The most expensive Cadillac yet, the Sixteen made an attention-grabbing debut at the 1930 New York Automobile Show. It also went on a promotional tour of Europe, a cavalcade of six cars visiting ten countries – stopping off at Cadillac in France even though there was no connection between town and car beyond the name.

The Sixteen was a sensation, offering over 30 different models when each body style and option was added up. This variety was possible because Cadillac had purchased coachbuilders Fleetwood and Fisher Body in order to offer buyers an in-house custom service, though a few Sixteens were sold in rolling chassis form to be bodied outside. As always, the rarer coupes, phaetons and convertibles are deemed most desirable today – though in truth every one of the 3,882 Sixteens built before 1938 looked fabulous, whatever the body style.

The company sold more than half the entire production run in the first six months of manufacture and estimated that it made a profit on not a one. Though this splendid series was a commercial disaster, today's classic car buffs regard original Sixteens as super-desirable (forget the lesser 1938-40 Series 90s) and any coming up for sale is priced accordingly. Expensive then, expensive now – but always offering drivers a refined experience as they change smoothly up through the three-speed synchromesh gear box then swiftly slow the stylish behemoth with servo-assisted brakes.

Surprisingly, the superb Sixteen was a commercial failure when first launched – though now anything but amongst the classic car collectors of America.

COUNTRY OF ORIGIN:
USA
FIRST MANUFACTURED:
1930 (until 1937)
ENGINE:
7.4 (452 cid) OHV V16
PERFORMANCE:
The sportiest models could reach 100 mph (161 km/h)
YOU SHOULD KNOW:
The possibilities for customizing these plush V16 models were endless – as illustrated by the fact that Prohibition-era gangster Al Capone was able to request a gun cabinet when ordering one (but not, unfortunately for Big Al, an in-built tax lawyer).

The low-slung styling of the Sixty-Special pointed the way to a look that would become commonplace in the 1940s.

Cadillac Sixty-Special

In the period when American automotive design was evolving from stuck-in-the-Depression-era styles towards the very different cars of the late 1940s, no vehicle was more influential in setting a new agenda than the Cadillac Sixty-Special. This derivative of the Series 60 entry-level Caddie was designed by Bill Mitchell, newly appointed head of styling at Cadillac and LaSalle.

GM bosses were sceptical about his creation, so radical was its understated styling in a notoriously conservative marketplace. This daring yet elegant four-door sedan without running boards looked like a convertible with a low ride height, built-in trunk, large windows with narrow frames, no belt-line trim and little chrome embellishment. But Mitchell proved to be a man of vision when the Sixty-Special outsold every other Cadillac in its debut year.

In 1939 there was some cosmetic updating, plus new options like a sunroof and sliding glass panel to separate driver and passengers. There was major evolution in the final two years of the Sixty-Special's first incarnation (the name would return on later models) when Cadillac's Fleetwood operation started building the bodies, allowing four styles to be offered – the basic touring sedan, an Imperial sedan and two formal Town cars with different finishes that allowed the roof above the driver to be removed and a glass partition raised to protect passengers and guarantee their privacy.

It is generally agreed that the 1941 Sixty-Specials – with a revised front-end design and skirted fenders – were the most attractive of all, before being superseded by a completely new model for 1942. Nearly 18,000 Specials were manufactured before this change, making it a huge commercial success. It may have started as an innovative low-end product, but as the years rolled by the Sixty-Special steadily climbed the Cadillac pecking order and has become a coveted drive for 1930s car enthusiasts.

COUNTRY OF ORIGIN:
USA
FIRST MANUFACTURED:
1938 (until 1941)
ENGINE:
5.67 l (346 cid) V8
PERFORMANCE:
Top speed around 90 mph (145 km/h)
YOU SHOULD KNOW:
The rarest Sixty-Specials were three one-offs dating from 1938 – two four-door convertibles owned by General Motors executives and a lone coupe. It is thought that there were no more than a dozen custom bodies fitted between 1938 and 1941.

Chevrolet Master

The Chevy has always been multi-marque General Motors' best-selling brand in the USA, and the Master was an honourable contributor to this rule during the 1930s. This popular public choice replaced the Master Eagle in 1934 and came in various styles – a four-door limousine, four-door sedan, two-door coach and two-door convertible, though these dropheads were soon abandoned. There were also improved Sport and DeLuxe versions for those willing to spend a little bit more. It was the senior vehicle in the twin-model line policy adopted by Chevrolet in 1933, its smaller sibling being the Standard.

The Master followed a trend for American cars of the period to have something of a European look. Buyers responded enthusiastically, to such good effect that the new model proved to be a runaway success, with the coach option outselling every other Chevrolet in 1934.

So the low-end Standard was abandoned and Chevy's twin-model offering became the Master and Master DeLuxe, with the latter doing best in sales terms. Each came in a choice of six body types – with the two-door town sedan proving the most popular. But owners of early models soon learned that the Master's revolutionary 'knee-action' shock absorbers designed to provide fewer rattles and a smoother ride were disastrous, frequently collapsing soon after meeting their first rough country road and leaving the front of the vehicle rubbing along on its suspension. Happily, the problem was soon remedied and early Masters remain a popular and affordable choice for enthusiasts who restore and drive 1930s American cars.

But Chevy didn't rest on its laurels. Although the established Master name was retained, the range was completely revamped by top designer Jules Agramonte in 1937. The designer of the stunning 1934 LaSalle completely changed the Master's look.

COUNTRY OF ORIGIN:
USA
FIRST MANUFACTURED:
1934 (until 1936)
ENGINE:
3.5 l (216 cid) Straight Six
PERFORMANCE:
Top speed of up to 85 mph (137 km/h) depending on model
YOU SHOULD KNOW:
Chevrolet's chosen slogans for early Masters included 'The most finely balanced low-price car ever built' and 'The only complete low-priced car' – posing the question of just what it was that vehicles supplied by the mass-market competition (especially Ford) failed to bolt on.

The colour of this modern survivor may not be to everyone's taste, but the Chevy Master is a 1930s classic.

Chrysler CL Custom Imperial

COUNTRY OF ORIGIN:
USA
FIRST MANUFACTURED:
1933
ENGINE:
6.3 l (385 cid) Straight Eight
PERFORMANCE:
Up to 100 mph (161 km/h)
YOU SHOULD KNOW:
This will be a really tough nut for
'must drivers' to crack – only eight of
the superb LeBaron Custom Imperial
phaetons are known to survive.

Wow! The Chrysler CL Custom Imperial must surely be one of the most impressive classic American car series ever, with the phaetons in particular being breathtakingly beautiful. Chrysler's luxury Imperial line was introduced in 1926 to challenge Cadillac and Lincoln at the top end of the market, and remained around in various shapes and forms for years. But enthusiasts are truly thankful for the 1931 revamp, which saw the second generation 'Imperial 8' with its new engine produced in four delightful standard body styles – a four-door limousine, a four-door sedan, a two-door roadster and a two-door coupe, all with signature wire wheels.

But four-door CL Custom Phaetons of 1933 with bodywork by LeBaron are the unchallenged Imperial superstars – and like all superstars they are certainly precious, as just 36 phaetons with bodies commissioned from the prestigious New York design-and-build company were included in the total of 151 Custom Imperials manufactured in 1933. With its endless hood and rounded trunk, this is a truly eye-catching vehicle. It was technically advanced, too, with Chrysler's 'Floating Power' system (added to the Imperial range in 1932) coupled with near-perfect weight distribution making a smooth ride even smoother, and ensuring that this large vehicle was a pleasure to drive.

However, a glass partition could be raised to separate front and back seats for those who preferred to let a chauffeur have the fun. Unfortunately, with The Great Depression in full swing, there weren't too many of these around to support continued production. So the flowing lines of the Imperial would soon be banished by Chrysler's more advanced, commercially successful but infinitely less appealing Airflow. Given the choice, today's classic car driver would choose the Imperial every time . . . hoping against hope that the magnificent machine would be an ultra-desirable Custom Phaeton.

The Chrysler Imperial was a notable – but by no means the only – casualty of the Great Depression's spending squeeze.

Citroen Traction Avant

The name of the game for Citroen in the mid-1930s was 'frontal traction', for the phenomenally successful Traction Avant was launched in 1934 and over three-quarters of a million would be sold before eventual discontinuation in 1957. As with many French cars over the years, both technology and design were innovative. The Traction Avant's looks were rakish and it had an arc-welded monocoque body – abandoning the traditional 'chassis with separate bodywork bolted on' approach in favour of an integrated unit . . . thus popularizing a method of car construction that became almost universal. Another advanced feature was the Traction Avant's independent front suspension.

This novel low-slung machine was daring indeed compared to its contemporaries. But unfortunately its high development costs bankrupted Citroen, which was taken over by Michelin – thus enabling production to continue, with the added benefit for the new owner that Traction Avants could be used to pre-test Michelin tyres. The original 7A model was a saloon with a small engine. This was quickly superseded by the 7B and 7C, each in turn having a slightly larger engine.

Later models were introduced with still larger engines, but the design hardly changed over two decades (though there was a rear-end tweak in 1952). Two-door coupes and four-door saloons were augmented with imaginative variants like the Commerciale, a clever hatchback with split tailgate. There was also a pleasing convertible and 'long' model with an extra row of seats, though plans for automatic transmission and a luxury V8-engined limousine version never came to fruition.

Traction Avants were not only built at the main Paris plant, but also in Belgium, Germany and England. These robust vehicles survive in large numbers, with owner-drivers regularly holding rallies all over the world and quite a few still in use as regular road cars.

The advanced Avant range lasted for many years and was produced in many countries.

COUNTRY OF ORIGIN:
France
FIRST MANUFACTURED:
1934 (until 1957)
ENGINE:
1,303 cc, 1,529 cc, 1,628 cc, 1,911 cc
Straight Four; 2,867 cc Straight Six
PERFORMANCE:
A mid-range engine could reach 70
mph (115 km/h)
YOU SHOULD KNOW:
The new monocoque body was treated with widespread suspicion when the Traction Avant was launched, with traditionalists believing it lacked strength – so to confound doubters Citroen arranged an impressive crash test in which the new vehicle remained in one piece after being pushed over a cliff.

It's easy to see why the in-your-face Cord became a real favourite with glamorous Hollywood film stars.

Cord 810/812

Sensation! So great was the impact created by the Auburn Manufacturing Company's Cord 810 at the 1936 New York Auto Show that eager visitors climbed on adjacent vehicles to try and see over the excited crowd around a stunning deco-style machine with a coffin nose and wrap-round louvers designed by the great Gordon M Buehrig. Front-wheel drive had already been pioneered on the Cord L-29 and this was retained for the 810, which also saw the debut of features like headlights operated by dashboard hand cranks that vanished into the front wings.

Unfortunately for those placing orders, the sought-after 1936 models (Westchester and Beverly four-door sedans, phaeton and convertible coupe) were not delivered until early the following year – and their handsome appearance was somewhat marred by mechanical unreliability. Problems included vapour locks in the fuel line and a tendency to slip out of gear. This was not untypical of ventures associated with the eponymous Erret L Cord – something of a snake-oil salesman who had a knack of producing truly stunning vehicles out of the hat, only for them to fail commercially. And that, indeed, was the ultimate fate of the 810 and its twin, the 812.

In fact, unsold 810s were rebranded as 812s and announced as the new 1937 model, which also saw an attempt to drum up sales by introducing a supercharged version with four dramatic chrome-plated exhaust pipes. With a total production run of around three thousand cars, the 810/812 didn't do badly but manufacture ceased after it was decided that the revised 1938 prototype could not be produced. Even so, this gallant failure remains one of the most distinctive cars designed in the 20th century – a sleek, low-slung vehicle that owners love, making the lucky pilot feel like American royalty.

COUNTRY OF ORIGIN:
USA
FIRST MANUFACTURED:
1936 (until 1937)
ENGINE:
4.7 l (289 cid)V8
PERFORMANCE:
Top speed of 93 mph (150 km/h)
YOU SHOULD KNOW:
A readers' poll in a well-regarded American classic car magazine awarded the title of the 'Single Most Beautiful American Car' to the hugely impressive Cord 810 sedan.

Delage D8S

Louis Delage was born two decades before the first automobile wheel turned in anger, but from 1910 this gifted engineer's cars were winning glory on the track – a process culminating in a world land-speed record in 1923 and victory in every major Grand Prix race of 1927. Naturally, track success was seen as a powerful incentive for discerning customers to purchase road cars, and Delage duly specialized in luxury saloons, tourers and roadsters for a rich clientele.

This policy led to the introduction of various evolutionary models throughout the 1920s, but it was not until the D8 model of 1929 that the company's cars really came of age, with the introduction of a superb eight-cylinder engine that replaced the earlier straight-six power plants.

This led on the Delage D8S, considered by many to be the most attractive French car made in the 1930s. It's easy to see why. A principal delight of the D8S is that top-flight coachbuilders like Chapron, Pourtout, Figoni, Fernandez & Darrin, Freestone & Webb, Letourneur & Marchand, Labourdette and Vanden Plas all applied their skills to cladding this low-slung beauty, ensuring a huge variety of mouth-watering styles, all with huge headlamps. There are saloons, sports coupes, tourers, cabriolets and roadsters to savour. But they're rare, with just 99 made in two years; though more D8SS models did follow and this lightweight machine was both nimble and sporty.

Is the Delage D8S a bit special? It looks that way. At least two people obviously think so – a spirited bidding war pushed the hammer price of a stunning white sports coupe to $3.4 million in 2007. This delightful roadster was originally shown at the Paris Motor Show in 1932, and obviously gave somebody a pretty serious attack of must-drive fever!

COUNTRY OF ORIGIN:
France
FIRST MANUFACTURED:
1931 (until 1933)
ENGINE:
4,050 cc OHV Straight Eight
PERFORMANCE:
An average speed of over 110 mph (175 km/h) was achieved by a lightweight model in a 24-hour endurance test in 1932. The 0-60 mph (97 km/h) time was 15 secs.
YOU SHOULD KNOW:
The Great Depression took its toll on many a specialist luxury car manufacturer and Delage folded in 1935, though the name lived on until 1953 on a Delage model made by the Delahaye company.

This fancy D8S's chauffeur didn't get soaked when it rained as his compartment sported a removable top.

Delahaye 135

COUNTRY OF ORIGIN:
France
FIRST YEAR OF MANUFACTURE:
1935 (until 1955)
ENGINE:
3,557 cc Straight Six
PERFORMANCE:
The fastest body styles were capable
of 100 mph (161 km/h), with a 0-60
mph (97 km/h) time of 10 secs
YOU SHOULD KNOW:
Production of Delahaye 135s
continued after World War II,
eventually taking the total number
produced to around the two
thousand mark – but despite
occasional delicious examples like
the Letourneur & Marchand cabriolet
of 1947, postwar models are not so
highly regarded as the 1930s
classics.

The Delahaye 135 is a grand representative of the hand-built luxury car for the wealthiest of patrons. Back in 1894 the Delahaye company had been one of the first to produce new-fangled automobiles, although as the business developed they specialized in trucks. But in the mid-1930s they decided to get back into cars, with some success. Indeed, it is accepted wisdom that Delahayes from this golden era are among the most handsome cars ever built.

The 135 arrived in 1935, when custom car-body design seemed more about creating rolling sculpture than practical motor vehicles – and indeed the rich buyers of these cars often demanded the most stylish of bodies simply in order to compete successfully in the popular Concours d'Elegance contests of the day, which demanded both the most impressive of contemporary body styling and stunning interiors.

This made the 135 a rich man's (and yes, woman's) expensive toy, but no matter. Some brilliant coachbuilders worked their magic on a rolling 135 chassis – including Figoni & Falaschi, Letourneur & Marchand, Saoutchik, Guillore, Chapron and Franay – and it's this fabulous selection of custom bodies that makes the Delahaye 135s

The Delahaye was the ultimate expression of luxury prewar French automobile manufacture.

so striking. But these cars weren't just pretty faces; their performance was also electrifying.

Indeed, with funding from American heiress Lucy O'Reilly Schell, a racing version of the 135 was built, winning the Monte Carlo Rally in 1937. An evolved 145 driven by Jewish driver René Dreyfus actually beat the fabulous race cars sponsored by Italian and German Fascist regimes, defeating a Bugatti in the 1937 'Million Franc Race' and Rudolf Caracciola's legendary Silver Arrow in the 1938 Pau Grand Prix – a victory that made Dreyfus and the Delahaye into national heroes. But that was the last hurrah, for World War II arrived to end the party.

Duesenberg SSJ

Barring a magnificent one-off, there could be nothing more exclusive than an open-top Duesenberg SSJ Speedster. Only two of these amazing machines were ever made, reflecting Hollywood friendships... or perhaps rivalry in the matinee idol stakes. For one was driven by Clark Gable and the other by Gary Cooper. The short-wheelbase SSJ Speedster is the stuff of Hollywood dreams, but for lesser mortals in search of an evocative drive, there just might be an opportunity to find a Duesenberg Model J (introduced in 1929), or better still a supercharged SJ (introduced in 1932).

Duesenbergs were the finest cars made in America between two World Wars, built to impeccable standards and including much cutting-edge automotive technology. The company went bust in the 1920s and became part of E L Cord's empire – a conglomerate that included Auburn Automobile and Cord Automobile. Cord bought the engineering expertise of the founding Duesenberg Brothers with a view to creating the ultimate in luxury automobiles. He succeeded to such an extent that exclusive customers ranged from European royalty to American billionaires, not forgetting that new Hollywood aristocracy.

As was the custom with quality interwar vehicles, the factory supplied a rolling chassis to a coachbuilder of the customer's choice, who then created unique bodywork that could double the price. This means that these superb vehicles come in an assortment of body styles reflecting the tastes of the day – but one thing every Duesenberg J, SJ or SSJ shared was awesome power, with a top speed approaching twice that of some rivals. And so good was Fred Duesenberg's chassis and engine that these unprecedented speeds were achieved in cars that could weigh up to three tons.

COUNTRY OF ORIGIN:
USA
FIRST MANUFACTURED:
1936
ENGINE:
6.9 l (420 cid) Straight Eight
PERFORMANCE:
A top speed of 140 mph (225 km/h) was claimed for the SSJ, with 0-60 mph in around 8 secs
YOU SHOULD KNOW:
Few of these classy Duesenbergs were made – the Great Depression damped down conspicuous consumption and only 470 Model Js, 11 SJs and the two SSJs were produced . . . but thanks to their prestige and build quality nearly 400 have survived.

The fabulous Duesenberg SSJ Speedster – only two of these awesome cars were ever built.

Ford Model T

COUNTRY OF ORIGIN:
USA.
FIRST MANUFACTURED:
1908 (until 1927)
ENGINE:
2.9 l (177 cid) Straight Four
PERFORMANCE:
Top speed was a stately 45 mph
(72 km/h)
YOU SHOULD KNOW:
'Must drivers' should know that the
throttle is the lever on the steering
wheel, the left foot pedal engages
two forward gears, the middle pedal
engages reverse and the right-hand
pedal is the brake, whilst the lever
beside the driver's seat is the parking
and emergency brake, also being
used to put the car into neutral.
Simple!

Cheerfully dubbed 'Tin Lizzie' or 'Flivver', the foundation of the Ford Motor Company's mighty automotive empire was the Model T, introduced in 1908. The world's first affordable automobile changed the face of America, kick-starting an industry that generated rapid economic growth in the USA (and beyond, for the Model T was manufactured in 11 other countries).

This phenomenal machine continued in production for nearly two decades, with each new car assembled in just 93 minutes. Over time the Model T did evolve, though Henry Ford was so fond of his soar-away success that he was reluctant to sanction too much development and allowed relatively few innovations. He had reason to believe in his baby – by 1918 half the cars in America were Model Ts and, though they were unsophisticated, with a throttle hand lever for acceleration and hand crank starting, the low prices achieved as a result of Ford's advanced production-line manufacturing techniques undercut the competition and ensured enduring success.

But when other companies started matching Ford on price, whilst offering better comfort and styling, Henry stubbornly refused to abandon the Model T and it lingered stoutly on through the 1920s, now with electric starter and coming in an assortment of body styles that included two-door tourers, roadsters, convertibles, coupes, pickups, trucks and wagons. Henry Ford may have famously said that customers could have any colour 'as long as it's black', but actually the Model T came in various colours before 1914 and again in 1926 and 1927.

Production ended on 26 May 1927, after 15,007,034 had been built (yes, someone was counting). The last innovation was to make wire wheels standard, with wooden wheels finally being discontinued. To service existing Model Ts the trusty engine was still manufactured until 1941, during which time another 170,000 were made.

Yes – this old beauty is the car that changed the world for ever.

Ford Model A

For all those innovative contributions Henry Ford made to 'the century of the automobile', he could be deeply resistant to change. The Ford Model A of 1903 had to wait nearly a quarter of a century to be reborn as the eventual successor to Henry's beloved Model T, which he stubbornly refused to replace for far too long. Indeed, the delay nearly ruined Ford, as the competition caught up and overtook.

The Model A arrived in the nick of time to rescue the stuck-in-the-past Ford company from imminent disaster.

But the new Model A revved to the rescue in the nick of time, becoming as important to the company as the Model T . . . perhaps more so, as it represented a bright future rather than the outmoded past. Buyers had almost infinite choice, with Ford fitting a huge selection of bodies onto the sturdy A ladder chassis. There were around 40 variations on the theme, inspired by Henry Ford's talented son Edsel. These included commercial vehicles like mail trucks, panel trucks, wood-panel delivery trucks, pickups and taxis that are hugely popular today. For car drivers the choice was bewildering, with numerous options among sedans, phaetons, coupes, roadsters and station wagons. Launch prices ranged from $385 for a basic roadster up to $1,400 for the plush Town Car. Oh, and the seven basic body styles came in a choice of four colours!

The recipe was successful. Everyone, from Hollywood stars, including Lillian Gish and Will Rogers, to politicians such as New York Governor (and future President) Franklin D Roosevelt, had to have one and nearly five million Model As were sold inside five years, dramatically setting Ford on the revival road. They were easier to drive than the Model T, with conventional controls and a three-speed gearbox.

COUNTRY OF ORIGIN:
USA
FIRST MANUFACTURED:
1927 (until 1931)
ENGINE:
3.3 l (201 cid) Straight Four
PERFORMANCE:
Top speed around 65 mph (104 km/h)
YOU SHOULD KNOW:
Those seeking a drive can find usable examples of the Ford Model A in many countries – as well as at 'home base' in Michigan, it was produced at Ford factories in Canada, France, Germany and Great Britain, and there was even a joint manufacturing venture with Soviet Russia.

This is but one of the many different body styles customers of the Model B/18 could choose.

Ford Model B/18

The first Ford Model B appeared in 1904 – one of the company's earliest products. The second coming of the Model B was in 1932, when Ford produced and sold around 118,000 of these typical Bonnie-and-Clydemobiles, developed from the Model A. The lesson of lingering with the Model T for too long – and relying for success on a single car – had finally been learned by Henry Ford.

The Model B made history by being the first to run alongside a concurrent model – the visually identical Model 18 (aka Ford V8) that differed only in that its engine was the awesome V8 destined to serve the company (and its customers) so well over the years ahead – though not before initial teething troubles were ironed out. But – despite relying totally on his trusty four-cylinder motor for decades – Henry Ford had become obsessed with his new engine and the Model 18 V8 was potentially so superior to its sibling (selling 224,000 in its launch year) that the four-cylinder Model B was phased out by 1934 (when the V8 was redesignated Model 40A).

In the meantime a mighty impressive selection included 18 different models, each with the option of a four- or eight-cylinder engine, making a total of 36 tempting choices for the buyer. The full range included two basic roadsters, three basic coupes, convertible sedan, cabriolet, Tudor sedan (two doors, get it?), Fordor sedan (you got it, four doors), DeLuxe roadster, DeLuxe coupe, DeLuxe phaeton, Victoria coupe, DeLuxe Tudor sedan, DeLuxe Fordor sedan and station wagon.

This serves as a reminder that Ford's 'one model' policy actually concealed a wealth of choice for car buyers. The number produced and availability of spares makes the B/18 an attractive option for restorers, and a large number are still enjoyed by weekend drivers.

COUNTRY OF ORIGIN:
USA
FIRST MANUFACTURED:
1932 (until 1934)
ENGINE:
3.3 l (201 cid) Straight Four (B); 3.6 l (221 cid) Flathead V8 (Model 18)
PERFORMANCE:
The Model 18 could reach 80 mph (129 km/h)
YOU SHOULD KNOW:
From the 1940s the Model B/18 became the most popular vehicle in a fashion that swept through America's testosterone-charged young men like wildfire – hot rodding – and the one customizers coveted above all others was the stylish 'Deuce coupe'.

Ford Model 48

This characteristic mid-1930s car marked the end of Henry Ford's love affair with the sturdy four-cylinder engine that had served the company so well for so long, and the triumphal confirmation of a new long-term partner. Ford's robust new V8 power plant would henceforth be in every car and truck the company manufactured.

The Model 48 continued the evolution that followed the relatively static Model T years, a process that would continue with new models in 1937 and a complete revamp of the line in 1941. This rapid development and continuous introduction of new models was a necessity to grab sales during the Great Depression, when car-buying dollars had to be tempted from cautious pockets.

The Model 48 was itself a major advance stylewise, with the grille pushed forward and made more prominent by smaller mudguards. There was also an integrated boot on trunkback saloons, more room inside and the comfortable new 'Center-Poise' seating arrangement. The overall effect was pleasingly modern to 1930s eyes – and today is much appreciated by those who like to be seen cutting a dash in affordable classics.

As usual, Ford offered many options within the range. The selection included a basic roadster (always the cheapest choice), convertible sedan, three-window coupe, five-window coupe, Tudor and Fordor saloons in trunkback or flatback and an imposing 'woodie' station wagon with birch or maple bodywork. There was also the new Model 51 truck. Within the general range two trim levels were offered, Standard and DeLuxe, and coupes came with or without rumble seats. For 1936 a cabriolet was introduced and the convertible sedan was uprated to trunkback. The Model 48 confirmed Ford's long commercial rehabilitation from the dark days of the late 1920s, briefly seizing market leadership from deadly rival Chevrolet.

COUNTRY OF ORIGIN:
USA
FIRST MANUFACTURED:
1935 (until 1936)
ENGINE:
3.6 l (221 cid) V8
PERFORMANCE:
Top speed of up to 85 mph
(137 km/h)
YOU SHOULD KNOW:
Despite finally going with the V8 engine, Henry Ford again showed stubborn conservatism by sticking to the old-fashioned suspension system inherited from the Model T, together with mechanical brakes, throughout the 1930s – again allowing the competition to gain a technical advantage.

Ford took a major step forward with the V8-powered Model 48.

Graham Blue Streak Eight

COUNTRY OF ORIGIN:
USA
FIRST MANUFACTURED:
1932 (until 1935)
ENGINE:
4.0 l (245 cid) Straight Eight
PERFORMANCE:
Supercharged versions reached
90 mph (145 km/h)
YOU SHOULD KNOW:
Despite their increasing commercial
problems throughout the decade,
Graham produced more
supercharged cars during the 1930s
than all the other US car
manufacturers combined.

*Graham models sported this
distinctive radiator badge.*

In 1927 brothers Joseph, Robert and Ray Graham purchased the ailing Paige-Detroit Motor Car Company. New Graham-Paige models initially did well, with a growing reputation for quality and around 73,000 cars shifted in Year One. The Paige part of the name was dropped for 1930, though trouble loomed for Graham as the Great Depression started to take fierce hold. Sales slumped and a new model, optimistically christened the Prosperity Six, singularly failed to live up to its name.

But the company continued to compete hard for market share, with a sensational design by Amos Northup and superb straight-eight engine introduced in 1932. This was christened 'Blue Streak', a title that so caught the public imagination that it was soon attached to cars powered by the new engine. The vehicles themselves were also technically advanced, with features like a clever 'banjo' chassis frame and side-mounted suspension that would eventually be copied by other manufacturers as late as the mid-1950s. Other novel ideas included enclosed mudguards and a radiator cap beneath the bonnet. Blue Streaks were (and still are) great to drive with terrific roadholding and a smooth engine.

These innovative machines represented a significant milestone in automotive history; their appearance set the trend for a decade of auto design as rival manufacturers scrambled to follow Graham's lead. First-series Blue Streaks came as sedans, three-window coupes and convertible coupes – a markedly limited choice compared to the likes of Ford – but could be distinguished by pearlescent paint jobs in striking colours. Models proliferated and a supercharger was added to boost performance (and hopefully sales) in 1934, but a revamp in 1935 proved disastrous, spoiling the sleek look of the car and seeing the end of the Blue Streak line, which ultimately failed to halt Graham's steady decline.

Hispano-Suiza J-12

This beautiful beast was a luxurious marriage of Swiss precision design, Spanish capital and French engineering expertise – a polyglot relationship that actually produced one of the finest cars ever made, well able to challenge top marques like Rolls-Royce on build quality and style. The J12 engine married to the Type 68 chassis succeeded the long-lived H6 model, launched in 1919 and so highly regarded that it lasted for a dozen years.

Unfortunately, it's hard to find a J12 Type 68 to drool over as they belong to that unique class of prewar vehicle inhabited by the likes of Duesenberg and the Bugatti Royale – luxurious custom-built automobiles for the super-rich that were therefore manufactured in very limited numbers. In fact, only 120 Hispano-Suiza J12s were created in eight years, fitted with a striking assortment of saloon, coupe, cabriolet and roadster bodies by leading coachbuilders of the day. Customers had a choice of four wheelbase sizes to ensure that there was one suited to the preferred body configuration.

There was no shortage of power for these weighty vehicles – the engine was developed from those the company had produced for fighter aircraft a decade earlier, and an even larger engine was offered alongside the massive incumbent from 1935, increasing fuel consumption that was already thirsty in the extreme.

Such was the prestige of Paris-based Hispano-Suiza under founder Mark Birkigt that the company never had to employ sales staff, for the company's reputation for producing the finest automobiles ensured that the orders kept on coming from European connoisseurs of luxury motor cars, keeping Hispano-Suiza's dedicated band of craftsmen busy even in the depths of recession. Anyone lucky enough to take to the road in a J12 today will enjoy the ultimate experience available only to the wealthiest of 1930s motorists.

The luxurious Hispano-Suiza became the ultimate status symbol for wealthy movers and shakers during the 1920s.

COUNTRY OF ORIGIN:
France
FIRST MANUFACTURED:
1931 (until 1938)
ENGINE:
9,424 cc or 11,310 cc OHV V12
PERFORMANCE:
Up to 120 mph (180 km/h) depending on body style
YOU SHOULD KNOW:
It was no idle boast when Hispano-Suiza J12s were compared favourably with Rolls-Royces, as contemporary Rollers incorporated patented Hispano-Suiza technology – notably the advanced braking system.

Isotta Fraschini 8/8A

During World War I the Italian car manufacturer Isotta Fraschini turned to the production of aircraft engines, but with the cessation of hostilities the company returned to exploiting a prewar development – their excellent eight-cylinder motor. The resultant 'Tipo 8' of 1919 was the first straight-eight engined car, soon becoming the darling of the world's rich and famous and establishing an enviable reputation in the all-important American market. There, Isotta Fraschini was second only to Rolls-Royce, testifying to the prestige of the Italian marque.

In 1924 came the Isotta Fraschini 8A, an evolution with revised chassis and suspension plus a larger engine. The standard chassis came with a very long wheelbase, but the needs of sportier drivers were served by models that had a shorter wheelbase designed to take a beefed-up motor and racier bodies. The 8A was a pleasure to drive, having so much torque that it could be started from a standstill in second gear (of three) and go from walking pace to maximum speed in third gear, though owners were more interested in the car's smoothness and reliability.

The 'Tipo 8A' featured a variety of stylish and elegant bodies meticulously crafted by great coachbuilders. Never were the results more aesthetically pleasing than in some of the delectable open-topped 8As from companies like Castagna and Fleetwood. One of the most impressive manifestations was the crouching Flying Star Roadster.

Production of the Tipo 8A ended in 1931 with the arrival of the more powerful Tipo B, but the Great Depression was hitting hard and it was no time to be trying to sell an automobile in the USA that actually cost more than America's finest, the Duesenberg. Sales flatlined and by the mid-1930s Isotta Fraschini had turned away from cars to concentrate on marine and aero engines.

COUNTRY OF ORIGIN:
Italy
FIRST MANUFACTURED:
1919 (until 1931)
ENGINE:
5,902 cc; 7,372 cc Straight Eight
PERFORMANCE:
Top speed was guaranteed to be at least 90 mph (145 km/h)
YOU SHOULD KNOW:
The ultimate stamp of approval in 1920s America was conferred by high-profile Hollywood stars; and they certainly loved the 8A – Clara Bow drove one and Rudolph Valentino had two.

Lagonda V12

When his company went bust in the early 1930s, W O Bentley soon bounced back, joining Lagonda to head the tech team after the company was rescued from bankruptcy in 1935. Ringing in his ears were the words of new Lagonda boss Alan P Good: 'We have to produce the best car in the world and have only two years'. This demanding ask was achieved, and if the Lagonda V12 wasn't the world's finest it was certainly one of the most interesting cars produced in the 1930s.

Bentley's team designed an innovative V12 power plant that delivered more horsepower than any comparable non-supercharged engine. The chassis was also special, with an advanced suspension system that delivered an ultra-smooth ride, always a major consideration with wealthy clients. Equally important was the fact that the chassis was available in three sizes – short, medium and long.

This enabled a discerning customer to choose any body style, with the long chassis perfect for grand limousine bodies and the shortest for speedy roadsters. Fabulous shapes were created in-house by Frank Feeley, reflecting the decline of independent coachbuilders, though some striking bodies were still constructed outside. Varieties included limousines, saloons, tourers, coupes and dropheads.

Two of the most attractive V12s were a pair hastily prepared to compete in the 1939 Le Mans 24 race. They performed brilliantly, finishing third and fourth overall with 'The Old Number Five' winning its class. Another lightweight version beat the lap record at the famous Brooklands circuit – setting a mark of 120 mph (190 km/h), ironically beating a Bentley in the process. Sadly, the outbreak of World War II saw an end to the brilliant Lagonda V12, which would surely have become an all-time great if W O Bentley had been able to continue its development.

COUNTRY OF ORIGIN:
UK
FIRST MANUFACTURED:
1938 (until 1939)
ENGINE:
4,480 cc V12
PERFORMANCE:
Top speed around 105 mph
(170 km/h)
YOU SHOULD KNOW:
These supreme machines are very exclusive, and still reserved for the wealthiest of drivers today – fewer than 200 Lagonda V12s were hand-built and they top many a classic-car wish list.

It's not hard to work out that the Lagonda V12 was designed by the former Bentley team.

Lancia Lambda

COUNTRY OF ORIGIN:
Italy
FIRST MANUFACTURED:
1922 (until 1931)
ENGINE:
2,119 cc, 2,370 cc or 2,568 cc V4
PERFORMANCE:
Top speed of up to 78 mph
(125 km/h) depending on model
YOU SHOULD KNOW:
Although the Lambda was essentially
an open-topped touring car, it came
with a soft top or a removable hard
top that transformed this low-slung
roadster into a square-looking sit-up-
and-beg saloon.

Jump into a major technical milestone (though it may simply seem like a fabulous 1920s sports car) and enjoy a road-hugging drive. In fact, the Lancia Lambda introduced the monocoque technique later put into mass production by Citroen . . . and now the cornerstone of modern car construction. Other innovations like independent suspension, brakes on all four wheels and a narrow V4 engine made for a sensational debut at the 1922 Paris Motor Show. The Lambda, with its torpedo body, open top and sweeping mudguards, was immediately recognized as something new and different.

It also proved to be a nippy race car, popular with privateers and capable of a 1-2-3 finish in Italy's famous Mille Miglia open road race – generating valuable publicity in the process, especially as MM race cars were little more than regular passenger vehicles with tuned engines. Race pedigree was appreciated by regular buyers, who liked the powerful engine and great roadholding. This was very much a driver's car that did not aspire to luxury status.

A product of Vincenzo Lancia's engineering genius, the Lambda would go through a decade of further refinement and nine separate series, with nearly 13,000 produced before production ceased. Engine size increased over time and three gears changed to four but the most significant development was the decision to offer a separate chassis option, as the unitary body did not take kindly to modification and the increasing numbers of affluent buyers tended to demand exotic bodies built to their personal requirements by external coachbuilders.

This move led to an increase in the variety of bodies found on surviving Lambdas, notably a late sedan option. Going with the flow, the factory introduced its own luxury model, the sumptuous V8 Dilambda, and sold the Series Nine Lambda as a rolling chassis.

*The Lancia Lambda was an
exciting open-top drive, and
also technically innovative.*

Lancia Aprilia

The last project undertaken by company founder Vincenzo Lancia before his sudden death in 1937 showed that he had lost none of his forward-thinking prowess. The Aprilia Berlinetta Aerodinamica was a final masterpiece. It was designed with the help of a wind tunnel and no production car had achieved such a low drag coefficient. The neat Berlinetta (saloon) body featured four pillarless doors and Lancia's all-new V4 engine, offering a perfect vehicle for an increasingly prosperous middle class as the 1930s recession slowly receded. It offered speed combined with economy and was easy to drive with a crisp gearbox, superb suspension, precise steering and great roadholding.

Although the Aprilia was a quality saloon for the family market, the second series from 1939 offered a *lusso* (luxury) option and later a stretched version was introduced. The advent of World War II saw the end of many 1930s cars, but the Aprilia soldiered on – literally, with production switching mainly to a militarised version, the Italian army's Torpedo Militare; the manufacture of civilian versions did not resume until 1946.

Lancia had learned the lesson that coachbuilders must be catered for back in the 1920s, when their introduction of unitary bodies closed off the lucrative custom market. So a rolling chassis was offered throughout the production run and about a quarter of all Aprilias came in this form. This guaranteed the appearance of many interesting body types, including tourers, cabriolets and some spectacular coupes that showed Italian stylists had lost none of their adventurous flair and love of dashing design. Striking 'specials' included a Carrozzeria touring convertible and a beautiful red Mille Miglia racing car.

The Aprilia was a great success, with some 28,000 produced in all. It was a fitting tribute to Vincenzo Lancia, who contributed so much to the formative years of automotive technology.

The Aprilia Berlinetta was Vincenzo Lancia's swansong.

COUNTRY OF ORIGIN:
Italy
FIRST MANUFACTURED:
1937 (until 1949)
ENGINE:
1,352 cc V4
PERFORMANCE:
Top speed of 80 mph (129 km/h)
YOU SHOULD KNOW:
The Aprilia followed the prewar convention of producing steering on the right for countries where driving on the right-hand side of the road made left-hand drive a more natural configuration – though demand for the latter option grew as traffic increased on the roads, necessitating frequent overtaking.

The LaSalle was the first design by the gifted Harley Earl, who went on to become General Motors' longtime design chief.

LaSalle

The open secret behind the rise and rise of General Motors – to the point where it swatted Ford off the top of the heap – was CEO Alfred P Sloan's clever policy of having a different brand for every segment of the car market, as opposed to Ford's single model with lots of options. Thus it came to pass that GM's entry-level marque was Chevrolet, with prices and prestige ascending through Oakland, Oldsmobile and Buick to Cadillac.

Then Sloan really got ambitious. Gaps appearing in the range of GM brands as each developed a more specific character were swiftly plugged with companion models. Pontiac was slipped between Chevy and Oakland, Viking and Marquette filled a widening gap between Olds and Buick . . . whilst LaSalle sailed in towards the top between Buick and Cadillac.

The superb LaSalle made its debut in 1927. Built by Cadillac and styled by Harley Earl as the first step on a 30-year journey as GM's style guru, it set new design standards others would be forced to emulate. Better still, Earl filled that market gap by creating an elegant alternative to the larger Cadillacs. For – despite an enticing echo of luxury marques like Hispano Suiza and Isotta Fraschini – his LaSalle was unlike any other car then in production. A range of bodies was offered, including a splashy two-tone roadster.

But Sloan's plan started unravelling with a little help from the Great Depression. Marquette and Viking soon folded, while canny buyers started trading down from Cadillac to LaSalle. The latter was swiftly revamped by Earl's team, becoming more Oldsmobile than Cadillac, but still played an important part in the success of GM's luxury division until 1940, after which LaSalle was quietly dropped with the 'affordable' Cadillac 61 successfully filling the junior luxury car slot.

COUNTRY OF ORIGIN:
USA
FIRST MANUFACTURED:
1927 (until 1940)
ENGINE:
5.0 l (303 cid) V8
PERFORMANCE:
Top speed around 95 mph (153 km/h)
YOU SHOULD KNOW:
One innovative feature of the later LaSalles was a sunshine roof, imaginatively promoted to the waiting world as a 'Sunshine Turret Top'.

Lincoln K-series

Henry Ford relished his acquisition of the bankrupt Lincoln Motor Company in 1922, for he had been forced out of his own Henry Ford Company in 1902 by Henry M Leland – the now-ruined boss of Lincoln. Leland had renamed the original Ford company Cadillac . . . ironically Lincoln's main competitor. The Lincoln was pitched at the luxury end of the spectrum and new ownership didn't change much.

Assorted body shapes were introduced in 1923 but the first real advance was the Lincoln K-series. Launched in 1931, it initially had a V8 engine, though this was swiftly upgraded to a V12 for added power and refinement. Further evolutions of this motor were introduced over time but failed to catapult the K-series to commercial glory. It never really caught the public's imagination and only two thousand were produced before the series was discontinued in 1939, finally being finished off by the introduction of its own stablemates – two phenomenally successful Lincolns – the Zephyr (1936) and Continental (1938).

This is unfortunate, as the hand-built K-series was very good indeed, especially after the introduction of the KB with the first V12 engine in 1932, though the KA line continued. These big machines came with different wheelbases allowing for a variety of interesting body styles produced both by the factory and external coachbuilders, including leading luminaries like Brunn and LeBaron. Amongst the favourites were formal town cars, four-door sedans, phaetons, convertible sedans, touring cabriolets and two-door convertibles.

In 1935 the KA and KB lines merged as the Model K, with a smaller but more efficient V12 power plant, but this failed to halt the sales slide. These handsome cars appeal mightily to the modern eye and they drive beautifully, so the problem can only have been price sensitivity during the Depression years.

COUNTRY OF ORIGIN:
USA
FIRST MANUFACTURED:
Launched as the KA in 1931
(until 1939)
ENGINE:
6.3 l (385 cid) V8; 7.3 l (448 cid),
6.3 l (382 cid), 6.8 l (414 cid) V12
PERFORMANCE:
Up to 95 mph (153 km/h) depending
on body style
YOU SHOULD KNOW:
One final – and impressive – Model K
built in 1939 (subsequently updated
in 1942) was the singular 'Sunshine
Special' convertible limousine
created especially for President
Franklin D Roosevelt.

The Lincoln K-series never quite lived up to the high expectations of the marque's new owner, Henry Ford.

Marmon Sixteen

COUNTRY OF ORIGIN:
USA
FIRST MANUFACTURED:
1931 (until 1933)
ENGINE:
8.0 l (491 cid) V16
PERFORMANCE:
Top speed of 105 mph (170 km/h)
YOU SHOULD KNOW:
Before being supplied, every Marmon
Sixteen was driven around the
Indianapolis Speedway for 210 miles
(338 km) – the last stretch at flat-out
speed – and this demanding test
included downshifting from top to
second at 80 mph (130 km/h)
without the gears clashing.

Just 400 were made, but this was justifiably described as 'The World's Most Advanced Car' upon debut in 1931. The Marmon Sixteen was the last of a line that began with machinery manufacture in the 19th century, saw experimental cars created in 1902, produced the winner of its inaugural home-town Indianapolis 500 race in 1909 (being first to use a rear-view mirror in the process) and the establishment of Marmon's reputation for producing quality cars.

Slumping sales marred Marmon's 1920s, but a reorganization that spun off the automobile operation from the core mill machinery business brought fresh hope. With impeccably bad timing, the straight eight Roosevelt model was launched in 1929 – and consigned to failure by the Wall Street Crash of that year. Undeterred, Howard Marmon continued to develop the sensational V16 engine conceived in 1927. Unfortunately, he couldn't fund production, and rivals Cadillac and Peerless both introduced V16 vehicles – each with an engine designed by an ex-Marmon employee.

In 1931, Howard Marmon did manage to build the superb Marmon Sixteen. His V16 engine was of aluminium construction with steel cylinder linings. The Sixteen was superior to the rival Cadillac, with a better power-to-weight ratio than any other contemporary car save the mighty Duesenberg and torque that provided phenomenal hill-climbing ability – no mean consideration as heavy luxury cars of the day often struggled on steep climbs.

The sleek styling of the Sixteen was adventurous, with clean lines that gave this innovative machine an appearance somewhat ahead of its time. Eight custom body styles from LeBaron were envisaged, but the Sixteen's timing was no better than the ill-fated Roosevelt's. It may have been the best luxury car on the market, but the Sixteen could not survive the worst year of the Great Depression, and the company folded in 1933.

A light aluminium body ensured that the Marmon Sixteen punched above its weight.

Maybach Zeppelin

The Maybach company produced airship engines for Zeppelins until the end of World War I, when legendary engineer Wilhelm Maybach and son Karl turned their attention to the production of luxury motorcars – succeeding to such good effect that they constructed some of the finest automobiles ever built. Such was the enduring reputation of Maybach that when Mercedes-Benz was developing a new top-of-the-range limousine in the 1990s the name Maybach was chosen, reviving a prestigious marque that vanished with the advent of World War II.

Inside twenty years Maybach, with its distinctive double-M logo, established an enviable reputation for producing superb bespoke vehicles that were among the most powerful production cars of their era. The most famous model was the Zeppelin, a name harking back to the company's roots. This enormous luxury limo was launched in 1928 as the DS7. The imposing Maybach flagship weighed in at a massive 6,600 lb (3,000 kg) or more, calling for a large V12 engine.

In 1932 came the Maybach Zeppelin DS8, an opulent extravagance of a car with an even larger motor. The company supplied some of Germany's finest coachbuilders – especially Hermann Spohn of Ravensburg – and the sort of bespoke bodies routinely commissioned by rich owners were duly added, including limousines, cabriolets, coupes and drophead tourers. Each one was an expensive work of automotive art.

Is this awe-inspiring classic a pleasure to drive? Not necessarily – despite advanced features like the lever on the steering wheel for clutchless gear changes and effective brakes, the steering is heavy, turning sharp corners is almost impossible and piloting such a large car through modern traffic is an ordeal. Never mind – anyone given the opportunity to try should grab it with both hands, for it's a motoring experience that can only be described as imperious.

The Zeppelin's distinctive radiator cap and badge.

COUNTRY OF ORIGIN:
Germany
FIRST MANUFACTURED:
1928 (until 1939)
ENGINE:
7,000 cc or 7,922 cc V12
PERFORMANCE:
The lightest variants were capable of 115 mph (185 km/h)
YOU SHOULD KNOW:
The Maybach engines that powered those huge Zeppelin cars so successfully also proved eminently suitable for propelling Germany's feared Panther and Tiger tanks in World War II.

Mercedes-Benz 540K

Following the creation of Mercedes-Benz in 1926, the merged company prospered by producing mass-market models. But it also maintained a prestigious niche as a supplier of fine custom-built vehicles to the European elite, who demanded superior build quality, high performance and exclusivity.

This earnest quest for automotive perfection reached incomparable heights in the mid-1930s with the creation of two superb models for the richest of customers. It must have been hard to imagine that the 500 series of 1934 could be improved upon – but this elegant sportscar was indeed bettered only two years later. Would-be buyers who were accustomed to the best of everything constantly lusted for more power, and Mercedes-Benz obliged by offering them the 540K.

The 540K was certainly exclusive – built only to order, each car was fabricated to the customer's exact requirements on an advanced chassis that featured four-wheel independent suspension for the smoothest of rides. There was enough power to suit the most demanding customers, too – K was for Kompressor, the supercharger that boosted output from the beautifully engineered straight eight engine.

Under 400 were produced, but body styles varied considerably. Popular choices included a two-door sports roadster, assorted two-door cabriolets, two-door tourers, two- and four-door fixed-head and convertible coupes and saloons. Most famous of all is the 'Spezial Roadster' designed by Hermann Ahrens and crafted (like almost all 540K bodies) by Mercedes-Benz's own custom bodyshop, Karrosserie Sindelfingen. These racy two-seaters can only be described as spectacular, with sweeping wings, external exhaust pipes, a recessed grille, raked windscreen and distinctive bonnet that make this an instantly recognizable masterwork.

If lovers of elegant 1930s speedsters could drive one vehicle of their choice, many would surely opt for a 540K (though Formula One guru Bernie Ecclestone was persuaded to part with his . . . for $8.25 million!).

The 540K was a prestige model that appealed to the most discerning customers.

COUNTRY OF ORIGIN:
Germany
FIRST MANUFACTURED:
1936 (until 1939)
ENGINE:
5,401 cc OHV Straight Eight
PERFORMANCE:
The fastest models reached 115 mph (185 km/h), achieving 0-60 mph (97 km/h) in 15 secs
YOU SHOULD KNOW:
It is said that after Jean Bugatti saw the early prototype of the sensationally streamlined 540K Autobahnkurier (only two made) he hurried home and immediately began work on the equally iconic Bugatti Type 57 Atlantic (only three made) – spot the similarity.

MG TA

Morris Garages were the car dealers in Oxford who customized existing cars, then began producing their own vehicles in the mid-1920s. This led to the establishment of the MG company in 1928 after successive moves to larger premises, culminating in the takeover of an old leather factory at Abingdon where MG remained until production controversially ceased in 1980.

Early output consisted of basic body-on-frame sportcars like the Speed Model Tourer, L2 Magna, NA Magnette Tourer and MG PB, though two-seater racers were also produced. This established an evolutionary line leading to the MG T series that made its first appearance in 1936 with the TA Midget, after MG merged with the Nuffield organization. This typically British open-top two-seater enjoyed considerable success in its own right and pointed the way to a postwar generation of sports cars that would include more MGs, Austin Healeys and Triumphs.

MG's existing chassis design was used but updated to take a Morris 10 engine that was tuned and teamed with twin SU carburettors to give the sort of nippy performance MG enthusiasts expected. But the introduction of hydraulic brakes and a synchromesh gearbox didn't please all MG addicts, despite making the TA easier to drive than its rough-and-tumble predecessors and opening up a wider general market for MG sportcars. Initially, two-seater open and closed versions were offered, the latter rejoicing in the name of 'Airline Coupe'. But this was soon replaced by the Tickford Coupe with its three-position folding soft top.

The MG TA Midget was replaced by the TB in 1939, the latter looking very similar but having a smaller, more modern engine, again borrowed from the Morris 10. But World War II spoiled the party and few TBs (only 379) were produced, though the postwar TC of 1945 hardly differed.

COUNTRY OF ORIGIN:
UK
FIRST MANUFACTURED:
1936 (until 1938)
ENGINE:
1,292 cc OHV Straight Four
PERFORMANCE:
Top speed of 79 mph (127 km/h)
YOU SHOULD KNOW:
Although the vast majority of the 3,000 or so MG TAs that were produced came with factory bodies, some very attractive customized TAs were constructed by top coachbuilders like Park Ward.

Everyone agrees that the prewar MGs paved the way for a series of great British sports cars.

Nash Twin-Ignition Eight

COUNTRY OF ORIGIN:
USA
FIRST MANUFACTURED:
1930 (until 1934)
ENGINE:
3.9 l or 4.9 l (1930-32); 4.3 l or 5.3 l
(1932-34) Straight Eight
PERFORMANCE:
Top speed of around 80 mph
(130 km/h) depending on body style
YOU SHOULD KNOW:
Perhaps it made sense that those
two great drivers of American
consumer-driven economic
expansion – cars and domestic
appliances – should be produced by
the same organization, so Nash
Motors duly merged with the
refrigerator-making Kelvinator
Appliance Company in 1937.

Nash Motors of Kenosha, Wisconsin was formed in 1916 when former General Motors president Charles W Nash purchased the Thomas B Jeffery Company, producer of Rambler and Jeffery cars since 1902. The new venture would prove to be an enduring success, selling mid-range vehicles to middle-class buyers using the slogan 'Give the customer more than he has paid for' (this being long before the era of political correctness).

The slogan was no idle boast, for Nash cars always delivered great value and bristled with innovations. One example was the company's twin-ignition system that offered two sets of plugs operating from a single distributor. Pioneered on the Twin-Ignition Six, the package was swiftly adopted for the Twin-Ignition Eight of 1930 – Nash's top-of-the-range model in an era of sumptuous styling. Other advanced features included proper in-car ventilation, dashboard starter button (when most starters were still floor pedals), shatterproof safety glass, downdraft carburettors and automatic chassis lubrication. Indeed, such was the Twin-Ignition Eight's quality that it was nicknamed 'The Kenosha Duesenberg'.

The well-built Twin-Ignition Eight came in five different wheelbases over its life and there were always two engine options to choose from, with an updated pair offered halfway through the run. The side-valve motor was for cheaper models, with a superior overhead-valve engine going into the more expensive vehicles. This allowed a wide variety of Twin-Ignition Eights to be constructed in all the popular body styles of the day – limousine, sedan, tourer, rumble-seat coupe, victoria, convertible cabriolet and roadster.

Some 30,000 Twin-Ignition Eights in all its forms were sold in just four years, ensuring that numerous examples of this beautifully styled vehicle remain on the road today, satisfying those dedicated owners who love being seen out and about in a 1930s classic that has the added bonus of great road manners.

Packard Twelve

The 1930s – constrained by The Great Depression – were a testing time for American car companies and several smaller players went to the wall. One of the keenest contests was in the luxury-car market, where Cadillac and Packard were both chasing top dollar from elite car buyers who had managed to retain serious purchasing power.

Everything began well for Packard. Their Twelve (launched in 1932 as the Twin Six, renamed Twelve in 1933) was technically brilliant, stylistically pleasing and beautifully built. It was also fast, earning the coveted title 'Boss of the Road'. Yet this was no racer, but a genuine

luxury car that could compete with America and Europe's finest when it came to comfort and ride quality – and did, comfortably outselling the stately (and more expensive) Cadillac Sixteen.

The rolling chassis had a splendid new V12 motor that was the secret of Packard's continuing success throughout the 1930s. During this period the Twelve went through 17 different series (actually 16, as 13 was omitted) as appearance was tweaked and mechanical improvements were introduced, allowing the Twelve to maintain its place as top luxury car. Early offerings included a wide range of custom bodies, though the choice was reduced somewhat as the decade unfolded. Every style had something in common, for all were delightful to look at.

In 1939, Packard management decided to discontinue the Twelve and focus on mass-market models, thus conceding a dominant position to Cadillac without a fight. It's perhaps understandable – half the workforce was occupied building Twelves, though these represented only a tiny fraction of the company's output. In eight model years fewer than 6,000 were manufactured, but they remain amongst the most prestigious of 1930s classics and robust build quality ensures that plenty have survived to be cherished by today's owners.

The Packard Twelve has become a desirable 1930s classic, with many surviving to this day.

COUNTRY OF ORIGIN:
USA
FIRST MANUFACTURED:
1932 (until 1939)
ENGINE:
7.3 l (445.5 cid) V12
PERFORMANCE:
Up to 100 mph (161 km/h) depending on model
YOU SHOULD KNOW:
Twelves had an innovative Ride Control feature, shock absorbers operated by a dashboard plunger that controlled the oil flow, and early models came with an engraved plate reading IN – HARD, OUT – SOFT, causing consternation amongst dealers and swiftly leading to revised wording.

Packard One Twenty

COUNTRY OF ORIGIN:
USA
FIRST MANUFACTURED:
1935 (until 1941, excluding 1938)
ENGINE:
4.2 l (256 cid) sidevalve Straight Eight
PERFORMANCE:
Sportier models could reach 85 mph
(137 km/h)
YOU SHOULD KNOW:
In World War II Packard turned to
aircraft engine manufacture,
licensing the Merlin engine from
Rolls-Royce, which was used in the
P-51 Mustang fighter – ironically
named 'Cadillac of the Skies' thus
confirming Packard's fall from luxury-
car grace.

Despite dominating the market niche for hand-built luxury cars, Packard could not survive the Great Depression on those alone. In 1933 the decision was taken to launch a mass-market model and – although quickly derided as a 'Junior Packard' by disgruntled owners of prestigious Packard Twelves and Eights – the One Twenty proved to be a company-saver.

A new plant was quickly established and the mid-market machine made its debut in 1935. In fact, the keenly priced One Twenty was great value for money and had advanced features not shared by the superior Packards, like hydraulic brakes and independent front suspension. But in order to cash in on the company's established prestige, the distinctive Packard bonnet and radiator remained the same.

This marketing ploy was an instant success. The kudos of Packard ownership was suddenly more widely available and thousands of buyers eagerly chose from the One-Twenty's full range of body styles that included two- and four-door sedans, tourers, various coupes and convertibles. Along the way a limousine, convertible four-door sedan and a wood-bodied station wagon appeared and two trim levels (C and CD) were offered as Packard launched even cheaper models.

After taking a year off, the One Twenty name returned to the Packard range in 1939 and lasted for three more years, still offering a full range of body styles. By the time it finally folded into the Six and Eight lines, the now-hyphenated One-Twenty had sold 175,000 units and shepherded this independent company through potentially lean years. It may have been a necessity, but the original One Twenty's appearance marked the beginning of the end of Packard's supremacy in the lucrative luxury-car market. Although Packard struggled on after World War II, it never really mastered the volume car market and the marque was finally abandoned in 1958.

The 'Junior Packard' managed to extend the marque's prestige during the Great Depression.

Pierce-Arrow Twelve

If only the Great Depression hadn't happened, Pierce-Arrow might still be making great cars. As it is, anyone lucky enough to have one is sitting on (or preferably in) a true thoroughbred. The company made prestigious cars that competed at the top end of the market, but lost focus after World War I and fell into the hands of the Studebaker Corporation in 1928.

This shotgun marriage was to mark Pierce-Arrow's last great flowering. Outmoded models were dumped and new engines replaced the company's venerable straight six. First came a powerful straight eight. Suddenly, demand picked up and production at the Buffalo, New York factory could hardly keep up with demand. But by 1932 sales slumped again as recession really took hold.

Next came V12 power plants, allowing the bold launch of the splendid Pierce-Arrow Twelve, which proved well able to compete with the likes of Cadillac, Packard and Lincoln for well-heeled customers still able to afford the best. The Twelve offered plenty of choice. It had the option of two engine sizes (after the first V12 was quickly superseded by more powerful units) and three chassis lengths. This allowed for an almost infinite selection of custom bodies to suit any requirement. The most eye-catching version was the streamlined fastback Silver Arrow, which was a sensation at the 1933 New York Auto Show, but so great was the price tag that only five were made.

Studebaker went bust in 1933 and though Pierce-Arrow was bought by a group of optimistic investors the end was nigh. The company lacked a mid-range model to generate cash flow, and despite considerable efforts to further improve the Twelve, the company closed its doors in 1938, ending production of one of the finest automobiles made in the 1930s.

This one made it, but the imposing (and expensive) Pierce-Arrow range failed to survive the Great Depression.

COUNTRY OF ORIGIN:
USA
FIRST MANUFACTURED:
1932 (until 1938)
ENGINE:
6.5 l (398 cid), 7.0 l (426 cid) sidevalve V12
PERFORMANCE:
The Twelve set many speed and endurance records, reaching 115 mph (185 km/h)
YOU SHOULD KNOW:
Build quality was so good that a number of Pierce-Arrows were converted into rail cars – effectively trucks or buses that ran on railway tracks – and the nickname for these strange hybrids was 'Galloping Goose' after their speedy progress and honking horns.

Rolls-Royce Silver Ghost

Ford wasn't the only company that clung to a model that served the company well, and – whilst it couldn't be further away on the automotive spectrum – the signature Rolls-Royce Silver Ghost was contemporaneous with Ford's famous Model T. There was a slight difference in numbers, with over fifteen million Model Ts sold as opposed to just 7,874 Silver Ghosts, but each defined its own market section and set a benchmark for others to chase.

As the Roaring Twenties got under way, the Silver Ghost was still the car of choice for most really wealthy buyers on both sides of the Atlantic, having been around for 15 years and established an enviable reputation for quality build, absolute reliability and a comfortable ride in the process. In fact, Rolls-Royce prosaically described this enduring icon as the 40/50 hp (horse power) series, and only one car initially had the name 'Silver Ghost' – which press and public soon attached to the whole series.

This was an aluminium-painted 40/50 with silver-plated fittings and open-top body by Barker that took part in the Scottish reliability trials of 1907 and then – packed with journalists – set endurance record after endurance record in the course of a punishing 15,000 mile (24,000 km) test over Britain's rough roads. Don't expect to drive that one – it's owned by Bentley Motors and insured for $35 million.

Reputation made, the series duly dominated the embryonic luxury car market, finally being officially named 'Silver Ghost' in 1925. In pioneering times when cars were unreliable, the Rolls-Royce 40/50 stood out as the exception to the rule. Its robust engine and sturdy chassis ensured enduring success, with no more than periodic technical updates. Its appearance never dated – buyers were able to select custom-built contemporary bodies in the style of their choice.

COUNTRY OF ORIGIN:
UK
FIRST MANUFACTURED:
1907 (until 1926)
ENGINE:
7,036 cc or 7,428 cc Straight Six
PERFORMANCE:
Late models with lightweight bodies reached 85 mph (137 km/h)
YOU SHOULD KNOW:
To take full advantage of the world's most important car-buying market, over 1,700 Silver Ghosts were produced at the Rolls-Royce company's American factory in Springfield, Massachusetts between 1921 and 1926.

Rolls-Royce Phantom III

After cheerfully sticking with the Silver Ghost for nearly two decades, Rolls-Royce started introducing new models on a regular basis in the 1920s and 1930s, splitting the enlarged range into two lines – standard and premium cars. The Phantom series was emphatically the latter, reaching a peak of luxurious development with the Phantom III. The Phantom series was introduced to replace the venerable Silver Ghost in 1925, the Phantom I being a handsome straight six built both in Britain and America and the Phantom II following in 1929, featuring a much-improved chassis.

In 1936, the Phantom III saw the introduction of Rolls-Royce's first V12 engine, an aluminium beauty with an unusual twin-spark ignition system that gave the car exceptional acceleration and a silky-smooth ride. This advanced machine had in-built jacking, a chassis lubrication system operated by internal lever, independent front suspension and servo-assisted brakes. It was unveiled at the 1935 Olympia Motor Show and lauded as the world's most technically advanced vehicle . . . a reputation maintained to this day with some experts boldly claiming that Henry Royce's swansong design was the best car ever made (he died in 1933).

The compact engine was arranged in a more forward position that on previous Phantoms, allowing greater space for an attractive range of custom bodywork. Some of the better-known Phantom III body styles include the Park Ward limousine, Mulliner saloon and Hooper sedanca de ville. But the ones that are really coveted today are the fabulous drophead coupes by the likes of James Young, for that ultimate 1930s wind-in-your-hair luxury motoring experience. Just 727 Phantom IIIs were built, but such was their quality that most are still rolling. Production ended when World War II broke out, and when car manufacture resumed in 1947 it was with the Silver Wraith.

COUNTRY OF ORIGIN:
UK
FIRST MANUFACTURED:
1936 (until 1939)
ENGINE:
7,338 cc OHV V12
PERFORMANCE:
Typical limousine-bodied cars could do around 90 mph (163 km/h) and go from 0-60 mph (97 km/h) in 17 secs
YOU SHOULD KNOW:
Despite introducing The Phantom III's highly successful V12 in 1936, it would be 1998 before Rolls-Royce returned to this engine format with the delectable Silver Seraph.

The pleasing Phantom III was Henry Royce's last design and proved to be an enduring classic.

Rolls-Royce Wraith

COUNTRY OF ORIGIN:
UK
FIRST MANUFACTURED:
1938 (until 1939)
ENGINE:
4,257 cc Straight Six
PERFORMANCE:
Top speed of 85 mph (137 km/h)
YOU SHOULD KNOW:
Field Marshal Bernard Montgomery was never one to hide his light under a bushel, and the great wartime commander liked to be seen out and about around Deep Cut army camp in his Wraith (vanity registration number FLD 99), which had a rare touring limousine body by Park Ward.

The Wraith was designed to be at the heart of the Rolls-Royce standard range, being introduced in 1938 as successor to the 20/25 of 1929 and 25/30 of 1936. It was built at the company's Derby factory and supplied to independent outside coachbuilders as a rolling chassis only, allowing them to design and build whatever body style might be specified by the customer.

As the smooth straight-six engine was designed for high-speed cruising, most body types were saloons with sharp art deco lines, notably the Park Ward limousine and saloon, but also the H J Mulliner four-light touring saloon and Hooper limousine. Other famous firms that produced distinctive bodies such as the occasional cabriolet, sedanca de ville (town car) or flowing roadster included Windover, Thrupp & Maberly and Youngs of Bromley.

Although it was a junior sibling of the Phantom III, the Wraith shared many of the latter's technical features, including the independent front suspension that made it superior to its predecessor, the 25/30 model. Build quality was as always excellent, ensuring that Rolls-Royce maintained its prestige despite offering a cheaper model, and the success of more affordable cars like the Wraith allowed the top-of-the-range Phantom to be offered at a very competitive price.

Around 490 Wraiths were produced before World War II put an abrupt end to production, but the highly regarded Wraith name lived on in a completely revamped model that was the first Roller to reappear after the war, this time with the added prefix 'Silver'. Because of the short production run, pre-war Wraiths are very rare and extremely desirable, as practically every example has classic late '30s lines that delight the eye and most survivors drive as well today as they did on the day they were made.

The stylish Wraith could cruise all day as it transported those lucky enough to own one.

Ruxton

Like a shooting star that flashed across the firmament and was gone, the extraordinary Ruxton was around for just four months, being constructed by the appropriately named Moon Motors for the New Era Motors Company. The Ruxton was truly revolutionary. The brainchild of design engineer and racing driver William Muller, this machine had an extraordinary appearance – long and low, with flowing wings and an absence of running boards that emphasized its sleek design and low ride height.

This was made possible by the Ruxton's front-wheel drive configuration – a system being introduced at the same time (without much success) by European manufacturers like Alvis and already incorporated into the American L29 Cord. After prototypes were built in 1928 and 1929, the Ruxton finally made it to the road in 1930, and some 500 examples were produced by an ill-funded consortium. Engines were Continental straight eights and bodies were mainly sedans built by Budd or open-tops by Rausing, though there were also town cars and phaetons. Striking paint jobs helped to stress the long, crouching look of these unique cars.

But this is a typical tale of the triumph of Depression over optimism. Quality manufacturer Marmon had agreed to build the Ruxton, but pulled out when the Wall Street Crash took place on deal-signing day. Moon Motors of St Louis was in trouble even before the production run began, so the work was split with the Kissel Motor Company in Wisconsin. But that, too, was struggling and recession took its inevitable toll, with too few buyers around to make an expensive machine offering innovative technology and no proven track record anything but a huge loss maker. Production ceased abruptly in a complicated mess of recrimination and law suits, ending one of the shortest and most bizarre chapters in American automotive history.

The garish but impressive Ruxton had a short life bedevilled by law suits.

COUNTRY OF ORIGIN:
USA
FIRST MANUFACTURED:
1930
ENGINE:
4.4 l (268 cid) Straight Eight
PERFORMANCE:
Top speed around 80 mph (130 km/h)
YOU SHOULD KNOW:
The Ruxton was named after potential investor Willam V C Ruxton, but the plan backfired in spectacular fashion when he not only failed to put up any money but also sued, to make it clear that he had nothing to do with the car or the shambles surrounding its construction and demise.

SS Jaguar 100

After cutting his engineering teeth on motorcycle sidecars and customized Austin Sevens, William Lyons moved on to his true life's work – the design and manufacture of Jaguar cars. But first the Swallow Sidecar company built a few SS cars,

Anyone lucky enough to own an SS Jaguar had a licence to be thrilled on the open road!

registering the SS Cars name in 1934. By combining beautiful styling with affordable prices, the company rode the Depression well. SS cars were available as coupes, tourers and saloons and the 1935 SS Mk II looked uncannily like a postwar MG.

In 1935 came the SS90 sportscar, so called because it boasted a top speed of 90 mph (140 km/h), but this pioneering model only lasted one year (with only 23 manufactured) before it was replaced by the SS Jaguar 100, the first use of this iconic name. One of the most attractive cars ever sculpted, this long, low flying machine was impressive to drive and stunning to look at. Two engine sizes were offered – the 2.5 litre and 3.5 litre – and as the name boldly suggested these streamlined beauties could top the magical 'ton' with the windscreen folded flat. Most SS100s were factory-bodied roadsters, but a single coupe was made and a few chassis were supplied to external coachbuilders.

SS continued to produce a bread-and-butter line of saloon cars, and after the pause in production caused by World War II the company returned as a maker of saloon cars, but the SS 100 was not revived and Jaguar would not resume production of sports cars until the splendid XK120 appeared in 1948 to adopt the mantle of its fabled cousin. Collectors of classic cars adore the SS100, but few get the opportunity to drive one – only 198 2.5 litre models and 116 of the 3.5 litre version were made, ranking these amongst the rarest and most desirable of prewar sportcars.

COUNTRY OF ORIGIN:
UK
FIRST MANUFACTURED:
1935 (until 1940)
ENGINE:
2,563 cc or 3,485 cc OHV Straight Six
PERFORMANCE:
Top speed of 101 mph (163 km/h);
0-60 mph (97 km/h) in under 11 secs
YOU SHOULD KNOW:
Although the SS 100 bore the model name Jaguar, it was only in 1945 that SS Cars officially became Jaguar Cars as the company was renamed after its popular pre-war model – a move dictated by the negative connotation of 'SS', which had become indelibly associated with Nazi horror.

Studebaker President Eight

A huge swathe of American automotive history is covered by the 'President' name for this (in various incarnations) was the premier model manufactured by the Studebaker Corporation of South Bend, Indiana from 1927 until 1942. It had such resonance that the name was revived in the 1950s. But the only true classics are the 'Eights' produced between 1929 and 1933.

Dynamic Studebaker president Albert Russel Erskine did well with mid-market cars but had a dream – to build America's best automobile. He bought the luxury Pierce-Arrow marque in 1928 and set about creating a premier Studebaker. His chosen vehicle was the President line, which made its debut as Studebaker's top-of-the-range offering in 1927, before getting a smaller but more powerful straight eight engine in 1928. Thus equipped, President Eights served as the basis of successful racing cars and set land speed records, some of which stood for years.

The Eight was reworked by the legendary Delmar G 'Barney' Roos in 1929, making it one of the most impressive vehicles of the early Depression years and the finest car ever to emerge from South Bend. These large, handsome vehicles came in a wide variety of attractive body styles, with impressive stretched sedans at one end of the range and sporty roadsters at the other. The engine was further improved in 1931, increasing horsepower and torque, but Erskine's drive for perfection was about to have a very unhappy ending.

His ambition to create America's best had delivered something special in the President Eight, but he sold these superior machines that were the equal of expensive marques like Cadillac, Chrysler and Packard for too little money. Though sadly the consequences were disastrous – Studebaker went bust in 1933 and Erskine committed suicide. The President lived on in a restructured company, but as a smaller and very different car.

COUNTRY OF ORIGIN:
USA
FIRST MANUFACTURED:
1928 (until 1933)
ENGINE:
5.5 l (337 cid), 4.0 l (250 cid) sidevalve Straight Eight
PERFORMANCE:
Up to 90 mph (145 km/h) depending on body style
YOU SHOULD KNOW:
One of the Studebaker model lines than ran alongside the President in the 1930s was the Dictator . . . a not altogether admirable choice of name at a time when Mussolini and Hitler were busy strutting their stuff in Europe.

The President Eight was a superior machine that set many long-lasting land speed and endurance records.

Studebaker Land Cruiser

COUNTRY OF ORIGIN:
USA
FIRST MANUFACTURED:
1934 (until 1936)
ENGINE:
4.0 l (250 cid) Straight Eight
(President); 3.6 l (221 cid) Straight
Eight (Commander);
3.4 l (205 cid) Straight Six (Dictator).
PERFORMANCE:
The President Land Cruiser could
reach 90 mph (145 km/h)
YOU SHOULD KNOW:
The centerpiece of Studebaker's
display at the Chicago World's Fair of
1933-34 was a massive model Land
Cruiser, painted yellow, that was
80 ft (24 m) long, 28 ft (8.5 m) tall
and 30 ft (9 m) wide . . . typifying the
imagination and marketing flair that
enabled the company to trade out of
bankruptcy.

The Streamlined Land Cruiser
caused a sensation when it was
first shown in New York, but
never made it into production.

Necessity is the mother of invention, and Studebaker was in need of inspiration after the financial collapse of 1933. The extraordinary Land Cruiser resulted, causing a sensation at the 1934 New York Auto Show. In fact, its creation had been stimulated by a rapturous reception received by the Silver Arrow at the previous year's event. That streamlined machine bristled with design and technical innovations and purported to come from subsidiary Pierce-Arrow, though the five prototypes were constructed at Studebaker's South Bend plant.

Though Studebaker could not afford to put this advanced design into production, an idea was born after the company received permission to trade out of trouble. The range was rationalized into three models – President, Commander and Dictator – and it was realized that a completely different body style with echoes of the Silver Arrow could be created without retooling. This was achieved by taking a standard four-door sedan and modifying the rear end.

The result was spectacular – creating a car that looked like a streamlined new model with advanced features including an integral trunk, wraparound four-light rear window and enclosed rear mudguards. The Land Cruiser body was Studebaker's prestige offering and was initially available only on Presidents, though it was later extended to the Commander and Dictator DeLuxe. As the most expensive body choice in each model, Land Cruisers were not big sellers in 1934-36 but they headlined marketing campaigns and made a vital contribution to the company's revival.

But no American auto manufacturer made a mass-market success of streamlined body shapes in the 1930s, despite many trying, and though the Land Cruiser continued as a periodic body option, evolving over the years, they were never made in large numbers and good drivable examples are rare today. But for all that it was one of the most important Studebakers ever made.

Studebaker Champion

If one car finally restored Studebaker's fortunes after the disastrous bankruptcy of 1933 it was the sensational Champion, introduced just as one decade was coming to its end and providing solid foundations for the next. This cleanly styled and well-engineered vehicle was offered as an economy business coupe, club sedan and four-door cruising saloon, immediately capturing the car-buying public's imagination.

Part of the Champion's appeal lay in the fact that it was an entirely new project (engineered by Roy Cole and Eugene Hardig) that allowed blue-sky thinking untrammelled by the need to use existing design features or components. The inspired result was achieved by putting particular emphasis on trimming down weight. This meant that a very economical small engine could deliver performance comparable with the larger Studebaker Commanders and Presidents, but at a bargain price. There had been a nationwide slump in 1938, leading to significant losses at Studebaker, but the Champ's buoyant reception the following year soon repaired the damage, with 34,000 units sold.

The next year small cosmetic changes were made, like Custom DeLuxe trim options and sealed-beam headlights, and a second coupe with rear 'opera seat' was introduced. Sales nearly doubled, to over 66,000, and further success followed a revamp by someone who had become very important to Studebaker – external industrial design consultant Raymond Loewy.

The Champ certainly lived up to its name, attracting 85,000 buyers in 1941 to become Studebaker's best-seller ever. Thanks to their outstanding fuel economy, Champions swiftly vanished from showrooms after all car production was suspended for the duration of World War II in February 1942, whilst used examples were like gold dust when gas rationing started to bite. Just as soon as hostilities ended, the Studebaker Champion was back – in the form of an all-new bullet-nosed beauty.

COUNTRY OF ORIGIN:
USA
FIRST MANUFACTURED:
1939 (until 1958)
ENGINE:
2.7 l (165 cid) Straight Six
PERFORMANCE:
Early models were capable of 78 mph (125 km/h)
YOU SHOULD KNOW:
So good was the straight six engine first used in 1939 Champions that it was fitted to the wartime Studebaker M29 Weasel cargo/personnel carrier and was still in use for the 1964 model year (after an OHV makeover in 1961).

The forward-looking Champion managed to deliver premium performance at a bargain price.

The iconic Bearcat became an unmistakable symbol of the have-fun Roaring Twenties.

Stutz Bearcat

It didn't take long for the new-fangled motorcar to become a symbol on the status totem – and right at the top for every red-blooded American male was the Stutz Bearcat. Although it became a cherished icon of the Roaring Twenties, the Bearcat had a much earlier genesis.

It was developed by innovative engineer Harry Stutz from the company's Bearcat Indianapolis racer and launched on the unsuspecting public in 1914. This powerful machine (along with the contemporary Mercer Raceabout) introduced the rugged sports car built for speed and thrills – and very little else. Indeed, production Bearcats could be (and frequently were) raced successfully straight out of the box.

The Bearcat formula was simple enough: large engine + low underslung chassis + minimal bodywork = high speed. Weather protection was not part of the equation, and the open-topped Bearcat offered nothing more than a folding 'monocle' windscreen. The public offering differed from all-conquering Bearcat 'White Squadron' race cars in having mudguards, lights and a trunk, plus a vivid paint job. They were for men only – clutches were brutally stiff and applying the brakes required real strength.

Ironically, by the time Bearcats became every college boy's dream and *de rigeur* with the flapper set, Harry Stutz had gone – selling up after a boardroom battle and departing to set up new ventures, producing fire engines and competing without much impact against his former company with look-alike HCS cars. His original Bearcats had ceased production in 1917, but the new Wall Street owners carried on with the well-known brand, cannily making the new Bearcats more user-friendly with the addition of bells and whistles like proper bodywork, chrome bumpers, full-size windscreens and fold-up tops. But the limited number produced and sold bore no relationship to the iconic status subsequently achieved by the Bearcat.

COUNTRY OF ORIGIN:
USA
FIRST MANUFACTURED:
1914 (until 1924)
ENGINE:
5.9 l (360.8 cid) T head Straight Four
PERFORMANCE:
The original Bearcat could reach 81 mph (130 km/h); 0-60 mph (97 km/h) in around 29 secs
YOU SHOULD KNOW:
A Bearcat set a coast-to-coast record in 1916, travelling from San Francisco to New York in 11 days over terrible roads – this feat became known as the Cannonball Run, inspiring both outlaw imitations and movies about outlaw imitations.

Stutz DV32

After the departure of Harry Stutz and the demise of his famous Bearcat, the Stutz Motor Car Company changed direction. The Bearcat was maintained into the 1920s, but when European-born Frederick E Moskovics arrived in 1925 he steered Stutz towards the luxury market. His beautiful new open and closed 'Safety Stutz' models offered improved handling and performance, setting the company's new tone.

At the heart of the reshaped line was a new straight eight engine, which the company called the 'Vertical Eight' and continued to develop into the 1930s. Moskovics departed in 1929, but the best was yet to come – the most sophisticated version of the Vertical Eight. This was the DV32 (as in 'dual valve') that came with a matching chassis, together forming the platform for Stutz's finest cars.

But times were hard. A cheaper six-cylinder LA model was introduced in an attempt to resist the ravages of the Great Depression but this failed, leaving only top-end machines on offer at a time when the market was sluggish. Stutz cars were beautifully made and it was possible to choose from around 30 appealing custom body styles from all the great coachbuilders of the era – such as LeBaron, Fleetwood, Rollston, Weymann, Brunn, Waterhouse and Derham – but buyers remained thin on the ground.

Stutz didn't go down without a fight, trying desperately to generate interest amongst potential customers. A well-proportioned Weymann Monte Carlo four-door sports sedan with aluminium body was created on the DV32 platform. Then the Bearcat name was revived in the form of a DV32 Super Bearcat short-chassis convertible coupe and boat-tailed speedster, both capable of outrunning the original. But it was all in vain. The DV32s may have been some of the best-built and most visually attractive cars of the 1930s, but they couldn't prevent Stutz's slide into bankruptcy.

The Stutz company made great cars but became yet another victim of the Great Depression.

COUNTRY OF ORIGIN:
USA
FIRST MANUFACTURED:
1931 (until 1936)
ENGINE:
5.3 l (322 cid) Straight Eight
PERFORMANCE:
Super Bearcat version had a top speed over 100 mph (160 km/h) while sedans reached 90 mph (145 km/h)
YOU SHOULD KNOW:
Despite the switch to luxury cars from the mid-1920s, Stutz still produced racers good enough to give Bentley a run for the money at Le Mans in 1928 and perform with distinction on the American stockcar circuit.

Could there be a more impressive example of the 1930s automobile as sculpture?

Talbot-Lago T150C SS

For slinky, streamlined looks that can more than hold their own against the Bugatti Type 57 Atlantic and Mercedes-Benz 540K Autobahnkurier, it would be hard to beat the Talbot-Lago T150C SS. This splendid French speedster emerged from the wreckage of the Depression-hit Anglo-French Sunbeam-Talbot-Darracq combine, which imploded in 1935, and is one of the most eye-catching production cars ever to hit the street.

The French end of the collapsed company was taken over by Anthony Lago. The new outfit changed its name to Talbot-Lago and introduced models designed by Walter Becchia. These featured independent suspension and included the two litre T11, three litre T17 and four litre T23. Lago was a clever engineer and developed the existing six-cylinder engine considerably. The resulting T150 served as the ideal power plant for the larger cars and acquired racing pedigree mounted on the T150C (for 'competition') chassis. This combo enjoyed great success on the track and spawned Talbot-Lago's SS (for Super Sport) road cars.

Bodies for these were made by leading coachbuilders like Saoutchik and Figoni & Falaschi . . . and the star was undoubtedly the latter's T150C SS coupe. This sensational machine was nothing less than mobile sculpture and was nicknamed the *Goutte d'Eau* (Teardrop) for its sensual curves. But this was no posturing dandy, for sensational looks were combined with terrific performance.

Two versions were made, though the sky-high price ensured exclusivity – five Teardrops with the so-called 'Jeancart' body (after the first owner) were made on the longer chassis, while eleven in New York Style were built on the short chassis. Although the overall look was the same, each car had exclusive design details specified by the wealthy purchaser. Teardrops had slightly heavy steering, but were still a dream drive – and high in the league table of desirable classic cars.

COUNTRY OF ORIGIN:
France
FIRST MANUFACTURED:
1937 (until 1939)
ENGINE:
3,966 cc Straight Six
PERFORMANCE:
Top speed around 115 mph
(185 km/h)
YOU SHOULD KNOW:
The Teardrop's competition potential was dramatically proved when a car straight from the showroom was placed third in the 1938 Le Mans 24 race – a huge achievement.

Volkswagen Beetle

After coming to power in 1933, the Nazi dictator Adolf Hitler wanted to produce a 'People's Car' (Volkswagen). Hitler told brilliant engineer Ferdinand Porsche to create this affordable vehicle – in an echo of Henry Ford's 'any colour as long as it's black' remark telling Porsche that the price could be anything he liked 'as long as it's under a thousand marks'. This was impossibly low and, despite Porsche's efforts, little progress was made until the German state threw its weight behind the project in 1936. American technicians were hired and mass-production know-how imported.

But in truth the People's Car, or Type 1 (nicknamed 'Beetle' for its shape, though the title was not used officially by Volkswagen until the New Beetle was launched in 1998) was merely a propaganda tool to impress the German people. No Beetles were delivered to the German citizens who had joined a savings scheme to purchase one, though Hitler was presented with a Type 1 cabriolet on his 49th birthday in 1938. As World War II loomed production at the purpose-built Wolfsberg factory (complete with new town for the workers) switched to an open-topped military version called the *Kübelwagen* (Bucket Car).

One of the world's great automobile success stories really started after the war, when the British occupation forces reopened the damaged factory in 1946. It finally ended in 2003, when production of Beetles was stopped in Brazil after 21,529,464 had been built over half a century. Along the way the Beetle hardly changed visually, retaining its unmistakable shape and trademark rear-mounted air-cooled engine – though there were plenty of technical modifications and a commercial version (including the famous camper van beloved by hippies and Aussies touring Europe) was introduced. So the Beetle is surely the easiest-to-find 'must-drive' car in the world, wherever you may be.

COUNTRY OF ORIGIN:
Germany (later also manufactured in Brazil)
FIRST MANUFACTURED:
1938
ENGINE:
985 cc eventually uprated to 1,303 cc (four sizes in between) Flat Four
PERFORMANCE:
The early Type 1s could reach 71 mph (115 km/h)
YOU SHOULD KNOW:
After World War II the Volkswagen factory was offered (free!) to American, British and French motor manufacturers. They all turned it down, Ford dismissing the car as 'not worth a damn' and Britain's Sir William Rootes describing the Beetle as 'too ugly and too noisy' . . . hindsight, anyone?

An early prewar Beetle – the beginning of the road for the world's best-selling car.

1940s

Alfa Romeo 6C 2500 Super Sport

COUNTRY OF ORIGIN:
Italy
FIRST MANUFACTURED:
1939 (until 1951)
ENGINE:
2,443 cc Straight Six
PERFORMANCE:
Non-competition models reached a top speed of 103 mph (165 km/h)
YOU SHOULD KNOW:
A rare handful of Competizione variants of the 6C 2500 were especially prepared for racing – one of which won the 1947 Mille Miglia, recording Alfa Romeo's last victory in Italy's famous road race.

The Alfa Romeo 6C appeared in 1925, launching cars powered by a new six-cylinder engine that gave the series its name. This proud title was attached to a succession of hand-built luxury cars, sports cars and racers that came out of Alfa's Milan factory for more than quarter of a century until the 1900 model superseded the 6C in the early 1950s.

Just before World War II came the 6C 2500, with a few examples built between 1939 and 1943. But the series didn't really get into its stride until postwar production commenced with various customized options. Numbers sold were still small, but these substantial vehicles were quality cars for those who could still afford them. Top of the range was a luxurious 6C 2500 Golden Arrow (purchased by the likes of Prince Rainier and King Farouk), but one of the most interesting versions was the 6C 2500 Super Sport.

This was descended from the exquisite open-topped Super Sport Corsa competition cars created in 1939 and 1940 and was introduced in 1947. Just 413 of these wonderful Super Sports were built in five years of production, but their handsome lines and legendary engineering made them firm favourites with elite buyers. The elegant Berlinetta coupe with super-light (*superleggera*) coachwork by Touring of Milan has become an enduring classic. In addition to fine build quality, it seated two occupants in great comfort and easily coped with sustained high-speed driving over long distances.

The few examples that found their way to the USA were lauded by serious American auto enthusiasts, who found the race-bred twin OHC (overhead camshaft) engines fascinating. This marked the start of America's love affair with Italian cars in the years after World War II, with 6C 2500s snapped up by trendsetting Hollywood luminaries such as Tyrone Power and Rita Hayworth.

The elegant Super Sport is a rare gem, with fewer than 420 built during the production run.

Allard J2/J2X

These custom-built flyers were the brainchild of South London car trader Sydney Allard, who produced an extraordinary assortment of innovative vehicles, manufacturing around 1,900 cars between 1936 and 1954. Of those, fewer than 180 were the Allard company's most sensational

The Allard's American V8 engine helped to make this British car a great success in the USA, where fancy European engines were regarded with suspicion.

machines – the brilliant J2 (90 built) and J2X (83 built) competition roadsters. These were the final fruit of Allard's prewar experiences building one-off cars for customers who wished to compete in trials events. Sydney Allard found that American V8 engines with massive torque were ideal for the rugged terrain encountered when trialling, setting a pattern for his postwar racing cars, the J2 and J2X.

The J2 was but one model launched by Allard after World War II (he also introduced the J, K, L, M and N road cars) – but proved to be the headliner. The American sports car market was wide open, and Allard's advanced J2 chassis with independent suspension (available as the J2X with a special enclosed LeMans body) was designed to take a succession of powerful American V8 engines, creating a high power-to-weight ratio that generated sensational performance. This not only made J2s potent competition cars, but also endeared them to American racers whose mechanics could work with familiar home-grown power plants rather than exotic European imports.

Success duly followed on both sides of the Atlantic, with many race wins recorded. A commendable third place in the 1950 Le Mans 24 was followed by a win in the 1952 Monte Carlo Rally, with Sydney Allard driving. But other manufacturers with more resources copied his cars and by the mid-1950s Allard's presence as a manufacturer effectively ended. Find one of the surviving J2/J2Xs if you can, because the effort will be worthwhile – driving one of these awesome machines just once in a lifetime should be every classic-car racer's dream.

COUNTRY OF ORIGIN:
UK
FIRST MANUFACTURED:
1949 (until 1954)
ENGINE:
Assorted American Ford V8s
3.6 l (220 cid) to 5.4 l (331 cid)
PERFORMANCE:
Top speed varied according to the engine, but was typically around 120 mph (193 km/h); 0-60 mph (97km/h) in 7.4 secs.
YOU SHOULD KNOW:
One American driver who raced an Allard was Carroll Shelby, who subsequently used the formula of light British sports car body teamed with beefy American engine to create the iconic AC Cobra.

The Armstrong Siddeley Hurricane was patriotically named after the famous World War II fighter aircraft.

Armstrong Siddeley Hurricane

After a succession of mergers, the Hawker Siddeley group emerged as the producer of Armstrong Siddeley cars – and when World War II ended one of the first models announced was the slinky two-door, four-seater Hurricane drophead coupe. The name shamelessly appealed to patriotic feelings generated by the exploits of the group's wartime Hurricane fighter planes (a companion saloon car was named after the Lancaster bomber).

So the stylish two litre Hurricane 16 appeared in 1945, with the Hurricane 18 following in 1949 – a similar model but fitted with a larger engine. The related Typhoon sports saloon (named after another Hawker fighter plane) was essentially a Hurricane with fixed hard top. The reason Armstrong Siddeley was the first British manufacturer able to resume postwar car production was that the company promised to put the emphasis on exports – and indeed the first two Hurricanes built were sent to America, where they completed an impressive coast-to-coast drive from New York to Los Angeles to generate favourable publicity.

One interesting feature of the Hurricane was the optional Wilson gearbox. This allowed gears to be preselected with a hand lever, and subsequently engaged with a 'change' pedal that replaced a conventional clutch. This made for smooth, fast gear changes and versions of this innovative system were used on buses, military vehicles and racing cars produced by other companies.

Just over 2,600 Hurricanes were built, but despite generally robust build quality only a few hundred survive – the chassis did tend to rust where it passed under the rear axle and the Hurricane had yet to acquire classic status when the Ministry of Transport (MOT) roadworthiness test was introduced in 1960. Sadly, as time passed plenty of Hurricanes went to the scrapyard – along with many other fine cars that their owners wish they still had today.

COUNTRY OF ORIGIN:
UK
FIRST MANUFACTURED:
1945 (until 1953)
ENGINE:
1,991 cc or 2,309 cc Straight Six
PERFORMANCE:
Top speed of 70 mph (120 km/h); 0-60 mph (97 km/h) in 29.7 secs (Hurricane 16)
YOU SHOULD KNOW:
Those driving Hurricanes on today's roads often use cars with retro-fitted overdrive gearboxes, as the low-geared originals are not ideal for high-speed cruising on dual carriageways and motorways.

Austin A90 Atlantic

Oops! The launch of the Austin A90 Atlantic at the 1948 Earls Court Motor Show in London was a gallant but misguided attempt to create a postwar export winner, by appealing directly to the American market with a car that looked vaguely . . . American. Unsurprisingly, the USA had plenty of American-styled cars of its own, and preferred imported vehicles to have the cachet of patently European design. Sadly for Austin, this meant that the Atlantic was successful on neither side of the Atlantic – despite heroic marketing efforts that included rally outings and record attempts – and production was ended in 1952 after fewer that 8,000 of these distinctive vehicles had been built.

It's a pity, because these streamlined two-door cars are certainly appreciated (and appreciating in value) today. The first Atlantics were convertibles with an interesting optional power-operated mechanism to close the hood. A hardtop sports coupe version followed in 1949 which had an unusual wind-down rear window. In fact, the styling wasn't truly American, but did include a rounded front end with five chrome strips and central fog lamp, plus bravura touches like a 'Flying A' mascot on each wing as well as the central Austin winged motif. Those teardrop wings swept down to a sloping tail with enclosed rear wheels. It also sported novel flashing traffic indicators rather than the more usual semaphore arms and offered optional hydraulically operated windows and an Ecko radio.

But the Americans still weren't convinced, and only a few hundred were sold in the States, though buyers in Europe and British Commonwealth countries were more easily impressed and nearly half the total production run was exported to Scandinavia and Australasia. Few examples of this interesting failure have survived, as handling was poor and rust-proofing wasn't a priority.

Despite its hopeful name the Atlantic was not a success in North America.

COUNTRY OF ORIGIN:
UK
FIRST MANUFACTURED:
1948 (until 1952)
ENGINE:
2,660 cc Straight Four
PERFORMANCE:
A top speed of 92 mph (148 km/h) was claimed, with a 0-60 mph (97 km/h) time of 16.6 secs
YOU SHOULD KNOW:
The A90 was not replaced when it was discontinued, though the engine lived on in the classic Austin Healey 100 sports car and another Austin A90 appeared in 1954 – though this was the entirely different Westminster model.

Bristol 400

COUNTRY OF ORIGIN:
UK
FIRST MANUFACTURED:
1947 (until 1950)
ENGINE:
1,971 cc Straight Six
PERFORMANCE:
Top speed of 82 mph (132 km/h);
0-60 mph (97 km/h) in 19.7 secs
YOU SHOULD KNOW:
Developed versions of the splendid
prewar BMW 328 straight six engine
would continue to power all Bristol
cars until the company switched to
Chrysler V8 engines in 1961.

When is a Bristol not a Bristol? In the case of the Bristol car company, which started production after World War II, the answer is 'when it's really a BMW'. For though the sinuous Bristol 400 touring car did indeed bear a Bristol badge, it borrowed heavily from the prewar BMW 328, which the German company had actually exported as a rolling chassis to Britain, where it was bodied and sold by Frazer Nash.

In 1945 Frazer Nash formed a joint venture with the Bristol Aircraft Company (maker of wartime Blenheim and Beaufighter aircraft) to explore the possibility of manufacturing luxury cars. Representatives of the new consortium visited the wrecked BMW factory in Munich during 1945, 'liberating' plans and engines before the Americans managed to ship the remains of the factory's contents and machinery Stateside. BMW chief engineer Fritz Friedel was swiftly recruited to continue developing the 328 engine and a prototype was constructed in 1946. BAC gained complete control of the venture in 1947, registered the name Bristol Cars and started production of the first series Bristol 400, which was replaced by the refined second series in 1948.

The BMW heritage was significant indeed. The rear suspension replicated that of the BMW 326, the body echoed the BMW 327 and the engine and front suspension came from the BMW 328, and even the distinctive BMW twin radiator grille was incorporated. The Bristol 400's appealing aerodynamic body came in various styles. The standard saloon had bodies designed by Touring and Zagato, whilst there was a drophead styled by Farina and built at Bristol. One or two custom examples were also built, including an extraordinary 'woodie' estate car by Hyde. The long, sloping boot had a characteristic raised circular housing for the spare wheel.

Finders keepers – the Bristol 400 owed more than a little something to the BMW 328.

Buick Super

The 'Super' description was no brash boast. In that automobile status league everyone understands, the Buick was a symbol of upper-middle-class prosperity, offering near-Cadillac quality at a thrifty discount. Buicks were big, comfortable and solidly made. The Super was Buick's mid-range straight eight – with the Special below and Roadmaster above – and the company's best-seller towards the end of the 1940s, helped by confident slogans like 'The Best Buy in Big Cars' or 'Buick's the Buy'.

Although first generation Supers were produced from 1940-42 and second generation models from 1946-1948, the third-generation cars introduced in 1949 were part of an entirely new Buick range. This major relaunch replaced postwar models that were continuations of those being manufactured when production was suspended in 1942. The new Super acquired the company's distinctive VentiPorts in the front wings, lots of chrome around Buick's characteristically toothy grille and the smoothly flowing lines so typical of late 1940s American cars. Body styles included Riviera and standard sedans, Riviera hardtop, estate wagon and convertible.

The Super was also offered with the primitive (by modern standards) Dynaflow automatic transmission system as an optional extra. This was a hydraulic pump-driven transmission with two speeds (low and high), altered either way by a shift lever. It did nothing to enhance performance – if anything it detracted – but nonetheless Dynaflow proved incredibly popular with innovation-hungry buyers and was soon fitted to the vast majority of new Buicks.

Having broken out of postwar shackles, Buick just kept right on enhancing the Super. The body was revamped again in 1950 and a fourth generation in 1954 saw an improved engine and more significant changes in the Super's look, to a squarish design that would be revamped yet again in 1957 before the Super finally bit the dust the following year.

The Buick Super was the aspirational buy for many a middle-class American family beginning to enjoy a new life in the burgeoning 'burbs.

COUNTRY OF ORIGIN:
USA
FIRST MANUFACTURED:
1940 (until 1958)
ENGINE:
4.3 l (263 cid) Straight Eight
PERFORMANCE:
Top speed approached 100 mph (161 km/h); 0-60 mph (97 km/h) in around 11 secs
YOU SHOULD KNOW:
Ford and Buick shared a 50th birthday in 1953, but whilst Ford celebrated its Golden Anniversary with a year of glitzy special events, Buick's sober approach was to introduce power steering, 12 volt electrics and the new OHV V8 Fireball engine for its Super and Roadmaster cars.

Cadillac Custom Convertible

COUNTRY OF ORIGIN:
USA
FIRST MANUFACTURED:
1940
ENGINE:
5.7 l (346 cid) V8
PERFORMANCE:
Top speed was around 95 mph
(153 km/h)
YOU SHOULD KNOW:
The surviving Cadillac Custom
Convertible was the subject of a full
ground-up restoration in 1990 and
this beautiful piece of automotive
history is now in immaculate
concours-winning condition.

By the late 1930s, the practice of supplying a rolling chassis to external coachbuilders that characterized the first decades of auto manufacture had been all but abandoned by mass market car companies, many of whom used in-house body shops to create different styles. So when Cadillac replaced its Series Sixty-One with the longer-wheelbase Series Sixty-Two in 1940, there was no intention of encouraging the outside production of custom-built bodies.

However, Pasadena's Bohman & Schwarz company knew a good thing when they saw one, having prospered in the 1930s by putting luxury bodies on Duesenbergs for Hollywood players. They decided the Sixty-Two provided a perfect base for their design-and-build skills, swiftly going to work on basic Cadillac coupes. The happy result was an all-time great, with emphasis on the 'an' (only two were made, one of which vanished from sight 50 years ago and may or may not still exist).

Lower, wider and rounder were the adjectives generally applied to the eye-catching Bohman & Schwarz Cadillac Custom Convertible – which was notable for its forward-looking 'torpedo' styling with curvaceous lines that gave this ample beauty an undeniably sexy look. The body was gently sectioned and a sloping cast-bronze split windscreen fitted. The door tops curved downwards before joining the beltline, paralleled by a chrome strip that ran from headlamps down to the skirted rear bumper with chrome gravel shield. This curving line separated two subtly different shades of rich red.

Detail included a diecast grille with bold horizontal bars, twin vents on each side of the bonnet, bullet headlamps and large tail lights. Lest street watchers might doubt this handsome machine's origins, Cadillac script adorned the bumpers. The Cadillac Custom Convertible still appears at concours meets, allowing admirers to see (but sadly not drive!) this stunning machine.

Cadillac Series Sixty-Two

Although Cadillac's entry-level Series Sixty-Two was manufactured for many years – from 1941 until 1958 – 1948 saw a distinct change of style for third generation Sixty-Twos, with the long wheelbase enjoyed by previous generations reduced to a shorter model that was virtually identical to that of the junior Series Sixty-One. This heralded the forthcoming demise of the latter (in 1951) and the consequent emergence of the Sixty-Two as Cadillac's sole 'budget' model. Budget or not, it was still an awful lot of motor for the money – and late 1940s examples are keenly sought as drivable classics.

There was little to distinguish the merging Sixty-One and Sixty-Two lines visually, though the Sixty-Two sported more chrome and was offered in convertible form (an option the Sixty-One lacked) as well as in two-door club coupe and four-door sedan style. This was the year that marked the start of Cadillac's inexorable drift towards the pronounced stylistic features that became the hallmark of late 1940s to late 1950s American cars – including huge tailfins and wrap-around windscreens. Cadillac brought the craze to a soaring climax in 1959 with a tailfin display that was never bettered, but initially 1948 models acquired more modest fins (albeit ambitiously inspired by the twin-boom tail assembly of the Lockheed P-38 Lightning fighter-bomber aircraft).

Just two years on, Sixty-Twos from General Motors' Fisher body shop got back a longer wheelbase and acquired the much-hyped new Cadillac OHV V8 engine and a more luxurious interior. New body options that year included a Coupe De Ville 'convertible hardtop', and soon there would be a top-of-the-line Eldorado luxury convertible, too. The fourth generation appeared in 1954, and in 1959 (though the cars remained the same) the designation changed to Series 6200, marking the end of the Sixty-Two, one of Cadillac's most successful lines.

COUNTRY OF ORIGIN:
USA
FIRST MANUFACTURED:
1941 (until 1958)
ENGINE:
5.7 l (346 cid) sidevalve V8 or
5.4 l (331cid) OHV V8
PERFORMANCE:
Top speed was up to 95 mph
(153 km/h), depending on model
YOU SHOULD KNOW:
During 1948 two fabulous custom-built Saoutchik Cadillac Sixty-Two drophead coupes were created in Paris costing $70,000 apiece (when the standard model sold for $2,837) – a black-and-violet beauty for a New York furrier and a glitzy white-and-violet number for Hollywood star Dolores del Rio.

The two-door coupe was a best-seller in the Sixty-Two range.

Chevrolet AK Pickup Truck

COUNTRY OF ORIGIN:
USA
FIRST MANUFACTURED:
1941 (until 1942)
ENGINE:
3.5 l (216.5 cid) or 3.8 l (235.5 cid)
Straight Six
PERFORMANCE:
Top speed was around 65 mph
(105 km/h) depending on engine and
gearing
YOU SHOULD KNOW:
One popular choice with country
boys was the Chevy Pickup with a
6.17:1 rear axle married to the more
powerful Load Master Six engine – a
meaty combination that carried a
self-explanatory 'Stump Puller'
nickname.

The pickup truck has long been an essential element of American rural life, and one of the best is Chevrolet's offering from 1941. This distinctive workhorse exuded a muscular sense of strength, with its long chrome-striped bonnet and wraparound horizontal chrome nose, above a massive radiator grille with vertical bars that clearly sat in front of a haul-anything engine. Bullet-shaped headlamps jutted purposefully from rounded front wings and the bumpers were nicely curved to deal with those minor shunts around the farm. The split windscreen could be opened for ventilation, though fancy additions like a second windscreen wiper for the passenger side or a radio were options rather than standard.

The Chevrolet Series AK Pickup was definitely a macho machine, though appearing streamlined compared with contemporary Ford and T-Series Dodge offerings. However, it was nothing like as sleek as International's K-line or the ever-so-handsome Studebaker M-series. The Chevy came in half- and three-quarter ton versions, the latter on a longer wheelbase. There was also a choice of two engines and three transmissions, depending on the buyer's requirements. The larger engine delivered significantly more torque for serious work, whilst the standard three-speed synchromesh gearbox could be replaced with a four-speed or sliding-gear four-speed box, the latter also designed for big workloads. The truck body was of heavy-duty steel, with a wooden floor protected with steel skid strips. The tailgate was reinforced with box girders.

The robust and hard-working AK Pickup would later become a custom-car favourite.

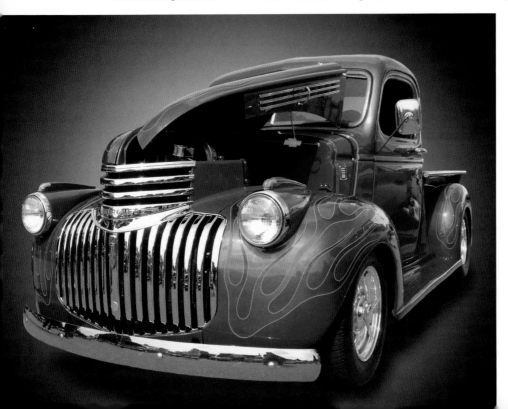

It was perhaps just as well that this great truck was built to last. The AK Pickup had been in production for less than a year when World War II put a lid on it, though Chevrolet would be the first manufacturer to introduce new pickup trucks after hostilities ceased, when the Advance-Design line appeared in the summer of 1947.

Chrysler Town & Country

Don't jump into a modern Chrysler Town & Country people carrier and think you're driving the real thing. That was introduced by the Chrysler Corporation in 1941, representing the company's entry into a burgeoning market sector that would – to the regret of many – last for barely a decade. For this was 'woodie' country and Chrysler's offering was the most elegant example ever – a station wagon with all-steel roof, plus varnished sides and twin side-hinged rear doors in contrasting wood (a light ash frame and darker Honduran mahogany panels). The rear was curved to mirror the design of contemporary saloons – indeed some describe it as the first hatchback sedan – and the whole thing was built to the highest quality and beautifully fitted out.

Like many new American models, the Town & Country made its debut in 1941 and had barely worked up a head of steam before production ceased by Government order early in 1942. In the case of this handsome wagon barely a thousand were made, though it was well received and sold fast in either seven- or nine-passenger form during the short period it was available.

Happily the Town & Country returned after World War II. The plan was to create extraordinary wood-trimmed luxury cars that represented a handsome blend of woodwork and metal, consisting of a sedan, brougham, convertible, roadster and pillarless two-door coupe. In the end the new offerings were trimmed to a four-door sedan (dropped in 1947) and two-door convertible – hand-built beauties that took an age to assemble and cost a fortune to buy, but were essentially a marketing tool whose sheer eye-appeal enticed potential customers into Chrysler showrooms.

Although 'woodie' production ceased in 1950, the Town & Country name was much too good to abandon and Chrysler has been using it on and off ever since.

The Chrysler 'woodie' station wagon was the top-of-the-line model in Chrysler's popular Town & Country range.

COUNTRY OF ORIGIN:
USA
FIRST MANUFACTURED:
1941 (until 1950)
ENGINE:
4.1 l (250.6 cid) Straight Six,
5.3 l (323.5 cid) Straight Eight
PERFORMANCE:
Top speed around 75 mph (120 km/h)
depending on model
YOU SHOULD KNOW:
The wooden body was too difficult for Chrysler's body provider to fabricate, and cynics suggest Chrysler boss Dave Wallace devised the Town & Country to keep the chosen external supplier in business – this was Pekin Wood Products of Arkansas (whose president happened to be a certain Dave Wallace).

Cisitalia 202

The ability to create successful racing cars has been part of the Italian genetic makeup since the dawn of the automobile age, and one of the lesser-known success stories is that of the Cisitalia D46, which flowered briefly in the years immediately following World War II. The D46 was designed and built by Dante Giacosa, using Fiat components modified for racing, and was intended for a series featuring only D46s where driver performance rather than the best car performance would be the decisive factor.

The Cisitalia 202 may have been very pretty but it attracted a mere handful of buyers.

Cisitalia also commissioned road cars from leading designers. Battista 'Pinin' Farina created a stunning shape for the handcrafted two-door Cisitalia 202 Gran Sport, a technical triumph and aesthetic *tour de force* that transformed postwar car design. This innovative masterpiece was chosen to feature in the New York Museum of Modern Art's first automobile exhibition in 1951. Built on a wooden frame, the 202's aluminium body was conceived as an integrated shell seamlessly incorporating the top, bonnet and wings with in-built headlights.

This created a look that would be followed by makers of high-performance GT coupes, like early Ferraris also designed by Pinin Farina. It was soon joined by a companion spider cabriolet by Vignale. The 202 was light, fast and fun to drive, but unfortunately the cost was prohibitive and too few sporty customers could be found in Italy, let alone beyond. Looks alone were not enough and only 170 examples were made, including just 17 cabriolets.

Variants of the 202 were built for competition purposes – including the famous red 202 SMM (for Spider Mille Miglia) roadster that starred in the 1947 race, driven by the great Tazio Nuvolari. It won its class and finished second overall, attracting enough attention to ensure that Farina produced some 20 examples for eager would-be racers.

COUNTRY OF ORIGIN:
Italy
FIRST MANUFACTURED:
1947 (until 1952)
ENGINE:
1,089 cc Straight Four
PERFORMANCE:
Top speed of 105 mph (169 km/h)
YOU SHOULD KNOW:
The Cisitalia business conglomerate was controlled by industrialist Piero Dusio, a sportsman who competed in the 1952 Italian Formula One world championship race driving one of his own Cisitalia D46s – but sadly he failed to qualify and attempts to create a proper Grand Prix car bankrupted the company.

Citroen 2CV

If you must drive this one (you must, you must!) the place to go is rural France. For this was not so much the French 'People's Car' as the 'French Country People's Car'. This versatile little machine was a godsend for rural folk, many of whom were still following a 19th-century way of life after World War II. The Citroen 2CV changed all that, serving as an affordable multi-function passenger car, van, pickup truck, off-roader and small livestock transporter.

The 2CV is one of Citroen's most iconic models, and the key to its success was brilliant simplicity. It had a light air-cooled engine that was easy to work on, soft suspension with adjustable ride height, high ground clearance and a canvas top that could be folded forward to accommodate larger loads. The winning nature of the formula may be judged by the fact that it remained in production for nearly half a century, with scarcely any modification along the way.

The design brief related directly to the target market, and would have made today's politically correct jobsworths shudder with horror. The new low-end vehicle should be an 'umbrella on four wheels' that could convey two large peasants (wearing clogs) and 100 kg (220 lb) of assorted goods to market along unpaved roads, and drive across a ploughed field with a full load of eggs without breaking any. And it did all that and more.

When production ceased in 1990, over 3.2 million 2CVs had been produced (plus 1.2 million examples of the camionette truck version) from factories in six countries. Sadly, the rapid advance of (relative) prosperity in the vast French countryside swiftly led to a situation where the once-ubiquitous 2CV was seen less and less in its homeland, to the point where this little Gallic gem has become something of a rarity.

COUNTRY OF ORIGIN:
France
FIRST MANUFACTURED:
1948
ENGINE:
375 cc Flat Twin
PERFORMANCE:
Top speed of early models was 39 mph (63 km/h)
YOU SHOULD KNOW:
The 2CV was so popular upon launch that there was soon a three-year waiting list, quickly rising to five years, ensuring that buyers who couldn't wait had to pay considerably more than the price of a new car for their coveted transport.

The 2CV revolutionized life throughout rural France by providing practical and affordable transport for a generation of country folk.

Crosley Hot Shot

COUNTRY OF ORIGIN:
USA
FIRST MANUFACTURED:
1949 (until 1952)
ENGINE:
0.75 l (45.8 cid) Straight Four
PERFORMANCE:
Top speed of 77 mph (124 km/h) for
models without a supercharger
YOU SHOULD KNOW:
When he first began marketing his
cars in 1939, Powel Crosley
distributed many of them through
the appliance stores that sold his
radios and refrigerators – with prices
for the basic economy models
starting as low as $299.

In the aftermath of World War II it wasn't just the United Kingdom that spawned low-cost sportcars built (and driven) by dedicated enthusiasts – America had the quirky Crosley Hot Shot. The love child of Cincinnati consumer-appliance magnate Powel Crosley Junior, the Hot Shot was the climax of his efforts, from 1939, to mass produce a small car intended to become the 'American Volkswagen'. Crosleys never reached those heights and when sales flagged, 1949 saw Powel Crosley switch to the FarmORoad utility vehicle and the sporty Hot Shot.

This extraordinary two-seater had cutaway sides without doors, a bulbous nose topped with staring freestanding headlights and a spare tyre hung on the stubby tail. Thanks to its lightweight construction, the Hot Shot's performance was good, with excellent roadholding and reasonable acceleration. When a new engine was introduced, this proved amenable to souping up, and supercharged versions gave a top speed of the magic 'ton'. If there was a problem, it was that earlier models had brakes that were prone to locking after they admitted road dirt. Once this problem was solved the Hot Shot became an admirable fun

It looked puny but the Crosley Hot Shot proved to be faster and tougher than it appeared.

drive that everyone could afford, with a price tag well below $1000 – half the price of competition like imported MG TCs and TDs.

In 1950 a superior version of the Hot Shot was introduced. The Super Sports was essentially a Hot Shot with doors added, and that year the new speedster won a class in the inaugural Sebring 12-hour race. In 1951 it nearly went one better, running prominently in France's hotly contested Le Mans 24 race before electrical problems ended this audacious bid for glory. Overwhelmed by competition from established manufacturers, Crosley production ceased in 1952 – marking the end of the only true sports car made in postwar America until the Corvette arrived in 1953.

Ferrari 166 Inter

For all that it was sporty, the Ferrari 166 Inter 2+2 fixed-head coupe was not the sort of growling supercar that later became the hallmark of the 'Prancing Horse' factory at Maranello. But then this was Ferrari's first road car, being based on the 125 S and 166 S racing cars with coachbuilt bodywork, and it was named to commemorate the 166's track victories. There was logic in the choice, for the 166 Inter shared both a chassis and Gioacchino Colombo-designed engine with the successful racer.

The world's first sight of this elegant new machine came at the Geneva Salon in 1949, where a Farina-bodied convertible appeared. At the subsequent Paris Motor Show a car wearing a handsome coupe body by Touring of Milan was shown. But well-heeled luxury car buyers weren't exactly seduced by Ferrari's first passenger car (just 37 were sold in two years), even though it had been created in response to persistent demand from followers of the Scuderia who were lusting after a road car to drive.

Each of the cars that came out of Maranello was unique. For in the fashion of the day Ferrari supplied a rolling chassis to the coachbuilder of the client's choice, who proceeded to design and fit custom bodywork. Companies thus favoured were Vignale (with forward-looking berlinettas and a coupe), Stabilimenti Farina with attractive coupes and cabriolets, whilst Ghia provided one adventurous coupe by Mario Boano. However, Touring remained responsible for the majority of 166 Inters, including ten berlinettas – the most popular body style – and the lone barchetta.

Enzo Ferrari may have been underwhelmed by the sales of 166 Inters, but he was sufficiently encouraged to take the next step along the supercar road with the 195 Inters and 212 Inters of 1950. The game was afoot!

The 166 was the first of Ferrari's fabulous road cars, though it appears a tad pedestrian compared to more modern models.

COUNTRY OF ORIGIN:
Italy
FIRST MANUFACTURED:
1948 (until 1950)
ENGINE:
1,995 cc V12
PERFORMANCE:
Top speed of 106 mph (170 km/h) with a 0-60 mph (97 km/h) time of 10 secs
YOU SHOULD KNOW:
The famous Ferrari Prancing Horse motif was originally the emblem of leading Italian World War I fighter ace Francesco Baracca – it was removed from the wreckage of his SPAD fighter plane after his mysterious death crash and acquired by Enzo Ferrari in 1923.

Ford V-8 Super DeLuxe Sportsman

COUNTRY OF ORIGIN:
USA
FIRST MANUFACTURED:
1946 (until 1948)
ENGINE:
3.9 l (239 cid) Flathead V8
PERFORMANCE:
Top speed was around 85 mph
(138 km/h)
YOU SHOULD KNOW:
Although production of the
Sportsman did not begin properly
until 1946, the very first car off the
line was delivered (with the loudest
fanfare Ford could muster) to
Hollywood Star Ella Raines on
Christmas Day in 1945.

It seemed that many American cars were inauspiciously launched for 1941, just before civilian car production was switched to war work. So it was with Ford, who stretched their two-line range to three, with the entry-level Special and superior DeLuxe joined by the most expensive of all – the Super DeLuxe. These were destined to return as Ford's postwar models, albeit with more powerful engines and a few cosmetic body tweaks.

However, one notable newcomer in 1946 was the Super DeLuxe Sportsman. This was a stylish convertible that – along with many other vehicles in the aftermath of World War II – made a virtue of steel-starved necessity by featuring wooden side panels and trunk. But there was also a strong element of self-promotion involved, with old Henry Ford figuring that his somewhat dated prewar cars needed a lift in the period before new models could be introduced, and getting the notion of extending the concept of the company's 'woodie' station wagons into a headline-grabbing road car.

Thus, the hand-built Sportsman Convertible became a major plank of Ford's marketing efforts, with that stunning body and luxurious art-deco inspired interior featuring heavily in dealer and corporate advertising. The marriage of painstaking craftsmanship, beautiful maple-and-mahogany bodywork and classic styling makes this one of the most collectable Fords ever made, as anyone lucky enough to slip behind the wheel of a Sportsman will testify.

The bodies were assembled alongside those of 'woodie' station wagons at Ford's Iron Mountain facility, starting with a basic convertible body that was carefully customized before being returned to the main factory to be put on a chassis. This meant numbers were limited and only a few thousand of these impressive convertibles were made before – job done – they were discontinued when the all-new 1949 Fords finally arrived on the scene.

Ford 1949 Custom

At last! Ford's 1949 model year saw the glitzy launch of a whole new range of cars at the Waldorf-Astoria Hotel in New York, effectively representing the company's first serious step forward for nearly a decade and once again bringing Ford level with the competition. This long-overdue move had been driven by Henry Ford II, who took over from his grandfather in 1945 and proceeded to modernize the somewhat hidebound giant – old Henry always having resisted change for far too long for Ford's own good.

The 1949s made a major design statement that emphasized changing times at Ford (albeit with a little help from Studebaker employees doing some sly moonlighting on the side), seeing the ageing three-line Custom, DeLuxe and Super DeLuxe cars replaced by a single model with two trim levels, Standard and Custom. The Custom name was used by Ford in the early years to suggest hand-built quality and the 1949 incarnation reinvented the theme, with the Custom being markedly superior to the Standard with better trim and extra models to choose from.

The 1949 Custom came as a Tudor and Fordor sedan, club coupe, convertible and station wagon. There were two engines on offer – an improved version of Ford's existing V8 engine and a cheaper six-cylinder motor. The coil-spring suspension was an advance on anything Ford had done before, build quality was fairly solid (though there were some teething problems with early cars) and there was lots of eye-catching chrome at the front. They were great cars to drive and a big hit with the car-buying public, effectively rescuing Ford as a major player on the American market.

Despite its importance to Ford's commercial survival, the plain old Custom had a short life, becoming the (admittedly not-so-very-different) Custom Deluxe in 1950.

COUNTRY OF ORIGIN:
USA
FIRST MANUFACTURED:
1949
ENGINE:
3.7 (226 cid) Straight Six;
3.9 l (239 cid) V8
PERFORMANCE:
Top speed was around 90 mph
(120 km/h) for the V8
YOU SHOULD KNOW:
Today's restore-and-drive enthusiasts generally feel that the 1949 Custom sedans are rather ordinary and much prefer the other body styles, which are highly sought after.

The full Custom range included sedans, coupes, this fine convertible and a sturdy station wagon.

Frazer Manhattan

COUNTRY OF ORIGIN:
USA
FIRST MANUFACTURED:
1947 (until 1951)
ENGINE:
3.7 l (226 cid) Straight Six
PERFORMANCE:
Top speed around 75 mph (121 km/h)
YOU SHOULD KNOW:
Kaiser-Frazer automobiles were built at Willow Run, the world's then-largest building, which had been constructed by the US Government and used by Henry Ford to build B-24 Liberator bombers – after the war Ford had no further interest in the facility and Kaiser-Frazer was able to secure a cheap lease.

What was the best thing ever to come out of Ypsilanti, Michigan? It may well be the Frazer, flagship of the senior automobile line built by the Kaiser-Frazer Corporation after World War II. Frazers were named after president Joseph W Frazer and designed by Howard 'Dutch' Darrin, to such effect that the cars were honoured with the Fashion Academy of New York Gold Medal for design excellence – perhaps reflecting the fact that (along with Crosley) Frazers were the first all-new vehicles styled and built after hostilities ended in 1945.

This helped Kaiser-Frazer's transition from Liberty-Ship builder to automobile manufacturer get off to a flying start, though both Frazers and the utilitarian front-wheel drive Kaisers came in two styles only – sedan and Vagabond hatchback. The devil was in the detail and the company introduced the semi-luxurious Frazer Manhattan in 1947. One cunning marketing ploy was to offer an unequalled array of interior and exterior colours, whilst a bulbous body and long wheelbase offered generous interior space. The Manhattan was powered by the Continental Red Seal six-cylinder engine, which continued to evolve throughout the 1940s. This delivered good fuel economy and the Manhattan was also noted for giving a smooth ride. On the down side, styling – despite innovative straight-through wings – was bland.

Nonetheless, early Manhattans enjoyed reasonable commercial success, with 41,000 sold in two years. But despite a cosmetic revamp sales started to decline and in 1949 a desperate attempt was made to revive interest by creating a convertible. This was hand built from a reinforced sedan shell with the top chopped off. The ploy was not a success – only 17 convertibles were produced and sales of the sedan plummeted below 10,000. J W Frazer left the company in 1951 and the Frazer name went with him, though partner Henry Kaiser carried on.

The Kaiser-Frazer company got round to making cars like the Manhattan after building Liberty Ships in World War II.

Healey Sportsmobile

In the immediate aftermath of World War II Donald Healey trod the path that also attracted fellow travellers like Colin Chapman in Britain and Frank Kurtis in America – the journey from successful race driver (and accomplished automobile engineer) to manufacturer of sporty road cars. The Donald Healey Motor Company obtained a factory in Warwick and set about marrying proprietary components like Riley's proven twin cam 2.4 litre four-cylinder engine and Lockheed hydraulic brakes with a light steel box-section chassis and suspension designed and built by Healey.

Production was never prolific – the best-seller among eight different models was the 200-unit Healey Tickford Saloon of the early 1950s, whilst the Healey Elliott Saloon was the success story of the 1940s with 101 produced – but Healey's innovative cars punched far above their commercial weight by establishing a great reputation for advanced engineering, thus influencing a generation of car designers. They were all variations on the same basic mechanical package, though there were two different versions of the chassis.

The third Healey off the line was the long, low Sportsmobile, first seen in 1948 and produced until 1950, during which time very few were actually made. This four-seater drophead coupe with winding windows was built on the B chassis and is sturdy rather than handsome – with its replacement, the Abbott Drophead, definitely being more attractive to look at. Nonetheless, the Sportsmobile was a prestigious four-seater tourer that was ahead of its time, offering outstanding performance in its class.

Unfortunately, it was held back and denied the success it deserved by the British Government's imposition of punitive purchase tax on all luxury cars costing more than £1,000 (when the Sportsmobile was more than double that), which badly affected Healey's sales and profitability.

The Sportsmobile was taxed out of production by the punitive levy on larger cars imposed by Britain's cash-strapped postwar Government to discourage the purchase of luxury items.

COUNTRY OF ORIGIN:
UK
FIRST MANUFACTURED:
1948 (until 1950)
ENGINE:
2,443 cc Straight Four
PERFORMANCE:
Top speed of 105 mph (164 km/h)
YOU SHOULD KNOW:
Bearing in mind that only 23 were ever made, the Healey advertising campaign for the Sportsmobile rather disingenuously stated that 'in spite of the demands of the export market a limited number of these superb cars is now available for home delivery.'

85

Healey Silverstone

COUNTRY OF ORIGIN:
UK
FIRST MANUFACTURED:
1949 (until 1950)
ENGINE:
2,443 cc Straight Four
PERFORMANCE:
Top speed of 113 mph (182 km/h);
0-60 mph (97 km/h) in 11 secs
YOU SHOULD KNOW:
Although almost all Silverstones came with Healey's enhanced 'fits everything' Riley 2.4 l four-cylinder engine, the inevitable quest to be faster than everyone else led to a few late models being fitted with a 3.0 l Alvis straight-six engine.

It's a moot point whether winning rally driver Donald Healey produced road cars to subsidize his true love – racing – or whether exploits on the track were regarded as a promotional tool to boost sales of road cars. Either way, the perfect player was the magnificent Healey Silverstone, named after the wartime bomber airfield that became a racing circuit in 1948.

The Silverstone delivered the best of both worlds, making its debut in 1949 with an advertising campaign featuring glowing testimonials from leading racing drivers of the day – and yes, they really did believe in the product. This was a proven racewinner with a sizzling top speed, rapid acceleration and great roadholding at a time when there was plenty of track and hill-climbing action on offer for owner-drivers, and the Silverstone was a car that could be driven to the meet and then used to compete – and win the day.

With its rounded contours, cycle mudguards and raked windscreen (both removable if necessary to improve race performance), there can be no mistaking the fact that the Silverstone was built for speed. This cigar-shaped sports car has cutaway doors and headlamps cutely concealed behind a vertical-bar grille to accentuate that naked racing look. The Silverstone even had signature portholes borrowed from contemporary Buicks and a spare tyre jutted jauntily out of the rear end, cleverly doubling as a bumper.

Just over a hundred of these dual-purpose 'ride-and-race' sports cars were

The clever doubling up of rear bumper and spare wheel was typical of Donald Healey's innovative thinking.

manufactured. They are regarded as the most desirable Healeys ever made, and with just over a hundred built in the two years of production scarcity value further ups the already steep 'wow factor' price. However, these robust racers rarely vanish into static collections. They were made to be driven, and those lucky enough to have one tend to campaign them regularly in classic sports car races.

HRG 1500 Aero

The HRG 1500's life as a macho British roadster was cut short by World War II, but there's no keeping a good car down. No sooner had VE day been wildly celebrated by a war-weary populace than the HRG 1500 was back, this time with a new body and impressive 'Aero' added to the name.

HRG was set up in 1936 by motor engineer Henry Ronald Godfrey (no prizes for guessing where the company name came from). Godfrey and Archie Frazer-Nash had made cycle cars together before World War I and formed a company in 1929 to supply the British forces, one notable product being the Frazer-Nash gun turret. But Godfrey also wanted to build cars for his Brooklands pals and created a wonderful 1.5 litre prototype in the best tradition of classic vintage sports cars.

Prewar examples had been resolutely old-fashioned even when new – but they appealed mightily to amateurs who liked to compete in the hill-climbs and road rallies that were then popular, perhaps with the odd track excursion thrown in. They were successful too, with their low-slung, lightweight bodies and tuned engines beating almost everything on those slippery hills.

The big wheeze for the postwar world was the 1500 Aero – the old chassis with an all-new aerodynamic teardrop body dreamed up (and hammered into shape) at HRG's Surrey factory. It outshone its spartan predecessor in terms of home comforts – it even had wind-up windows – but sporty buyers were dismayed by a tendency for the bodywork to shake off during hill climbs and imbalance caused by fitting the fuel tank into a front wing. Some of the 35 Aeros HRG built were returned to be fitted with the traditional body, whilst the originals became a quirky footnote in the tale of British sports cars.

COUNTRY OF ORIGIN:
UK
FIRST MANUFACTURED:
1945 (until 1947)
ENGINE:
1,496 cc Straight Four
PERFORMANCE:
Top speed of 100 mph (161 km/h)
YOU SHOULD KNOW:
HRG also made an 1100 version of their fabled competition car, with tuned engines borrowed from Singer's Nine Tourer (the 1500 engine came from the Twelve Saloon) and though only some 250 cars were made during two decades their build quality may be judged by the fact that some 225 are still around.

The 1500 Aero appeared in 1945 as an uprated version of the prewar HRG 1500 speedster.

Hudson Commodore Eight

COUNTRY OF ORIGIN:
USA
FIRST MANUFACTURED:
1941 (until 1952)
ENGINE:
4.1 l (254 cid) Straight Eight
PERFORMANCE:
Top speed of 91 mph (146 km/h)
YOU SHOULD KNOW:
Those third generation 'step-down'
Commodores were very well built
and still drive beautifully today,
representing great value for money
as drivable classics with good
original examples available for well
under $50,000.

The luxurious Hudson Commodore was the Detroit outfit's top-of-the-range model from 1941 to 1952, with the inevitable production break during World War II. The debut line consisted of two wheelbases – short for coupes and convertibles, long for the sedan. There was also a choice between the straight six and straight eight engines, though the 'Eight' was always the star. The convertible was particularly impressive with its bold bonnet, V-shaped grille and fancy chrome bumpers, and is highly prized today.

In common with most US manufacturers, postwar offerings were tweaked versions of the 1941 line and second generation Hudsons weren't very different from the first. But the choice of coupe styles was reduced to one (club), with the sedan and convertible also remaining in production. To their credit, Commodores were better fitted than the competition, with neat features like sealed-beam headlights, twin air horns, double wipers, stop lights, arm rests, lockable glove box and pile carpeting.

In 1948, everything changed with the arrival of the third generation. If a picky film director ordered a classic late-1940s sedan from Central Casting, he would have been ecstatic if a road-hugging Commodore arrived. Hudson introduced an aerodynamic 'step-down' body that placed the passenger compartment within the chassis, so there was no need for the running boards that helped people step up into a raised compartment, allowing for stunning low styling and great roadholding. The Commodore again came with a host of features that others only fitted as extras, and had a fabulous dashboard.

Unfortunately, the simple step-down styling of the Commodore was quickly overtaken by the dash for flash as soaring wings and chrome in Wurlitzer quantities started to appear. Despite selling 60,000 units in two years, the 1951-52 model proved to be the last, as Hudson disastrously abandoned class and switched to compacts.

The aerodynamic third-generation Commodore Eights were classic examples of late 1940s American styling.

Humber Hawk

The Humber car company had an illustrious history, being one of the manufacturers who produced horseless carriages in the late 19th century. By World War I, Humber was the second largest carmaker in Britain and afterwards expanded into commercial vehicle production with the acquisition of Commer. Hillman was taken over in 1928 but in 1931 Humber itself became a takeover victim as it was swallowed by the Rootes Group.

Still, Humber continued to operate at the smart end of the Rootes spectrum throughout the 1930s, and with the advent of war switched to sturdy staff cars, sturdier armoured cars and military utility vehicles. But Humber was ready to resume car production when the war ended and – in keeping with lean times – introduced the new four-cylinder Humber Hawk rather than immediately relaunching the six-cylinder Super Snipe. Despite its name, the Hawk lacked either the grace or speed of a stooping raptor – and had the dubious advantage of being a typical British car of the immediate postwar period. In truth the snazzy name fooled nobody. The new Humber was an old prewar Hillman 14 by any other name, with a lame sidevalve engine dating back to the early 1930s.

No matter. Rationing and a general shortage of cash ensured that few consumers could afford a new car, but Humber's reputation for nicely appointed interiors and good build quality ensured that plenty of bureaucrats and businessmen were happy to splash out other people's cash for this solid four-door saloon with three window lights on each side and a sunshine roof as standard. The Mk I became the Mk II in 1947, but the only noticeable difference was that the gear lever migrated from the floor to become a column change. By 1948 Humber was able to introduce the Mk III, a genuinely fresh model.

The lumbering Humber Hawk was in fact almost identical to the prewar Hillman 14.

COUNTRY OF ORIGIN:
UK
FIRST MANUFACTURED:
1945 (until 1949)
ENGINE:
1,944 cc Sidevalve Straight Four
PERFORMANCE:
Top speed of 65 mph (105 km/h)
YOU SHOULD KNOW:
The Hawk went on to better things after humble beginnings, continuing to evolve as a genuine premium brand within the Rootes stable – the last big revamp coming in 1957, with Series I to IVA Hawks continuing until Rootes finally abandoned luxury car production a decade later.

Jaguar XK 120

Having wowed sporting drivers before World War II with the SS Jaguar 100, the company (now officially named Jaguar) impressed them even more in 1948 when it introduced the fabulous XK 120. For it was positive public reaction to the sensational concept car shown at the Earls Court Motor Show that year which persuaded Jaguar chief William Lyons to put his beautiful machine into full-scale production.

The first XK 120s were hand built, though Jaguar soon got a regular production line going to meet buoyant demand.

The first few hundred completed in 1948 had to be hand built with aluminium bodies over ash frames, but buoyant demand saw the introduction of pressed-steel bodies early in 1949. The 'XK' stood for Jaguar's advanced 3.4 litre six-cylinder engine, which in modified form would continue in production into the 1980s. The '120' represented the top speed – exceptional performance for a road car at the time. With the windscreen removed, ceiling speed was 136 mph (220 km/h), comfortably confirming the XK 120's status as the world's fastest production car.

This streamlined speedster was eventually produced in three body styles – first an open-top roadster, with a fixed-head coupe added in 1951 and a convertible coupe available from 1953. The roadster's detachable sidescreens and canvas top stowed behind the seats whilst the windscreen could be removed and performance-enhancing aeroscreens fitted. The convertible had a hood that folded back onto the rear deck, wind-up windows and fixed windscreen. A Special Equipment (SE) version offered a tuned engine, stiffer suspension and twin exhausts.

This high performer was a natural racer, enjoying considerable track success and setting numerous speed records. Needless to say, these sublime postwar sports cars were coveted then as now, and anyone lucky enough to pilot one gets to experience the ultimate 1940s driving experience. There's a good chance – over 12,000 were built, making the XK 120 a great British success story.

COUNTRY OF ORIGIN:
UK
FIRST MANUFACTURED:
1948 (until 1954)
ENGINE:
3,442 cc DOHC Straight Six
PERFORMANCE:
Top speed of 125 mph (201 km/h) in road trim; 0-60 mph (97 km/h) in 10 secs
YOU SHOULD KNOW:
The best place to chase an XK 120 is America – over three-quarters of the production run consisted of left-hand drive versions destined for the car's admirers (including Humphrey Bogart and many other Hollywood stars) in the United States.

90

Kurtis Sport

Frank Kurtis was a gifted pioneer of the sports racing car. This talented chassis designer created a series of brilliant racers from the 1920s onwards, many of them nimble dirt-trackers powered by the flathead Ford V8. All that racing know-how came to an impressive climax with ultra-competitive Indy cars that won the Indianapolis 500 four times between 1950 and 1955.

Along with other great racecar builders like Carroll Shelby and Colin Chapman, Frank Kurtis dreamed of building the ultimate road car. The result was the Kurtis Sport from Kurtis-Kraft, a good-looking sports car that appeared to great reviews in 1948. It was a pleasing two-door roadster with a rounded nose, sloping rear end and broad chrome rub rail to protect the bodywork. Understated double bumpers straddled an unobtrusive grille and the windscreen was raked. The well-furnished cockpit featured a full display of instrumentation and an ahead-of-its-time adjustable steering column. The Sport came with both a hard and soft top, with rather awkward clip-on side windows.

Customers could opt for anything from a build-your-own kit to a completed car, with various stages in between, as most of the components were proprietary items. However a Kurtis Sport came together, the finished article did just what it said on the box. It had undeniably sporty looks, accelerated like a rocket, had a high top speed ('faster than a Jaguar XK 120' was Frank Kurtis's proud boast), stuck to the road like glue and was highly manoeuvrable.

Unfortunately, it just wasn't possible to hand build enough Sports to make the project financially viable and Frank Kurtis sold out in 1950. The new owner tried stretching the Sport into the Cadillac-powered four-seater Road Jet but that venture failed too, consigning the Kurtis Sport to automotive history.

COUNTRY OF ORIGIN:
USA
FIRST MANUFACTURED:
1948 (until 1950)
ENGINE:
Mostly the 3.9 l (239 cid) Ford V8 (but other motors could be and were fitted)
PERFORMANCE:
Top speed of up to 140 mph (225 km/h) depending on engine
YOU SHOULD KNOW:
Frank Kurtis tried again in the mid-1950s, producing a few 500M production sports cars, based on his 1953 Indy-winning design, that were mostly given fibreglass roadster bodies – but sadly they didn't catch on and Kurtis was to end his automotive days building lumbering airport service vehicles.

The Sport was a build-your-own kit car, though it was possible to buy a factory-built example for a few dollars more.

Land Rover Series 1

COUNTRY OF ORIGIN:
UK
FIRST MANUFACTURED:
1948 (until 1958)
ENGINE:
1,595 or 1,997 cc Straight Four
petrol; 1,997 cc Straight Four diesel
PERFORMANCE:
Up to 65 mph (2 litre models)
YOU SHOULD KNOW:
Nobody at Rover ever actually said it,
but the message must have been
glaringly obvious to buyers of early
Series 1 Land Rovers – you can have
any colour you like as long as it's
Army-surplus green.

From sturdy acorns mighty oaks may grow – and that's certainly what happened in the case of Land Rover. For the inspired Series 1 was the forerunner of a vehicle type that would reach its zenith half a century later when the SUV (Sports Utility Vehicle) became the transport of choice for millions.

Back in the aftermath of World War II the British economy was wrecked and rationing ruled, Rover's Coventry factory had been bombed and materials for consumer goods (especially cars) were in short supply. But dispensation was available for useful products, especially anything with export potential, and chief designer Maurice Wilkes used that to advantage. A surplus wartime Willys Jeep chassis and Rover P3 car engine went into a prototype that was a cross between light truck and tractor, with the PTO (power take off) feature that allowed it to drive farm machinery.

This satisfied the 'useful' requirement and production began in 1948. Better still, buyers paid no purchase tax as this was a 'commercial' – even though the machine launched at the Amsterdam Motor Show had become less tractor-like. The clever four-wheel drive stopgap before normal car manufacture resumed was so well received that the proposed two-year production run never ended, with the Land Rover outselling revived Rover road cars.

The Series I Land Rover was a rugged off-roader that beat the ban on road-car manufacture.

The original Series I was so basic that window panels and a roof of metal or canvas were optional extras, but various improvements were made before the major revamp that saw the introduction of the Series II a decade later. Larger engines were fitted (including a diesel) and long- and short-wheelbase variants appeared. But the essential character remained the same and it's not hard to find a Series I for some off-road fun – nearly three-quarters of these robust workers are still chugging on.

Lincoln Continental

It's nice to own a major car company, and Henry Ford's son Edsel was happy to take advantage. He commissioned a custom-built car for his 1939 spring vacation, turning to Lincoln (Ford's up-market brand since 1922). Chief designer Eugene 'Bob' Gregorie obliged, working from the Lincoln Zephyr to create a stylish convertible (the boss was off to sunny Florida). This impressive machine had a long bonnet covering the Lincoln V12 engine, sweeping wings and a short boot with the covered external spare tyre that would become the Continental's signature.

Henry's boy was delighted and his wealthy Florida friends were so impressed that Edsel claimed that he intended to put the newly minted Continental into production all along. A few were swiftly ordered and put into production, with bodywork hammered by hand. Most were convertibles like Edsel's, but a few coupes were essayed. One or two cars were completed in 1939, known as 1940 Continentals after the year when production started in earnest.

Around 400 were built in the first year, with the new coupe outselling the original convertible cabriolet by roughly two to one over the production run. Early examples had hand-made bodywork, as machine pressing did not begin until 1941. Production stopped after the attack on Pearl Harbour brought America into World War II, but resumed in 1946.

Like all its Ford and Lincoln brethren, the Continental was essentially unchanged from 1941 – though, like most, it had extensive extra trimming to create the illusion of a revamped model. First series Continentals are amongst the newest to be awarded full classic status by the notoriously strict Classic Car Club of America, testifying to their outstanding character and build quality – though in truth they're not that great to drive. Production ceased in 1948, but resumed nine years later.

COUNTRY OF ORIGIN:
USA
FIRST MANUFACTURED:
1940 (until 1948)
ENGINE:
4.8 l (293 cid) V12
PERFORMANCE:
Top speed of barely 70 mph (113 km/h)
YOU SHOULD KNOW:
Edsel Ford was so pleased with the reaction to his custom-built Continental that he brashly claimed that he could sell a thousand instantly – but in fact when production of the first series ended in 1948 just over two thousand had been made, though World War II may have had something to do with the shortfall.

The Continental started life as a one-off created for Edsel Ford's 1939 Florida vacation and turned into a coveted luxury car after World War II.

Maserati A6

After the Maserati family sold out to Adolfo Orsi and the factory moved from Bologna to Modena, World War II intervened and car production was suspended. But Maserati returned vigorously to the postwar fray with exclusive cars that were built around the company's powerful straight six engines. The A6 Sport (also known rather more laboriously as the Tipo 6CS/46) was a barchetta (open-top two-seater racing car) prototype by Ernesto Maserati and Albert Massimino. This was transformed into the A6 1500 two-door berlinetta (coupe) by Pininfarina first shown at the Geneva Motor Show in 1947. Only 59 of these low-slung, stylish machines were ever built, along with just two of the spider convertible versions shown at the 1948 Turin Motor Show. The line was discontinued in 1950.

A further development was the introduction of the two-seater A6GCS, with a larger two litre engine. The company's real emphasis was on producing engines and chassis that would succeed on Europe's racing circuits, and various manifestations of the CGS (including single-seaters and cycle-wing versions) duly obliged, becoming one of the great race cars and laying firm foundations for Maserati's track success that continued through the 1950s, with the heroic red-trident badged machines repeatedly being driven to victory by such luminaries as Juan-Manuel Fangio. A typical CGS racing car was capable of 130 mph (205 km/h) with blistering acceleration to match. Just 16 of these cars were produced before they were superseded by the iconic A6GCS/53.

But a sideline in road cars was maintained, and the early 1950s saw the basic A6G rolling chassis with alloy engine being supplied to the likes of Pininfarina, Zagato, Bertone, Pietro Frua, Vignale and Carrozzeria Allemano, who created a few stylish coupes and roadsters to maintain the Maserati A6's road-going credentials.

The pacy Maserati A6 was produced in various open-topped versions from 1947 until the line was discontinued in '53.

COUNTRY OF ORIGIN:
Italy
FIRST MANUFACTURED:
1947 (until 1953)
ENGINE:
1,488 cc (A6 1500), 1,980 cc (A6GCS)
Straight Six
PERFORMANCE:
Top speed of 95 mph (153 km/h).
YOU SHOULD KNOW:
During World War II an unseemly race developed between Maserati and Volkswagen to develop the first prestigious V16 town car for their respective dictators, Benito Mussolini and Adolf Hitler – but neither succeeded.

Mercury 1949

Edsel Ford created Mercury in 1939, to fill the gap between Ford's regular models and the company's Lincoln luxmobiles. The two divisions were merged after World War II to create the Lincoln-Mercury Division, to stress the fact that the Mercury should be seen as a 'junior Lincoln' rather than 'senior Ford'. The Mercury's soaraway decade would be the 1950s, with a succession of big winners, but the trend started in 1949 when the Mercury new-look integrated body was introduced, updating a tired line that had mainly been styled in the early 1940s.

The rounded number newcomer with its flush wings became known as the 'inverted bathtub', echoing the modish styling of contemporary Hudsons and Packards. The well-built Mercury had a solid presence, yet appeared streamlined with clean, pleasing lines. Four body styles were offered – a four-door sport sedan, coupe, convertible and a two-door station wagon with much less wood than its predecessor.

Along with the Mercury 1949's attractive looks came a beefed-up engine sitting on a new chassis with independent front suspension and longitudinal leaf springs at the rear that (at last) superseded old Henry Ford's beloved but somewhat insensitive single transverse leaf system. The result was a fast, comfortable machine that did indeed establish Mercury's luxury credentials and even offered Touch-O-Matic overdrive as a tempting option. Other tasty possibilities included power windows (standard on the convertible), power seats, a heater, two-tone paintwork and whitewall tyres.

There were new models added to the line-up in 1950 (a starter coupe and limited edition Monterey coupe), whilst the eagerly awaited Merc-O-Matic automatic transmission arrived in 1951. Impressive all-new styling appeared in 1952 to oust the classic Bathtub Mercurys and capitalize fully on the marque's proven appeal in a new decade, but not before over 900,000 1949-1951 units had been sold.

COUNTRY OF ORIGIN:
USA
FIRST MANUFACTURED:
1949 (until 1951)
ENGINE:
4.2 l (256 cid) V8
PERFORMANCE:
Top speed of 105 mph (169 km/h)
YOU SHOULD KNOW:
From the start, one of the chief selling points of Mercury cars was their high performance, echoing the model name (Mercury was the speedy winged messenger of Greek mythology) and easily outrunning Fords V8s with the same motor, as a result of Mercury's careful engine-tuning programme.

The high performance of the Mercury engine was a major selling point of the 1949.

Morris Minor

COUNTRY OF ORIGIN:
UK
FIRST MANUFACTURED:
1948 (until 1971)
ENGINE:
918 cc Straight Four (Series I)
PERFORMANCE:
Series 1 had a top speed of
60 mph (97km/h)
YOU SHOULD KNOW:
The names Morris Minor (and later
Minor Thousand) undoubtedly have
a familiar ring but they might well
have sounded strange to modern
ears had the original name been kept
– the prototype was known as the
'Morris Mosquito', though this was
wisely dropped.

Reviving the name of a 1920s competitor to the Austin 7, Morris Motors came up with a small saloon that would turn the tables on that formidable prewar rival, for Austin entirely failed to match the success of the Morris Minor, which thrived for over two decades following its launch at the Earls Court Motor Show in 1948 – an event that saw many of Britain's first all-new postwar cars presented to an eager public.

Later to become famous for creating the Mini, Alec Issigonis was responsible for the Minor's innovative design. It was conceived as a vehicle for the mass market at a very reasonable price for the build quality. There were three versions in Series I – two- and four-door saloons and a convertible tourer. Plans to use a flat four motor were scrapped late in the day and a straight four sidevalve was substituted. Around a quarter-of-a-million Minors were built in under four years, with the convertible taking a third of sales.

Series II in 1952 saw the fitting of a smaller but more powerful OHV engine (from the competing Austin A30, as Austin and Morris had merged to form the British Motor Corporation). Three new body styles appeared, too – the van, pickup and Traveller with its signature wooden frame. Series II lasted until 1956.

Cosmetic modifications were made for Series III, including a further uprating of the engine and in 1961 the Morris Minor became the first British car to sell more than one million units. An even larger engine was introduced the following year but it was the beginning of the end. The 1960s saw a steadily declining sales graph until the convertible went in 1969 and the saloon in 1970. The last of the line were Travellers made in 1971. Sadly, the Minor's replacement was the eminently forgettable Marina.

The postwar Morris Minor was the first of the cars designed by innovative Alec Issigonis.

Nash Airflyte

When you design a car with the help of a wind tunnel, 'Airflyte' might seem like a good name for the result. Nash-Kelvinator certainly thought so, for that's what engineering boss Nils 'Wally' Wahlberg christened their 1949 model, which represented the first radical design advance after World War II.

It was as though every manufacturer was singing from the same song sheet (the one warbling the praises of streamlined World War II aircraft), for most opted for the 'inverted bathtub' look for 1949. Even so, no other offering was more strikingly different from anything that had gone before than the Airflyte, which was wide and low with smoothly rounded contours. The slab-sided design involved flat wings that enclosed the wheels, further improving an already impressive drag coefficient. The end product was a roomy car that was both comfortable and quiet.

The comfort dimension was emphasized by an interior finish that allowed the passenger compartment to be dubbed the 'Super Lounge'. Design was uncluttered to match the sleek exterior, with instruments mounted in a 'Uniscope' pod atop the steering column. The front seats could even be laid back to create a bed for three (don't ask). Two models shared identical styling – the 600 (later Statesman) and Ambassador. There was little variety of body style, with just two- and four-door sedans on offer, though buyers could choose between Super, Super Special and Custom trim level. The public loved this advanced machine, which lifted Nash production to levels never seen before (or subsequently), with profits to match.

Strangely, the bathtub design – though all the rage with most major car companies as the 1940s turned into the 1950s – lasted barely two years. The Airflyte was no exception, being completely redesigned for 1952 and acquiring a fancy new name – the Golden Airflyte.

Streamlining was the key to the creation of the striking Airflyte that was a prime example of 1940s 'bath tub' styling.

COUNTRY OF ORIGIN:
USA
FIRST MANUFACTURED:
1949 (until 1951)
ENGINE:
2.8 l (171 cid) (600/Statesman);
3.8 l (232 cid) (Ambassador)
Straight Six
PERFORMANCE:
Top speed of 89 mph (143 km/h);
0-60 mph (97 km/h) in 17.4 secs
YOU SHOULD KNOW:
The first thing anyone who drives an Airflyte today discovers is that enclosed wheels can only swivel so far, resulting in a very wide turning circle and difficulty in negotiating hairpin bends – and salesmen in 1949 even had a job persuading would-be buyers that flat tyres could be changed.

The Futuramic 88 wasn't slow to make the boldest of statements in gleaming chrome.

Oldsmobile Futuramic 88

A lot happened on the American automobile scene in 1949, and Oldsmobile's contribution was the overhead-valve Rocket V8 engine, which replaced the company's elderly flathead straight eight. This awesome power plant was a great selling point and Olds swiftly put their new baby in cars that did it justice. This annoyed General Motors stablemate Cadillac/LaSalle (hitherto offering GM's only V8) but Oldsmobile pressed on regardless, forcing Cadillac to upsize their own V8 in order to remain top dog.

Oldsmobile's Futuramic range had been launched in 1948, before the new engine was available, but when the Rocket arrived it was dropped into the Futuramic 88, a last-minute addition to the '49 lineup. The result was a breathtaking car that set new performance standards. Though the newly developed Rocket was also fitted to the top-of-the-range Futuramic 98, the 88 left the heavier car breathing tyre smoke.

The 88's outstanding performance was complemented by a handsome appearance, with a range of body styles. It was offered as a four-door sedan, four-door town sedan, two-door club sedan, two-door club coupe, convertible and four-door station wagon, the latter having an all-steel body with imitation wood trim to maintain a traditional wagon look. America took to this special car big time, with a tad short of 100,000 units sold in 1949. The following year a two-door Holiday hardtop was added and the word was really out, with overall sales more than doubling.

The 88 also dominated NASCAR stock-car racing, underlining its competitive edge. It was revamped for 1951 but the winning name was too good to lose and the evolving model remained in production until 1999. This 1949 muscle car is still a pokey ride today, so the modern driver can appreciate the impact made when it first appeared half a century ago.

COUNTRY OF ORIGIN:
USA
FIRST MANUFACTURED:
1949 (until 1950)
ENGINE:
5.0 l (303 cid) OHV V8
PERFORMANCE:
Top speed of 90 mph (km/h); 0-60 mph (97 km/h) in 12.2 secs
YOU SHOULD KNOW:
Valuable publicity was always given to the pace car selected for the high-profile Indianapolis 500 race at the historic Brickyard – and in 1949 that honour went to an Oldsmobile Futuramic 88.

Porsche 356

Though it was no slouch, this was Porsche's first production car and some way from the higher-performance models that were to come. The Porsche 356 was based on Volkswagen Beetle running gear with flat four engines also borrowed from the People's Car, albeit subject to serious tuning. This compact sports car was designed by Ferdinand 'Ferry' Porsche and – like his father's Beetle – was a rear-engined, air-cooled, rear-wheel drive car with monocoque construction in coupe and cabriolet styles.

The first few Porsche 356s were fabricated in Austria with hand-built aluminium bodywork, but production soon switched to Germany and bodies made of pressed steel. This advanced-for-its-time machine was a slow burner, with but a handful made in the first two years – mostly sold in Germany and Austria. But excellent build quality, aerodynamic shape and great roadholding were gradually noticed by serious motoring enthusiasts on both sides of the Atlantic and by 1955 nearly 8,000 had been sold.

One of the last variants was the desirable Speedster, introduced for American consumption in 1954. This had a raked windscreen, bucket seats and a skimpy folding top, falling into the 'ride-and-race' category beloved of sporting types who would drive to the meet, remove the windscreen and start racing. The Speedster was popular in California, but its introduction marked the way forward. The basic 356 had had its day, and the future lay with evolution models.

These continued in production for another decade, starting with the 356A in 1955, followed by the 356B in 1962 and finally by the 356C of 1964, which was capable of a very respectable 125 mph (201 km/h). Meanwhile, the first Porsche 911s hit the road and the 356 series was discontinued in 1965, by which time a grand total of 76,000 356s had been sold.

COUNTRY OF ORIGIN:
Germany
FIRST MANUFACTURED:
1949 (until 1955)
ENGINE:
1,131 cc, 1,286 cc or 1,488 cc
Flat Four
PERFORMANCE:
Top speed increased with engine size, but for early models was 84 mph (135 km/h); 0-60 mph (97 km/h) in 12.5 secs
YOU SHOULD KNOW:
The car in which James Dean died in 1955 was a Porsche 550 Spyder, a car that was actually derived from the 356 Speedster – whose track successes had prompted Porsche to develop the 550 specifically for racing purposes.

The first 356s founded a classy sports car dynasty that would eventually rise to rule the German automobile industry.

Riley RM

After a long and honourable existence as an independent manufacturer going back to the dawn of the motoring era and beyond (starting with bicycle manufacture), the various Riley companies went bust in the 1930s. Despite producing the successful Brooklands racing car in the late 1920s and early 1930s, together with a range of attractive road cars, Riley was subsumed into the Nuffield Organisation before World War II.

But the marque remained alive and in 1945 new RM Rileys appeared, though engines were unchanged from the company's robust prewar offerings. These were to be the company's last independently produced cars, though the name lived on in subsequent corporate offering from the British Motor Corporation (BMC). The RM series consisted of the RMA (later RME) saloon, the larger RMB (later RMF) saloon and the delightful and rare RMC (a convertible RMB) and RMD (a drophead coupe). There were two wheelbase lengths, the shorter to take Riley's famous 1.5 litre engine and the longer for the 2.5 litre 'Big Four'. The last of the 'real' Rileys was the Riley Pathfinder, which superseded the RMF.

That sounds like a lot of different vehicles, but actually the family resemblance is close and the flowing lines of these fine motor cars makes them instantly recognizable today. The RMs, with sturdy chassis and ash-framed bodywork, were among the last traditional British cars to be made in reasonably large quantities. Steering was by a precise rack-and-pinion system and the front suspension was wishbone and torsion bar. The interior was comfortable and well appointed, whilst handling was good and performance brisk. These attributes made the RM series popular in the 1940s and early 1950s – and extremely desirable to classic car buffs today – but sadly the era of the quality hand-build car was drawing to a close, taking Riley with it.

Well built and with good performance, the RM remains a firm favourite at modern British classic car rallies.

Rolls-Royce Silver Dawn

Rolls and Bentley cars saw the introduction of standardized production between the two marques with the appearance of the handsome Silver Dawn.

At last the days of custom-bodied Rolls-Royces were (nearly) over. The introduction of the Silver Dawn at the end of the 1940s marked the arrival of the company's first model to be sold with a standard steel body – though 64 'escaped' to be fitted with coachbuilt bodies and these are the most desirable Silver Dawns, especially soft tops like the drop-dead-gorgeous Park Ward convertible coupe. This at least confirms one traditional virtue – there was a separate chassis (riveted until 1953, welded thereafter) capable of taking either standard steel or hand-built bodies.

To reflect the hard times Britain's postwar economy was experiencing, the first Silver Dawns to emerge from the Crewe factory were left-hand drive cars destined for export. Not until the R type arrived in 1953 would these fine cars be available to home buyers. Whisper it if you dare, but the Silver Dawn was actually a Bentley with a Rolls-Royce radiator, bonnet and badge. At least Rolls-Royce was moving with the times by standardizing components between its luxury marques. Not only were Silver Dawn bodies standard production numbers that had much in common with the Bentley Mk VI, but the chassis was also shared with the Bentley Mk VI (until 1952, when the R chassis was shared by both).

Unfortunately, the great export plan was undermined by one fatal flaw – the Silver Dawn had a manual column gear change and this simply wasn't good enough for the vital American market where wealthy buyers expected (and were only willing to pay for) automatic transmission. The fault was finally remedied with the introduction of an automatic version in 1953, but by then the damage was done – only 761 Silver Dawns were ever built.

COUNTRY OF ORIGIN:
UK
FIRST MANUFACTURED:
1949 (until 1955)
ENGINE:
4,257 cc or 4,566 cc Straight Six
PERFORMANCE:
Top speed of 94 mph (151 km/h);
0-60 mph (97 km/h) in 15.2 seconds.
YOU SHOULD KNOW:
Thanks to inexperience with pressed-steel bodywork, coupled with the poor quality of postwar materials available to car makers, the legendary Rolls-Royce build quality was somewhat compromised and (shock, horror!) Silver Dawns were prone to serious rust problems.

The 1949 P4 was the first model in a range that would retain this unmistakable shape for many years to come.

Rover P4 75 'Cyclops'

The maker of the Victorian Rover Safety bicycle started producing motor cars at the dawn of the 20th century and became one of the most famous – and enduring – names in the pantheon of British motor manufacturers. Rover moved up market in the 1930s, and maintained its appeal to middle-class motorists after World War II. But in common with many cars on both sides of the Atlantic, the old-fashioned Rover P3 of 1948 was very much a prewar revival that filled the gap before new models could be introduced.

When it came, the Rover P4 four-door saloon was mould-breaking. The modern styling had more than a hint of new-fangled American streamlining about it. Indeed, the P4 owed more than a little something to the contemporary Studebaker Champion, two examples of which had been studied closely at the Rover works. This audacious piracy was not to everyone's taste but time would tell – the ongoing P4 series lasted for 15 years and became a firm favourite with the conservative target market.

The 'P4' was actually a factory designation not in popular use. Owners would normally have referred to their 'Rover 75', but the P4 75 quickly acquired the nickname 'Cyclops' for a fog lamp mounted on the radiator grille (ironically, this feature was soon dropped as it interfered with cooling). The engine came from the Rover P3, but the addition of twin carburettors improved performance.

Around 33,000 original P4 75s were sold, though when the evolution 60s, 75 Mk IIs, 80s, 90s, 95/110s, 100s and 105R/105Ss were added the grand total for the P4 series was over 130,000 units. With all those different models, it might be assumed that there was considerable change during the life of the evolving P4. but in fact that iconic design remained virtually unaltered to the end.

COUNTRY OF ORIGIN:
UK
FIRST MANUFACTURED:
1949 (until 1954)
ENGINE:
2,106 cc Straight Six
PERFORMANCE:
Top speed of 85 mph (137 km/h);
0-60 mph (97 km/h) in 21.6 secs
YOU SHOULD KNOW:
The Rover P4 75 chassis and engine were used by two ex-Rover engineers to create the two-seater Marauder sports car – but they failed to make a success of it and only 15 roadsters and coupes were actually produced in two years from 1950 before the chastened would-be entrepreneurs rejoined Rover.

Saab 92

For a car powered with a transversely-mounted, water-cooled, thermo-syphon, two-cylinder, two-stroke engine of modest proportions, the Saab 92 was influential beyond any reasonable expectation. It was not the sort of offering anticipated from a Scandinavian company that had never made a car before and was developing jet fighters for the Swedish Air Force – although the 92 certainly had a slithery shape, with an aerodynamic coefficient that was better than that of (to name but one) a Ferrari F40. Although it looked futuristic in its day, this eye-catching machine can be claimed by the 1940s – production began in December 1949.

It proved to be an immediate winner (not quite literally) when finishing second in its Swedish Rally class weeks later. This was the starting point for several years of competition success, albeit with the help of a highly tuned engine. This compact two-door coupe was also a huge hit with the Swedish car-buying public. Just 1,246 were produced in the first year, all offered with no choice of colour (dark green it had to be). But there was a waiting list of 30,000 because these sturdy machines were solid, reliable and capable of dealing with the harsh Swedish winters for which they had been designed.

There were various mechanical enhancements and the 92B arrived in 1953 with a larger rear window and increased luggage space – plus a choice of colours, a box that converted the car into a small van and a bed kit that transformed the interior into a double bed. Buoyed by continued demand, production built up and laid the foundations for the most successful car company to start from scratch after World War II. The Saab 93 arrived to supersede the 92B in 1955, but the two models were produced side by side until early 1957.

COUNTRY OF ORIGIN:
Sweden
FIRST MANUFACTURED:
1949 (until 1957)
ENGINE:
764 cc Flat Twin
PERFORMANCE:
Top speed of 65 mph (105 km/h); 0-60 mph (97 km/h) in 26.6 secs
YOU SHOULD KNOW:
When America's mighty General Motors made a list of their all-time great cars in 2008 the humble Saab 92 finished (wait for it) . . . in first place.

The 92 was the first in a long line of Saab coupes that scored numerous rally victories.

Sunbeam Talbot 90

COUNTRY OF ORIGIN:
UK
FIRST MANUFACTURED:
1948 (until 1954)
ENGINE:
1,944 cc or 2,267 cc Straight Four
PERFORMANCE:
Top speed of 85 mph (137 km/h);
0-60 mph (97 km/h) in 20.2 secs
YOU SHOULD KNOW:
Although production of the Sunbeam
Talbot 90 officially ceased in 1954, it
effectively continued for another
three years in the near-identical form
of the Mk III, which carried a
Sunbeam Supreme badge.

For those enamoured with well-built British cars, there couldn't be a better example of a postwar sports tourer. In 1948 the Sunbeam Talbot 90 was launched by the Rootes Group amidst considerable fanfare. Tuned 90s were subsequently entered into various rallies to garner valuable publicity – with considerable success. But actually the car was very popular with the buying public anyway, for its innate build quality. There was a rather pallid junior version of the 90 that wasn't, lasting just two years (the Sunbeam Talbot 80, with a Hillman Minx engine).

But the 90 went on to become an established success story. The last of the Sunbeam Talbots was a solid, graceful car built on a massively strong chassis using many Humber components. The body was a modern four-door saloon envelope with vertical grille, sweeping front wings, flat sides and a nicely rounded shape. In keeping with a habit caught from America, the early models had a column gear change, though a floor change and overdrive option appeared later. This was a stable, well-behaved vehicle with excellent road manners.

The Mk I with its none-too-impressive sidevalve engine derived from a prewar Humber came with the choice of the saloon or a pleasing two-door drophead coupe. Improvements were made to the Mk II, which appeared in 1952. A larger overhead-valve engine was fitted and the somewhat basic suspension was much improved. Twin air inlets appeared on each side of the radiator grille and the headlights were raised. The final revamp came in 1952 with the Mk IIA, whose tuned engine and higher top speed required bigger brakes, which were cooled by pierced wheels.

Around 20,000 of these upstanding machines were manufactured, so there's always a chance of enjoying a rewarding spin in this great postwar British classic.

The Talbot 90 was a fine British touring car that enjoyed rally success in the postwar years.

Triumph Roadster

How do you challenge a fabulous machine like the SS Jaguar 100? That was the question facing Sir John Black of the Standard Motor Company, who assumed the awesome Jaguar would be back after World War II (he was right, though sadly for him the resulting XK 120 was even better than its predecessor). Still, Black's hopeful answer was to task the newly acquired Triumph Motor Company with the job of producing a competitor. The plans that emerged were to evolve into the postwar Triumph Roadster which – though it never did manage to be any sort of competition for the new Jaguar – has become a classic in its own right.

Retro styling harked back unapologetically to those great 1930s coachbuilt classics, and the 1800 was launched at the Earls Court Motor Show in 1947. A bench seat was designed to accommodate three (necessitating a column change) whilst two more could perch on the rear dickey (reached via a step on the back bumper). This pair was protected by a folding windscreen, but forever remained outside the Roadster's folding soft top. The car's sweeping front wings were slightly bulbous and the headlamps appeared to hang in midair, whilst the grille was set well back from the front bumper. All of which added up to a very attractive – but unsuccessful – car.

The 1800 was succeeded by the 2000 Roadster with its larger engine, but the old-fashioned styling that so appeals to modern taste was not much appreciated in the early 1950s, when people were looking forward to an exciting new 'you've never had it so good' world. Coupled with the ruinous level of purchase tax on larger cars, this sentiment killed the Roadster in 1949. Sadly, this child of the 1930s born in the 1940s never got the chance to grow up.

The quirky Roadster was one of several cars that were killed off (at least in part) by the high purchase tax levied on big cars.

COUNTRY OF ORIGIN:
UK
FIRST MANUFACTURED:
1946 (until 1948)
ENGINE:
1,775 cc or 2,088 cc Straight Four
PERFORMANCE:
1800 – top speed of 75 mph
(121 km/h); 0-60 mph (97 km/h)
in 34.4 secs
2000 – top speed of 77 mph
(124 km/h); 0-60 mph (97 km/h)
in 27.9 secs
YOU SHOULD KNOW:
Jersey detective Bergerac managed to drive one of these handsome cars on TV, but emulating him isn't easy. Only some 2,500 1800s and a symmetrical 2,000 2000s were made and those that survive are jealously guarded by besotted owners.

Triumph Mayflower

The Mayflower had a striking body shape, but the poor engine and bad engineering ensured that the car was a notable flop.

'The Watch Charm Rolls-Royce' sounds impressive, but what a name to live up to. Sadly, the car in question didn't. The Triumph Mayflower was a postwar curiosity, with its side-valve engine and angular bodywork. This was a conscious attempt to produce a luxury small car that would ring up valuable American sales. There was a rapid increase in US car production as the 1950s loomed but demand still exceeded supply and a willingness to take wafer-thin profits in exchange for desirable dollars made British exporters competitive.

The Mayflower was conceived to exploit this situation, with a resonant name boldly borrowed from American history. And knife-edge styling was intended to put potential transatlantic buyers in mind of coachbuilt luxury cars like the Rolls-Royce that were so prestigious in the USA – though by way of insurance lip service was paid to the envelope style that had become all the rage in the late 1940s, with integral headlamps and flowing wings.

It was not (despite positive press coverage following the Mayflower's launch at the 1949 Earls Court Motor Show) a happy marriage. The car had a reasonable trim level but was woefully underpowered, had an awkward gearbox and rolled dramatically when cornering at anything near its modest maximum speed. Unsurprisingly, Americans hated it and Triumph threw in the towel after four painful years.

The world was then (and is now) sharply divided between a minority who love the Mayflower and those who believe it is the ugliest car ever made – the latter cruelly suggesting that 34,000 were sold only because there was such a shortage of cars that a soapbox with a lawnmower engine would have sold well. There's one positive aspect to this polarized thinking – the Mayflower is a very affordable entry-level classic car for weekend drivers, especially those who can't afford a real Roller.

COUNTRY OF ORIGIN:
UK
FIRST MANUFACTURED:
1949 (until 1953)
ENGINE:
1,247 cc Straight Four
PERFORMANCE:
Top speed of 63 mph (101 km/h)
YOU SHOULD KNOW:
Despite aiming squarely at the American market, Triumph actually managed to ship more Mayflowers to relatively undeveloped Sri Lanka (then Ceylon) than they ever managed to sell in the United States.

Tucker '48 Sedan

On Christmas Eve in 1946, Alex S Tremulis was hired by entrepreneur Preston Tucker and given six days to finalize the design of an all-new car. Tucker had kicked around the racing circuits of America before World War II and saw Federal support of smaller manufacturers after the conflict as a great opportunity to hit the jackpot by getting into serious automobile manufacture.

Tucker's ideas were revolutionary. The design brief encompassed modern styling coupled with high safety levels, plus innovative features like a flat-six rear engine, fuel injection, magnesium wheels, disc brakes, a swiveling spotlight at the front, padded dashboard and instrumentation on the steering wheel. Not all these daring notions made it off the drawing board, but Tremulis did his bit.

A final design was approved by Preston Tucker on New Year's Eve and the Tucker Torpedo was born. This extraordinary sedan was wide and low with streamlined fastback styling and a passenger cabin that narrowed gracefully where it met the sedan's broad rump, which had vertical air intakes for the rear-mounted engine. The prototype was ready for June 1947 and a huge launch was organized – but actually the car wasn't ready. The suspension broke and it wouldn't move, though Tucker saved the day by ad-libbing to 3,000 people for two hours until the Torpedo was fixed and could be unveiled to thunderous applause. But it was a portent of things to come.

His revolutionary flat six engine failed, but he found another (for helicopters) that fitted and ironed out transmission difficulties. Fifty pre-production cars joined the prototype and made triumphant national tours generating huge excitement and massive acclaim wherever they went. But sadly for all those who placed orders, the Preston Tucker Company folded amidst allegations of fraud and surviving Tucker '48 sedans are mostly valued museum pieces.

COUNTRY OF ORIGIN:
USA
FIRST MANUFACTURED:
1948
ENGINE:
5.5 l (335.6 cid) Flat Six
PERFORMANCE:
Top speed of 120 mph (193 km/h);
0-60 mph (97 km/h) in around
10 secs
YOU SHOULD KNOW:
Some of Tucker's problems – notably the damaging official investigation into his Accessories Programme that raised money by selling accessories on cars as yet unbuilt to eager would-be buyers – were instigated by Detroit's 'Big Three' car manufacturers who feared Tucker's formidable new challenger.

The Tucker '48 was a complete wild card that never made the grade despite its undoubted technical brilliance.

Willys MB Jeep

COUNTRY OF ORIGIN:
USA
FIRST MANUFACTURED:
1941
ENGINE:
2.2 l (134 cid) Straight Four
PERFORMANCE:
Top road speed of 55 mph (89 km/h)
YOU SHOULD KNOW:
The original prototype that evolved into the Jeep was created by American Bantam, the reorganized outfit that emerged after the bankruptcy of the American Austin Car Company, the US manufacturing arm of Britain's Austin Motor Company.

Hundreds of war movies must have featured the Willys Jeep. Forget the Sherman tank – if one vehicle symbolizes American participation in World War II it's that iconic Jeep, which usually comes bouncing along at a critical moment containing the hero, or the one person the hero doesn't want to see.

It began when the US War Department invited tenders for 'a general purpose personnel or cargo carrier especially adaptable for reconnaissance or command'. Willy-Overland was a car manufacturer whose heyday had been before World War I, though by the mid 1930s the company was on its knees. But new chief executive Joseph W Frazer had arrived from Chrysler with brilliant engineer Delmar 'Barney' Rood from Studebaker and they were up for the challenge.

The Army ran exhaustive tests on prototypes from three manufacturers (Willys-Overland, American Bantam and Ford) and Willys eventually emerged victorious, largely on the strength of a fine engine that acquired the nickname 'Go Devil'. Production of the four-wheel drive Willys MB began in 1941 and before the war ended around 650,000 had been built. Willys-Overland couldn't cope with demand alone and the design was licensed to Ford whose GPW was effectively a Willys. The functional Jeep certainly looked the part with its angled mudguards, fold-down windscreen and lack of doors – repeatedly proving its rugged military capabilities on battlefields all over the globe.

There's no definitive explanation for the 'Jeep' name (unofficial until trademarked by Willys after the war). The best explanation is that it's a corruption of the GP (General Purpose) designation, though others claim the word was used by soldiers to describe unproven equipment and appeared in a press feature on the new machine, or even that it was named after the happy Eugene the Jeep character in popular Popeye cartoons. Whatever, the name stuck!

The Jeep became an iconic symbol of the American participation in World War II.

Wolseley 6/80

The Wolseley Motor Company wasn't particularly fast out of the starting gate when British car production resumed after World War II, sharing the problems of all manufacturers when it came to obtaining raw materials. When the first postwar Wolseleys were finally rushed into production, two models were launched at the Earls Court Motor Show, both based on Morris cars. They were built alongside the Morris Oxford at the Morris Motor Company's Cowley factory, Wolseley having been a Morris subsidiary since 1927. The smaller of the two new Wolseleys was the 4/50, whilst the larger was the 6/80 (strictly speaking the Six Eighty) – these designations being a combination of the number of cylinders and the horsepower of each.

The Wolseley 6/80 was well equipped and looked impressive. It had an unmistakably Morris-style rounded rear end, but the front sported an upright Wolseley grille that was very different. But there was more than a radiator to differentiate the 6/80 from its Morris Six clone. The six-cylinder engine sported twin SU carburettors and there was a four-speed gearbox operated by a column change. The enhancements added up to lively performance and these sturdy 6/80s were used extensively as police cars, as anyone familiar with the numerous black-and-white British crime films made as supporting features in the postwar era will know.

As the Nuffield organization's luxury model, the Wolseley 6/80 benefitted from enhancements like leather upholstery, a wooden dash and door cappings, carpeting throughout, rear courtesy lights, twin fog lights, built-in reversing lamp and a red warning light inside the boot lid. The Wolseley 6/80 was a great success story. Over 25,000 were made, with nearly a third going abroad (mostly to Australia) to earn vital export revenue for Britain. The Wolseley 6/90 replaced it in 1954.

COUNTRY OF ORIGIN:
UK
FIRST MANUFACTURED:
1948 (until 1954)
ENGINE:
2,215 cc Straight Six
PERFORMANCE:
Top speed of 85 mph (138 km/h);
0-60 mph (97 km/h) in 21.4 secs
YOU SHOULD KNOW:
Unfortunately, despite widespread use as a police car, the Wolseley 6/80 had an unfortunate habit of running hot and consuming its own exhaust valves after being driven hard, thus tending to spend too much time in the police MRD (Motor Repair Depot).

All the Wolseley cars had this signature illuminated badge.

1950s

AC Ace

COUNTRY OF ORIGIN:
UK
FIRST MANUFACTURED:
1953 (until 1963)
ENGINE:
1,991 cc, 1,971 cc or 2,553 cc
Straight Six
PERFORMANCE:
Top speed of 103 mph (166 km/h);
0-60 mph (97 km/h) in 11.4 secs
YOU SHOULD KNOW:
Even as it was developing and
manufacturing high-powered cars
after World War II, AC's bread-and-
butter line was a single-seat invalid
carriage with a BSA motorcycle
engine – a lucrative Government
contract that would last until the
mid-1970s.

AC Cars (originally Auto Carriers) was one of the first independent car manufacturers in Britain. But the company went bust at the end of the 1920s and production did not get going again until the mid-1930s. Following World War II, AC bounced back with a new 2 litre model that was traditionally built using an underslung chassis and ash-framed, aluminium bodywork offered in saloon and drophead form.

The revitalized company prospered and the impressive AC Ace roadster appeared in 1953. This had a chassis designed by John Tojeiro and was initially fitted with an evolution version of the elderly AC six-cylinder engine that had first come off the drawing board just after World War I (and would remain in production until 1963). The Ace's light weight made it a potent performer – but racing driver Ken Rudd soon fitted his own competition car with a smaller but more powerful engine derived from the prewar BMW straight six motor subsequently developed by Bristol.

In 1957, this superior combination was put into production as the AC Ace-Bristol and enjoyed considerable track success, including creditable outings in the punishing Le Mans 24 race in 1957 and 1958. The original AC engine remained an option, but in 1961 Bristol stopped producing engines and this time the ever-inventive Ken Rudd suggested using a Ford Zephyr engine. Unfortunately, this wasn't an easy option, involving a chassis modification and redesigned front end. But the result was sensational, with many regarding the AC Ace 2.6 as the best ever. It could certainly shift, with a top speed of 125 mph (201 km/h), though sadly for lovers of macho sports cars only 37 were made.

Other variations on the 'Ace' theme included the Aceca closed coupe unveiled in 1954 and a four-seat Greyhound built on a stretched Ace chassis.

The splendid AC Ace saw a number of different engines fitted in succession as the production run unfolded.

Alfa Romeo Giulietta

Anyone who dreams of winning a lottery prize to secure the car of their dreams is following a well-trodden path – for the wonderful Alfa Romeo Giulietta came about as a result of just such dreams. After World War II, Alfa decided to move towards a mass-market operation. By 1952 they even had a new small saloon ready to go, but lacked financial resources to build the Giulietta Berlina.

Alfa's solution was inventive. They sold interest-bearing bonds with the promise that 200 lucky bond holders would each win a brand-new Berlina, once production began. The scheme was a success but by the appointed launch date no cars had appeared, after body-building problems. Again, Alfa's solution was ingenious – wrapping a simple sports car body around the Berlina engine and chassis to placate anxious bondholders, by showing them a real car.

The result – designed by Franco Scaglione – was a sensation. Four examples of the Giulietta Sprint coupe were completed and shown at the Turin Motor Show in 1954, with enough bodies ordered from Bertone to satisfy winning bondholders. To Alfa's surprise (and delight) their knocked-together car proved to be a huge hit.

The original Sprint coupe was swiftly followed by a Berlina saloon and a delicious open two-seater Spider designed by Pininfarina. As production continued, variants of the Sprint were produced – the Sprint Veloce, Sprint Special by Bertone and Sprint SZ by Zagato – the latter pair capable of over 120 mph (193 km/h). Carrozzeria Boneschi bodied a few Weekendina estate cars, whilst Colli also produced a small number of estates. The Giulia was introduced in 1952, essentially the Giulietta with a punchy 1,570 cc engine.

The nimble Giuliettas are great fun to drive, with good acceleration, sticky roadholding and more than enough oomph to leave any speed camera blinking in disbelief.

Is this the most stylish Italian sports car of them all?

COUNTRY OF ORIGIN:
Italy
FIRST MANUFACTURED:
1954 (until 1965)
ENGINE:
1,290 cc DOHC Straight Four
PERFORMANCE:
Top speed of 103 mph (166 km/h);
0-60 mph (97 km/h) in 13 secs
YOU SHOULD KNOW:
Question: When is a Spider not a Spider? Answer: When it's a Spyder. Italian manufacturers couldn't agree on the standard description of an open-top roadster, with Alfa opting for the former and Ferrari the latter (Porsche siding with Ferrari).

The DBR1 remains a potent competitor in classic car races.

Aston Martin DBR1

Sliding into the car that carries the registration plate XSK 497 is to sit in (and hopefully drive) the most valuable Aston Martin in the world – the DBR1/2, which still participates in classic road races. The 'R' stands for Racing, and the DBR wasn't remotely like the company's production models, though experience gained in building them did contribute to Aston Martin's custom-built 1950s racers, the DB3S and the DBR1. The latter had various incarnations with the engine, space-frame chassis and rear transaxle specially made to be teamed with components like disc brakes and suspension from the earlier DB3S. Five were built.

Initially, the DBR1 had a 2.5 litre engine – made for a new formula introduced after a tragic accident at Le Mans in 1955, when Pierre Levegh's Mercedes-Benz 300 SLR hurtled into the crowd, killing both driver and 80 spectators in the world's worst-ever motor racing disaster. After gearbox failure in the 1956 race, the DBR1 acquired a larger engine in the hope of challenging the Jaguar D-types, Maserati 450Ss and Ferrari 250s – and the car did indeed enjoy modest success in 1957. The return of gearbox problems blighted the 1958 campaign, but all that changed in 1959.

Ten years after he bought Aston Martin, David Brown saw a long-held ambition fulfilled. After an engine upgrade, XSK 497 sped to victory in the prestigious Le Mans 24 race, driven by Carroll Shelby and Roy Salvadori. Aston Martin went on to clinch the 1959 World Sportscar Championship by winning the final race of the series at Goodwood when the DBR1 of Shelby, Stirling Moss and Jack Fairman triumphed. Having reached this peak of achievement, David Brown withdrew Aston Martin from competition and set about cashing in on newly acquired racetrack reputation by creating a series of superb road cars.

COUNTRY OF ORIGIN:
UK
FIRST MANUFACTURED:
1956 (until 1959)
ENGINE:
2,493 cc or 2,992 cc DOHC
Straight Six
PERFORMANCE:
Top speed of 180 mph (290 km/h)
when slipstreaming
YOU SHOULD KNOW:
When Aston Martin clinched the
1959 World Sportscar Championship
at Goodwood the car driven by
Stirling Moss went up in flames,
putting the official pit out of
commission – privateer Graham
Whitehead then scratched his DBR1
to allow the factory entries to refuel,
Moss switched to another car . . .
and drove to victory.

Aston Martin DB4/DB4GT

The DB4 was an innovation and distinctly un-English sports car, designed by Carrozzeria Touring of Milan and manufactured in Aston Martin's recently acquired Newport Pagnell factory. Using the *superleggera* (super-light) tube frame technology pioneered by Touring, together with rack and pinion steering and a powerful new 3.7 litre engine designed by Polish engineer Tadek Marek, Aston Martin constructed a landmark car – capable of 0–100 mph (161 km/h) in a mere 21 seconds, it was the first production car to hit the ton in under 30 seconds. Altogether 1,110 DB4s were produced, in five distinct 'series' with various style changes and improvements over the course of its five-year run, of which 70 were convertibles, first introduced in 1962.

Buoyed by the success of his DBR1 in the World Sportscar Championship, Aston Martin's boss David Brown didn't hesitate to milk the DB4 for all it was worth. In 1959 he produced a beefed-up GT version on a shortened wheelbase for lower weight and better handling. Only 100 DB4 GTs were produced, 25 of which were sent as rolling chassis to Zagato in Milan where talented young Ercole Spada, later to be Zagato's chief designer, was given his first gig: turning out a spin-off limited edition with which to challenge Ferrari on the race circuits.

The 1960 GT Zagato was the ultimate evolution of the DB4. Spada installed a 314 bhp engine and effectually transformed the GT from a road car that could be raced into a racing car that could be driven on the road. Is the DB4 GT Zagato the most desirable Aston Martin ever? A price tag of £3.5 million when one comes up for sale suggests it is. Only 19 are in existence so don't expect to be driving one any time soon.

COUNTRY OF ORIGIN:
UK
FIRST MANUFACTURED:
1958 (until 1963)
ENGINE:
3,670 cc DOHC Straight Six
PERFORMANCE:
The GT Zagato had a top speed of 153 mph (246 km/h); 0-60 mph (97 km/h) in 6.1 secs
YOU SHOULD KNOW:
Four DB4 'Sanction II' cars were officially given GT Zagato status at the Milan factory in 1991 – Zagato had to disassemble an original to remind themselves of the body-building technique they had used on these iconic machines back in the early 1960s.

The DB4 Zagato proved very capable of pushing Ferrari to the limit in sports car races.

Austin-Healey 100

The quirky Austin A90 Atlantic gave birth to a rather attractive child, though not without a lot of help from midwife Donald Healey. For he it was who took an A90 engine and chassis as the basis for his prototype Healey 100 (that seductive figure representing the car's ability to top

The attractive Austin Healey 100 was a hit at the 1952 Motor Show in London, leading to a production deal with BMC.

the 'ton') which he proudly showed at the Earls Court Motor Show in 1952. The owner of the parent Austin Atlantic, BMC, was so impressed with Healey's streamlined roadster that it decided to sponsor a production run.

The BN1 model that resulted was built by Jensen Motors at West Bromwich and finished at BMC's Longbridge plant in Birmingham. The BN1 had a well-tuned A90 engine and drivetrain with modified manual transmission – a three-speed box with overdrive on second and top gears. There was independent front suspension and Girling drum brakes were fitted all round. These classics with their fold-flat windscreens and clean-cut lines with few embellishments hit the market in the summer of '53 and proved to be a popular buy, vindicating BMC's decision to back Donald Healey's vision. Better still, the Austin-Healey 100 sold well in America, establishing the marque as a serious contender in the international sports car market.

The BN2 appeared in 1955, offering a four-speed gearbox, new rear axle and a choice of natty paint jobs – for the first time including a two-tone option. To satisfy those sporty buyers who wanted extra performance, a modified 100M version was created. This could be distinguished by its louvred bonnet (complete with strap). A small number of aluminium-bodied 100S (for Sebring) cars were also made. These lightweight speedsters were the most powerful 100s of all, and the first production cars in the world to have disc brakes front and back.

COUNTRY OF ORIGIN:
UK
FIRST MANUFACTURED:
1953 (until 1957)
ENGINE:
2,660 cc Straight Four
PERFORMANCE:
Top speed of 106 mph (171 km/h);
0-60 mph (97 km/h) in 11.2 secs
YOU SHOULD KNOW:
The final '100' models became 100-6s with the fitting of a smaller straight six engine and were the 2+2 BN4 of 1956 and the two-seater BN6 of 1958. These were marginally slower than the original four-cylinder 100s but offered better acceleration.

Austin-Healey Sprite

Buoyed by the success of the Austin-Healey 100, partners BMC and Donald Healey came up with a clever new concept. The innovative 1958 Austin-Healey Sprite was designed to appeal to increasing numbers of youngsters with good incomes who were excited by the idea of open-top motoring but couldn't afford the expensive roadsters driven by their well-heeled elders. It proved to be an inspired thought.

This time the Sprite's major 'donor' was Austin's well-proven A35, with help from the Morris 1000. The engine acquired twin carburettors and the body was simplicity itself, with no external boot access or door handles. Trim was minimal and the one fancy element – pop-up headlights set into the bonnet lid – was soon abandoned as too complicated. However, fixed headlights substituted, giving this neat little sports car its characteristic appearance and quickly earning the nickname 'Frogeye Sprite' ('Bugeye' in America). The front end, wings and all, was hinged to fold forward and give access to the engine compartment. This was also the first production sports car to use integrated construction where body panels provide the vehicle's structural strength.

These nippy little cars were ideal competition material and were campaigned by the BMC Competition Department, almost immediately securing a class win at the 1958 Alpine Rally. Many privateers appreciated the Sprite's competitive qualities and the ultimate development was the Sebring Sprite built by Williams & Pritchard under the direction of rally champion John Sprinzel. This was accepted by the FIA (Fédération Internationale de l'Automobile) as a separate model in its own right.

Many Sprites are still driven for pleasure or in competition today, maintaining that early intention that they should be the most accessible of sports cars. The early 'Frogeyes' are considered more desirable than later Mk II, III and IV evolutions with more conventional styling.

COUNTRY OF ORIGIN:
UK
FIRST MANUFACTURED:
1958 (until 1961)
ENGINE:
948 cc Straight Four
PERFORMANCE:
Top speed of 83 mph (133 km/h);
0-60 mph (97 km/h) in 20.5 secs
YOU SHOULD KNOW:
MG with their Midget subsequently imitated the 'junior sports car' idea and the two junior sports cars are referred to collectively as 'Spridgets' (both were built at the MG factory in Abingdon). Triumph also jumped on the bandwagon with their 1962 Spitfire.

Any idea why the Sprite was nicknamed 'The Frogeye'?

Austin-Healey 3000

The 'Big Healey' appeared in 1956 when the 100-6 was introduced, continuing in production for a dozen years. The name was coined to differentiate between large and small Austin-Healeys after the Frogeye Sprite appeared, applying retrospectively to the 100-6 as well as the Austin-Healey 3000 that superseded it (with the number of cylinders replaced by cubic capacity to distinguish old from new as both models looked almost identical).

The 3000 Mk I had a larger engine than its predecessor and was built between 1959 and 1961. The BN7 version was an open two-seater and the BT7 a hardtop 2+2. Equipped with twin SU carburettors, the

3000 had Girling front disc brakes. The signature wire wheels were extra, as was the popular two-tone paint finish.

The Mk II (1961-1963) saw the fitting of triple carbs (soon dropped) with cosmetic changes like a new front grille. The BJ7 was introduced, featuring wind-up windows and a curved windscreen, though just two (trouble-free) carburettors. From 1963 the Mk III BJ8 – the most powerful and well-trimmed of all Big Healeys – was the only option. This 2+2 had a walnut-veneered dashboard, proper windows and servo-assisted brakes all round.

So much for the rugged road cars, of which over 40,000 were made – a great success story at a time when a coveted 3000 cost going on for double the annual salary a university graduate might expect. But that's only half the story. The Austin-Healey 3000 became a famed competitor on top racing circuits around the world, such as Le Mans and the Sebring International Raceway in Florida. Works versions of the 3000 were fitted with aluminium bodywork whilst privateers devised numerous performance-enhancing modifications, and large numbers still compete in classic sports car races. The Austin-Healey 3000 remains ultra-desirable, lasts well and still drives beautifully.

COUNTRY OF ORIGIN:
UK
FIRST MANUFACTURED:
1959 (until 1967)
ENGINE:
2,912 cc Straight Six
PERFORMANCE:
Top speed of the Mk I BT7 was 115 mph (185 km/h) with 0-60 mph (97 km/h) in 11.7 secs
YOU SHOULD KNOW:
After Donald Healey parted company with British Leyland in 1966 he went on to become Chairman of Jensen Motors, where (among other achievements) he produced the Jensen-Healey to fill the void left by the Austin-Healey 3000's discontinuation.

The Austin-Healey 3000 is generally regarded as the most desirable of the great British postwar sports cars.

Each and every one of the high-performance Continentals was custom bodied by one of the UK's leading coachbuilders.

COUNTRY OF ORIGIN:
UK
FIRST MANUFACTURED:
1955 (until 1959)
ENGINE:
4,887 cc F-head Straight Six
PERFORMANCE:
Top speed of around 120 mph
(192 km/h); 0-60 mph (97 km/h)
in 12.9 secs
YOU SHOULD KNOW:
When Rolls-Royce built something it
was meant to last, and the engine
that went into the Bentley S1 was
the final evolution of the R-R straight-
six motor that had been introduced
in 1922 to power the Rolls-Royce
Twenty series.

Bentley S1 Continental

When the Bentley marque enjoyed a healthy revival after World War II, parent company Rolls-Royce was heavily into badge engineering – the Bentley S1 was identical to the Silver Cloud I, with no more that the distinctive R-R radiator distinguishing the two luxury cars. They both used the same six-cylinder engine and had a four-speed automatic gearbox (though a manual was available until 1957).

This duopoly also represented the first standardization of pressed steel body styles by Rolls, but as far as the S1 went that was far from the whole story. The vast majority of S1s were indeed factory-built saloons, but around 150 escaped to receive the distinctive accolade of handcrafted bodywork, whilst a dozen long-wheelbase versions were also custom bodied. The tale didn't end there, for six months after the S1 appeared in 1955 the Continental made its bow. This featured a tuned engine and other performance tweaks enabling Bentley to claim that the company's new speedster – helped by a switch to lightweight aluminium bodywork – was the world's fastest production car.

None of the Continentals (431 were built) were factory bodied, which led to the creation of some exquisite body shapes and showed that the great British tradition of fine coachbuilding was alive and in rude health. The likes of Hooper, H J Mulliner, Park Ward and James Young produced some to-die-for S1 Continentals that included stunning two-door fastbacks, two-door saloons, dropheads and four-door sports saloons. Quite a number of these were left-hand drive cars destined for wealthy admirers in the United States. Even Italy's famous Pininfarina got in on the act with a distinctive fastback coupe.

The Continentals may represent the crown jewels, but with only 3,538 S1s produced each and every survivor is a cherished classic that offers serious bragging rights and is still a stately drive.

Bentley S2 Continental

The Bentley Continental S1 had done well for Rolls-Royce – as did the companion Silver Shadow I – but times they were a-changing. In particular, the bell tolled for the venerable straight-six F-head, for Rolls introduced a 6.2 litre aluminium V8 that immediately went into uprated Bentley S2s and Rolls-Royce Silver Cloud IIs.

These powerful grand tourers were ideal for their era. Motorways, autoroutes, autobahns and autostrada were proliferating all over Europe with speed limits no more than a cloud on the horizon. The large, heavy S2 was more than capable of taking full advantage, cruising at high speed for hours on end – an attribute appreciated by wealthy owners and envied by drivers of most contemporary mass-produced cars. But the new engine was teamed with an old-fashioned chassis and servo-assisted drum brakes (at least now boasting four shoes) reminiscent of the Edwardian era. It would not be long before the S3 arrived to address some of those deficiencies.

In the meantime, that old-fashioned chassis allowed the S2's Continental derivative to enjoy the stylish addition of hand-build custom bodywork, though creative coachbuilders were coming under pressure from the rise and rise of monocoque construction. But they could still deliver the goods. H J Mulliner offered traditional elegance, producing the famous 'Flying Spur' – a six-light design considered to be one of the most handsome large saloons ever. Mulliner was equally at home with the two-door coupe, though Park Ward specialized in attractive fixed and drophead coupes and other coachbuilders like James Young gatecrashed the Continental party.

The S-series would be the last real opportunity for these superb coachbuilders to strut their stuff, and the S2 Continentals are regarded as the best of the best – having more power and flexibility than S1s without the added weight of S3s.

The super S2 Continental confirmed that classic British custom coachbuilders were alive and well – just.

COUNTRY OF ORIGIN:
UK
FIRST MANUFACTURED:
1959 (until 1962)
ENGINE:
6,230 cc OHV V8
PERFORMANCE:
Top speed of 120 mph (185 km/h);
0-60 mph (97 km/h) in 11.4 secs
YOU SHOULD KNOW:
Rolls-Royce could have its cake and eat it with the S2 Continental – for both the coachbuilder entrusted with creating the closed bodies (H J Mulliner) and the company tasked with developing the open bodies (Park Ward) were actually owned by Rolls-Royce.

121

BMW-Isetta

In the aftermath of World War II the extraordinary Isetta made an appearance – a tiny minicar capable of meeting the need for affordable transport at a time when raw materials (and money) were scarce. This unmistakable vehicle was introduced in 1953 and with its hinged front, teardrop shape and small proportions was unlike anything seen before. It swept the world, being licensed in various countries – Belgium, Brazil, Britain, France, Germany and Spain – acquiring assorted nicknames like 'bubble car', 'rolling egg' and 'yogurt pot'. The most graphic was Brazil's 'FNM's soccer ball' (FNM being a heavy truck). In the latter context, and the happy event that anyone survived a head-on crash, the Isetta's occupants were supposed to exit through the canvas sunroof.

Postwar austerity saw the phrase 'bubble car' enter the language as the innovative Isetta provided affordable wheels.

Having obtained the licence to manufacture the Isetta in Germany, BMW, with Teutonic efficiency, quickly set about improving the basic design. In came a fan-cooled, four-stroke BMW motorcycle engine, the front suspension was reworked, headlights were repositioned and a larger sump installed. The big Dynastart combination generator-starter unit was retained, along with the complex drive train that turned two closely spaced rear wheels. In 1956 the Isetta Moto Coupe DeLuxe was introduced, the 'DeLuxe' element being new sliding windows and protruding front crash bars. This became the BMW-Isetta 300 with a larger engine that improved acceleration and aided hill climbing.

The BMW 600 was an enlarged Isetta stretched to contain four seats, with an unchanged front, two side doors and a 582 cc twin-cylinder motorcycle engine – it was made from 1957 to 1959 but wasn't a success as customers were by then clamouring for real cars. However, production of the 300 continued until 1962 to service the financially challenged and by the time the last hinged front slammed shut in the factory over 161,000 of the handy little roadrunners had been built.

COUNTRY OF ORIGIN:
Germany
FIRST MANUFACTURED:
1955 (until 1962)
ENGINE:
247 cc or 298 cc Single Cylinder
PERFORMANCE:
Top speed of both models was
54 mph (87 km/h)
YOU SHOULD KNOW:
Original Italian Isettas were entered in the legendary Mille Miglia road race in 1954 and took the top three places in the economy class, with the winner averaging nearly 45 mph (72 km/h) during a punishing run that lasted for some 22 hours.

BMW 507

After nearly going bust in the late 1950s, BMW recovered to become a giant of the international automobile industry, but it was a close-run thing. The car that did the damage and pushed the Bavarian outfit to the brink was the BMW 507. It all started innocently enough in 1954. American importer Max Hoffman saw a niche for a $5,000 sports car and was confident he could sell several thousand a year in the USA.

This ambitious project was duly undertaken by BMW, with the prototype 507 TS (for Touring Sport) making its debut at New York's Waldorf-Astoria Hotel in the summer of 1955. The idea was to produce a high-performance two-door roadster that could compete with Mercedes-Benz and Jaguar on the race track, thus reminding everyone of BMW's racing pedigree and gaining valuable publicity for mass-market road cars.

With its inward-slanting grille and curvaceous lines, the 507 TS was almost shark-like. It was based on a modified platform from the BMW 503, the handsome 2+2 coupe and cabriolet model also introduced in 1955. Albrecht von Goertz designed both sporty models and each was powered by the company's lightweight OHV V8 engine, as borrowed from the BMW 502, and fitted with twin Solex Zenith carburettors.

The 507's body was hand-crafted in aluminium, with the result that no two cars were identical. There was a removable hardtop available, but if ordered it was made to fit the car in question and these hardtops are not interchangeable. The result of all this detailed work was a price tag double that originally envisaged by Max Hoffman, a virtually unsaleable car, massive accumulated losses for BMW and discontinuation of both loss-making sports cars in 1959. Only 252 507s and 414 503s were built – making these rare 1950s BMWs ultra-collectable.

COUNTRY OF ORIGIN:
Germany
FIRST MANUFACTURED:
1956 (until 1959)
ENGINE:
3,168 cc OHV V8
PERFORMANCE:
BMW claimed a top speed of 140 mph (225 km/h) and 0-60 mph (97 km/h) in around 10 secs
YOU SHOULD KNOW:
Elvis Presley bought a white 507 TS whilst on Army service in Germany, but rather crassly replaced the engine with a Ford V8 after returning to the States – he later gave the car to actress Ursula Andress.

The superb build quality of the 507 took BMW to the very brink of terminal financial collapse.

Borgward Isabella

Carl Borgward was an innovative German engineer who made his mark in the 1920s with the *Blitzkarren* (Lightning Cart) – a tiny three-wheeled delivery van. Cars followed in the 1930s and production was resumed after World War II with the Borgward Hansa 1500, a striking modern saloon car that made its debut in 1949 – the first all-new postwar model to appear in Germany.

In 1954 the Isabella superseded the Hansa, though initially the name was not changed. The Isabella proved to be a winner, and remained in production for the rest of the company's short life. Named after Carl Borgward's wife, this medium sized two-door saloon car was a huge success, despite early models being affected by teething troubles. These were in part due to innovative features like a swing rear axle, coil spring suspension all round, a hydraulic clutch and four-speed box with synchromesh on all gears. The Isabella retained the 'three box' body style that Borgward pioneered with the Hansa, which became a manufacturing norm in Germany.

1955 saw the introduction of an estate-car version, and a cabriolet that required considerable modification of the monocoque body and was therefore expensive. Carl Borgward continued to innovate and the Isabella's looks were improved with an attractive coupe model that was introduced in 1957, utilizing the cabriolet's more powerful engine. This in turn found its way into the upmarket saloons and estate cars by 1958.

Isabellas continued to sell well, but there was trouble in store. In 1961 Borgward was liquidated, despite Carl Borgward's insistence that the company was solvent. He was proved right, but by then a manufacturer who might have become another great German automotive success story had been forced out of business. Borgward's machinery was sold to Argentina where more Isabellas were produced.

COUNTRY OF ORIGIN:
Germany
FIRST MANUFACTURED:
1954 (until 1962)
ENGINE:
1,493 cc Straight Four
PERFORMANCE:
Top speed around 81 mph (130 km/h)
YOU SHOULD KNOW:
The untimely demise of Borgward allowed BMW to launch its stylish 1500 line in 1962, to plug a big gap left by the vanished Isabella – a lucky break that is said to have rescued BMW from possible bankruptcy and laid the foundation for future success.

Buick Limited

Back in 1942 when World War II rudely interrupted American car production, the massive Buick Limited models were the most expensive this mid-market company produced, riding sedately on the longest wheelbase and having lavish interiors. The 'Limited' designation was appropriate, as these exclusive limousines and touring sedans sold in small numbers.

Fast forward to 1958, when a Buick Limited series was revived as the ultimate Buick, designed as a top-end luxury challenger to smartly restyled Chryslers – and with its stretched rear end the Limited was the biggest car on the market, outgunning the rival Imperial by several inches. Size (at least in the minds of car makers) definitely mattered.

Junior Buicks for the new model year saw the application of flashy chrome and indubitable styling excesses, and the classy Limiteds were hardly more restrained. They had the extraordinary Fashion-Aire Dynastar front end consisting of 160 chrome-plated squares, each with four concave faces, that ensured the grille constantly sparkled. And Limiteds (which were essentially upgraded Roadmasters) flaunted more chrome and polished steel than any car ever made, earning nicknames like 'Rhinestone Cowboy' and 'Wurlitzer on Wheels'.

Limiteds have quad headlights, acres of sparkling brightwork and U-shaped rear side panels with vertical hatching. Three models were offered – a four-door Riviera sedan, a two-door Riviera coupe and the luscious convertible. Interiors were finished to the highest standard and some even swore the big Buick was better than its Cadillac rivals. But badge perception is hard to beat; the established luxury marque massively outsold the Limited and that was that – after just one year the revived Limited expired again. It was replaced by the less impressive (and cheaper) Electra 225. However, that makes these glittering gems both rare and very desirable today, when Limiteds are seen to represent the very soul of excessive late-1950s American auto-culture.

COUNTRY OF ORIGIN:
USA
FIRST MANUFACTURED:
1958
ENGINE:
6 l (364 cid)V8
PERFORMANCE:
Top speed around 85 mph
(138 km/h)
YOU SHOULD KNOW:
Limited models had Buick's hugely complicated automatic Flight-Pitch Dynaflow transmission, which delivered a terrifically smooth ride but was heavy on fuel – around 11 miles per gallon on a run and less in the city.

Car or work of art – or is it simply a Wurlitzer on Wheels?

Chevrolet Bel Air

COUNTRY OF ORIGIN:
USA
FIRST MANUFACTURED:
1953 (until 1975)
ENGINE:
Numerous options, usually the
3.9 l (235 cid) Straight Six or
4.3 l (265 cid) V8
PERFORMANCE:
Varied by model and engine, but
the '53 launch model was capable of
87 mph (140 km/h)
YOU SHOULD KNOW:
1955 was the year when the
50-millionth car built by Chevrolet
finally rolled off the line . . . and by
accident or design it turned out to be
a Bel Air hardtop that was especially
trimmed in gold to mark the
momentous milestone.

The Bel Air name appeared in 1950 but did not become a distinct series until 1953, when it was designated as Chevrolet's premium offering, pitched at growing numbers of middle-class buyers who were migrating to leafy suburbs. Lavish trim and heavy chromework distinguished spanking new Bel Airs from lesser Chevys, with two- and four-door sedans, a sports coupe and convertible offered to eager buyers.

Dealers were delighted to find (with over half a million sold) that demand was brisk. An eight-seat Townsman station wagon was added for 1954, whilst the following year saw an all-new contemporary look for six Bel Air body styles, plus strikingly colour-coordinated interiors and the chance to select the fabulous new V8 Turbo-Fire engine. Other optional extras included air conditioning, power steering and electric windows. Although the stylish Nomad station wagon was nominally part of the Bel Air family, the wagon that did serious business was the Townsman four-door model.

In 1956 a new four-door Sport Sedan was introduced and the Bel Air range had a facelift. This saw a reworked grille, revised wheel apertures and two-tone paint jobs – all combining to give these big cars a sense of speed, even at rest. A masterly reworking in 1957 made cars that were effectively unchanged mechanically look completely different, with sharp fins and aluminium trim panels.

Classic mid-1950 Chevrolets are considered to be among the most attractive the company ever made, with the '55, '56 and '57 Bel Airs (commonly called TriFives) being those most eagerly sought by collectors – especially convertibles. In 1958, the Impala arrived to share senior status with the Bel Airs, which thereafter – though retaining great mid-range status and selling in large numbers – slowly started sliding down the totem, finishing up as no-frills fleet cars in the 1970s.

The Bel Air was not just any old Chevy, but a rather superior model that aimed higher than the marque's traditional blue-collar buyers.

Chevrolet Nomad

In most series that feature coupes and convertibles, these are the most sought-after body styles. But one exception to the rule is the famous Chevy Nomad, described by one authority as 'the prettiest station wagon ever made'. This may display just a trace of hyperbole, but there's no doubting the enduring appeal of this handsome vehicle – though in truth its reputation has largely been established with the benefit of hindsight.

The Nomad was hastily introduced in 1955 after the prototype received a great reception – perhaps too hastily. It was nominally part of Chevrolet's Bel Air line but differed in most respects – not least in being the most expensive Chevy ever, which didn't help sales. Neither did the fact that it had but two passenger doors, a slanting tailgate that was both heavy and prone to admitting rainwater, inadequate interior ventilation and a nasty habit of sucking in exhaust fumes when the engine was running with the tailgate open.

Even so, the Nomad offered excellent performance and many people were seduced by its looks. So it returned for 1956, albeit with some of the more expensive trim features dispensed with, putting the Nomad in line with comparable Bel Air models. Chevrolet hoped that sales would take off, but even with production economies the price went up and the ambitious target of 10,000 sales proved to be a forlorn hope. Plans for an uprated 1958 version were therefore quietly abandoned.

The name lingered on, but the 'true' Nomad expired after just three years, a victim of its status as a flawed upscale vehicle with a hefty price tag to match. But the 1955-57 Nomads remain coveted classics, with their undoubted beauty more than overcoming some beastly faults in the eyes of Chevy enthusiasts.

Grandly tagged as the prettiest station wagon in the world, the Nomad was also the most expensive – causing its demise.

COUNTRY OF ORIGIN:
USA
FIRST MANUFACTURED:
1955 (until 1957)
ENGINE:
4.3 l (265 cid) V8
PERFORMANCE:
With the 'Super Power Pack' engine, a top speed of 120 mph (km/h); 0-60 mph (97 km/h) in 8.1 secs
YOU SHOULD KNOW:
The Nomad prototype was one of three concept cars based on the Corvette shown at the 1954 General Motors Motorama at New York's Waldorf Astoria Hotel – intended as no more than a 'halo car' to showcase Chevy's design abilities, the reaction was so positive that this racy station wagon was hurried into production.

The DS is a leading contender when it comes to choosing the most innovative car of all time.

Citroen DS

The debut of the Citroen DS series at the Paris Salon in 1955 was sensational. Some humorously suggested Flaminio Bertoni's design was so futuristic that aliens must have invaded his drawing office and sketched out a 23rd-century machine, but the point was well made. No other car before or since has provoked so much comment, for this was truly unlike any other car seen before or since. The European reaction was replicated when the DS 19 appeared in New York, billed as 'the dream car of tomorrow, on the road today'. This aerodynamic marvel boasted a 'Citro-Matic' hydraulic system that controlled the suspension, steering, brakes, clutch and gear change.

It followed a grand tradition of French cars that broke the mould, and would go on to enjoy two successful decades of automotive life. Throughout that period it remained the world's most technically advanced car, packed with amazing innovations. The DS was a machine that divided opinion into 'love it' and 'hate it' camps and whilst technical wizardry delighted supporters, detractors seized upon the car's complexity as a disadvantage.

But some even worshipped this slinky car – its DS designation denoted *Desiree Speciale*, but these letters are pronounced the same way as the French *déesse*, which means goddess. So 'Goddess' the DS became, and remained. Even those who disliked the car had to admit that roadholding, ride quality, handling and braking were exceptional. A station wagon and rare convertible were introduced, and further enhancements throughout the production run ensured that the DS remained at the cutting edge with styling updates in 1962 and 1967, plus the introduction of features like electronic fuel injection, five gears, automatic transmission and headlights that turned with the steering. Though relatively few sold in America (just 38,000) nearly 1.5 million DS models were produced.

COUNTRY OF ORIGIN:
France
FIRST MANUFACTURED:
1955 (until 1975)
ENGINE:
1,911 cc OHV Straight Four
PERFORMANCE:
Top speed of 98 mph (158 km/h);
0-60 mph (97 km/h) in 21.2 secs
YOU SHOULD KNOW:
A junior (more affordable) look-alike version of the DS was introduced in 1957, without many of the DS's advanced features – though it too had a punning model name in ID (as in *idée* for idea).

Daimler SP250 (Dart)

Launched in New York as the Dart, Daimler's first sports car was officially renamed the SP250 after Dodge claimed copyright. The car was a barefaced attempt to ride the wave of popularity for British sports cars in America, and it looked much more transatlantic than the Triumph or MG competitors on which its chassis was based. Daimler's boldness, and hurry to enter the market, resulted in confused styling. From the front, the fibreglass moulded lines curl sinuously down to the wide grille. From the rear three-quarter view, the futuristic horizontal and vertical lines forming the SP250's outrageous fins seem to belong to another car.

Even so, the awkward design looks sexy – but it is the authoritative throaty rumble from the SP250's twin exhausts that confirms it. Powered by a 2.5 litre V8 engine, the SP250 is a joy to drive. Once initial problems of the chassis (the doors on the original 'A' spec version had a tendency to fly open on tight bends) had been ironed out, the car began to fulfil its destiny as a two-door, open-topped king of the road. It was, and is, fun. Its responsive acceleration appeals as strongly to enthusiasts as it once did to the British police, who fielded a number of automatic versions as high-speed pursuit vehicles.

The real surprise is that Daimler ever made the SP250 (Dart). For decades the company had been associated firmly with upmarket family saloons and limited production of luxury limousines (clientele included the British Royal Family). The SP250 is really a delightful aberration. Its oddity, as well as its success, marks it as a product of a very specific, late 1950s social climate.

COUNTRY OF ORIGIN:
UK
FIRST MANUFACTURED:
1959 (until 1964)
ENGINE:
2,548cc OHV V8
PERFORMANCE:
Top speed of 123mph (198 km/h);
0-60 mph (97 km/h) in 9.2 secs
YOU SHOULD KNOW:
Take a head-on look at the SP250 (Dart) engine grille, and you won't be surprised that some enthusiasts call it 'the Catfish'

You're nicked, sunshine – the British police used SP250s to pursue speeding motorists on the then-new M1 motorway.

Daimler Majestic Major

COUNTRY OF ORIGIN:
UK
FIRST MANUFACTURED:
1959 (until 1968)
ENGINE:
4,561 cc V8
PERFORMANCE:
Top speed of 120 mph (193 km/h);
0-60 mph (97 km/h) in 9.7 secs
YOU SHOULD KNOW:
Jaguar Cars purchased Daimler in
1960 and experimented by putting
the 4.5 litre Daimler V8 engine from
the Majestic Major into a Jaguar
Mk X – and thus equipped the lighter
car proved capable of reaching a top
speed of 130 mph (209 km/h).

The Daimler Majestic 101 was launched in 1958, in the hope that there was still demand for a sturdy saloon in the best traditions of this famous marque. The Majestic was mechanically advanced but had a traditional coachbuilt body on a heavy chassis that made this large car hard to manoeuvre – though a lusty 3.8 litre engine meant the Majestic could sail past 100 mph (161 km/h). Barely a year after the Majestic hit the street, the Majestic Major appeared in 1959.

The two models ran concurrently until 1962 and were virtually impossible to tell apart. The difference was beneath the bonnet, where a new hemi-head V8 engine lurked. This was both lighter and more powerful than the old straight six, considerably improving the Majestic Major's performance. Ironically, more Majestics than Majestic Majors were sold, despite the fact that the former was available for five years and the latter for nearly a decade.

The Majestic Major was certainly a high-performance luxury car that could reasonably hope to attract executives who had not quite reached Rolls-Royce or Bentley status, but still liked the thought of being seen in a prestigious car. But perhaps it was stylistically old before its time, with more modern alternatives having better curb appeal for a new generation of businessmen. And despite an impressive top speed, advanced Borg Warner automatic transmission and servo disc brakes all round, this clumsy machine had a huge turning circle and power steering was not standard until 1964. It was not successful, with fewer than 1,200 built.

A stretched DR450 limousine based on the Majestic Major appeared in 1961, for those with chauffeurs and the carriage trade. It was also adapted into a hearse, many examples of which are still doing stately service today – definitely not the version you want to ride.

Launched just before the Swinging Sixties, Daimler's sturdy Majestic Major managed to look old before its time.

Ferrari 250 GT Spyder California

Maranello's racing success in the mid 1950s happened in such a flurry of technical and design innovation that for several years the latest Ferrari race cars had no roadgoing versions. The Ferrari 250 Cabriolet Series I, an open version of Pininfarina's lovely 250GT Coupe, launched in 1957 to meet the demand, growled satisfactorily on the road, but lacked the dual purpose characteristic of Ferrari's earliest open sports racing cars. Even so, Ferrari's American customers were slavering for it, and the biggest dealer in Southern California begged his friend Enzo Ferrari to raise his quota.

Enzo did his friend proud. He created the Ferrari 250 GT Spyder California. The 'Cal Spyder' was vintage racing Ferrari, at the sharp end of automotive progress but – somehow – both street legal and a work of art (with consummate grace, Scaglietti and Pininfarina each credited the other for the stunning design). California took it to its glossily competitive heart. Stars like Paul Newman, Steve McQueen, James Coburn and Clint Eastwood returned Enzo's compliment, and raced for real; but common sense (as ever, many buyers wanted the look, not the danger) dictated that some Cal Spyders intended for road use were more steel than aluminium, and were gradually invested with carpets and other touches of luxury. There were constant mechanical upgrades like disc brakes. Most significant of all was the introduction of the short wheel base (SWB) chassis, which greatly improved rigidity and handling. The 250 GT Spyder California SWB is the apotheosis of genuine dual-purpose open-air Ferraris, and the last of them.

All the more surprising that in 2009, Ferrari revived the name California Spyder for a car that may be a marvellous luxury sports car, but owes much more to Hollywood than to racing.

The Cal Spyder started as a pure racer for the American market, but soon became the car that everyone on the West Coast wanted to be seen in.

COUNTRY OF ORIGIN:
Italy
FIRST MANUFACTURED:
1957 (until 1963)
ENGINE:
2,953 cc V12
PERFORMANCE:
Top speed of 155 mph (250 km/h);
0-60 mph (97 km/h) in 7.2 secs
YOU SHOULD KNOW:
The rarity and desirability of the Ferrari 250 GT Spyder California (only around 100 were ever made) makes it one of the most treasured vehicles on earth. In 2008, a black 1961 SWB Spyder Cal formerly owned by the actor James Coburn (*The Magnificent Seven; The Great Escape* etc) was sold at auction for $10.894 million.

The Super America was one of Ferrari's most impressive shots at the vital US market.

Ferrari 410 Super America

Though Europe was still struggling back to its economic feet in the early 1950s, its enthusiasm for glamour was already shaping Ferrari's success. Of course, only a chosen few, even among the wealthy, could hope to drive one of the stream of fabulous race and road cars the company produced; and most of them were more than happy to own one or another version of the Ferrari 250GT like the Boano or the Ellena. But from the very beginning, Enzo Ferrari had been careful to foster the cream of his clientele by continuously upping the ante on his own success. For the discerning (targeted) elite, and with an eye on the much wealthier, emerging US market, he created a series of big V12 touring models with customized coachwork. The Ferrari America was one of them. It had beauty, luxury and high performance – but it still wasn't exclusive enough. In 1955 the 375 Ferrari America chassis was re-conceived as the wider, heavier and yet more muscular Ferrari 410 Super America.

In just four years, the 410 Super America appeared in three

versions, and the 5 litre Lampredi V12 engine could be tuned up to 400 horsepower. They came as coupe or cabriolet, with swooping curves that spoke insouciantly of elegance and speed. The very best coachbuilders (Ghia, Scaglietti, Boano) designed at least one, and Pininfarina worked his magic on the rest. Of the total of 35 Ferrari 410 Super Americas, the only features common to all are the signature low front grille, and the side vents behind the front wheels. They are not just ultra-exclusive. When the cars were made, they were reassuringly expensive – double the price of the contemporary Mercedes-Benz 300SL 'Gullwing', enough to satisfy the exalted status of owners including the Aga Khan, Gianni Agnelli and Nelson Rockefeller.

COUNTRY OF ORIGIN:
Italy
FIRST MANUFACTURED:
1955 (until 1959)
ENGINE:
4,962 cc V12
PERFORMANCE:
Top speed of 162 mph (261 km/h);
0-60 mph (97 km/h) in 5.8 secs
YOU SHOULD KNOW:
It's easy to confuse the 410 SA with
the Ferrari 400 Super America,
introduced in 1959 after the 410 SA.
The 400 SA was given an uprated
4.0 l version of the refined and
generally more reliable Colombo V12
engine, which never matched the
Lampredi's power.

The Cinquecento – Fiat's minicar appealed across all social classes and became a major feature of the Italian streetscape.

COUNTRY OF ORIGIN:
Italy
FIRST MANUFACTURED:
1957 (until 1975)
ENGINE:
479 cc, 499 cc, 594 cc Straight Two, air-cooled
PERFORMANCE:
Top speed of 59 mph (95 km/h)
YOU SHOULD KNOW:
There's an all-electric Fiat 500 made by NICE Car Co and the Italian firm Micro-Vett. Powered by lithium ion batteries, it has a range of 55 mi (89 km) and a top speed of 55 mph (89 km/h) – plenty for a typical day in the city.

Fiat 500

The Fiat 500 is an adorable bubble of a car conceived by a philosophy so successful that in 2007 it was relaunched in its umpteenth incarnation. The philosophy was originally dictated by post-World War II economics. Fiat took its prewar 500 (the 'Topolino', of 1936) and created the first true 'city car', capable (just) of carrying four people in completely basic, no-frills, pitifully low-powered, rear-engined, bony discomfort. The 'Nuova 500', designed by Dante Giacosa, instantly became the definitive 'Cinquecento'. Never mind it was necessarily small, cheap and utilitarian. It was reliable, and almost as basic to maintain as the scooters it replaced. Most of all it was loved because it was insanely cute.

The Cinquecento did for Italy what the 2CV did for France. It was classless, meaning you got jounced about on Italy's cobbled streets and uneven tarmac just as much on a romantic date as you did packing the family to market; and its appeal has endured as much as the simple purity of its engineering and styling. Between 1957 and 1975, Fiat introduced at least six versions, losing the 'suicide doors', switching the engine from rear to front, experimenting with chrome add-ons, and calling the 500 the 'Bambino'. But as any owner will confirm, it eventually proved more fun to keep your old, battered friend on the road than to buy new.

Only in 2004, with the 'Trepiuno', did Fiat rediscover its original 500 magic – the radically modern redesign looks much more like a descendant of the classic Cinquecento than anything in between; and the 500 Abarth, the Sports version based on the Trepiuno, caused a sensation in 2007 for marrying low cost to fabulous performance, comfort and sporty looks. If any car has a philosophical pedigree – of doing a simple thing with brilliance and flair, cheaply – suited to the economic climate, it's the Fiat 500.

Ford Thunderbird

Think the Pacific surf thundering in, and the Coast Highway glinting silver, snaking past the sunsplashed canyons. The Thunderbird – the 'T-Bird' of legend – was born to the infectious upbeat of Jan & Dean and the Beach Boys, synonymous with youth and fun and the fulfilled promise of a comfortable post World War II America. In fact it was devised as the first 'personal luxury' car to be available at a mass market price. It only looked like a sports car, its two-seater bodywork slung low, but with a longer, heavier body, just enough tailfin and features borrowed from bigger family cars to give it its characteristic, solid sleekness. No mere sports car of the era could match the T-Bird's standard fittings (power steering, brakes, windows; radio; heater; choice of transmission; and five possible colours) at the price.

The original Thunderbird was thought to be a little soft and loose to drive; but it was the perfect ride for America's growing Interstate Highway system, and when its V8 was on song, its performance easily matched the beautiful styling, at speeds well over 100 mph (160 km/h). More than 50 years later, riding a T-Bird still feels just as thrilling: the interior is a microcosm of the 1950s USA, once described as 'like a contemporary juke-box, stylized and brash'.

Since the day it was first shown (on which orders for 4000 were placed!) the Thunderbird legend has grown steadily. Its evolution has gone full circle from two-seater to four-seater, luxury and Continental luxury, two-door sport coupe and back to 'retro' two-seater, in just thirteen generations spanning every automotive development. But no technology can recreate the spirit in which the 1955 Thunderbird was conceived, received and driven. The gods still smile at the thought.

COUNTRY OF ORIGIN:
USA
FIRST MANUFACTURED:
1955 (until 2005)
ENGINE:
4.8 l (292 cid) Y-block (OHV) V8
PERFORMANCE:
Top speed of 110 mph (177 km/h);
0-60 mph (97 km/h) in 9.5 secs
YOU SHOULD KNOW:
Only an accident of good taste prevented the car from being named the 'Hep Cat' or the 'Beaver' – serious suggestions before 'Thunderbird' saved the day.

The T-Bird's glitzy interior shared distinctive styling cues with contemporary jukeboxes.

Ford Zephyr Mark II

COUNTRY OF ORIGIN:
UK
FIRST MANUFACTURED:
1956 (until1962)
ENGINE:
2,553 cc OHV Straight Six
PERFORMANCE:
Top speed of 89 mph (143 km/h);
0-60 mph (97 km/h) in 17 secs
YOU SHOULD KNOW:
A factory-modified Mk II rallying
version had a top speed over
101 mph (163 km/h) and achieved
0-60 mph (97 km/h) in less than
10 secs.

By the middle of the 1950s Ford of Britain was reaching its industrial zenith. Success at every market level was maintained by constant innovation and improvement. With its Consul/Zephyr/Zodiac range, Ford had already struck gold in both sales and motorsport. A Mk I Zephyr (originally known as the Zephyr Six) had won the Monte Carlo Rally in 1953 and the East African Safari in 1955, enhancing the car's reputation for good value. Problems of understeer and limited performance were overcome with easily made modifications that improved handling and added as much as 20 mph (32 km/h) to the top speed.

Success bred success. In 1956 the new Mk II Consul/Zephyr/Zodiac models were acclaimed as 'the three graces', thanks to their stunningly family-friendly new lines. The Mk II Zephyr benefited most. Longer, heavier, wider and more powerful, its popularity as the biggest mass market family car was assured – considerably helped by a run of competition successes crowned by winning outright the 1959 RAC Rally.

It was the Mk II Zephyr which opened the door for Ford's later adventures with the Cortina and the Escort. Many are still competing in Classic and other events: and drivers' reports of powering a Mk II up a snowy mountain pass, or controlling the well-behaved heavyweight hurtling through mud-clogged forest lanes, continue to excite everyone who has ever dreamed of their family car transforming into a supercar. The Zephyr Mk II is the car that proves you don't have to be rich to be a winner.

The Zephyr Mk II sought to bring the American look that was all the rage to Britain.

Ford Anglia 105E/123E Super

The Anglia, with its slanting rear window, had revolutionary styling for the time.

Although it was designed, according to the philosophy of its era, to fit into an existing range of Ford cars, the Anglia 105E was all new. As a two-door, four-seater family saloon it broke completely with traditional styling. The wind-tunnel tested and streamlined smoothness of its swept-back nose and flat roof line, the muted tailfins, and reverse-raked rear window (like contemporary Lincolns and Mercurys) suggested American glamour even in the standard budget version. Most people opted for the 105E Deluxe, with a full width grille, chrome side strips and rear light surrounds, and two-tone trim.

Equally exciting was the innovative 105E engine, a gleaming 997cc OHV (overhead valve) straight four which became the basis of Ford engines for many years. Easy to tune, and as 'tweakable' as the styling (Ford Marketing supplied a never-ending selection of add-ons), the Kent engine quickly became beloved of hot-rodders. In fact the 105E was so successful on all counts that in 1962 Ford introduced what it believed to be the car's apotheosis – the Anglia 123E Super. It had more chrome, more comfort, more power and more flash; and corresponded exactly to a national mood.

The 105E/123E is what people mean by an Anglia. It has never been out of style. As one generation of drivers enjoyed it and moved on, another discovered its motor sport potential. It's instantly recognisable on the track or in the street, an icon of a peculiarly British vision of modernity. Now it's loved for its retro-chic and adaptability at every level. A blue 105E featured (airborne, and magically customized to hold nine people!) in the film Harry Potter and the Chamber of Secrets, demonstrating conclusively how the Anglia is cherished.

COUNTRY OF ORIGIN:
UK
FIRST MANUFACTURED:
1959 (105E); 1962 (123E) (until 1967)
ENGINE:
997cc (105E), 1,198cc (123E) OHV
Straight Four
PERFORMANCE:
Top speed of 74 mph (119 km/h)
YOU SHOULD KNOW:
In 1962 a Ford Anglia 105E was driven for seven days and nights at the Montlhery circuit near Paris, at an average speed of more than 83 mph (133 km/h). It set six new world records for a car under 1,000 cc.

137

The Hudson radiator badge signified strength, integrity and the spirit of adventure.

Hudson Hornet

Hudson cars were one of the early US auto building success stories. Hudson's history of big, powerful models made the company competitive with its giant Detroit neighbours like Ford and Chrysler. It survived the Depression, and bounced back from war production in 1948 quicker than almost everybody else – and with a brilliant Big Idea for its first totally new postwar model, the Commodore. It was called 'step-down' design: passengers 'stepped down' to a floor pan recessed into the car's unitary frame. The lower centre of gravity improved handling, and made for a more comfortable and spacious ride that still made the most of the Commodore's powerful engine.

The Hudson Hornet introduced in 1951 was really an upgraded Commodore, but it looked and felt like its own boss. Low-slung, with enclosed rear wheels, it looked sleek and muscular rearing up from the inverted 'V' chrome grin of its front grille, over the bulbous hood to the split windscreen and tapering off towards the rear. This was Hudson's advertised new 'Skyliner Styling' and it came with a 'Custom-Luxury' interior spacious enough for six people. What made the car truly outstanding was the huge new 'H-145' engine, in which the 4.3 litre inline six of the Commodore was increased to 5.0 litres. Its performance alerted Hudson to the Hornet's racing potential, and suitably tweaked versions won 79 races between 1951-54, including NASCAR championships in '51,'52 and '53, and AAA championships in '52, '53 (12 out of the 13 races) and '54.

The Hornet was Hudson's finest hour. It handled like a dream despite its size. It looked terrific. It even fulfilled its advertising claims of having 'a definite look of the future' and, thanks to its 'engine sensation', 'blazing getaway-activity'. If only.

COUNTRY OF ORIGIN:
USA
FIRST MANUFACTURED:
1951 (until 1954)
ENGINE:
5.0 l (308 cid) 'H-145' Straight Six
PERFORMANCE:
Top speed of 99 mph (160 km/h); 0-60 mph (97 km/h) in 14.5 secs
YOU SHOULD KNOW:
The NASCAR and AAA Hudson racing team drivers were the legendary stock car aces Marshall Teague, Herb Thomas and Tim Flock. Their cars were emblazoned with 'Fabulous Hudson Hornet', and one of them can be seen, fully restored, at the Ypsilanti Automotive Heritage Museum in Michigan.

Jaguar XK150

Though Jaguar is now a subsidiary of Ford, the marque is still esteemed for its pre- and post-World War II reputation for luxury saloons and competitive sports cars. In 1948, Jaguar had thrilled the motoring world with its XK120, still sought after and enjoyed for its mean, lean, sporting lines. Nine years and the XK140 later, the company's wealth of racing and marketing experience was poured into the XK150, the last and most glamorous of its species. Obvious family resemblances were misleading: the XK150's subtly improved, but still old world styling incorporated extensive modernization that paved the way for both the stylistic Great Statement of the E-Type and the mechanical glories of the XK engine-powered sports saloons of the 1960s.

In fact the first XK 150s were not as quick as their predecessors. Their beefed-up curves (with the new one-piece windscreen, wider bonnet and wing line raised almost to door level, the heavier car still looked as athletically poised and dangerous as the leaping mascot itself!) relied on the XK140's standard 3.4 engine. But from 1958, the 3.4 and (later) 3.8 litre versions could be tuned to 'S' form, restoring real performance to match the car's aura of stylish menace. You could have a Fixed Head Coupe (FHC), a two-to-three seater like the Drop Head Coupe (DHC), or the Roadster.

In the XK150's short production life (to October 1960), almost 10,000 owners succumbed in equal measure to the magic of the three versions. Subsequently, in his first film as actor/director, Clint Eastwood immortalized one of them in *Play Misty For Me*. In every way, the XK150 bears the hallmarks of discriminating taste: like so many Jaguars, it talks quietly, and walks the walk effortlessly, on demand.

COUNTRY OF ORIGIN:
UK
FIRST MANUFACTURED:
1957 (until 1960)
ENGINE:
DOHC Straight Six (available as 3.4/3.4S and 3.8/3.8S)
PERFORMANCE:
A 3.4 l XK150S FHC achieved a top speed of 132 mph (212 km/h) and 0-60 mph (97 km/h) in 7.8 secs.
YOU SHOULD KNOW:
What we now know as Jaguar Cars was founded in 1922 as the Swallow Sidecar Company. After World War II, the company had to change its name because of 'associations' with the initials forming its previous logo – SS.

The XK150 was the final incarnation of Jaguar's truly awesome XK sports range.

Jaguar Mark II

COUNTRY OF ORIGIN:
UK
FIRST MANUFACTURED:
1959 (until 1967)
ENGINE:
2,483 cc, 3,442cc, 3,781 cc DOHC
Straight Six
PERFORMANCE:
Top speed of 125 mph (201 km/h);
0-60 mph (97 km/h) in 8.5 secs
YOU SHOULD KNOW:
The Jaguar Mark II's most enduring
cultural success is probably as the
car driven by Inspector Morse in the
internationally successful TV series
based on the novels of Colin Dexter.
Although the car used in the TV
series was the less desirable
2.4 version, and somewhat battered,
it was sold in 2005 after restoration
for over £100,000.

Jaguar hit the jackpot in 1959 when it redesigned the company's first monocoque (body and chassis as single unit) four-door saloon. The Mark II's bigger windows created an impression of airy brightness, and minor changes to the trim, instrument panel and external styling all added up to a handsome car that drivers felt to be 'adult'. It made much more of the existing 2.4 and 3.4 litre engines – but the star of the range was the new 3.8 litre version of the legendary XK. Ensconced in serious leather-and-walnut comfort (that subsequently became one of Jaguar's hallmarks), Mark II drivers discovered how easily the 3.8 could embarrass contemporary sports cars in both acceleration and speed. With a slightly wider rear axle, the improved road-handling was impeccable; and even the optional wire wheels had an additional, useful function in providing extra cooling for the now standard disc brakes.

The Mark II catapulted Jaguar into the role of style leader for sports saloons. In practice, its speed and manoeuvrability made it first choice both for old-style criminals in need of a getaway car, and for the police chasing them. Featured in lots of British films and TV shows of the early 1960s, the Mark II has always retained its image of quirky individualism. It still does. It even transcends the usual barriers of class and wealth: owners were and are just as likely to be wage-earners as aristocrats. More than fifty years after it was first launched, its unceasing popularity among connoisseurs makes the Mark II the perfect expression of its originator's (William Lyons, Jaguar's Chairman) desire to build a car of 'grace, space and pace'. Its combination of luxury and performance made it a paragon of aspirational sophistication that may have been equalled, but never surpassed.

Along with many an upwardly mobile but honest Brit, armed robbers tended to go for a speedy top-of-the-range Jaguar 3.8

Lagonda 3.0 Litre

The Lagonda was a marque of automotive aristocracy more than equal to its luxury sports car competitors, Bentley, Invicta and Railton. When Rolls-Royce bought him out, W.O.Bentley in fact chose to move to Lagonda, which was acquired in 1947 by the industrialist David Brown at much the same time as Aston Martin, for whose salvation he depended on Bentley's legendary engineering. Brown put the available 2.6 litre Bentley engine first into his Aston Martin DB2, and only in 1948 into his first Lagonda, a wonderful but old-fashioned, somewhat stately magnificence. It was 1953 before he announced the new 3 litre Lagonda, powered by a revised Bentley engine capable of topping the magic 100 mph (161 km/h), and featuring the advanced design of a cruciform-braced chassis and all-round independent suspension. Initially, though seating four, it came only as a two-door closed saloon or a convertible drophead coupe (styled by the Swiss coachbuilder, Graber). Though fast, the column-change gearbox detracted from its sporty appeal.

By 1954, the gear change was floor mounted, and drivers could feel they were truly participating in one of the era's great motoring experiences. The saloon appeared with four doors, and the drophead coupe just got better. You bathed in leather and walnut, with every available extra installed as standard in a vehicle of supremely discreet elegance, while the engine effortlessly dealt with the solid weight of genuine luxury. Five people could be comfortable in a 3 litre Lagonda; and even with the ample boot filled with luggage, the car fulfilled its fastest specs.

HRH the Duke of Edinburgh thought so, too, and had his 3 litre Lagonda Drophead Coupe finished in Edinburgh Green with Battleship Grey upholstery. He even persuaded his bride, HM The Queen, to use it in 1959 on the occasion of the official opening of Britain's first motorway, the M1.

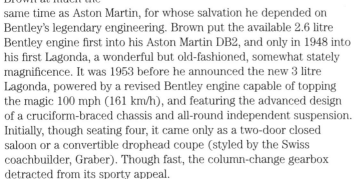

The Lagonda was a convertible drophead coupe beloved by the well-heeled British upper classes.

COUNTRY OF ORIGIN:
UK
FIRST MANUFACTURED:
1953 (until 1958)
ENGINE:
2,922 cc DOHC Straight Six
PERFORMANCE:
Top speed of 104 mph (167 km/h);
0-60 mph (97 km/h) in 12.9 secs
YOU SHOULD KNOW:
This beautiful car was unfortunately more expensive than its obvious rivals, and only 270 were ever made including all its configurations. It was succeeded in 1961 by the Lagonda Rapide, another super luxury saloon – but after that Aston Martin had to go it alone.

141

Lancia Aurelia B20 GT

The Aurelia may have looked like a pussycat, but classic styling concealed a tiger's bite.

Before and after World War II, Lancia never introduced a new car without an accompanying strategy to develop a series. The company was expert at demographic subdivision, and ultra-sensitive to the sudden shifts in public taste. The Aurelia series as a whole, and the Aurelia B20 GT in particular, typified the success of their vision.

At its inception in 1949, the Aurelia was the most advanced production car anywhere, and it was styled by Vittorio Jano following his colossal success at Alfa Romeo. Its sleek, fastback lines embodied the aesthetic of modernity; and it was the first Lancia to get a V6 engine. It appeared either as a four-door berlina (sedan) or as a limousine. Both were solid and comfortable, if a little short on true luxury and acceptable performance. By 1951 both problems had been addressed – and the triumphant solution emphasized by the introduction of what has often been called 'the first true Gran Turismo (GT)', the sporty, two-door Aurelia B20 GT. The coupe's wheelbase was shortened in the hands of designer Gian Paolo Boano (son of the owner of Ghia), and the V6 upgraded to 2 litres, tuned for excitement by production boss Pininfarina.

With such an Italian 'dream team' as midwives, the Aurelia B20 GT was recognized instantly as a classic. It was rapidly improved, in line with Lancia's willingness to respond to its customers, eventually appearing in six official series to fulfil the demand spurred by the Aurelia's persistently excellent results in races like the Mille Miglia during the early 1950s. It had speed, the power to dig in its heels, and finesse. Best of all, it brought some of the best Italian design and engineering within financial reach of the relatively many.

COUNTRY OF ORIGIN:
Italy
FIRST MANUFACTURED:
1951 (until 1958)
ENGINE:
1,991 cc V6
PERFORMANCE:
Series I had a top speed of 100.5 mph (162 km/h)
YOU SHOULD KNOW:
By its final Series 6 version, the Aurelia B20 GT's early, aluminium, sporty exhilaration was restrained by around 600lbs extra of refined luxury (chromed brass trim and other features essential to maximum comfort); and though much more powerful, the Series 6 handled more like a sedan than the sporting superstar it had been.

142

Lotus Elite

Its streamlined elegance flabbergasted the motoring world when it was unveiled at the London Earls Court Motor Show of 1957. The Lotus Elite's fibreglass monocoque engineering was the very first combination of its kind. It was also the first 'regular', roadgoing, production sports car created by the maverick engineering genius, Colin Chapman and his team, even if the first line-produced car was not made until mid-1958 (and bought, incidentally, by the celebrated jazz musician, Chris Barber). Though there was a steel subframe to support the engine, suspension and essentials like the door hinges, the Elite's featherweight and advanced aerodynamic construction balanced on four-wheel independent suspension, made it a dream to handle. It was a wonderfully quick car. In fact to begin with, the 1.2 litre engine made it almost overpowered – but it provided the Elite with the authentic sports car performance that gained it, among many triumphs, six class victories in the Le Mans 24 hour. The interior had carefully matching, stylish practicality – including a metal dashboard shaped exactly like the Elite's exterior profile.

There were major problems. The drive was bolted directly to the monocoque without even rubber cushions. The noise was horrendous. Forget 'opening the windows': curved on two planes so they couldn't wind down into the doors, the only option was to remove them completely and stow them in special pockets behind the seats. Worse, the glass fibre bodywork was liable to crack.

Not even shifting body manufacture to the Bristol Aircraft Company resolved the Elite's shortcomings. Yet its performance belied its fragility – and when you see one today, zipping along with fluid elegance, it's impossible to forget that the Lotus Elite is a car whose subsequent influence entitles it to be universally lauded as a genuine ancestor.

COUNTRY OF ORIGIN:
UK
FIRST MANUFACTURED:
1957 (prototype); 1958 (production)
(until 1963)
ENGINE:
1,216 cc Straight Four
PERFORMANCE:
Top speed of 115 mph (185 km/h);
0-60 mph (97 km/h) in 12.2 secs
YOU SHOULD KNOW:
If you enjoy automotive mathematics, investigate the Lotus Elite's incredible drag coefficient. Those gentle, delicate curves contain nothing superfluous. The Elite's beauty is dedicated to achieving its coefficient of 0.29, brilliant today, and simply unheard of in 1957.

The Lotus Elite was attractive, but was beauty enough to compensate for bad manners?

Lotus Seven

COUNTRY OF ORIGIN:
UK
FIRST MANUFACTURED:
1957 (until 1972)
ENGINE:
1,172 cc Flathead Straight Four
PERFORMANCE:
Top speed of 85.5 mph (136.8 km/h);
0-60 mph (97 km/h) in 14.3 secs
YOU SHOULD KNOW:
Under British tax laws in 1957, you
didn't have to pay Purchase Tax on a
car kit as long as it did not contain
assembly instructions. So Chapman
included disassembly instructions
which you followed in reverse – a bit
of lateral thinking typical of
Chapman's whole subversive ethos.
In 1973 when the tax advantage
loophole was plugged, Lotus sold the
licence to build kits and complete
Sevens to Caterham Cars.

The maverick automotive genius of Britain's Colin Chapman was in overdrive in 1957. For nearly ten years (including his RAF service) the engineering visionary had been refining increasingly successful versions of his super-lightweight sports race cars. He was close to achieving his goal of creating a Formula One contender, and every move was the subject of fascinated public scrutiny. The public loved his Lotus 6, a genuinely low-cost, street-legal competitor that they could drive to the track or hillclimb, compete, and go home in afterwards. They wanted more – and they thought they could see it in the one-off Lotus Seven fitted with a Coventry Climax engine, de Dion rear suspension and disc brakes that slaughtered the hillclimb and sprint season opposition of that year. Chapman, pressed for a road version, gave them a prototype classic instead, still in production according to its virtually original design more than fifty years later, and the blueprint for dozens of imitators around the world.

The Lotus Seven of legend first appeared in kit form. It was a stroke of minimalist genius, using readily available parts that would fit into the radical geometry of its lightweight, tubular and steel panel frame. De Dion was ousted for the solid beam axle of a Nash Metropolitan. The tiny engine was taken from the genteel Ford Prefect and Anglia (though when it began selling complete cars in 1958, Lotus offered the Climax or the BMC 'A' series from the Austin Sprite). There were some real problems (a tendency for rust to eat into the tubular chassis, causing sudden, terrifying collapse!), and the Lotus Seven was so Spartan, unadorned and basic that it was described as 'like driving a motorized roller-skate'. Enormous fun, in fact. The Seven is about sporty performance, brilliant handling, and – all but literally – driving by the seat of your pants.

The Lotus Seven was produced by the speed-obsessed Colin Chapman as the best possible budget driver's car.

MG TD

The traditions that dominate the evolution of MG sports cars include the company's reluctance to introduce radically new styling while its existing models still have a steady market. All kinds of technological developments might take place under the hood or in and around the chassis, but visible changes suggest annual tweaking rituals rather than re-styling ambition. MG's 'T' series was introduced in 1936. A new engine, hydraulic brakes and synchromesh on the top gears justified the new designation, but the styling was itself an evolution of the 'PB' series it replaced. Its successor (after 'TB' and 'TC') the MG TD still belonged to the same archetype of prewar 'British-look' sports cars. It was a two-door roadster, wider and sleeker than its narrow, straight-backed forebears, but with the same big grille and sporty, flowing lines. The running boards were tweaked a little further forward as a civilizing gesture, and other changes (like the bumpers, newly mandatory in the US, MG's prime market at the time) all demonstrated MG's awareness of its customers' developing stylistic sophistication and demand for comfort. Within a few months, the MG TD Mk II included yet more improvements – but the essential driving experience remained the same.

It was fun. It was fast. It was reliable. It was a car to fall in love in (and very often, with). With or without a passenger, it was a racer. Many owners did race – especially in the USA, which gobbled up roughly 23,500 of the 30,000 TDs ever made (only 149 right-hand drive cars were made for British buyers) – but its exhilarating road-holding and nippy characteristics were equally evident on the open road. Though an improved 'TF' followed, the 'TD' was the most popular of its series. It stands proudly on the cusp of old and new, in the place of honour.

The TD was the last in a line of MGs that offered classic prewar styling, soon to be superseded by a more modern look.

COUNTRY OF ORIGIN:
UK
FIRST MANUFACTURED:
1950 (until 1953)
ENGINE:
1,250 cc Straight Four
PERFORMANCE:
A 1952 road test by The Motor magazine saw the MG TD achieve a top speed of 77 mph (123 km/h), and 0-60 mph (97 km/h) in 18.2 secs.
YOU SHOULD KNOW:
This beautiful, classic car has such a perennial hold on motoring enthusiasts' imaginations that in 1998, all manufacturing and associated rights in the MG TD were vested in TD Cars company in Malaysia, to reproduce the original as TD2000.

145

The unmistakable rounded grille of the MGA – first in a new generation of MG cars.

MG MGA

After 20 years of the highly traditional 'T' series sports car, MG appeared to break with its usual *modus operandi'*. The MGA came to its public as an unknown Adonis, the first MG with a full-width body and streamlined curves. In fact, though the styling was indeed radically new, it had (as always with MG) been evolved over four years from a prototype shell based on the 'TD' series, and progressively refined. The engine was a BMC B series already chosen for the MG Magnette sports saloon. Its size meant the hood line could be lowered, reducing the drag coefficient. Mutterings about 'underpower' were stilled when the MGA (suitably handicapped) totally outperformed its predecessor and stablemate, an MG TF 1500. The MGA's stylish aerodynamics alone were shown to add just under 10 secs to its top speed.

The MGA faced the future squarely. Traditionalists were disappointed, but the company was firmly fixed on innovation and improvement. Almost immediately the engine was uprated (from 68 to 72 bhp). Then came a 'bubble-top' coupe version with the sports car luxury of wind-up windows, and the first of a procession of stylistic adjustments throughout the car's production. The Twin-Cam of 1958 looked normal, but revelled in a competitive ability to hit 114 mph (183.5 km/h) or more. In anything but expert hands, it was unreliable. In its place came the MGA 1600 Mark I & II, which did most of the same things, and stayed on their respective feet. Finally, every development was incorporated into a few, leftover, twin cam chassis and designated the MG MGA 1600 Mk II Deluxe. It was now a brilliant, beautiful, high-performance sports car (with a really snappy name!), but its time had passed. Luckily, the MGB was waiting in the wings.

COUNTRY OF ORIGIN:
UK
FIRST MANUFACTURED:
1955 (until 1962)
ENGINE:
1,489 cc OHV Straight Four
PERFORMANCE:
Top speed of 98 mph (157 km/h);
0-60 mph (97 km/h) in 15 secs
YOU SHOULD KNOW:
Besides starring in a 1970s Kellogs Corn Flakes commercial on Golden Gate bridge, the MGA has an excellent Hollywood pedigree. Among other films, it features in *Animal House* (1978) and *Guess Who's Coming to Dinner* (1968). Most conspicuously, Elvis Presley liked the red 1960 MGA 1600 Mk I roadster he uses throughout *Blue Hawaii* (1961) so much that he bought it. You can see it at Graceland.

Mercedes Benz 300 SL

At least one major poll declared the Mercedes 300 SL 'Gullwing' to be 'Sports Car of the [Twentieth] Century'. And it's true: more than fifty years after its introduction, its aerodynamic finesse has the undimmed, futuristic beauty of a timeless thoroughbred; and its original ergonomic brilliance still makes it one of the most pleasing cars you will ever drive.

New York City saw the Gullwing first, at the 1954 Auto Show. The two-seater closed sports car was the road model of Daimler-Benz's hugely successful 300 SL racing car. It was the company's response to urgent prompting by their official US importer, who accurately foresaw an eager market for a top quality Mercedes sports car. It was a sensation. The importer immediately ordered a thousand. The aerodynamic streamlining spoke of muscular sophistication, and the visual drama of the unfolding gullwing doors released the full potential of the car's inherent panache.

Performance depended not just on the light weight of its aluminium skin, but on the rigidity of the tubular frame, which necessarily reached much higher than usual up the side. Normal doors were impossible – and so was any proposal for an open-top version. Instead, customers could choose from five rear-axle ratios for their preferred balance between straight line speed and acceleration, all of which benefited from the Gullwing's revolutionary new direct fuel injection system, another first for a petrol-powered production car and not even installed in the Gullwing's race-only predecessor.

Climbing in was an adventure. Once there, the ergonomic lay-out, like everything else, was years ahead. The road-holding and handling were precise but effortless. Steering was direct, power instantaneous. This dazzling automobile cloaked you in its own charisma, and it still does.

COUNTRY OF ORIGIN:
Germany
FIRST MANUFACTURED:
1955 (until 1957)
ENGINE:
2,996 cc Straight Six
PERFORMANCE:
Top speed of 146-162 mph (235-260 km/h) according to axle ratio; 0-60 mph (97 km/h) in 10 secs
YOU SHOULD KNOW:
1. To squeeze beneath the Gullwing's remarkably flat bonnet profile, the engine had to be tilted more than 45 degrees to the left. 2. Gullwing owners could make the most of their car's space by ordering a set of luggage made to measure.

Despite gullwing doors, the 300 SL couldn't actually fly – though it may have seemed that way at max speed.

Messerschmitt KR200

COUNTRY OF ORIGIN:
Germany
FIRST MANUFACTURED:
1955 (until 1964)
ENGINE:
191 cc air-cooled Fichtel & Sachs
2-stroke
PERFORMANCE:
Top speed of 62 mph (100 km/h)
YOU SHOULD KNOW:
To reverse the KR200, you stop the
engine, push the ignition key in
further than usual, then re-start,
going backwards. This means you get
4 gears in reverse as well as forward
– a clever wheeze.

*Those who felt like a fighter
pilot in their Messerschmitt
cockpit doubtless checked the
side-mounted rearview mirror
from time to time in case there
was an Armstrong Siddeley
Hurricane on their tail.*

The 'KR' stands for *Kabinenroller* (Cabin Scooter). After World War
II, the German Messerschmitt company was forbidden to
manufacture aircraft. Instead, it sought to stay in business by making
auto parts for others, and its own economy vehicles for a mass
market. It had already produced the KR175, a primitive but quite
effective two-seat (in tandem), an all-weather, three-wheel version
of a scooter with handlebar steering. It was deficient in so many
different ways that Messerschmitt felt it was betraying the
company's reputation for excellent aircraft and precision technology
in general; pride and a *faut-de-mieux* curiosity prompted a genuine
desire to do the job well, if at all and if it could.

The KR200 is called a 'microcar', but nobody who appreciates it
thinks of it as anything but an airplane cockpit somehow given
independent motion. The plexiglas bubble canopy tilts over for
access. With the pilot/driver and navigator/passenger seated in line,
the cabin tapers towards the back; and with the (single) rear-wheel
drive, the arrangement makes for good handling. There is no wheel
to turn. You push the steering bar: it's connected directly to the
track rods on the front wheels, which means, just like a fighter
aircraft, the response is so direct that anything but little, directional
twitches magnifies the
intended effect dramatically.

Having thought seriously
about the KR200's design,
Messerschmitt abandoned it
to make aircraft at the first
opportunity in 1956. The
vehicle's designer, Fritz
Fend, continued to develop
'sport', 'roadster', and even
'luxury' versions for a few
years under the FMR
company, but its (resolutely
democratizing) time had
passed. Even the KR200's
biggest export customer,
the UK, where the economy
was not nearly so buoyant
as in Germany in 1962,
could afford the new Mini
instead.

If you ever, ever get the
chance: it really is
disturbingly like flying to
drive the KR200.

Mini Cooper

In 1959 the Austin/Morris Mini changed the face of motoring. Just 3 m (10 ft) long, it was the most efficient and effective use of road space ever seen. The apparent miracle of Sir Alec Issigonis's design was to create a front-wheel drive, two-door, four-seat economy saloon that sacrificed nothing to exact steering, superb handling, and super-agile response. At the time of its first launch, BMC (which included Austin and Morris, and marketed the Mini under both to keep the names before the public) lent a Mini to John Cooper, whose racing cars were then approaching the peak of their success (in several formulae, including two Formula 1 World Championships). He was immediately fascinated. By 1961 his 'idea' for a hot Mini had been researched, tested and produced – to a tidal wave of public and professional applause.

It was a social revolution as much as anything. The Mini Cooper, brilliant on the track and multi-winner of Monte Carlo Rallies, was the car of Britain's about-to-be 'swinging 60s' elite. In London the unofficial race track was Belgrave Square (there was much less traffic than today). The manic screeching of tyres at night is said to have only been tamed when a local policeman got his own Mini Cooper to give chase.

The Mini Cooper, and of course the even snappier Cooper 'S', have added to their legendary exploits with every incarnation. Like the Mini itself (and the MINI, as current owners BMW distinguish their versions), the Cooper has appeared in dozens of configurations, from economy to super-deluxe and back again. It has always guaranteed and delivered pure thrill; and that's why so many people continue to admire and drive one more than fifty years on.

If one car looked to the future it was surely the brilliantly fast Mini Cooper, that appeared in 1959 before accelerating into the new decade.

COUNTRY OF ORIGIN:
UK
FIRST MANUFACTURED:
1959
ENGINE:
997 cc Straight Four
PERFORMANCE:
Top speed of 85 mph (137 km/h); 0-60 mph (97 km/h) 17.5 secs
YOU SHOULD KNOW:
Customized Minis or Mini Coopers were stars in films like The Italian Job, A Shot In The Dark, and the Beatles' Magical Mystery Tour. Owners included Steve McQueen, Enzo Ferrari, Marianne Faithfull, all four Beatles, and Peter Sellers (whose Mini had wicker side-panels designed by the Rolls-Royce coach builder, Hooper). The Legend continues.

150

Morgan 4/4

The company was famous for its three-wheelers when Morgan announced its first '4-4 – four wheels and four cylinders' cars in 1936. It returned from war production in 1950 with its Plus-4, a commercial success but a demographic step too far upmarket for the marque's core enthusiasts. So in 1955 Morgan introduced the Morgan 4/4 Series II (note the subtle change from 4-4 to 4/4) as a lower-powered, lightweight, nippy return to the company's original principles. Ever since, through succeeding generations of power plants and every kind of technical evolution, the car has existed in a category of its own.

Sturdy but light, built from aluminium on an ash frame, the Morgan 4/4 has survived many experiments in modern materials, and innumerable cycles of fashionability. In effect, the experience of providing fast, fun, recreational transport at the lowest practicable cost, to which the original Henry Morgan devoted himself in 1910, locked the company into a way of doing things which it has never been able to change without compromising the reasons for its success. Owners and drivers of the Morgan 4/4 of any era get particular pleasure from tinkering. Closed factory systems and computerized technology inhibit it, so Morgan avoids them where it can. The outward, still 1930s, styling is a hallmark of the 4/4's longstanding promise of keen handling and performance characteristics that can readily be modified to suit an individual's requirements (or expectations). The Series II, and every subsequent version, comes with all the technical mod cons of the day – but it always looks and drives like you've just roared in, rimed with dust where your goggles sheltered your eyes, from the Mille Miglia or the Indy 500, or even Box Hill. The Morgan 4/4 is, par excellence, the sports car of Everyman's imagination. That's why it's still going strong.

COUNTRY OF ORIGIN:
UK
FIRST MANUFACTURED:
1955 (Series II) (until 1959)
ENGINE:
1,172 cc flathead Straight Four Ford 100E
PERFORMANCE:
Top speed of 75 mph (121 km/h); 0-60 mph (97 km/h) in 26.9 secs
YOU SHOULD KNOW:
You get a very direct ride in a Morgan 4/4, but the car has never been built for raw power. Its success is the result of decades of cunning, balancing the least available power to the least available structural weight.

The ash frames of Morgans have always been produced using traditional hand-crafted methodology, as they are now.

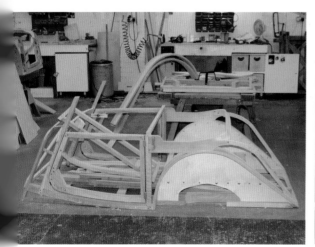
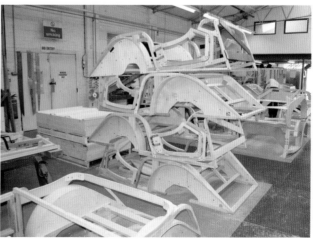

The ladies loved it, but the strangely styled Metropolitan managed to miss the boat in both Britain and the USA.

Nash Metropolitan

It was to sail like a tiny boat through the waves of suburban America. With a wheelbase shorter than a VW Beetle, the Nash Metropolitan was conceived as an ideal city 'stopping and shopping' car. It grew, via several years of committee discussion, from a genuine desire to create an American economy car, allied to Nash's determination to use its advanced and available 'Airflyte' technology, into a gloriously eccentric mess. Its monocoque construction sat heavily on its tiny frame, wholly enclosing not just the wheels but a host of standard features that anywhere else would have been optional. Innumerable 'surviews' (survey + preview) imposed demands that could only be fulfilled economically if the entire car was made and assembled in Britain, and shipped back for sale in the USA. By 1954, when it was introduced, it was already an anachronism. America was launched on its postwar mind-set of big-finned, bouncy-riding, long-distance highway languor, and the Nash Metropolitan wasn't it.

Nevertheless, like one third of nearly everything worth treasuring, the Nash Metropolitan achieved greatness – but only in hindsight. Every idea it encapsulated was ahead of its time, like its size, urban convenience, and interior fittings. Initially, it was slow, unwieldy, and unreliable (most of its innards were doctored from existing British Austin components); and it looked lumpy and dumpy in both its hardtop and convertible options. By 1957 when it was released in Europe, it was vastly improved (unless you attempted taking an 'S' bend at speed when it rolled like a drunken sailor), but its styling proved too *outré* for a society still too fractured by war and restraint to enjoy it.

Now we recognize it as a stylistic benchmark of its era, and a brave attempt to live the future before it arrived.

COUNTRY OF ORIGIN:
USA (built in UK)
FIRST MANUFACTURED:
1954 (until 1961)
ENGINE:
1,200 cc OHV Straight Four
PERFORMANCE:
Top speed of 70 mph (113 km/h);
0-60 mph (97 km/h) in 28-30 secs
YOU SHOULD KNOW:
The Nash Metropolitan's notoriously adorable 'cuteness' has always appealed to society's rebels, including Jimmy Buffet, Jay Leno, Paul Newman, Elvis Presley, HRH Princess Margaret, 'Weird Al' Jankovic, Kenneth McKellar and Alma Cogan. Other 'enthusiasts' have converted the car to anything from a stretch limo to a twin-track snowmobile. Style is everything.

Nissan Skyline

For years, the Nissan Skyline GT-R series has starred in road and track races, and in some of the world's most successful video games, like Gran Turismo. Its latest incarnation, the Nissan GT-R (the 'Skyline' got dropped in 2007) R35 uses 'launch control' to achieve 0-60mph (97 km/h) in 3.2 secs, and blasts on to a top speed of over 192 mph (309 km/h). Appropriately for a Japanese car, it owes much to its ancestors, the Nissan Skyline ALSI-1 and ALSI-2 first introduced in 1957.

Back then, what we know retrospectively as the Nissan was actually a Prince Skyline, made by the Japanese auto manufacturer that merged with Nissan-Datsun. It was a luxury four-door sedan or a five-door station wagon, updated within its first year with a more powerful engine and the first quad headlights arrangement ever seen on a Japanese car. It had all the virtues of contemporary cars designed for Middle America, on which it was based, but not many of their vices. In terms of automotive history, its success was not just its virtuous good looks or its well-mannered competence (it agreed politely when you wanted to accelerate, then took off, gracefully), but the mere fact of its existence. The Nissan Skyline set a benchmark by establishing Japanese capability to match worldwide technical and aesthetic auto evolution. Since the ALSI-1, the Skyline's genealogy has included sports and super sports cars, pick-up trucks, luxury sedans, and one of the finest families of GT cars ever made anywhere. You still see lots of Nissan Skyline GTs from each of the last three decades, barely resembling anything of their lineage except pure quality of design, and inspirational – sometimes titanic – technology under the hood.

COUNTRY OF ORIGIN:
Japan
FIRST MANUFACTURED:
1957 (until 1963)
ENGINE:
1,482 cc, 1,862 cc OHV Straight Four
PERFORMANCE:
Top speed of 87 mph (140 km/h)
YOU SHOULD KNOW:
Though you won't see it badged on Nissan cars, the Prince marque still exists within the Nissan company. After the Tachikawa Aircraft Company turned from making World War II fighter planes to making electric cars in 1947, it moved on to make petrol-driven cars in 1954 – simultaneously changing its name to Prince Motors to honour the Japanese Crown Prince Hirohita. It still does.

The Skyline proved that Japan could make a good, reliable car that was the equal of anything offered by American and European car manufacturers.

Packard Hawk

COUNTRY OF ORIGIN:
USA
FIRST MANUFACTURED:
1958
ENGINE:
4.7 l (289cid) OHV V8
PERFORMANCE:
Top speed of 125 mph (201 km/h);
0-60 mph (97 km/h) in 12.0 secs
YOU SHOULD KNOW:
It's hard to overstate the shock felt
in the USA at the demise of Packard.
Since 1899, the company had grown
big on its high standards of
engineering and luxury fittings. It was
also Packard who built the V12
engines of the World War I Liberty
airplane – a power unit that allegedly
'distinguished itself in rum-running
boats after the war'.

At the time it looked like automotive suicide – and there is certainly a direct relationship between the Packard Hawk's outrageous styling and the final demise of the company. Packard had been one of the great prewar American car manufacturers, but lost their way in the superheated market competition of the 1950s. A 1956 merger with Studebaker – also dying on its feet – attempted to blend the companies' car styles as well as the ledgers. Both were disasters, and the Packard Hawk is their final memorial.

It's a tough one. You love it for its over-the-top fins, scoops, and 'features', and devastating power-to-weight ratio (its groundbreaking use of fibreglass made it extremely fast); or you hate the ridiculous add-ons of a wind scoop on the hood and a pointless, fake continental tyre bulge on the trunk, the compressed 'fishy' grin of the front grille, and the total lack of aesthetic unity that insulted the respective histories of both Packard and Studebaker. The Hawk's seats were leather, with matching Naugahyde trim around the instruments crowded on the dashboard. There were vinyl armrests outside the windows, presumably for super-relaxed driving. The finesse of Studebaker's early 1950s Starlight and Starliner coupes was stretched into the fishy rictus of Packard's desperate attempt to make the Hawk attractive – to someone, somewhere. It was said, wonderingly, that the Packard Hawk was 'the swan [that] had become the ugly duckling'.

The hybrid was so depressingly contrived it was contemptuously dismissed as a 'Packardbaker'. Yet its Studebaker V8 engine, supercharged, made it the fastest production car ever made by Packard; and stylistically, if only in retrospect, the Packard Hawk's marriage of form and function is only as overwrought as Le Corbusier's buildings. Like them, it now looks more robustly effective, if just as strange.

It was the last gasp of a failing manufacturing conglomerate, and plenty of critics suggested that the Hawk deserved to die.

Panhard Dyna Z/Panhard PL 17

Though actually rather large and roomy inside, the Panhard managed to look like a small car.

Halfway through its development of the Dyna Z sedan, the Panhard Car Company was partially integrated with Citroen. By the time the car had evolved into the Panhard PL17, that merger was evident in the modified styling, and you can see the future of Citroen's most famous profiles emerging.

Stylistically, the Panhard Dyna Z tells the story of French car design in the 1950s. When it was launched in 1953, it was a comfortable but economic six-seater mid-range saloon, still made of aluminium (which evaded the postwar proscription on steel for cars) on a front and rear steel tube subframe. With characteristic *élan*, Panhard created a smooth, rounded (even slightly bulbous), futuristically sleek profile. The Dyna Z looked good, and novel. By 1956, the bodies were made of steel, and the suspension improved to take the weight – but the car remained light enough to lift a back wheel on tight corners, or slide the passengers across the bench seats if it didn't.

Reliability was dealt with while Citroen used their influence on the design for the Dyna Z's successor. The Panhard PL17 of 1959 (the 'L' referred to Levassor, Panhard's original partner) looked like a new model, but was the Dyna Z in all important technical senses. The PL17 flattened the Dyna Z's curves into streamlined simplicity, but left the fairly extreme curvature of the front of the hood in what we now recognize as a prototype of later Citroens. Even at the time, it was a radical aesthetic, but over half a century later, the Panhard PL17 still holds its own as a progressive profile. In the light of the revolutionary engineering being developed by Citroen, perhaps it shouldn't be surprising that the Dyna Z engine was never developed to match, and this was almost Panhard's last car.

COUNTRY OF ORIGIN:
France
FIRST MANUFACTURED:
1953 (until 1959 Dyna Z; 1965 PL17)
ENGINE:
848 cc-851 cc Flat-twin
PERFORMANCE:
Dyna Z – top speed of 81 mph
(130 km/h)
Dyna Z 'Tigre'/PL17 – top speed of
90 mph (145 km/h)
YOU SHOULD KNOW:
While the column shift made the Panhard Dyna Z more spacious, other controls were less obvious. Since the brake lights had a dual function as reversing lights, you could start the car without a key – in reverse with the brake on.

155

Pegaso Z102B

COUNTRY OF ORIGIN:
Spain
FIRST MANUFACTURED:
1951 (until 1958)
ENGINE:
2,816 cc V8
PERFORMANCE:
Top speed of more than 100 mph
(160 km/h)
YOU SHOULD KNOW:
Pegaso was dogged by really bad
luck, with accidents and technical
misfortunes outside its control that
deterred its backers. Even its world
speed record only lasted a few
weeks before a Jaguar XK120
(described as 'mildly modified' which
doesn't help) blitzed the 'Flying Mile'
at 173 mph (278 km/h).

In 1953, for a few brief weeks, the fastest road car in the world was all-Spanish. The Spanish designer Wilfredo Ricart had fled the Spanish Civil War to Italy, where he was Technical Director and worked with Enzo Ferrari at Alfa Romeo. By the end of the 1940s, he was back in Spain working for the government bus and truck company ENASA (Empresa Nacional de Autocamiones SA). Franco's government sensed a PR coup and backed Ricart's proposal for a Spanish supercar to dominate all European rivals. They even gave him the former Hispano-Suiza factory to work in.

The Pegaso Z102 began as a demonstration of technical and engineering brilliance. Ricart's forte was engines, and he created a fire-breathing hellhound out of a mere 2.5 litre V8 upstart (though he allowed for it to be increased to 2.8 and even 3.2 litres) using four Weber carburettors (one of very few non- Spanish parts) to suck in the necessaries. Ferrari's horse pranced. The winged Pegasus flew. The Pegaso Z102 was all but a Grand Prix lion dressed as a frisky lamb. The trouble was that nobody could actually see the technological beauty under the relatively lumpen exterior – ENASA, with the best will in the world, was still accustomed only to making trucks and buses. On his second visit to the Paris Salon, Ricart finally attracted at least professional interest by showing the Z102 with a clear perspex body, revealing his inmost secrets.

For styling, he turned to Superleggera Touring in Milan, and Saoutchik of Paris, who made the handful of cars we think of when we think of Pegaso. Touring made perhaps the most beautiful, the one-off Z102B 'Thrill'; but Saoutchik made the two-seat cabriolet and two/three seat Berlinetta whose surviving examples conjure up the same passion and excitement as their inspirational ancestor, Hispano-Suiza.

Spain's ultra-fast Pegaso sadly concealed its special technical excellence beneath a relatively mundane outer skin.

Plymouth Fury

1956 was the year of 'The Forward Look', when Plymouth sought to amaze its competitors and the US public with tailfin 'developments' and a series of ingenious in-car devices. In addition to the V8 'Hy-Fire' engine from the previous year, the 1956 Plymouths could have push-button 'Powerflite' automatic transmission and 'Highway Hi-Fi', a record player designed to keep the stylus in the platter's groove while you avoided potholes in the road. Plymouth marketing was a cameo of the economic optimism of the era – but it couldn't prepare the company for the kind of enthusiasm that greeted the summer launch of its new hardtop coupe, a limited edition to crown its range: the first Plymouth Fury.

It only came in white, with a gold stripe worked down each side to emphasize the high fins looming over the twin exhausts that spoke of the 240 bhp inside. It was beautiful, fast, and difficult to get your hands on. It raised the profile of every Plymouth model, and the company began its most successful era. The Fury's role as high-performance standard-bearer for Plymouth increased with its staggering tail size. Its proven reliability and performance even endeared it to US Police forces (who also, apparently, greatly admired its unexpectedly soft ride). By 1959, the Fury's name was attached to most Plymouth high-end models (pushing the Belvedere, Savoy etc down the marketing pecking order); and a new 'Sport Fury' was created as a limited edition with numerous options for making it even more flashy (it already came with a trunk lid appliqué intended to look like an exterior spare tyre, but resembling a trash-can top). In the giddy euphoria of the day, the ruse worked, and went on working. The Plymouth Fury is a marketing milestone as well as one of America's hottest 1950s cars.

Any colour you like – as long as it's white with a flashy gold stripe and whitewall tyres.

COUNTRY OF ORIGIN:
USA
FIRST MANUFACTURED:
1956 (until 1959)
ENGINE:
5.0 l (303 cid) V8
PERFORMANCE:
Top speed of 110 mph (177 km/h);
0-60 mph (97 km/h) in 10 secs
YOU SHOULD KNOW:
Since 1961, the name 'Fury' has been attached to several generations of Plymouth models and series. The villain of Stephen King's novel *Christine* is a psychopathic, demoniacally-possessed 1958 Plymouth Fury which manipulates two rather odd people to fall in love, and slaughters anyone who gets in the way.

Pontiac Bonneville

COUNTRY OF ORIGIN:
USA
FIRST MANUFACTURED:
1959 (until 1961)
ENGINE:
6.0 l (370 cid) V8
PERFORMANCE:
Top speed of 120 mph (193 km/h);
0-60 mph (97 km/h) in 8.1 secs

Launched in 1957 as a low-slung, sexy, convertible limited edition at the top of the Pontiac range, the Bonneville was flashy and fast. It was good enough to pace the 1958 Indianapolis 500 (a first for any Pontiac), but it missed its intended mark. That was a blessing: a necessary redesign coincided with Pontiac's Wide Track policy on all its models, and the 1959 Bonneville benefited more than any of them. It became emblematic of Pontiac's resurgence. Already low, the extra inches on the wheelbase banished any suggestion of top-heaviness. It looked even more glamorous, handled with precision, and cornered more tightly than any other full-size car. Motor Trend Magazine made it their 1959 'Car of the Year'.

The 1959 Bonneville also carried the Pontiac flag for the styling edict that applied to every Pontiac model of that year. It was the

first appearance of the signature split grille and integrated arrowhead emblem that has characterized Pontiacs ever since, and the Bonneville's styling carried the idea through to the detail, blending it into the flamboyant features beloved of the era. From any angle, the Bonneville looks sleek, broad and powerful. From the rear, you can see how the body line resolves into a three-dimensional 'V'-shaped fin, with the rear brights a round circle at its point; and the inner facets of the 'V' are all chrome! Other options include power brakes, steering, windows and bucket seats; signal-seeking radio; and interior luxury trim.

The Bonneville was no longer a limited edition in 1959. It was far too popular. Pontiac re-drew its rather stodgy pre-1957 image with its dramatic styling and technology; and the 1959 Bonneville is important historically as the car which integrated glitz and good taste, on the cusp of yesterday and tomorrow.

YOU SHOULD KNOW:
Since 1959, Pontiac have regularly revived the Bonneville marque for their high-end limited editions and series. The most recent, the Bonneville GXP of 2004-5 uses Cadillac's 4.6 l Northstar V8 engine giving it an acceleration of 0-60mph (97 km/h) in 6.5 secs, but the split grille is still a giveaway.

Flashy, fast, big, comfortable and finned – the Bonneville was a true monument to American automotive excess.

The Dauphine was one of the first mass imports to Britain where buyers were not put off by its shoddy workmanship.

Renault Dauphine

In 1956, Renault came up with a brilliant marketing strategy – out with the good (the successful Renault 4C) and in with the bad (the hugely successful Dauphine).

For despite being underpowered and suffering from very poor build quality, the Renault Dauphine would become a rewarding decade-long commercial success story for the French company. This neatly rounded four-door, four-seater saloon of single-shell monocoque construction was visually attractive. However, it was prone to a variety of mechanical problems and notoriously slow – an ironic weakness as the name chosen by Renault for the new baby was 'Corvette', which was abandoned when Chevrolet's flying sports car appeared first. Happily for Renault, the car's shortcomings didn't deter buyers (who seemed to love the feminine Dauphine), or dampen international acclaim.

Amazingly for a car that almost entirely lacked redeeming features, a huge number were produced in France – and beyond. Dauphines were assembled or built under licence in far-flung corners of the globe like Japan, Argentina, Brazil, Mexico, the USA, Israel, Italy (by Alfa Romeo alongside the altogether more satisfactory Alfa Giulietta), Ireland, Spain, Australia and South Africa. This cheap and cheerful little car was also the first model to be imported to the United Kingdom in significant numbers – to challenge a British car manufacturing industry that would soon be struggling to compete with more agile overseas constructors. Anyone for a Dauphine? Believe it or not with the benefit of hindsight, well over two million purchasers said 'yes please' before this notoriously unreliable machine ceased to be.

Various efforts were made to gild the lily. A luxury Ondine model was marketed from 1960 to 1962 and there were two speedier versions. The Gordini was engineered to reach a zippy 81 mph (130 km/h) whilst the 1093 (adorned with go-faster blue stripes) could in the fullness of time hit 87 mph (140 km/h). Awesome!

COUNTRY OF ORIGIN:
France
FIRST MANUFACTURED:
1956 (until 1967)
ENGINE:
845 cc OHV Straight Four
PERFORMANCE:
Top speed of 70 mph (113 km/h);
0-60 mph (97 km/h) in 32 secs
YOU SHOULD KNOW:
If you must drive a Dauphine, diligent searching may be required – these cars weren't built to last for 40 years, and one commentator sourly observed that you could actually hear a Dauphine rusting away . . . before you put your foot down and it went through the floor.

Riley 1.5

Throughout the 1930s and 1940s Riley was numbered among Britain's most successful manufacturers of sports cars, sporting saloons, and even luxury limousines. Their characteristic, slightly raffish and aristocratic styling did not survive the 1952 merger of the Nuffield group (including Riley) with Austin, which formed BMC. It took five years for the merger to bear fruit: twin replacements for the Morris Minor 1000, to be launched as the Wolseley 1500 and then later, the Riley 1.5.

The classic 1950s Riley 1.5 couldn't quite make up its mind what it was supposed to be.

It was a radical change for the Riley. Fifty years of sporting elegance was replaced by a four-door, mid-size family saloon on which awkward curves vied uncomfortably with straight lines. The Riley 1.5 looked like it couldn't decide if it wanted to look American, or just a little like a Jaguar, if only by its suggestive grille shape. It was safe, solid, comfortable, and at least it was more powerful than the Wolseley, with which it shared so many Morris Minor components. Both were fitted with the BMC B-series engine, but the Riley's twin SU carburettors gave it substantially more clout. It also had some of the same attention to interior detail of its more magnificent Riley predecessors, like the walnut veneer and extensive dial arrangement of the fascia.

The Riley 1.5 was successful enough to warrant a Mark II version, an almost entirely cosmetic style-tweak that enabled it to be sold in a sporty duo-tone version; and in 1961, a Mark III, with lower suspension. In fact, BMC's Australian-built Riley 1.5s incorporated more changes than were ever made in Britain. In its place of origin, the Riley 1.5 is a monument to motoring decency. Impeccably behaved, and both comfortable and speedy, it belongs neither to the past nor the future. It's in the middle.

COUNTRY OF ORIGIN:
UK
FIRST MANUFACTURED:
1957 (until 1965)
ENGINE:
1,489 cc Straight Four
PERFORMANCE:
Top speed of 84 mph (135 km/h);
0-60 mph (97 km/h) in 24.8 secs
YOU SHOULD KNOW:
The Riley 1.5 had a high final drive in the axle, which meant it could cruise comfortably at speed. For a small car, it also proved surprisingly lively in contemporary races and rallies. Its Riley ancestors would have approved.

Rolls-Royce Silver Cloud II

COUNTRY OF ORIGIN:
UK
FIRST MANUFACTURED:
1959 (until 1962)
ENGINE:
6,230 cc V8
PERFORMANCE:
Top speed 117 mph (188 km/h);
0-60 mph (97 km/h) in 10.8 secs
YOU SHOULD KNOW:
The Rolls-Royce Silver Cloud is the
car which prompted the immortal
advertising slogan 'At 60 miles an
hour, the loudest noise in this new
Rolls-Royce comes from the
electric clock'.

*How else could the good and
the great possibly get around?*

The Rolls-Royce Silver Cloud II is the last of the illustrious marque
of which the motoring world could agree: 'This is the best car in the
world'. It performed better than any previous Rolls-Royce; and
every model that followed (starting with the re-styled Silver Cloud
III) marked a further compromise on a long road to relative
mediocrity.

The Cloud II shared its fabulous grandeur with Cloud I. There
were minor cosmetic changes, but only in the cause of technical
improvement or greater luxury, like the improved headlights and
the addition of adjustable fresh air vents to the fascia. Cloud II also
had more body styles, adding a two-door convertible and two-door
coupe to the range. Like Cloud I, Cloud II had the 'standard steel'
sedan body, its mighty wings rolling backwards in a wave of refined
elegance to meet their rear echo, and every subtle curve and scoop
in harmony with the whole. As always with Rolls-Royce, there were

long-wheelbase limousines (299 of 2,417) with handcrafted coachwork and a division window, but the Crewe standard was an international hallmark of complete excellence.

The Silver Cloud II took that excellence to new technical heights. It was the first Rolls-Royce to be powered by a V8. With or without General Motors' excellent automatic transmission (R-R and Bentley had used them for years), Cloud II was faster, quieter, accelerated much better, and now had power steering as standard to make it much easier to handle and respond. The only faults you could possibly find with it are retrospective: in its day, high fuel consumption was not an issue, and if the chassis or bodywork proved prone to rust fifty years later, frankly, big deal. It's the only car that feels as good to be driven in as it does to drive.

Studebaker Golden Hawk

The Studebaker Starlight and Starliner coupes of 1953 were among America's most beautiful cars. Low on the ground, sleek and fast, they were designed by Raymond Loewy, a hero of contemporary US auto engineering. Three years later and still guided by Loewy's ideas, including the fabulous 1955 Studebaker President Speedster, they became the basis of Studebaker's last great production series.

In 1956 Studebaker simultaneously announced its new Flight Hawk and Power Hawk coupes, the Sky Hawk hardtop, and a two-door, pillarless hardtop coupe for the top of the line, to be called the Studebaker Golden Hawk. It was to be America's first, family-size sports car, and it was a serious contender. The massive hood reared to a pointed nose truncated by a nearly vertical, 'egg-crate' front grille; and the shallow curve of each wing swept back to a graceful echo in the muted fins, but neatly contrasted with a chrome strip straight along the bodyline from the headlights to the centre of the vertically-stacked rear light cluster. The wraparound rear window helped give the Golden Hawk the profile of a beast (or bird) of prey, poised on its haunches. So did the bump of the air intake on the hood, especially knowing it housed the McCulloch supercharger on the 5.8 litre V8 that could fling the big car forward to 60 mph (97 km/h) in 7.8 secs.

The heavy engine gave the Golden Hawk a power-to-weight ratio good enough to threaten Chrysler's more expensive 300 B model, a street-legal NASCAR combatant. It was nose heavy, and difficult to handle, but a series of acceleration and sprint tests by racing professionals saw it shrug aside Ford's Thunderbird and Chevrolet's Corvette. Respect. The Studebaker Golden Hawk is one of the true godfathers of the Muscle Cars of the following decade.

COUNTRY OF ORIGIN:
USA
FIRST MANUFACTURED:
1956 (until 1958)
ENGINE:
5.8 l (352 cid) V8 (1956); 4.7 l (289 cid) supercharged V8 (1957)
PERFORMANCE:
Top speed 125 mph (201 km/h); 0-60 mph (97 km/h) in 7.8 secs
YOU SHOULD KNOW:
Studebaker was America's oldest vehicle maker, and celebrated its centenary in 1952. Five brothers started the company, and turned it into the world's biggest producer of horse-drawn vehicles, before creating some of the best and best-looking of US cars. The company closed down in 1966.

Tatra 603

Throughout the 1930s and 1940s Tatra cars were celebrated for their exceptionally slippery streamlining, accentuated by the often huge and always bizarre dorsal fin on the car's sloping rear. After nationalization in 1948, the Czech company's car production was run down until it was left with nothing but trucks. Tatra's talented engineers honed their skills instead by making a series of racing prototypes, including a sports car (T602), a small racing car (T605) and a Formula One single-seater (T607). The experiments enabled them to develop a new engine, ready for the new, four-door sedan they were ordered to design by the Czechoslovak government for the use of senior officials. First shown at the1955 International Motor Show at Zlin, but not produced until 1957, the T603 was immediately recognizable as a Tatra.

Early T603s picked up where Tatra had left off. They were just as quirky, but on a more modest scale. The dorsal fin was reduced to a vestige between split rear windows, but the swooping rear streamlining remained, bounded by air louvres to cool the rear-mounted engine. The front looked like a typically bulbous postwar design with a split windscreen – except that gathered in the centre of the bulge, beneath the cosmetic windscoop, three headlights were grouped close behind a single glass window. For a thumping great luxury car, they were very stylish. They were also reliable and dependably quick, and the V8 engine (tested and refined for so long) received only one upgrade, in 1963.

From then on, the Tatra 603 had its stylistic character gradually assassinated. The curves withdrew to sharper angles, the front headlights separated into two pairs and Tatra's stylistic extravagance was tamed to conformity. By 1975, you couldn't recognize the T603 except by its long-serving engine. It was about the only component not subject to bureaucracy.

The Tatra 603 provided typical Soviet-era transportation for Communist Party high-ups and favoured Government officials.

COUNTRY OF ORIGIN:
Czechoslovakia (now Czech Republic)
FIRST MANUFACTURED:
1955 (until 1975)
ENGINE:
2,472 cc V8
PERFORMANCE:
Top speed of 100mph (160 km/h)
YOU SHOULD KNOW:
Private individuals were not allowed to own the Tatra 603, and low demand dictated that Tatra's engineers and designers build most of the cars by hand – especially to begin with. In its first 7 years, only 5992 Tatra 603-1 cars were made. These were the models with the real magic.

Triumph TR2

The Triumph TR2 was a triumph of willpower. The forerunner of one of Britain's most successful sports car series, it was created by Sir John Black, head of the Standard Motor Company and of Triumph. Standard had supplied engines to the fledgling Jaguar Company, and Black desperately wanted to share or compete with Jaguar's success. His first efforts, the Triumph 1800 and Triumph 2000, were classic British sports cars, but already stylistically outmoded. Then Jaguar pre-empted his plans with the fabulous XK120. The ingenious Sir John spotted a gap in the market. Necessity for strict economy in development and production drove the inspired invention of a truly beautiful, small open roadster. It hit the bullseye.

The TR2's witches' brew of components defied identification in the glorious finished product. The new car was based on unused frames from the prewar Standard Flying Nine. The engine was devised from the 2.1 litre four used in both the Standard Vanguard and the Ferguson tractor. The suspension and rear axle came from the Triumph Mayflower sedan (you couldn't make this up!). To save costs on stamping compound curves, the panels were beaten and welded; and the depth of the front intake hid a simple mesh instead of a formal grille. The designers even abandoned their idea for retractable headlight pods, and installed the fixed pods that completed the TR2's 'frog-eye' front.

For something out of nothing, the TR2 was a tour de force. America loved it, too, and the car won many Sports Car Club of America events. A team of TR2s also did well in the Mille Miglia and the 24 du Mans. The car was the least expensive model capable of over 100 mph (160 km/h). For style and sheer chutzpah, it matched the very best.

COUNTRY OF ORIGIN:
UK
FIRST MANUFACTURED:
1953 (until 1955)
ENGINE:
1,991 cc Straight Four
PERFORMANCE:
Tests by Motor magazine gave a top speed of 107.3 mph (172.8 km/h), and 0-60 mph (97 km/h) in 12.0 secs.
YOU SHOULD KNOW:
You may come across a car called a 'long door' Triumph TR2. These were the 1953 and early 1954 line production models, with doors that extended to the very edge of the car. A shorter door style was introduced in the autumn of 1954, which appears on the majority of TR2s.

The TR2 was a very successful combination of assorted components that included a prewar Standard chassis and a modified Ferguson tractor engine.

Vauxhall PA Cresta

COUNTRY OF ORIGIN:
UK
FIRST MANUFACTURED:
1957 (until 1962)
ENGINE:
2,262 cc Straight Six ('pushrod' OHV
until 1960)
PERFORMANCE:
Top speed of 90 mph (144 km/h)
with acceleration of 0-60 mph
(97 km/h) in 16.8 secs
YOU SHOULD KNOW:
Ironically, despite (or maybe because
of) the PA Cresta's rock 'n' roll
image, the Queen of England had a
rare estate version for her own
personal use.

Few cars are so evocative of Britain's late '50s obsession with American culture as the PA range. The introduction of the PA Cresta was the culmination of several years' gradual Americanization of the Vauxhall marque and the drift away from the small-car market with which it had been associated in the prewar years. General Motors (Vauxhall's parent company) had given the first subtle signs that the marque was evolving in a new direction with the introduction of the Wyvern family saloon in 1948, and by 1954 understated echoes of American styling had become apparent in Vauxhall's Velox and Cresta saloon range, indicating the start of a new era in design that paved the way for the 1957 launch of the PA Cresta, a deluxe version of the PA Velox.

The PA's flashy tailfins, clustered rear lights, whitewall tyres and wrap-around windows were blatantly transatlantic, emulating the brash good looks of the Buicks and Cadillacs rolling off General Motors' Detroit assembly line. Its paintwork came in bright (optional two-tone) colours with plenty of gleaming chrome trim while the plush interior was fitted with leather upholstery and pile carpet, and included the luxury of a fitted heater as standard. Three people could easily sit together along the front benchseat, with the handbrake neatly stowed under the dashboard and the gearshift mounted on the steering column, leaving the floor completely clear for feet. A beautifully designed tri-sectioned rear screen gave panoramic visibility while the all-sync three-speed gearbox and independent front suspension ensured a smooth ride.

If the starchier members of the establishment considered the PA too *outré* for words, it was certainly the prestige statement car that every hip '50s glamour-seeker aspired to. More than 81,000 PA Crestas were built and today it is a highly sought-after classic.

The semi-transatlantic Cresta appeared when General Motors decided that Britain was ready to embrace rock 'n' roll styling.

Volkswagen Type 2 (Camper)

The Type 2 *KombinationsKraftWagen*, or 'Kombi', was originally intended as a utilitarian commercial transporter for the numerous new business enterprises that sprang up after World War II. It was built on a modified Type 1 (Beetle) platform and almost as soon as it was introduced it became clear there was a market for a passenger version with removable seats – the campervan was born. The split-windowed early models, known as 'splitties', had various styles of interior layout and degrees of luxury, of which the best-known are the thousand or so original 'westies' produced by Westfalia, VW's official coachbuilders.

From its inception, the Type 2 was recognised as a uniquely versatile new type of vehicle. The novelty of its very un-American low-powered, air-cooled rear engine and space-saving boxy shape appealed enormously to the US market and in the 1960s it was adopted by the counter-culture as the ultimate fashion accessory for living out the hippie dream – the epitome of wanderlust chic. The VW Camper's great attraction lies in the fact that it is extraordinarily easy to drive with excellent visibility and easy steering and, although it has the acceleration of a snail and is neither particularly comfortable nor very economical, these are small prices to pay in return for the towering sensation of power you feel at the wheel – a veritable king of the road.

Over the years, the Type 2 has evolved through a multitude of styles to come almost full-circle: the latest model is a retro second generation 1970s 'breadloaf' version but with more power, a water-cooled engine and a vintage price tag. Too much to hope, though, for a remake of the original classic 'splittie' – it is destined to remain a rusty collector's piece for dreamers.

This is how Kombis looked before the hippie generation painted flowers all over them and hit the road to heaven.

COUNTRY OF ORIGIN:
Germany (also produced in Brazil and Mexico)
FIRST MANUFACTURED:
1950 (Split-screen until 1967)
ENGINE:
Depending on model, ranges from 1,131 cc to 2,000 cc Flat Four (air-cooled until 1984)
PERFORMANCE:
Top speed of 60 mph (97 km/h); 0-60 mph (97km/h) in 75 secs
YOU SHOULD KNOW:
The VW Type 2 Camper has acquired almost as many nicknames as it has had incarnations. As well as 'kombi', 'westie', 'splittie', and 'hippie van/bus', you may hear it referred to as a 'microbus', 'bulli', 'loaf', 'bay' or 'vee-dub'.

Volkswagen Karmann-Ghia

COUNTRY OF ORIGIN:
Germany (and also built in Brazil)
FIRST MANUFACTURED:
1955 (until 1974)
ENGINE:
1,192 cc Flat Four
PERFORMANCE:
Early models could hit a top speed of
76 mph (122 km/h) which improved
to 85 mph (140 km/h) in later years.
YOU SHOULD KNOW:
A variant of the Karmann-Ghia, the
Type 34 was introduced in 1961. It
had considerably more power than
the original but was less strikingly
attractive and never achieved
anything like the sales, although
today it has become something of a
collector's item simply for its
rarity value.

Having hit the jackpot with its 'People's Car', the utilitarian and reliable Type 1 (Beetle), VW repeated its success with the Karmann-Ghia. As the world started to recover from postwar austerity and aspire to upwardly mobile, image-enhancing lifestyle statements, VW cannily responded to the zeitgeist with a stunningly attractive, and attractively priced, 2+2 coupe that brought the dream of owning a sports car within the grasp of the ordinary person in the street. The coupe was an instant hit, followed amost immediately by an equally popular convertible version.

The K-G was constructed on a Type 1 platform using the Beetle engine and backbone chassis with a slightly widened floorpan. The impeccably styled body emerged from the Italian design house Carrozzeria Ghia and was produced by Karmann coachbuilders. Backed by VW's well-established reputation for sound engineering and a famously punchy advertising campaign, the K-G soon became the leading import car in the US and over the years almost half a millon were produced. Although a right-hand drive version was built, the K-G never really took off in Britain because restrictive import duties made it prohibitively pricey.

The K-G was unbeatable in its price class for looks, quality and comfort. And even though it didn't have anything like enough power to be classified as a true sports car, it was a superb tourer – a perfect combination of Teutonic technology and Italian glamour. The light steering, low-slung body and bucket seats give the illusion of being in a nippy little sports car and even though the K-G is not really much speedier than the Beetle, it is really good fun to drive – a timeless classic that is eminently affordable with easily obtainable spare parts.

The slinky Karmann-Ghia cleverly managed to look much faster than it actually was.

Volvo 'Amazon' 120 Series

Arguably the car with which Volvo established its reputation as a manufacturer of safe, solid and attractive mid-range cars, the Amazon is perhaps the most famous and easily recognisable car that Volvo has ever produced. Designer Jan Wilsgaard's take on the classic Chrysler tailfins and bull nose was influenced by Italian and British design as much as American; the Amazon has a restrained elegance about it that still impresses today.

The Amazon was designed to be the sophisticated, up-to-the-minute successor to the rugged but staid postwar PV series, but almost as soon as it went on the market a problem arose: its name. Sole title had already been registered by a German motorbike manufacturer which meant that Volvo's use of it was restricted to the Baltic countries. Throughout the rest of Europe the car had to be marketed by model number alone. Despite this marketing gaffe, the car quickly gained a reputation for reliability and durability and Volvo soon also demonstrated concern for safety, offering fitted front-seat safety belts as standard on its 1959 sports version.

The basic model (known as the 121) was a three-speed manual with rear-wheel drive, fitted with a single Stromberg carb, 1.6 litre engine. In 1958 a four-speed, twin carb sports version (122S) was produced. Further models and more powerful (1.8 and 2 litre) engines continued to be introduced and by the time production ended you could have chosen from a selection of two- and four-door saloons as well as estate versions, with a number of engine options.

The 120 series was a bestseller for Volvo for more than a decade and nearly half the Amazons sold in Sweden are still on the road today. Their astoundingly good condition attests to Volvo's quality production.

The chunky Amazon was solid and tough, but surprisingly quick in its rally versions.

COUNTRY OF ORIGIN:
Sweden
FIRST MANUFACTURED:
1956 (until 1970)
ENGINE:
1580 cc, 1778 cc, 1896 cc OHV Straight Four
(Volvo B16, B18 or B20 engines)
PERFORMANCE:
Top speed of 108 mph (174 km/h)
YOU SHOULD KNOW:
Volvo's numbering system for the 120 series is notoriously confusing, depending partly on which country the car was marketed in. In theory, four-door saloons are designated 120s, two-door saloons as 130s and estates as 220s; and an S on the end indicates a sports model. However, they are by no means always badged according to this system. To establish beyond doubt what a particular model is, it is best to consult the type number in the engine compartment.

1960s

AC Shelby Cobra

COUNTRY OF ORIGIN:
UK/USA
FIRST MANUFACTURED:
1961 (until1967)
ENGINE:
4.2 l (260 cid); 4.7 l (289 cid);
7 l (427 cid) V8
PERFORMANCE:
Top speed of around 163 mph
(262 km/h) in standard model and
180 mph (290 km/h) in competition
model; 0-60 mph (97 km/h)
in 4.2 secs
YOU SHOULD KNOW:
In 2006, Carroll Shelby's own Cobra
sold at auction in Arizona for a
record $5.5 million.

One of the top 1960s sports cars, renowned for both speed and looks, the Cobra is a winning combination of lightweight British roadster and hefty high-torque American Ford V8 engine. Whether you regard it as a British or an American car depends entirely on which side of the Atlantic your loyalty lies. Texan racing star Carroll Shelby certainly considered it his baby – he even declared that the name 'Cobra' had come to him in a dream, and after AC went bankrupt in 1967 he sued for rights and won acknowledgement that he was the maker of every Cobra in the USA, even though they had indisputably been designed and partly built in AC's Thames Ditton workshop.

The Cobra story starts in 1961. Shelby expressed interest in fitting a V8 engine into AC's Ace competition roadster, which had hitherto been equipped with a straight six. A prototype was produced and the Cobra was born. The first 75 were fitted with a Ford 260 HiPo 4.2 litre engine while another 51 had the larger 289 (4.7 litre). At the end of 1962, Alan Turner, AC's chief engineer, made major modifications and fitted new steering using a VW Beetle column. About 530 of these Mark II versions were produced but they were outperformed on the race track and in 1965 the Mark III was designed to be powered by a whopping 'side-oiler' Ford 427 7 litre engine. AC sent some 300 rolling chassis to Shelby and at the same time produced a narrow-fendered AC 289 version for the European market.

The Cobra was almost too fast for its own good. Legend has it that racing driver Jack Sears reached 185 mph (298 km/h) on the M1 in 1964, supposedly a contributory factor in the government's decision to introduce speed limits on British roads.

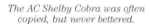

The AC Shelby Cobra was often copied, but never bettered.

Alfa Romeo T33 Stradale

For some years Alfa Romeo competed successfully on the race track by using modified production cars, but in 1967 the company adopted a new approach – the 2 litre Tipo 33 racer was built from scratch. This prototype was to become the basis of the legendary Stradale, a roadster born from racing car technology that not only vies for title of most beautiful car ever made but also performed in the same league as any supercar of the day.

Technically, the Stradale was virtually identical to the T33 racer but with a longer wheel base and a lower-tuned engine, a custom-built, powerful but compact, lightweight alloy shortstroke V8 designed by Alfa's racing engineer, Carlo Chiti, and a Valerio Colotti six-speed transaxle gearbox. The cars were assembled individually entirely by hand at coachbuilder Carrozzeria Marazzi of Milan to a daring futuristic design of Franco Scaglione. The beautifully sculpted aluminium body had the first butterfly doors (opening upwards and outwards) to be found in a production car and side windows that arched seamlessly into the bubble roof. The finished product oozed sex appeal in a way that was far ahead of its time.

Anyone lucky enough to get behind the wheel of a Stradale is in for the experience of a lifetime. The car literally begs you to let go and give in to your lust for speed. But dream on! You've got about as much chance of driving one of these gorgeous million dollar roadsters as you have of going to the moon. Only 18 were ever made and even they were outside the grasp of any but the very deepest pocket – the Stradale was one of the most expensive cars on the market, selling at $17,000, more than five times as much as the average car at that time.

COUNTRY OF ORIGIN:
Italy
FIRST MANUFACTURED:
1968 (until 1971)
ENGINE:
1,995 cc V8
PERFORMANCE:
Top speed 162 mph (260 km/h);
0-60 mph (97 km/h) in 5.4 secs
YOU SHOULD KNOW:
You can see an Alfa T33 Stradale in the Alfa Romeo Museum in Arese near Milan, Italy.

A light aluminium body helped to give the T33 neck-snapping performance figures.

Alfa Spider Series I

Made famous by Dustin Hoffman in the film *The Graduate*, the Spider was launched at the Geneva Motor Show in 1966, just when the era of the 'muscle car' was reaching its height. Based on the chassis of the Giulia 105, a lightweight car with a powerful engine, it was designed and built by Battista Pininfarina. It was to be the last car he worked on – he died only a month after the Spider's introduction.

Like Pininfarina's masterpiece, the iconic Cisitalia 202, the Spider was a monocoque (all-in-one body). It was fitted with Alfa's all-alloy twin cam four-cylinder engine and had five-speed manual transmission, disc brakes and independent front suspension. Initially called the Duetto, it soon acquired the nickname *Osso di Seppia* (Cuttlefish Bone) after its distinctive rounded rear tail. Its raunchy Italian styling encapsulated the liberated spirit of the approaching 'summer of love' and today it is considered a design classic of the swinging '60s.

In 1967 the Duetto was replaced by the beefed-up 1750 Veloce version, manufactured with two twin carburettors for the European market and fuel injection for the US. The Veloce looked more or less identical to the Duetto but it was fitted with a more powerful engine and modified suspension, brakes and electrics. At the same time a less exclusive, pared-down Junior 1300 version was produced.

The Spider is an absolute joy to drive – pure unadulterated fun. It is the ideal roadster – nippy, easy to control (four-wheel disc brakes and rack-and-pinion steering make for excellent handling) and comfortable enough for long journeys. And it had staying power – with only minor modifications, the Spider went through four iterations, remaining in production for the best part of 30 years, by which time some 124,000 had been built.

COUNTRY OF ORIGIN:
Italy
FIRST MANUFACTURED:
1966 (until 1969)
ENGINE:
Duetto 1,570 cc, Veloce 1,779 cc,
Junior 1,290 cc DOHC Straight Four
PERFORMANCE:
Duetto – top speed of 109 mph
(175 km/h); 0-60 mph (97 km/h)
in 11.3 secs
Veloce – top speed of 116 mph
(187 km/h); 0-60 mph (97 km/h)
in 9.2 secs
YOU SHOULD KNOW:
Altogether there were four
generations of the Alfa Spider –
the *Ossa di Seppia* or Roundtail
(1966-69), the *Coda Tronca* or Kamm
Tail (1970-81), the *Aerodinamica* or
Duck Tail (1982-89) and finally the
1,962 cc Type 4 (1990-1993).

Alpine A110 Berlinette

The Alpine A110 is the rally car *par excellence*, the embodiment of one man's pioneer spirit and passionate dedication to the world of motor racing. Born in Dieppe in 1922, the son of a Renault engineer, Jean Rédéle grew up tinkering with cars and fascinated by the race track. He started to enter competitions in a self-modified Renault 4CV, winning his class in the Mille Miglia.

Rédéle became the youngest Renault dealer in France and, with unlimited access to parts, he started to design his own lightweight sports coupes. He founded the Alpine company in 1954 and in 1960 showed his A108 2+2 closed coupe (berlinetta) at the Paris Autosalon. It had a fibreglass body on a steel backbone chassis and was fitted with an 850 cc rear-mounted Renault Dauphine engine. Rédéle named it the 'Berlinette Tour de France'. This was the car which, when fitted with a more powerful Renault 8 engine, morphed into the legendary A110 Berlinette, unveiled in 1963. Rédéle carried on tinkering and the Berlinette kept evolving. What had started out as a little 956 cc 51 bhp coupe ended up as an 1,800 cc with 180+ bhp, and was available both as a coupe and a cabriolet.

Year after year, the latest version kept winning all the most prestigious prizes and thrilling the rally-driving world. By 1968 Renault was pouring the whole of its racing budget into Alpine with the inevitable consequence that in 1970 Rédéle's company was swallowed up by his powerful patron. The economic downturn of the 1970s eventually brought about Alpine's demise in 1977.

The Berlinette was never intended to be anything other than a rally car and as such has never really been equalled. This light, lowslung car drives like a dream. There won't be another like it in a hurry.

COUNTRY OF ORIGIN:
France
FIRST MANUFACTURED:
1962 (until 1977)
ENGINE:
Displacement ranging from 1,108 cc to 1,647 cc OHV Straight Four
PERFORMANCE:
Top speed 133 mph (215km/h)
YOU SHOULD KNOW:
In 1971 Ove Andersson won the Monte Carlo Rally in an Alpine A110 and the same year the A110 won the International Rally Championship; in 1973 it became the first World Rally Champion.

Jean Rédéle went from car dealer to race winner driving the Renault cars he created.

Alvis TF21

COUNTRY OF ORIGIN:
UK
FIRST MANUFACTURED:
1966
ENGINE:
2,993 cc Straight Six
PERFORMANCE:
Top speed of 120 mph (193 km/h)
YOU SHOULD KNOW:
Founded in Coventry by engineer
T G John (1880–1946) originally a
naval architect, Alvis made exclusive
cars for 47 years (1920–1967) which
are renowned for their character and
the high quality of their
workmanship. They have survived
well and are still driven in
competition racing. A TF21 drophead
coupe in good condition can cost
around $65,000.

Alvis had a 'good' World War II, switching from the specialist car market to the manufacture of aero engines thus ensuring a healthy profit. But the war had shaken up society, creating a more egalitarian climate in which the minority privilege of elite sports cars and luxury tourers had no place. This top-end specialist market had been Alvis's customer base so it isn't surprising that the company folded; the only wonder is how it was able to give such a long-lasting swansong.

Alvis's final cars were an imaginative line of 3 litre saloons and drophead coupes, starting with the TA21 in 1950 and ending with the TF21 in 1966 – the last-ever Alvis car. Alvis's short-stroke six-cylinder 3 litre engine supplied plenty of power whatever the revs (150 bhp in the TF21) but carriagework was a dying art and Alvis were only able to go into production by going abroad – to renowned Swiss coachbuilder Hermann Graber. Together with Mulliner Park Ward, by now a subsidiary of Rolls Royce, Graber saved the day. He built some stupendous one-off models while Mulliner produced the rest in batches to his modified design.

The TF21 was the model with which the company closed its doors on the car industry for good, with not a whimper but, rather, a thundering great bang. Though it is generally agreed that the apotheosis of the 3 litre series was a remarkably beautiful Graber-inspired TD21, there is something incredibly special about the TF21. Only 106 were ever made and the experience of sitting behind the wheel of this luxurious motor easily beats driving a contemporaneous Jaguar or Bentley. Alvis faded from the car market with its reputation still at its height. Sadly the company was swallowed up by British Leyland in 1967 and reverted to general engineering.

The TF21 was the last in a long and illustrious line of fine gentleman's sports tourers with a 'Made in Britain' label.

AMC
AMX

By the late 1960s the American Motor Company (AMC) was in deep trouble financially. It was the era of the 'muscle car', when Ford, General Motors and Chrysler were engaged in ferocious rivalry for market dominance. AMC didn't have the resources to keep up with the Big Three but, in a last-ditch bid to snatch back some market share, it produced the AMX.

An acronym of American Motors eXperimental, The AMX was not a true 'pony car' in the mould of the iconic 1964 Ford Mustang but AMC certainly marketed it as a car in the GT (*Grand Turismo*) tradition – a rear-wheel drive, high-performance two-door coupe designed for long-distance travel. With its long-hooded sleek design, dual exhausts, four-speed manual transmission and heavy-duty suspension, reclining bucket seats, carpet and woodgrain trim, the AMX pulled all the right strings – power, glamour, comfort – to fulfil anyone's macho dreams. It fitted neatly into the gap between domestically produced pony cars and expensive import models; and it was the only steel-bodied domestic two-seater sports car on the market – the first since the 1950s Ford Thunderbird – its only competitor being the much pricier fibreglass Chevrolet Corvette.

The car was economically manufactured using AMC's existing unibody technology and engine sizes were based on their standard 290, stepping up to the 343 and 390. The basic price was a very reasonable $3,245. In 1969 and again in 1970 the AMX won the title of Best Engineered Car. The 1970 model was the last true AMX. In three years, just over 19,000 had been sold – not enough to make it cost effective. But it had done its job of promoting AMC as an upbeat, youthful company, putting it back in the running. The name AMX was attached to a version of AMC's Javelin instead.

The AMX was conceived as a muscle car, and boosted the American Motor Company's street cred as a go-ahead maker.

COUNTRY OF ORIGIN:
USA
FIRST MANUFACTURED:
1968 (until1970)
ENGINE:
4.8 l (290 cid); 5.6 l (343 cid); 5.9 l (360 cid); 6.4 l (390 cid) V8
PERFORMANCE:
Top speed of around 130 mph (209 km/h); 0-60 mph (97 km/h) in 6.9 secs
YOU SHOULD KNOW:
In 1968 racing champion Craig Breedlove set 106 world speed records in an AMX, and a highly desirable limited edition of 50 red, white and blue 'Breedlove' models were manufactured to celebrate his achievement. In the same year, AMC presented Playmate of the Year Angela Dorian with a specially painted 'Playmate Pink' AMX. Its numberplate displayed her vital statistics.

*Unluckily for drivers of the
standard DB5, it lacked the
James Bond machine guns that
would have made the onset of
road rage seriously interesting.*

Aston Martin DB5

Possibly the most successful ever example of car product placement,
the DB5 achieved film star status in its own right in the hands of
Sean Connery as James Bond's over-the-top set of wheels in the film
Goldfinger. The must-haves for the car chase in the hills above
Monte Carlo included twin pop-out 30 calibre Browning machine
guns, a three-way revolving front number plate, smokescreen
generator, spiked nail dispenser, oil-slick spray nozzle to dispatch
tailgaters and a passenger-seat ejector for the instant removal of
unwanted company. The car's starring role in the film led to sales of
over a thousand DB5s – a record for the Aston Martin company. The
DB5 was the epitome of style and if your sights were trained on Miss
Moneypenny, the DB5 was the unchallenged transport of delight.

The DB5 replaced the relatively long-lasting DB4, in two-door,
four-seater coupe, convertible or estate versions. The DB4's 3.7 litre
engine was revved up to 4 litres for the DB5. Earlier models
maintained the DB4's four-speed manual transmission plus optional
overdrive, or the three-speed automatic alternative but these
systems were soon superseded by a standard five-speed manual
gearbox. The three SU carburettors of the earlier DB5 model
produced a top speed of about 140 mph (225 km/h). The Aston
Martin Volante, introduced in late 1964, was slightly more powerful.

While its price/performance ratio couldn't match such
contemporaries as the Jaguar E-Type (at about half the price tag),
the DB5's classic design was infinitely more refined than the E-Type's
blatantly vulgar appearance. With its leather upholstery and classy
wood interior fittings (though without power steering), it was a
machine for the financially inoculated to die for, or even use as their
licence for thrills.

COUNTRY OF ORIGIN:
United Kingdom
FIRST MANUFACTURED:
1963 (until 1965)
ENGINE:
3,995 cc Straight Six
PERFORMANCE:
Top speed of 140 mph (225 km/h);
0-60 mph (97 km/h) in 8.1 secs
YOU SHOULD KNOW:
The Aston Martin DB series was
named after David Brown, its
managing director. He bought the
company in 1947 and sold it in 1972.

BMW 3200 CS

Designed as the successor to the BMW 503, the exceedingly handsome 3200CS four-seat sports tourer was BMW's top-range model in 1962. The body was designed and built by Italian car stylist Gruppo Bertone then freighted to BMW in Germany for mounting on the 503 chassis. It was the first BMW to be fitted with front disc brakes, and it had twin Zenith carburettors, a tweaked V8 engine, four-speed transmission and rear-wheel drive.

The coupe body, a typically distinctive Bertone design, introduced a new style feature – the 'Hofmeister kink' (named after BMW's director of design). This is the sharp-angled forward bend (or 'kink') towards the base of the C-pillar (the roof-support strut that separates the rear side-window from the rear windscreen) which has become the signature design of the BMW marque. Look at any BMW model sideways-on and your eye is automatically drawn to the C-pillar. The design philosophy at BMW has always been 'form should follow function' and the purpose of the Hofmeister kink is not simply to look pretty but to subliminally indicate that the drive lies in the rear wheels. The Hofmeister kink has since been incorporated into many different makes of car but it is still primarily associated with BMW.

The launch of the 3200CS was overshadowed by the simultaneous appearance of the BMW New Class 1500 sedan, one of a series of saloons designed to fill a gap in the market between mass produced cars and luxury designer models. In its two-door version, the 1500 was so successful that BMW was barely able to keep up with production so the company dropped the 3200CS in 1995 after only three years. Sadly, it was to be the last of the big V8 BMWs.

COUNTRY OF ORIGIN:
Germany (and partly Italy)
FIRST MANUFACTURED:
1962 (until1965)
ENGINE:
3,168 cc OHV V8
PERFORMANCE:
Advertised top speed 124 mph
(200 km/h)
YOU SHOULD KNOW:
Bertone designed and built a one-off convertible version of the 3200CS for BMW boss Herbert Quandt, the wealthy German industrialist who saved BMW from being swallowed up by Daimler-Benz in 1959. This unique car still exists and was exhibited to the public at the classic car show, Techno Classica 2003.

The 3200 CS coupe was at the top of BMW's top range, but it only lasted for three years.

BMW 2002

COUNTRY OF ORIGIN:
Germany
FIRST MANUFACTURED:
1968 (until 1976)
ENGINE:
1,990 cc Straight Four
PERFORMANCE:
Top speed for the 2002 of 112 mph
(181 km/h); top speed for the 2002Tii
of 115 mph (185 km/h)
YOU SHOULD KNOW:
The 2002 and 2002Tii are classic cars
for tinkerers. BMW are not unaware
of the nostalgia value of their
charismatic car and have made it
extremely easy for legions of
dedicated 2002 enthusiasts to obtain
spare parts.

The 2002 is a seminal car. It not only saved BMW from insolvency but put the BMW marque on par with top German manufacturers like Volkswagen. The world (and especially the US) was already primed for high-powered but nimble small sports saloons and BMW filled the niche to perfection with the 2002. It was synonymous with modernity: a two-door economy car that fulfilled practical everyday requirements – space for four people to travel in comfort (independent suspension with MacPherson struts) with room for luggage too – but which drove like a racer – speedy, agile and quick off the mark, handling better than just about any other small car on the market.

The 2002 evolved out of BMW's New Class sedans, first introduced in 1961. These were powered by BMW's four-cylinder M10 engine designed by one of the company's founding fathers, Baron Alex von Falkenhausen. Although the M10 was a 1.5 litre engine, it was cunningly designed so that it could easily be expanded to 2 litres. Von Falkenhausen and BMW's Planning Director Helmut Werner Bonsch discovered by chance that they had both independently put a 2 litre M10 into their own personal two-door New Class 1600s and been thrilled by the result. They decided to make a joint formal proposal for its production. And thus the BMW 2002 was born.

Based on BMW's New Class 1600, the 2002 was a sound economic proposition. BMW also introduced a hatchbacked three-door model, the 2002Ti (Touring international) and finally its star model, the 2002Tii (Touring international injection) fitted with a Kugelfischer fuel injection pump. With the introduction of the 2002Tii, BMW firmly established itself as a reputable quality manufacturer and set the standard for the entire class of small, high-performance cars, paving the way for the models on the road today.

This was the first of many small sports saloons from BMW.

Borgward P100

Nothing illustrated the brilliance of Carl Borgward as an automobile engineer better that *Der Grosser* Borgward (Big Borgward) introduced in 1960. The P100 was an exciting model that replaced the big six-cylinder Hansa 2400 Pullman, which had not been a notable commercial success. Borgward's all-new large saloon car was presented at the Frankfurt Motor Show in 1959 and had an angular contemporary design with panoramic rear window and small tail fins, reminiscent of the look Pininfarina was developing at the same time for cars like the Fiat 1800 in Italy.

The P100 (also known as the Big Six) had the same type of integral three-box monocoque chassis as the company's successful Isabella model, and was powered by an evolutionary version of Borgward's own six-cylinder engine. It had revolutionary self-levelling air suspension (which the company christened Airswing), some time before this feature was introduced by rival Mercedes-Benz – the Stuttgart leviathan that was firmly in Borgward's sights when the new saloon was introduced. The P100's marketing campaign made much of advanced engineering features like that pneumatic suspension, underlining the fact that Mercedes now had some serious competition at the luxury end of the market.

Unfortunately, the Big Six suffered from an old Borgward drawback – unexpected mechanical problems that only surfaced after a car had been launched, rather than being sorted beforehand. Even so, when Bremen-based Borgward was unjustly forced into liquidation by its own state government (conspiracy theorists suggest with some covert encouragement from other German car companies seeking to suppress a feisty rival) over 2,500 P100s had been produced, suggesting that this fine car was on course to penetrate the market for big six-cylinder cars that had been dominated by Mercedes-Benz throughout the 1950s. But sadly it was not to be.

The now-forgotten Borgward was a luxury car that briefly proved to be a genuine rival to Mercedes-Benz models.

COUNTRY OF ORIGIN:
Germany
FIRST YEAR OF MANUFACTURE:
1960 (until 1961)
ENGINE:
2,238 cc Straight Six
PERFORMANCE:
Top speed of 100 mph (161 km/h);
0-60 mph (97 km/h) around 16 secs
YOU SHOULD KNOW:
The hard-done-by Carl Borgward didn't live to see the resurrection of the P100 in Argentina, using the Borgward production line. Devastated by the loss of his company, he died a broken man in 1963.

COUNTRY OF ORIGIN:
USA
FIRST MANUFACTURED:
1961 (until 1963)
ENGINE:
3.5 litre (215 cid) V8
PERFORMANCE:
Top speed of 107 mph (172 km/h);
0-60 mph (97 km/h) in 10.2 secs
YOU SHOULD KNOW:
The Skylark name regularly appeared
on Buick cars, always denoting a
step up in power or comfort from
whatever series preceded it. The
name is attached to numerous
special editions and to whole series
of cars. It still is – but every Skylark
model has fulfilled its initial promise,
at least to begin with.

*Special it was – and also pretty
good for a spot of skylarking.*

Buick Special Skylark

You could base a social history on the Buick Special Skylark. It was
conceived as a conventionally cynical exercise in the idiom of
contemporary supermarket salesmanship. The Buick Special had
performed reasonably well for the company, which wasn't quite
ready to launch a whole new series of models. The Special Skylark
was going to pep up the existing range, and prepare America for the
next one. Using the same chassis as the Chevrolet Corvair, Pontiac
Tempest and Oldsmobile F-85, Buick based the new car's styling on
the 1960 Buick Special two-door coupe. The Buick Special Skylark
was launched in mid 1961 with a vinyl roof, lower body side
mouldings, new rear light cluster, and the crucial, unique Skylark
badging. Inside it was luxurious and well-made: a four-star rather
than five-star car, with all-leather bucket seats as optional.

Buick's real target was the wannabe 'Wild Ones', 'the younger
generation' just beginning to make the connection between rock 'n'
roll and the highway ethic of
'the endless grey ribbon'. All
the other manufacturers
were chasing them but it was
the Special Skylark that hit
the spot. Improvements to
the V8 engine gave it
substantially more muscle
than other comparable cars –
a higher compression ratio
and a four-barrel carburettor
boosted it from 155hp at
4600 rpm to 185 hp. With its
other features, the Special
Skylark was something new
– a sporty compact with a
big-car feel. It was a pioneer.

By 1962, the transition
from Special was deemed
successful, and the identical
car became simply the
Skylark. This was available
as a two-door convertible
coupe as well as a hardtop.
In 1963, the frame was made
bigger, the engine became
even more muscular – and
the pioneer was absorbed
into the next cycle of
automotive marketing.

Buick Riviera

The Riviera was Buick's answer to the Ford Thunderbird – a 'personal luxury' car that gave the Thunderbird its first real competition and became a long-running success story. The 'Riviera' tag had first been coined in 1949 to describe a two-door pillarless hardtop. Buick was the first marque to put the style into mass production with its 1956 Roadmaster version and it had proved so popular that it was offered as an alternative body style on other Buick lines over the next few years. But the Riviera of '63 was the first time that the tag became a model in its own right. It soon became Buick's flagship car. Sales in the first three years topped 112,000.

The 1963 Riviera is considered a benchmark in car styling: a two-door pillarless hardtop sports coupe with frameless door windows (a completely new concept). Its streamlined elegance broke the mould and started a new era in American styling that introduced elements of sophisticated European design to large cars so that they appeared more than mere brash behemoths. The Riviera sold 40,000 in its first year – a huge success

Buick used a modified version of its standard chassis – slightly shorter and narrower – and fitted a standard Buick V8 engine and brakes, power steering and twin turbine automatic transmission, thus investing the Riviera with the same power as the larger Buick models for impressive overall performance. The bucket-seated interior was equipped with every conceivable luxury and a range of optional extras, including power windows and seats, cruise control, air conditioning and a tilt steering wheel. In 1964 the 401 engine was dropped and the car acquired its distinctive stylized 'R' badge that was to last until the end of the run 36 years later, by which time well over a million of these beauties had been produced.

The Riviera's streamlined look seemed almost European in concept, and pointed the way ahead for American auto design.

COUNTRY OF ORIGIN:
USA
FIRST YEAR OF MANUFACTURE:
1963 (until 1999)
ENGINE:
6.5 l (401 cid), 6.9 l (425 cid) V8
PERFORMANCE:
Top speed of 115 mph (184 km/h);
0-60 mph (97 km/h) in 8 secs
YOU SHOULD KNOW:
There were eight generations of this fabulously successful car each very different both externally and mechanically from the one before. The most sought-after versions date from 1963 to the early 1970s.

Cadillac Eldorado

COUNTRY OF ORIGIN:
USA
FIRST MANUFACTURED:
(Fourth generation) 1967 (until 1970)
ENGINE:
7.0 l (429 cid), 7.7 l (472 cid) or 8.2 l
(500 cid) V8
PERFORMANCE:
Top speed of 120 mph (193 km/h);
0-60 mph (97 km/h) in 8.9 secs
YOU SHOULD KNOW:
The personal luxury car was a
creature of the 20th century –
although the Eldorado lingered on
into the 21st century (just!)
competitors like the Oldsmobile
Toronado, Ford Thunderbird, Lincoln
Mark and Buick Riviera had perished
in the 1990s, predeceased by the
Chrysler Cordoba in 1983.

The Eldorado is an automotive institution, having been a stylish presence for the second half of the 20th century. The name appeared in 1953 and had covered a multitude of models before the last Eldorado rolled off the line in 2002. However, they all had one thing in common – they were Cadillac's pampered playboys in the personal luxury car segment of the market. That was a strange but lucrative niche reserved for image-conscious buyers who wanted a smack-you-in-the-eye luxury car with oodles of style, at the expense of trifling practical concerns like boot space and good leg room for back-seat passengers.

This egocentric market was booming in 1967, when the fourth generation Eldorado was radically reworked. It shared a GM E-body with the Olds Toronado and also had that model's front-wheel drive system and Powerplant Package. The launch saw a car with an endless bonnet covering a hefty 7 litre engine, a short cabin and stubby rear end. The headlights were hidden and the front end sported a jutting triangle in the centre, giving this crouching speedster an aggressive appearance. And speedy it was, capable of rocketing well past the 'ton' with blistering acceleration to match. As would be expected by those please-themselves owners, handling and roadholding were exceptional, too.

Next year, there were cosmetic styling tweaks – and an even larger V8 motor. The 1969 advances saw the hidden headlamps appear, along with flashy options like a (then sensational) vinyl roof and a power sunroof. For the last year before another major revamp, the Eldorado acquired the ultimate boy's toy – a massive 8.2 litre engine that remained exclusive until it was adopted by the other big Caddies in 1975. This was the biggest production V8 ever made, and its cachet ensured that Eldorado sales remained brisk.

It's tempting to suggest that the Eldorado required a master's ticket rather than a driver's licence, as this massive machine with its fancy cabin and rolling suspension was a true ship of the road.

Chevrolet Corvette Sting Ray

Chevy's Corvette (designed by the legendary Harley Earl and launched in 1953) had been a sizzling success, but by the early 1960s a completely reworked model was in the pipeline. After an exhaustive design process the C2 (officially named the Corvette Sting Ray) took its first bow in 1963 – to thunderous applause. Public reaction was so positive that the St Louis factory had to run a double shift and still couldn't meet demand. A waiting list built up and eager buyers were willing to pay well over list price for a nearly new Sting Ray. So what made this car so special, and desirable?

Had Bill Clinton been asked to answer that question, his answer would have been 'It's the design, stupid'. For the Sting Ray was stunningly beautiful, with two styles to die for – a purposeful coupe with a distinctive split rear window (a feature dropped in 1964) and a roadster that simply cried out to be driven for thrills. As the production run unfolded, the fabulous open-topped version sold best, though the coupe eventually reached annual parity just before the next model update, which saw the C3 'Shark' introduced in 1968.

In addition to breathtaking styling, the Sting Ray had mechanical enhancements like independent rear suspension, also retaining expensive options like fuel injection. Further development took place during the production run, delivering disc brakes all round and options like a telescopic steering wheel and external exhaust pipes. But the big news (literally) was in the engine department. A big-block 6.5 litre V8 appeared in 1965, followed by a massive 7 litre power plant in 1966. To drive the best, go for the tuned L-88 version of the latter – found only in the most collectable Sting Rays that carry a price tag around the million dollar mark.

The all-new Corvette was a sensational addition to the performance car scene.

COUNTRY OF ORIGIN:
USA
FIRST MANUFACTURED:
1963 (until 1967)
ENGINE:
5.35 l (327 cid), 6.5 l (396 cid)
or 7.0 l (427 cid) V8
PERFORMANCE:
With 7.0 l engine – top speed of 147 mph (237 km/h); 0-60 mph (97 km/h) in 6.1 secs
YOU SHOULD KNOW:
Around 110,000 C2 Sting Rays were produced and they are considered to be amongst the most collectable Corvettes built during the model's 50+ years of life – and the Sting Ray regularly comes out towards the top in polls that rank 'Best Sports Cars of the 1960s'.

Chevrolet Chevelle SS 396

It may have looked like a typical medium-sized saloon, but the Chevelle packed a seriously powerful punch.

In 1964 Chevrolet launched a new midline model – the Chevelle – which was destined to be a great success for parent General Motors. It also provided an opportunity to gatecrash the burgeoning muscle-car market, ignited by the concurrent appearance of the Pontiac GTO. Chevy's attention-grabbing riposte – codenamed Z16 – was the storming Chevelle Malibu SS 396 that appeared in early 1965. The SS stood for Super Sport and the 396 for a new big-block engine that would give this medium-sized car sensational performance. Just 201 were made (including one now-vanished custom convertible) and they catapulted the Chevelle SS to the forefront of muscle car production.

In 1966, Chevrolet cashed in with the Chevelle SS 396 becoming a distinct series in its own right. This sports coupe was equipped with tuned engine options and special features like enhanced suspension, transmission and brakes to handle that serious high performance capability. But the Chevelle SS 396's distinct identity would last for just three years, though all the goodies that made up the SS package were henceforth available as an option. This deal had already been offered on the '66 and '67 El Camino, but the formal El Camino SS 396 was available for one year only, 1968.

That exclusive SS badge still guaranteed grunt after the Chevelle SS 396 series was discontinued, but times they were a-changing. The 1970s saw the American auto industry start to ease back from over-the-top performance cars, with many engines being detuned to run on low-lead fuel.

In 1973, General Motors marques underwent an across-the-board revamp so – though the name remained the same – that year's Chevelle was effectively a new model. The SS custom option lingered on, though it no longer indicated the raw power of previous incarnations, and the Chevelle itself reached the end of the line in 1977.

COUNTRY OF ORIGIN:
USA
FIRST MANUFACTURED:
1965 (until 1968)
ENGINE:
6.5 l (396 cid) V8
PERFORMANCE:
Top speed of 120 mph (km/h);
0-60 mph (97 km/h) in 6.6 secs
YOU SHOULD KNOW:
From 1970 GM dropped a rule banning engines larger than 400 cid from mid-sized cars, and the SS package first acquired a 6.6 litre (402 cid) option, then a truly monstrous 7.4 litre (454 cid) power plant that cemented the Chevelle's reputation as an awesome muscle car. .

Chevrolet Camaro

The Ford Mustang set the pony-car agenda at just the right time, when the Sheiks turned off the oil taps and gas guzzling became bad news, but Chevrolet's response was swift and impressive. The Camaro followed the required long-bonnet-short-rear-deck pony-car principle, but its styling was in no way imitative and the new equine runner was an instant winner.

The Camaro 'personal car' (Chevy's description) came as a sleek 2+2 coupe or convertible. From the beginning the Camaro tempted buyers seeking that heady combination of performance and style. The 3.8 litre straight six was the standard engine, but a larger straight six and succession of five V8s rising to a potent 6.5 litre monster would eventually be offered. A popular first addition to the range was the mid-year SS-350 performance version, with bee-striped nose and a 295 bhp V8. There was also a Rally Sport package featuring concealed headlamps. Beyond the choice of body style and engine, a host of optional extras allowed buyers to personalize their new wheels. Did they respond well? You bet – over 220,000 were sold in Year One, more than half with a macho V8 engine.

The Camaro story would be one of constant evolution, and 1968 models saw improved suspension with front disc brakes, plus through-flow Astra ventilation for a sales tally of 235,000. In 1969 an extensive facelift introduced new bumpers and grille – creating a sleek long, low look that earned a 'Hugger' nickname and 243,000 sales.

A second generation Camaro appeared in 1970, with all-new fastback coupe styling, and this special speedster went on to become something of an institution, going through four generations and remaining in production until the early 21st century, before returning in 2009 as a fifth generation retro-styled machine that represents a stunning revival of the iconic Camaro brand.

COUNTRY OF ORIGIN:
USA
FIRST MANUFACTURED:
1967 (until 2002)
ENGINE:
Various, from 3.8 l (230 cid) Straight Six to 6.5 l (396 cid) V8
PERFORMANCE:
SS-350 model – top speed of 142 mph (229 km/h); 0-60 mph (97 km/h) in 6.3 secs
YOU SHOULD KNOW:
There was never any doubt where Chevrolet's sights were set – at the press conference where the Camaro name was unveiled to the eager motoring press, one journalist asked 'But what is a Camaro?' – to which enquiry came the swift reply 'A small, vicious animal that eats Mustangs'.

Chevrolet described the Camaro as a 'personal car', which was autospeak for 'have some seriously macho driving fun'.

Daimler DS420

COUNTRY OF ORIGIN:
UK
FIRST MANUFACTURED:
1968 (until 1992)
ENGINE:
4,235 cc V8
PERFORMANCE:
Top speed of 110 mph (177 km/h);
0-60 mph (97 km/h) in 10.5 secs
YOU SHOULD KNOW:
Jaguar supremo John Egan obviously
had faith in his own products – it is
said that in the mid-1980s his DS420
was a mobile boardroom fitted with
a TV, computer with printer and the
inevitable drinks cabinet.

The venerable Daimler company had gone as an independent entity but the new owner – Jaguar– let the name live on. In 1968 the last 'real' Daimler – the stately DR450 limousine – was replaced by the Daimler DS420. An unmistakable Daimler fluted grille remained, but the front end was given Jaguar four-headlight treatment and the new limo was built on a stretched Jaguar 420G floorpan at the Vanden Plas works. It also had a 4.2 litre straight six Jaguar engine.

However, the DS420's aspirations were altogether more upmarket. For this was Jaguar's cheeky attempt to take on the Rolls-Royce Phantom VI – a contest that wasn't entirely one-sided. The two luxury limousines were the same size with automatic transmission, independent suspension and disc brakes all round ensuring that the Daimler's ride was smooth and safe. Better still, it was half the Roller's price.

Various trim levels were available – from luxurious to opulent – and the DS420 had a glass screen allowing back-seat passengers to ride in splendid isolation from the chauffeur – suggesting the target market consisted of up-and-coming company directors who liked to travel in style. It was also popular at senior Government level (home and abroad) and used by top hotels to pamper premium guests. Last but not least it was much used in the matched-and-dispatched trade, sweeping brides to church (in white) or transporting grieving relatives

This stately limousine really was a child of the Sixties, albeit a decidedly well-bred one.

and (suitably modified) the dear departed to funerals (in black).

Over the years around 4,100 DS420s were built, suggesting that Jaguar's ambitious plan was not without commercial merit. Production transferred to the company's Coventry plant in 1979, but the only change came in the shape of larger bumpers and a new rear numberplate surround. The enduring quality of these hand-built beauties is such that most are still around to delight dedicated drivers of a distinguished modern classic.

De Tomaso Mangusta

It's nearly as familiar a story as boy meets girl – racing driver decides to build ultimate roasters. And so it was when Argentinian racer Alejandro de Tomaso migrated from the USA to Italy with his American wife in the late 1950s. He played around with assorted racing cars but really wanted De Tomaso Automobili to create stunning sports cars. After suffering various failed prototypes and false starts he finally came up with his first winner – the Mangusta.

This innovative but spartan two-seater had one great selling point – lots of bang for the buck. The Mangusta was wide and sat low to the ground, coming with disc brakes all round and alternative engines – a big V8 for Europe and an even bigger one for America. It had distinctive gullwing doors that opened above the rear engine and luggage compartments but it wasn't exactly comfortably appointed and didn't even drive that well, being hard to handle and suffering from instability at high speed. But buyers didn't care about the shortcomings, because the mighty Mangusta's performance was nothing less than awesome.

This was not intended to be a well-appointed GT car, instead being designed with a view to creating powerful appeal for enthusiasts who liked the exhilarating notion of driving a racing car on the road. Muscular macho character did not deliver a vast pool of buyers, but there were certainly enough out there to ensure that 80 Mangustas were sold in each of the production run's five years.

This added up to commercial success and allowed Alejandro de Tomaso's company to thrive and prosper in the coming decades. There are thought to be around 200 Mangustas out there somewhere, each still capable of pinning its driver to the bucket seat when the pedal is metalled.

COUNTRY OF ORIGIN:
Italy
FIRST MANUFACTURED:
1967 (until 1971)
ENGINE:
Europe – 4,728 cc V8;
USA – 4.9 l (302 cid) V8
PERFORMANCE:
With 4.9 l engine – top speed of
155 mph (249 km/h); 0-60 mph
(97 km/h) in 5.9 secs
YOU SHOULD KNOW:
The Italian word *mangusta* translates
as 'mongoose', renowned enemy of
cobras – the car being so named
because a consignment of Ford
engines intended for De Tomaso
instead went into Shelby Cobras.
May the best creature win!

*The fiery Mangusta was a GT
sports tourer that could
compete with the muscle cars*

Dodge Charger

COUNTRY OF ORIGIN:
USA
FIRST MANUFACTURED:
First generation 1966 (until 1967)
ENGINE:
Ranged from 5.2 – 7.0 l
(318 – 426 cid) V8
PERFORMANCE:
NASCAR versions top speed around
150 mph (241 km/h); 6.3 l road car –
0-60 mph (97 km/h) in 6.4 secs
YOU SHOULD KNOW:
The Charger wasn't just a boy racer's
dream – despite the high-quality
interior finish this was also a very
practical vehicle, with rear seats
that would fold flat to create a long
load space.

Flex your biceps and leap into a 1966 Dodge Charger. It wasn't the first muscle car on the block, but rather a hasty midyear introduction to compete in a market crowded with performance cars like the Pontiac GTO, Chevelle SS 396, Buick Gran Sport, Olds 442, Plymouth Barracuda and Ford Mustang. A concept car had been presented at auto shows in 1965, which Dodge claimed would only be built if interest was high. But that was a gimmick – production was already approved and, having been slow away, Dodge was soon up to top speed.

The wide, low Charger with its sweeping fastback had a beautiful state-of-the-art interior with bucket seats front and back and a console that reached to the back seat, plus a choice of V8s going all the way up to the 7 litre Chrysler 426 Street Hemi plant developed for NASCAR racing. This connection was no accident – national stock car racing was (and is) the premier American motorsport.

The Charger was the first production car to boast a rear 'spoiler', added to make it competitive – race cars had to be based on production models which were so streamlined that they acted like an aircraft wing and lifted at speed. It worked – a Charger secured a NASCAR win in 1966. This made it a big seller – success on the track immediately translating into brisk sales that topped 37,000.

Few changes were made for 1967, but competition was always cut-throat in America and the plethora of existing muscle cars were soon joined by the Chevrolet Camaro. Novelty value exhausted, Charger sales started to slide and a major revamp was ordered for 1968. This produced the 'Coke bottle' Charger whose sinuous lines replicated the famous beverage container, and the Charger series would continue through numerous modifications until 1978.

As a testosterone-charged example of a muscle car, the Charger couldn't be bettered.

Facel Vega II

This magnificent French car was boldly advertised as 'the fastest four-seater coupe in the world', and was Facel Vega's last throw of the dice – the company was facing bankruptcy and hoped the Facel II would be a big winner. It was certainly an imposing hand-built car, and the use of American V8 engines ensured that European refinement was complemented by brute power to create the ultimate luxury grand tourer.

The choice of engines lay between the Chrysler Typhoon and larger Chrysler Hemi-V8, whilst the transmission was three-speed automatic or four-speed manual. Despite the weight of its stylish four-seater body, the Facel II could match two-seater lightweights from Ferrari, Mercedes Benz and Aston Martin for pace.

This head-turning car was impressive, and so was the price. But that only increased the allure for status-conscious purchasers. Included on the glittering owner's roll of honour were Royalty (including the Shah of Persia and Princess Grace of Monaco), aristocracy (among them Prince Poniatowski, Lord Brabourne and the Marchionesses of Tavistock and Huntly), Hollywood stars (Tony Curtis, Frank Sinatra, Anthony Quinn, Debbie Reynolds, Joan Fontaine, Ava Gardner, Joan Collins), racing drivers (Stirling Moss, Tony Vandervell, Rob Walker and Maurice Trintignant) and assorted luminaries like Pablo Picasso, Christian Dior, Lionel Bart, François Truffaut, Ringo Starr, Sir Mortimer Wheeler and Herbert von Karajan. In short, the Facel II was the car that the influential movers and shakers of the early 1960s most wanted to be seen in.

So did that final gamble pay off? Sadly it didn't, with Facel Vega collapsing in 1964; though the Facel II was a great way to go – as anyone lucky enough to own one of these elegant automobiles will testify. Not many are so blessed – only 180 were built, making them the most desirable of 1960s grand tourers.

Facel Vega is hardly a household name nowadays, but in its time this luxurious machine was the chosen car of stars and royalty.

COUNTRY OF ORIGIN:
France
FIRST MANUFACTURED:
1961 (until 1964)
ENGINE:
6,286 cc or 6,767 cc Chrysler OHV V8
PERFORMANCE:
With 6.3 litre engine – top speed of 133 mph (214 km/h); 0-60 mph (97 km/h) in 7.8 secs
YOU SHOULD KNOW:
Playboy industrialist Jean Daninos created Facel Vega in 1954 and lit up the world of custom-built luxury cars like a shooting star, but it was his rash move into volume-car production with the small and troubled Facellia sports car that finished the company.

The thrustful 250 GTO has become one of the most coveted (and valuable) Ferraris ever.

Ferrari 250 GTO

This red car is a blue-chip investment – for in the excessive world of classic-car investment the Ferrari 250 GTO is as valuable as they come. It falls into that glamorous category of racers that can be driven on the road by those lucky enough to afford one. Actually it should never have made the track, being designed for the GT series that required a hundred of the relevant model to be manufactured before it was eligible.

Enzo Ferrari obviously had all the right numbers in his phone book, for the 250 GTO was allowed to race despite the fact that only 36 were made. And race it did – finishing second on debut in Florida's Sebring 12 Hour race and winning the World Manufacturers' Championship in '62, '63 and '64. In so doing, it was one of the last successful front-engined racing cars, for the era of mid-engine supremacy was nigh.

The 250 GTO was developed from a short-wheelbase 250 GT chassis fitted with a 3 litre engine from the 250 Testa Rossa, whilst Sergio Scaglietti designed the slippery body. The five-speed manual gearbox had the metal gate that subsequently became a Ferrari signature, and there could be no doubt that this was a serious racing car rather than a fancy rich man's toy. Instrumentation was basic and switches came from the mighty Fiat 500. It is even rumoured that the first seats were covered with overall cloth, so hastily was the 250 GTO rushed into production.

Some may disagree with the premise that the Ferrari 250 GTO is the greatest sports car ever made, but few dispute the fact that it represents a perfect marriage of form and function – one of the most beautiful shapes ever to grace a Ferrari chassis and a winner to boot.

COUNTRY OF ORIGIN:
Italy
FIRST MANUFACTURED:
1962 (until 1964)
ENGINE:
2,953 cc V12
PERFORMANCE:
Top speed of 175 mph (282 km/h);
0-60 mph (97 km/h) in 5.8 secs
YOU SHOULD KNOW:
Not just anyone with $18,000 to spare could phone up Maranello and order a 250 GTO – every prospective purchaser was vetted personally by Enzo Ferrari before being allowed to join the waiting list for one of his precious sports racers.

192

Ferrari 275

After production of the soaraway Ferrari 250 GTO ended in 1964, the 275 series arrived to delight admirers of the Prancing Horse. First to gallop was the shapely 275 GTB coupe with a flowing body designed by Pininfarina and produced by Carrozzeria Scaglietti. The twin cam engine came with a choice of three or six Weber carburettors.

But this was to be an evolution series. A slightly redesigned GTB appeared in 1965, whilst Pininfarina built a couple of hundred 275 GTS roadsters between 1964 and 1966, primarily intended for the American market. These Spyders had completely different bodywork from the sports coupe that inspired them.

In 1965 a few lightweight 275 GTB racing versions were produced. These had the smaller 3 litre engine from the 250 GTO. The following year a dozen 275 GTB/C cars were built, of which two were released for road use. Although appearing almost identical to the 275 GTB road cars, they were completely different beneath the skin with a special lightweight chassis. As an interesting historical footnote, these would be the last Ferraris to have wire wheels.

An updated four cam 275 GTB/4 was introduced in 1966. The engine was substantially reworked to offer improved performance, with a new valve set-up, dry-sump design and six carburettors as standard issue. Refinement of the suspension and drive package led to better handling, noise suppression and a reduction in vibration at high speeds.

The last – most exclusive – version of this splendid series was the 275 GTB/4 NART. The NART stood for North American Racing Team, run by Ferrari importer Luigi Chinetti. He begged Enzo Ferrari and Sergio Scaglietti to create a Spyder version of the 275 GTB/4, and they obliged their important partner by sending ten of these fabulous sports cars to America in 1967 and 1968.

COUNTRY OF ORIGIN:
Italy
FIRST MANUFACTURED:
1964 (until 1968).
ENGINE:
3,286 cc V12
PERFORMANCE:
Original 275 GTB coupe – top speed of 165 mph (265 km/h); 0-60 mph (97 km/h) in 6.7 secs
YOU SHOULD KNOW:
Racing was in Enzo's blood and the specially constructed 275 GTB/C was finally approved as a GT racer, with the few examples that were manufactured going on to enjoy many victories and continuing to be competitive in endurance races until the mid-1970s.

The 275 smoothly continued Ferrari's inexorable march towards supercar greatness.

Pininfarina designed the Daytona and was Ferrari's long-time design partner.

Ferrari Daytona

Everyone calls it a Ferrari Daytona, but of course they're wrong – it's really the 365 GTB/4. Daytona it is, then. This late 1960s stunner was just that, representing a radical departure from everything that went before. The Daytona was created by long-time Ferrari collaborator Pininfarina and introduced at the Paris Motor Show in 1968. But to the dismay of many it was not like the slinky Pininfarina curves adored by aficionados. Instead, it had sharp-edged looks that reminded doubters of – whisper it if you dare – a Lamborghini.

Unlike the latest Lambo, however, the Daytona retained one traditional Ferrari characteristic – an engine up front, this time a meaty 4.4 litre DOHC V12 with six twin carburettors. But even this was a disappointment as Ferrari's racers had already gone mid-engined. With all that not going for it, the Daytona turned out to be rather successful and even (eventually) quite well liked. Around 1,400 were built.

The majority were left-hand drive GTB/4 coupes, though around 150 right-hand drive versions were made. The factory also issued 122 GTS/4 Spyders converted from coupes by Daytona bodybuilder Scaglietti. A mere seven of these were RHDs. The open-topped cars are so desirable that a number of Berlinetta coupes have magically turned into Spyders over the years, but these ringers can be distinguished from the real thing because the windscreen is more steeply angled. A total of 15 special lightweight competition Daytonas was also constructed.

There were a couple of related evolutions that don't have genuine 'Daytona' cachet. The 365 GTC/4 used an identical chassis and had a 2+2 coupe body by Pininfarina. The 365 GT4 2+2 was another four-seater with an angular look that had vague resemblance to a true Daytona, reiterating an angular style that Ferrari would use for cars like the Mondial in the 1980s.

COUNTRY OF ORIGIN:
Italy
FIRST MANUFACTURED:
1968 (until 1973)
ENGINE:
4,390 cc DOHC V12
PERFORMANCE:
Top speed of 150 mph (241 km/h); 0-60 mph (97 km/h) in 5.4 secs
YOU SHOULD KNOW:
All hell broke loose when Ferrari discovered that TV cops Crockett and Tubbs were driving a replica Daytona (built on a Corvette chassis) in the *Miami Vice* TV series – but the offending machine was conveniently destroyed in an action sequence and thereafter a gen-u-ine Ferrari Testarossa scorched the screen streets of Miami.

Ferrari Dino 246 GT/GTS

When is a Ferrari not a Ferrari? Answer – when it's a Dino. Old Enzo Ferrari's son Alfredo (aka Dino) was an accomplished engineer who was to be his father's successor at Maranello, but sadly muscular dystrophy carried him off in 1955 at the age of 24. Enzo was heartbroken, but carried on ruling his company with a rod of iron for three decades.

A dozen years after Dino's death Ferrari flirted with an 'affordable' model to challenge best-selling sports cars like the Porsche 911. A mid-engined prototype was designed by Sergio Pininfarina around the V6 engine first mooted by Dino Ferrari. Partly in his son's memory – and to differentiate the cheaper car from expensive V12s – Enzo called it the Dino. The marque got off to an auspicious start with the Dino 206 S receiving an enthusiastic reception at the Paris Motor Show in 1965. Another prototype with smoother styling was shown at the Turin Show in 1966 and a pre-production model at the same event in 1967. This had a 2 litre engine and went on sale in 1968.

But Ferrari rarely stood still for long, and the final refinement was the shapely Dino 246 GT in 1969. It appeared identical to the 206, save for a discreet Prancing Horse on the fuel-filler flap, but was actually slightly larger than its predecessor with a steel body replacing aluminium and a bigger engine. The result was a superb performer that had reviewers raving. The only other significant advances before the 246 was discontinued were the debut of the 246 GTS with its removable targa top panel and a Spyder convertible option from 1971. These 'Junior Ferraris' were brilliant cars that did full justice to Dino's memory, looking (and sounding) as good today as they did when new.

COUNTRY OF ORIGIN:
Italy
FIRST MANUFACTURED:
1969 (until 1974)
ENGINE:
2,418 cc V6
PERFORMANCE:
Top speed of 148 mph (238 km/h);
0-60 mph (97 km/h) in 7.1 secs
YOU SHOULD KNOW:
The Dino series sold well from the 206's launch to the discontinuation of 246 models in 1974, with almost 4,000 units built and the concept of a mid-engined volume car so well established that the idea of a separate marque was abandoned, with replacement 308 models reverting to the Ferrari name.

Enzo Ferrari named the Dino in memory of his son, who tragically died young with his undoubted promise unfulfilled.

Fiat 850

COUNTRY OF ORIGIN:
Italy
FIRST MANUFACTURED:
1964 (until 1973, saloon)
ENGINE:
817 cc, 843 cc or 903 cc OHV
Straight Four
PERFORMANCE:
Basic saloon – top speed of 78 mph
(126 km/h); 0-60 mph (97 km/h) in
25.5 secs
YOU SHOULD KNOW:
Though it did not make the same
impact behind the Iron Curtain as the
Fiat 124, the 850 was definitely the
hors d'oeuvre – it was assembled
from kits as the Pirin-Fiat by a state
cooperative in Bulgaria between
1967 and 1971.

This small rear-engined car was an important step in Fiat's long march towards fully paid-up membership of the international car manufacturers' club. The two-door Fiat 850 was introduced in 1964 to run alongside and eventually succeed the Fiat 600, that hugely successful Seicento city car produced between 1955 and 1969.

In fact, the 850 saloon was an evolution of the 600, with a bored-out engine that came in two versions – standard and super, with the latter being only slightly more powerful than the former. But that wasn't the only variation on a theme, because several body styles were wrapped around the same mechanics.

The 850 Special was a sports saloon introduced in 1967. It had a tuned engine, better trim and front disc brakes. Another variant was the Familiare, an early people carrier with a boxy body and three rows of seating. It claimed to accommodate seven, though truthfully didn't add the words 'in comfort'. The Familiare lasted longer than its parent, remaining in production for three years after the saloon was discontinued.

A Sports Coupe with tuned engine appeared at the Geneva Motor Show in '65, and that year also saw the Bertone-designed 850 Spider make a welcome entrance. This little roadster could zip to 90 mph (145 km/h) with good acceleration along the way. The Spider featured flowing lines and a clever hood that easily folded beneath a rear flap.

Last but not least was the 850 Abarth. Don't attempt to drive one unless you're tired of life, because it can be a brute. The engine size was nearly doubled and twin carbs helped punch out far more power than the car could comfortably handle. The Abarth therefore suffers from understeer and becomes unstable under braking or at speed, which could be 131 mph (210 km/h). Scary!

The 850 was designed to be produced in many countries.

Fiat 124

Fiat certainly started something with the 124, which went on and on – and formed the basis of Russia's basic Lada models.

It hasn't actually been spotted around, but the ideal bumper sticker for a Fiat 124 would be MY OTHER CAR IS A LADA. For it's the 124's rebirth as Russia's Lada BA3-2102/Zhiguli (later wisely shortened to Lada 1200, then Lada Riva) that puts the Fiat 124 series close to the top of the all-time bestseller chart with going on for 15 million units sold. It wasn't just Russia that jumped on the 124 wagonette, either, for these acclaimed cars were also made in Bulgaria, Egypt, India, Korea, Spain and Turkey.

This hugely successful mid-sized family saloon appeared in the mid-1960s and was an immediate hit, scooping a European Car of the Year award. The simple square design allowed for ample interior space whilst lightweight construction and a relatively small engine made it economical to run. Coil spring rear suspension and disc brakes all round added to a very satisfactory package.

The 124 platform was not only used throughout Europe, but also by Fiat to create evolutionary versions. A five-door station wagon was introduced, and in 1967 came the 124 Coupe. The first AC model went through upgrades to BC and CC with progressively larger engines, though knowledgeable collectors swear by the AC.

Fiat also commissioned a two-seater convertible design from Pininfarina, which was introduced at the Turin Motor Show and continued to sell well for nearly 20 years and become an affordable classic that's ideal for top-down summer driving. Pininfarina had to shorten the floorpan and wheelbase in creating the Fiat 124 Sport Spider. The Cambiano-based outfit actually manufactured the monocoque for the Spider, making the venture a major commercial success for them. Over the long production run the Spider's engine size crept up from 1.4 litres to 2 litres, though the body remained unchanged.

COUNTRY OF ORIGIN:
Italy
FIRST MANUFACTURED:
1966 (until 1974)
ENGINE:
1,197 cc, 1,438 cc or 1,592 cc
OHV Straight Four
PERFORMANCE:
With 1.2 l engine – top speed
of 87 mph (140 km/h); 0-60 mph
(97 km/h) in 13.3 secs
YOU SHOULD KNOW:
The Fiat 124-derived Lada Riva
was introduced in 1980 as an
evolution of the earlier Lada 1200 –
and is still in production at the ZAZ
factory in the Ukraine and the
Suzuki plant in Egypt.

197

Fiat Dino

There's no getting away from it – the word 'homologate' had to be mentioned sooner or later, inevitably in a context involving Ferrari. Maranello was besotted with racing, but formulae in which Ferrari wished to compete required homologation – approval by the governing body (FIA) that a particular car is eligible to race. As getting the nod invariably depended on a specific number of road cars being produced, Ferrari often struggled as the company tended to concentrate on expensive custom racing cars with just a few offered for sporting road use.

And so to the Fiat Dino Spider. This stylish sports car was the forerunner of GT cars that Ferrari would market under the Dino name from 1968, and the two are sometimes confused. The purpose of the Fiat Dino Spider was to homologate Ferrari's 2 litre (and later 2.4 litre) engine for Formula Two racing by producing the required 500 road cars. This was the V6 power plant initially proposed by Enzo Ferrari's son Dino before his untimely passing at the age of 24. It came to fruition a decade after his death and enjoyed a successful run in cars that bore Dino's name.

Fiat went along with Enzo's co-production request and the delectable 2 litre Fiat Dino Spider was introduced at the Turin

COUNTRY OF ORIGIN:
Italy
FIRST MANUFACTURED:
1966 (until 1973)
ENGINE:
1,987 cc or 2,418 cc V6
PERFORMANCE:
Top speed of 130 mph (210 km/h);
0-60 mph (97 km/h) in 8.7 secs
YOU SHOULD KNOW:
Ferraris they are not, but the association is there – allowing financially challenged fans of the Prancing Horse to drive something that looks quite like a Ferrari and has a Ferrari engine . . . and is almost affordable.

Motor Show in 1966, with a crisp four-seater coupe following a year later at the Geneva Motor Show. The Spider was designed by Pininfarina and the coupe by Bertone. The engine was at the front and was mated to triple Weber carburettors. These stylish Dinos sported a five-speed manual gearbox and had a live axle suspended by leaf springs. In 1969 engine size was increased and coil-sprung independent rear suspension introduced. Over 7,500 Dinos were made (all variants), amply justifying homologation, with around three-quarters of these being coupes.

Ford Galaxie Starliner/Sunliner

Ford's big Galaxie first appeared in 1959 as the model line for Ford's top-of-the-range, full-sized cars. All sorts of Galaxies would appear over time, from high-performance muscle cars down to solid family saloons, but 1959 was a bad year to launch a new model, marking the last convulsions of over-the-top auto design in late-1950s America. So the six Galaxie models (updated versions of the ageing Fairlane) duly dripped chrome, flashed big fins and came with the inevitable two-tone paint job.

But all that was outdated almost before it hit the street, and the following year the Galaxie underwent major surgery. Out went the fancy stuff and in came a more futuristic look, with Sunliners and Starliners leading the way. They were longer and wider than their predecessors, with a choice of engines and famously smooth ride quality. The styling was restrained compared to previous excesses – featuring a plain grille beneath a sloping bonnet, wings with clean, straight lines and discreet 'bat-wing' tailfins.

The Starliner was a two-door pillarless coupe with a trim fastback look and curving rear window. It might have been designed for the racetrack, and indeed performed with distinction in that sphere. Nearly 70,000 Starliners were sold, making this clean-cut machine a reasonable commercial success. The Sunliner convertible version was very pleasing on the eye, with its swoopy styling, selling nearly 45,000.

The following year saw the introduction of a concave grille, a more rounded body and big circular tail lights. But in 1961 Ford rashly restyled the Starliner to create a more conventional coupe, sales bombed and that was that. The Starliner was cancelled for 1962, dragging the Sunliner down with it, even though convertible sales had held up well. This short lifespan and their attractive appearance make Starliners and Sunliners highly collectable today.

COUNTRY OF ORIGIN:
USA
FIRST MANUFACTURED:
1960 (until 1961)
ENGINE:
3.7 l (223 cid) Straight Six;
4.8 l (292 cid), 5.8 l (352 cid)
or 6.4 l (390 cid) V8
PERFORMANCE:
Varied according to engine –
typically a top speed of around
100 mph (161 km/h)
YOU SHOULD KNOW:
After 1966 the Galaxie line was
knocked from Ford's big-model top
spot by the LTD, which made its
debut as the most expensive Galaxie
in 1965 before becoming a separate
model in 1967 – the Galaxie was
then forced to battle on in second
place until the name was dropped
in 1974.

Ford Cortina Mk I

COUNTRY OF ORIGIN:
UK
FIRST MANUFACTURED:
1962 (until 1966)
ENGINE:
1,198 cc or 1,498 cc Straight Four
PERFORMANCE:
With 1.5 l engine – top speed
of 85 mph (138 km/h); 0-60 mph
(97 km/h) in 21 secs
YOU SHOULD KNOW:
The Cortina's name was derived from
the glamorous Italian ski resort of
Cortina d'Ampezzo in the Italian
Dolomites (which was cheeky, as
Triumph had first used the Dolomite
name in 1934) – and a notorious
Ford publicity stunt saw Cortinas
driven down the resort's fearsome
bobsled run.

*Its Y-shaped rear lamp cluster
was the Cortina's signature.*

As the Swinging Sixties got into gear, Ford was smarting from the mauling it was receiving from the trendy car of the moment – BMC's iconic Mini. Ford couldn't afford to retool to produce a competitive small car, so the company went with what it knew best – a new family saloon. The Cortina Mk I duly appeared in 1962 to take on Vauxhall Victors and Morris Oxfords.

Initially this angular car with tapering flutes along the sides and signature 'Y' rear light clusters was the Consul Cortina, but a cosmetic facelift in 1964 saw the Consul bit quietly buried. The Cortina had arrived, and would be around for some time. It came with two or four doors, there was a choice of engines (1.2 litre or 1.5 litre) and trim levels (standard and deluxe).

It wasn't long before the Cortina family started reproducing. The 1500 Super arrived in January 1963, identified by tapered chrome strips along the flutes. A GT model with twin carbs, front disc brakes and modified suspension followed a month later. An estate car in deluxe or super made its debut in March, with the latter sporting fake wood panelling on the sides and tailgate. Over a million Mk Is would be sold, laying the foundations for what followed.

The Cortina just went from strength to strength. A Mk II version appeared in 1967, followed by the Mk III in 1970. The Mk IV occupied the 1975–1979 slot and the Cortina 80 was the last of the line, the very final one being a silver Crusader that rolled off the Dagenham line in the summer of 1982. It had been a more-than-modest success along the way, becoming the UK's bestseller from 1967 until 1981, with 4.35 million units sold during the extended production run.

Ford Lotus Cortina

Although it was technically a variation on the Ford Cortina Mk I theme, the brilliant Ford Lotus Cortina deserves an entry all its own. This was one of the most interesting British saloon cars of the 1960s, making its debut in 1963 as the result of a partnership between Ford and Lotus Cars.

Lotus supremo Colin Chapman had developed a twin-cam version of the Ford Kent engine for racing purposes. Ford's competition department asked Chapman to fit this into a thousand Ford saloons, so they could rally and race in Group 2. The deal was swiftly done and the Type 28 was born. Ford called it the Cortina Lotus, but for once the little guy won out and the world remembers this splendid custom car as the Lotus Cortina – which undoubtedly had a better ring to the target market of boy racers. Lotus did the mechanical stuff while Ford handled distribution and marketing.

A reinforced two-door Cortina shell provided innocent-looking wrapping around a potent 1.6 litre twin-cam Lotus engine that belted out 105 bhp. Lowered and revised suspension plus servo-assisted disc brakes ensured that the Lotus Cortina handled well, with wide road wheels and tyres providing limpet-like grip. Nobody who tried to beat one of these stylish sprinters away from the traffic lights had any doubts about what they'd just run up against – but just in case someone thought this special sports saloon was any old Cortina, a white paint job and green side flash proclaimed the Lotus Cortina's exclusive parentage.

Ford wanted to continue with the cooperative venture when the Mk II Cortina appeared, but Lotus declined and the Lotus Cortina Mk II was produced entirely by Ford from 1966 until 1970, with the Lotus badge being replaced by a bland 'Twin Cam' announcement after a few months.

COUNTRY OF ORIGIN:
UK
FIRST MANUFACTURED:
1963 (until 1966)
ENGINE:
1,558 cc DOHC Straight Four
PERFORMANCE:
Top speed of 108 mph (174 km/h);
0-60 mph (97 km/h) in 10.1 secs
YOU SHOULD KNOW:
The aim of creating a great sports racer was successful, with the Lotus Cortina enjoying many race victories. Unfortunately, it was prone to mechanical problems when used as a road car, but was so exciting that besotted owners easily forgave its faults.

Naughty, naughty – the Lotus Cortina was really a powerful street-legal racing car.

The GT40 dominated the Le Mans 24 race in the late Sixties.

Ford GT40

Every competitive carmaker in the 1960s wanted to poke the all-conquering Maranello boys in the eye. Ford was no exception, fuelled by Enzo Ferrari's abrupt termination of negotiations to sell his company to Ford. Whilst the decision to go head-to-head with Ferrari came from slighted Henry Ford II in America, design-and-build work took place in Britain.

The sensational result was the Ford GT (later named the GT40). Ford's attack on the international endurance race circuit was not entirely motivated by pique – for sustained track success was the best advertising money couldn't buy. The development team included Eric Broadley, owner-designer of the advanced Lola GT mid-engined racecar, and a new factory was established at Slough. The prototype was unveiled in April 1964.

This was powered by a 4.2 litre Ford Fairlane engine and – though not a winner – put in track time that helped finalize the Mk I's design. This had a 4.7 litre engine and 50 were built to satisfy production sports car regulations. But it still wasn't a winner, so the Mk II saw the introduction of a monstrous 7 litre engine that had been tried and tested on American racetracks, together with bodywork tweaks to accommodate it.

Ford had cracked it – the GT40 Mk II secured a 1-2-3 finish at Daytona. In 1966 there was a prestigious 1-2-3 in the Le Mans 24 ahead of Ferrari and Henry Ford II's mission was accomplished. Meanwhile, a Mk III was built for road use, fitted with a 4.7 litre engine, but this wasn't a success (seven produced). Still, Le Mans fell to a GT40 Mk IV in 1967 and two more Le Mans wins would follow in 1968 and 1969. And there, sadly, the extraordinary GT40 story effectively ended – its successor was the evolutionary G7A, built and campaigned in America.

COUNTRY OF ORIGIN:
UK
FIRST MANUFACTURED:
1965 (until 1968)
ENGINE:
4.2 l (256 cid), 4.7 l (288.5 cid) or 7.0 l (427 cid) V8
PERFORMANCE:
Mk III road car – top speed of 160 mph (257 km/h); 0-60 mph (97 km/h) in 5.3 secs
YOU SHOULD KNOW:
Ford's attempt to stage a dead-heat at the end of the 1966 Le Mans 24 race came unstuck when, despite the neck-and-neck finish, Bruce McClaren and Chris Amon were declared the winners, having started further back down the track than second-placed Ken Miles – who was thus denied a heroic hat trick of GT40 wins at Sebring, Daytona and Le Mans in the same year.

Ford Bronco

This gallant 30-year veteran was finally pensioned off in 1996, but not before going through five evolutionary stages. The first generation half-ton Ford Bronco lived from 1966 to 1977, and – choose your acronym – this compact ORV (Off-Road Vehicle) or SUV (Sports Utility Vehicle) was launched as a competitor for the Jeep CJ and Harvester Scout.

The four-wheel drive Bronco was an original design that – unlike most Fords – owed little to any other model, though axles and brakes came from the 4WD Ford pickup truck. Unlike later SUVs it was intended to be a genuine rural workhorse. The two-door Bronco had robust suspension (though a heavy-duty option was available for real backwoodsmen) and the choice of a straight six or V8 engine. Low range gearing for heavy work was standard.

Simple, boxy styling made for economical manufacturing and a budget ticket price, with the Bronco offered as a wagon, popular half cab or roofless roadster (the latter soon dropped). Despite the affordable price, a long list of extras encouraged buyers to trade up from the base model. Apart from genuine treats like bucket seats or CB radio, these add-ons tended to be the sort of helpful tools appreciated by rural folk – towbar, winch, post-hole digger, power take-off for assorted farm machinery, snow plough and the like.

The 'Early Bronco' was a steady rather than spectacular seller, with around 231,000 shifted in a dozen years. The first major revamp in 1978 saw the Bronco evolve into an altogether larger vehicle to compete with the Dodge Ramcharger, Chevy Blazer and Jeep Cherokee – SUVs setting the trend towards luxury transport for the city and suburbs that were happy to go off road during vacations. Thereafter, until the model line ended in 1996, these big boys were known as 'Full-size Broncos'.

COUNTRY OF ORIGIN:
USA
FIRST MANUFACTURED:
1966 (until 1996)
ENGINE:
2.8 l (170 cid) or 3.3 l (200 cid)
Straight Six; 4.7 l (289 cid)
or 4.9 l (302 cid) V8
PERFORMANCE:
Varied according to engine – typically top speed of 75 mph (121 km/h); 0-60 mph (97 km/h) in 21 secs
YOU SHOULD KNOW:
Yes, there was a racing version – the Baja Bronco was prepared by Bill Stroppe for cross-country road races south of the border, like the Baja 500 and Mexico 1000. It had a roll cage, wide tyres and tuned engine. Stroppe cars tasted success and the sport's popularity spread to the USA in the early 1970s.

The Bronco was more of a farmyard friend than a suburban status symbol.

Ford Mustang

COUNTRY OF ORIGIN:
USA
FIRST MANUFACTURED:
1964 (until 1973) Series 1
ENGINE:
Ranged from 2.9 l (170 cid) Straight
Six to 7.0 l (427 cid) V8
PERFORMANCE:
1965 Mustang 4.7 l V8 – top speed
of 120 mph (193 km/h);
0-60 mph (97 km/h) in 8.3 secs
YOU SHOULD KNOW:
Although the Mustang's cinematic
debut was in the James Bond film
Goldfinger, its best-ever role was
starring alongside Steve McQueen in
Bullitt when a 1968 Ford Mustang
Fastback (actually two identical cars)
driven by Lieutenant Frank Bullitt
chased two baddies in a Dodge
Charger to a fiery grave through the
streets of San Francisco.

The first generation Mustang was a revelation. Despite an inspired promotional campaign, Ford's most successful launch since the Model A in the 1920s still gave the Dearborn behemoth a pleasant surprise as 'Mustang Mania' swept the nation. Year One-and-a-half projections (the launch came midway through the 1964 model year) anticipated sales of 100,000 units, but the runaway Mustang sold 1.5 million inside 18 months.

Best of all, the Mustang was basically a humble Ford Falcon in fancy dress, and its soaring success created a new class of vehicle – the pony car. These were compact performance cars with long bonnets and short rear ends – and those mega-Mustang sales soon

spawned imitators like Chevy's Camara and AMC's Javelin.

As with most Ford lines one model could be many, with different body styles, a wide choice of engines, extras and trim levels allowing almost endless permutations. The Mustang launched with a hardtop and convertible, with a semi-fastback 2+2 coupe arriving in September '64 for the official start of the 1965 model year. There was a major first generation revamp in 1967 that produced all sorts of mechanical upgrades (including a new big V8 engine option) and also one of the most desirable manifestations of the Mustang – the full fastback. The Mustang Fastback has acquired iconic status over time and made a major contribution to establishing the Mustang as America's best-loved sporty car.

First generation Mustangs are the true classics, for when the second generation arrived for 1974 it was both smaller and heavier than the original 1964 car, thanks to new regulations that included pollution control laws. The Mustang series continues to this day but only fond memories – and lots of cherished cars – remain to commemorate the 'Golden Decade' when this mould-breaking car was at its very best.

The Fastback was built to have Steve McQueen at the wheel.

Ford Escort Mk I

COUNTRY OF ORIGIN:
UK (also assembled in Belgium, then Germany)
FIRST MANUFACTURED:
1967 (until 1974)
ENGINE:
940 cc (rarely), 1,098 cc, 1,298 cc and 1,558 cc Straight Four
PERFORMANCE:
1300 Sport – top speed of 98 mph (158 km/h)
YOU SHOULD KNOW:
The Escort Mk I's reach was long – it was not only built at Halewood and Saarlouis in Germany, but also assembled in Australia and New Zealand.

Although used to identify an estate car version of the Ford Anglia 100E, and appearing on various Ford cars sold in North America, the Escort name started writing a long chapter in the history of European motoring with the debut of the Ford Escort Mk I in late 1967. The long-running Ford Anglia's replacement had to be fit for mass-market purpose, and was.

First up was a two-door saloon with a curving waistline and characteristic 'dog-bone' front grille with headlamps at either end. A three-door estate appeared in spring 1968 and a tradesman's van followed a year later. The four-door saloon did not arrive until 1969. There was the usual Ford options package – different trim levels (De Luxe and Super) and a choice of engines (1.1 litre or 1.3 litre). It wasn't long before a specialist performance version appeared in the form of a 1300GT with tuned engine and Weber carburettor. A further variation with the same engine set-up was the Sport, with flared front wings, which in turn spawned the 1300E with fancy executive touches like a wood-trimmed dashboard.

Ford was a great believer in the power of race wins when it came to selling road cars and the Escort Twin Cam was a high-performance competition model fitted with a 1.6 litre engine tweaked by Lotus Cars and assembled at Ford's AVO (Advanced Vehicle Operation) facility at Aveley. The investment was shrewd, with Escort Mk Is sweeping all before them on the rally circuit and going on to become one of the most successful rally cars of all time.

That contributed to the Escort's massive commercial success, especially in Britain where it comfortably outsold its General Motors competitor, the Vauxhall Viva – though to be fair GM hit back in Europe where the Opel Kadett won out.

The Escort had something to offer everyone, from working man to racing driver.

Ford Capri Mk 1

The European idea of a perfect pony car (long front, short back) was the Ford Capri – or more accurately it was Ford Europe's idea. The recently created conglomerate launched this trendy car in 1969, hoping to emulate the Mustang's success in North America. The Capri was based on the Cortina platform and had common styling but different engine specs for Britain and the Continent.

Ford wanted to produce a fashionable car that would appeal to the widest possible market (or to put it another way, every pocket). Thus a variety of engines was offered. The initial UK options were 1.3 litre or 1.6 litre versions of the Ford Kent straight four, with a 2 litre Cologne V6 topping the offering. Before long, Brits with lots of dosh could choose sports versions like the 3000 GT with the Ford Essex V6 engine. That's the one that always featured in memorable car chases in 1970s TV series like *The Professionals*, frequently ending in a slewing handbrake emergency stop followed by a bonnet roll and brisk gunplay.

Competition glory was never far from Ford's mind, and a souped-up Capri duly appeared in 1971, powered by a 2.6 litre version of the Cologne V6 assembled by Weslake and featuring alloy cylinder heads. This was the Capri RS2600, which would prove to be a star of the European Touring Car Championship in the early 1970s. Never slow to appreciate the powerful aphrodisiac properties of track success, a luxury road-going version with a detuned engine and double-barrel Solex carb was available.

Business was encouragingly brisk, but Ford still gave the Mk 1 a facelift in 1972, introducing better suspension, more comfortable seats, rectangular headlights and enlarged tail lights. A significant revamp saw the larger Capri Mk 2 arrive in February 1974, complete with hatchback rear door.

What's good for America is worth trying in Europe, thought Ford, and were duly rewarded when their Capri pony car hit the spot.

COUNTRY OF ORIGIN:
UK (also built in Belgium and Germany)
FIRST MANUFACTURED:
1969 (to 1974)
ENGINE:
1,298 cc or 1,598 cc Straight Four, 2,550 cc or 2,994 cc V6
PERFORMANCE:
3000 GT – top speed of 122 mph (196 km/h); 0-60 mph (97 km/h) in 8.4 secs
YOU SHOULD KNOW:
The original choice of name for the Capri was the Ford Colt – but Mitsubishi had cleverly trademarked that iconic American title so Capri it became, revisiting the not-altogether-different Consul Capri of the early 1960s and borrowing a model name used by various Ford-owned marques in America.

Ginetta G4

Who says there was no room for the start-up automobile entrepreneur in postwar Britain? The four Walklett Brothers certainly managed to found a successful car manufacturing business in 1958 (in the wilds of Suffolk) and ran it until their retirement in 1989.

The Ginetta G4 was an early introduction, in 1961. It had a fibreglass convertible roadster body that sported tailfins and was fitted with a Ford 105E engine. Unlike its immediate predecessors, the G4 was not designed specifically for competition use, though it was successful in that sphere. It was a classic 'drive to the track and race' car, which was equally at home on a motor-racing circuit or strutting its stuff to admiring glances when used as a road car.

The G4 offered the evolutionary choice of many Ford engines during its production run.

This lightweight car had a space-frame chassis with double wishbones, coil springs and dampers in the front. Rear suspension consisted of a Ford live axle and there were drum brakes. Over the years the G4 enjoyed considerable evolution and improvement. A selection of Ford engines was offered, including a 1.3 litre Classic, 1.6 litre X-flow and a 1.5 litre Cortina GT power plant.

With the introduction of Series II in 1963, the roadster was joined by a coupe, which was essentially the same car with an add-on hardtop. At the same time a BMC rear axle replaced the Ford live axle. The tailfins were dropped and enhancements like disc brakes were introduced to improve all-round handling and performance. The G4 Series III took over in 1966, though the only obvious change was then-modish pop-up headlights that rested on the front bumper when not in use.

Around 500 of these zippy sports racers were built in the 1960s and they still compete regularly at classic meets, piloted by enthusiastic drivers who appreciate unmistakably British motoring heritage.

COUNTRY OF ORIGIN:
UK
FIRST MANUFACTURED:
1961 (until 1969)
ENGINE:
Various, but originally a 997 cc
Straight Four
PERFORMANCE:
1 litre engine – top speed of
105 mph (169 km/h)
YOU SHOULD KNOW:
This great British sports car rides again in the form of the contemporary DARE Ginetta G4 – a sleek sports racer with a 1.8 litre Ford Zetec that delivers a top speed of 130 mph (209 km/h) and a 0-60 mph (97 km/h) time of 5.8 secs.

Hillman Imp

BMC's Mini caused a sensation in 1959, and rival manufacturers were caught on the hop by the popularity of that innovative new small car. But they all wanted a piece of the action and the Rootes Group's belated response was the Hillman Imp, which appeared in 1963.

It was a huge gamble. Rootes had little experience of small-car production and the Imp (codenamed 'Apex') required a new factory, as further development at the company's Ryton base was impossible. The chosen site (after government arm-twisting and provision of generous grants) was Linwood near Glasgow. This necessitated a long round-trip for Linwood parts finished at Ryton, and involved a militant Scottish workforce prone to striking first and talking later. An added difficulty was the fact that the Imp's aluminium engine was another leap into the unknown.

All that considered, the Imp turned out to be an interesting and popular car. There were teething troubles after the daring design was rushed into production, but despite that the distinctive Imp was well received, being cheap to buy and economical to run. A lightweight engine was mounted behind the rear wheels and this required sophisticated rear suspension to counteract an inevitable tendency to oversteer.

The original Imp was a two-door saloon with a rear hatch. A coupe version was added in 1965. That year also saw the introduction of a van and estate car (effectively a van with windows), though these were discontinued in 1970. The Imp got a major revamp in 1966 to iron out early mechanical problems and Rootes continued to improve this attractive little car throughout its life. Around 440,000 were built, and they're as much fun to drive today as they were then. But ultimately the Rootes gamble failed – the expensive Linwood venture eventually ruined the company.

COUNTRY OF ORIGIN:
UK
FIRST MANUFACTURED:
1963 (until 1976)
ENGINE:
874 cc Straight Four
PERFORMANCE:
Top speed of 80 mph (129 km/h);
0-50 mph (80 km/h) in 14.7 secs
YOU SHOULD KNOW:
Rootes produced some special Imp derivatives like the Imp Californian, and nifty badge engineering transformed the Basic Imp into desirable alternatives like the Singer Chamois, the Sunbeam Stiletto and Sunbeam Sport with its tuned twin-carb engine.

Rootes' chirpy rival to BMC's Mini was troubled by logistics and strikes but still sold well.

Honda S800

COUNTRY OF ORIGIN:
Japan
FIRST MANUFACTURED:
1966 (until 1970)
ENGINE:
791 cc Straight Four
PERFORMANCE:
Top speed of 97 mph (156 km/h);
0-50 mph (80 km/h) in 9.4 secs
YOU SHOULD KNOW:
The S800 did its job by establishing
Honda's credentials as an innovative
car maker. Following its
discontinuation in 1970 – as the
company concentrated on
motorcycles and conventional
passenger cars – there wouldn't be
another Honda sports car for three
decades, until the Millennium saw
the launch of the S2000.

Japanese car manufacture after World War II was initially shaped by regulations that favoured the smallest of cars. Motorcycle maker Honda was keen to move into car production and showed a tiny S360 two-seater concept car at the 1962 Tokyo Motor Show. Officials decided it was too sporty to merit coveted 'light car' status, so Honda recklessly put in a 531 cc engine and launched the S500 anyway. They were rewarded with good sales figures and pressed on to marginally bigger and better things, introducing the petite S600 in 1964, that contained a brute of a 601 cc motor.

But it didn't stop there. At the urging of New Zealand racing drivers Bruce McLaren and Denny Hulme, Honda upped the power again. The S800 was previewed at the 1965 Tokyo Motor Show and would succeed the very successful S600 in 1966. The dinky S800 sports car was available in roadster or coupe form, with standard or SM trim levels, and extended the Japanese company's growing reputation for technical innovation, wringing extraordinary performance and impressive economy from a 791 cc engine.

At first the S800 employed chain drive and independent suspension, but Honda soon switched to a more conventional live rear axle. The next upgrade involved front disc brakes, followed by a major reworking in 1968 aimed at opening up the American market. This involved creating the S800M in an attempt to meet US regulations. This had lean carburettion, dual-circuit brakes, safety glass, reconfigured tail lights, outside marker lights and flush door handles. Amazingly (considering all those massive V8s propelling home-bred American cars), the S800's tiny but high-revving engine failed to meet US emission control standards. With entry to the most important export market in the world thus barred, Honda quietly ended manufacture of the S800 in 1970, after some 11,500 vehicles had been built.

The S800 was the last in a line of seriously impressive small Honda sports cars.

Imperial LeBaron

This was an expensive, luxurious oddity. Chrysler had turned its Imperial models into a separate marque in 1955, to compete with Ford's up-market Lincoln brand, so these grand cars were aimed at the pricey end of the market. In 1960 the *crème de la crème* was the range-topping four-door Imperial LeBaron. This mighty machine sported four headlights, acres of chrome, flying wing trim and a lengthy rear end with sloping trunk lid (complete with raised spare wheel housing). The sci-fi ensemble was completed by soaring fins with gunsight tail lights and wide expanses of curved glass front and back.

Was there ever a more extraordinary monument to excessive American car design? Unlikely. A pillared saloon offered in 1960 was soon axed, leaving a choice of one – the sumptuous Southampton hardtop sedan. This ornate masterpiece had a pampered interior featuring impressive touches like (optional) leather upholstery in contrasting colours and a bright dashboard laden with buttons, complemented by an odd squarish steering wheel facing a generously padded high-backed driver's seat.

But time was running out for the flamboyant LeBaron's creator, design boss Virgil Exner. Chrysler was after a new look and poached Ford style guru Elwood Engel. Exner departed in 1963 and Imperials underwent major work for 1964. Out went flash fins and 1950s frippery and in came straight-line styling that produced rectilinear cars not unlike the latest Lincoln, which had evolved from the Engel-designed Continental of 1961.

Only some 5,000 of the 1960-63 Imperial LeBarons were produced, which makes them rare survivors – now cherished by those who like to preserve and drive the emblematic giants that characterize America's mid-20th century love affair with big, in-your-face luxury cars. The two-door Imperial Crown hardtop looks similar but is less desirable, but those who prefer open-top motoring love the brash Crown convertible.

COUNTRY OF ORIGIN:
USA
FIRST MANUFACTURED:
1960 (until 1963)
ENGINE:
6.8 l (413 cid) V8
PERFORMANCE:
Top speed of 102 mph (km/h);
0-60 mph (97 km/h) in 12 secs
YOU SHOULD KNOW:
Imperials were unsportingly banned from that popular American autofest, the demolition derby – they retained a substantial chassis after others had gone over to monocoque construction and drivers equipped with lesser makes simply bounced off them.

Iso Grifo

Iso Autoveicoli was founded in 1953, as successor to a company that made refrigerators before switching to scooters, motorcycles and three wheelers after World War II. The founder was engineer Renzo Rivolta, whose new venture took off when he developed the successful Isetta Bubble Car, which was produced in many countries.

Thus fortified, Renzo produced the modestly named Iso Rivolta IR 300, an elegant 2+2 coupe presented at the Turin Motor Show in 1962. Modest or not, it was an excellent vehicle that was well engineered and drove well. Sales were low but provided a stepping-stone to the next development – a stunning Grifo A3L prototype coupe styled by Bertone that appeared at Turin in 1963.

By the time the Grifo went into production two years later, it had been refined from the low-slung speedster shown at Turin. With a steel body and rigid chassis this large, shapely fastback had a long bonnet, air intakes on the front wings and a double grille sporting four headlights. The Grifo shared Corvette running gear and suspension with its predecessor but the Chevrolet engine was more highly tuned. Over time, engine size progressively increased to 7.4 litres, delivering frightening performance. This solidly built GT handled well, accelerated fast, had a stratospheric top speed and stopped quickly.

But sadly, despite its undoubted class, the Grifo failed to attract enough wealthy buyers, who preferred to be seduced by the prestigious badge appeal of Ferraris and Maseratis (and were perhaps a little sniffy about American mechanicals). Around 400 Grifos were made and their sound build quality means most have survived. They are eminently collectable, but rare enough to ensure that it's hard to even see one, let along enjoy the privilege of a high-speed drive in one of the most elegant GT cars ever made.

COUNTRY OF ORIGIN:
Italy
FIRST MANUFACTURED:
1965 (until 1974)
ENGINE:
5.4 l (327 cid), 5.7 l (351 cid), 7.0 l (427 cid) or 7.4 l (454 cid) V8
PERFORMANCE:
7.0 l engine – top speed of 171 mph (275 km/h); 0-60 mph (97 km/h) in 6.1 secs
YOU SHOULD KNOW:
The Iso Rivolta's chassis (also used for the Grifo) was designed by freelance consultant engineer Giotto Bizzarrini, who developed the celebrated 250 GTO at Ferrari – after parting company with Iso he went on to develop his own version of the original A3 prototype, which became the Bizzarrini 5300 GT.

Jaguar E-Type

The golden era of Jaguar Cars got off to a great start with the XK120 and XK150, but the company really hit the jackpot with the E-Type (XK-E in America). This is regarded as the finest-looking sports car of all time ('The most beautiful car ever made' was Enzo Ferrari's verdict) and also the most influential – leading the way for many fabulous brethren that made the 1960s a seminal decade for super sports cars.

Series 1 was launched in 1961, consisting of two-door convertibles and coupes with a 3.8 litre engine carried over from the XK150S. The cars featured torsion bar front ends with independent rear suspension and disc brakes all round. A 4.2 litre engine was introduced in 1964, along with styling changes. The 2+2 version with a stretched coupe body appeared in 1966 and further modifications followed to meet American requirements, sufficient to justify the Series 1.5 tag applied by some.

Series 2 followed in 1968, retaining the 4.2 litre engine and all three body styles. Modifications towards the end of Series 1 were extended to meet US regulations, which also required the triple-carb UK engine to be detuned. Headlights had lost glass covers, a wraparound rear bumper appeared and the cooling system was improved. New seats added comfort, whilst air conditioning and power steering were optional extras. Series 2 carried the E-Type forward into the 1970s.

Series 3 ran from 1971 to 1975, and saw the introduction of a 5.3 litre V12, discontinuation of the short-wheelbase coupe and switch of the convertible to the longer 2+2 floorpan. The cars acquired an aggressive slatted grille, flared wheel arches . . . and boastful V12 badge. With 15,000 Series 3s completing an overall production run of 70,000, it was a fitting climax to 15 years of breathtaking sporting motoring.

COUNTRY OF ORIGIN:
UK
FIRST MANUFACTURED:
1961 (until 1975)
ENGINE:
3,781 cc, 4,235 cc Straight Six;
5,344 cc V12
PERFORMANCE:
Series 1 with 3.8 litre engine – top speed of 149 mph (238 km/h); 0-60 mph (97 km/h) in 7.1 secs
YOU SHOULD KNOW:
The rarest E-Types are either those from the first batch of 500, which have flat floors and external bonnet catches (after which the floors were swiftly modified to provide more leg room and bonnet catches were repositioned internally) or the few Series 3 cars built using the old 4.2 litre straight six engine. Take your pick!

The E-Type was a genuine world beater – enough said?

Jaguar Mk X

COUNTRY OF ORIGIN:
UK
FIRST MANUFACTURED:
1961 (until 1965)
ENGINE:
3,718 cc or 4,235 cc Straight Six
PERFORMANCE:
With 4.2 litre engine – top speed of
123 mph (198 km/h); 0-60 mph
(97 km/h) of 10.4 secs
YOU SHOULD KNOW:
After all that effort put into
producing a BIG car pitched at the
American market, it did not sell well
in the States. Just a small percentage
of the 19,000 Mk X/420Gs built
actually crossed the Atlantic.

This top-of-the-range luxury car was completely different from its Mk IX predecessor and a bit of a monster by European standards – fully six feet (two metres) wide. That was because it was principally designed for the United States market where big was beautiful and petrol consumption immaterial.

Jaguar's big saloon had independent suspension and a 3.7 litre engine, which was replaced by a 4.2 litre plant in 1964. Triple carburettors helped to deliver performance comparable with American V8 engines twice the size, and for all its bulk the Mk X was a speedy car when pedal hit metal. Perhaps that isn't too surprising, as the engine was borrowed from the E-Type Jag. Power steering was standard, which ensured that this gargantuan car wasn't hard to handle.

The Mk X was the first car to have the signature Jaguar face of four headlights set into rounded wings, and the sumptuous old-fashioned interior was notable by the ultimate wood finish. There was timber everywhere – dashboard, around windows, housing various controls – and even the handy tables that folded down behind the front seats were stoutly constructed of matching wood.

Technically, production of the Mk X ended in 1965 with the introduction of the Jaguar 420G (not to be confused with the 420 compact sporting saloon produced between 1966 and 1968, which was virtually the same as the Daimler Sovereign). But in fact this was merely a name change and the rebadged 420G was effectively a Mk X Series 2. There were cosmetic design changes and a stretched version was offered to permit the installation of a glass screen – and the floorpan was lengthened further when the Daimler DS 420 was launched in 1968, with the two luxury limousines effectively being badge-engineered non-identical twins.

The Jaguar Mk X was big,
but sadly not very beautiful.

Jaguar XJ Mk 1 Series 1

Jaguar's strenuous efforts to make the grade as an upmarket volume purveyor of quality saloon cars took a step forward in 1968 with the introduction of the all-new XJ Series 1. The launch of the XJ (from Xperimental Jaguar) Series consolidated the company's saloon car offering into a single range. New XJ models provided a superb replacement for existing Jaguars (S-Type Mk 2, 420 and 420G, plus their Daimler counterparts) and the line would continue to be produced into the 1990s.

First out of the box was the XJ6 Mk 1. These comfortable saloons came with a choice of two straight sixes – 2.8 litre and 4.2 litre versions of Jaguar's renowned twin-cam XK engine. The former was considered to be somewhat underpowered and the latter outsold it by three to one. Power steering was standard and there was a choice of manual or automatic transmission. With either engine the XJ6 was famous for silky-smooth performance and crisp handling.

The particularly graceful styling was classic 'four-headlamp' Jaguar and the interior was lavishly appointed with wood and leather upholstery in the marque's finest traditions. A long-wheelbase version of the 4.2 litre XJ6 appeared towards the end of the run, offering more rear legroom, as did the top-of-the-range XJ12 with its powerful 5.3 litre V12 engine.

Around 82,000 Series 1 XJs were produced, plus another 16,000 of the Daimler equivalents of each Jaguar type, so there are still plenty around for anyone who owns a petrol station to drive and enjoy. Series 2 appeared in 1973 and did not acquire the best of reputations, with allegations of shoddy build quality said to stem from Jaguar's absorption into the British Leyland Group. The cars themselves weren't so different from Series 1 examples, but were modified to meet US regulations.

COUNTRY OF ORIGIN:
UK
FIRST MANUFACTURED:
1968 (until 1973)
ENGINE:
2,790 cc or 4,235 cc Straight Six;
5,343 cc V12
PERFORMANCE:
With 2.6 litre engine – top speed
of 118 mph (190 km/h); 0-60 mph
(97 km/h) in 10.5 secs
YOU SHOULD KNOW:
During the initial launch campaign
Jaguar boss Sir William Lyons
described the XJ6 as 'the finest
Jaguar ever' – but he would say that,
wouldn't he? Actually, he knew a little
something – Series 1 cars are
universally considered to have the
best build quality and are definitely
the most collectable XJs.

*The Series 1 Jaguar XJs were
sleek and fast, a combination
that brought commerical success.*

Jensen Interceptor and Jensen FF

COUNTRY OF ORIGIN:
UK
FIRST MANUFACTURED:
1966 (until 1976)
ENGINE:
6,286 cc or 7,212 cc V8
PERFORMANCE:
With 6.3 l engine – top speed
of 133 mph (214 km/h); 0-60 mph
(97 km/h) in 7.3 secs
YOU SHOULD KNOW:
Despite frequent strikes at the
factory, a penchant for rapidly rusting
and a relatively high ticket price,
nearly 6,500 Interceptors were
produced in 10 years, which
compares extremely favourably with
anything the competition managed
to achieve.

*The Interceptor not only looked
stunning, but also delivered a
superb level of performance.*

Jensen Motors was founded by brothers Richard and Alan, who made
vehicle bodies before World War II and were soon producing their own
cars. The first Interceptor appeared in 1949 – a coupe with an Austin Six
engine and a pioneering fibreglass body. The Jensen 541 replaced it in
1953, despite the demands of a major contract to produce bodies for the
Austin Healey sports cars. In 1961, production of bodies for Volvo's P1800
was added and the booming company introduced the Jensen CV-8.

But the CV-8 soon looked dated, and Jensen decided to compete with
big boys like Aston Martin and those luscious Latins. Although the CV-8's
updated chassis, Chrysler V8 engine and TorqueFlite automatic
transmission were up to the job, Italian styling was called for. A design by
Carrozzeria Touring was realized by Vignale, who created the first
production bodies. This stunning new fastback bore the revived
Interceptor name and its look was distinctive, with a squarish front and
rounded rear topped by a huge curved rear window that was also a
hinged hatchback. The interior with its wood and leather was, however,
reassuringly British.

Despite intense competition in the luxury GT market, the Interceptor
sold well throughout the '60s and into the mid-1970s, despite build-quality
problems and serious commercial pressures created by the collapse of

Jensen's core body-building business. The Mk II arrived in 1969 and the Mk III in 1971 with a bigger engine. A yummy convertible was introduced in 1974 and a coupe in 1975.

The stylish Interceptor is deserving of a more-than-honourable mention in the book of British automotive success stories, but in many respects its importance is outweighed by that of a commercially unsuccessful companion model. Jensen Motors had been working with Harry Ferguson (of Massey-Ferguson tractor fame) since the early 1960s, and the innovative Irish engineer was intent on producing an effective four-wheel-drive system for race and road cars.

In 1961 the Ferguson P99 Climax scored a notable first and last. In the hands of Stirling Moss it became the first four-wheel-drive car – and last front-engined car – to win a Formula 1 race. On the road front, the joint venture led to the Jensen CV-8 FF shown at the Earls Court Motor Show in 1965. This was the debut of the FF road-car system (FF stood for Ferguson Formula) and it anticipated the world's first four-wheel drive supercar.

This was the Jensen FF, which deployed Ferguson's four-wheel drive system to great effect, also offering Dunlop Maxaret anti-lock braking, traction control and power steering. It shared Chrysler TorqueFlite transmission and 6.3 litre V8 motor with the Interceptor. To all intents and purposes both models were identical, though in fact the FF had a slightly longer wheelbase and an extra cooling vent in the front bumper. But technically it was a world ahead and was better to drive than the Interceptor, adding leech-like roadholding to its sibling's many qualities.

Unfortunately, mechanical complexity made it difficult – and expensive – to produce. Jensen FFs were built to order only, and the steep price ensured that relatively few were sold – some 320 in six years. And when Jensen started struggling in the early 1970s, the innovative FF was reluctantly discontinued – a classic example of a great car that was ahead of its time.

An attempt to enter the sports car market with the Jensen Healey was made after Donald Healey joined the company in the early '70s, but none of these moves could revive Jensen's fortunes and the company was dissolved in 1976, leaving the splendid Interceptor as a lasting memorial.

This massive rear hatch window was a characteristic design feature of the Interceptor.

COUNTRY OF ORIGIN:
UK
FIRST MANUFACTURED:
1966 (until 1971)
ENGINE:
6,286 cc V8
PERFORMANCE:
Top speed of 130 mph (210 km/h);
0-60 mph (97 km/h) in 7.7 secs
YOU SHOULD KNOW:
A drawback that inhibited the Jensen FF's commercial viability was a serious design fault – because of the transmission set-up and steering geometry it couldn't be converted to left-hand drive for the important American luxury GT market. Oops!

The Rapide was definitely exclusive, as it harked back to former times by only being built to order.

Lagonda Rapide

In 1947 entrepreneur David Brown answered a small ad in The Times offering 'High-class motor business for sale' . . . and bought Aston Martin. His spending spree didn't stop, for he also acquired Lagonda . . . which cost more than twice as much as Aston Martin. In fact, the bargain buy would be the winner and Lagonda an also-ran.

At first everything went well. The first postwar Lagonda engine – designed by the legendary W O Bentley – not only appeared in the handsome Lagonda 2.6 litre drophead coupe of 1948 but would also power the great Aston Martins of the 1950s. The 2.6 was succeeded by the 3 litre coupe (fixed or drophead) and saloon in 1953, but when that was discontinued in 1958 and not replaced it was generally assumed the Lagonda marque was toast.

But no! David Brown may have been busy winning races with his Astons, but he found time to develop another Lagonda – the elegant Rapide, styled by Touring in Milan, launched in 1961 and based on the Aston Martin DB4. This long, low saloon was every bit as elegant as its predecessors. It had a 4 litre engine, lightweight chassis and aluminium body. There were servo-assisted disc brakes all round and an automatic four-speed gearbox. The interior featured a mandatory burr walnut dashboard and leather upholstery. It lived up to its name with an impressive top speed as David Brown tried to resurrect the four-door performance GT format.

He was delighted with the result, but sadly cash-rich buyers were slow to appreciate the opportunity they were missing. The Rapide was built to order, and only 55 of those were taken in four years. The last Lagonda was hand-built in 1964 and if you don't already own one don't bother to go looking.

COUNTRY OF ORIGIN:
UK
FIRST MANUFACTURED:
1961 (until 1964)
ENGINE:
3,995 cc Straight Six
PERFORMANCE:
Top speed of 130 mph; 0-60 mph (97 km/h) in 10.2 secs
YOU SHOULD KNOW:
The combined price David Brown paid for both Aston Martin and Lagonda in 1947 was less than £75,000 – which in turn was only half the average price of ONE Aston Martin Lagonda, the stunning supercar launched 30 years later.

Lamborghini 350 GT

Could it be true? Rumour has it that self-made Italian industrialist Ferruccio Lamborghini had trouble with his Ferrari, complained to old Enzo personally and was brusquely rebuffed by Il Commendatore. Suitably insulted, he decided to try and geld the Prancing Horse by creating a sharp new breed of performance cars. True or not, Lamborghini certainly did produce glamorous cars that undoubtedly went on to hijack many sales from Ferrari.

The first offering from the new factory at Santa'Agata was the Lambo 350 GT of 1964, a dashing two-seater coupe with a superb V12 engine designed by (poke, poke) ex-Ferrari engineer Giotto Bizzarrini. Better still, youthful Lamborghini boss Giampaolo Dallara had worked for both Ferrari and Maserati, giving him impeccable supercar credentials. The result of their joint effort must have come as a nasty surprise to Maranello when it appeared at the Geneva Motor Show in March '64, for the somewhat angular prototype seen the previous year had been rounded off by Carrozzeria Touring and the sleek debutant looked very sexy.

It was also a sensational performer, with the magnificent engine delivering brutal acceleration and an awesome top speed. The ride was good, with independent suspension all round, roadholding was tenacious and power-assisted Girling disc brakes stopped it efficiently from high speed. After a slowish start the word got out, and production of the 350 GT grew rapidly through '65 and into '66.

That year Lamborghini introduced the 400 GT – essentially an improved version of the earlier car with a larger engine – and after a period of co-production in 1966–67 the 400 GT had a year on its own before being replaced by the Islero. These special GTs represented an auspicious start to Ferruccio Lamborghini's bold new venture, which would go from strength to strength.

COUNTRY OF ORIGIN:
Italy
FIRST MANUFACTURED:
1964 (until 1967)
ENGINE:
3,464 cc DOHC V12
PERFORMANCE:
Top speed of 156 mph (251 km/h);
0-60 mph (97 km/h) in 6.4 secs
YOU SHOULD KNOW:
If anyone doubts the story of Ferruccio Lamborghini's slighting by Enzo Ferrari, the former's intentions in setting up his manufacturing operation may perhaps be judged by his choice of badge for the Lambo – the Rampant Bull.

The 350 GT was Ferruccio Lamborghini's first warning shot across Enzo Ferrari's bows.

Lamborghini Miura

If Ferrari hadn't already received a wakeup call, the arrival of Lamborghini Miura must have rattled Maranello's rafters. When it first appeared in 1965 at the Turin Motor Show the Miura was just a bare chassis – but that didn't stop wealthy aficionados putting down deposits without knowing precisely (or even vaguely) what form their purchase would eventually take. They felt the spectacular chassis spoke for itself, with a layout derived from contemporary sports racers with a transversely mounted V12 engine in the middle that simply shrieked performance.

Nobody asked for their money back when they saw the finished article at the Geneva Motor Show. The word 'sensational' may be over-used, but was entirely appropriate to describe the motoring world's reception of the first true supercar. This was a young man's dream machine – engineered by a team under Lamborghini's brilliant 24-year-old Giampaolo Dallara and designed by the equally youthful Marcello Gandini at Bertone.

The electrifying Miura was a slim, low two-seater coupe with a curving front end and aerodynamic rear, punctuated by businesslike vertical air scoops at the rear of the cabin. That tough steel chassis carried a flamboyant aluminium body that included unusual clamshell-opening bonnet and boot (for access to the engine and a tiny luggage compartment).

The first Miuras to be built were designated as P400 (*Posteriore 4 Litri*) models. Although they were expensive by the standards of the day, P400s sold well. But the refined P400S was shown at Turin in November 1968, featuring some external trim modifications, electric windows, a tuned engine and various internal enhancements. Last but not least – in fact considered best of the best – the P400SV appeared in 1971, with an even more powerful engine and slip differential. If you can only afford to drive one Miura, make it a P400SV.

The Miura undoubtedly earned the right to be described as the world's first genuine supercar.

Lamborghini Espada S1

Long, wide and low are three words that spring to mind when describing the Lambo Espada S1 sports coupe that lit up the latter part of the 1960s, before the S2 and S3 versions carried the Espada through most of the 1970s. This typically Latin Grand Tourer was based on Lamborghini's Marzal concept car, designed by Bertone and shown at the 1967 Geneva Motor Show. With some additional styling notes borrowed from Bertone's sensationally reworked Jaguar E-Type Piranha, the Espada filled a gap in the Lamborghini range. It was a true two-door 2+2 four-seater and there was obviously demand for such a car, for the Espada became Lamborghini's best seller of the period.

The Espada had fully independent suspension and disc brakes all round. Five-speed manual transmission was standard but an unusual automatic option was available – the three ratios were drive, first and reverse. The car was front-engined and – despite its flamboyant styling – did not have the pop-up headlamps beloved by designers of GT cars at the time. The interior trim was first-class and the only complaint was that rear-seat passengers were somewhat cramped. The Santa'Agata factory was a hive of activity as Ferruccio Lamborghini challenged Ferrari on all fronts, and the head-turning Espada was definitely a major gauntlet.

The Espada S2 appeared in 1970, and was in turn succeeded in 1972 by the S3 that lasted until 1978. Power output from the V12 was increased from series to series and the interiors saw major revamping, but there was little external change of appearance – though the S3 did acquire the ugly rubber bumpers required by new US regulations. Over 1,200 Espadas were built over the model's 10-year life – a sales record that added up to lots of lovely lira.

Drivers and passengers needed to be pretty supple to enter and exit the long, low Espada.

COUNTRY OF ORIGIN:
Italy
FIRST MANUFACTURED:
1968 (until 1970)
ENGINE:
3,929 cc 2 x DOHC V12
PERFORMANCE:
Top speed of 150 mph (241 km/h);
0-60 mph (97 km/h) in 7.9 secs
YOU SHOULD KNOW:
Granted the length and slim profile of the Espada, the name seems entirely appropriate – in Spanish espada is the sword used by a matador to dispatch the bull at the climax of a corrida de toros, ideally with graceful efficiency and dashing style. Presumably Lambo's Rampant Bull was the one that got away.

Lancia Fulvia

The 1963 Geneva Motor Show saw the introduction of a car that would win its spurs in the competitive world of international rallying and enjoy long life and considerable fortune as a road car. But for all that it couldn't prevent its parent from being consumed by Fiat in 1969, though happily the proud Lancia name was allowed to live on. The Lancia Fulvia was initially offered as the Berlina four-door saloon with a coupe following later. There was also a Sport coupe produced by Milan's renowned Zagato concern as a dashing alternative to the factory offering. The Fulvia replaced Lancia's rear-wheel drive Appia but was itself a front-wheel drive car, following the route pioneered by Lancia with the launch of the Flavia in 1961.

Indeed, the Fulvia closely replicated the Flavia's general mechanical configuration, though the two models had very different engines. The Fulvia had a brand-new narrow-angle DOHC V4 designed by Zaccone Mina that was destined to be the last in the famous line of such engines created by Lancia since the early 1920s. This was mounted longitudinally in front of the transaxle and would eventually be made in six different capacities as the model line expanded.

An almost endless succession of new and evolutionary options appeared during the Fulvia's long production run, and the styling gradually evolved from the rather severe sharp-edged appearance of the earlier cars to a much rounder look. The basic Berlina went through several changes, including uprating to GT and GTE status. Nine or ten versions of the factory coupe were created during the long production run, whilst Zagato's Sport coupe went through three series, the last being the fastest road-going Fulvia ever – the Sport 1600 with its top speed of 118 mph (190 km/h) – a fitting climax to the impressive Fulvia story.

With the Fulvia, Lancia hit the commercial jackpot as many and various models were produced for a decade and more.

COUNTRY OF ORIGIN:
Italy
FIRST MANUFACTURED:
1963 (until 1976)
ENGINE:
Six variants from 1,091 cc
to 1,584 cc V4
PERFORMANCE:
With typical 1,216 cc engine –
top speed of 97 mph (156 km/h);
0-60 mph (97 km/h) in 15.7 secs
YOU SHOULD KNOW:
The one that own-and-drive collectors all chase after is the Lancia Fulvia Coupe HF, first offered in 1965 – this is a supremely elegant compact coupe that spawned a whole line of high-performance Rallye coupes.

Lincoln Continental

The first Lincoln Continental appeared before World War II, with postwar production resuming until this big and exclusive automobile was discontinued in 1948. Then the Continental reappeared in 1956 as a separate one-model Ford-owned marque, but it was not until 1961 that the Lincoln and Continental names were reunited in an iconic design by the great Elwood Engel – a design considered by many to be his great masterpiece. The car's understated elegance won design awards and was soon copied by envious rivals such as Buick and Cadillac.

The Lincoln Continental was smaller than previous versions, but still very much at the luxury end of the Ford family spectrum. If there was one distinctive design feature, it was that the back doors were rear hinged and opened from the front – the so-called 'suicide doors' common on prewar cars but hardly seen after 1945. With a few minor internal and external changes, the rectilinear design would last until the next Continental generation was launched in 1970, though it was stretched slightly in 1964 to give more rear-seat legroom.

The initial Continental offering was restricted to a pair of four-door models – the sedan and convertible – though a two-door coupe appeared subsequently in 1966, at which point a larger engine was introduced. In 1968 the Lincoln Continental Mark III coupe appeared but this famous car (as a result of being used on film to smuggle heroin in *The French Connection*) was sufficiently altered to be considered a completely different model. It was discontinued in 1971.

Despite enjoying great success throughout the 1960s, the Lincoln Continental nearly didn't happen – Elwood Engel's splendid design was originally intended for a new Ford Thunderbird, until an inspired decision was made to tweak and enlarge the car to create a revived Lincoln Continental.

COUNTRY OF ORIGIN:
USA
FIRST MANUFACTURED:
1961 (until 1969)
ENGINE:
7.0 l (430 cid), 7.5 l (460 cid) or 7.6 l (462 cid) V8
PERFORMANCE:
Top speed of 110 mph (177 km/h); 0-60 mph (97 km/h) in 12.4 secs
YOU SHOULD KNOW:
The open-top parade limousine in which John F Kennedy was assassinated in 1963 was custom built from a Lincoln Continental convertible – codenamed SS-100-X, it was subsequently armour-plated and fitted with a bulletproof roof, after which it continued in White House service for many years.

This convertible version had the Continental's signature back-hinged rear 'suicide doors'.

Lotus Elan

COUNTRY OF ORIGIN:
UK
FIRST MANUFACTURED:
1962 (until 1975)
ENGINE:
1,558 cc Straight Four
PERFORMANCE:
Top speed of 118 mph (190 km/h);
0-60 mph (97 km/h) in 7.6 secs
YOU SHOULD KNOW:
Nobody could ever accuse the
Japanese of being copycats, but it is
known that Mazda bought,
disassembled and closely studied a
couple of first generation Lotus Elans
– though of course the close
resemblance of the subsequent
Mazda MX-5 is a complete
coincidence.

The Lotus Elan roadster was a welcome debutant in 1962 – welcome to the manufacturer because it replaced the expensive-to-build Elite and welcomed by sporting drivers who appreciated performance-packed possibilities. It was even embraced by those who weren't minted but could wield a mean spanner, as the Elan was initially offered in kit form like the successful Lotus Seven.

The Elan was an uncompromising manifestation of Colin Chapman's lightweight design philosophy and delivered acceleration and top speed far ahead of its time for this class of sports car. The power came from a 1.6 litre evolution version of the sturdy Ford Kent engine that had been fitted with a Lotus-designed Cosworth twin-cam alloy head (the engine also used in the punchy Lotus-Cortina). The Elan boasted independent suspension and disc brakes all round long before these became widely used standard features. It had a steel chassis and fibreglass body that kept the weight right down.

With its streamlined shape and pop-up headlamps, this modern-looking roadster was an instant hit. The Elan's favourable reception was complemented by the swift appearance of a hardtop option in 1963 and a two-seater coupe in 1965. The Elan's commercial success was finally cemented by the arrival of the handsome long-wheelbase Elan Plus Two in 1967. This was a genuine 2+2 coupe with a roomy cabin, which retained all the speed and agility of its predecessors – in fact it was even a tad faster, thanks to a slippery aerodynamic shape. The Plus Two continued in production until 1975, two years after the roadster and coupe were discontinued.

The Lotus Elan would be born again in the late 1980s for a six-year production run – differentiated from its illustrious ancestry by an M100 tag and lauded as a technical masterpiece in the finest traditions of advanced Lotus engineering.

Initially a kit-car in classic Lotus mode, the Elan soon proved to be a sporty factory-built winner with buyers.

Marcos 1800 GT

The Marcos biography covers a succession of bankruptcies interrupted by interesting cars, starting with the company's foundation in 1959 by Frank Costin and Jem Marsh. Their first effort was a GT that appeared in 1960 with then-fashionable gullwing doors and an odd four-piece windscreen. Nine examples made in the next couple of years had assorted Ford engines teamed with Standard/Triumph steering and suspension. Their most unusual feature was the fact that the chassis was fabricated from laminated plywood – an idea suggested by Costin, who worked on the wood-framed Mosquito fighter bomber in World War II.

After the Adams brothers came aboard they refined the original design and in 1963 the classic 1800 GT coupe was introduced, with hints of E-Type Jaguar in its racy look and long body shape. This was a very pretty car that would continue to be produced for years, through various comings and goings of the Marcos marque. The engine was bought in from Volvo and was the same power plant used in the iconic Volvo P1800 of 1961. Later in the 1800 GT's run various different engines were offered as options.

In 1969 the GT effectively became a different car as a steel chassis was introduced, enabling Marcos to fit a range of more powerful engines, including the 3 litre Ford Essex V6 or the similarly sized Volvo straight six. But production ended with the first 'bust' in 1971, when the money ran out as a result of problems getting export clearance for the USA coupled with the crippling development costs of the new Mantis.

Today, surviving Marcos 1800 GTs are prized as classic racing cars, with well-maintained track versions fetching high prices – for they are still great fun to drive and very competitive more than 40 years after they first burst onto the scene.

COUNTRY OF ORIGIN:
UK
FIRST MANUFACTURED:
1963 (until 1968)
ENGINE:
1,778 cc Straight Four
PERFORMANCE:
Top speed of 116 mph (187 km/h); 0-60 mph (97 km/h) in 8.2 secs
YOU SHOULD KNOW:
The Marcos 1800 GT named for its engine size should not be confused with the company's other '1800' – the Mini Marcos of 1965 that had a wheelbase of just 69 inches (1800 mm) and proved to be popular in Japan and quite a little track star in Europe.

Many different engines were offered during the production run of the handsome 1800 GT.

Maserati Ghibli

Maserati quit racing in the 1950s to concentrate on producing road cars, but failed to come up with a real winner until the mid-1960s. But the debut of the fabulous Ghibli coupe at the Turin Motor Show in 1966 changed all that. Eager customers had to wait until 1967 to get their hands on one of these low,

The fabulous Ghibli with the trident badge made famous on Europe's racing circuits was Maserati's first great road car.

streamlined beauties with their twin fuel tanks, a characteristic shark-like nose, pop-up headlights, alloy wheels and a luxurious leather interior.

In the early 1960s many makers were turning to fibreglass bodies in order to reduce weight and thus boost performance, but Maserati opted for a traditional steel body designed by Giorgetto Giugiaro at Ghia. The Ghibli did not seem to be disadvantaged by being made of old-fashioned heavy metal, with searing acceleration and a top speed around the 150 mph (241 km/h) mark. The transmission was either three-speed automatic or five-speed manual, with the former appealing to Americans and the latter to Europeans.

Whatever their choice of gearbox, those first customers were so satisfied with their beautifully designed and well-built GTs that they told their rich friends, with the result that the Ghibli actually outsold formidable rivals like the Ferrari Daytona and the Lamborghini Miura. Encouraged by this commercial success, Maserati created the convertible Ghibli Spyder in 1969.

These are rare, as Ghibli production ceased in 1973 to make way for the Maserati Khamsin, designed by Bertone. Even rarer is the more powerful Ghibli Spyder SS – only 25 were made, making them the most desirable of Ghiblis. Not that the others are short of admirers – the coupe (around 1,150 made) and the regular Spyder (125 made) are amongst the most sought-after of classic 1960s Italian GTs, of which there are many. But the Ghibli's star quality certainly remains undimmed.

COUNTRY OF ORIGIN:
Italy
FIRST MANUFACTURED:
1966 (until 1973)
ENGINE:
4,919 cc DOHC V8
PERFORMANCE:
Top speed of 154 mph (248 km/h);
0-60 mph (97 km/h) in 6.8 secs
YOU SHOULD KNOW:
Many a car manufacturer has decided that there's no keeping a good name down, and Maserati is no exception – after a 20-year holiday the Ghibli returned in 1992 as a refined but conservative two-door, four-seater luxury coupe with performance that matched the original's but without any of the original Ghibli's raw supercar appeal.

Mazda Cosmo 110S

The one manufacturer to make a real go of the rotary engine originally designed by Felix Wankel was Mazda, and the Japanese company's first rotary-engined car was the Cosmo 110S, a GT car intended to headline the company's drive into mass-market car production.

The Cosmo 110S was first seen at the Tokyo Motor Show in 1964 and pre-production models were extensively tested before the Series I L/10A Cosmo 110S was released – thus avoiding the trap that NSU fell into by hastily launching its Wankel-engined Ro80, which acquired a destructive reputation for engine failure. Mazda even went to the length of running a couple of 110S cars in an 84-hour endurance race in Germany.

This rather angular coupe had a twin-chamber rotary engine with two spark plugs per chamber, each with a distributor. A four-speed manual gearbox was standard. Suspension was independent at the front with a live rear axle and leaf springs at the back. The braking system consisted of front discs and rear drums. Considering that this was effectively a cross between a test bed and a marketing device, Series I sales of around 350 in two years can't have been too disappointing.

Serious business began in 1968 when the Series II L/10B was introduced. This offered increased power output from an enhanced engine, servo-assisted brakes all round, larger wheels and a longer wheelbase. There were also cosmetic styling changes that differentiated between the two versions, including a new grille with two additional air vents. The later Cosmo 110Ss were seen as an altogether better buy and Mazda sold nearly 1,200 before production was ended in 1972. Driving one today is nearly impossible – with the exception of a few that went to America, hardly any escaped from Japan.

COUNTRY OF ORIGIN:
Japan
FIRST MANUFACTURED:
1967 (until 1972)
ENGINE:
982 cc Twin-chamber Rotary
PERFORMANCE:
Series II – top speed of 120 mph (193 km/h); 0-60 mph (97 km/h) in 9.3 secs
YOU SHOULD KNOW:
The Cosmo name reappeared several times for Mazda – the Cosmo AP (from 1975) was known as the RX-5 for export purposes, the HB Cosmo ran through the 1980s and the Eunos Cosmo, with the distinction of a triple-rotor engine, was Mazda's top-of-the-range 2+2 coupe from the early 1990s.

The Cosmo had a rotary engine that actually worked well.

Mercedes-Benz 230 SL

COUNTRY OF ORIGIN:
Germany
FIRST MANUFACTURED:
1963 (until 1967)
ENGINE:
2,308 cc Straight Six
PERFORMANCE:
Top speed of 124 mph (200 km/h);
0-60 mph (97 km/h) in 10.5 secs
YOU SHOULD KNOW:
The 230 SL is the least desirable of
the three 1960s SLs, as the smaller
engine offers less impressive
performance than later brethren, but
this means that (despite a marked
tendency to rust underneath) there
are plenty around for anyone who
fancies stylish pagoda-top motoring.

The 230 SL was lovely to look at, but lacked the power to match its sporting appearance.

The racing-derived Mercedes 300SL coupe with gullwing doors was the must-have sports car of the mid-1950s. It was the first of the SL (Sport Leicht = Light Sports) class that has continued to the present day, though subsequent SLs haven't quite recaptured the glamour of the sensually rounded 300SL – also offered as a roadster and voted one of the top sports cars of all time.

But Mercedes certainly tried hard. The 300SL's companion car was the smaller but similar-looking 190SL. Together they comprised the W198 SL class, discontinued during 1963 after the W113 SL class appeared in the form of the 230 SL. This marked the debut of the famous 'pagoda roof" SL with its six-cylinder fuel-injected engine and aluminium body panels, which reduced weight and improved the performance of this solidly built car. The 230 SL was a Coupe-Roadster, with an in-built soft top stored in a well behind the two seats and a removable coupe hardtop that enabled either configuration to be used.

There was a 230 SL California Coupe. It came with the coupe top only, though this could still be removed for open-top motoring – presumably in the ever-reliable California sun. In the space normally occupied by the soft top was a drop-down bench seat, but this was virtually useless and the 2+2 wasn't a hit.

The heavier R107 SL class superseded the W113 SLs in 1972, but not before the 230 SL had evolved, though this was not apparent visually as the main difference was larger engines. The 250 SL was offered in 1967 and 1968, whilst the 280 SL ran from 1968 to 1971. The production run of the three models was around 49,000, ensuring that these classics are not rare, with about 20,000 original 230 SLs produced.

Mercedes-Benz 600

A newly minted Merc hit the road in 1963, specifically designed to compete with Rolls-Royces and the finest top-of-the-range American limousines. The Mercedes-Benz 600 was a large, luxurious car that was intended to be chauffeur driven, as most models had a powered divider window that separated the driver and passenger compartments. This awesome car was also meant to illustrate the fact that Mercedes was capable of delivering unbeatable engineering excellence.

Two types of 600 were produced. There were short-wheelbase four-door saloons that came with or without the divider. But the true splendour of this magnificent machine was seen in the long-wheelbase Pullmans. These came in three forms, all with divider. There was a four-door limousine that had two rear-facing seats in addition to the main passenger bench. Secondly there was the six-door limousine, which also had extra seating, and finally ultra-rare landaulets – six-door Pullmans with a convertible rear section designed for ceremonial use by royalty or heads of state in the days before open cars were deemed a potentially lethal security risk.

The 600 was, of course, massive. The sheer size of the car necessitated the use of a huge 6.3 litre V8 power plant that was specially developed. This not only enabled the weighty limo to outperform pretty much everything up to Porsche 911 level, but also supported an array of hydraulic-powered features that included ultra-smooth air suspension (the 600's body almost touched ground before the engine was started), windows, moveable seats and automatically closed doors and boots.

Although a few 600s continued to be made until the official discontinuation date of 1981, production effectively ended in 1972 when the oil crisis made these thirsty monsters seem a trifle ostentatious and therefore somewhat unfashionable. The 600 was not replaced until the Maybach appeared in the 21st century.

COUNTRY OF ORIGIN:
Germany
FIRST MANUFACTURED:
1963 (until 1981)
ENGINE:
6,332 cc V8
PERFORMANCE:
Top speed of 127 mph (205 km/h);
0-60 mph (97 km/h) in 9.4 secs
YOU SHOULD KNOW:
The Mercedes-Benz 600 naturally appealed to celebrities, with typical owners including the likes of Aristotle Onassis, Hugh Hefner, John Lennon, Elvis Presley and Elizabeth Taylor – but it was also very popular with heads of state in former British colonies who did not wish to be seen in Rolls-Royces for political reasons.

The Pullman was really a car for heads of state, though many a film star thought they had equal status and bought one.

In true German style, the 280 SE was technically advanced and beautifully engineered.

Mercedes-Benz 280 SE 3.5

COUNTRY OF ORIGIN:
Germany
FIRST MANUFACTURED:
1969 (until 1971)
ENGINE:
3,499 cc V8
PERFORMANCE:
Top speed of 127 mph (204 km/h);
0-60 mph (97 km/h) in 8.9 secs
YOU SHOULD KNOW:
Unlike many classics, the Mercedes
280 SE seems like a thoroughly
modern car when used as every-day
transport – still handling well and
driving beautifully, with the heavy
cost of petrol unlikely to deter the
celebrities and media types who like
to be seen gadding around town in
this exclusive automobile.

The super-luxurious 280 SE 3.5 made its debut at the Frankfurt Motor Show in 1969, giving convincing evidence of the Stuttgart company's increasing self-confidence as it advanced towards major international status by offering its first V-powered sporty car. There were two versions of this rather traditional but handsome machine – a coupe and cabriolet – with the old-fashioned look explained by the fact that the 280 SE was based on the 220 SE of 1961 with only the smallest of style changes. Even so, the '*Flachkuler*' is thought by many classic car enthusiasts to be one of the most beautiful and elegant coupes ever made, well able to stand alongside the best of contemporary competitors in the minds of those who could afford the best.

But the real innovation was found beneath the bonnet, where the most advanced engine ever produced by Mercedes could be found. It had transistorized ignition, three-phase generator and a Bosch electronic fuel injection system. This brand-new V8 had a cast-iron block with an aluminium head. It hardly weighed more than the standard Mercedes six-cylinder engine but gave the 280 SE rapid acceleration and an impressive top speed. In 1971 it would be uprated to 4.5 litres, especially for the American market.

The superb 280 SE had standard features such as servo-assisted brakes, four-speed automatic transmission with a column change (there was a manual option), air conditioning, electric windows and Becker Europa stereo radio. The luxurious interior featured leather upholstery and specially selected wood trim.

The original price was steep, reflecting the high cost of manufacture, which means that just 4,500 of these collectable cars were manufactured to an extraordinary standard of craftsmanship. They are the last of the hand-built Mercedes cars, making them especially rare and desirable, with good examples fetching serious money today.

Mercury Monterey Custom S-55

Ford's entry-level luxury marque was missing something, and the wide, long low, well-chromed Mercury Monterey Custom S-55 arrived in mid-1962 to rectify the omission. The general intention was to grab a piece of the action that was developing around sportier models in the early '60s and the particular task was socking it to the successful Pontiac Grand Prix, which was just such a car.

This was the first of the big-bucket-seat Mercurys that sought to profit by stretching and lowering Ford platforms. The Monterey Custom S-55 came with a base 6.4 litre engine, but Dearborn's new 406 enlargement was available as a go-faster option with two levels of tuning – both engines were called Marauders when dropped into a Mercury. The Monterey was similar to the Ford Galaxie 500XL that arrived at the same time with a similar mission statement.

The Custom S-55 had beefed-up suspension and mostly came with three-speed Multi-Drive Merc-O-Matic automatic transmission coupled with the smaller engine, as the objective was fast roadwork rather than track prowess. The interior was nicely appointed with thin-shell bucket seats, plenty of vinyl trim and a bright-metal floor console with shift lever and storage compartment. But '62 turned out to be a bad year, with just over 4,000 sold.

Undeterred, the Custom S-55 was back in '63 with an enlarged range, consisting of four body styles. There was a two-door convertible, two-door Marauder Hardtop, four-door Breezeaway Hardtop and the two-door Breezeaway Hardtop. The hardtops had a distinctive backward-raking sloped rear window and there was a choice of three-speed automatic transmission or a four-speed manual gearbox plus a third, even-bigger engine. The styling did not please everyone, though combined sales did rise to around the 7,500 mark. It was not enough, however, and the Custom S-55 was immediately discontinued.

COUNTRY OF ORIGIN:
USA
FIRST MANUFACTURED:
1962 (until 1963)
ENGINE:
6.4 l (390 cid), 6.7 l (406 cid) or 7.0 l (427 cid) V8
PERFORMANCE:
With 7.0 l engine – top speed of 120 mph (193 km/h); 0-60 mph (97 km/h) in 7.7 secs
YOU SHOULD KNOW:
Although the Monterey Custom S-55 line was dropped after just two years, the S-55 designation would later reappear as a high-performance 'Sports Package' option on other Mercury cars.

Mercury Cougar

COUNTRY OF ORIGIN:
USA
FIRST MANUFACTURED:
1967 (until 1973)
ENGINE:
Various, from 4.7 l (289 cid)
to 7.0 l (429 cid) V8
PERFORMANCE:
With 5.8 l engine – top speed of
104 mph (km/h); 0.60 mph (97 km/h)
in 7.6 secs
YOU SHOULD KNOW:
The Cougar works team competed
with honour – and considerable
success – in the 1967 Trans-Am road
racing series for production sedans,
though it failed to topple the
all-conquering Mustang and was
rather mysteriously withdrawn from
the following year's Trans-Am.

Blessed was the carmaker who invented a niche market which proved incredibly profitable. In the early 1960s that left Ford smirking, for their Mustang had become the first ponycar. This had involved the creation of a stylish compact capturing the free 'n' easy spirit of the age at an affordable price. Of course in the cutthroat world of US auto manufacture a unique niche soon became a genre with virtually every Detroit player trying to run a winning 'pony'.

Ford was greedy, and decided it might be possible for its Mercury marque to clamber aboard the bandwagon, even though Mercury cars were big. The answer was obvious – a bigger ponycar that might find its own niche within a niche. The thinking was sound. When the Cougar finally appeared in 1967 after a long development process it was an instant hit, with the elegantly designed standard hardtop and punchy XR-7 with their well-appointed interiors and huge options package selling well from Day One.

The Cougar ponycar would go on to enjoy an eight-year run that saw the introduction of various evolutionary models, including a convertible from 1969 when range styling was updated for a second generation. Along the way there would be a choice of many engines, although sales declined steadily and never replicated the stunning success of the launch year.

The Cougar lasted as a ponycar until 1973, but enjoyed a much better run than some of Mercury's efforts to chase specific market share – around 615,000 of the various versions were sold over the years, and the Cougar pony has become a much-appreciated cherished car that has developed a cult following. The third generation was relaunched as a personally luxury car and the feline name is still in use.

The Cougar was a long-lasting (and large) manifestation of the enduring ponycar craze.

Mercury Marauder

The Marauder name appealed to the good folk at Mercury, for they chose it for the big Ford engines the company used in the 1960s. Suitably enthused, they also applied the name to some early 1960s fastback versions of the Monterey, Montclair and Park Lane models. And in 1969 they went all the way, launching the Mercury Marauder as a fully-fledged model in its own right.

This large, two-door coupe was a hopeful entry into the personal luxury car market, where self-indulgent quality cars tended to offer long fronts, short tails with fastback styling, luxury cabins and high performance. There were two types – those with big engines in smallish cars or alternatively big engines in biggish cars. The latter category included speedsters like the Ford T-bird, Buick Riviera and Pontiac Grand Prix and they were the ones in Mercury's sights.

The roomy Marauder certainly conformed to the latter stereotype, with a choice of versions – the standard offering having a 6.4 litre engine and the X-100 a larger 7 litre alternative. Despite being based on the Mercury Marquis – the pair had the same thrusting front end and shared interior components – the Marauder had a distinctive back end with fake side air intakes. It could be made more individual by ordering options like rear fender skirts (standard on the X-100), vinyl roof, bucket seats and a floor console for the gearshift.

Sadly (and not for the first time when Mercury was trying to cash in on perceived market trends) the Marauder failed to hit the spot, because the market for full-sized sporty cars had already started to evaporate – fast. Just 15,000 Marauders were sold in 1969, with the figure slumping to 6,000 the following year. Two years were enough for embarrassed management, and the Marauder swiftly passed into history.

The Marauder was a late entry in a market segment that was running out of gas and sadly missed out on the money.

COUNTRY OF ORIGIN:
USA
FIRST MANUFACTURED:
1969 (until 1970)
ENGINE:
6.4 l (390 cid) or 7.0 l (429 cid) V8
PERFORMANCE:
With 7.0 l engine – top speed of 126 mph (km/h); 0-60 mph (97 km/h) in 7.5 secs
YOU SHOULD KNOW:
Ford resurrected the Marauder name from 2003 to 2004, when it became the badge worn by a high-performance version of the Mercury Grand Marquis line, which was marketed as a 'muscle sedan'.

MGB

COUNTRY OF ORIGIN:
UK
FIRST MANUFACTURED:
1962 (until 1980)
ENGINE:
1,799 cc Straight Four
PERFORMANCE:
Top speed of 103 mph (166 km/h);
0-60 mph (97 km/h) in 12.2 secs
YOU SHOULD KNOW:
For MGB purists, the last year that
really counts is 1973 – for that's the
last year the car was produced with
traditional chrome bumpers, rather
than the large, black rubber
monstrosities introduced the
following year to comply with
US regulations.

The rather voluptuous lines of the MGA were starting to look dated as the Swinging Sixties dawned, but the British Motor Corporation was ready with one of its few great success stories – the MGB. This brilliant sports car with its clean lines would be around for nearly twenty years and well over half a million MGBs (and derivatives) would be manufactured, making it the best-selling British sports car of all time.

The two-seater roadster was introduced in 1962, and this neat convertible was joined in 1973 by the hatchback MGB GT coupe – nominally a 2+2, though the rear seating would only have been adequate if Snow White were driving. This version would continue to be produced in virtually unchanged form until it was dropped in 1974, though a meaty V8 evolution was offered from 1973 to 1976.

The roadster had a comfortable interior with wind-up windows and a parcel shelf behind the seats. The car featured a four-cylinder 1.8 litre engine and – unlike the MGA it replaced and the Triumph TRs with which it competed – had monocoque rather than body-on-chassis construction, which reduced weight and costs allowing the MGB to be sold at an attractive price. It was an instant success with sporty drivers because the MGB was (and is) a joy to drive, with good acceleration, excellent roadholding and an ability to top the 'ton' when flat out.

The roadster was upgraded as the Mk II in 1967, with an all-synchromesh gearbox and the option of automatic transmission. Various other cosmetic changes took place until the Mk III was introduced in 1972. This had a better heater and new fascia, and would be the final evolution. The last MGB rolled off the line at Abingdon in 1980, to end the era of mass-produced Great British sports cars.

A classic example of the chrome-bumpered roadster.

MGC

Mechanically speaking, the MGC's biography is not really so very different from the heart-warming MGB story, for the two models appear to be virtually identical. But that superficial likeness conceals considerable differences. Produced for just three years (1967 to 1969), the MGC was more than a performance-enhanced MGB fitted with a 2.9 litre straight six. It was intended as a replacement for parent company BMC's Austin-Healey 3000, which was discontinued in 1967.

Considerable modification of the MGB platform was required to accommodate the 2.9 litre Morris C-series engine with its polished aluminium head and twin SU carburettors. This took the form of a revised floorpan and bonnet with a characteristic bulge to allow for a raised radiator, plus a neat teardrop for the carburettors. There was a special torsion-bar suspension system with telescopic dampers and the standard gearbox was a four-speed manual. Overdrive or three-speed automatic transmission were options. The wheels were bigger than those on MGBs.

Very much following the MGB formula, both an MGC roadster and MGC GT were offered, but these powerful sports cars never really fired the public imagination. Despite their extra grunt and performance that far exceeded that of the four-cylinder car, the heavy engine adversely affected the nimble handling that had made the MGB so popular. However, the factory did produce a few lightweight MGC GTS racing models, and these competed with some success. The GTS cars were very attractive with flared wings and an aggressive bonnet bulge.

With around 9,000 produced during the shortish production run, the MGC is far rarer than its 'common' relation and therefore much sought-after by MG enthusiasts and collectors of classic sports cars. Happily, modern tyres and a little suspension tweaking can iron out those original handling problems to the complete satisfaction of today's owner-drivers.

Though both bigger and more powerful than the MGB, the MGC was not a nimble car.

COUNTRY OF ORIGIN:
UK
FIRST MANUFACTURED:
1967 (until 1969)
ENGINE:
2,912 cc OHV Straight Six
PERFORMANCE:
Top speed of 120 mph (193 km/h);
0-60 mph (97 km/h) in 10 secs
YOU SHOULD KNOW:
Sadly, the MGC would be the last all-new model to be created and produced by this great maker at the company's famous Abingdon works before it was closed in 1980.

Morgan Plus 8

Some people just refuse to move with the times – and thank goodness for that. At least so say the fans (there are many) of the Morgan Motor Company. Founded in 1909, Morgan is based in rural Worcestershire and hand-assembles fine British sports cars that are so coveted that there is inevitably a (sometimes lengthy) list containing the names of those who have put down deposits and can't wait (but must) for their brand-new Morgan to be ready.

Having made a prewar name with classic three-wheelers, Morgan had launched the company's first 4-4 car (four cylinders, four wheels) in 1936, and it was a derivation of this that appeared as the traditional Morgan Plus 4 sports car in 1950 – a car that would continue to be produced as it evolved steadily into the 21st century.

The next big development was the arrival of the Morgan Plus 8 in 1968 (nothing to do with the number of wheels, but rather the new Rover V8 engine). Plus 4 and Plus 8 looked similar, but the latter's performance was superior. Indeed, the V8 gave it deceptive oomph, with blistering acceleration and a surprisingly high top speed. To the considerable satisfaction of enthusiasts, Moggies (as Morgans are affectionately known) have never departed from the traditional construction method of steel chassis, ash frame and hand-crafted body – and the resultant lightweight sports car has always offered relatively high performance for an open roadster.

The Plus 8 was continued in production until 2004 (with various engine upgrades along the way), by which time over 3,500 had been produced. They remain collectable British classics that are robust enough to enjoy taking to the road day in, day out (especially in summer with the top down) – and sufficiently rare to ensure that second-hand values remain high.

COUNTRY OF ORIGIN:
UK
FIRST MANUFACTURED:
1968 (until 2004)
ENGINE:
3,532 cc V8
PERFORMANCE:
Top speed of 124 mph (200 km/h);
0-60 mph (97 km/h) in 6.7 secs
YOU SHOULD KNOW:
The Plus 8 is fast, but its successor leaves it standing – the retro-styled Aero 8 can scorch from rest to 60 mph in just 4.4 seconds and zip on to a top speed of 170 mph (270 km/h) – not bad for a wooden car!

NSU Wankel Spider

The long-established NSU car company was sold to Fiat in the 1930s, but the name was revived in World War II for production of the SdKfz 2, better known as the *Kettenkrad* – a small half-tracked all-terrain vehicle with a motorcycle front end. After hostilities ended, NSU restarted as a motorcycle manufacturer. Its innovative machines were very successful and NSU became a world leader in motorcycle production by the mid-1950s. This encouraged the company to start building cars.

The first four-wheeled offering was the small Prinz saloon, launched in 1957, but NSU might have become a footnote in postwar automobile history had it not been for the extraordinary Wankelspider. At first glance there was nothing very special about the plainly styled but attractive little convertible that appeared at the Frankfurt Motor Show in 1964, based on NSU's four-year-old Sport Prinz coupe.

The special secret lay beneath a shallow luggage locker at the back – an innovative Wankel rotary engine positioned over the rear axle. This was an incredibly efficient single-cylinder power plant developed by the gifted German engineer Felix Wankel. A rolling rotor turned within the single combustion chamber converting combustion pressure directly into rotary movement, eliminating energy loss experienced in a conventional piston engine when reciprocating movement is converted into rotational movement. The result was a very compact high-revving engine that generated enormous excitement and was initially hailed the next great advance in automotive technology. It wasn't, but that's another story.

The little Wankel Spider was something of a test bed for the new engine, and NSU was not overly concerned with sales. The company was more interested in pioneering the engine concept that was intended to make its fortune, and only some 2,400 units were produced before the little roadster was discontinued in 1966. And after that the fun really began.

COUNTRY OF ORIGIN:
Germany
FIRST MANUFACTURED:
1964 (until 1966)
ENGINE:
498 cc Single-rotor Wankel
PERFORMANCE:
Top speed of 92 mph (148 km/h); 0-60 mph (97 km /h) in 16.7 secs
YOU SHOULD KNOW:
Despite the many licences issued to produce the Wankel engine, the only manufacturer to have overcome the technical problems and use it consistently in production cars has been Mazda, in such niche performance cars as the RX-7 introduced in the late 1970s.

This pretty little roadster was a test bed for the Wankel engine.

NSU Ro80

COUNTRY OF ORIGIN:
Germany
FIRST MANUFACTURED:
1967 (until 1977)
ENGINE:
995 cc Double-rotor Wankel
PERFORMANCE:
Top speed of 112 mph (180 km/h);
0-60 mph (97 km/h) in 14.2 secs
YOU SHOULD KNOW:
The aerodynamic Ro80 (designed in
the mid-1960s) was indeed ahead of
its time – as anyone who compares
it with the 1983 Audi 100 will
confirm. The two cars have a virtually
identical body shape.

Having pioneered use of the revolutionary Wankel rotary engine in the Wankelspider roadster, NSU hoped to make a killing by producing a passenger car that would take full advantage of this exclusive engine. The result was the Ro80. It was a beautifully designed four-door saloon with an aerodynamic body, advanced engineering, superb performance and excellent handling. As well as that super-smooth engine, the Ro80 featured front-wheel drive, independent suspension all round, power steering and disc brakes, making it a really advanced vehicle.

Sounds too good to be true? Sadly, it was. NSU did not have the resources to undertake a thorough test progamme on the new, twin-chamber rotary engine developed from the single-chamber version in the Wankel Spider. This proved to be a terminal weakness, though the patient would linger on for a decade.

It was quickly apparent that engine components were not up to the stresses placed upon them. Some rotaries even imploded, but mostly they just started losing power. Amongst other faults, chamber walls could distort and rotor tips wore rapidly, causing oil leaks. A service would sometimes correct the problem, but engines often needed a rebuild or even replacement after two or three years. Added to that was the fact that Ro80s were heavy on fuel and dealers found difficulty understanding the new technology. It all added up to a ruinous reputation.

NSU tried valiantly to save the Ro80 (and the company) by instituting a generous warranty programme, and actually sorted most of the engine problems by 1970. But the damage was done. NSU was acquired by Volkswagen and merged with Audi. The Ro80 was allowed to fade away, with production ending in 1977 after some 37,000 had been made. But some are still going strong, offering a unique driving experience.

The Ro80 was great to look at, but the revolutionary engine proved to be an ongoing disaster.

Oldsmobile Starfire

The Starfire was a futuristic 1953 Olds concept car that never made it into production, though the name was then used for the most expensive Oldsmobiles of the 1950s – Model 98 Starfire convertibles. It was not until 1961 that the name borrowed from a Lockheed jet fighter plane was used for a stand-alone line.

In the confusing world where cars were created to serve all sorts of real or imagined market segments, the new Starfire was Oldsmobile's bold tilt at producing a personal luxury car. Unlike Ford's competing Thunderbird, it was part of the Olds full-size lineup, sharing a body and wheelbase with the Oldsmobile 88s. A convertible was the first to appear, with a whopping price tag to cover a wealth of standard equipment. This included Hydra-matic transmission with floor-mounted shift, brushed aluminium side panels, power steering, electrically adjustable driver's seat, electric windows, leather bucket seats and a centre console with tachometer. The engine was the most powerful available – the 6.5 litre Skyrocket.

In 1962 a two-door hardtop with a convertible roofline doubled the Starfire range and comfortably outsold the original soft-top. There was a styling update in 1963 but the Starfire's appeal was weakened by the debut of the Buick Riviera, which had the added appeal of unique styling that compared favourably with the Starfire's one-of-many-similar-Oldsmobiles appearance.

The Starfire limped through 1964, further weakened commercially by sharing a bodyshell with the cheaper Jetstar I. A major revamp across the Oldsmobile range in 1965 offered hope, with Starfire buyers getting the option of a larger engine and four-speed manual transmission. But the convertible was discontinued and many former standard features became options, to give a lower headline ticket price. It was all in vain. After 1967 the Starfire's flagship status went to the Toronado.

The glam name may have been borrowed from a jet fighter, but the Starfire was all car.

COUNTRY OF ORIGIN:
USA
FIRST MANUFACTURED:
1961 (until 1966)
ENGINE:
6.5 l (394 cid) or 7.0 l (425 cid) V8
PERFORMANCE:
With 6.5 l engine – top speed of 105 mph (km/h); 0-60 mph (97 km/h) in 9.7 secs
YOU SHOULD KNOW:
To ensure some element of exclusivity, Starfire buyers could mix 'n' match 15 exterior colours with four interior colours (blue, fawn, grey, and red) – with a further six colours to choose from when it came to convertible tops (black, blue, fawn, green, red and white). Welcome to Glitzville, USA!

Oldsmobile F-85 Cutlass

COUNTRY OF ORIGIN:
USA
FIRST MANUFACTURED:
1961 (until 1972)
ENGINE:
3.5 l (215 cid) V6; 3.7 l (225 cid) V6;
4.1 l (250 cid) Straight Six;
5.4 l (330 cid) V8; 6.6 l (400 cid) V8;
7.5 l (455 cid) V8
PERFORMANCE:
With mid-range 5.4 litre V8 – top
speed of 111 mph (179 km/h);
0-60 mph (87 km/h) in 9.4 secs
YOU SHOULD KNOW:
The co-production deal with
specialist customizer Hurst
Performance allowed the Hurst/Olds
Cutlass Supreme coupe and club
coupe introduced in 1968 to use the
7.5 l Rocket V8 engine – a power
plant that General Motors normally
banned from their intermediate
cars, restricting them to 6.6 l or
smaller engines.

Nobody was guiltier of confusing buyers with its model-naming policy than Oldsmobile – and one of the worst cases in point was the Cutlass. The name was first used on a prototype sports coupe in 1954, reappeared in the early 1960s as a sub-model of the F-85 series and thereafter rode triumphantly through three decades as a popular but confusing nameplate that appeared on a variety of different cars.

But all that lay in the future when Oldsmobile's new 'senior compact' car appeared in 1961. The F-85 with its 3.5 litre engine was the cheapest Olds, but sales were slow until the F-85 Cutlass appeared. This pillared two-door sports coupe had special exterior trim, a tuned engine and interior features like bucket seats and a centre console associated with performance cars.

It was a hit, turning into a pillarless coupe in 1962 with a convertible version added. Another new offering was the turbocharged Cutlass Jetfire, but this only lasted two years. The F-85s were enlarged in 1964, though body styles remained the same. There was further evolution in 1965 with styling changes and yet more engine options, always a feature of American model life as manufacturers liked to start cheap and give customers the choice of spending more on increasingly expensive options and extras.

The Cutlass remained a best-selling F-85, with the introduction of a Supreme saloon in 1966 and a Turnpike Cruiser option in 1967. A major revamp in 1968 saw the Cutlass coupes and convertibles acquire a fastback roofline and long back end.

A high-performance Hurst/Olds Cutlass Supreme was offered, and by 1970 the Cutlass name extended to all seven body styles, though the end was nigh for the F-85 line, which ceased in 1972. But the popular Cutlass name lived on as its successor.

The Cutlass was another classic 1960s drophead that cut a dash.

Oldsmobile Jetstar I

The Jetstar I was a falling meteor that burned out fast.

Nobody could accuse Oldsmobile of resting on its laurels, for the company was constantly messing with model names, revamping, uprating, relaunching and introducing new models to keep a constant sense of excitement and innovation swirling around the brand name. Of course this was not a unique approach, applying to most other American manufacturers, but Olds was a master proponent of the black art.

The policy was not always an unqualified success and sometimes a downright disaster. It isn't easy to decide which of these epithets applies to the Jetstar I, but it's certainly one of them. The car appeared in 1964 as the marketing gurus chased a double benefit. The Jetstar was a full-size high-performance car that would compete directly with the Pontiac Grand Prix – and offer a cheaper alternative to the company's own Starfire which was laden with luxurious standard features and therefore expensive. To leave the Starfire with some exclusivity, the Jetstar did not offer a convertible version, though they shared an engine.

Year One was hardly a triumph – Pontiac's Grand Prix outsold the Jetstar by four to one, and a hole was gobbled in Starfire sales by canny buyers who chose options that pushed the cheaper Jetstar towards the superior Starfire spec. Undeterred by these minor setbacks, Oldsmobile substantially reworked the Jetstar I for 1965, along with the rest of its full-size range.

In came curvy 'Coke bottle' styling, a more rounded roofline and a new engine – the 6.5 litre Rocket being replaced by the powerful 7 litre Starfire V8. And out went elderly Roto Hydramatic transmission in favour of the vastly improved Turbo Hydramatic system. The 1965 Jetstar I was actually a gem of a high-performance car, but it was all in vain. The 'Poor Man's Starfire' still failed to hit the sweet spot and was promptly discontinued.

COUNTRY OF ORIGIN:
USA
FIRST MANUFACTURED:
1964 (until 1965)
ENGINE:
6.5 l (394 cid) or 7.0 l (425 cid) V8
PERFORMANCE:
Top speed of 105 mph (km/h);
0-60 mph (97 km/h) in 9.5 secs
YOU SHOULD KNOW:
Remember that Oldsmobile weakness for muddying the minds of consumers? Pay attention – the Jetstar I (1964-65) should not be confused with the Jetstar 88 (1964–66) which was the Olds entry-level line (complete with fins on the front) that had no relationship whatsoever to the more expensive Jetstar I.

Oldsmobile Toronado

COUNTRY OF ORIGIN:
USA
FIRST MANUFACTURED:
1966 (until 1970)
ENGINE:
7.0 l (425 cid) or 7.6 l (455 cid) V8
PERFORMANCE:
Top speed of 130 mph (209 km/h);
0-60 mph (97 km/h) in 8 secs
YOU SHOULD KNOW:
The booming 1960s stretched limo
market saw the Toronado
customized as the 28 ft (8.5 m) ACQ
Jetway 707 – it could comfortably
seat a dozen people, had eight doors,
six wheels, two axles, an enclosed
cargo area and unique raised roof
with side windows. It is thought that
around 100 were made.

The demise of the Starfire left a hole at the top of the Oldsmobile range, which was swiftly filled with a new speedmobile. The Toronado two-door fastback coupe was a good example of a practice that would later become common – making up a model name that meant nothing but had a vaguely feelgood ring. Later on, of course, marketing consultancies would be paid millions for thinking up suitable words, but this one was all General Motors' own work – and better still recycled, having been previously used for a concept car from GM stablemate Chevrolet.

The choice of 'Toronado' must have been inspired, or made by the boss, because it stayed around until the 1990s. This meant several complete reinventions, but first generation models stayed around for the rest of the 1960s. Olds were sanctioned by GM to build a full-size personal luxury car to compete with the Buick Riviera and Ford T-Bird. The resulting Toronado shared a platform with the Buick Riviera and Cadillac Eldorado, though styling differed and the Olds has one unique selling point – front-wheel drive.

This bold leap had necessitated lengthy development, as Oldsmobile couldn't risk a stain on its corporate escutcheon. The preparation paid off, with the Toronado's UPP (Unitized Power Package) working like a dream. For standardization purposes it could not have an engine bay larger than that of a comparable rear-wheel drive car. The job was done, even though the power plant was a 7 litre Super Rocket V8. This was teamed with new Turbo-Hydramatic transmission to deliver fantastic performance for a heavy car, though the drum brakes were suspect and a disc option swiftly appeared. An enhanced W-34 option pack was offered from 1968, as was a larger engine, but otherwise the Toronado remained virtually unchanged until the entirely restyled second generation appeared in 1970.

Oldsmobile made up a name for their new fastback that none too subtly suggested it had the power of a tornado.

Panhard 24

Panhard & Levassor (established 1887) was one of the world's first car manufacturers. The company thrived and innovated in the early years of motoring, becoming a significant player by World War I. Between the wars Panhard produced various interesting models and broke speed records, but it never quite regained its prewar eminence. After World War II a range of light cars was produced, often bodied in aluminium to get around the steel shortages. From the mid-1950s Panhard and Citroen started integrating their operations, a process that was finally completed a decade later.

The Panhard 24 was the final throw of the dice for this long-established French maker, soon to be swallowed by Citroen.

One of the most eye-catching postwar cars was the pretty Panhard 24, launched in 1963 and in production from 1964. This small two-door car had an air-cooled two-cylinder boxer engine at the front, with a low, waisted body reminiscent of a contemporary Chevy Corvair. It had an independent chassis and strong steel bodywork. The swooping nose had four headlamps, each pair behind a glass shield.

Various versions of the Panhard 24 were produced. The 24 C was a four-seater and the 24 CT was a pretty 2+2 coupe. The former – with a somewhat basic interior – did not prove popular and was soon dropped. In 1964 a long-wheelbase floorpan was introduced, allowing the 24 B and 24 BT to be made. These were simply scaled-up versions of the smaller cars, but as sales of the three well-appointed 24s sagged an attempt was made to capture mass-market sales with the cheap and cheerful 24 BA. It was not a success and production of the 24 ended in 1967.

Sadly, the 24 was the last of the Panhards. For the company ceased car production in 1967 to concentrate on making military vehicles and the passenger car business was complete absorbed by Citroen with the loss of the historic Panhard marque.

COUNTRY OF ORIGIN:
France
FIRST MANUFACTURED:
1963 (until 1967)
ENGINE:
848 cc Flat Two
PERFORMANCE:
Top speed of 86 mph (138 km/h);
0-60 mph (97 km/h) in 23.9 secs
YOU SHOULD KNOW:
There's a reasonable chance of enjoying a drive – a fair proportion of the 25,000 24s produced are still around (mostly in France), cherished by owners who like to be seen out and about in something completely different.

Peel P50

Advertised as being for 'one adult and a shopping bag', the Peel P50 was designed as a convenience microcar for nipping around town. When it was launched at the 1962 Earl's Court Motor Show, it caused a stir on two counts: it was the only car ever to have emanated from the Isle of Man, and it was unlike anything else on the road. The Peel P50 holds the title for smallest-ever production car: a mere 117 cm (46 in) high, 135 cm (53 in) long and 99 cm (39 in) wide, it weighs just 59 kg (130 lb).

The Peel was great for parking but not recommended when it came to a rear-end shunt.

COUNTRY OF ORIGIN:
UK
FIRST MANUFACTURED:
1963 (until 1964)
ENGINE:
49 cc Two Stroke DKW
PERFORMANCE:
Top speed of 38 mph (61 km/h)
YOU SHOULD KNOW:
Fewer than 50 Peel P50s were made, in three choices of colour: red, white or blue. It is estimated that there are only around 20 still in existence, valued at between £35,000 and £50,000. Two original P50s are on the Isle of Man – you can see one in the Peel Transport Museum.

This cute little three-wheeler, running on an air-cooled Zweirad Union moped engine, was designed by Cyril Cannell, boss of the Peel Engineering Co. The tubular steel frame and GRP body were largely hand-assembled. It had only one door, one headlight and one windscreen wiper and there was no starter motor – you used a crank lever to get it going – and no speedometer – it was considered unnecessary since you had to go flat out to break the 30 mph speed limit. It had three forward gears and an innovative means of reversing – you just got out and hauled the car backwards by its rear-attached chrome handle. In a 15 mile road test round London the P50 triumphed – reaching the finish 30 minutes before any other car.

The Peel P50 was not a great success: it had poor suspension, tipped over rather too easily and generally felt a bit of a death-trap. However, it was very cheap (under £200) and incredibly economical on fuel. And there was no problem about finding a parking space – you just picked it up and slotted it into any available gap. Ahead of its time, perhaps?

Plymouth Road Runner

In 1968, Mr Muscles met Road Runner, with Plymouth paying Warner Brothers a handsome fee to use the name of that speedy cartoon character who never quite gets caught by Wile E Coyote. Plymouth even developed a signature 'beep beep' horn for their lean new beast, which was introduced because muscle cars were getting plump with the passage of time.

Plymouth's own GTX of 1967 underlined the point, being billed as a 'gentleman's muscle car'. In fact, it was no more than a beefed-up Satellite with special suspension, and Plymouth shrewdly guessed that all those who loved no-frills muscle cars might respond better to something that more closely adhered to the original 'cheap and fast' concept. They were not wrong.

The Road Runner outsped and outsold its more expensive stablemate, swallowing the GTX (a mere option package on the Road Runner after 1971). Plymouth's idea was simple – leave out anything non-essential to performance and crank up everything else. The Road Runner was based on the mid-range Belvedere and had a spartan interior with no external embellishments. The first style was a pillar coupe, later joined by a pillarless coupe.

There was a choice of engines. The base motor was the 6.3 litre V8, with a 7 litre 426 Hemi available for a (good) few dollars more. A convertible appeared in 1969, along with a distinctive 'Air-Grabber' scoop on the bonnet. The Six-Pack Road Runner version with a 7.2 litre engine was produced to qualify for Super Stock racing. In 1970 came the aerodynamic Superbird with goalpost rear spoiler. The Road Runner exceeded all Plymouth's sales expectations and continued through a revamped second generation (from 1971) before running out of sales oomph and being demoted to a tweaked version of the short-lived Volare line from 1976 until 1980.

COUNTRY OF ORIGIN:
USA
FIRST MANUFACTURED:
1968 (until 1976)
ENGINE:
6.3 l (383 cid), 7.0 l (426 cid) or 7.2 l (440 cid) OHV V8
PERFORMANCE:
With 6.3 l engine – top speed of 107 mph (172 km/h); 0-60 mph (97 km/h) in 7.6 secs
YOU SHOULD KNOW:
Nothing better illustrated the very spirit of the American muscle car than the 1970 Road Runner's Air-Grabber bonnet feature – operated from within the car, it opened to reveal a menacing sharklike grin consisting of fearsome zig-zag teeth in lurid colours.

The Superbird was a muscle car that didn't leave it there, but overdosed on steroids.

Pontiac Grand Prix

Many American model lines involve confusing nomenclature – especially when names continue for decades – and so it is with the 1960s Pontiac Grand Prix, which made its debut in 1962 and has been around ever since. But first series cars belong squarely to the Swinging Sixties, as the second series (from 1969) dropped the Grand Prix from Pontiac's upmarket full-size range into the mid-range.

The initial offering was developed from the Pontiac Catalina coupe, without its predecessor's excessive chromework and with sporty interior trim that included a centre console and bucket seats. This was designed to make the Grand Prix the personal luxury car for those who preferred to be seen in (and drive) a quality high-performance model, to which end numerous fancy extras were offered. The stratagem worked well, for the Grand Prix sold well until it was demoted.

First generation cars were fitted with a 6.4 litre V8 from the companion Bonneville, though various tuned versions were available and a larger 6.9 litre option was offered. The engine choice remained the same until 1967, when two improved versions of the old power plants appeared at 6.5 and 7 litres respectively. The Grand Prix's appearance evolved over the decade, too. The initial convertible-style roofline was squared off with a concave rear window, and a major restyle in 1965 saw all Pontiac models acquire the more rounded 'Coke bottle' look that was then modish. However, the Grand Prix did not change as drastically as most.

Further styling changes were implemented in 1967, along with the introduction of a convertible Grand Prix. But the end was nigh, and though 1968 saw a new beak-nosed grille and bumper, the convertible was swiftly discontinued and this would be the Grand Prix's last year as a member of the full-sized Pontiac club.

COUNTRY OF ORIGIN:
USA
FIRST MANUFACTURED:
1962 (until 1968)
ENGINE:
6.4 l (389 cid) or 6.9 l (421 cid) V8;
6.5 l (400 cid) or 7.0 l (428 cid) V8
PERFORMANCE:
Varied according to engine – but typically top speed of around 130 mph (209 km/h); 0-100 mph (161 km/h) in 12 secs
YOU SHOULD KNOW:
The Grand Prix's sporty profile was down to John DeLorean, Pontiac's head of advanced engineering – who would become notorious as the founder of Northern Ireland's DeLorean Motor Company, which went spectacularly bust in the early 1980s after making 9,000 gullwing DeLorean sports cars.

Pontiac GTO Judge

When John DeLorean, Pontiac's chief engineer in the 1960s, named the first Pontiac GTO after the Ferrari 250 GTO, it was considered almost sacrilegious. The letters stand for Gran Turismo Omologato, that is, homologated (accredited) for GT racing. General Motors had banned advertising that associated their marques with racing, a keystone of Pontiac's strategy. DeLorean sidestepped the ban by creating the GTO as a performance 'option' of Pontiac's LeMans and Tempest models, a wily subterfuge senior management could collude with. By 1969, the GTO was still competitive, but Pontiac wanted a low-cost version, stripped of its accretion of luxury and 'performance enhancement' gimmickry. The Judge was born.

Almost immediately, economy was forgotten. Pontiac's raging desire to create the ultimate in street performance and muscular image made the GTO Judge more expensive than any other version. For the money you got a true muscle car, which reached its apotheosis at the end of 1970 when the long-stroke 455 engine became an option. Its top speed wasn't as high as other GTO Judge versions, but it wasn't particularly temperamental at low speed either. The Ram Air hood scoop was more style statement than functionally useful, like the rear spoiler, and for a short time it even had VOE (Vacuum Operated Exhaust) – in case people hadn't noticed the car when you pulled up, the VOE knob trebled the exhaust volume. Self-advertisement wasn't an issue. With its wide wheels, beefy front end and speed-whipped lines, the Judge was power incarnate in its day – and (though you could choose any colour) the Judge-exclusive, standard factory Orbit-Orange with blue/pink stripes made sure everyone saw it and knew it. As Road Test magazine noted, it was 'not for people who are shy about being looked at'. The Judge was a young man's dream.

COUNTRY OF ORIGIN:
USA
FIRST MANUFACTURED:
1969 (until 1971)
ENGINE:
6.6 l (400 cid) or 7.5 l (455 cid) OHV V8
PERFORMANCE:
Top speed around 130 mph (209 km/h) according to engine tuning; 0-60 mph (97 km/h) in 6.1 secs
YOU SHOULD KNOW:
The Pontiac GTO series was produced from 1964 to 1974 by which time emissions requirements had sent performance and hence sales into decline. To the surprise of GTO fans (or 'Goats' as they call themselves) the name was reintroduced in 2004. The GTO Judge was named in honour of Rowan & Martin's Laugh-In TV show catch-phrase 'Here comes the Judge'. Seventeen convertible Judges were made which are the rarest of all the GTOs.

Most American road-goers shared this rear view of the super-fast Pontiac GTO Judge.

Porsche 904 Carrera GTS

COUNTRY OF ORIGIN:
Germany
FIRST MANUFACTURED:
1963 (until 1964)
ENGINE:
1,966 cc DOHC Flat Four
PERFORMANCE:
Top speed of 160 mph (257 km/h);
0-60 mph (97 km/h) in 5.3 secs
YOU SHOULD KNOW:
The 904 was the first in a line of
sports racers that would culminate in
the 917, which gave Porsche its first
outright wins in the Le Mans 24
(1970 and 1971) – this awesome
beast hit 60 mph (97 km/h) in less
than 2.5 seconds on the way to a top
speed of 255 mph (410 km/h).
Phewwhatascorcher!

*This is the beauty that first
drove Porsche to fame and then
on to considerable fortune.*

After easing out of F1 Grand Prix racing in the early 1960s, Porsche refocused on sports car racing. The versatile mid-engined Porsche 718 had featured in various classes since its debut in 1958, and was briefly replaced by the flying silver Porsche 804, which secured the company's only F1 victory in the 1962 French Grand Prix. But ending F1 involvement freed up funds to improve Porsche's competitiveness in the GT class.

The current GT competitor was the 356 Carrera 2, a modified road car that was looking tired compared to shiny stars being introduced by the likes of Alfa Romeo and Abarth. A new car was required, with a road-going version to secure homologation. One hundred would have to be produced to meet the rules, and the Porsche design team started with a blank sheet of paper. Lead designer was Ferry 'Butzi' Porsche, the founder's grandson.

His innovative solution was the first 'plastic' Porsche, with a very attractive fibreglass coupe body bonded to a steel chassis, which perforce carried a tuned four-cylinder engine from the Carrera 2, as the intended flat six was not ready. After testing, the stunning Porsche 904 Carrera GTS was revealed to the waiting world in November 1963. Waiting it was – Porsche's canny plan to get a 'free' sports racer worked out perfectly, with the vast majority of 90 cars allocated for public sale ordered within weeks. This ensured that the homologation rules were fully satisfied by the following spring, leaving Porsche 30 cars with which to go racing.

This exclusive machine duly enjoyed considerable all-round track success – including outright Targa Florio victory, class wins at Le Mans and second place in the Monte Carlo Rally. Porsche's 904 Carrera GTS remains the company's only true dual-purpose road/race car and is rightly regarded as one of the finest cars they ever made.

Porsche 911S

Think Beetle, then think bigger, finally decide to create the world's most profitable car company – that was the audacious Porsche family plan, and how well it worked. The patriarch was Austrian engineer Ferdinand Porsche, designer of the Volkswagen Beetle before World War II, who would subsequently be imprisoned for alleged war crimes. But his son Ferdinand 'Ferry' Porsche operated Porsche AG and his grandson Ferdinand 'Butzi' Porsche was intimately involved in the development of the Porsche 911 – the car directly descended from the VW Beetle that would establish the company as a world-famous purveyor of superlative sports cars.

The classic 911 coupe was first shown in late 1963 at the Frankfurt Motor Show and went into production the following year. Like its mass-market Beetle ancestor, the 911 was a distinctive rear-engined, air-cooled car that would retain its characteristic aerodynamic shape for decades. The boxer flat-six motor was teamed with a four- or five-speed manual gearbox for electrifying performance, steering was precise – though roadholding was best described as sporty.

But this would be an evolutionary series, and the first advance came with the 911S (for Super) that was introduced in 1966. Nothing looked very different, apart from the signature five-spoke Fuchs 'flower-petal' alloy wheels, but the engine had been uprated and the Weber carburettors tuned. Chassis improvements – including ventilated disc brakes all round, Koni shocks and a second roll bar – ensured the extra power was harnessed.

The first Porsche 911S was the sensational model that really established the line's performance credentials, though initially there were faults like plug fouling. But improvement and refinement would characterize the 911S at every stage of its long life, with a second generation (filling the next slot between 1969 and 1971) boasting a larger engine. But that was just the beginning of the success story – don't go away!

The 911 evolved over several decades without a serious change to the famous shape.

COUNTRY OF ORIGIN:
Germany
FIRST MANUFACTURED:
1966 (until 1969)
ENGINE:
1,991 cc Flat Six
PERFORMANCE:
Top speed of 131 mph (211 km/h);
0-60 mph (97 km/h) in 8.3 secs
YOU SHOULD KNOW:
The Porsche 912 is the almost-forgotten companion model of the 911, manufactured from 1965 to 1969 – it was Porsche's entry-level model and looked very similar to its big brother, the main difference being that it had a four-cylinder engine.

This workmanlike mid-sized convertible from American Motors was not destined for a long and happy production run.

Rambler American Convertible

In the late 1950s American Motors revived a name from the recent past, recycling the Rambler name from the Nash and Hudson compacts of the mid-1950s. The resulting Rambler American would last for 10 years. This workaday line had three distinct lives. The first generation was rather old-fashioned and consisted of a two-door coupe, two-door station wagon and four-door sedan. The dated look was hardly surprising – AMC had reused tooling dating back to the early 1950s.

The second generation looked sharper. Although American didn't retool, there was major restyling of the old bodies. In 1961 the three existing models were joined by a four-door station wagon and a very pleasing convertible. An attractive pillarless hardtop coupe was added in 1963, along with a 440-H sports special with bucket seats and tuned engine.

Of the six body styles, there can be no doubt which one best captures and holds the modern eye. The second generation Rambler American Convertible is considered to be something of a minor design classic, in that a new skin brilliantly disguised elderly mechanics and the clean, simple lines entirely escaped from the rounded 'bath-tub' look of previous cars, also eschewing the flashy fins popular at the time. With around 17,500 built, the Rambler American Convertible has a loyal modern following of weekend owner-drivers.

From 1964 to 1969, third generation Rambler Americans were very different after being completely redesigned. The range was trimmed to five body styles as out went the two-door station wagon and in came a wide range of engine options. The third generation ultimately saw eight different power plants ranging from the old 3.2 litre straight six up to a meaty 6.8 litre V8. There was, of course, a new convertible – which is also quite well regarded as a collectable (and affordable) 1960s ragtop.

COUNTRY OF ORIGIN:
USA
FIRST MANUFACTURED:
1961 (until 1963)
ENGINE:
3.2 l (196 cid) Straight Six.
PERFORMANCE:
Top speed of 90 mph (145 km/h);
0-60 mph (97 km/h) in 12.9 secs
YOU SHOULD KNOW:
The Rambler American was the last series to bear the Rambler brand name in North American markets – though the marque lived on into the 1980s in far-flung countries like South Africa, Iran, Mexico and Argentina.

Reliant Scimitar GTE SE5

It all began in 1935 when bicycle company Raleigh decided to discontinue its three-wheeler delivery van. The van's designer was T L Williams, who founded Reliant to take over production. This led to a series of three-wheelers culminating in Reliant Robin economy cars and the extraordinary Bond Bug. However, the company also became active at the opposite end of the performance spectrum. First up was the punchy Reliant Sabre, but this was soon followed by the company's innovative Scimitar.

The Scimitar SE4 appeared in 1964 as a two-door booted coupe. With around a thousand sold, the SE4 was successful enough to encourage the Scimitar's next evolution, which saw the completely redesigned SE5 model introduced late in 1968. With its sturdy chassis and cute fibreglass body, the SE5 was a head turner.

This four-seater GT was based on a design by British consultancy Ogle, which came up with a racy estate car with ample fold-flat rear load space accessed through the hinged, sloping rear window. The only car that came close to a similar layout was the Volvo P1800 estate, but the Reliant True Brit was the preferred repository for the muddy green wellies of sporty country types (famously, the Scimitar would acquire at least one high-profile fan, with the young Princess Anne rarely seen driving anything else).

There was a choice of straight six or V6 engines, but the latter was more powerful and proved the popular choice, leading to the former being dropped. Performance was excellent. The Scimitar had a snappy four-speed manual gearbox that later acquired overdrive, and Borg-Warner automatic transmission was offered as an option. Fewer than 2,500 SE5s were hand-built at Tamworth, but the upgraded SE5A (1972 to 1975) would be the best seller in a long line of Scimitars stretching ahead to 1995.

COUNTRY OF ORIGIN:
UK
FIRST MANUFACTURED:
1968 (until 1972)
ENGINE:
2,553 cc Straight Six or 2,994 cc V6
PERFORMANCE:
With the V6 engine – top speed of 121 mph (195 km/h); 0-60 mph (97 km/h) in 8.9 secs
YOU SHOULD KNOW:
Many cars on both sides of the Atlantic were named after the sleek fighter aircraft of World War II, but it was surely a coincidence that the 1960s Reliant Scimitar shared a designation with the SE5 – that fine British biplane that duelled with the Red Baron's Fokker Triplane in World War I.

Like the Robin, the Scimitar had a fibreglass body, but it actually boasted four wheels.

Renault 4

COUNTRY OF ORIGIN:
France
FIRST MANUFACTURED:
1961 (until 1993)
ENGINE:
747 cc OHV Straight Four
PERFORMANCE:
Top speed of 75 mph (120 km/h);
0-60 mph (97 km/h) in 38 secs
YOU SHOULD KNOW:
The Renault 4 is also known as
the 4L – pronounced *Quatrelle*, which
in French sounds like "Four Wings".
In France the car is also called 'the
hen coop on wheels'. In Colombia,
one of 16 countries where the
Renault 4 has been produced, it is
affectionately called *Amigo Fiel*
("Faithful Friend"). In Argentina and
Chile it's the *Renolata* – a play on the
Spanish *camioneta* ("truck") and a
dig at the 2CV, known as the
Citroneta in consequence.

Renault had already tried direct competition with Citroen's 2CV. The company believed it could go one-better in 1961 with the Renault 4, a notionally more up-market car with very real improvements in power, space and capacity. Renault's chairman declared its first front-engine, five-door, new runabout to be 'an everyman's car . . . a woman's car, a farmer's car, a city car . . . suitable for motorists round the world'. He got that right, then.

Hindsight tells the story of global, enduring success. It was based on common sense practicality, logic and simplicity, but it took some getting used to. Though the rear door revealed plenty of boot space, seats tipped, folded or removed to create room for unfeasibly large loads, making the Renault 4 the first true hatchback. You could look directly at the bonnet lid through the mesh over the face-high fresh air 'vent' (a hole in the car's skin). Economy dictated rubber mats, press-down flaps fashioned from the cutouts in the door panels instead of handles, sliding windows (no winding machinery) and heating with four controls all positioned out of useful sight. The biggest economy of all was continuity. The Renault 4 was barely developed throughout its long production run. Its size and shape never changed at all. The engine was perked from 747 cc to 845 cc from 1963, and only replaced with a smaller version of Renault's 1978 new 1108 cc engine in 1986.

The Renault 4 was basic and proud of it. It was remarkably comfortable to ride in. Its dash-mounted gear lever (thanks to 2CV) made much more space available; and if it might roll on cornering, it certainly never wallowed. It was classless, and it still is, though descendants like the Dauphine and Clio might argue otherwise. No wonder it sold over eight million, the fifth biggest-selling car in the world.

Like the Mini, the Renault 4 was completely classless.

Rolls-Royce Silver Shadow

Neatly bisecting the 1960s, the Rolls-Royce Silver Shadow was introduced in October 1965 and would continue in production for more than a dozen years, becoming the most successful Roller ever made. The Silver Shadow had been in development for a considerable time and when this signature model appeared it incorporated many modern features that finally consigned some hitherto sacred Rolls-Royce design principles to history – along with the unwanted perception that Rolls-Royces were becoming rather old fashioned.

The superb Silver Shadow proved to be the most successful Roller to date, doing extremely well commercially.

The new model no longer employed the traditional chassis beloved of custom coachbuilders, instead using monocoque construction. Suspension consisted of independent springing on all four wheels and four-wheel disc brakes to ensure smooth and effortless stopping power, even from the Silver Shadow's impressive top speed. This was achieved using the powerful 6.2 litre aluminium V8 carried forward from the Silver Cloud, coupled to an improved four-speed automatic gearbox, soon to be replaced with all-new three-speed torque transmission. There was an advanced hydraulic system (licensed from Citroen) that offered dual-circuit braking and self-levelling suspension, guaranteeing excellent ride quality. Naturally, the interior was discreetly palatial with the finest hide upholstery available in a choice of eight colours to tone with the 14 bodywork shades offered.

A long-wheelbase variant, sometimes with internal glass divider, was introduced in 1969. There was also a two-door fixed-head coupe model by Mulliner Park Ward or James Young, the latter much scarcer. A convertible followed in 1967 and this desirable model was given its own identity in 1971 as the Corniche. Much later, a Pininfarina coupe was built on the Shadow's platform and christened the Camargue, which was then the most expensive Roller of all, with a higher price than the Phantom VI limousine. Corniches and Camargues comfortably outlived their parent, with the last examples built in 1986.

COUNTRY OF ORIGIN:
UK
FIRST MANUFACTURED:
1965 (until 1976)
ENGINE:
6,230 cc V8 (until 1970)
PERFORMANCE:
Top speed of 120 mph (193 mph);
0-60 mph (97 km/h) in 10.9 secs
YOU SHOULD KNOW:
Rolls-Royce produced a shared-platform Bentley T version that shadowed the Shadow all the way, also offering coupes and convertibles from Mulliner Park Ward and James Young – the only difference was the radiator grille, with the cheaper-to-make Bentley grille ensuring that the Silver Shadow was ever-so-slightly more expensive.

The P5B seemed British through and through, but actually had a modified Buick V8 engine.

Rover P5B

The Rover P5 appeared in 1958, replacing the much-loved but elderly P4 (then a tired 25-year-old). The P5 was a larger car that took the Rover line up market, appealing as it did to senior businessmen and civil servants. It was also a very good car, soon becoming established as one of Britain's best-selling luxury motors of the 1960s.

The Mk I was powered by a 3 litre straight six. This solid four-door saloon had independent front suspension, whilst servo-assisted front discs soon became standard. Automatic transmission, overdrive on the manual box and power steering were options. A minor upgrade in 1961 saw front quarter lights introduced, but that was just a holding operation until the Mk II appeared in 1962. This featured better suspension and a tuned engine, also offering the choice of a coupe version with sporty lowered roofline. The Mk III of 1965 was little changed, though the styling was updated and the engine's power output further tweaked.

In 1967 the best P5 of all appeared – the P5B. The B stood for Buick, for Rover had taken the American company's unsuccessful lightweight aluminium V8 and improved it out of all recognition (indeed, evolutionary versions would remain around for decades). This engine gave the P5B lots more grunt, which was teamed with standard Borg-Warner automatic transmission and power steering. Not much changed externally, but a pair of fog lamps gave the front a magisterial four-light look and (lest anyone should doubt that this was the new model) chrome Rostyle wheels were complemented by prominent '3.5 Litre' badging.

The P5B has become a collectable modern classic, and still gives drivers a superior feeling as they glide effortlessly amongst lesser vehicles. The saloon was produced in the largest numbers, making the coupe rarer and therefore more desirable.

COUNTRY OF ORIGIN:
UK
FIRST MANUFACTURED:
1967 (until 1973)
ENGINE:
3,528 cc V8
PERFORMANCE:
Coupe – top speed of 113 mph
(182 km/h)
YOU SHOULD KNOW:
The P5 may have remained as an aspirational purchase for the British middle classes, but was classy enough to be acceptable to Royalty and Prime Ministers – Queen Elizabeth II used one, as did PMs Harold Wilson, Edward Heath, James Callaghan and Margaret Thatcher.

254

Rover 2000

The P6 would be the last of Rover's P-classification model lines but – even after it was finally discontinued – not many people knew that, because the three P6 models were invariably known by their engine size – 2000, 2200 or 3500. The Rover 2000 replaced the P4 in 1963 and was an entirely new design. The somewhat angular shape was very different from its comfortably rounded predecessor but was very much in tune with the times, being voted European Car of the Year in 1964.

This was in part due to advanced features like an all-synchro gearbox, four-wheel disc brakes and de Dion tube rear suspension. The 2 litre overhead-cam engine had been specially designed for the P6 2000 with a flat Heron head that had combustion chambers let into the piston heads. This would be redesigned and fitted with twin SU carburettors for the 2000 TC, upping the power output by a quarter. This performance version had competed in rally competition and was primarily intended for export to America, though it was available on the home market from late '66.

The next evolution was the Rover 3500, which was launched in 1968 with the powerful aluminium V8 engine already used to good effect in the Rover P5. Both 2000 and 3500 were offered side by side, jointly seeing a major revision in 1970 with a Mk II version that delivered minor styling changes and an enhanced interior. The battery was moved to the boot, further encroaching on already limited luggage space.

The 2000 continued in production until the Rover 2200 appeared in 1973 with a bored-out version of the 2000 engine, allowing the 2000 to be honourably retired. Production of the entire P6 series finally came to an end in 1977 after a long and commercially successful run.

COUNTRY OF ORIGIN:
UK
FIRST MANUFACTURED:
1963 (until 1973)
ENGINE:
1,978 cc Straight Four
PERFORMANCE:
Rover 2000 TC – top speed of 112 mph (180 km/h); 0-60 mph (97 km/h) in 9.9 secs
YOU SHOULD KNOW:
The rarest of P6s are the fewer than 200 that were converted to Estoura estate cars with Rover's blessing, the work being undertaken by H R Owen and Crayford Engineering – though it is thought that a minority of these were actually based on Rover 2000s.

The Rover 2000 was a part of the last successful model line produced by a great British manufacturer that failed to move with the automotive times.

Saab 96

COUNTRY OF ORIGIN:
Sweden
FIRST MANUFACTURED:
1960 (until 1980)
ENGINE:
750 cc, 841 cc or 819 cc Straight
Three; 1,498 cc V4
PERFORMANCE:
With 0.8 litre engine – top speed of
79 mph (127 km/h); 0-50 mph
(80 km/h) in 14.7 secs
YOU SHOULD KNOW:
Don't assume that cherished Saab 96
was actually built in Sweden – a
large number (including the last ones
made) were fabricated by the
state-owned Valmet Oy in
Uusikaupunki in Western Finland.

Most Brits had only seen pictures of Saab cars (if they were even aware the Scandinavian marque existed) until the unique 96 burst onto the scene in 1960, becoming the first Saab officially exported from Sweden to the United Kingdom. In truth, it did not look very different from its predecessor, the Saab 93, but this distinctive coupe was still a novelty in Britain. By the time the 96 was canned 20 years later, nearly 550,000 would have been built.

Considering the apparently puny three-cylinder two-stroke engine, the Saab 96 performed brilliantly on the rally circuit in the early 1960s, winning the RAC Rally three years running (1960–1962) and the prestigious Monte Carlo Rally twice in succession (1962 and 1963), driven by Erik Carlsson. Of course the Saab Sport was modified, but racing success put the 96 on the map and established a reputation for robust reliability.

The original two-stroke engine displaced a mere 750 ccs, but lest this was considered parsimonious Saab soon cranked it up to 841 ccs, though it would later drop back to 819 ccs to dodge tough US emission regulations. It was the largest of the three that was used in Sport and Monte Carlo models, with oil injection and triple carbs. The two-stroke was available until 1968, lingering on for just one year after the 96 was treated to a 1.5 litre Ford Taunus V4 engine.

The intended replacement for the 96 – the Saab 99 – hit the road in 1969. But the old faithful outlived its successor, continuing in production until 1980 by which time the 99 was well and truly kaput. The 96 was accompanied all the way by its estate-car twin, the Saab 95, and both were valued then as now for their distinctly quirky character, the old-fashioned column change and Saab's unique freewheeling device.

Unusually for a sporty European saloon, the 96 sported a column gear-change.

Shelby GT

One sure-fire certainty in America is that every time a muscle car is produced, someone thinks they can 'improve' it by cranking up the performance. In the case of the new Ford Mustang, the 'someone' was racing driver and talented engineer Carroll Shelby, who had already established a formidable reputation for turning fast cars into much faster ones. He went to work with the support of Ford, who hired him to customize a line of cars that would enable Mustangs to run against the factory-sponsored Chevy Corvettes in sports car races.

The very special Mustang variant that resulted was the Shelby GT 350, launched in 1965 and much modified from base semi-fastback 2+2 Mustangs by the inventive Carroll Shelby. It was a hit and went into production, while the race version became a multiple competition winner.

For 1967, the uprated Shelby Mustang was the GT 500, though the GT 350 continued. Now that factory cars were offering a 6.6 litre V8 option, Shelby had to do better – and did, with the frightening tuned 7 litre Police Interceptor power plant. At the same time, a certain level of refinement crept in, as customers seemed willing to sacrifice raw performance for a few creature comforts like power steering and air conditioning. The GT 500 was more like a proper grand tourer that its race-bred predecessor, but buyers loved it and were happy to pay a premium for the satisfaction of obtaining big-block muscle-car status (often complete with white Le Mans racing stripes that were a must-have extra).

From 1968 the Shelby Mustang appeared, though Shelby's co-production deal with Ford was terminated in 1969 leaving a stock of face-lifted 1969 GT 350s (with a new 5.8 litre engine) and 500s that were sold off as '69 and '70 Shelby Mustangs.

The Shelby was a thoroughbred track car that was available to buy in the showroom.

COUNTRY OF ORIGIN:
USA
FIRST MANUFACTURED:
1965 (until 1970)
ENGINE:
GT 350 – 4.7 l (289 cid) or (302 cid)
V8; GT 500 – 7.0 l (429 cid) V8
PERFORMANCE:
Top speed range of 120 mph
(193 km/h) to 135 mph (217 km/h);
0-60 mph (97 km/h) range from
6.5 to 4.8 secs
YOU SHOULD KNOW:
One thousand Shelby GT 350H cars were made for Hertz to rent out – when early manual examples started coming back with burned-out clutches the spec was changed to automatic transmission, but these Hertz cars (much sought-after today) were still hired to race, sometimes even coming back with different engines.

257

Sunbeam Tiger

The first car to bear the stand-alone Sunbeam name for more than 30 years was the old-fashioned Sunbeam Alpine roadster introduced by the Rootes Group in 1953 to cash in on the postwar British appetite for open-top motoring, but it didn't last long. The Alpine really came into its own after a complete revamp saw its launch as a new sports car in 1959. This had clean modern lines and would zip through the Swinging Sixties.

However, it was primarily intended for the important US export market, and a canny American sales executive suggested beefing up the basic 1.6 litre Series II Alpine to create something closer to high-powered muscle cars like the Shelby Cobra, then becoming popular in the States. This initiative saw Carroll Shelby himself create a prototype that contained the Cobra's 4.3 litre Ford Windsor V8 engine. A second example was created by Shelby associate Ken Miles and Rootes was persuaded that the idea could fly.

Further testing by Jensen Motors confirmed that the engineering sums added up, and the Sunbeam Tiger (built by Jensen at West Bromwich) made its growling appearance in 1964. It didn't look so very different from the gentler Alpine, but of course performance was in a different league.

Sadly, the Tiger adventure would not last long. Chrysler took over the Rootes Group in 1967, was not prepared to sell a car that had a Ford engine but couldn't provide a suitable Chrysler alternative. After just four years – and some 7,000 cars – production came to an end. Only some 500 of these were the second series Mk II cars with a larger engine, which are consequently the most desirable. But anyone lucky enough to catch any Tiger by the tail will appreciate how special this fast feline was.

COUNTRY OF ORIGIN:
UK
FIRST MANUFACTURED:
1964 (until 1967)
ENGINE:
4,261 cc or 5,306 cc V8
PERFORMANCE:
With 4.3 l engine – top speed of 116 mph (187 km/h); 0-60 mph (97 km/h) in 9.5 secs
YOU SHOULD KNOW:
The name 'Tiger' was chosen for the beefed-up Alpine because it harked back to a great V12 Sunbeam racing car of the 1920s – driven by Sir Henry Seagrave, the Sunbeam Tiger was the first to exceed 150 mph (240 km/h), becoming a proud holder of the World Land Speed Record.

Toyota Land Cruiser FJ40

The famous World War II Willys Jeep continued after 1945 as the civilian CJ model, offering a no-frills, rugged four-wheel drive vehicle. Toyota certainly thought it was a good idea, after building Jeeps to a Willys spec for American troops to use in the nearby Korean War. In the mid-1950s these Toyota Jeep clones evolved into the Land Cruiser, which would become the company's enduring four-wheel-drive flagship offering. After various developments of the Jeep format, the 40 series appeared in 1960 and would last for a quarter of a century.

This Land Cruiser line would establish Toyota's off-roaders as the toughest and most reliable money could buy – especially appreciated by Aussies who lived in the daren't-break-down Outback. The compact two-door FJ40 was the new generation's firstborn, with fresh body styling and low-range gearing. Mind you, the designer must have loved his set square, as the body was remarkably box-like with lots of precise straight lines.

The FJ40 was the short-wheelbase option, with fold-flat windscreen. Larger mid-wheelbase (BJ43) and long-wheelbase (HJ45) versions were offered later. The FJ had a petrol engine whilst the larger pair were diesel-engined. The FJ40's transmission evolved over time from three-, to four- and finally a five-speed automatic. Petrol engines also changed, from the F 3.9 litre (until 1974) to the 2F 4.2 litre (from 1974 to 1984). Body types over time would be two-door soft and hardtops, two-door pickup and four-door wagon.

Early FJ40s can be hard to find, especially in America, as the customizers love to fit them with alternative engines (and pretty much everything else) in order to indulge in the gravity-defying automobile art of rock crawling. But originals are appreciated as Toyota's true classic off-roaders, before the SUV started its inexorable drive into refined suburban streets.

COUNTRY OF ORIGIN:
Japan
FIRST MANUFACTURED:
1960 (until 1984)
ENGINE:
3,878 cc, 3,955 cc or 4,230 cc
Straight Six
PERFORMANCE:
Varied according to engine and transmission – top speed typically 85 mph (138 km/h); 0-60 mph (97 km/h) in 29 secs
YOU SHOULD KNOW:
Classification of the Land Cruiser series involved an engine series designation (eg F = original petrol engine) and body style (eg 40 = original two-door short wheelbase) separated by a J for Jeep. The Land Cruiser Series 40 contained literally dozens of different variations, with a raft of letter codes to describe individual characteristics; this system can help pin down the exact model type.

The Land Cruiser greedily ate into Land Rover's export markets.

Toyota 2000GT

COUNTRY OF ORIGIN:
Japan
FIRST MANUFACTURED:
1967 (until 1970)
ENGINE:
1,988 cc Straight Six
PERFORMANCE:
Top speed of 137 mph (220 km/h);
0-60 mph (97 km/h) in 8.4 secs
YOU SHOULD KNOW:
Don't go looking for a convertible to
dash around in – the two
scrumptious roadsters that featured
in the James Bond film *You Only Live
Twice* were factory-produced custom
specials – sadly Toyota never actually
offered a convertible version of the
2000GT for sale.

Although cynics suggest this rare-as-hen's-teeth sports car borrowed a little something from the lauded E-Type, that is unfair. Of course everyone had seen and admired the stunning Jaguar, but the Toyota 2000GT was an impressive two-door sports coupe in its own right that has come to be recognized as something of an original design classic.

It wasn't just a pretty face, either – for in best secret agent traditions the 2000GT had a vital mission. This was to show the wider world that Japan was capable of producing a supercar capable of rivalling anything produced in Europe. It was certainly successful in demolishing a perception that Japanese car manufacture was just about creating boring four-wheel passenger transport from A to B. Ironically the company to do so was Toyota, regarded as Japan's most conservative automaker.

The 2000GT was designed by Toyota's Satoru Nozaki, who went for a long, low car with flowing lines sculpted in aluminium. It had pop-up headlights teamed with a pair of large spots behind Plexiglas, which was prone to damage as the 2000GT lacked a serious front bumper (and any rear bumper at all). The engine was a 2 litre straight six borrowed from the top-of-the-range Toyota Crown saloon. This was teamed with triple carburettors. There were nine MF-12 specials built with a 2.3 litre engine. The 2000GT had servo-assisted disc brakes all round, a five-speed manual gearbox and limited-slip differential – a first for Japan. The well-trimmed interior was slightly cramped by European standards, but very well-appointed with nice touches like a rosewood dashboard.

Toyota 2000GTs were exported in small numbers to many countries, in keeping with the mission to inform, with around 350 built over a four-year period. They are admired by collectors and have started fetching high prices at auction.

The 2000GT proved that the Japanese could build a sports car that was seriously good.

Triumph Spitfire Mk I

The Austin Healey Sprite proved there was a market for small British sports cars and the bandwagon springs were soon creaking as first the MG Midget and then the Triumph Spitfire climbed aboard – both would outlast their inspiration, with the late-arriving Spitfire doing best with nearly 315,000 sold in 18 years. It evolved considerably during that run, but it all began with the Mk I (sometimes called the Spitfire 4) in 1962.

In fact, Standard-Triumph had been planning their baby sports car for some time, having commissioned a design in the late 1950s. It was based on the Triumph Herald saloon, which had a separate chassis that was easily modified to carry a sports body without the need for expensive retooling. Even so, the company couldn't afford to launch the Spitfire until Leyland took over.

The new owner discovered the traditionally styled prototype with its pleasing lines lurking in the Standard-Triumph factory and promptly sanctioned production. This basic sports car had advantages – like a tilt-forward front end that offered excellent access to the 1.1 litre engine – and disadvantages like swing-axle rear suspension that was liable to cause violent oversteer. Trim was basic, though the Spitfire had wind-up windows (unlike contemporary Sprites and Midgets) whilst wire wheels and a hard top were options.

The Triumph Spitfire went through several evolutions. There was a GT6 coupe from 1966 to 1973. The Spitfire Mk II (1965–1967) saw a relatively minor interim upgrade. The Mk III (1967–1970) had a serious facelift with a bigger engine. The Mk IV (1970–74) saw a major upgrade with significant style changes. The last version was the Spitfire 1500, with the largest engine of all, which ran from 1974 to 1980, though not without problems – completing a series that offered fun-packed open-top motoring on an affordable budget.

The Spitfire offered fun open-top motoring on a tight budget.

COUNTRY OF ORIGIN:
UK
FIRST MANUFACTURED:
1962 (until 1980)
ENGINE:
1,147 cc Straight Four
PERFORMANCE:
Top speed of 92 mph (148 km/h);
0-60 mph (97 km/h) in 17.3 secs
YOU SHOULD KNOW:
The final demise of the Triumph Spitfire in 1980 ended an era, as Standard-Triumph's historic works at Canley, Coventry, was closed shortly afterwards – and after passing through various hands the Triumph name finished up being owned by BMW, which kept the name after selling on the Rover Group.

Triumph Vitesse Mk II

COUNTRY OF ORIGIN:
UK
FIRST MANUFACTURED:
1968 (until 1971)
ENGINE:
1,998 cc Straight Six
PERFORMANCE:
Top speed of 100 mph (140 km/h);
0-60 mph (97 km/h) in 11.2 secs
YOU SHOULD KNOW:
Just over 9,000 Vitesse Mk IIs were
produced in four years, with the
saloon selling around 5,600 and
convertible some 3,500 – and there
is a definite scarcity of earlier
Vitesse cars as many have been
cannibalized for spares to keep the
ultra-desirable Mk II compact sports
models going.

By the late 1950s Standard-Triumph was experiencing financial difficulty, though TR sports cars were thriving, as the company's small Standard saloons had never sold well. So the Triumph Herald was introduced to replace those ageing Standards. Italian Giovanni Michelotti designed the pretty little two-door saloon with lots of glass, which had an old-fashioned rolling chassis to which the body was bolted. This had the advantage of allowing different body styles to be used without much difficulty and a coupe, convertible, estate car and van soon appeared.

If there was one problem it was that the Herald – with its small engine – was not the zippiest of performers. Standard-Triumph's answer was to create the Vitesse 6. Also by Michelotti, it mostly used Herald body panels and had a distinctive front with two pairs of slanting headlights. Power was supplied by a 1.5 litre straight six, modified from the Standard Vanguard Six engine. Saloons and convertibles were offered and the level of interior trim was high. The compact Vitesse 6 appeared in 1962 and was soon being uprated. The first big evolution was the Vitesse 2 Litre of 1966, but the more powerful car highlighted a generic weakness in Triumph's performance models – rear suspension that caused serious oversteer under hard driving.

Triumph finally solved this problem – and created an excellent car – with the Vitesse Mk II, launched in 1968. The new suspension system guaranteed leech-like roadholding and the tweaked engine delivered performance that could put the enhanced handling to a proper test. Again, there were both saloon and convertible versions, and it was the latter that represented terrific value for the sporting motorist who liked the thrill of open-top driving. It was a handsome four-seater that could easily outperform contemporary sports cars like the MGB, and remains very collectable to this day.

The Vitesse represented terrific value for the sporting motorist, combining style with power and great roadholding.

Triumph TR6

'Rattly, draughty, unpredictable in the wet, prone to disintegration . . .' That's how celebrity car buff, James May described the TR6. And coming from him, the words were glowing praise; for it is the sheer, unadulterated blokishness of the TR6 that was the secret of its success – a hunky machine, modelled along the lines of a classic British roadster but with the promise of high-performance tearaway thrills. When it came onto the market it immediately hit the spot, and by the time production ended in 1976 the TR6 was Triumph's best seller – more than 94,500 had been built.

The TR6 was the consummation of a series which had evolved steadily through each model. Mechanically more or less identical to the TR5 (which itself was simply a TR4 with a pushrod six-cylinder engine) the TR6 had a classy new body, styled by Karmann. Its flowing lines gave it a beautiful old-fashioned shape and the interior had touches of opulence: pile carpet, wooden dashboard and comfortable bucket seats with plenty of leg room. A steel hardtop was included as an optional extra for instant conversion to a sports coupe. Built in Triumph's Coventry factory using the traditional body-on-frame construction method rather than the mass-production unibody technology that by then had become the norm, the TR6 had four-speed manual transmission with optional overdrive, rack-and-pinion steering and a fuel-injected engine – which gave so much power that Triumph had to detune it from 150 bhp to 125 bhp to make it more manageable.

The TR6 is a brilliant hobbyist's car for weekend tinkerering. Spare parts are readily available and inexpensive, the electrics are straightforward and there is enough room around the engine to wield a spanner with ease. And on the road, it fulfils every criterion of those boy racer dreams – a superb heritage toy.

COUNTRY OF ORIGIN:
UK
FIRST MANUFACTURED:
1969 (until 1976)
ENGINE:
2.498 cc Straight Six
PERFORMANCE:
Top speed of 118mph (191 km/h);
0-60 mph (97 km/h) in around
9.5 secs
YOU SHOULD KNOW:
The TR6's fuel-injected engine failed
US emissions requirements so
models for export to America were
a somewhat strangulated
twin-carburetted version.

263

Vanden Plas Princess 4 Litre

COUNTRY OF ORIGIN:
UK
FIRST MANUFACTURED:
1960 (until 1968)
ENGINE:
3,995 cc or 3,909 cc Straight Six
PERFORMANCE:
Princess 4 Litre R – top speed of
106 mph (171 km/h)
YOU SHOULD KNOW:
The only other model Vanden Plas
built in its own name was the
Pininfarina-designed car simply
known as the Vanden Plas Princess
– it was a luxury four-door saloon
built from 1960 to 1964 that had a
2.9 litre engine and was based on
the Austin A99 Westminster.

Vanden Plas was a coachbuilding company that originated in Belgium and was licensed in the United Kingdom from 1910. After various ups and downs the British company built Bentley bodies in the 1920s, then worked for various makers including Alvis, Daimler and Rolls-Royce in the 1930s. After World War II Vanden Plas was acquired by Austin, who gave Vanden Plas the job of fitting bodies to the upmarket A135 Princess. From 1960 Austin successor BMC decided that Vanden Plas should be a stand-alone marque, so the Austin Princess turned into the stately Vanden Plas Princess 4 Litre.

This hand-built luxury limousine went through two generations before the Vanden Plas marque was abolished, with the name subsequently being used for top-of-the-range models by various companies within the merged British Leyland Motor Corporation from 1968, including Jaguar. The Princess 4 Litre had a relatively short life before being replaced by the Daimler DS420, Leyland's sole limousine offering.

The first Vanden Plas Princess 4 Litre was the former Austin Princess IV, which had been restyled in 1956 to eliminate the car's dated look though mechanicals were not much changed. These ceremonial limos were never big sellers (just 200 in nine years), but the Vanden Plas Princess 4 Litre R was a different story, with nearly 7,000 made between its launch in 1964 and the demise of Vanden Plas as independent marque.

This was an interesting vehicle as the Princess 4 Litre R had a Rolls-Royce straight six under the bonnet (signified by the 'R'). It possessed more rounded styling than its predecessor and lost the tail fins. It had the distinction of being the only mass-produced passenger car ever to have a Rolls-Royce engine and was something of a favourite with politicians, senior government officials and up-and-coming businessmen.

The Princess was beautifully made, had a super-comfortable ride and came with the added bonus of a Rolls-Royce engine.

Volvo P1800

Forever associated with the TV Saint, the Volvo P1800 was well publicized by its appearance as Simon Templar's wheels in The Saint, starring Roger Moore. In fact, Volvo supplied several P1800 coupes for the long-running production, each in turn wearing the numberplate ST 1, after Jaguar refused to offer an E-Type. This canny move certainly enhanced sales of the P1800, which first appeared in 1961 after Volvo decided to enter the sports car market again (the 1950s P1900 roadster had been a disaster).

After various problems locating a suitable supplier, Volvo contracted Jensen Motors who agreed to do the business, using bodies from Pressed Steel at Linwood to produce this classic 2+2 notchback coupe designed by Carrozzeria Pietro Frua in Italy (where the designer who worked on the new car happened to be Pelle Pettersson, son of Volvo engineering consultant Helmer Pettersson).

Nepotism duly justified by a brilliant result, the first P1800s appeared to great public excitement in 1961. The engine was a specially engineered version of Volvo's reliable B18 plant with dual SU carburettors that gave ton-topping performance with brisk acceleration via a manual four-speed gearbox (optional overdrive available).

After 6,000 of the contracted 10,000 P1800s had been built, Jensen ran into problems and production was transferred to Sweden in 1963, at which point the name was changed to 1800S (S = Swedish assembly) and the engine was improved. The next big shake-up came in 1970, when the P1800E was introduced. This had a bigger fuel-injected engine and disc brakes all round. The last version appeared in 1972 – a striking hatchback estate car version designated P1800ES. This would be the only model built in the last year of production, 1973. Around 47,000 P1800s were produced and they are usable classics well up to the rigours of modern motoring.

This Scandanavian beauty was actually made at the Jensen factory in West Bromwich to an Italian design using Scottish-built bodies, until production transferred to Sweden in 1963.

COUNTRY OF ORIGIN:
Sweden (initially built in the UK)
FIRST MANUFACTURED:
1961 (until 1973)
ENGINE:
1,778 cc or 1,986 cc Straight Four
PERFORMANCE:
1800E without overdrive – top speed of 118 mph (km/h); 0-60 mph (97 km/h) in 7.1 secs
YOU SHOULD KNOW:
For some reason the B18 Volvo engine has a reputation as being rather robust and well built, perhaps because one Volvo P1800 has done over 2.7 million miles (4 million kilometers) – and counting – on its original B18 engine. Okay, so it IS rather robust and well built.

1970s

AC 3000ME

COUNTRY OF ORIGIN:
UK
FIRST MANUFACTURED:
1979 (until 1984)
ENGINE:
2,994 cc OHV V6
PERFORMANCE:
Top speed of 120 mph (193 km/h);
0-60 mph (97 km/h) in 8.5 secs
YOU SHOULD KNOW:
The last AC 3000MEs were built
north of the border after the AC
name and car were licensed to the
AC (Scotland) company formed for
the purpose – but only 30 more cars
were built at the factory in Hillington,
Glasgow, before the new enterprise
failed in 1985.

Go looking for a crock of gold at the end of the nearest rainbow and you'll probably find it just before you manage to locate an AC 3000ME – just one hundred of these low-slung cars were built and they tended to rust. It all came about because AC boss Derek Hurlock was looking for a small custom-built luxury car with which to tackle the fuel-starved 1970s, and found the one-off Diablo prototype built by racing privateers Robin Stables and Peter Bohanna around an Austin Maxi engine. AC bought the rights and started developing it as the 3000ME.

After somewhat prematurely showing an 3000ME mid-engined concept car containing the Ford Essex V6 engine at the 1973 Earls Court Motor Show in London, AC hit trouble when new regulations called for a crash test – which the 3000ME failed in 1976 at the very point when it was ready for sale. A major reworking of the chassis secured an A+ in the crash test, but AC's limited resources meant that the uprated car – now called the 3000ME – did not go to market until 1979. When it did, the wait must have seemed worthwhile for those lucky enough to secure one.

With its thrusting wedge-shaped front end, distinctive air intakes and advanced features, this was a handsome high-performance coupe with exceptional roadholding in best AC traditions. It had pop-up headlamps, five-speed gearbox, independent suspension and disc brakes all round. AC also included goodies like adjustable steering column, electric windows, sunshine roof, sun-dym laminated windscreen and windows, through-flow ventilation, electric aerial, alloy wheels and stainless steel exhaust. This was a terrific little car, but production delays meant the 3000ME arrived too late – the problem of competing with the formidable Lotus Esprit was insurmountable and production ceased at the Thames Ditton facility in 1984.

Technical difficulties and new regulations delayed the arrival of the 3000ME for years.

Alfa Romeo Junior Zagato

The 1970s opened in style for lovers of sporty Alfa Romeos, who had been metaphorically licking their lips since the Junior Zagato was presented at the Turin Motor Show in November 1969. It was part of Alfa's 105 series and shared a floorpan – and lots of components – with the Giulia Spider, although the Junior Z was altogether more exclusive. Its public availability from the beginning of 1970 extended the 105 series GT Junior range, which had already sold well to those who wanted a stylish coupe that handled well and was fairly sporty – whilst also having a small motor to beat high Italian taxation on large engine capacities.

The GT 1300 Junior was made from 1965 until 1977, with a GT 1600 Junior added in 1972. But those with a nose for something special got really excited when the 1300 Junior Zagato hit the streets, for that added another dimension to their motoring pleasure. The Junior Z was a very different animal from the standard Junior 1300, with a classic short-tailed sporting coupe body aerodynamically crafted by Ercole Spada for Zagato of Milan, purveyor of fine automobile design to the likes of Aston Martin, Lancia and Maserati.

This was a fairly exclusive offering, with a strictly limited number built, and added excitement was generated amongst Alfa aficionados because it was very reminiscent of Giulietta Sprint Zagatos which had previously raced with great success, although the wedge-shaped 1300 Junior Z was not itself intended as a track star. Two years later this splendid little coupe was no more – but only because it was replaced in 1972 by the equally dashing 1600 Junior Zagato with its longer back end and improved performance. This would remain a low-production offering until 1976, when the new Alfetta range took over.

The arrival of Alfa's Junior Z was eagerly awaited after adoring afficionados saw the prototype at the Turin Motor Show.

COUNTRY OF ORIGIN:
Italy
FIRST MANUFACTURED:
1970 (until 1976)
ENGINE:
1,290 cc or 1,570 cc Straight Four
PERFORMANCE:
Top speed of 118 mph (190 km/h); 0-60 mph (97 km/h) in 11.2 secs
YOU SHOULD KNOW:
It won't be easy to find a Junior Z to drive: Zagato (despite stretching production facilities to the limit) only built 1,108 1300 JZs and a mere 402 1600 JZs – though the effort did put Zagato on a par with other carrozzeria like Bertone and Pininfarina in terms of its commercial relationship with Alfa.

269

The Alfa's big V8 motor ensured it was a serious performance car.

Alfa Romeo Montreal

The first production Montreal was shown at the Geneva Motor Show in 1970 and attracted crowds of admirers – and no wonder. Alfa had come up with a very distinctive 2+2 coupe that seemed to tick all the boxes. For a start, it was a handsome, classically styled two-door sports coupe in the best Italian tradition, designed by Bertone. But the real appeal lay beneath the bonnet, where a fuel-injected 2.6 litre V8 lurked, capable of pumping out 200 bhp. With the help of a five-speed ZF gearbox and limited-slip differential this meant the Alfa Romeo Montreal was a mean performer, with rapid acceleration and an impressive top speed.

The chassis and suspension of the Montreal came from the Giulia GTV coupe and the engine was a bored-out version of the 2 litre, four-cam V8 from the 33 Stradale, the road-going version of Alfa Romeo's Tipo 33 racing car. The Montreal's front end had four headlights mounted beneath unusual grilles that retracted when the lights were switched on. The fake air duct on the bonnet is in fact a necessary extension created as a power bulge. The prominent horizontal slats to the rear of the doors did work, but only as cabin vents.

Sadly, for all the initial excitement the Montreal failed to capture the hearts and wallets of many buyers. It undoubtedly suffered from entering a 'junior supercar' sector that was already looking crowded, not least by other sporty Alfas. Although it was not officially discontinued until 1977, Alfa had long ceased production and merely waited until the generous stick of unsold cars was finally shifted before announcing the Montreal's demise, with around 4,000 sold in eight years. It was a sad end for a rather impressive car that has happily received belated recognition from modern classic car collectors.

COUNTRY OF ORIGIN:
Italy
FIRST MANUFACTURED:
1970 (until 1977)
ENGINE:
2,594 cc V8
PERFORMANCE:
Top speed of 138 mph (222 km/h);
060 mph (97 km/h) in 7.5 secs
YOU SHOULD KNOW:
The concept car's first appearance was at Expo 67 in Montreal, Canada – the two prototypes had no name and were very different from the production model, but motoring press and public had christened this potentially exciting car 'The Montreal' and Alfa shrewdly went with the popular name.

AMC Rebel Machine

The Rebel name had been around since the late 1950s as a 'special' with a big engine and the American Motors Corporation's mid-sized Rambler bore the name from 1967 until 1970. And that was the one-and-only year the extraordinary AMC Rebel Machine was offered to the performance fraternity. The great champion of economy cars for the masses had finally caught muscle-car fever after dipping a toe in the water with the 1969 SC/Rambler developed with Hurst Performance.

The first examples of the racy Rebel Machine coupe had a garishly patriotic red-white-and-blue paint job, though this mercifully vanished from later examples and became a $75 option. The sporty interior was black with bucket seats separated by an armrest upholstered in (wait for it) red, white and blue vinyl, which never did vanish.

Colour scheme apart, AMC did a pretty good job – the Rebel Machine was an impressive performer thanks to a ram-air 6.4 litre V8 tuned to produce 340 bhp, assisted by a huge air scoop on the bonnet that fed the greedy engine via a vacuum-controlled butterfly valve. The engine was AMC's most powerful and came with modified heads, valve train, cam, intake and exhaust, plus a four-barrel carb. There was a four-speed manual gearbox with a floor shift from Hurst Performance, who had helped with the development programme.

The car had stiff suspension giving the Rebel Machine an elevated rear end and somewhat menacing raked look that more than hinted at its capabilities. It was street legal all right, though often used for drag racing. Around 2,300 were sold in 1970 and – whilst many were burnt out and bit the dust – there is still an enthusiastic band of supporters dedicated to restoring and preserving The Machine whilst revelling in its muscular All-American performance.

COUNTRY OF ORIGIN:
USA
FIRST MANUFACTURED:
1970
ENGINE:
6.5 l (390 cid) V8
PERFORMANCE:
Top speed of 125 mph (201 km/h); 0-60 mph (97 km/h) in 6.4 seconds
YOU SHOULD KNOW:
AMC really liked that colour scheme, and sold it hard just like this: 'What makes The Machine so unique? Let's start with the paint job. Red . . . white . . . and blue. Complete with stripes that glow in the dark, matching racing mirrors plus THE MACHINE decals inside, outside and on the back. Pretty wild.'

The Rebel Machine was a big car from a small manufacturer.

AMC Matador Coupe

COUNTRY OF ORIGIN:
USA
FIRST MANUFACTURED:
1974 (until 1978)
ENGINE:
4.2 l (258 cid) Straight Six; 5.0 l
(304 cid), 5.9 l (360 cid) or 6.6 l
(401 cid) V8
PERFORMANCE:
With 5.9 l engine – top speed
of 116 mph (187 km/h); 0-60 mph
(97 km/h) in 8.9 secs
YOU SHOULD KNOW:
A copper-coloured Oleg Cassini
Matador coupe with its black interior
appears in the James Bond film *The
Man with the Golden Gun*, where it
features rather dramatically as 'the
flying car'.

Would a car manufacturer ever tell a little white lie? AMC's marketing campaign certainly did in 1971, assuring the world that the Matador was an all-new car when it was a face-lifted 1970 Rebel. There was, however, a wide choice of engines and four body styles – two-door hardtop or coupe, four-door saloon and station wagon. Echoes of AMC's recent muscle-car adventures remained, with The Machine option package available on the two-door hardtop.

But wait! In 1974 AMC really did redesign the Matador, with second generation cars finally approaching that original 'all new' claim. The saloon and station wagon saw major changes, with a revamped front end that had a protruding section following the front bumper, earning the nickname 'coffin noses'. But the real surprise was the two-door's reincarnation as a completely different, radically styled coupe.

Although this streamlined car with its long bonnet and short rear deck won a 'Best Styled Car of 1974' award, the stretched fastback atop a short wheelbase with tunnel headlights was not to everyone's liking, though part of AMC's intention in producing this in-your-face machine was to create an aerodynamic something that could go NASCAR racing, and indeed it won five races. So in consequence the Matador Coupe was pretty speedy.

There was a choice of three engines over the production run, with a fourth big one added for 1974 only. Several trim levels were offered, along with a succession of 'designer' models – Oleg Cassini (1974–75), Barcelona 1 (1976) and Barcelona 2 (1977–78) – that had luxurious interiors. These (somewhat bizarre examples of 1970s kitsch) have become quite collectable, though it's fair to say that the Matador Coupe has never entirely captured the hearts of those of today's enthusiasts who look back to that generation of mighty 1970s American cars with affection.

Though it was both quick and stylish, the Matador Coupe was not to everyone's taste.

AMC Pacer

The oil crisis of the early 1970s put the boys from Kenosha in their element. For AMC was all about producing affordable cars for the masses and swiftly came up with a compact to suit the mood of the moment. The futuristic Pacer had curvaceous

lines, lots of glass and a handy hatchback, contrasting with the boxy offerings of most other makers. The little car quickly acquired the nickname 'Jellybean'.

The term 'compact' was relative – the Pacer was wider than a Rolls-Royce Silver Shadow and the smallest of three engine options was a 3.8 litre straight six, paradoxically giving very poor fuel economy compared with imported compacts flooding in from Japan. An unusual feature was a passenger side door that was longer than the driver's to facilitate back-seat access. The car certainly fulfilled the design brief of being unique and the car-buying public responded well, shelling out for around 280,000 Pacers over time.

However, 145,000 of those sales were in the first year, and AMC was soon casting around for ways to bolster sales. Performance of the first edition was poor, with either straight six engine, so a more powerful version of the larger engine was offered in 1976, then a V8. Although rear seats folded flat to give load space, little remained with the seats up, so a station wagon version appeared in 1977.

AMC also started a hopeful drift from economy compact to luxury compact by offering various upgrade packages. The X was sporty, the D/L was a minor upgrade that became standard in 1978 and the Limited was a leather-upholstered offering loaded with extras that appeared in 1979. There were even specials like The Sundowner (for California) and a Levi's Package with blue denim interior trim and fender logos. It was all in vain, for this 1970s icon expired with the decade.

The Pacer may have been billed as a compact, but it still had a large and thirsty engine.

COUNTRY OF ORIGIN:
USA
FIRST MANUFACTURED:
1975 (until 1980)
ENGINE:
3.8 l (232 cid) or 4.2 l (258 cid)
Straight Six; 5.0 l (304 cid) V8
PERFORMANCE:
With V8 engine – top speed of
96 mph (154 km/h); 0-60 mph
(97 km/h) in 14.8 secs
YOU SHOULD KNOW:
The Pacer was originally designed to
have a Wankel rotary engine but
when preferred supplier General
Motors canned their Wankel
development programme AMC had
to hastily modify the Pacer to take
their own straight six motor.

The Vantage V8 looked the part and delivered on its promises.

Aston Martin Vantage V8

It was quite a responsibility to be named as 'Britain's First Supercar', but the 1977 Vantage V8 was up for it with the ability to beat a Ferrari Daytona to 60 mph (97 km/h) from a standing start and stratospheric top speed. Aston Martin had used the Vantage name before, usually to indicate a high-performance version of an existing model, and the Vantage V8 was ia souped-up version of the regular Aston Martin V8 – itself effectively the DBS V8 relaunched in 1972.

However, this time the Vantage was classified as a model in its own right. Tadek Marek's excellent V8 engine was tuned to deliver 438 bhp with increased compression, large inlet valves, special camshafts, new manifolds and enlarged carburettors – a set-up that would remain until an engine upgrade in 1986.

The Vantage was recognizable from the standard V8 by its rear spoiler, blanked-out radiator grille and closed-off bonnet without an air scoop. The Vantage also had flared wheel arches and side skirts (though Prince Charles ordered one without the latter embellishments, setting a minor fashion). There were various small styling and wheel changes throughout the Vantage V8's long life. Two versions were offered – the saloon (313 produced) and the fabulous Volante convertible (115 built), the Volante not being introduced until 1987.

And yes, James Bond did indeed drive an imaginary Aston Martin Vantage V8 in *The Living Daylights*. It was actually three cars meant to be one – a V8 Vantage Volante convertible and two non-Vantage V8 saloons – with bulletproof windows, fireproof bodywork, retractable outriggers, wheel lasers, heat-seeking missiles, an afterburner, tire spikes and a self-destruct system. All that said, most people would love to slip behind the wheel of any old Aston Martin Vantage V8 and have a license to be thrilled.

COUNTRY OF ORIGIN:
UK
FIRST MANUFACTURED:
1977 (until 1989)
ENGINE:
5,340 cc V8
PERFORMANCE:
Top speed of 170 mph (274 km/h);
0-60 mph (97 km/h) in 5.3 secs
YOU SHOULD KNOW:
Aston Martin V8 Vantages were sold into the American market but looked slightly different, with a flattened bonnet, and performance was toned down to meet US regulations – so these American examples lacked the awesome power of the real thing.

Audi 100 Coupe S

Volkswagen bought Auto Union from Mercedes-Benz in 1965 to acquire the Ingolstadt factory, a new production facility that could be used meet booming orders for Beetles. Consequently, the first instruction from Wolfsburg banned development of Auto Union or Audi models. But designer Dr Ludwig Kraus turned a deaf ear, continuing to develop the Audi 100 in secret. To the credit of VW bosses, they accepted the subterfuge with good grace and sanctioned production when Kraus produced his prototype with a flourish. It was a good decision that played a major part in securing VW's future. When demand for the rear-engined Beetle declined, Volkswagen could respond with front-engined, water-cooled cars thanks to their Audi experience.

A pet project of the good Dr Kraus was a lightweight sporting version of his Audi. The 100 Coupe S appeared at the Frankfurt Motor Show in late 1969 and went on sale a year later. It was a low, streamlined 2+2 fastback coupe on a shortened Audi 100 subframe with a bored-out engine fitted with twin carburettors to give punchy performance via a four-speed manual gearbox. Front disc brakes were a necessary adjunct, for this was a very fast car. It has a likeness to the Aston Martin DBS, with a similar back end and matching detail like the rear light clusters and side louvres, whilst there is also marked similarity to the handsome Fiat Dino coupe.

No matter where the design inspiration came from, the new Audi 100 Coupe S was a solid hit with the buying public, who purchased sufficient numbers to sustain a good production run. There was a revised version in 1972, with an engine modification to increase fuel consumption and reduce emissions ahead of new American regulations. Production of this beautiful car finally ceased in 1976.

COUNTRY OF ORIGIN:
Germany
FIRST MANUFACTURED:
1970 (until 1976)
ENGINE:
1,871 cc Straight Four
PERFORMANCE:
Top speed of 116 mph (185 km/h); 0-60 mph in (97 km/h) 10.6 secs
YOU SHOULD KNOW:
Sadly, it seems that rust prevention was not a priority on the production line. So while over 30,000 Audi 100 Coupes were built very few survive to be enjoyed by modern drivers who like to cut a classic dash.

The 100 Coupe S should have been the car that never was after Audi was swallowed by VW.

Bitter CD

COUNTRY OF ORIGIN:
Germany
FIRST MANUFACTURED:
1973 (until 1979)
ENGINE:
5,354 cc V8
PERFORMANCE:
Top speed of 130 mph (209 km/h);
0-60 mph (97 km/h) in 9.4 secs
YOU SHOULD KNOW:
After the Bitter CD was discontinued
its successor was the Bitter SC,
based on Opel's large Senator model,
which would be produced for
another 10 years until the practice of
major manufacturers using
commissioned suppliers to produce
their custom performance cars went
out of fashion.

Ex-racing driver Erich Bitter produced cars in Germany (and later Austria) from 1973 after the failure of a joint venture with Italian outfit Construzione Automobili Intermeccanica of Turin. Entrepreneurial Erich's first self-build venture was the Bitter CD, a splendid three-door fastback sports coupe with a long, sloping rear hatch based on the Opel Diplomat platform.

In fact, the Bitter CD was effectively an Opel-sanctioned production version of a concept car shown by Opel at the 1969 Frankfurt Motor Show. The Opel CD (standing for 'Coupe Diplomat') got a great reception and the company liked the idea of putting a road version into production. The great Pietro Frua was commissioned to modify the CD prototype and his evolution was shown at Frankfurt in 1970. The following year Opel design boss Dave Holls asked Erich Bitter to build the new car, and he set up a company to do just that.

With a lot of technical help and support from Opel, Erich Bitter further refined the Frua design before commissioning the experienced Baur of Stuttgart to build body panels, assemble the shell, fit it to Opel running gear and trim the interior. The stylish flyer was fitted with a grunty Chevrolet 5.4 litre V8 engine from parent General Motors that used three-speed automatic transmission to deliver potent performance. It appeared at Frankfurt in 1973 to general acclaim, with over 175 orders taken. Sadly, the oil crisis intervened and many were cancelled.

Some 400 Bitter CDs were built, so they are quite rare, though the surviving examples are relatively cheap at auction. That gives anyone who likes to be seen driving an unusual semi-supercar lots of eye-catching bang for their bucks. The odd combination of Italian design with an indestructible American engine and German engineering prowess makes for a pretty reliable ride.

The Bitter CD could not have been built without the active support of Opel but even so, relatively few cars ever got to burn rubber.

BMW 3.0CSL

In order to participate in Group 2 European Touring car racing, BMW had to homologate the big six-cylinder CS coupes for track use, and therefore created the 3.0 CSL series, with the L standing for 'lightweight'. The high-performance road-going version made no concession to comfort. The car was based on the pillarless steel body shell built by Karmann. But the 3.0CSL had thinner body panels, Plexiglas side windows, alloy-skinned doors and bonnet, no front bumper and a fibreglass rear bumper. The interior was very basic, the suspension was stiff and the car had fat alloy wheels with chrome wheel-arch extensions to keep them street-legal. Black go-faster stripes distinguished the CSL from the 3.0CS/Csi models.

An uprating after a year saw the engine size increased slightly, with Bosch fuel injection replacing the twin Zenith carburettors. A further engine enlargement took place in 1973 to homologate the engine used in the works racing coupe. The 3.2 litre CSL had a prominent spoiler and most cars were supplied with the positively decadent Town & Country option pack that included electric windows made of real glass, Bilstein gas-pressure shocks plus genuine metal bumpers front and back.

Exactly one thousand BMW 3.0CSL Coupes were made, 500 each in left-hand and right-hand drive. Perhaps the most famous version was that which was equipped with aerodynamic spoilers and prominent tail fins, causing it to be swiftly nicknamed the 'Batmobile'. It is generally accepted that just 37 of these famous cars were built, all left-hand drive examples.

The BMW 3.0CSL was certainly in the superhero category when it came to performance – this was a phenomenally successful track performer, winning six European Touring Car Championships during the 1970s, remaining competitive and winning races long after the road-going version had served its purpose and been discontinued.

It's not too hard to understand why the 3.0CSL was swiftly nicknamed 'The 'Batmobile'.

COUNTRY OF ORIGIN:
Germany
FIRST MANUFACTURED:
1971 (until 1975)
ENGINE:
2,985 cc, 3,003 cc or 3,153 cc
Straight Six
PERFORMANCE:
Top speed of 134 mph (216 km/h);
0-60 mph (97 km/h) in 7.8 secs
YOU SHOULD KNOW:
German buyers who fancied a Batmobile found their racing kit coyly hiding in the boot when their new car was delivered, as the spectacular appendages were not actually legal for road use in Germany.

BMW 6 Series

The first BMW 6 series appeared in the mid-1970s to replace the 2800 CS, 3.0 CS and 3.0 CSi coupes. The new E24 chassis was introduced in 1976 and that first 6 series would remain in business until the late 1980s. The clean, crisp styling by Paul Bracq was certainly up to the job, remaining virtually unchanged throughout and looking as pleasingly modern at the end of the production run as it had at the beginning.

The forward-leaning front end with familiar twin-kidney grille imparted a strong sense of purpose, supported by a wide bonnet, raked windscreen and rear window and neat boot. The side glass was divided by thin B-pillars that were unobtrusive. The cars had independent suspension and disc brakes all round, together with variable power steering for good road feel and the pioneering Check Control system that monitored engine systems, fluid levels and bulbs. The interior was luxurious, with twin bucket seats at the back separated by the extended front console, which joined the impressive angled 'Cockpit Design' dashboard.

There would inevitably be engine changes during the life of any such extended production run, but the 6 Series had more than most other long-lived European lines as the models evolved. The 630CS had a 3 litre carburetted six, whilst the 633CSi was fitted with a 3.2 litre six with Bosch fuel injection, adding serious power to style. The 1970s lineup was completed by the 2.8 litre 628CSi and 635CSi, each with fuel injection. The latter was fitted with an uprated 3.4 litre engine in 1982, and the final model was the awesome M635CSi introduced in 1983. These cars were so well built and satisfying that many are still in everyday use, driving as well today as when they came out of the box.

BMW's 6 Series saw quite a few engine changes over a decade and more, but all the models were commercially successful.

COUNTRY OF ORIGIN:
Germany
FIRST MANUFACTURED:
1976 (until 1989)
ENGINE:
Various, from 2,788 cc to 3,453 cc
Straight Six
PERFORMANCE:
630CS – top speed of 131 mph
(211 km/h); 0-50 mph (80 km/h)
in 5.9 secs
YOU SHOULD KNOW:
There can be slight confusion about model identification because BMW released just one 6 series car at a time in markets with tough emission controls like Japan and the USA, so the 630CSi sent there was actually a standard 630CS with a fuel-injected 2,986 cc engine.

BMW M1

The only mass-produced mid-engined BMW to be manufactured –
and the first of the company's famous 'M' cars – owed its public
availability to that demanding master, homologation. BMW had
entered into an arrangement with Lamborghini to produce sufficient
road versions to homologate a competition car for Group 5 sports
car races. Prototypes were designed and built by Lamborghini, who
were unfortunately unable to honour their production contract, so
these special cars were then hand-built by BMW's Motorsport
division using chassis and bodies fabricated in Italy.

The throaty 3.5 litre engine had four valves per cylinder and six
separate throttle butterflies. It could comfortably propel the M1
beyond 150 mph (241 km/h) – and that was just the road-going
version. This classic wedge-shaped GT design was by Giorgetto
Giugiaro, following the lead set by BMW's 1972 Turbo concept car.
The wide, shallow front end had BMW's signature twin-kidney grille
motif, though the overall design was a tad heavy around the back
end. The M1 had disc brakes and independent suspension all round.
The three versions were the road car, a Group 4 racer and a Group 5
racer with turbocharged 3.2 litre engine that kicked out 850 bhp.

Ironically, after all that effort to achieve homologation the M1
enjoyed limited racing success – a change in the rules meant it
didn't qualify for Group 5 racing until it was no longer competitive,
so its main claim to racing fame was as a short-lived support series
to Formula 1, where all the drivers used similar M1 cars from the
total of 56 built, so driving skill alone could determine the outcome
on the day – winners included Niki Lauda and Nelson Piquet. But
sadly BMW had lost interest in the M1's racing progress before it
really got a chance to realize its massive potential.

COUNTRY OF ORIGIN:
Germany
FIRST MANUFACTURED:
1978 (until 1981)
ENGINE:
3,453 cc DOHC Straight Six
PERFORMANCE:
Road-going version – top speed
of 162 mph (260 km/h); 0-60 mph
(97 km/h) in 5.6 secs
YOU SHOULD KNOW:
Survivors amongst the 399 refined
road-going examples are much
appreciated as top-quality sports
cars that go like the wind and are
ranked in the top dozen supercars of
the 1970s, with comprehensive
equipment including air conditioning
and full carpeting to enhance the
driving experience.

*Compared to conventional road
cars, the M1 was super-fast.*

Buick GSX

COUNTRY OF ORIGIN:
USA
FIRST MANUFACTURED:
1970 (until 1972)
ENGINE:
7.5 l (455 cid) V8
PERFORMANCE:
Top speed of 145 mph (233 km/h);
0-60 mph (97 km/h) in 6.2 secs
YOU SHOULD KNOW:
A total sale between 1970 and 1972
of less than a thousand GSX 455s
seems an unfair reflection on a great
car, but is good news for anyone
fortunate enough to have one of
these rare muscle cars, which is
now widely acknowledged as an
all-time-great.

The hot Buick mid-sized Gran Sport (GS) muscle cars of the 1960s were about to expire in the face of oil shortages and an inexorable trend towards high-performance pony cars, but they didn't go down without a last, fierce firefight. The 1968 two-door Buick GS 350 was completely restyled and the engine size was slightly increased, creating a handsome car that ran alongside the unchanged GS 400, which acquired a souped-up Stage 1 option for an even better vroom factor.

But the writing was on the wall, and owner General Motors' last throw of the Gran Sport dice involved lifting the ban on large engines in intermediate models. Buick responded instantly by dropping in its big-car 7.5 litre V8 and changing the model name to GS 455 to namecheck the exciting big block news. But Buick hoped the really thrilling development would be the arrival of the GSX, a headline version of the GS 455 that had spoilers front and back, four-speed manual transmission with floor shift, bonnet-mounted tachometer, bucket seats and wide tyres – plus the inevitable black stripes outlined in red that shouted 'catch me if you can' to rival road users.

The GSX came in standard or uprated Stage 1 form, and in either guise it was a formidable machine. The first cars were either bright yellow or white, with additional colour choices arriving the following year. For all that it was an impressive performer, the GSX was an expensive option that was out of time before the race started. It did not sell well, despite sensational reviews from the motoring press. This pattern was not broken when the GSX package was offered on all Gran Sport cars, and the GSX was soon discontinued, subsequently becoming a feeble options package on lesser models.

The reviews were sensational, but the formidable GSX never made the sales grade and was soon consigned to history.

Cadillac Seville

The Seville name graced hardtop versions of the Cadillac Eldorado in the 1950s (notably in '59, setting a world record for tail-fin size), before going into storage. Cadillac always operated on the belief that 'big is beautiful' when prosperous Americans were choosing quality automobiles. But by the mid-1970s it had become apparent that – shock, horror! – American tastes were changing, with smaller imported European cars grabbing an ever-increasing share of the market for luxury cars.

General Motors counter-attacked in 1975 with an all-new Cadillac Seville, just when the word 'downsizing' was reluctantly entering Detroit's vocabulary. This inverted previous policy by making the smallest car in the range the most expensive, to compete with those classy Mercs and BMWs that were turning American heads. It was a pretty good move – the Seville would go through five generations into the 21st century.

The first generation was based on an extensively modified Chevy Nova platform, but humble origins were concealed by a smart body with clean lines that pointed the way ahead for American auto design. The public certainly liked Cadillac's efforts as the car's reduced size, huge selection of standard features and smooth performance made it a smash hit.

Initially there was little choice, in best Henry Ford tradition (remembering that Chrysler grew from the first Ford company in 1902 after Henry threw his spanners out of the pram). There was one body style (a four-door sedan) with one engine (a super-smooth Oldsmobile V8 with electronic fuel injection). At first there was even but one colour (though it was silver). A full colour palette was soon offered and a diesel version of the engine appeared in 1978, proving unpopular. Luxury packages (Elegante in 1978 and Gucci for 1979) were offered, and a considerably revamped second generation Seville appeared in 1980.

The smooth Seville represented an American effort to roll back the tide of luxurious European imports – mostly from Germany.

COUNTRY OF ORIGIN:
USA
FIRST MANUFACTURED:
1975 (until 1979)
ENGINE:
5.7 l (350 cid) (petrol or diesel) V8
PERFORMANCE:
Top speed of 110 mph (177 km/h); 0-60 mph (97 mph) in 11.5 seconds
YOU SHOULD KNOW:
In 1979 only, the Seville offered a feature that would eventually become an industry standard – the trip computer. This served as an electronic fuel gauge and speedometer, and also performed calculations like miles remaining to empty and journey arrival time (if the destination was programmed in).

Chrysler 300 Hurst

Despite the bold '300' in the title, this was no return of the fabled Chrysler 300 letter series of luxury cars that had been produced from 1958 to 1965 (or to put it another way, from A to L), though some consider the Chrysler 300 Hurst to be an honorary member of the elite 300 club. What is indisputable is that Chrysler press releases at the time did boldly refer to the 'Chrysler 300H'.

If anything, the Hurst was even more exclusive than its sought-after predecessors, for this co-operative venture between Chrysler and famed customizer Hurst Performance appeared five years after the original series ended and was offered for just one year. Around 500 cars were produced, mostly hardtops with a couple of special convertibles thrown in for promotional purposes.

The two-door Hurst was a high-performance version of the large Chrysler 300, a car with a seemingly endless boot lid. The Hurst was identifiable by the fact that it was painted in Spinnaker White and Satin Tan (very close to gold). It also sported a scooped bonnet with fake power bulge and boot lid with moulded spoiler, both in fibreglass. There was no choice of engine – it was the 7.2 litre TNT V8 or nothing. This beast breathed through a dual-snorkel air cleaner and had booming twin exhausts, requiring beefed-up Torque-Flite transmission to put the power down and stiffened suspension to cope. All the Hursts had saddle-coloured leather interiors borrowed from the Chrysler Imperial, and featured bucket seats and a pull-down armrest.

Unfortunately, a communications failure between Chrysler and Hurst left each party thinking that the other would be handling promotion, so hardly anybody knew this muscular flyer was available. The 2,000-unit production target was not reached and the Chrysler 300 Hurst was not invited back for '71.

The 300 Hurst was a terrific performance car, but Chrysler and Hurst got their wires crossed and neither promoted this awesome custom special.

COUNTRY OF ORIGIN:
USA
FIRST MANUFACTURED:
1970
ENGINE:
7.2 l (440 cid) V8
PERFORMANCE:
Top speed of 120 mph (193 km/h);
0-60 mph (97 km/h) in 7.1 secs
YOU SHOULD KNOW:
It isn't easy to cut the mustard in a Chrysler 300 Hurst nowadays – of the original production run it is thought that around 250 of these huge muscle cars survive, the vast majority still in North America.

Chrysler Cordoba 300

The Chrysler Corporation was going through a bad patch in the 1970s, and cast around for new ideas to revive fast-flagging fortunes. In the 1960s Chrysler had very publicly declared that the company would never, ever produce anything less than a full-size car. Promises, promises! But by the time a new decade rolled round with an accompanying oil crisis it was a case of needs must.

So in 1975 the Cordoba made its debut, as Chrysler's smallest-ever model – designed to slot into the increasingly popular intermediate personal luxury car category. For a while this about-face and blatant attempt to cash in on Chrysler's reputation for top-of-the-range quality cars seemed justified, but sales fell off rapidly towards the end of the decade after a revamp and growing awareness that build quality wasn't all it should be.

Thus the 1979 Chrysler Cordoba 300 was a rather desperate one-year-only attempt to recapture the former glories of the famous letter-series 300 luxury cars in particular and Chrysler in general. Sadly, the Cordoba 300 was somewhat inferior to its illustrious predecessors. Reviving the famous 300 name was not a successful ploy, with just 2,500 Cordoba 300s built in the year, perhaps because they were simply too expensive.

The two-door Cordoba 300 was basically a pricey option version of the standard car, thought up at the last minute in an attempt to boost Cordoba sales. This big coupe came with a white paint job, a revived 300-style cross-hair grille, non-functional bumper vents, red-white-and-blue pinstripes, red-leather interior, bucket seats, leather steering wheel, dashboard with engine-turned appliqués, tachometer and opera windows. Mandatory Torque-Flite transmission was teamed with power steering, beefed-up suspension and a four-barrel 5.9 litre V8 engine – Chrysler's most potent power plant in the '79 model year.

COUNTRY OF ORIGIN:
USA
FIRST MANUFACTURED:
1979
ENGINE:
5.9 l (360 cid) V8
PERFORMANCE:
Top speed of 115 mph (185 km/h)
YOU SHOULD KNOW:
The Cordoba 300 was replaced by the even less-memorable and further-downsized Cordoba LS, before the unlamented model series finally bit the prairie dust in 1982.

The Cordoba made nonsense of Chrysler's vow never to make anything but full-sized cars.

Citroen GS

COUNTRY OF ORIGIN:
France
FIRST MANUFACTURED:
1970 (until 1979)
ENGINE:
1,015 cc, 1,129 cc, 1,222 cc or
1,299 cc Flat Four
PERFORMANCE:
With 1.0 l engine – top speed of
92 mph (148 km/h); 0-50 mph
(80 km/h) in 11.7 secs
YOU SHOULD KNOW:
Citroen persisted with its Wankel
dreams and launched the two-rotor
GS Biorotor model in 1973 – but it
proved to be a nightmare with just a
few hundred sold . . . and Citroen
was forced to buy those back in
order to avoid the expense of
producing spare parts.

Better late than never – the arrival of the GS in 1970 plugged a gap that had cost Citroen dear over time. This four-door family car belatedly slotted between the Ami and 2CV economy cars and the luxurious DS – a vital market segment where rivals had been cheerfully cleaning up since Citroen discontinued the famous Traction Avant in 1957.

At least Citroen's response met the standards of technical innovation and excellence for which the company was famous. When launched, the GS may well have been the world's most technologically advanced set of new wheels, with great aerodynamics and numerous safety features. It was an instant hit with the car-buying public, too, confirming in the nicest possible way what Citroen had been missing for all those years.

The in-house styling was typically French – which is to say unlike anything else on the market. It was a fastback saloon with an enormous amount of boot space, the spare wheel having been cunningly placed on top of the engine. There were two trim levels – GS Club and the superior GS Pallas. A van and estate car were quickly added to the range, though a hatchback did not appear until the uprated GSA series arrived in 1979. If the GS had a fault, it was that all four engines offered were rather feeble for the job.

Unfortunately, Citroen had let things slide too far, despite the success of the GS. A number of factors combined to bankrupt the company in 1974 – the expensively aborted development of a Wankel engine, the effort of launching the GS, the cost of a new factory to build the CX replacement for the ageing DS and the catastrophic impact of the 1973 oil crisis. However, a shotgun marriage to Peugeot presided over by the French government saved the day.

The GS finally gave the Citroen range a mid-market family car.

Citroen CX

Voted European Car of the Year in 1975, the Citroen CX was the last car built by this quirky French maker before a forced merger with Peugeot ended the company's famed independence of thought and deed. In common with Citroen's other new offerings in the early 1970s, the CX was designed in house by Robert Opron. The car's flowing lines are derived from those of the Citroen GS and the CX's fastback shape contributed to extremely aerodynamic contours that allowed the car to achieve performance comparable with that of vehicles with bigger engines.

The CX was Citroen's entry in the lucrative executive car market and – *naturellement* – this meant a mechanically advanced vehicle, with transverse engine and the company's unique self-levelling suspension system, plus speed-sensitive power steering. The interior featured a 'spaceship' dashboard with rotating speedometer and an extraordinary steering wheel with a single half-spoke that allowed the driver to operate key controls with both hands on the wheel. These large saloons had wonderful roadholding and offered the smoothest of rides. There was a Safari estate car version and a stretched Prestige limo for those who wanted to be chauffeured.

Sadly, the CX's build quality left something to be desired, though this improved over time, but the car was originally designed for a compact rotary engine. When this was abandoned the CX's engine bay was too small for the six-cylinder engine the car deserved, so it was therefore fitted with a succession of four-cylinder engines that left the car somewhat underpowered.

In 1985 the styling was revised to create the Series 2, and the CX series was finally discontinued in 1991. By that time, over one million of these innovative cars had been produced to guarantee an honourable place in the pantheon of postwar French cars.

COUNTRY OF ORIGIN:
France
FIRST MANUFACTURED:
1974 (until 1991)
ENGINE:
Various, including 1,995 cc, 2,165 cc, 2,347 cc or 2,500 cc Straight Four
PERFORMANCE:
With 2.1 litre engine – top speed of 114 mph (184 km/h); 0-60 mph (97 km/h) in 9.7 secs
YOU SHOULD KNOW:
Citroen's hydropneumatic self-levelling suspension system was possibly the most efficient ever made – so good that it was licensed for use in the Rolls-Royce Camargue and top-of-the-range Mercedes luxury cars.

The CX was underpowered and the build quality was variable.

Citroen SM

COUNTRY OF ORIGIN:
France
FIRST MANUFACTURED:
1970 (until 1975)
ENGINE:
2,670 cc Quad-cam V6
PERFORMANCE:
Top speed of 142 mph (229 km/h);
0-60 mph (97 km/h) in 8.3 secs
YOU SHOULD KNOW:
There are two explanations of the
SM model name, neither confirmed.
Was it SM for 'Sport Maserati'? Or,
more romantically, did the letters
stand for *Sa Majesté* – French for
'Her Majesty' and an entirely
appropriate extension of the DS's
punning nickname *La Déesse*
(The Goddess)?

Citroen had purchased Maserati in 1968, with a view to combining its own advanced suspension system with Maserati engines to create a GT version of the upmarket Citroen DS. The result went on show at the Geneva Motor Show in 1970 as Citroen's headliner, destined to keep the company's name in lights alongside the likes of Porsche, Jaguar, Lotus, Alfa Romeo . . . even Ferrari and Aston Martin. It was an odd market sector for the French mass-marketeer to chase, but the pursuit was both enthusiastic and stylish.

The two-door SM 2+2 was designed in-house by Robert Opron and this big front-wheel drive car had a slippery fastback shape with a wide front and tapering rear. Every aspect of the car was engineered with aerodynamic efficiency in mind, done so well that the SM was literally sucked down onto the road at high speeds. The SM still appears futuristic today, four decades on, so the impact in 1970 was nothing short of sensational.

Good looks were enhanced by the SM's advanced technology, which included self-levelling pneumatic suspension, lights that swivelled with the power steering, self-centreing steering, advanced disc brakes delivering extraordinary stopping power and a wiper system that was rain sensitive. Despite this, the SM's very complexity created problems, as there were technical teething troubles and the cars required specialist attention from dealers with expertise in Maserati engines. In a country where most villages still had a mechanic, this didn't go down well.

Still, the interior was luxurious and performance was excellent. In pre-speed-limit days the SM's ability to cruise for long periods at 120 mph (193 km/h) on trans-European journeys was impressive. It wasn't enough. Sales fell sharply and, following Citroen's collapse in 1974, new owner Peugeot sold Maserati and called time on the brilliant but commercially unsuccessful SM.

The Citroen SM was a beautiful but complex machine, the latter aspect causing various problems.

Datsun 240Z

COUNTRY OF ORIGIN:
Japan
FIRST MANUFACTURED:
1970 (until 1978)
ENGINE:
2,393 cc Straight Six
PERFORMANCE:
Top speed of 125 mph (201 km/h);
0-60 mph (97 km/h) in 8.3 secs
YOU SHOULD KNOW:
To help ensure continuing American
interest in the 240Z, Nissan ran an
imaginative programme in the late
1990s whereby the company
purchased as many cars as possible,
had them professionally restored and
then sold them through dealerships.

It had various different designations, ranging from Fairlady Z to the S30 Nissan/Datsun, but most people seem happy to agree on Datsun 240Z. This was the first of the company's Z-series sports cars, designed by Yoshihiko Matsuo. The rear-wheel drive, fixed-head coupe had clean and simple fastback lines with a sloping rear hatch. The six-cylinder engine was teamed with four- or five-speed manual transmission (or three-speed automatic box), whilst the 240Z had independent suspension, front disc brakes and rear drums. Internal trim was excellent, with reclining bucket seats, full instrument pack, radio and wall-to-wall carpeting. Air conditioning was available as an optional extra.

Performance was first class, with impressive top speed, crisp handling, tenacious roadholding, comfortable ride quality and notable reliability, adding up to a refined sports car that delivered unheard-of value in the price bracket. It made the Datsun 240Z a massive international success with Nissan unable to keep up with demand.

The main export market was the USA, where Nissan introduced the Datsun 240Z in 1970 – breaking out of the stereotype that Japanese imports were all boxy economy cars. Keen pricing undercut sporty imports like Jaguar and Porsche, ensuring that the 240Z was a huge hit with the American car-buying public, with the car's profile raised by considerable success on the racetrack. Regular upgrades were made over the years to conform to tightening American regulations.

A modified 240ZG was introduced in 1971 to homologate the 240Z for Group 4 racing. The two models were very similar, though 240ZG was sold only in Japan and had modified bodywork, notably an extended nose. There were various other evolutions of the standard Datsun 240Z – the high-performance Z432 and Z432R, the 260Z and 280Z. These well-made sports cars all combine stylish good looks with excellent performance, and they're fast becoming collectable classics.

The sporty 240Z has become very collectable over time.

De Tomaso Pantera

If anyone were foolish enough to claim that the De Tomaso Pantera (a Panther in England) came from any country but Italy, they would instantly be branded as a liar – this stylish flyer is quite clearly a quintessentially Italian sports car. But appearances can be deceptive. Beneath that wedge-shaped fastback body lurked a powerful Ford Cleveland V8 engine, so the Pantera represented a unique cross between cutting-edge Italian styling and American muscle-car performance. Introduced in 1970, it would remain in limited production for more than two decades, initially aided and abetted by a formal tie-up with Ford of America that sold Panteras through the Lincoln-Mercury network.

American muscle – Italian style

The design was by Ghia (a company also controlled by Alejandro de Tomaso), with American Tom Tjaarda taking the lead. Unlike its predecessor, the Mangusta with its conventional chassis, the Pantera was of all-steel monocoque construction, with a mid-engine powertrain layout. There was independent suspension all round and the 5.8 litre V8 was teamed with five-speed manual transmission. The bodies were fabricated by Vignale in Turin and Panteras were assembled at De Tomaso's Modena factory.

It all started rather well, with a thousand cars shipped in Year One. Shortcomings soon surfaced – the cabin was cramped and tended to overheat rapidly, the driving position was rather strange and build quality left much to be desired – but these were offset by a combination of blistering performance, Italian supercar prestige and a low ticket price. But it ended badly. Despite shifting around 6,000 Panteras in the USA by 1974, De Tomaso had paid little heed to upcoming regulation changes. Reworking the car to meet them would have been prohibitively expensive, and the oil crisis was dampening demand for greedy cars. No Panteras were exported to America thereafter, though they continued to be made and sold into European markets.

COUNTRY OF ORIGIN:
Italy
FIRST MANUFACTURED:
1970 (until 1991)
ENGINE:
5,763 cc V8
PERFORMANCE:
Top speed of 159 mph (km/h);
0-60 mph (97 km/h) in 5.5 secs
YOU SHOULD KNOW:
Build quality of early Panteras wasn't great – a triumph of style over substance – and celebrity owner Elvis Presley once became so frustrated when his yellow Pantera wouldn't start that he blasted it with a gun.

Dodge Challenger

Those who know always go for the original 1970 Challengers as these were the cream of the crop – closely followed by the '71s.

COUNTRY OF ORIGIN:
USA
FIRST MANUFACTURED:
1970 (until 1974)
ENGINE:
Various, from 3.2 l (198 cid) Straight Six to 7.2 l (440 cid) V8
PERFORMANCE:
With 7.2 litre V8 – top speed of 125 mph (201 km/h); 0-60 mph (97 km/h) in 6.2 secs
YOU SHOULD KNOW:
If at first you don't succeed . . . The second generation Challenger was the Dodge-badged version of the imported Mitsubishi Galant Lambda coupe (Plymouth's identical car was called the Sapporo) – this time the big idea was to give the Challenger a sportier feel than the Sapporo with bright paint colours and go-faster stripes.

If you've got a good name, flaunt it – that was clearly Dodge's thinking regarding the Challenger tag, which has featured on three distinct generations of car. The first two appeared in the 1970s and early 1980s, and the name returned with a bang in 2008. Granted the fact that all three incarnations were completely different, it is maybe unsurprising that the rationale behind the first generation was not altogether clear.

Perhaps the reasoning process went something like this. Better late than never – we'd just love a piece of the lucrative ponycar action begun by the Ford Mustang and Chevy Camaro. Plymouth came up with the clever idea of challenging those small ponycars with the slightly bigger, more luxurious Barracuda. We'll launch a new model called the Challenger (to make our intentions plain) that goes wheel to wheel with the Barracuda. We'll market the Challenger as the most potent pony car ever and offer a choice of eight engines and two body styles and endless option packs so everyone can be happy, especially us.

Whatever, it wasn't a brilliant plan, though ironically the car was excellent. The basic body styles were both two-door versions – hardtop coupe and convertible – though engine selection and choice of various option packs made for a formidable number of variations on the theme. But they all shared a classic wide, low, long-bonnet, short rear-deck ponycar appearance. The performance model was the R/T (Road/Track).

Once Year One novelty wore off, annual sales plunged from a respectable 77,000 to 23,000 in 1972, after which the multiple choice approach was canned leaving just the V8 hardtop for the dying years of '73 and '74, after which the first generation Challenger was discontinued. Muscle-car movers agree that the '70 Challengers were awesome, the '71s were great and the rest came nowhere.

Ferrari Berlinetta Boxer

The Berlinetta Boxer (BB) series produced by Ferrari from 1973 to 1984 marked a major policy shift at Maranello. Much like another autocratic automobile supremo before him – Henry Ford – Enzo Ferrari could stubbornly refuse to sanction a progressive move. So it had been with the thorny question of mid-engined road cars. Even after Ferrari had been forced to introduce mid-engined race cars to remain competitive on the track, Enzo stubbornly clung to the belief that mere mortals would be unable to handle such high-strung thoroughbreds on the road.

His engineers had long tried to persuade Il Commendatore to relax this unbending stance, and managed a partial victory when he agreed that lesser Dino road cars could use the controversial layout. But the new Ferrari Daytona launched in 1968 had the traditional front-engine configuration and it was not until 1971 that Enzo finally gave in and allowed the 365 GT4 BB to be shown at Turin. It shared a designation with the Daytona, but was completely different. Further refinement meant that this angular wedge with pop-up headlamps designed by Pininfarina did not go into production until 1973 and just 387 were built, making it the rarest and most desirable of Berlinetta Boxers. It was also the fastest.

In 1976 the 512 BB replaced the 365, borrowing the name of the 512 racecar discontinued in 1970. The engine was slightly larger and there were minor external differences like a new front spoiler, side air vents and a remodelled rear lamp cluster. There were 929 512s built in six years. The final Berlinetta Boxer appeared in 1981. The fuel-injected 512i BB was the most successful of the series commercially, with over a thousand produced before the BB series was superseded by the famous Ferrari Testarossa.

COUNTRY OF ORIGIN:
Italy
FIRST MANUFACTURED:
1973 (until 1984)
ENGINE:
4,390 cc or 4,942 cc Flat 12
PERFORMANCE:
365 GT4 BB – top speed of 181 mph (291 km/h); 0-60 mph (97 km/h) in 5.4 secs
YOU SHOULD KNOW:
Ironically in view of Enzo Ferrari's long-held objections to producing a mid-engined road car – based on the assumption that customers would find such a machine too hot to handle – his engineers had been right all along . . . the 365 GT4 BB was voted the sweetest-ever road-going Ferrari by the motoring press.

The Berlinetta Boxer was the first of Ferrari's mid-engined production cars.

Fiat 130 Coupe

COUNTRY OF ORIGIN:
Italy
FIRST MANUFACTURED:
1971 (until 1977)
ENGINE:
3,235 cc V6
PERFORMANCE:
Top speed of 123 mph (198 km/h);
0-50 mph (80 km/h) in 7.5 secs
YOU SHOULD KNOW:
The 130 Coupe's body design proved
to be a long-term winner –
Pininfarina recycled it for the
Peugeot 604 (1965) and Peugeot 505
(1979) while its final use was for
505 coupe and convertible
prototypes developed in the USA
for the American market, a dozen
years after the Fiat 130 Coupe
first appeared.

The pleasing Fiat 130 was introduced at the end of the 1960s. This large four-door saloon replaced the company's previous top-of-the-range offering, the Fiat 2300. Fiat thought the 130 had everything required of a modern executive car – refined good looks, independent suspension, disc brakes all round, a smooth 2.9 litre V6 engine, three-speed automatic transmission (manual optional), power steering – but unfortunately it entirely failed to hit the Mercedes/BMW sweet spot. Among other faults, the interior was an uninspiring expanse of black plastic, the exhaust boomed annoyingly and the 130 was hard to start when hot. The general consensus was that Fiat had rushed the car into production so it was something of an unfinished masterpiece – or simply unfinished.

However, the 130 had a raffish relative that was altogether more interesting. The two-door Fiat 130 Coupe appeared at the Geneva Motor Show in 1971 to gasps of admiration. It was designed by Pininfarina, who duly received a prestigious award for an eye-catching effort. The body was completely different, with sharp rectangular lines that could blur over time as individual panels lifted. The engine was larger than the saloon's, but the 130 Coupe's true glory was its extraordinary interior – a luxurious confection with wood-veneer dash, door panels and central console. This was complemented by extraordinary orange velveteen upholstery, sporty dials with white needles and fibre-optic illumination, Autovox stereo, adjustable seats and steering wheel. Aircon was optional.

It was enough to secure the ultimate endorsement, with Enzo Ferrari acquiring a Fiat 130 Coupe for his long-distance road trips. Today, build-quality issues mean that very few of these unusual cars have survived in reasonable original condition, with good examples being eagerly sought by specialist collectors. Just 4,300 of the distinctive 130 Coupes were built, so today's would-be owners are fishing in a small pond.

It was a beautiful car, but the 130 Coupe had mechanical problems and never caught on.

Fiat X1/9

It was nicknamed 'The Flying Wedge' and the X1/9 was a huge hit for Fiat . . . in spite of itself. This two-seater sports roadster was designed by Bertone and had the stylish good looks of many larger – and infinitely more expensive – Italian mid-engined GT cars. Indeed, one motoring journalist's crisp summary was 'A baby Ferrari'. Like larger GTs, it had pop-up headlights, also featuring a removable targa top that could be stored in the front boot.

The X1/9 broke new ground by using the front-wheel drive Fiat 128's engine and gearbox in a mid-mounted rear-wheel drive configuration, an elegant solution that helped create an affordable mid-engined sports car – later copied by other manufacturers. The X1/9 started life as the Autobianchi Runabout concept car shown in 1969, and the response was so positive that Fiat hurried out a production version. The performance wasn't that great, with a relatively heavy body designed to meet US crash test standards propelled by a small engine, but handling was crisp and the image positive for sporty drivers.

Unfortunately, Fiat moved too quickly. As a result the X1/9 had shortcomings. The engine compartment was too small to permit easy maintenance, also causing overheating. The car rusted quickly and reverse gear often failed. Weight distribution was not perfect and excellent dry-road handling deteriorated markedly in wet conditions.

Considering these flaws the X1/9 enjoyed a long life, with Bertone taking over manufacture and upping the engine size in 1982. The reason was simple – for all its shortcomings the X1/9 was a joy to drive, with many enthusiastic owners fitting more powerful engines and better brakes to further enhance their motoring pleasure. After all, it's unlikely that the final production figure of 200,000 X1/9s would have been achieved unless there was something very appealing about this pocket speedster.

COUNTRY OF ORIGIN:
Italy
FIRST MANUFACTURED:
1972 (until 1989)
ENGINE:
1,290 cc or 1,498 cc Straight Four
PERFORMANCE:
With 1.3 l engine – top speed of 105 mph (169 km/h); 0-60 mph (97 km/h) in 11.8 secs
YOU SHOULD KNOW:
The X1/9 name should never have made it to the press launch, for the new sports roadster should have been introduced as the Fiat 128 Spider – but instead someone shrewdly decided that the car's X1/9 development tag (X1 = passenger car, 9 = ninth project in the 1960s series) sounded much better.

'The Flying Wedge' proved to be popular with young drivers.

Ford Escort Mexico

One of the clever evolutions of the Ford Escort Mk 1 was the Mexico road car. The works team's Ford Escort RS1600s won the Daily Mirror World Cup Rally and also finished third, fifth and sixth. The winning car was driven by Hannu Mikkola and Gunnar Palm who conquered a gruelling 16,000 mi (25,750 km) course through Europe and South America, starting at London's Wembley Stadium in mid-April and finishing in Mexico City during late May.

This extraordinary event attracted massive public interest, and Ford was a past master at turning motor-racing victories into hard cash by selling road cars that exploited the cachet of competition success. It was therefore no surprise to anyone when the distinctive Escort Mexico started appearing in showrooms up and down Britain. In fact, this custom version wasn't really so very different from any old Escort Mk 1, but that didn't stop it becoming a popular buy with dedicated motorsports enthusiasts.

The Escort Mexico did have the robust Ford Kent OHV engine, and shared the competition RS1600's strengthened two-door body shell, plus Rallye Sport suspension and brakes. Buyers obviously wanted to trumpet the fact that they had a special car, so the Mexico sported bucket seats and wide body stripes that contrasted with the rest of the paintwork. Extras like alloy wheels and four rather ostentatiously covered rally-style spotlamps on the front usually completed the impressive picture.

Escort Mexicos have become very desirable amongst those who like to own, maintain and drive collectable British cars from the 1970s. They are affordable, robust, easy to work on and still drive well. And with fewer than 10,000 produced during the four-year production run, the Mexico stands out from the large crowd of Escort Mk 1s that have dodged the scrapyard.

Ford won the gruelling World Cup Rally in 1970 and soon cashed in with a successful road car that ticked all the right commercial boxes.

COUNTRY OF ORIGIN:
UK
FIRST MANUFACTURED:
1970 (until 1974)
ENGINE:
1,599 cc OHV Straight Four
PERFORMANCE:
Top speed of 100 mph (161 km/h);
0-50 mph (80 km/h) in 7.9 secs
YOU SHOULD KNOW:
The Mk 2 Escort Mexico was produced between 1975 and 1978 and is much rarer than its predecessor, having to compete with the Escort 1600 Sport and the pokey Escort RS2000 – just 2,500 examples were built at Saarlouis in West Germany.

Ford Escort RS1600

Technically this may be a variation of the Escort Mk I, but the Ford Escort RS1600 is a distinctive predator that would feel insulted to be lumped in with its decent but undoubtedly tamer siblings. For this was the fearsome competition car that battered the opposition into almost total submission from the early 1970s.

It was fairly obvious that the RS1600 was not designed for gently commuting to the station.

And it was the first car to wear Ford's RS (for Rallye Sport) badge of honour, which would frequently speed to race wins in the decades ahead. Some 20 wildly different cars have been RS-badged since the Escort RS1600 appeared in 1970 – but the accolade is not awarded lightly, strictly reserved for competition-hardened thoroughbreds. Ford tries to ensure that road-going RS cars offer advanced technology, great performance, terrific roadholding and value for money.

This winning formula was pioneered by the Escort RS1600, the first Ford to use a 16-valve twin overhead-camshaft engine. It was also first to be assembled at the company's new AVO (Advanced Vehicle Operation) factory at Aveley. The impressive hat trick was the RS1600's status as the first car to be sold through a specialist network of Rallye Sport dealerships.

The RS1600 was developed from the Escort Mk 1 twin-cam and was fitted with a 1.6 litre BDA 16-valve engine. Stiffened body shells, sports suspension and front disc brakes helped cope with the rigorous demands of long-distance rallies. In fact, for the longest events 1860 pushrod X-flow engines replaced the BDAs, as the robust replacement never suffered mechanical failure. Road versions were detuned compared to works racers, but still offered (and still do offer) high speed coupled with punchy acceleration to thrill sporting drivers.

With the advent of the Escort Mk 2 in 1976, the RS1600 morphed into the RS1800 – an even more potent machine that would consolidate Ford's hard-earned racing reputation.

COUNTRY OF ORIGIN:
UK
FIRST MANUFACTURED:
1970 (until 1975)
ENGINE:
1,599 cc DOHC Straight Four
PERFORMANCE:
Road version – top speed of 113 mph (182 km/h); 0-50 mph (80 km/h) in 6.4 secs
YOU SHOULD KNOW:
Impressive competition scalps lifted by the awesome RS1600 included the East African Safari Rally of 1972, three RAC Rallies and the European Touring Car Championship of 1974.

Ford Torino GT Convertible

COUNTRY OF ORIGIN:
USA
FIRST MANUFACTURED:
1970 (until 1971)
ENGINE:
Various, from 4.9 l (302 cid) to
7.0 l (429 cid) V8
PERFORMANCE:
With 7.0 l engine – top speed of
128 mph (206 km/h); 0-60 mph
(97 km/h) in 6 secs
YOU SHOULD KNOW:
One of the more unusual options
on the Ford Torino GT Convertible
was a pair of broad reflective laser
stripes that ran back along the front
wings and across the doors before
terminating, giving extraordinary
colour effects as the light played
on them.

One of the hardest tasks in American life during the 20th century must have been choosing a new car – especially a Ford. American manufacturers in general and Ford in particular delighted in being cavalier with the use of model names and loved offering endless permutations that must have left potential buyers with spinning heads. Nothing illustrates the point better than the Ford Torino.

In 1968 and 1969 the Torino was an upmarket sub series within the intermediate Ford Fairlane range. In 1970 the Torino became Ford's intermediate car with the Fairlane becoming the sub series. There were 13 models, five engine options, three transmission packages – and that's before even thinking about colour choice. Ah well, tens of thousands of happy campers managed to make a decision in the end, so perhaps Ford-buying wasn't that hard after all.

Certainly the top choice for someone looking to join the performance party was the 1970 Torino GT Convertible. This wide, low machine was sleekly styled with a distinctive egg-crate grille with hideaway headlights and full-width rear light panel. The comfortable cabin sported a raked windscreen, bucket front seats and simple dashboard. The really good bit was the great big lump under the bonnet – a 7 litre Cobra Jet engine. This put the GT Convertible right at the top of the muscle-car class at a time when these sporting bruisers were at the height of their popularity, before the impending oil crisis banished them to the world of happy memories.

With buyers spoiled for muscle-car choice, the Torino GT Convertible sold just under 4,000 units, making this speedy ragtop the rarest Ford intermediate. Today, scarcity value coupled with the fact that the GT was a terrific car in the first place has made this an ultra-collectable '70s icon.

Catch a collectable Torino ragtop if you can – it's the rarest of Ford intermediates.

Ford Granada Mk I

The Ford Granada was launched in 1972 as a large executive saloon and/or capacious family car, replacing both the Zephyr and Zodiac in the UK and Taunus 20M and 26M in Europe. It was a truly European production number, being made both at Dagenham in the United Kingdom and Cologne in Germany.

To add to the complexity of an apparently simple tale, entry-level Mk I models were badged as Ford Consuls until 1975, when they all became Granadas. In 1976 British production ended, leaving Germany to carry on alone. There was a choice of seven engines, some available in the UK only, some available in Europe only and some shared by both. There were four body styles – two- and four-door saloons, a two-door coupe and a five-door estate car. Some variations were not sold in the UK (like the fastback coupe with 'Coke bottle' styling), though a revised coupe was sold in the UK, but only as a Ghia option. Clear as mud!

Despite the Granada being yet another typically complex Ford model offering, the bottom line was simple enough – Ford had created another pleasingly designed, well-built car that went down a storm with the public and quickly became the sturdy mainstay of many a commercial fleet, hire car business, taxi operator, undertaker and police force.

The Granada Mk II appeared in 1977, with straight-line design and a square look. This lasted until 1985 when the Mk III appeared, though this was really a different car – called the Ford Scorpio everywhere but the UK and Ireland, where the Granada name was so potent that it was retained for the new model. There's no doubting the affection in which the Granada is held – there are well-supported owners' clubs and thousands of weekend drivers dedicated to keeping the Granada legend rolling.

The well-loved Granada was a considerable success for Ford's integrated European operation.

COUNTRY OF ORIGIN:
Germany/UK
FIRST MANUFACTURED:
1972 (until 1977)
ENGINE:
1,993 cc Straight Four; 1,699 cc or 1,996 cc V4; 2,293 cc, 2,494 cc, 2,551 cc or 2,994 cc V6
PERFORMANCE:
With 3 l engine – top speed of 111 mph (179 km/h); 0-50 mph (80 km/h) 8.4 secs
YOU SHOULD KNOW:
If the car's the star, the Ford Granada's finest hour was *The Sweeney*, that tough 1970s TV cop show that saw Inspector Jack Regan and Sergeant George Carter of Scotland Yard's Flying Squad pursuing assorted villains all over London with the help of a succession of seriously abused but ever-willing Granadas.

Honda Civic

COUNTRY OF ORIGIN:
Japan
FIRST MANUFACTURED:
1972 (until 1979)
ENGINE:
1,169 cc, 1,237 cc or 1,488 cc
Straight Four
PERFORMANCE:
With 1.5 litre engine – top speed of
99 mph (160 km/h)
YOU SHOULD KNOW:
Smog-plagued California had
America's toughest anti-emission
regulations, but the state was an
important source of business –
so Honda developed the 1.5 litre
'clean' CVCC (Compound Vortex
Controlled Combustion) motor that
became compulsory for all Civics
sold in California.

The Honda Civic name has been around for a long time, with the badge adorning a basic sub-compact car from the early 1970s until the mid-1990s and thereafter a more luxurious compact. The first generation Civic was launched in 1972 and lasted until 1979, with a redesigned second generation model carrying the evolutionary series forward into the 1980s.

Although widely exported, the Civic's success – and the inexorable rise of Honda as a major international carmaker – was about felicitous timing. At the very moment that enraged Middle Eastern suppliers pointed the oil weapon at the West for supporting Israel in the Yom Kippur War, the handy little Civic was on hand to meet the American buying public's sudden demand for fuel-efficient small cars. Home manufacturers were stuck in the era of heavy metal, with some popular muscle cars gulping a gallon of petrol for every six or seven miles of town driving.

The little Civic was positively parsimonious by comparison, and affordable to boot. The first generation started with a neat little 1.2 litre transverse four-cylinder engine, cleverly marketed using the slogan 'We make it simple'. Simple indeed, but brilliantly so – the well-built Civic had independent suspension all round and front disc brakes, whilst the interior had comfortable bucket seats. Standard transmission was four-speed manual, though there was an automatic version as an optional extra. Body styles (not always available in all markets) were the two-door coupe, three-door hatchback, four-door saloon, five-door hatchback and five-door station wagon. The first generation Civic was tweaked as the decade unfolded, with some small style changes and the introduction of larger engines.

The Civic was just the ticket when the oil crisis bit motorists.

American small cars such as the Ford Pinto and Chevy Vega just couldn't compete and Civic sales boomed, along with those of Datsun and Toyota. The Japanese invasion was finally in full swing.

MLA 993P

Honda Prelude

Throughout the 1960s Honda's quirky little S800 sports car had provided a touch of performance frivolity against the solid backdrop of the well-built economy cars that were the Japanese company's stock in trade. The 1970s proved the value of that sober approach, establishing Honda as a major international exporter, but with that job safely done the Prelude was introduced in 1978 to compete with the successful Toyota Celica and broaden a Honda product range that then consisted of the sub-compact Civic and the mid-sized Accord.

The design of this neat two-door notchback coupe reflected that of the other two models, though the Prelude also had distinct echoes of the Mercedes-Benz SL. It was described by Honda as a sports compact and one unusual feature was the standard sunroof. Another was found on the dashboard, which featured a concentric speedometer/tachometer combo, with the former encircling the latter.

First generation 2+2 Preludes had excellent build quality, good fuel consumption and were a pleasure to drive, though back-seat accommodation was cramped. They came with one of two overhead-cam four-cylinder engines (depending on which country they were sold in), the larger of which came out of the Honda Accord. Drive options were initially a five-speed manual gearbox or two-speed Hondamatic automatic transmission, though a more conventional four-speed automatic soon appeared. The Prelude had independent suspension all round and rack-and-pinion steering, giving excellent roadholding ability and nimble handling. It's fair to say that performance was brisk rather than outstanding, with early cars not quite capable of hitting the 'ton' and not therefore appealing to the sportiest of drivers.

The first generation was only produced until 1982, but set the scene for future progress. Thereafter four more generations would carry the Prelude triumphantly into the 21st century.

The Prelude's arrival saw Honda move in on the sporting saloon sector – needless to say scoring another success with an evolutionary brand that would be around for decades.

COUNTRY OF ORIGIN:
Japan
FIRST MANUFACTURED:
1978 (until 1982) (First generation)
ENGINE:
1,602 cc or 1,751 cc Straight Four
PERFORMANCE:
With 1.6 l engine – top speed 98 mph (158 km/h); 0-60 mph (97 km/h) 11.3 secs
YOU SHOULD KNOW:
Early Preludes remain great fun to drive and are becoming quite collectable, but it's important to look for a solid example that is rust-free (a generic problem) and has manual transmission (automatic transmission saps performance).

Jaguar XJ-S Mk I

Replacing a 20th-century icon when the E-Type was finally discontinued was always going to be a thankless task – and so it proved. Jaguar's replacement for its phenomenal sports car was a very different animal – the XJ-S Mk I. This 2+2 coupe was based on the XJ Saloon and was more of a luxurious grand tourer than out-and-out sports car, though a fuel-injected 5.3 litre V12 engine inherited from the E-Type ensured that the XJ-S had supercar performance.

Even so it never captured the public's affection as its predecessor had, perhaps because the styling was not to everyone's taste. Although it was a big car, the XJ-S was loosely designed along American ponycar lines – low and wide, with a long bonnet and short rear deck, divided by a fastback cabin. At first the XJ-S Mk I came with a manual gearbox option but that sporty choice was soon discontinued, leaving three-speed automatic transmission as standard.

The XJ-S may have been different from the E-Type, but it certainly delivered within its own terms of reference. Many now consider it to be the best GT of its generation, with superb ride quality and impeccable handling. The combination of strong performance and effortless refinement was seductive, and the XJ-S sold well.

Around 14,800 XJ-S Mk Is were built before the Mk II arrived in 1981, with its improved high-efficiency V12 and 3.6 litre straight six variant. The early cars went through hard times as they worked their way down the used-car pyramid from luxury grand tourer to expensive-to-run rust bucket. But the passage of time has been kind to perception of those that remain. Although still not as popular as the Mk II cars with their targa and convertible variations, early Mk Is are starting to be collected and restored as future classics.

COUNTRY OF ORIGIN:
UK
FIRST MANUFACTURED:
1975 (until 1980)
ENGINE:
5,344 cc V12
PERFORMANCE:
Top speed of 150 mph (240 km/h);
0-60 mph (97 km/h) in 6.9 secs
YOU SHOULD KNOW:
Responding to criticism that the XJ-S was a somewhat dull successor to the slender E-Type visually, Jaguar commissioned Pininfarina to design the Jaguar XJ Spider concept car, but never put this flamboyant machine into production.

Jensen-Healey

When the Austin Healey 3000 was discontinued, Kjell Qvale was disappointed. The entrepreneurial Californian had built up a massive business importing and selling British and European performance cars in the USA. As such he was an influential player, managing to persuade Donald Healey and Jensen Motors to design and build a sports car to fill the hole left by the late, lamented 3000.

The project was actioned and the result appeared in 1972. The Jensen-Healey was a traditional roadster, created with sourced components like running gear from the Vauxhall Firenza, Sunbeam Rapier transmission and front brakes that originated from the truly awful Morris Marina. The suspension was simple but effective – live rear axle with coils and trailing arms coupled with double wishbone and coil springs at the front. The car had drum brakes at the rear and discs up front. Interiors were functional.

After experimenting with various different engines, it was decided that the Jensen-Healey should use the brand-new Lotus 907, a DOHC 16-valve all-alloy motor. This was teamed with a four- or five-speed manual gearbox to deliver impressive performance – though as always the package had to be detuned to meet US emission control regulations. It was also an American requirement that unattractive rubber bumpers should be fitted (from 1974).

Kjell Qvale did his part, ensuring that the sporty Jensen-Healey sold well in the States. But all was not well on the home front. The 1973 oil crisis had virtually killed off the thirsty Jensen Interceptor, and the company scrambled to fill the void by developing the Jensen GT, a sporting estate-car version of the roadster. This was a terrific little speedster, but only a few hundred were made before Jensen folded in 1976, leaving behind a legacy of around 10,000 Jensen-Healey models to tempt future sports car collectors.

COUNTRY OF ORIGIN:
UK
FIRST MANUFACTURED:
1972 (until 1976)
ENGINE:
1,973 cc DOHC Straight Four
PERFORMANCE:
Top speed of 119 mph (192 km/h); 0-60 mph (97 km/h) in 7.8 secs
YOU SHOULD KNOW:
A factory-sponsored Jensen-Healey team went sports car racing in America during 1973 and 1974, winning the SCCA (Sports Car Club of America) D Production Championship in both years. But this commendable effort ended in 1975 ahead of Jensen Motors' collapse.

Poor build quality severely compromised Jensen-Healey's commercial prospects.

Lamborghini Countach

COUNTRY OF ORIGIN:
Italy
FIRST MANUFACTURED:
1974 (until 1989)
ENGINE:
3,929 cc, 4,754 cc or 5,167 cc V12
PERFORMANCE:
With 4.0 l engine – top speed of
175 mph (282 km/h); 0-60 mph
(97 km/h) in 5.6 secs
YOU SHOULD KNOW:
Ironically for a car that attracted
such admiring press coverage when
launched, rearward visibility from the
Countach's cabin was virtually nil,
the engine tended to overheat, the
windows only opened a few inches
and the car's aerodynamics were
lousy – and still everyone drooled
over it.

The words 'instant' and 'legend' can but rarely be combined when it comes to describing a new car's impact, but are truly justified in the case of the Lambo Countach's arrival in the world of exotic automobiles. Perhaps the reason was a persistent rumour that this was the fastest production car ever, or maybe it was the fact that this was the ultimate example of stylish Italian supercar design (and to hell with the practicalities).

Crafted by Marcello Gandini of Bertone, the LP500 prototype shown at the Geneva Motor Show in 1971 certainly contributed to the hype surrounding the extended run-up to the Countach's official launch in 1974. This extraordinary white machine was often pictured from behind and above, to emphasize the fact that it was more like a 23rd-century starfighter than a mere car. It pioneered the extreme wedge shape and cabin-forward approach that would soon become *de rigeur* for high-performance supercars.

But numerous detail changes were made before the prototype metamorphosed into the first production Countach LP 400, though the overall look and signature upward-opening cabin doors remained much the same. The 400 had the Miura's 4 litre V12 mounted longitudinally behind the driver, equipped with six Weber carburettors. The Countach had a lightweight aluminium skin over a racing-car style tubular space frame to keep the weight down.

In 1978 further tweaking gave the Countach LP 400S a rather more aggressive look with wheel arch extensions. There was an improved engine and the option of a rear spoiler that many thought ugly, but most buyers chose it anyway. A more powerful engine arrived in 1982, bedded in the LP 500S, shortly before the Countach 5000QV was launched with a 5.2 litre V12. The final evolution came in 1988 with the 25th Anniversary Countach, celebrating Lamborghini's first quarter century.

The Countach was not the most practical mode of transport, but that's not what supercars are all about.

Lamborghini Silhouette

Rare as hen's teeth? Sure is! If you find one of these in a Palladian shed at the bottom of someone's country estate, it will increase the number of Lamborghini Silhouettes known to exist from 31 to 32 (out of an original production run of just 54 cars). These two-door, two-seater coupes had a removable targa lid for those who liked the wind in their hair, making this the first Lambo open-top. It was a refined development of the not-very-good Lamborghini Urraco 2+2 coupe designed by Bertone to compete with Ferrari's Dino and the Porsche 911, produced throughout the 1970s.

Bertone also styled the Silhouette, which was an attempt to improve on the Urraco. The Silhouette had much softer lines than the angular Urraco and was altogether kinder on the eye. It also had revised suspension and a more powerful engine, making it lighter and faster. But the two models were so close in terms of what they offered the buying public that it hardly seems surprising that there was room for only one in the Lambo product range – if there is a surprise involved, it's that the Silhouette failed to displace the Urraco.

If the Silhouette failed, it was because the car had been created to target the US market, which required modifications like the fitting of a catalytic converter and various regulation requirements like plastic bumpers. This was a good car, but for good reasons (like poor build quality and the company's high-profile financial difficulties) American buyers regarded Lamborghini with suspicion and the project died. Still, all the effort that went into creating so few Silhouettes wasn't wasted – it contributed mightily to the altogether more successful Lamborghini Jalpa, launched in 1981 and destined for a seven-year run that would see over 400 units produced.

With the targa top removed, the rare Silhouette was the first Lambo that let the occupants enjoy the wind in their hair.

COUNTRY OF ORIGIN:
Italy
FIRST MANUFACTURED:
1976 (until 1979)
ENGINE:
2,996 cc V8
PERFORMANCE:
Top speed of 158 mph (255 km/h);
0-60 mph (97 km/h) in 7.6 secs
YOU SHOULD KNOW:
One concept car based on the Lamborghini Silhouette was built by Bertone and shown at the 1979 Geneva Motor Show – it was an elegant two-seater roadster that unfortunately never went into production.

Lancia Stratos HF

The Lancia Stratos HF (HF = High Fidelity) was developed for the purpose of rallying, and very successful this extraordinary machine proved to be. Lancia had enjoyed great success on the rally circuit during the 1960s, but the Fulvia coupe was starting to struggle and a new contender was required.

Happily, the recent takeover of Lancia by Fiat (who also bought a half share in Ferrari) provided the ideal opportunity to create something special. Bertone had presented a stunning Stratos Zero concept car based on the Fulvia at the 1970 Turin Motor Show, and this provided both a name and starting point for the new rally car that would be styled and built by Bertone. Out went Fulvia foundations and in came the midships drive train from Ferrari's Dino 246 GT. This was complemented with purpose-built independent suspension, crisp rack-and-pinion steering and disc brakes on all four wheels.

Around this potent mechanical package Bertone wrapped a short, wide coupe body with flared wheel arches, a louvered wedge of a bonnet and aircraft-style cockpit with wraparound glass – surely one of the most striking designs ever from the Grugliasco-based *carrozzeria*. No more than the 500-odd examples needed to homologate the Stratos HF for racing were built, and those that went for road use immediately acquired cult classic status. They made no concessions to private buyers, with strictly practical interiors and the edgy handling that made them fearsome rally cars.

The Stratos HF duly swept all before it, winning the World Rally Championship in 1974, 1975 and 1976, whilst also securing a notable consecutive three-timer in the prestigious Monte Carlo Rally from 1975. It would continue to win rallies in the hands of privateers into the 1980s, after Fiat pulled the factory plug in favour of its own-name Fiat 131 rally car.

COUNTRY OF ORIGIN:
Italy
FIRST MANUFACTURED:
1972 (until 1974)
ENGINE:
2,418 cc V6
PERFORMANCE:
Top speed of 143 mph (230 km/h);
0-60 mph (97 km/h) in 6 secs
YOU SHOULD KNOW:
One avid collector likes the Lancia Stratos so much that he has around a dozen of the original cars – and became professionally involved in the project to create a revival NewStratos that culminated in the debut of a brilliant concept car at the Geneva Motor Show in 2005.

Lancia Montecarlo

The takeover of Lancia by all-conquering Fiat led to some strange anomalies – one of which was undoubtedly the appearance of the Lancia Montecarlo in 1975. This mid-engined sports car came in two versions – a two-door coupe and a two-door convertible, the latter with an unusual roll-back targa-style top operated by hand.

The odd thing about the Montecarlo is that it was never intended to emerge from the Lancia stable. The car was Fiat's X1/8 development project, based on the prototype Abarth 030. It was always intended to be a larger version of the company's hugely successful small mid-engined X1/9 sports car (which actually retained its project tag after commercial production began). The Montecarlo had a much roomier interior than the cramped X1/9, plus larger engine and a slightly more conventional fastback coupe appearance, with a side-opening rear-access panel.

For some reason Fiat lost interest in the car, and passed it on to Lancia. Original design consultant Pininfarina was retained to refine the new model for production, and the Turin outfit also secured the contract to build the Montecarlo. The S1 version had faults – like a tendency for the front brakes to lock up in the wet – and this was sufficiently serious to see production suspended in 1978, although it returned in 1980 as the enhanced S2, which was in turn discontinued in 1981. In short, it was never a huge success, and perhaps vindicated Fiat's decision to step aside.

A turbocharged racing version of the Montecarlo did, however, compete successfully in Group 5 races in the early 1980s. The Montecarlo also served as the genesis for Lancia's splendid 037 Group B rally car, although in truth this used little more than the original centre section, and even then the engine was mounted longitudinally rather than horizontally as it had been mounted in the Montecarlo.

COUNTRY OF ORIGIN:
Italy
FIRST MANUFACTURED:
1975 (until 1981)
ENGINE:
1,995 cc Straight Four
PERFORMANCE:
Top speed of 118 mph (190 km/h); 0-60 mph (97 km/h) in 8.6 secs
YOU SHOULD KNOW:
There was a detuned and rebadged version of the Montecarlo made for export to the USA with a smaller 1.8 l engine – called the Lancia Scorpion, it was a feeble shadow of the European car and was sold only in 1976 and 1977 before being discontinued.

The Montecarlo proudly bore a Lancia badge but the car was actually a recycled Fiat project.

Leata

The car world has more than its fair share of eccentrics but few can compare with Don E Stinebaugh of Post Falls, Idaho. A man of many ideas (he patented all of 48 inventions) but little business acumen, he built himself a small fibreglass ATV which was much admired locally. The positive reaction from his neighbours encouraged him to set up the Stinebaugh Manufacturing Co to build bigger versions fit for the road. So the Leata (named after his wife) was born.

Stinebaugh bought in mechanical parts, mainly from Ford, had custom frames made for him by a racing-car builder, fitted a Ford Pinto 2.3 litre engine and commandeered his sons into helping him construct the hand-laid fibreglass body. But the Leata was no kit car; being put together with perfectionist zeal and professional skill to an original design that gave more than a passing nod to Stinebaugh's favourite car, the 1939 Lincoln Continental. This accounts for the Leata's peculiar anachronistic looks – a small two-seater based on old-fashioned big car styling which from a side-on view appears simply to have had the back hacked off. Athough undeniably cute and packing a frightening amount of power for its size, the Leata was ultimately a heroic failure.

Stinebaugh didn't bother to advertise. He reckoned that word of mouth would give him all the business he could handle at a production rate of one car a day, selling for under $3,000. In the event, he couldn't build more than a car a week and the price went up to $3,295 – several hundred dollars more than a four-seater Ford Pinto. The Leata was doomed, and less than 100 were built. But Don Stinebaugh was unbowed – he carried on investing in self-designed cars, and carried on losing money hand over fist.

Lotus Esprit

The long-running success story that was the Esprit started as a production spin-off from a concept car designed by Giorgetto Giugiaro. It was among the first of his renowned 'folded paper' cars, a clean-lined, sharp-angled wedge in the forefront of fashion. Colin Chapman, with the luxury supercar market in mind, immediately snapped up the design for Lotus. When the Esprit first appeared in 1976 it was somewhat disparagingly labelled a 'poor man's Ferrari' but it soon acquired snob appeal by appearing as James Bond's vehicle in *The Spy Who Loved Me* (1977) epitomising British seventies glamour – powerful, exclusive, stylish, and (not least) a lot more reliable than a Ferrari.

The Esprit S1 was a mid-engine, high-performance two-door coupe with a GRP (glass-reinforced plastic) body built on a steel backbone chassis, weighing in at less than 1000 kg (2200 lbs). Lotus used pre-existing parts to keep costs down and fitted a Lotus 907 lightweight alloy 2 litre engine with twin cams and 16 valves. From the start the car was praised for its superb handling, though there was the occasional gripe about insufficient power, especially in the USA where the engine was downrated to comply with emissions regulations.

Over the years, the Lotus Esprit went through several incarnations with a couple of major revamps. The body was restyled with rounder features in 1987 and was remodelled again in 1993, and throughout the 28 years of its production, continual mechanical improvements were made to enhance performance. All these tweakings have added to the original Giugiaro model's legendary status. The very last model was the 1999 Sport 350, which could do 0-60 mph (97 km/h) in less than 5 secs, but it is the 1976 Giugiaro S1 design that will be remembered as the iconic supercar of its era.

YOU SHOULD KNOW:
Altogether 10,675 Esprits were produced over the course of its 28-year run. Some models are extremely rare. To celebrate Lotus's success on the racetrack, an exclusive gold and black JPS (John Player Special) model was produced in a run of less than 150, and a mere 45 special red, blue and chrome 'Essex' versions of the 1980 turbocharged Esprit were made.

It's true, it's true – the great British Esprit proved that Italy didn't have a supercar monopoly.

Marcos Mantis M70

From its inception in 1959, Marcos had been associated with the race track rather than the road. The company's founders, engineers Jem Marsh and Frank Costin made a name for themselves among the racing fraternity by building cars that, although not always beautiful, performed outstandingly well. Costin's experience in the aero industry gave the company an edge in pioneering wooden-chassised unibody technology to produce remarkably powerful lightweight cars.

The first Mantis was built in 1968: a mid-engine racer that was a one-off. It was an apt name – the futuristic design was reminiscent of nothing so much as a giant predatory insect. After racing it only once, Jem Marsh fitted it with a new engine suitable for road use before selling it in the USA. But the name was too good to waste on a single car that had disappeared to the other side of the Atlantic so when Marcos decided to branch out into mainstream car manufacture with its 2+2 road tourer, the 'Mantis' label was recycled. The Mantis M70 was unveiled at the 1970 Earl's Court Motor Show to be met with gaping stares. Nobody knew quite what to make of its startlingly brazen design – a fantastical long-nosed monster built in GRP and fitted with a Triumph TR6 fuel-injected engine.

Who knows whether the Mantis would have been a triumphant success under different circumstances but Marcos was plagued by production problems and financial difficulties which led to the company's collapse after only 32 of these amazing sports coupes had been built. The Mantis M70 was the only four-seater car that Marcos produced. If you even glimpse one you're lucky, and if by some amazing good fortune you get a chance to have a go in it, grab the opportunity for the rarity value alone.

COUNTRY OF ORIGIN:
UK
FIRST MANUFACTURED:
1970 (until 1971)
ENGINE:
2,498 cc Straight Six
PERFORMANCE:
Top speed of 120 mph (193 km/h);
0-60 mph (97 km/h) in 8 secs
YOU SHOULD KNOW:
Over the years the Marcos company was beset with financial difficulties and after two relaunches it finally folded for good in 2007.

308

Maserati Bora (Tipo 117)

After the runaway success of the Ghibli, in order to stay ahead in the game, Maserati set its sights on the production of a mid-engined sports car. Chief engineer Giulio Alfieri was over the moon – he had long dreamed of building an RMR-layout road car and here was his chance. Giugiaro, designer of the Ghibli, was asked to style a two-seater that would be 'innovative but not revolutionary'. Between the two of them, they came up with a masterpiece.

The Tipo 117 was a steel monocoque with independent, all-round coil spring suspension and anti-roll bars. Alfieri used a 4.7 litre quad cam V8 engine, positioning it just in front of the rear axle and linking it to transaxle transmission in-line behind, containing the whole in a tubular steel sub-frame. Production conveniently coincided with Citroen's takeover of Maserati, giving the design team access to Citroen hydraulics technology, which they incorporated into the car's gadgetry with gay abandon: hydraulic pop-up headlights, hydraulic disc brakes, a steering wheel that hydraulically tilted and telescoped and – for the first time on a road car – a hydraulic pedal box. Instead of the driver having the bother of adjusting the seat into position, the pedals automatically slid back or forward to engage comfortably with the foot. Visually the car was a stunner. Giugiaro's *tour de force* was to give definition to the roof and A-pillars by making them of brushed stainless steel.

The Tipo 117 was eventually called Bora – the name given to a powerful wind that gusts down the Adriatic coast; it certainly blew away the spectators at the 1971 Geneva Motor Show. It had everything that the public had come to expect from Maserati: style, solidity, reliability, comfort and effortless speed. It was the ultimate in Maserati road cars.

COUNTRY OF ORIGIN:
Italy
FIRST MANUFACTURED:
1971 (until 1979)
ENGINE:
4,719 cc V8
PERFORMANCE:
Top speed of 170 mph (273 km/h); 0-60 mph (97 km/h) in 6.5 secs
YOU SHOULD KNOW:
The Maserati 4.7 l engine was not homologated in the USA so a slightly larger 4.9 l engine (which met with emissions requirements) was fitted on export models to America and later became standard. Altogether, 524 Boras were built of which 289 were 4.7 l versions.

Maserati put everything they knew into creating the Bora, the company's ultimate road car.

Maserati Khamsin

COUNTRY OF ORIGIN:
Italy
FIRST MANUFACTURED:
1974 (until 1982)
ENGINE:
4,930 cc V8
PERFORMANCE:
Top speed of 160 mph (258 km/h);
0-60 mph (97km/h) in 5.6 secs
YOU SHOULD KNOW:
Like the Ghibli and Bora before it, the
Khamsin is named after a
Mediterranean wind. (The word
khamsin comes from 'fifty' in Arabic.
The wind blows from the Sahara for
50 days).

At last, even if not by intention, a woman's supercar – a high-powered car that didn't need the strength of Hercules to handle it. It can take real brawn to operate the hefty clutch in a high-performance car because the pressure needed increases directly in relation to torque; but, thanks to Citroen hydraulics, the Khamsin's clutch could be engaged with the lightest of touches. The rack-and-pinion steering was also power-assisted (using the same recently developed DIRAVI system that was in Citroen's flagship SM model). All this hydraulic help ensured that the Khamsin was eminently handleable by any competent driver.

Styled by Marcello Gandini at Gruppo Bertone, the Khamsin was an exceptionally low, long-nosed unibodied steel wedge with crisp lines and Gandini's trademark asymmetric bonnet vents. The back panel below the rear window was glass (a repeat of Gandini's design for the Lamborghini Espada) which gave unusually good reverse visibility. The engine was the same 4.9 litre quad cam V8 as some Bora models but this time it was front-mounted. The only slight niggle in the design is that although the Khamsin is notionally a 2+2 GT coupe, in reality back passengers are squashed into an unrealistically narrow, cramped perch.

Like all Maseratis, the Khamsin is a sensational drive. The exhaust emits a knee-trembling roar as you take off from standstill to 100 mph (161 km/h) in less than 14 secs, and you could (if it were legal) cruise quite happily at 140 mph (225 km/h) without feeling remotely out of control. But just as the Khamsin went into production the oil crisis hit Europe, threatening to bring Maserati juddering to a halt and precipitately ending the vogue for supercars. Only 421 of these exquisite machines were ever built and they are beginning to be regarded as highly desirable collectors' cars.

The Khamsin was very fast, but easier to drive than most 'supers'.

Mazda RX-7

The oil crisis of the early 1970s nearly put Mazda out of business. The Wankel rotary engine which had been such a success in the Cosmo may have been renowned for its smoothness but certainly wasn't for its fuel economy. Although theoretically the company was totally committed to the Wankel, in practice the only way it was going to sell cars during a fuel shortage was by producing conventional piston-engined ones. Plans for a rotary-engined sports car had to be shelved. But they were not entirely jettisoned; as soon as oil started to flow again, Mazda introduced the fabulous RX-7, a car that was so successful it went through three generations and eight series.

The RX-7 was designed to be an affordable sports car, which meant making do with second-best: drum brakes instead of discs; recirculating ball steering rather than the more expensive rack-and-pinion. But, despite this parsimony, the RX-7 became the best-selling rotary-engined car of all time (getting on for half a million of the first generation alone) and in later series the penny-pinching mechanics were rectified. The FMR layout – a compact, lightweight twin-rotor Wankel front-mounted but set behind the front axle so that the car's centre of mass was positioned for optimum stability and rear-wheel drive so that the load was balanced – made for exceptionally safe and easy handling. The smoothness of the rotary engine eliminated juddering giving such an effortless glide at high revs that a warning buzzer was fitted at the tachometer's red line.

People loved the RX-7. Even though it might not have been the fastest sports coupe in the world, it was a really neat car with superb braking and acceleration – just the job for roller-coastering along mountain roads.

The RX-7 continued Mazda's passionate and long-lasting love affair with the rotary engine.

COUNTRY OF ORIGIN:
Japan
FIRST MANUFACTURED:
1978 (until 2002)
ENGINE:
1,146 cc Rotary (Wankel 12A)
PERFORMANCE:
Top speed of 125 mph (201 km/h);
0-60 mph (97 km/h) in 9.2 secs
YOU SHOULD KNOW:
The RX-7 won a place in the 'ten best' list of *Car and Driver* magazine five times.

The SLC fixed hardtop two-door coupe was slightly longer than the two-seater SL roadster.

Mercedes-Benz R107 SLC

The official Mercedes codename for its 1970s *Sports Leicht* was 'R107' but in the trade it was nicknamed the *Panzerwagen* because, although somewhat lighter than a tank, it weighed around 1,550 kg (3,400 lbs) – 140 kg (300 lbs) more than the 1960s Pagoda 230SL. It was only marginally lower, longer and wider than the Pagoda but its sophisticated Bruno Sacco styling gave the illusion of an altogether broader car. The R107 was a success right from the start and can still claim to be the longest-running of all Mercedes-Benz car series (not including the G-Wagen).

The R107 came in two versions: the SL two-seater roadster with optional attachable hard roof, and the slightly longer SLC, a fixed hardtop two-door coupe with small but functional rear seats. Mercedes used the chassis from their mid-size W114 first with the 2.8 litre straight six engine from the Pagoda and then the new S-class sedan's fuel-injected 3.5 litre V8 (except in North America where it had a larger 4.5 litre V8 engine yet, confusingly, was still designated 350).

In 1973 the 4.5 litre V8 engine was made available everywhere (and the model numbering was rationalized). To attempt to follow the numerous minor modifications, different engine sizes and model designations over the years is to wade through a mire of Teutonic complexity. Suffice it to say that the SLC was offered as an alternative to the SL only for the first ten years of the R107's 18 year run.

The SLC is the only fixed-roof Mercedes coupe to have stemmed from a roadster not a sedan. As soon as you drive one you can see why it was so successful. Although not renowned for its agility, its solidness and ease of handling wrap you in a protective comfort zone that inspires absolute confidence.

COUNTRY OF ORIGIN:
Germany
FIRST MANUFACTURED:
1972 (until 1981)
ENGINE:
2,746 cc Straight Six; 3,499 cc, 3,818 cc, 4,520 cc or 4,973 cc V8
PERFORMANCE:
With 2.8 l engine – top speed of 129 mph (207 km/h)
YOU SHOULD KNOW:
The last R107 ever made was a silver 500SL. You can see it in the Mercedes-Benz museum, Stuttgart.

Mercedes-Benz G Class W460

If you're thinking of driving into a war zone, the *Geländewagen* (rough terrain wagon) is just what you're after. It owes its distinctly military appearance to its origins as an army car. Supposedly, the G Class emerged out of a proposal from the Shah of Iran, who wanted a military vehicle (maybe because he was having a dicey time as absolute ruler). Production facilities were set up in Graz in collaboration with the Austrian firm Steyr-Daimler-Puch and G-Wagens were (and still are) assembled largely by hand, produced to order for military-equipment purchasers. Over the past 30 years countless custom versions have been produced for high-profile clients. Even the 'Popemobile' has sometimes been a G-Wagen in disguise.

From 1979, Mercedes started to manufacture the G-Wagen as a sturdy SUV for off-road enthusiasts. The first version, the W460 was rear-wheel drive with a manual selector for switching to 4WD when the going got rough. It had either manual or automatic transmission and four engine variants, ranging from 72 to 156 hp. It came as a short wheelbase convertible or a short or long wheelbase (two-door or four-door) wagon and either petrol or diesel powered.

More than 50,000 were built in the first ten years and in 1983 a G-Wagen won the gruelling Paris to Dakar rally. However, its military aura ensured that the G-Wagen never succeeded in joining the ranks of luxury 4x4s. Although you feel pretty all-powerful at the wheel, in much the same way as you would if you were driving a tank, and it has an efficient German ruthlessness about it, the G-Wagen couldn't be described as a car of character, and it lacks a certain oomph. Having said that, there's nothing quite like it for transporting you across desert and mountain (or muscling your way along crowded roads) unhindered.

COUNTRY OF ORIGIN:
Germany
FIRST MANUFACTURED:
1979 (until 1991) (First generation)
ENGINE:
Petrol – 2,307 cc Straight Four or
(from 1982) 2,299 cc Straight Four,
2,996 cc Straight Six
Diesel – 2,399 cc Straight Four or
(from 1987) 2,497 cc Straight Five,
2,998 cc Straight Five
PERFORMANCE:
Top speed of 85 mph (136 km/h) to
97 mph (155 km/h)
YOU SHOULD KNOW:
There have been three G-Wagen models for the general market: the W460 (1979–91); the W461 (1991–2001), almost identical to its predecessor but with fewer engine choices (and from 1997 only as a 290 turbo diesel automatic); the W463 (1990–) with a wide choice of engines and transmission, heavy-duty suspension and full-time 4WD.

The sturdy G-Wagen is the longest running Mercedes series.

Panther de Ville

COUNTRY OF ORIGIN:
UK
FIRST MANUFACTURED:
1974 (until 1984)
ENGINE:
4,235 cc Straight Six or 5,343 cc V12
PERFORMANCE:
Top speed of 150 mph (241 km/h);
0-60 mph (97 km/h) in 6.5 secs
YOU SHOULD KNOW:
The Panther de Ville was – naturally –
the transport of choice of Cruella de
Vil (played by Glenn Close) in
Disney's films *101 Dalmatians* and
102 Dalmatians.

The growing 1970s trend for replicas was largely confined to smaller kit or factory-built sports cars, until the English manufacturer Panther Westwinds set a new trend for powerful, luxury automobiles styled on the panache of the 'Golden Age' of the 1930s. Panther's first car was the J72, a replica of Jaguar's SS100. Its phenomenal success persuaded Panther to attempt something even more spectacular. The Panther de Ville four-door saloon of 1974 was a glorious whiff of a 1930 Bugatti Royale. It was no imitation – but the de Ville gave a brilliant impression of a Bugatti, with the long sweep of its wings and running boards culminating in an imposing arch of a front grille, enormous headlights, and a sporty tilt to the windscreen. Only the design of its two-tone paintwork was actually copied from Bugatti. What you can't see immediately is the Jaguar underneath that made the Panther de Ville so easy to drive, so quick, and such fun. The giant wheelbase carried Jaguar suspension, power steering and automatic transmission, and a choice of either 4.2 litre or 5.3 litre engine. Hawk-eyed car buffs will also notice that the doors come from an Austin Maxi (BMC 1800).

If it was cobbled together, the Panther de Ville was meticulously hand-crafted to the highest standard. The interiors went beyond lavish to theatrical, with walnut and silver-appointed bars (including ice-maker) and TV, and a catalogue of refinements that encapsulated the ostentation of the era. Its opulence was worthy of an emperor (it was bought by Sir Elton John among others); yet it had a rakish, dangerous splendour like its Bugatti inspiration. Only 60 were made, including seven two-seat convertibles – and just one, six-door, turbo-charged, pink and gold limousine, festooned with headlights. Nicknamed 'The Golden Eagle', it was made for a Malaysian prince.

Panther hoped to create a niche market for the de Ville but only 60 were ever made.

Plymouth Duster 340

The US motor corporations' 1960s philosophy of 'planned obsolescence' meant that every one of them felt compelled to challenge every model of every series produced by a rival. Intense competition combined with rapid technical evolution often led to 'junkyard styling' – creating a 'brand new' car out of existing, disparate components. The Plymouth Duster is proof that it could work, and brilliantly. With no money for a sporty, two-door compact to replace the Barracuda (the performance version of a Plymouth Valiant now elevated to a series of its own) Plymouth took the Valiant A-body platform, re-styled the rear as a semi-fastback, dropped in a hot, 340 cu in LA-series V8 – long proven for its power and reliability in Darts and early Barracudas – and hit their market bullseye.

The Plymouth Duster 340 made real muscle available to the masses. Lighter, more spacious and faster than much more expensive cars, the 340 was the performance leader of the Duster range, all of which shared its characteristics in proportion to their engine option. Plymouth's 'Rapid Transit System' allotted it the full armoury of performance enhancers at little extra cost – but apart from a pistol-grip for the four-speed manual option, dual exhausts and some discreet decals, there was nothing obvious to advertise the Duster 340's blazing capability.

You just had to drive one. The suspension was a little stiff, the ride punishing, and the economy trim devoid of excess comfort. On the other hand, it rode corners with contempt, and powered away with a throaty snarl. Even years later, when high speeds were curbed by the emissions rules, the 1970 Duster 340 still gave you more bang for your buck than its dozens of 'editions' or imitators from other companies. Quite probably, it was the most successful big 'something' ever to come from nothing at all.

COUNTRY OF ORIGIN:
USA
FIRST MANUFACTURED:
1970 (until 1976)
ENGINE:
5.6 l (340 cid) OHV V8
PERFORMANCE:
Top speed of 127 mph (205 km/h);
0-60 mph (97 km/h) in 6.2 secs
YOU SHOULD KNOW:
The name 'Duster' was intended (allegedly) to suggest the 'dust' you left in your speedy wake. Even more questionable monikers were given to subsequent versions, including the 'Twister' (it was: it looked exactly like a dolled-up 340, without the powerful 340 engine), the 'Space Duster' and the 'Feather Duster'.

The Duster was capable of wiping up muscle-car rivals.

The 'Cuda was the ultimate muscle car and good examples fetch megabucks today.

Plymouth Hemi 'Cuda

In 1970, Chrysler launched the third generation of its Plymouth Barracuda. Originally developed from the Plymouth Valiant to challenge Ford's success with the Mustang, the 1970 Barracuda finally got its own platform and exclusive styling. It had Chrysler's new, wider and slightly shorter E-body. It was a frame for a pugnacious automotive warrior, but only two-door coupes and convertibles were made available, in standard and luxury (Gran Coupe) versions, and a high-performance version was marketed separately as the Plymouth 'Cuda. Until 1970 the limitations of the A-body had prevented Chrysler exploiting the dramatic power potential of some of its big block engines and, although in 1968–9 the company had put its 7 litre Hemi into 50 fastback Barracudas, the cars were restricted to Super Stock drag racing – 0.25 mi (0.4 km) in just over 10 secs! The E-body had a bigger engine bay; for the first time, Chrysler could use the big-block Hemi in a street legal vehicle – the 1970 Plymouth Hemi 'Cuda.

True to its deceptively relaxed styling, the Hemi 'Cuda is no screaming racer. It powers up like an aircraft: you baby it through an accelerating glide to about 50 mph (80 km/h), floor the pedal so the featured 'Torqueflite' drops into second gear and the carburettors open, and take off with the effortless pull of a jet liner. Innocuous apart from the ominous 'shaker hood', the Hemi 'Cuda's styling belies this thrilling capacity to 'haul ass and burn rubber'.

Much admired at the time, the 1970 Plymouth Hemi 'Cuda is now legendary as a prince of American muscle cars. It lasted only two years before Federal emissions controls killed big block engines and tamed the beast. Just 652 Hemi 'Cudas were made for 1970; and a mere 14 Hemi 'Cuda convertibles. Surviving examples change hands for millions of dollars.

COUNTRY OF ORIGIN:
USA
FIRST MANUFACTURED:
1970 (until 1971)
ENGINE:
7.0 l (426 cid) OHV V8
PERFORMANCE:
Top speed of 117 mph (188 km/h);
0-60 mph (97 km/h) in 5.8 secs
YOU SHOULD KNOW:
1970-71 Plymouth Hemi 'Cudas are so rare and valuable that it's not unusual for very cleverly disguised clones to be offered for sale. *Caveat emptor* – you'll need to look well beyond 'obviously' matching parts' serial numbers.

Pontiac Firebird Trans Am

It was John Z. DeLorean who had brought the Firebird to the American public in 1967. Super-sensitive to the steady clamour for muscle cars, his vision extended to fostering the Firebird's Trans Am performance version – but no sooner had its teething problems been solved for the launch of the Trans Am's second generation (known as the 1970-1/2 model), than the new Federal emissions regulations drew the fangs of every muscle monster on US highways. Pontiac's mega-punchy Super Duty 455 V8 engine, intended for the 1973 Trans Am, was a damp squib. Although it was constructed so that it could easily be converted for high-performance racing, its massive power was de-tuned to a street-legal whimper. Pontiac decided to kill it for 1975 – the year they re-drew the Trans Am's speedometer dial to show a maximum speed of just 100 mph (160 km/h) instead of its previous, 'Oh-my-lord!' 160 mph (258 km/h). The 1975 Firebird Trans Am arrived as a glorious, snarling, but apparently emasculated thug: the enormous firebird decal splashed across the hood was known as the 'Screamin' Chicken'.

Everyone wanted one. By 1975 it was the last muscle car around. Its engine options, the standard 400 V8 and the big block 455 V8 (re-introduced in the mid-year as the 'HO455', as carried by the sedate Pontiac Bonneville, but a big block just the same), were authentic, and so was every other potentially racing component. Pontiac contributed by improving visibility and handling. If they couldn't sell it as a rocket, they could and did make sure that within the legal limits the Trans Am was the last remaining tiger, poised, lethally quick at low speeds, and joyous to drive.

The 1975 Trans Am has been called the 'Soul Survivor' of the 'Big Cube Birds'. Treasure it – it's the real deal.

COUNTRY OF ORIGIN:
USA
FIRST MANUFACTURED:
Second Generation 1970 (until 1981)
ENGINE:
7.5 l (455 cid) V8 (with catalytic converter)
PERFORMANCE:
Top speed around 120 mph (193 km/h) according to engine tuning; 0-60 mph (97 km/h) in 7.8 secs
YOU SHOULD KNOW:
The Firebird Trans Am is most famous in the black and gold livery of the 1976 Limited Edition. It had gold Honeycomb wheels, grille, steering wheel spokes, body stripes and badging. A very few also had black chrome exhaust tips, and are relatively very valuable. Rising prices mean you now have to beware of clones for these and for all Firebird Trans Ams of the period.

The 'Screamin' Chicken' was the last muscle car on the block.

Porsche 911 Turbo

COUNTRY OF ORIGIN:
Germany
FIRST MANUFACTURED:
1975 (until 1989)
ENGINE:
2,993 cc Flat Six Turbo
PERFORMANCE:
Top speed of 153 mph (246 km/h);
0-60 mph (97 km/h) in 5.2 secs
YOU SHOULD KNOW:
Following the unforeseen success of the Porsche 911 Turbo, every subsequent 911 generation has featured a turbocharged version distinguished by its roadgoing modifications of authentic race car technology

The first production turbocharged Porsche 911 (known as the Porsche 930 in America) made its debut at the Paris Motor Show in 1974. It was Germany's fastest road-going sports car.

Though turbochargers had long been used in motor sport, the 911 Turbo was the first production car to tame the beast. Its genesis was almost accidental. Porsche disbelieved its own ability to sell the 400 GT sports cars it was required to produce for GT racing accreditation. There weren't 400 racing drivers to buy them. Instead, the company installed creature comforts and safety measures well beyond the demands of street legality, and aimed at a production run of 1000. Even after a decade of the 911, the new Turbo made experienced Porsche enthusiasts gasp. Every aspect of the technical and design expertise the company had gleaned from its successes in motor sport had been put to good use.

The 911 Turbo body-shape was totally distinctive. The wheel arches were flared to fit the wider tyres; and the rear spoiler was so unfeasibly big it became known as the 'whale tail' (in the early models – when it was later shrunk, the nickname changed to 'tea-tray'). If you learned to manage the alarming turbo lag, and to control the quite stupendous transfer of power from the wheels to the road, the acceleration was moon-shot exhilarating. The car satisfied the new US regulations on emissions and impact bumpers, but seemed to defy them by opposing convention. Other cars got heavier and slower. The Porsche 911 Turbo used the new minimum weight for GT racers as a convenient guide, and produced power not just to compensate, but to take flight. For a 3 litre engine, its performance stretched credulity – and driving it is one of the greatest thrills you can have outside an aircraft.

The 911 Turbo was all about power and drivng pleasure.

Porsche 924

With the 924 – much to the company's surprise – Porsche discovered that front-engined cars can actually work well.

After Volkswagen cancelled its contract to design 'something' from available VW spare parts, Porsche bought back the rights in 1976 and produced the car anyway – making VW assemble it at the Neckarsulm Audi factory. The Porsche 924 was a perfectly adequate, upmarket sports coupe, with components refined or modified from the Audi 100 and VW's Golf, Scirocco and Super-Beetle. Tweaking the interior trim and any number of less visible changes failed to make it a 'proper' Porsche, and the company rapidly introduced a number of versions to help them establish the parameters of what was for them an unfamiliar market. The Martini Edition (1977), the Limited Edition (1978), the Sebring Edition (1979) and constant upgrades of brakes, springs, torsion bars, shocks, swaybars and engine power, in conjunction with increasing attention to comfort and luxury, gradually won the 924 respect worthy of its parental name.

For Porsche, the 924 was a radical leap into the unknown. It was the company's first front-engined car, and their first to have no racing antecedents. But it was a bridge to a whole new – and initially reluctant – market. When international success did come in 1977, the 924 achieved another, linguistic, first. Porsche wasn't used to being praised for 'neutral balance', 'poised steering' or 'sweet gearchange' by sources which considered moderation to be admirable. The 924 needed a touch of the fierce glamour surrounding its stablemates. Porsche made their point by revamping the 924's Audi 100 engine by hand at their own factory, and launching the 924 Turbo in 1979 as final proof of the car's familial worthiness. The 924 Carrera GT followed on its heels, burying conclusively the notion that the 924 was 'too soft' to be a Porsche. Since its inception, each generation of the standard car has proved the best entry-level Porsche drive you can get.

COUNTRY OF ORIGIN:
Germany
FIRST MANUFACTURED:
1976 (until 1985)
ENGINE:
1,984 cc Straight Four
PERFORMANCE:
Top speed of 142 mph (229 km/h);
0-60 mph (97 km/h) in 7.7 secs
YOU SHOULD KNOW:
The stock 924 of 1976/7 is now celebrated as a true sports car that responds well to being driven hard. While some people sneered at its hybrid status, the Porsche 924 proved nothing so much as 'nothing destroys a good status symbol like affordability'.

The 928 was built over nearly two decades and offered owners luxurious grand touring combined with outstanding performance.

Porsche 928

If any model deserves to be placed at the top of the Porsche range, it is the Porsche 928. As explosive as anything and as much fun as the 911, the big, luxury grand tourer does it all, but with grace and subtlety as permanent options.

Its very existence was challenged by the oil crisis of the mid-1970s, and its design programme threatened by Ralph Nader's invective about the safety of rear-engined cars (Nader's book Unsafe At Any Speed was highly influential among US politicians). Porsche's only experience with anything else was restricted to the Porsche 924, but that was enough to set Porsche engineers on an experimental path of such rigorous testing that the outcome could only be all or nothing. The 928 launched with a big front-mounted, water-cooled V8 driving the rear wheels, and an astounding 50:50 weight distribution that made featherlight handling of its capacious 2+2 interior. Jaws dropped at the 1977 Geneva motor show prototype, and the Porsche 928 was voted European Car of the Year for 1978. It remains the only sports car to have won the accolade.

The fabulous body shape sat low and broad on all sorts of technical innovations. Apart from the aluminium engine block and heads, the Weissach axle was a revolutionary design that reduced oversteer by involving the rear suspension in self-adjustment during cornering. It was adapted for use across the whole Porsche range, and eventually Porsche created a special 928 Weissach edition of 205 cars painted 'champagne gold' and with matching brushed gold alloy wheels (and a hugely coveted, exclusive three-piece Porsche luggage set).

The Porsche 928 was born as crown prince to an automotive aristocracy. From the start, and through all its many editions, its speed, acceleration and compliance earned the car its star ranking.

COUNTRY OF ORIGIN:
Germany
FIRST MANUFACTURED:
1978 (until 1995)
ENGINE:
4,474 cc V8
PERFORMANCE:
Top speed in range of 138-171 mph (221-275 km/h); 0-60 mph (97 km/h) in range 5.1-7.7 secs
YOU SHOULD KNOW:
The Porsche 928 is also known as the 'Land Shark' (because it gobbles up road miles with smooth amiability). It features the world's longest timing belt (toothed, Gilmer-type) in a production vehicle. Laid out, it measures 2.1 m (7 ft).

Range Rover Classic

If ever there was an accidental success story it's that of the Range Rover Classic. It was introduced in 1970 for the English county set, in the belief that a robust four-wheel drive vehicle that was more comfortable than the utilitarian Land Rover would go down well with those who rode horses, shot birds, hunted, attended agricultural shows and were always surrounded by wet dogs. As such, the first Range Rovers had vinyl seats and plastic dashboards that could be hosed down after green wellies tramped mud into the car.

Early two-door Range Rovers were built to deliver real cross-country ability. They had permanent four-wheel drive with low range for off-road work. Rover's V8 petrol engine was teamed with a four-speed manual gearbox. Advanced independent suspension offered coil springs all round with disc brakes front and back. To British Leyland's credit, they soon realized their new rural transport was appealing to a wider market, meeting the dual requirement of looking good and operating well both on and off the road.

This would mark the start of enhancement and uprating that would last for decades, resulting in the creation of the ultimate luxury SUV that European manufacturers like BMW, Volkswagen and Porsche eventually felt they had to challenge with their own awesome off-roaders primarily intended for imposing road use by wealthy drivers.

During the 1970s the Range Rover saw refinements like power steering introduced, but it was not until the early 1980s that significant change happened – including a four-door body and automatic transmission option. There were further style tweaks in the 1980s, plus innovations like the availability of diesel engines. A luxurious Vogue special edition was offered from 1983, and a stretched LSE model appeared in 1992. After 25 great years, second generation cars finally superseded the Range Rover Classic in 1996.

COUNTRY OF ORIGIN:
UK
FIRST MANUFACTURED:
1970 (until 1996) (First generation)
ENGINE:
3,532 cc, 3,947 cc or 4,197 cc V8;
2,393 cc or 2,499 cc Straight Four
Diesel; 2,495 cc Straight Four
Turbo-Diesel
PERFORMANCE:
With 3.5 l engine – top speed
of 96 mph (154 km/h); 0-50 mph
(80 km/h) in 11.1 secs
YOU SHOULD KNOW:
The series name was devised with
the benefit of hindsight – Range
Rover Classic was the tag used for
first generation cars that briefly
continued to be built alongside
second generation cars in the 1990s,
and Rover liked the name so much it
retro-fitted the 'Classic' designation
to all first generation Range Rovers.

The Range Rover soon moved from the county set's favourite mode of transport to a more cosmopolitan appeal.

Reliant Bond Bug

COUNTRY OF ORIGIN:
UK
FIRST MANUFACTURED:
1970 (until 1974)
ENGINE:
701 cc OHV Straight Four
PERFORMANCE:
Top speed of 75 mph (121 km/h)
YOU SHOULD KNOW:
When a new 750 cc Reliant Robin was launched in 1973, the Bond Bug 700s were dropped in favour of 750 E and ES versions. Apart from the larger engine, these were more or less identical to the earlier models. It is estimated that there are fewer than 900 Bond Bugs of any sort still in existence.

Plastic, orange and short of a wheel – but at least drivers didn't need a full car licence.

The Reliant Robin, Regal and Rialto three-wheeler cars have a certain air of eccentricity, a peculiarly British charm that is inextricably linked with 'characters' like Mr Bean, or Del Boy in the TV series *Only Fools and Horses*. Reliant was keen to dissociate three-wheelers from this rather whimsical image and wanted to promote them instead as sporty, fun cars for the young. With this in mind, the company commissioned Tom Karen of Ogle Design to work on a prototype. When, in 1969, Reliant took over its rival, the Bond Motor Co, it immediately stopped production of Bond cars and used the Bond factory solely to manufacture its own Ogle car. Although the Ogle was soon moved to Reliant's own workshops, the company marketed its new model under the Bond name.

The Bond Bug was a triangular fibreglass wedge built on a modified Reliant Regal chassis with the same mechanics and 0.7 litre part alloy engine. Instead of doors, the top of the car (including the side frames) was a hinged overhead canopy for people to climb in and out like pilots. The Bug came in three versions: the 700 – a very basic model without sidescreens; the 700E, which made slightly more concessions to comfort; and the 700 ES, a de luxe version with a higher compression engine, racing steering wheel, mud flaps and wing mirrors, and the generous inclusion of a spare wheel. In terms of power, the Bug matched a small four-wheeler but it was pricier than the Mini, which meant it was bound to fail. Only 2,268 Bugs were built (all painted a virulent shade of tangerine except for the six white versions that were made as a special promotion for Rothman's cigarettes). Unsurprisingly, this quirky little car now has a fanatical following and is much sought after.

Renault-Alpine A310 V6

Renault's close association with Alpine was rooted in a shared racing philosophy. Until 1971 the collaboration was restricted to nimble, rear-engined coupes that broke easily and lacked both space and comfort. They were terrific for racing or rallying, but not a lot of fun for normal driving. The advent of the Alpine-Renault A310 in 1971 changed the perception of both companies, and the driving public. It was longer, wider, and roomier than its predecessors, though still conceived to the same Alpine-Renault formula of a rear-mounted engine set into a steel skeleton chassis and a separate fibreglass body. It was also faster, but unreliable. Only in 1976, when Renault had bought Alpine outright to redeem the company from financial catastrophe, did the A310 fulfil its destiny. With its new, 90-degree V6 engine, it became the only serious challenger to the Porsche 911 as the fastest rear-engine production car in the world.

It looked the part. A single aerodynamic line swept up and over from the front windscreen – but every curve was bitten off by a geometrically-severe, angular ridge. The A310 V6 needed its new, little black rear spoiler to control its new capability; and with the wheel rims newly-styled to look like the old, four-inch, reel-to-reel tape drums, it resembled a mobile, flattened bullet. Inside it retained Alpine's excellent driving position, but Renault now added a wholly unexpected level of comfort. It had grown up in every way, and it sold.

The A310 V6 soaked up punishment and it was reliable, but it was still a relatively lightweight, rear-engined sports car with every reason to fishtail when pedal hit metal. That, and Guy Frequelin's victory in the 1977 French Rallye, made it specially attractive to a younger and mostly male generation. The car's acceleration might snap your neck, but it was enormous fun.

Ambitious but true – the A310 V6 challenged the Porsche 911 as the fastest rear-engined car.

COUNTRY OF ORIGIN:
France
FIRST MANUFACTURED:
1976 (until 1984)
ENGINE:
2,664 cc V6
PERFORMANCE:
Top speed of 137 mph (221 km/h);
0-60 mph (97 km/h) in 7.5 secs
YOU SHOULD KNOW:
The A310's V6 engine was a joint development between Peugeot, Renault and Volvo. Throughout the late 1970s and 1980s it powered dozens of different marques and models, including the DeLorean.

Rolls-Royce Corniche

COUNTRY OF ORIGIN:
UK
FIRST MANUFACTURED:
1971 (until 1982 Coupe);
(until 1987 Convertible)
ENGINE:
6,750 cc V8
PERFORMANCE:
Top speed of 125 mph (201 km/h);
0-60 mph (97 km/h) in 10.2 secs
YOU SHOULD KNOW:
When Rolls-Royce first experimented
with what would become the
Corniche, the celebrated
coachbuilder James Young designed
his own version alongside that of
MPW. It never went into production,
and the few Rollers made to Young's
imaginative genius are among the
rarest of the rare.

The Corniche had a late baptism in 1971. The monocoque construction of the 1965 Silver Shadow range made it virtually impossible for traditional coachbuilders to practice their calling: there was no separate chassis on which to fit panel work. Rolls-Royce faced the problem by increasing their stake in Mulliner Park Ward (MPW), already their in-house specialist partner, in order to develop a two-door coupe (1966) and two-door convertible (1967) based on the Silver Shadow. By 1971, with Rolls-Royce in the throes of splitting the company into separate divisions to solve a financial crisis, the time was ripe for the publicity splash of a new model. Both coupe and convertible were revamped and powered up, and launched as the Rolls-Royce (and, of course, Bentley) Corniche.

MPW learned how to press panels and weld them to the Silver Shadow floor-pan. After technical assembly by Rolls-Royce in Crewe, which included the major modifications that justified the Corniche as an independent series, MPW completed the cars back in London. The hand-built quality showed, even if the 1971 'production' car didn't look very different. The sumptuous luxury extended to the finest detail, like the power-operated soft top which, alone, took as long as two weeks to make, fit and adjust.The bodyline still had the dip over the rear wheel arch that suggested the sporty monster sitting, poised on its athletic haunches.

You couldn't see many internal changes, but you could drive them. The Corniche wasn't about top speed, but about shifting its magnificent bulk with incomparably smooth ease, no matter what kind of road, throughout the low, mid and upper-mid ranges. Its stylish, measured glide became the benchmark of comfortable cruising. It was, literally as well as figuratively, designed for the Corniche. Monte Carlo and California absolutely adored it.

It was true what they said – if you had to ask the price of a Corniche you probably couldn't afford to buy one.

Rolls-Royce Camargue

The magnificently luxurious Camargue was the ultimate Roller.

The Camargue stands slightly apart, and indeed aloof, from other Rolls Royce series and models. The company had been inspired by a 1968 Bentley T unmistakably designed by that genius of Italian sports car styling, Pininfarina. Submerged in financial crisis during the early 1970s, Rolls-Royce needed a dramatic statement car. For the first time since World War II, a production model was not to be designed in-house. The new, top-of-the-range Rolls-Royce flagship was to be a really exclusive, two-door saloon styled with Pininfarina's impeccable elegance and sporty Italian panache. Longer and wider than the Corniche (long since available), the Camargue was nevertheless beautifully proportioned. The front grille was especially broad, and for the first time it was set at an oblique angle (7 degrees) to match the snappier inclines of the front and rear screens. The window glass itself was curved – another first for Rolls-Royce, along with the revolutionary automatic split-level air-conditioning (which cost as much as a Mini, took 8 years to develop, and had the cooling capacity of 30 refrigerators) envied throughout the automotive world.

Mechanically, the Camargue was much the same as the Corniche and Silver Shadow. It was a little more powerful – but it was still a coupe, albeit the largest and most luxurious ever built. It was a car for the newly-adventurous among film stars, royalty, and blue-blooded aristocracy, owner-drivers prepared to ditch the chauffeur and the Rolls-Royce Phantom VI limousine that the Camargue replaced at the top of the family tree.

In its day, the Rolls-Royce Camargue was the most expensive production car in the world – but its production standards were so high that during eleven years, only 530 (535 including prototypes and a single, specially commissioned, Bentley Camargue) were made. It was a car from which to rule the world.

COUNTRY OF ORIGIN:
UK
FIRST MANUFACTURED:
1975 (until 1986)
ENGINE:
6,750 cc V8
PERFORMANCE:
Top speed of 120 mph (193 km/h); 0-60 mph (97 km/h) in 11.3 secs
YOU SHOULD KNOW:
Not everyone liked the Camargue's angular, chiselled, Italian sleekness, or even the exotic dashboard styled by Sergio Pininfarina to suggest an aircraft cockpit. But the attention to comfort included super-wide doors to allow easy access to the rear seats and a second door handle inside, placed so that a passenger didn't have the bother of leaning forward to open it to get out again.

Rover P6B 3500S

COUNTRY OF ORIGIN:
UK
FIRST MANUFACTURED:
1971 (until 1977)
ENGINE:
3,528 cc V8
PERFORMANCE:
Top speed of 124 mph (200 km/h);
0-60 mph (97 km/h) in 9 secs
YOU SHOULD KNOW:
Often called the P6 NADA ('North
American Dollar Area' – an acronym
dropped officially in 1967), the
left-hand drive Federal 3500S
combined Mark I and II features,
and was the best of the lot. Alas!
Wraparound bumpers, air scoops
on the hood, air-conditioning and
'Icelert' sensors on the grille (to warn
you of falling outside temperatures)
didn't compensate for unreliability.

In the mid 1960s, when Rover discovered that Buick had developed
a compact V8 which proved unsuitable for their own, US Interstate-
cruising sized saloons, they bought it. The small-block, aluminium
3.5 litre engine generated some 50% more power than Rover's
existing staple. Proudly, after improving the engine in house, and
successfully testing it in their P5 model, the company spelled out its
new P6 version as the Three Thousand Five in 1968. By 1970, the
year Rover re-vamped its entire P6 range as the Mark II, or 'B'
(officially – but it's often known as the Series II) it was plain 3500;
and in 1971, the addition of a four-speed manual version was
designated the Rover P6B 3500S.

Everything came together. The P6 had been designed from
scratch in 1963. It had de Dion tube suspension at the back, four
wheel disc brakes, full synchromesh, and a unitary construction

'inspired' by the Citroen DS. It also had a clutch of industry safety awards. A fortuitous feature was the front suspension, designed among other things to maximize the space in the engine compartment. The Buick V8, when it arrived, squeezed in – but the Mark II upgrades included reshaping the hood to improve the fit and the air intake, and a new radiator grille. Inside, 1971 brought smart piping to the leather trim and a plethora of circular gauges and rotary switches (for Rover at the time, 'old' was linear, and old-style circular was 'new'). The lighter (than the P5B), more powerful and faster P6B 3500S was now top of the Rover range. Police forces loved it.

With a top speed of 124 mph (200 km/h), Rover hoped the car's otherwise adult solidity would entice drivers as an alternative to BMWs and Alfa Romeos. But for the unreliable gearbox, it was a worthy ambition.

Plenty of V8 power made this Rover something of a favourite with the British Police.

The SD1 was handsome, but a leading contender when it comes to choosing the British production car with the worst-ever build quality.

Rover SD1

The Rover SD1 of 1976 inspired either ecstasy or apoplexy. As a member of the new British Leyland group, Rover now had major in-house competitors like Triumph and Jaguar, with whom it expected to share parts and develop discrete elements of the company's extended range. It also had a brand-new factory of its own to produce the fruits of its Specialist Division – but that couldn't happen until the Division had learned the lessons of compromise from its early efforts.

The SD1 went into production on a wave of infectious optimism shared by industry critics and the public. It was fast and safe – crash-tested, crumple-zoned, ergonomically brilliant and innovative. With the ever-versatile and seemingly endless tuneability of the 3.5 litre Buick V8 (though perhaps after more than a decade it could be called Rover's own), it made the most of its low weight. People spoke admiringly of its sporty handling, composed ride and modern design. It looked a little like a Ferrari Daytona (check the front end light assembly) with a hatchback designed by Pininfarina; and until Rover introduced a range of smaller engines some time later, it had a performance to match. The executive market for which it was intended glowed with reflected glory at its racing and rallying success. Mrs Thatcher's Cabinet Ministers all wanted one, and it was photographed underneath Concorde's needle nose as the 1976 Car of the Year.

Unfortunately, the new icon of postwar British car design was a manufacturing crock. Initial reaction had made favourable comparison with Jaguar and its ilk. Instead of upgrading the SD1, its price and build quality to match, Rover tried to give it a more 'economy' feel. Simultaneously, the first batch of cars began to rust, break down, and fall apart. Conceived as a world contender, the SD1's future literally rotted away.

COUNTRY OF ORIGIN:
UK
FIRST MANUFACTURED:
1976 (until 1986)
ENGINE:
3,528 cc V8
PERFORMANCE:
Top speed of 130 mph (208 km/h);
0-60 mph (97 km/h) in 7.7 secs
YOU SHOULD KNOW:
In its lifetime, the SD1 was never marketed by that name. The 14 different versions (including the Vanden Plas and Vitesse of the 1980s) were identified by their engines.

Saab 99 Turbo

The actual Saab 99 Turbo launch car was an almost iridescent pearl white. It stunned the 1977 Frankfurt Auto Show. The unique body colour dramatized Saab's revolutionary solution to every auto manufacturer's problem of maintaining performance in the teeth of increasingly strict emissions controls, in Europe and more importantly, the USA. The new model wasn't just turbocharged for high speed like a sports car. It was turbo tuned for low speed torque in a proper sedan intended for daily, including urban, driving. After a decade of upping the power of the Saab 99's Triumph Slant Four engine (always suitably doctored by Saab's own Zenith-Stromberg CD carburetor), and brief tests using the Triumph Stag's V8, Saab was the first manufacturer to dare this holy grail. Turbocharged cars (like the Porsche 911) were notoriously difficult to handle at low or variable speeds - but Saab devised the first 'closed loop' catalyst system, monitored by an oxygen sensor, to control the fuel injection on its existing 2 litre engine.

The Saab 99 Turbo's acceleration pattern had never been seen. There was no jerk when the Turbo cut in at just 1500 rpm, and though it went faster and faster as the boost increased, the really dramatic effects were on overtaking and mini-sprints from street or highway corner to corner. The 99 Turbo shrugged off the kudos of accelerating from a standing start and substituted stability and inspired handling at practical mid-speeds. It was a fundamental change of attitude, and brilliant engineering.

The Saab 99 Turbo wasn't pretty or even fashionable. It was striking in a *'jolie laide'* kind of way, right down to its extraordinary 'Inca' alloy wheels. First-time drivers stepped out, puzzled by their own ease and comfort with such power at their disposal. They stayed struck, and delighted.

COUNTRY OF ORIGIN:
Sweden
FIRST MANUFACTURED:
1977 (until 1980)
ENGINE:
1,985 cc turbocharged Slant Four
PERFORMANCE:
Top speed of 123 mph (198 km/h); 0-60 mph (97 km/h) in 8.9 secs
YOU SHOULD KNOW:
The Saab 99 Turbo was designed as a three-door 'Combi coupe' – among the first family cars to be turbocharged since the 1963–4 Oldsmobile Turbo Jetfire – but in due course two (only) turbo limousine versions were produced (as part of a long wheelbase special edition), and called the Saab 99 Turbo Finlandia.

The powerful 99 Turbo was technologically advanced and had distinctive styling.

Saab 900 Turbo Classic

COUNTRY OF ORIGIN:
Sweden
FIRST MANUFACTURED:
1979 (until 1993)
ENGINE:
1,985 cc turbocharged Slant Four
PERFORMANCE:
Top speed of 120 mph (193 km/h);
0-60 mph (97 km/h) in 8.9 secs
YOU SHOULD KNOW:
The extent of the Saab 900 Turbo
Classic's 'boat-shaped' cool is
demonstrated by its selection as
James Bond (007)'s car in the 1981
Bond novel *Licence Renewed*.
Crucially different as always, Bond's
version gets a staggering 175 bhp
from the same 1,985 cc engine
allowed to mere mortals; a top speed
of 145 mph (233 km/h); and
0-60 mph (97 km/h) in 7.8 secs.
And pigs fly.

The flagship of the Saab 900 Classic series, the 900 Turbo Classic demonstrated just how effectively Saab shared the automotive and aviation experience within the company. Though it derived, like all 900s, from the Saab 99, the 900 Turbo Classic was a revelation. According to what you wanted it to be, it was a four-star luxury car, a fast and spacious family car, or a sporty executive saloon. Two, three, four or five doors, the shell was essentially the same – a big but aerodynamic oddity which could look sleek or clunky depending on the viewing angle. Its beauty grew in direct proportion to familiarity with the details of its design, engineering, finish and performance.

Like most major manufacturers, Saab habitually borrowed from other companies – but the 900 Turbo Classic is the most purely Swedish car it made, before or since its takeover by General Motors in 1993. The car's aviation heritage was evident in its wind tunnel-tested, swooping aerodynamics: the longer nose, the deep, wraparound windscreen curve, and the endless dashboard with its instruments sited like an ergonomically refined aircraft cockpit to minimize driver distraction. Saab applied the same, stringent notions of safety required for aircraft to the car's unseen engineering, too, as it had for the 99 Turbo. The 900's floor was reinforced by box-section steel beams. It had the world's first side-impact bars and super-strong rolled steel windscreen pillars; energy-absorbent bumpers and (low) front and rear spoilers made of resilient thermoplastic rubber; and the first pollen and pollution air filter ever created for a car cabin. Even the seats were orthopaedic!

The Saab 900 Turbo Classic brought rally-standard handling and supercar performance to a mass market. Now, its styling looks timeless, and the durability of its innovative engineering continues to make it one of the world's most enjoyable cars to drive.

The 900 Turbo Classic has become a timeless style icon.

Suzuki SC100 GX 'Whizzkid'

The Suzuki name is now garlanded with accolades from two-wheel motor sports. Such success was inconceivable when, in 1952, the company abandoned its long history of making industrial looms for weavers, and gambled everything on motorizing some of Japan's 97 million people. Early experience with mopeds and motorbikes encouraged Suzuki to explore ways of minimizing four-wheel transport for domestic and commercial use. In 1955 it was the first to launch a 'Kei' ('very small') car (aka plain 'K'), ideal for the appalling snarl-ups of Japanese conurbations, and which attracted tax and parking benefits for their owners. For twenty years Suzuki made the best Kei cars, but were unable to challenge the relative sophistication of Toyota, Nissan and other major Japanese car manufacturers at home. Only in 1979, with a network of overseas co-manufacturers and agents (for their off-road vehicles and vans) in place, did the company put all their thwarted expertise into an internationally-competitive Kei passenger car.

The Suzuki Cervo (SC) 100 was released in 1972 as a 2+2 coupe version of the rear-engine Suzuki Fronte saloon. It was a tiny 3.2 m (10.5 ft) long, pushed along in Japan by a 539 cc two-stroke engine to a maximum of 65 mph (105 km/h). In 1979 the export model launched in Holland and the UK as the SC100 GX (there were never any other options) put it to shame. The SC100 GX was thrust by a rear-mounted four-cylinder Alto engine which raised its parental 28 bhp to 47 bhp. It flew, and the power in the tail made driving enormous fun. It had zip. It had zing. It had more lavish equipment than any European carmaker could offer at the price. It was a brilliant city car, amply fulfilling its fond UK nickname of 'Whizzkid'.

This little nipper was a perfect town car – but not for cruising.

COUNTRY OF ORIGIN:
Japan
FIRST MANUFACTURED:
1979 (until 1982)
ENGINE:
970 cc Straight Four
PERFORMANCE:
Top speed of 85 mph (137 km/h);
0-60 mph (97 km/h) in 16.5 secs
YOU SHOULD KNOW:
Despite being a bargain, sporty smash hit, under 5,000 Whizzkids were sold because Suzuki failed to anticipate the demand or respond to it. The Whizzkid's stock has been rising ever since. In 2005 Suzuki re-used the Cervo name for a new luxury Kei-car: it helped Suzuki to attain its longstanding though conventional ambitions, but left no room in the kid for renewed whizz.

Beware of the Talbot Sunbeam Lotus – a true wolf in innocent-looking sheep's clothing.

Talbot Sunbeam Lotus

The Talbot Sunbeam Lotus is Hannibal Lecter garbed in the fluffiest of white woolly fleeces. If you're racing against it, rallying or just taking off informally from a contested red light, this car will rip your throat out before parking neatly to offer you Elastoplast therapy. If, on the other hand, you are the driver, you may wear your smirk with vicarious pride for the many who would love to be in your place.

There's a thoroughly professional construct underlying the corporate and political face-offs that surrounded the car's genesis. Chrysler inherited Hillman's Imp and Avenger when it acquired Britain's Rootes Group with a subsequent governmental condition that it maintain the Linwood factory in Scotland. To satisfy many competing demands, including its own to create a serious Group 4 racing contender, Chrysler (by now Chrysler UK and Europe), developed the agreed new supermini, the Sunbeam, from existing Imp and Avenger parts, as a fairly conventional three-door hatchback. The Sunbeam's shortened Avenger wheelbase was, of course, a highly exploitable rear wheel drive. Lotus, invited to the party after the 1977 launch, installed their own 2.2 litre twin cam engine and managed to create one of the fastest rallying-potential cars of the era.

Lotus did much more, modifying the suspension and brakes to make the live axle more effective, and insisting on a five-speed ZF gearbox (with 1st gear canted over to the left in true racing style!). Visually, apart from sills above the wheel arches, there wasn't much to reveal its lightning secrets; and the Chrysler Sunbeam Lotus was presented at the Geneva Motor Show of 1979. By then, Chrysler had sold itself to Peugeot, and the road-going version was delivered as the Talbot Sunbeam Lotus.

Never mind the politics. It won the 1980 Lombard RAC Rally and the 1981 World Rally Championship. Its apparent innocence makes you shiver. It's magnificent.

COUNTRY OF ORIGIN:
UK
FIRST MANUFACTURED:
1979 (until 1981)
ENGINE:
2,174 cc Slant Four
PERFORMANCE:
Top speed of 121 mph (195 km/h);
0-60 mph (97 km/h) in 7.4 secs
YOU SHOULD KNOW:
Very seldom has a race or rally car been conceived, designed, tested, homologated and raced
(with success) as quickly as the Talbot Sunbeam Lotus.
Ultra-professionalism extended to works drivers including Henri Toivonen, Guy Frequelin, Tony Pond and even Stig Blomqvist.

Toyota Celica A20/35 1st Series

During some 35 years of success, seven generations of the Toyota Celica have never deviated far from the principles which governed the genesis of the first series. The Celica A20/35 was profiled as a four-seat, pillarless, hardtop coupe that filled the gap between Toyota's 2000GT supercar and the family-oriented Carina saloon. In October 1970 at the Tokyo Motor Show, the Celica promised to be a 'personal car' reflecting the owner's stylish accomplishment and enjoyment of driving; by December five versions were in domestic production. The broad demographic of affordability was sliced into subdivisions by the ruthless logic of ergonomics and engineering. You got what you could pay for – but the Celica concept allowed you lots of room to decide how you wanted to characterize yourself.

There were two distinctive models in the first series, the slant nose and 'facelift' straight nose of 1973-4. Each might come with any of four engines and three kinds of trim. Export choices re-arranged the combination possibilities. In 1973 Japan got the three-door, straight-nose Liftback (often known as the 'Mustang' shape), in which, despite the absence of a 'B' pillar, the rear windows are not made to roll down – even in the US export model (1976) supposed to carry the full trimmings. Throughout the Celica's first series, every bulge in the hood, new light configuration, change in the ratio between rubber and chrome in the bumpers, wheel style, or addition (or subtraction) of vents – or any combination thereof including versions of versions of engines – meant a new code and new badging.

But you could barely tell the difference, because Toyota's ethic was to give even its economy models the gauges, radio and touches like cigar lighter which were then legitimate luxuries. The Celica was a bitter lesson for US and European manufacturers. It sold 1.5 million.

COUNTRY OF ORIGIN:
Japan
FIRST MANUFACTURED:
1970 (until 1977)
ENGINE:
1,588 cc – 2,189 cc Straight Four
PERFORMANCE:
Top speed of 102 – 112 mph
(164 – 180 km/h)
YOU SHOULD KNOW:
The Toyota Celica GT was the only first generation model to be instantly recognizable. It had its own grille, underbody spoilers, tinted windows, distinctive hood flutes, power windows, air conditioning, and oil pressure and ammeter gauges (instead of economy models' mere warning lights). Plus of course, the other, standard 'luxuries'.

The one standard thing about the Celica was that nothing was standard – a cunning but unoriginal marketing ploy.

Triumph Stag

The Triumph Stag was launched as British Leyland's four-seat, fully convertible, sporting grand tourer challenge to the Mercedes-Benz 280SL. It was the culmination of Italian designer Giovanni Michelotti's long collaboration with Triumph, who insisted that Michelotti's wholly original ideas should not be compromised by the 1968 merger of BMC and Leyland-Rover-Triumph. Like the hero of a Greek tragedy, the Stag came into being bearing the seed of its own destruction.

The Stag was a great favourite with sporty drivers and is still loved by classic car fans.

COUNTRY OF ORIGIN:
UK
FIRST MANUFACTURED:
1970 (until 1977)
ENGINE:
2,998 cc DOHC V8
PERFORMANCE:
Top speed of 118 mph (190 km/h);
0-60 mph (97 km/h) in 9.3 secs
YOU SHOULD KNOW:
The Triumph Stag made *Time* magazine's 'All-Time Worst Cars' list, characterized as 'a despicable, rotten-to-the-core mockery of a car', though 'lively and fun to drive, as long as it ran'. *Time* also judged that the effect of the chrome-framed windows was 'to put the driver in a shiny aquarium'.

British Leyland took over shortly after the Stag's development was up and running. Already, the car was seen to be creating a niche overlooked by its competitors: a posh, 'gentleman's tourer' (later pinpointed, amusingly, as 'a sort of British Thunderbird'), powered by its own, British, V8 engine. Rover already had a masterly 3.5 litre V8 – but Rover were Triumph's arch-rivals, and their parents' shotgun marriage was not to permit them to wrestle Triumph's baby away. The Stag's bespoke engine block went ahead. In essence, two Triumph 1.5 litre Slant Four engines were joined on a common crankshaft to create the Stag's double overhead camshaft 3 litre V8. With the water pump mounted too high in the 'V' of the cylinder heads, the coolant level quickly dropped. Blown gaskets and overheating wrecked dozens of engines.

When it worked, the Stag was a refined cruiser with great handling and impeccable style, but long before its launch it had been subverted by Leyland bean-counters. They demanded cheap versions of every component and fabric. Allied to poor build and laughable quality control, British Leyland's every action devalued Michelotti's fabulous concept. Some problems were resolved in the 1973 Mark 2, but it was too late to affect public confidence.

The Triumph Stag's demise broke hearts, but history holds it dear (*Classic & Sports Car* magazine noted it was 'the most stolen classic car'). And so it should.

Triumph Dolomite Sprint

The affectionate nickname 'Dolly Sprint' is a measure of the respect aficionados have for the car. Triumph's Dolomite Sprint was a very fast, very clever creation. Its Jekyll was a four-door, traditionally manicured, upmarket saloon calculated to reassure corporate managers of their status, and to persuade them by association of its genteel suitability as an executive-level company fleet vehicle for their colleagues. Its Hyde was invisible engineering that gave the Sprint blistering acceleration and the high-speed stamina to win the British Saloon Car Championships (in 1975 and 1978).

The Sprint was the 2 litre performance version of the Triumph Dolomite luxury saloon – but the Sprint's engine was technically much more original than the usual upgrade. Len Dawtrey, one of Spen King's dedicated design team, found a way to actuate 16 valves off a single camshaft. His method sited the plugs centrally in the cylinder head, the ideal position to create real gains in horsepower from the available engine. Now it sounds simple. Then, it was revolutionary, and the cylinder head won a British Design Council award in 1974. Everything else had to be improved to tame the dramatic increase in power. In overdrive, Sprint Jekyll cruised with smooth refinement; but when push needed a shove, Sprint Hyde responded with brusque urgency and violence that really did seem to belong to a different character. Otherwise sharp handling was prone to understeer on tight corners – but drivers got used to it, and enjoyed the Sprint's dual nature.

A walnut fascia, thick carpeting, armchair comfort and every conceivable facility added to the pleasure (and distractions) of driving a car which demanded focus and concentration; but the real enemy was British Leyland's pennypinching and slapdash quality control, which brutalized the Sprint's reputation. Happily, surviving Sprints are still terrorizing the world of motor sports.

COUNTRY OF ORIGIN:
UK
FIRST MANUFACTURED:
1973 (until 1980)
ENGINE:
1,998 cc Straight Four
PERFORMANCE:
Top speed 118 mph (190 km/h);
0-60 mph (97 km/h) in 8.4 secs
YOU SHOULD KNOW:
In 1975, the British specialist car maker Panther created a 'mini Rolls-Royce' version of the Triumph Dolomite Sprint. The Panther Rio has hand-beaten panelwork and flaunts an interior of sybaritic leather and walnut luxury – at not much more than three times the price.

The Dolomite was great fun to drive, with a luxurious interior.

The 3000S was a joy to drive for anyone who was lucky enough to get hold of one.

TVR 3000S

Since 1947, every TVR sports car has been the love child of one of the company's various owners, all of whom have devoted themselves to their passion with a usually reckless regard for its cost in any form. It's magnificent – it has always been – but it's not car manufacturing. The TVR 3000S exemplifies the company's totally individualistic approach to design; and it is a landmark, the ultimate expression of that approach, pointing both backwards at TVR's history of achievement, and forwards to the way ahead. Almost literally.

The TVR 3000S only happened because the company's then-current owner wanted a convertible. Since every TVR is hand-made, his car wasn't just a decapitated 3000M coupe, though it shared everything mechanical. The windscreen was dropped. Every body panel to the rear of the hood had to be re-cut to lower the doors for a racier feel, and to fulfil the redesigned rear section to include (for the first time) proper boot-space. The side windows could be removed, but not rolled down, and the hood was a vintage-style foldaway. The dashboard had to be re-organized round the transmission tunnel: which made the speedometer on right-hand drive models invisible to the driver, and the rev counter hidden on left-hand drives. Lower, sleeker, and (with the 'M' hood unchanged) meaner by far than the coupe or its hatchback Taimar version, the production TVR 3000S incorporated the company's past and future. It is mystifying that no-one had previously tried it.

They certainly loved it. Its performance was already proven, and it got better. Turbo versions achieved 145 mph (233 km/h). TVR's California agent was terrified by crowds brandishing wads of dollar bills in the hope of securing one, but TVR could only make 258 in two years. Its vicissitudes continued - but the first production convertible saw TVR through the 'coma years', and secured its future.

COUNTRY OF ORIGIN:
UK
FIRST MANUFACTURED:
1978 (until 1979)
ENGINE:
2,994 cc V6
PERFORMANCE:
Top speed of 133 mph (214 km/h);
0-60 mph (97 km/h) in 7.5 secs
YOU SHOULD KNOW:
Finding replacement parts for the TVR 3000S (or any of the TVR M series) is a matter of 'automotive archaeology', because the company was completely dependent on raiding the parts boxes of other manufacturers in the first place. Whether it's a door latch, windscreen, or even engine part, identical models often have different, frequently untraceable, components.

Volkswagen Scirocco Mark I

The Volkswagen Scirocco arrived with a dual purpose. It was intended to replace the Karmann Ghia as the affordable sports coupe in VW's range, and to share a major company image makeover with the forthcoming VW Golf. The VW Beetle was thirty years old. Moving with the zeitgeist, VW wanted to demonstrate how economy cars could be modified for excitement and performance; but they believed their immediate future success lay in the economy runaround represented by the Golf, so they launched the Scirocco first as a test-bed for any snags that might need to be resolved before the Golf hit the world at large. After all, both cars were based on the same front wheel drive, water-cooled, transverse-engined A1 chassis.

VW should not have been surprised that the Scirocco very quickly established its own personality. It was styled by Giugiaro, fresh from the Lotus Esprit and VW's own Passat. Low-slung and sleek, the Scirocco's crisp lines were judged more attractive than other, rather half-hearted 'super coupes' beginning to appear (naming would be invidious); and its performance was well beyond respectable, with good reason. Though visually it struck a clever balance between safe, quotidian utility and a dash of hands-on, open-road fun, Karmann was in charge of production. All the bits that mattered were given a sporty engineering twist, and each of the three power options (1.1, 1.5 and 1.6 litre - a fourth, the later 1.7 litre, was restricted to North America) performed above its weight.

There were frequent tweaks during the seven years of the Mark I Scirocco, such as the 1975 quad headlamps, the 1976 single wiper, and the 1978 wraparound black bumper. VW had its mind on other things – and meanwhile the Scirocco was reinforcing its instant classic status by selling half a million.

COUNTRY OF ORIGIN:
Germany
FIRST MANUFACTURED:
1974 (until 1981)
ENGINE:
1,093 cc – 1,588 cc Straight Four
PERFORMANCE:
Top speed of 103 mph (166 km/h);
0-60 mph (97 km/h) in 10.3 secs
YOU SHOULD KNOW:
If ever a car had its cool status ratified publicly, it is the Scirocco Mark I featured in George A. Romero's 1978 humdinger of horror Zombie film classic *Dawn of the Dead* – where it is seen dodging frantically between the zombies in the shopping mall.

VW was as surprised as anyone when this became an instant hit.

Volkswagen Golf GTI Mark I

COUNTRY OF ORIGIN:
Germany
FIRST MANUFACTURED:
1976 (until 1983)
ENGINE:
1,588 cc Volkswagen Straight Four
PERFORMANCE:
Top speed of 112 mph (180 km/h);
0-60 mph (97 km/h) in 8.7 secs
YOU SHOULD KNOW:
As it had done so often before, VW
tested its forthcoming technology in
public, but without telling the public:
so you can find late Mark I Golf GTIs
fitted with the 1800 cc engine
planned for the GTI Mark II. The
difference in performance at lower
engine speeds did a lot to raise the
'Golf GTI hype' to fever pitch.

The mid-1970s was a heady era for Volkswagen. The company was flourishing after the runaway success of both the Scirocco and the Golf. In fact VW had sought to copy Ford's marketing strategy of boosting economy model sales by association with the sporty character of a close automotive relative, and chosen the Scirocco for the job. It was some time before anyone realized VW had missed a trick: nobody thought of the Scirocco as a 'sporty Golf' any more – it was out there pursuing its own destiny. There was room for a new, high-performance model derived from and named specifically after the Golf, even if VW's top brass couldn't see it, and reluctantly agreed only to keep their eager (and brilliant) engineering team happy. The production run was to be confined to 5000, and the car's name was not to mention 'sport' in any way, in case it was a disappointment.

Call it serendipity. The letters 'GTI' were chosen before the Golf's traditional carburettor was ditched in favour of the Bosch K-Jetronic Fuel Injection system to which VW gained access when the company absorbed Audi and NSU. People would believe what they wanted to believe, especially once they sat in the car and discovered how smoothly it started, and felt the instantaneous throttle response. But there were dozens of other engineering modifications besides fuel injection that contributed to the 57% increase in power over the standard 1600 Golf; and dozens more suggestions (like spoilers,

The first of the hot hatch generation set pulses racing.

airdams and ailerons) that were rejected for fear of detracting from the Golf GTI's subtle good looks.

Word-of-mouth marvelled at the GTI's discreetly contained oomph, and swiftly outran all of VW's frantic post-launch PR and advertising. Production was quickly reassessed at 5000 per month. The Golf GTI heralded the 'hot-hatch' revolution and spawned a host of imitators.

Volvo 1800ES

A sports station-wagon with an all-glass tailgate, the 1971 Volvo 1800ES was the final version of the P1800 sports car first presented publicly at the 1960 Brussels Motor Show. Age had not withered its Karmann-influenced, shark-like nose, though after eleven years custom had staled public response to a design born from 1950s futurism. It had its admirers, but the charisma of its timeless elegance has grown organically as others have tried to match its blend of practicality and performance.

Though Volvo always admired American auto design, in the long aftermath of World War II anything but a small or three-quarter (i.e. European) size car was domestically doomed. Instead, like nearly every manufacturer, Volvo sought the association of Italian glamour. The P1800 was sketched out by Frua, an Italian affiliate of Karmann, and actually designed by Pelle Petterson, a Swede who worked for them (even if Volvo never acknowledged his role for fear of diluting the car's 'Italian-ness'). The unibody steel shell was contracted out to Jensen in the UK (until 1963, when production moved to Gothenburg and 1800S denoted 'Swedish assembly').Year on year, the authentically fabulous coupe was progressively upgraded. By 1970 it had four-wheel disc brakes, a revised camshaft and a fuel-injected 2 litre engine producing 130 bhp without surrendering fuel economy.

Modern critics suggest that the 1800ES 'Sportwagon' that followed was just a response to sporting estates of comparable price and pedigree like the MGB GT, Reliant Scimitar, or even Jensen Interceptor. A derisive snort is permitted. Aside from the advanced ergonomics and interior comforts, and the Volvo's well-made, well-mannered handling over long distances at speed, the 1800ES has, if anything, greater elegance and panache than the coupe just for carrying its size and practicality in such a wonderful package. Even today, it looks like tomorrow's car.

COUNTRY OF ORIGIN:
Sweden
FIRST MANUFACTURED:
1971 (until 1973)
ENGINE:
1,985 cc Straight Four
PERFORMANCE:
Top speed of 112 mph (180 km/h); 0-60 mph (97 km/h) in 9.9 secs
YOU SHOULD KNOW:
In 1971, Intel launched the world's first microprocessor; Joe Frazier defeated Muhammad Ali at Madison Square Garden; Louis Armstrong died; and Volvo could advertise its new Volvo 1800ES with the suggestion that the extra space would be 'good for hunting equipment or golf clubs'.

With its futuristic good looks, the 1800ES soon became a favourite with trendy buyers.

1980s

Alfa Romeo GTV6

COUNTRY OF ORIGIN:
Italy
FIRST MANUFACTURED:
1981 (until 1986)
ENGINE:
2,492cc V6
PERFORMANCE:
Top speed of 132 mph (212 kph):
0-60 mph (97 km/h) in 8.4 secs
YOU SHOULD KNOW:
Giorgetto Giugiaro, the man behind
the GTV's body design, was also
responsible for that of the DeLorean
DMC-12, the car made famous by its
appearance as a time machine in the
Back to the Future trilogy.

*Alfa's GTV6 was a serious
contender on the rally circuit
and a serial winner of the
European Touring Car
Championship in the early '80s.*

Alfa Romeo's reputation could never be said to rest on reliable engineering. Alfas have always been about looks and speed – cars that are built to impress rather than to last. By the late 1970s, this notorious lack of dependability was beginning to seriously affect sales of the popular Alfetta four-cylinder rear-wheel drive saloon. Rather than deal with the reliability issue, Alfa's solution was simply to introduce more fab-looking fast cars to its range. It had already produced GT and GTV versions of the Alfetta. In 1981 a more powerful 2.5 litre fuel injected V6 coupe model was added to the range and, at the same time, the name Alfetta was dropped.

Based on the Alfetta's elegant Giugiaro design, the GTV6 had a distinctive bulge in the bonnet, necessary to accommodate its large engine but also a distinguishing feature that added a touch of macho flamboyance to the otherwise restrained simplicity of its sharp Italian lines. This was a car to stir the soul – fast, responsive and elegant. The GTV6 performed beautifully whatever the conditions. The rear transaxle transmission ensured a perfectly balanced weight distribution – making for superb handling – and its low gear ratio gave instant acceleration. It glided smoothly even on poor surfaces, could fly along the twists and turns of mountain roads and swoop round wide open bends, always producing that extra bit of oomph when overtaking other drivers. It was a fantastically successful rally car and won the European Touring Car Championship four years in succession (1982-5).

Admittedly the GTV6 has some rather frustrating niggles – a slightly awkward driving position and unreliable electrics for a start. But let's be honest, who cares how well the wipers work when you're sitting behind the wheel of a car that offers such pure driving heaven?

Alfa Romeo 164

Fiat took over Alfa Romeo while the Alfa 164 was in development, so the car is considered the last independent model of that illustrious marque. In fact Fiat's influence anticipated the 164's genesis by years, because in 1978 Alfa Romeo had agreed to co-build the Type Four chassis with Fiat, who made it their Croma model, Lancia (Thema) and Saab (Saab 9000). By the time it appeared, the Alfa 164's design had benefited from each of the others, just as it had from the Ferrari Testarossa, the project Sergio Pininfarina completed before designing the Alfa 164. With his habitual genius, Pininfarina synthesized all of this, adding references to Alfa Romeo's own, earlier Alfetta (famous for its 'long nose, square light'), and created the best, four-door, executive saloon ever made to that date by Alfa. It was a smack in the eye for the Mercedes, BMW and Audi club.

The Alfa Romeo 164 was front-wheel drive fun. Its 3 litre V6 engine said so, growling loudly. At the same time, no function, system, gadget or executive motoring toy was ignored in the 164's attention to driver and passenger comfort. Everything was power-adjustable, remote-controlled, pushbutton-sensitive, or merely tinted to attract unwanted paparazzi. What wasn't electronic in the engineering was computer-guided, and its surefooted road handling and agility defined the 164 as an exemplar of Alfa Romeo's best traditions. It was even good enough to override Alfa's reputation as the stylish buffoon broken-down by the side of the highway – though undeniably there were still problems, if not with the magnificent engine.

The 164 set a standard for development testing that everyone else had to imitate; and while Pininfarina made sure that its styling would become a landmark in automotive design, it was one which could never quite be followed.

COUNTRY OF ORIGIN:
Italy
FIRST MANUFACTURED:
1988 (until 1997)
ENGINE:
2,959 cc V6
PERFORMANCE:
Top speed of 139 mph (224 km/h);
0-60 mph (97 km/h) in 8 secs
YOU SHOULD KNOW:
The 'Pro Car' series was a 1980s Formula One race curtain-raiser, in which famous drivers raced a 'silhouette' (i.e. more-or-less body shell) car based on a high performance road car. When the BMW M1 ceased production, a new 'silhouette' car had to be chosen to be modified. Alfa Romeo's racing division built a 'silhouette' 164 with the only Alfa Romeo V10 engine ever built – and its bodyshape made its top speed of 210 mph (338 km/h) quicker than the F1 cars! It never raced.

The 164 finally buried Alfa's reputation for unreliability.

Alfa Romeo SZ (ES-30)

Almost as rare as the Yeti and just as powerful, 'Il Monstro' ('The Monster') was a limited edition collaboration between Alfa Romeo and the design wizard Andrea Zagato. It was a high performance super coupe with the underlying menace of an aggressive bulldog.

In effect, Zagato was *capo dei capi* of a number of high performance and racing design teams who had contributed to the SZ.

It's an Alfa all right, but not exactly from the usual mould.

COUNTRY OF ORIGIN:
Italy
FIRST MANUFACTURED:
1989 (until 1991)
ENGINE:
2,959 cc Alfa Romeo V6
PERFORMANCE:
Top speed of 153 mph (246 km/h);
0-60 mph (97 km/h) in 6.7 secs
YOU SHOULD KNOW:
Immediately after Alfa Romeo SZ production ended, production began of a small number of convertible versions, called the RZ. It didn't even compare to the coupe. The chassis wasn't reinforced, and the car was heavier. The RZ's handling was irredeemably compromised, and it only looked the promised part.

Using the Alfa Romeo 75 saloon as a basis for most of the mechanics, Fiat's own design studio came up with the controversial 'flying wedge' styling, rigidifying and stabilizing the chassis by bonding the GRP composite body to the steel frame. The head of the Lancia rally works team modified the Alfa 75's suspension, and Koni produced the SZ's hydraulic damper system. Zagato brooded, and tweaked. The rear-mounted transmission on the shortened wheelbase created perfect weight distribution. With the dampers to adjust the drive height for every condition, and aerodynamics refined by the ground effect underbody and carbon-fibre rear spoiler, the SZ's inherent balance provided featherweight handling but kept the car glued to the road at real speed. Drivers literally laughed with pleasure at the experience, and the smooth, smooth engine roared back its shared delight.

The sacrifice was top speed and acceleration, neither of which matched eager expectations. Being 'as good as' anything else wasn't enough for stopwatch anoraks, who also criticized the short, stubby departure from Alfa design norms. They failed to realize that the SZ's elegance lay in its integration of form and function: on real roads, in real conditions, this car could get from A to B quicker and more safely than anything comparable. The SZ was Zagato's Alfa swansong, and a monster of a legacy.

Aston Martin V8 Zagato

The lightning of inspiration can indeed strike twice. Twenty years after collaborating on one of motoring history's most desirable cars, the DB4 GT Zagato, Aston Martin and Zagato hatched a new plot to raise the bar on their competitors' supercars. The new car would obviously be about stunning looks and rarity – but in fact it's a story about naked, street-legal horsepower. Between them, they would create the fastest car in the world without surrendering any of the luxury people expected from an Aston Martin. With astonishing chutzpah, they even dared to announce their objective before the design was complete, and promptly sold all 50 planned cars from the drawings.

The V8 Zagato was a coupe based on Aston Martin's already slightly *passé* Vantage chassis. Zagato shortened the wheelbase, discarded the rear seat and designed a lighter, composite body with a frontal area 7% less than the standard Vantage. It was the crucial element in reducing the overall drag. With 165 kg (364 lb) pared away, 58% of the car's still heavy weight was put over the front wheels, encouraging the notion that the V8 Zagato was a super-quick GT and not a sports car. But achieving the 186 mph (300 km/h) promised at the outset was impossible with fuel injection, and Zagato included a pronounced bulge on the hood to accommodate the old-fashioned, twin-choke Weber carburettors (enlarged for the purpose!), which did the job instead. Larger valves, faster cams and Cosworth pistons combined to raise the output from the 370 bhp of the Vantage to 432 bhp, more than the Ferrari GTO.

Zagato's angular planes and geometric lines (he took real liberties with Aston Martin's traditional grille) exactly matched the 'power-dressing' big-shouldered clothes of the 1980s, but nobody could mistake his trademark 'double-bubble roof'. This Aston Martin kept all its promises.

The V8 Zagato was another contender for the coveted title of 'world's fastest production car'.

COUNTRY OF ORIGIN:
UK
FIRST MANUFACTURED:
1986 (until 1988)
ENGINE:
5,341 cc V8
PERFORMANCE:
Top speed of 186 mph (300 km/h);
0-60 mph (97 km/h) in 4.8 secs
YOU SHOULD KNOW:
The years 1985-1990 saw the peak of 'silly money' supercars. Most of the 50 Aston Martin V8 Zagatos produced were bought by investors who merely stored them in the expectation of huge profits (prices reached £500,000). Consequently, the car is a very rare sight indeed. Those buyers missed the point completely – the V8 Zagato is enormous fun, a true driving machine.

Aston Martin Virage

COUNTRY OF ORIGIN:
UK
FIRST MANUFACTURED:
1988 (until 1994)
ENGINE:
5,341 cc V8
PERFORMANCE:
Top speed of 157 mph (253 km/h);
0-60 mph (97 km/h) in 6.0 secs
YOU SHOULD KNOW:
The Aston Martin Virage, like all its
predecessors, continued to save
money by borrowing parts from
other cars. Among many small
components too expensive to
manufacture independently, the rear
light clusters came from the VW
Scirocco and the headlamps from
the Audi 100.

The Virage of 1988 was Aston Martin's first new production car for eighteen years, and it still used the trusty V8 engine that had powered so many of its extended family. As a new flagship, it was fresh, modern, and understated; clearly a heavyweight supercar but. in contrast with a succession of increasingly flamboyant competitors from different manufacturers, it still embodied a gentlemanly elegance forever associated with Aston Martin. Some critics called it 'lacklustre'. In fact its design was both beautiful in its own right, and a practical base for a whole raft of versions, developments and editions that were either already on other people's drawing boards, or at least a steady gleam in an automotive parent's eye. These would emerge during the Virage's official production life as a Lagonda, Volante, Shooting Brake and yet another Vantage performance version, among others, many of which continued in production after the V12 Vanquish displaced the Virage.

The 5.3 litre V8 engine got a makeover, too. The Connecticut tuning specialists Callaway Engineering improved aspiration by developing new cylinder heads with four valves per cylinder. This overcame the inevitable drain in power from using the catalytic converter already mandatory in the US, and allowed the use of lead-free petrol in any country. With computers now refining structural, engineering and transmission elements, the Virage was quieter, more comfortable, smoother and quicker for less outlay than its predecessors. And if that wasn't good enough for people expecting ostentation for their admittedly big money, by the time production orders could be fulfilled there was a 6.3 litre Volante version (March 1992) with a top speed of 174 mph (280 km/h) and 0-60 mph (97 km/h) time of 5.4 secs. It was, nevertheless, a Virage.

Audi Quattro

The Audi Quattro is often referred to as the 'Ur-Quattro' (German for 'Original Quattro') to avoid confusion with subsequent four-wheel drive Audis. Designed in the late 1970s, the Quattro really stood out from the crowd at the Geneva Motor show in March 1980. It was the first car to combine 4WD with a turbocharged engine – a giant leap forward in automotive design. Under the watchful eye of Dr Ferdinand Piëch (eldest grandson of Ferdinand Porsche) Audi's engineers developed the lightweight Quattro 4WD system that would bring instant success in the World Rally Championship, as well as start an international craze for high performance, all-drive road cars.

The power in 4WD cars was split between the front and the rear of the car by a weighty transfer gear behind the gearbox which locked the front and rear drive shafts so that they shared torque from the engine. This was only practical in large off-road vehicles – the extra weight made it unviable in a road car. Audi invented an ingenious system: a hollow gearbox output shaft connected to a central differential contained an inner drive shaft to return power to the front axle, while a prop shaft running off the same centre diff transferred its share of torque to the rear axle. This compact, lightweight system gave permanent all-wheel drive. Audi had achieved the impossible – created a 4WD sports car. And with its muscular features and flared wheel arches, the Quattro wasn't just one for the science geeks either.

The Ur-Quattro gave Audi a whole new image, transforming it from a company known for being dependable but dull to one of the most exciting marques in the car industry. The Quattro 4WD system has become a standard option for most Audi models and the 'Ur-Quattro' is a collector's item.

COUNTRY OF ORIGIN:
Germany
FIRST MANUFACTURED:
1980 (until 1991)
ENGINE:
2,144 cc Straight Five
PERFORMANCE:
Top speed of 120 mph (193 km/h);
0-60mph (97 km/h) in 8.8 secs
YOU SHOULD KNOW:
In 1981, Michele Mouton became the first female ever to win a world championship rally. She was piloting an Audi Quattro.

The Quattro dominated the rally scene for years.

347

BMW M3

COUNTRY OF ORIGIN:
Germany
FIRST MANUFACTURED:
1986 (until 1992)
ENGINE:
2,302 cc Straight Four
PERFORMANCE:
Top speed of 143 mph (230 km/h);
0-60 mph (97 km/h) in 7.6 secs
YOU SHOULD KNOW:
Homologation specials continued to
appear regularly as the E30 M3 race
car was improved. The road car just
became more and more impressive,
too; and its popularity means you still
see (and hear) them frequently at
anything from events to shows to
the supermarket. No other race car
ever proved so genuinely versatile,
and such fun.

The BMW M3 is the most successful example ever of racing homologation creating an internationally-acclaimed road car. Its genealogy is straightforward. The M3 is a high performance version of the BMW 3-series compact, based on the E30; but its racing engine has a broad pedigree in BMW motorsport. The engine's basic block layout derives from the M10 familiar from the earlier BMW 2002 and 320 series, overbored to resemble the specifications of the BMW M88 Straight Six. In fact the M3 uses a four-cylinder engine because it derived from their Formula One engine of the day. The roll-call of influences is an evolutionary history of motorsport – and no car has added to it more than the M3, which has won more road races than any other model in history, and dominated Group A Touring Car racing throughout its years of production.

The M3 doesn't look especially like the E30 whose soul it shares. Only the hood and roof panels are interchangeable, and the M3's obviously improved aerodynamics are emphasized rather stylishly by the famous 'box flared' fenders essential to accommodate the wider track and wheels. The stiffer body shell permits improvements to the suspension and power steering that, combined with the five-speed Getrag gearbox, add up to truly extraordinary road handling characteristics which more than compensate for a slight loss of top end speed. The trade press fairly worshipped it. *Classic & Sports Car* spoke lyrically of 'its beautifully balanced chassis, razor sharp steering, and sweet singin' twin-cam four'. *Car and Driver* described in awe how 'the M3 leaps through corners like a cat, its feisty engine spinning and spitting until you snatch another gear or the rev limiter grabs it by the tail'.

The M3, everyone without exception agrees, is the ultimate definition of 'a driver's car'.

M3s were seriously performance-enhanced 3-series BMWs.

BMW Z1

The glaring eccentricities of the BMW Z1 are a wonderful testament to the confidence of the company. For the Z1 was conceived with no rationale other than to test new ideas which might later prove to be valuable. A two-seater compact roadster at first seems to limit opportunities

for research, but the Z1 merely miniaturized a trunkload of theories about aerodynamics, aspiration, structure loads, ratios of ratios, and plain interesting new ways of doing things.

The most obvious is the 'doors'. There aren't any. Instead, you push a button and on either side, the window glass withdraws into the body panel as the panel itself withdraws into the lower body, leaving a gap like a boat's entry port. The sill is still fairly high, and getting in and out a clamber; it's even been suggested that BMW have not tried very hard to solve the difficulties of getting out of the car in a skirt.

The Z1 does fascinating things. Body panels can be substituted far more readily than on a normal car. A skilled technician is said to be able to 'change the colour of the car' in a day, just by panel swapping. The Z1's structure is in any case unique: the smooth body contours and flat composite undertray covering the bottom of the car draws air towards an integral rear diffuser, generating 'ground effect' and sucking the car towards the ground. At speed, the Z1 remains stable – without significant spoilers. So familiar now, ground effect was unique to BMW when the Z1 appeared, and the car incorporates several major engineering enquiries to which the solutions would later appear in many different vehicles.

The Z1's only real problem was its high price. It was a lovely, tough little roadster, if too heavy to be quick – definitely a one-off classic to treasure.

The Z1 startled uninitiated observers by lacking doors.

COUNTRY OF ORIGIN:
Germany
FIRST MANUFACTURED:
1988 (until 1991)
ENGINE:
2,494 cc BMW Straight Six
PERFORMANCE:
Top speed of 136 mph (219 km/h);
0-60 mph (97 km/h) in 7.9 secs
YOU SHOULD KNOW:
The 'Z' of the BMW Z1 is said to stand for the German word *Zunkuft*, meaning 'Future'; or perhaps for the Z-axle rear suspension it used, and which was being tested for the forthcoming E36 BMW 3-series. Or perhaps neither, because the Z1's successor, the Z3, was retro-styled instead of futuristic, and re-used a much older form of suspension. But *Zunkuft* is what the Z1 was truly about.

The Grand National's all-black finish underlined this powerful machine's aggressive nature.

Buick Regal Grand National

At the time they called it 'the winningest facelift in history'. After a restyling for 1981 improved its aerodynamics so much that it swept the NASCAR Grand National race championships, the Buick Regal was the 'it' car of the USA. It reflected well on the perception of Buick's entire range. Seizing the moment, in 1982 Buick introduced an option package of a limited edition, charcoal and silver grey, red-pinstriped, 4.1 litre V6 engined coupe, dubbed the Buick Regal Grand National. That year, a Buick Regal won 25 of 30 races in the Manufacturer's Championship, a further 12 races to win the Grand National Championship, and provided seven of the first eight, including the winner, at the Daytona 500. The 215 Grand National options sold out.

By now Buick had resolved the reliability problems of its turbocharged V6 engine, which it had not wanted to inflict on the super prestige Grand National edition. Instead of an edition, the (from now on mandatory) all-black Buick Regal Grand National with the fuel-injected turbocharger straining at the V6 leash was a production model of its own.

Seen in any quantity, the GNs looked like the legion from hell, their glossy blackness set off by the small amount of chrome in the wheels. They were mean, fast and redefined the term 'muscle car', forgotten for more than a decade. They dazzled with their apparent air of self-entitlement: in the era of George Lucas's *Star Wars*, the sinister Grand National was called 'Darth Vader's car'.

It could lift its rear wheels in a drag race, and for three years its power was increased. Then, as Buick dissipated all its individuality in other models, the Regal Grand National was neutered into automotive memory.

COUNTRY OF ORIGIN:
USA
FIRST MANUFACTURED:
1982 (until 1987)
ENGINE:
3.8 l (231 cid) turbocharged V6
(1984 production model)
PERFORMANCE:
Top speed of 142 mph (229 km/h);
0-60 mph (97 km/h) in 5.4 secs
YOU SHOULD KNOW:
Major car manufacturers don't get starry-eyed about their product. In their 1982 Dealers' Bulletin, Buick bluntly stressed that the objective in producing 'Grand National' Regals was 'to offer an attraction that will stimulate sales of all Buicks. We also want to capitalize on the momentum and take advantage of magazine coverage to increase Buick's penetration of the enthusiast market'.

Cadillac Allante

It was to be the finest ultra-luxury coupe the world had ever seen. Cadillac's first two-seat roadster since 1941 would combine 'European elan' with 'American muscle', and 'grandpa' General Motors would accept no compromise to its offspring's tour de force. Witnesses to the Cadillac Allante's unveiling in 1986 acclaimed its sleek, dramatic lines, and basked in the aura of rarified luxury emanating from the ten-way, power Recaro sport bucket seats trimmed in the same hand-stitched saddle leather that framed the dazzling electronic displays on the dashboard. It even smelled of freshly-harvested wads of $100 bills.

Freed from conventional budgetary restraints, Sergio Pininfarina was thrilled to be commissioned, and designed an aerodynamic wedge of minimal drag and surpassing elegance. Its apparent simplicity belied the technical innovation it incorporated. The Allante was so beautifully balanced it appeared to be poised in mid-flight. To be certain it stayed that way, Pininfarina built it as well. General Motors had a fleet of Boeing 747s fitted out as 'air bridges' to carry fully-assembled and painted Allante body shells, 56 at a time, to Hamtramck, Michigan, to be fitted with their engines, transmissions and mechanicals, and for final testing.

Wags called it 'the world's longest assembly line'. The joke turned sour when, inevitably, divided responsibilities diminished quality controls. The Allante only justified its price if it remained as perfect as it left the showroom. It didn't. Trivial faults were magnified by ebbing consumer confidence, until not even discounting could shift the backlog. By the time the Allante was – reliably – restored to its glamorous perfection, its moment had passed. In 1993 it sold more than in any previous year, but General Motors had itself given up the Allante's ghost. But it was no lemon. It was, in the end, a luxury contender with no purpose.

COUNTRY OF ORIGIN:
USA
FIRST MANUFACTURED:
1987 (until 1993)
ENGINE:
4.0 l (249 cid) V8
PERFORMANCE:
Top speed of 125 mph (201 km/h);
0-60 mph (97 km/h) in 9.5 secs
YOU SHOULD KNOW:
When Cadillac finally changed the Allante's engine to the 279 cid DOHC Northstar V8, the car realized the super-sensational GT potential it had always promised, with a top speed just under 150 mph (241 km/h), and 0-60 mph (97 km/h) in 6.5 secs.

The Allante was a bold attempt to combine European style with good old American muscle.

Chevrolet Citation

COUNTRY OF ORIGIN:
USA
FIRST MANUFACTURED:
1980 (until 1985)
ENGINE:
2.8l (173 cid) V6
PERFORMANCE:
Top speed of 108 mph (174 km/h);
0-60mph (97 km/h) in 9.6 secs
YOU SHOULD KNOW:
It's a measure of how good the
Citation looked when it was first
introduced that *Motor Trend*
magazine declared it to be 1980
Car of the Year.

*The Citation was the exact
opposite of a success story.*

History was firm but fair to the Chevrolet Citation. It was a great car, the biggest-selling car in America in its first year; but when it got found out, it had to pay the price of public failure.

General Motors' new generation of modern, front-wheel drive cars was known as the 'X-family'. Pontiac, Oldsmobile, Buick and Chevrolet all created models that shared a basic mechanical layout – an efficient unibody with a transverse four- or six-cylinder engine – but Chevrolet offered more body styles of its come-hither Citation. Olds and Buick kept the four-door sedans for themselves, while the Citation had the three- and hugely popular five-door hatchback.

The Citation was a generational change, of car and market. For example, it was much shorter than the compact Nova it replaced, but had much more room inside; and to direct its appeal more specifically to a younger buyer, Chevrolet gave its coupe and three-door hatch added value as the X-11 models, with a considerably improved suspension package (so the said buyer could kid him or herself that he or she was being thoughtful) and 'bold exterior graphics' (beads and Manhattan come to mind). It wasn't so very different from other Citations, but then they were very good cars to begin with.

The point is that with targeted marketing proving so successful, the smug manufacturers became a bit careless. The Citation's transmission hose was liable to leak, and a number of engine fires prompted the recall of 225,000 cars. It was the first of many, until the Citation became one of the most recalled cars in history. Beefing-up the X-11's engine stemmed the tide, but not for very long. Serious faults kept surfacing, reinforcing the sense of waste – and General Motors didn't really help themselves by sending specially-engineered models for professional testing, deliberately concealing major problems that existed in the production vehicles.

In fact, the story of the Citation is worthy of Aesop.

Chevrolet Corvette C4

With good reason, Chevrolet took no chances. Not since 1968 had there been a complete rethink of the iconic Corvette. Designed and made in 1982, a new car was ready to roll off the production line by March 1983, but Chevrolet preferred to test the 50-odd prototypes to the limit before permitting sales of the C4 1984-designated model year. By October the look was right. It was leaner and more purposeful than its flamboyant predecessor. It had a 'birdcage' unibody of galvanised steel with a one-piece removeable roof panel, rear hatch window, and a front-opening 'clamshell' hood. Shorter but wider, and still heavy despite all its lightweight components, the C4 was an enormous aerodynamic improvement on the past. It looked race-ready, even if you were only going to the mall; but its thundering 5.7 litre V8 was constantly thwarted by General Motors' temperamental new 'Crossfire Injection' fuel system, and the suspension (influenced by Britain's Lotus, to make it feel more 'European') was in fact bruising on the school run.

1984 came good in 1985. The C4 Corvette now incorporated dozens of refinements to safety and comfort inspired by real-world ergonomics, particularly the ride. The L83 engine was replaced with the much more technologically-advanced L98 as standard. Its tuned-port fuel injection, allied to a mass airflow sensor and new filters, delivered 10% more power for 10% better fuel economy. The Corvette was back, updated and reliable, ready to thrill another whole generation.

Car and Driver magazine noted in 1985 that the C4 Corvette was now America's 'fastest production car', with the best acceleration and (alongside the current Porsche) the tightest roadholding. Chevrolet merited the applause (and the sales). Once again, the Corvette was a thoroughly desirable, all-American sports car re-born to the siren song of the open highway.

The leaner, meaner C4 was a sleek American statement.

COUNTRY OF ORIGIN:
USA
FIRST MANUFACTURED:
1984 (until 1996)
ENGINE:
5.7 l (350 cid) V8
PERFORMANCE:
Top speed of 149 mph (240 km/h);
0-60 mph (97 km/h) in 5.8 secs
YOU SHOULD KNOW:
Rolling Thunderz designs otherwise street-legal race and drag-race cars. The company once modified a 1986 Corvette C4 that became a multiple race record holder in the American Supercar Challenge Corvette and Viper drag race series. Naturally aspirated, the car had a top speed of 182 mph (293 km/h) and achieved 0-60 mph (97 km/h) in 2.4 secs. Using nitrous oxide, it did 0-60 mph (97 km/h) in 1.7 secs.

Surprisingly, the Laser and its sister car – the Dodge Daytona – were not promoted hard enough to communicate their virtues.

Chrysler Laser XT

They were near-identical twins. Built on Chrysler's G platform (a shorter version of their old warhorse K platform), the new Dodge Daytona and Chrysler Laser launched simultaneously in 1984 to replace the Chrysler Conquest. Their restrained but eager styling made them two of the best-looking sports coupes ever made in America, an appreciation they have never relinquished. The Daytona already knew its target market of street performance-mad boy racers. The Laser was conceived as an upmarket version with the feel of European luxury comparable to increasingly popular imports. Initial performance matched aesthetics – but 1985 brought important mechanical changes that included the creation of the Laser XT version. Chrysler's own publicity never even mentioned the XT until 1986. By then, word of mouth had confirmed the XT's credentials as a supremely well-appointed powerhouse, an unlikely blend of menace and elegance that was beautiful.

It looked fast, standing still. The sharp rake of the nose was repeated in the windscreen, and balanced by the wraparound rear glass hatch with its attached spoiler. Louvres on the hood discreetly advertised the XT's turbo (an option on the basic Laser), but not the XT's improved power. Inside, a pleasuredrome of soft leather faced ranks of electronic dials and gauges (preferred over the digital instrument cluster of the XE, the XT's nearest relative); and hours of fun were guaranteed by disobeying the voice-activated warning system or the electronic 'navigator'. In fact just about the only extra you could add to the XT was a jeweller's hallmark.

The mystery is why Chrysler didn't make more of its masterpiece. It was fast, handled very well, and matched or outperformed anything else remotely near its price range. But it vanished, as it appeared, in silence. Finding one is like boarding a luxury *Marie Celeste*.

COUNTRY OF ORIGIN:
USA
FIRST MANUFACTURED:
1985 (until 1986)
ENGINE:
2.2l (135 cid) Turbocharged Straight Four
PERFORMANCE:
Top speed of 115 mph (185 km/h); 0-60 mph (97 km/h) in 8.05 secs
YOU SHOULD KNOW:
The noiseless disappearance of the Chrysler Laser XT makes a kind of sense since sales of the Dodge Daytona Turbo Z option, so similar to the XT of 1986 (except for the 'Swiss-cheese' wheels), justified its promotion as a model in its own right. But logic defies the resurrection of the Laser name for the 1990 Plymouth Laser, Chrysler's tedious collaborative variant of Mitsubishi's Eclipse.

DeLorean DMC-12

The story behind the DMC-12 is a scandalous tale of over-reaching ambition and ultimate ruination. Its production was surrounded by a murky aura of shady deals and sleaze, which involved Lotus Cars and the British government and ended in the arrest and trial of ex-Pontiac engineer, John Z DeLorean on charges of cocaine smuggling.

In the 1970s, DeLorean fell out with General Motors and trawled for high-profile backers to finance the setting up of his own company. His stated aim was to make an 'ethical' car. He commissioned Giugiaro, no less, to design a gullwinged-door body and sought technical inspiration from former GM engineer Bill Collins, who had a radical vision of using new materials technology to create a simple, super-safe high performance car. But DeLorean abruptly sidelined Collins and talked Colin Chapman of Lotus into getting involved. The entire direction of the car changed. The DMC-12 ended up being built on the Esprit platform with a hotch-potch of proprietary parts and complicated electrics. Even though the car was targeted at the US market, De Lorean persuaded the British government into bank-rolling a purpose-built factory in Northern Ireland and after endless delays the DMC-12 finally started to roll off the production line.

The unpainted stainless steel body and gullwing doors looked slick enough but the rear-mounted 2.8 litre PRV (Peugeot-Renault-Volvo) V6 engine could only produce 130 bhp, the drivetrain was nothing to write home about and the retail price of $28,000 was more than twice as much as had been anticipated. The DMC-12 was underpowered and overpriced. Sales never matched expectations, and there were serious quality problems. DeLorean's reputation finally hit rock bottom when he was arrested by the FBI for cocaine smuggling. He was eventually found not guilty but by then his company was bankrupt and his name mud.

COUNTRY OF ORIGIN:
UK (Northern Ireland)
FIRST MANUFACTURED:
1981 (until 1982)
ENGINE:
2,849 cc V6
PERFORMANCE:
Top speed of 110 mph (177 km/h);
0-60 mph (97 km/h) in 10.5 secs
YOU SHOULD KNOW:
Two customised gold-plated versions of the DMC-12 were produced and a DMC-12 features as the time machine in the *Back to the Future* series of films. Around 9,000 DMC-12s were built, some of which were sent out of the factory in 1983, after DeLorean had gone bust, in a hopeless attempt to recoup some of the British taxpayers' losses.

Underpowered, overpriced but great to look at – and an unmitigated commercial flop.

Ferrari Testarossa

COUNTRY OF ORIGIN:
Italy
FIRST MANUFACTURED:
1984 (until 1991)
ENGINE:
4,943 cc Flat Twelve
PERFORMANCE:
Top speed of 181 mph (291 km/h);
0-60 mph (97 km/h) in 5.2 secs
YOU SHOULD KNOW:
A unique, official, Testarossa Spider
(convertible) was created as a
present for Gianni Agnelli, then the
head of Fiat. It was silver, with a
white magnolia leather interior
featuring a dark blue stripe above
the black sills, and a silver Ferrari
logo. Despite thousands of pleading
requests, Ferrari refused to make
any more.

The Testarossa is in contention
as the most desirable Ferrari of
all time, but then quite a few of
Maranello's masterpieces fall
into that crowded category.

With a pedigree as exalted and refined as any Arab stallion, the Ferrari Testarossa is one of the most beautiful and memorable cars ever made. Its name honoured the spirit of Ferrari's fabulous 1957 sports racer, the Testa Rossa ('Red Head'), and it replaced the 4.9 litre 512 BB (Berlinetta Boxer) of 1973, with the engine of which the Testarossa shared the capacity and a passing resemblance, but very few actual parts. But the Testarossa wasn't motivated just by evolution: it was built to cock a snook at Lamborghini, whose visually amazing Countach had surprised Ferrari, and at Porsche, whose creations threatened what Ferrari had always felt to be its pole position as supercar supremo.

The Testarossa shows Pininfarina at his most inspired and lateral-thinking. He kept the rear mid-engine, rear-wheel drive layout, lengthened the wheelbase, and increased the width to a mighty 1,976 mm (78 ins). Then he added the Testarossa's signature feature, the side-strakes that changed car design for ever, and simultaneously solved three major technical problems. Instead of a single radiator in the front, there were twin radiators at the back, cooled much more efficiently via the strakes. The arrangement also solved the Boxer's problem of cabin overheating at a stroke. Thirdly, the strakes made the car wider at the back than at the front, improving its handling and stability. With its balletic balance, aerodynamics that gave negative lift (obviating the need for external spoilers), and despite its size, the Testarossa was fingertip light and agile to drive.

In an age of decadence, the Testarossa became synonymous with a social revolution, too. Everyone drooled – but Yuppies made it their ultimate status symbol as an icon of style, speed and plain wealth. Long after they got their come-uppance, the Testarossa remains immortal, a landmark among the best sports cars of all time.

Ferrari F40

It was the ultimate swansong. Conceived and named to celebrate Ferrari's forty glorious years of production, it was the last Ferrari built under Enzo Ferrari's direct supervision. Enzo, of course, determined that it would be the world's fastest production car, and it was. Completely street-legal, you could drive it to the racetrack, compete and (probably) win. It was the definitive 1980s sports car.

Beauty was not the point. Nor was luxury. Inside, it was sparse, furnished for survival during the pursuit of the hitherto unbroken 200 mph (322 km/h) barrier. Nothing was used unless it contributed to that goal. There was no power steering or brakes, nor even a carpet or radio; and all the windows except the actual windshield were plexiglass. The F40 shared the longitudinal, mid-mounted, twin turbocharged V8 configuration with the Formula One Ferrari 288 GTO on which it was based, and was built on a similar tubular steel frame chassis. Combined with carbon fibre, the frame achieved a rigidity that matched race car standards, and Kevlar and other advanced composite panels contributed greatly to overall weight reduction.

The challenge for Pininfarina was not just to make the F40 fly (he did that by modifying the 228 GTO's V8 engine to generate a spectacular 478 bhp) but to make the F40's speed and behaviour predictable and stable for road use. He cloaked it with wings, vents, air scoops and spoilers, and reduced the frontal area to smooth the airflow and gain maximum downforce. He made the F40 a master-class in aerodynamics, showing how the correct checks and balances could harness what was effectively contemporary Formula One technology and tame it. The F40 was a brilliantly futuristic design, but no dream. It was an uncompromising race car you could take home – providing only that you could afford the stratospheric ticket price.

In its day the F40 was the world's fastest production car.

COUNTRY OF ORIGIN:
Italy
FIRST MANUFACTURED:
1987 (until 1991)
ENGINE:
2,936 cc DOHC V8 Twin Turbo
PERFORMANCE:
Top speed of 201 mph (324 km/h) (NB from 1987-89, this was the world speed record for a street-legal production car); 0-60 mph (97 km/h) in 3.8 secs (road) or 3.2 secs (track)
YOU SHOULD KNOW:
The F40's rated top speed was publicly confirmed in 1992 when the owner of a Japanese dealership filmed himself – and the speedometer – on a freeway. He sold over 10,000 copies of the videotape before being arrested after selling one to an undercover policeman. In 2006 at Bonneville Speed Week, Amir Rosenbaum of Spectre Performance modified his F40 air intake and achieved 226 mph (364 km/h).

Fiat Strada Abarth 130 TC

It was born in Italy as the Ritmo, but in Britain and North America it was called the Strada. For several years from 1978, this small family car appeared in equally dull versions whose only real claim to fame was that,

The Abarth looked very similar to the production Strada but packed surprising performance.

COUNTRY OF ORIGIN:
Italy
FIRST MANUFACTURED:
1982 (as Ritmo) 1984 (as Strada)
(until 1988)
ENGINE:
1,995 cc DOHC Straight Four
PERFORMANCE:
Top speed of 121 mph (195 km/h);
0-60 mph (97 km/h) in 7.8 secs
YOU SHOULD KNOW:
The Fiat Strada Abarth 130TC was the only 1980s hot hatch that never used or switched to fuel injection. Instead, it came with twin carburettors, either twin Solex ADDHE or Weber DCOE40, and electronically controlled ignition timing.

thanks to Fiat's pioneering investment in automated assembly, it could be advertised as 'handbuilt by robots'. There was one exception, the 105TC sports model of 1981, intriguing enough to bring tuning and sports specialists Abarth into a collaboration with Fiat that produced the 2 litre Ritmo Abarth 125TC. It was good, but Abarth quickly saw it could be better. By 1982 they created the 130TC, a seriously hot hatchback with performance figures to see off contemporaries like the VW Golf GTi and Ford Escort XR3i.

The Fiat Ritmo/Strada Abarth 130TC was not an easy option. It had to follow where the standard Fiat Ritmo led, since so much of it (and all of the shell) was shared. Apart from the discreet spoiler on the hatchback, the wheels and interior trim, you couldn't tell that a veritable tiger was lurking under the bonnet. The Ritmo (Series 2) body was both blessing and curse. It was lightweight – the Ritmo's appeal had always been based on keeping it cheaper to produce than other comparable cars – so little of its power was dissipated just carrying, and its speed and acceleration were amazing. But the same manufacturing economies made it difficult to handle. Improved suspension and other tweaks couldn't compensate for the lack of rigidity or cornering balance needed to easily control the available surge of energy.

Britain in particular loved it. The Strada Abarth 130TC came with Recaro seats as standard, and that, together with the minor 1985 facelift, was good enough for the boy racers who made its tyre-shredding screech their calling card.

Ford Sierra Cosworth RS500

In 1982, Ford dumbfounded the motoring world by replacing the ultra-conventional and best-selling Cortina with the relatively refined Sierra. In 1985-6, it produced further shocks by reviving its association with race-engine manufacturers Cosworth, to make competitive rally and Group A racing versions, designated RS. In 1987, Ford and Cosworth found what they were looking for – having perfected the Sierra RS Cosworth's handling characteristics, they now found the extra power to make it worthwhile.

The development car went to Aston Martin's Tickford racing specialist team for the conversion. They called it the Sierra Cosworth RS500, because only 500 were built to homologate it for rallying and racing; and because in its race tuning, the aggressive, pug-nosed car produced over 500 bhp. It looked rather unprepossessing: a three-door saloon with bonnet vents, air intakes beneath a bumper stretched wide across the front, and an enormous 'whale tail' spoiler stuck on the back. The 'big wing' was declared the 'automotive equivalent of [1980s] shoulder-pads' (presumably making the RS500 the Joan Collins of the motoring world).

First impressions were confounded when it roared into action. The RS500 behaved like a brilliantined thug. The road version, powered up to 224 bhp (from 203 bhp in the original Cosworth RS), appeared in your rear-view mirror as though from nowhere, all wide arches and pumping energy – unmistakably quick – and sailed disdainfully past. On the race-track, the RS500 swept all before it.

It was the most successful Touring Car in the world. The RS500 won the World Touring Car Championship in 1987, and was so authoritatively dominant that the WTC/FIA changed the rules to outlaw it. Even so, it won countless races world-wide, and still holds the unbeaten record of 40 straight wins in the British Touring Car Championships.

COUNTRY OF ORIGIN:
UK
FIRST MANUFACTURED:
March, 1987 (until August, 1987)
ENGINE:
1,993 cc DOHC Straight Four Turbo
PERFORMANCE:
Top speed of 154 mph (248 km/h); 0-60 mph (97 km/h) in 6.1 secs
YOU SHOULD KNOW:
Roughly half the Ford Sierra Cosworth RS500 models made still exist. They are highly sought-after. Most of the original 500 were black, but a few were white or a special 'Moondust Blue'. Find one of those and you're in the money.

The RS500 was not only a great track car, but also something of a motorway monster.

Honda CR-X Si

COUNTRY OF ORIGIN:
Japan
FIRST MANUFACTURED:
1988 (until 1991)
ENGINE:
(USA) 1,590 cc Straight Four;
(Europe & Japan) 1,590 cc
DOHC Straight Four
PERFORMANCE:
Top speed of 135 mph (217 km/h);
0-60 mph (97 km/h) in 8.2 secs
YOU SHOULD KNOW:
The 1988 Honda CR-X Si was named
one of the 'Ten Best Cars of All Time'
by *Road & Track*. Spurred, if only in
hindsight, by this plaudit, Honda
began production in 2009 of a new
compact sports car, the CR-Z
(standing for 'Compact Renaissance
Zero'), designed visually and
functionally to recall the spirit of the
CR-X ('Civic Renaissance X').

The regularity with which US motor trade papers honoured Japanese cars during the late 1980s is professional testament to the technical prowess that Japanese engineers brought to contemporary design. *Motor Trend* named the Honda CR-X Si 'Import Car of the Year' for 1988. The praise was worthily won. The whole CR-X series was a category-busting new genre.

A sports compact launched as the Honda Ballade Sports CR-X and extensively redesigned in 1988, its combination of super-light weight, stunning fuel economy, nimble response and relative power reached its most balanced expression in the CR-X Si model of that year. It wasn't technically the best at anything specific, but it was a summary of Honda's consistently improving technology, and its awareness – in a crowded and cut-throat market – of what people wanted before they knew it themselves.

In 1988, people wanted to have fun, and the Honda CR-X Si gave it to them, free of guilt and nearly as cheap to run. The CR-X Si was the performance model of the range (though there were differences between the US engine and the Japanese and European versions), and while it didn't match the US market's CR-X HF (High Fuel) model economy figures of 41 mpg (urban) and 50 mpg (highway), it wasn't far off. In the USA it was a two-seater, which virtually guaranteed its agility. Europe and Japan got a 2+2 option, and a shade more power to deal with it. Fully independent wishbones all around encouraged owners to enjoy pushing it to the limit.

The other wonderful characteristic of the CR-X Si (and the range in general) was its potential for tuning and upgrading. It inspired a still-flourishing sub-industry of transformation among admirers who see in the CR-X their realizable, automotive dream: it's a thrill thing.

By general agreement the CR-X Si was a great sports compact.

Jeep Cherokee XJ

The Cherokee claimed the honours as the first of the SUVs.

Though its name suggests membership of a venerable lineage of existing off-road vehicles, the Jeep Cherokee XJ was completely new. It was a compact, and the first unibody sports utility vehicle; and it set the standard for all the SUVs that followed. It was introduced in 1984 without special fanfare after a massive (over $215 million) design and production investment by AMC (then Jeep's owners) in conjunction with Renault. Research and Development had got it right: 78,000 were sold in its first year, as word spread of the XJ's superlative off-road accomplishment – and an on-road performance that could take the place of a regular car.

Narrower, lower, and shorter overall by 53 cms (21 ins) than its predecessor, the huge, four-door, truck-based, four-wheel drive Cherokee Wagoneer, the Cherokee XJ was also lighter and far easier to handle. Off-road, the XJ benefited from not one, but two four-wheel drive systems, 'Command-Trac' and the full-time four-wheel drive operational option of 'Selec-Trac'. Just as novel, and perhaps more important, was the 'Quadra-Link' suspension system that proved adaptable to almost every situation.

With its clean, straight lines accentuated by strong wheel-arch flares, the Cherokee XJ had the beauty of functionalism. The cabin was upright, giving good, all-round visibility; and there were no fussy details to detract from its companionably 'alert' air. Automobile magazine praised it as 'possibly the best SUV shape of all time . . . the paradigmatic model to which other designers have since aspired'. It must have been. For all the dozens of different versions of trim, seating configuration and power train, the Cherokee XJ changed very little during its production life, in the USA or in China – and modification packages for it are still being made.

Better SUVs have been made since, but only in the potent shadow of the Cherokee XJ.

COUNTRY OF ORIGIN:
USA
FIRST MANUFACTURED:
1984 (until 2001 in USA; until 2005 in China)
ENGINE:
2.5 l (153 cid) Straight Four
PERFORMANCE:
Top speed of 108 mph (174 km/h); 0-60 mph (97 km/h) in 12.8 secs
YOU SHOULD KNOW:
Enthusiasm for the Cherokee XJ ensured that it rapidly became more and more powerful. By 1987 a new 4.0 l inline six-cylinder Jeep engine known as the 'Power-Tech Six' could raise 177 hp, enough power to tow 5,000 lbs – or for a Jeep Cherokee XJ to sprint from 0-60 mph (97 km/h) in just under 9 secs.

Lancia Delta HF Integrale

COUNTRY OF ORIGIN:
Italy
FIRST MANUFACTURED:
1987 (until 1994)
ENGINE:
1,995 cc DOHC Straight Four
PERFORMANCE:
Top speed of 134 mph (215 km/h);
0-60 mph (97 km/h) in 6.4 secs
YOU SHOULD KNOW:
Lancia liked the HF Integrale so much
that it produced several special
editions over the years, often
celebrated with an in-car plaque –
these included the 5 World Rally
Champion, 6 World Rally Champion,
Pearl White, Blue Lagos and
Edizione Finale.

The Lancia Delta appeared in 1979 and this small family car's first generation would be around until 1994, proving to be a great commercial success. Road cars always did well on the back of Lancia's legendary rallying prowess – established in the 1960s with the Fulvia and continued in the 1970s with the Stratos – and the Delta would be no exception.

The new Delta range was initially topped with Delta HF Turbo and the rally version was the S4. But in 1986 Lancia launched the four-wheel drive Delta HF, a sports model with turbocharged 2 litre engine. The following year this evolved into the Lancia Delta HF Integrale – one of the most awesome rally cars the planet has ever seen. With more aggressive styling to highlight its competitive character, this hot hatch dominated the World Rally Championship with 46 outright victories, six successive Constructors' Championships (1987 to 1992) and four individual Drivers' Championships.

Lancia enthusiasts naturally wanted their share of the action, and the company was happy to oblige. In any event it was necessary to homologate the new HF Integrale model, but sales of road-going versions far exceeded the minimum requirement for racing approval. Before the series was discontinued in 1994 over 44,000 Integrales were sold – an impressive total.

This is perhaps not surprising, for the HF Integrale's rally success was reflected in the fact that this five-door hatchback was a very practical road car, with enough unique styling touches to let everyone know it was special. Permanent 4WD coupled with a sophisticated torque splitter made for clingy roadholding, complemented by rally suspension and ultra-efficient brakes. The fuel-injected twin-cam engine made for scorching acceleration and stratospheric top speed – performance that was even better with the advent of a 16-valve version. This really was (and is) the ultimate driver's car. Enjoy!

Maserati Biturbo Spyder

COUNTRY OF ORIGIN:
Italy
FIRST MANUFACTURED:
1984 (until 1991)
ENGINE:
1,995 cc V6 Twin Turbo
PERFORMANCE:
Top speed of 135 mph (217 km/h);
0-60 mph (97 km/h) in 6.7 secs

The decision was bold, brave and as it turned out, almost catastrophic. After 50 years of success in building fast and fancy GT and race cars, in the 1980s Maserati risked its reputation by attempting to straddle the line between mass production and hand-crafted luxury. The Maserati Biturbo sought to blend Ferrari-standard technology and style with BMW practicality, at the price of a superior Fiat or Alfa-Romeo.

The Biturbo was first introduced as a 2 litre 2+2 coupe in 1981, when high fuel costs and a plethora of increasingly tough emissions controls had created a sort of turbo arms race between manufacturers. The engine, although completely new, was developed on the platform of the Merak V6. The twin turbos gave the Biturbo real performance edge, but the 2 litre version (governed by Italian tax laws of the time) had to be raised to 2.5 litres for the all-important US market.

In Europe, the Maserati Biturbo became a family of cars, with a range of engines and body styles to suit almost everyone. The Zagato-designed 2 litre Spyder convertible, on a shorter wheelbase, appeared to great acclaim at the 1984 Turin Motor Show – but it too had to be modified for the 2.5 litre engine before America got it in 1986, along with the four-door sedan Quattroporte version.

So the beautiful, luxurious Spyder, chock-full of inspirational technology, became associated with the same mountain of criticism that the US market heaped on the Biturbo in general. The engines were brilliant, but the rest of the car had been developed on a comparative shoestring budget, and it showed. Wiring fell apart. Breakdown was endemic. Maserati withdrew completely from the USA, leaving the Maserati Biturbo Spyder as the definitive survivor of its production ambitions. If only in retrospect, America loves it.

The Biturbo's build quality was very poor – and that's actually the polite way of saying it.

Mazda MX-5 Miata

COUNTRY OF ORIGIN:
Japan
FIRST MANUFACTURED:
First generation 1989 (until 1998)
ENGINE:
1,598 cc DOHC Straight Four
PERFORMANCE:
Top speed of 117 mph (188 km/h);
0-60 mph (97 km/h) in 8.5 secs
YOU SHOULD KNOW:
'Spec Miata' is 'a class of racing car
used in Sports Car Club of America
(SCCA) and other US motor sport
organizations. The strict rules enable
people to race their MX-5 Miatas in
various classes on level terms, and
as safely as possible. Races include
sprints and endurance competitions.

Few cars have been conceived with a more persuasively ambitious philosophy. Mazda wanted to revive the glamour and glorious fun associated with 1930s and 1940s British two-seater roadsters. They sought to recreate what fighter pilots called 'flying by the seat of your pants', and Mazda called *Jinba ittai* or 'Rider and horse one-ness'. In the spirit of the project, they held an intra-company competition between their design teams in Tokyo and California, the winner to be the design that best expressed the exhilaration of 'pure driving'. Introduced at the 1989 Chicago Auto Show, the finished MX-5 Miata (aka 'Eunos' in Japan, and just 'Miata' or 'MX-5' depending on wherever else you were) literally raised squeals of joy. From that very first appearance, the MX-5 Miata revolutionized the affordable, two-seater roadster market, long dormant and thought to be dead. Ten years later, it was in the Guinness Book of Records as the most popular roadster the world had ever seen.

The MX-5 Miata became an immediate cult, still growing and evolving more than two decades later. To begin with, it was the physical sensation of driving: there were no unnecessary frills, but the seats, cabin and mechanicals – notably the clever suspension – combined to relay accurate information back to the driver. Even in 1989 modern comforts routinely insulated people from the reality of driving; the MX-5 restored it, along with the wind and road noise that went with the genre. It was never the fastest car, but it was the most responsive, agile, reliable, and once you'd come to an understanding, sweetly impeccable at speed. Gradually, that cult of pure driving has evolved. Now it embraces democratic competition, with a hugely popular 'Spec Miata' driver-to-driver race championship. It's the ultimate expression of *Jinba ittai*, and of the MX-5 Miata's enduring success.

The MX-5 was not the fastest animal in the jungle but it became a firm favourite with the midlife-crisis set.

Mercedes-Benz 500 SEC

Every CEO's favourite – unless he happened to be in charge of a rival car manufacturer.

The 'S' stands for 'Sonderklasse' ('Special Class'), and the 'C' for 'Coupe'. Everything else stands for the Mercedes-Benz W126 flagship series launched in 1979. The 500 SEC is the five litre, two-door coupe version of the W126 launched in Europe in 1981, and in North America in 1984. It was Mercedes' most expensive car, and top of the line in every way. You would like to drive one. You really would.

Now that we justifiably take standards of comfort, safety, and even onboard toys for granted, it's hard to imagine the round-eyed gawping that the 500 SEC inspired. It was much better-looking than anything else in the W126 range. Its profile was lower and sleeker, and it reeked of *ancien regime* luxury, poised athletically to whisk you away on some languidly mysterious Grand Tour. Ergonomically-contoured individual buttons powered reading lights, heated and reclined seats, tilted the steering wheel, adjusted armrests and climate control, and – rather dramatically – replaced the centre rear seat with a burr walnut inlaid centre console for greater 2+2 comfort. The safety features included another lists of 'firsts'. Airbags, traction control, pre-tensioning seat-belts, crumple zones and anti-locking brake systems weren't Mercedes' inventions, but their appearance in the 500 SEC had the wow factor of total novelty.

The 500 SEC was just as innovative technically. The automatic transmission even had a 'topographical sensor' which monitored the car's position on an incline and replicated the appropriate response that you would choose with manual transmission (for example, holding back acceleration while going downhill). Equally thoughtful was the 'limp-home mode' button on the transmission, in case of electronic failure.

But Mercedes were clever. The Mercedes-Benz 500 SEC may be a cocoon of impossible, wonderful luxury, but it's still a thoroughly practical driver's car. That's sheer class.

COUNTRY OF ORIGIN:
Germany
FIRST MANUFACTURED:
1981 (until 1990)
ENGINE:
4,973 cc DOHC V8
PERFORMANCE:
Top speed of 140 mph (225 km/h); 0-60 mph (97 km/h) in 7.9 secs
YOU SHOULD KNOW:
The favourite gadget for many drivers of the 500 SEC is the seat-belt: when the engine is started, a motorized arm pops up from the door and flips through 90 degrees over the driver's shoulder, enabling the driver to take the seat belt and fasten it. It marks the beginning of onboard valet service.

Mercedes-Benz 380 SL

This is one of the all-time great roadsters, part of the celebrated Mercedes-Benz R107 series produced from 1971 to 1989. Like all Mercedes series, models and versions came and went. The 380 SL was introduced in 1980 as a two-seater convertible with a standard soft and hard top. It gave rise to a stretched version, the fixed roof 380 SLC with which it has been confused, and which was popular in its own right – but only the 380 SL could give you that '. . . through Paris, with the wind in your hair' feeling of glamour and sophistication.

In 1981, the 380 SL found its feet with an engine retuned for efficiency and better fuel consumption compatible with the US market. It lost some power in the process, but its already slightly underpowered magic wasn't about speed – it was about style. And the 380 SL had loads of it. Its production run came at the end of the longest uninterrupted run in Mercedes history, and it benefited from all the minor changes and technological advances of its predecessors. That it still looked so similar to earlier roadsters was a tribute to Mercedes-Benz design. Spoiled for choice, people continued to choose to spend a lot of money on the 380 SL as a statement. It conferred membership of an international club as distinctively as a kilt identified a Scot – and owners gained the extra kudos of association with the great Mercedes SL models of history, including the 1950s Gullwing itself.

If it was a status symbol, the 380 SL was more affordable than most. By the end of its production, its profile was so familiar it almost seemed conventional. With the advantage of hindsight, it's obvious that it never was. The Mercedes-Benz 380 SL purred to its own tune.

COUNTRY OF ORIGIN:
Germany
FIRST MANUFACTURED:
1980 (until 1986)
ENGINE:
3,818 cc V8
PERFORMANCE:
Top speed of 110 mph (177 km/h);
0-60 mph (97 km/h) in 11.5 secs
YOU SHOULD KNOW:
For a long time after the introduction of R107 models they were referred to as *der Panzerwagen* ('the armoured car') because of their great solidity and weight compared to their 1960s sporting predecessors. But the series sold over a quarter of a million cars, very many of which are still on the roads today.

MG Metro Turbo

The MG Metro Turbo came at a difficult time. MG's Abingdon factory had recently closed, and mourning was still *de rigeur* among MG enthusiasts, who resented the use of the MG sports car marque badge on a three-door family hatchback. But the revival of the MG badge on the MG Metro so soon after the final withdrawal of the MGB was not a 'badge engineering' scam – the MG Metro 1300 handled and performed better than the MGB; and the Turbo was wholly different again, loaded with parts and modifications unique to the new model. The MG Metro Turbo was a real credit to MG's history in sporting cars – and it is unfortunate that its mundane mall boxiness, increasingly fashionable in an era of compact hatches, should be compared to the romance of an open-top two-seater with a Spitfire crackle and a leather belt round the engine. It was progress.

Looking beyond the poor building standards endemic to all Metros, the MG Metro Turbo's specs and performance were exceptional for its day. With the guidance of Lotus Engineering, the engine was comprehensively strengthened on race car principles, with specially-made cylinder head, pistons crankshaft, block and sodium-filled exhaust valves among dozens of improvements that made light work of the Turbo's declared 93 bhp (later, race-tuned versions pushed a massive 200 bhp – from a 1,300 cc

engine!). The only problem was that this powerful engine sat on top of the four-speed gearbox. This anachronism (every other hatch with pretensions to power was using a five-speed) almost ruined the car, but the complex boost process developed to compensate not only worked (for a while, until the gearbox broke) but proved a valuable technological forerunner of current turbo equipment.

The MG Metro Turbo was such a 'Definitely maybe' sort of car. And nippy with it.

The Metro had a great little engine that delivered nippy performance, but everything else rather let the side down.

COUNTRY OF ORIGIN:
UK
FIRST MANUFACTURED:
1983 (until 1990)
ENGINE:
1,275 cc OHV Straight Four Turbo
PERFORMANCE:
Top speed of 112 mph (180 km/h); 0-60 mph (97 km/h) in 9.4 secs
YOU SHOULD KNOW:
The phrase 'built-in obsolescence' acquired really sinister meaning when applied to the durability of parts and assembly of all forms of Metro. One fearless reviewer declared of MG Metro Turbo cars in particular that 'they rust with the speed that ice melts in summer sun'. The poetry wasn't mutual.

MG Maestro Turbo

COUNTRY OF ORIGIN:
UK
FIRST MANUFACTURED:
1988 (until 1989)
ENGINE:
1,994 cc Straight Four Turbo
PERFORMANCE:
Top speed of 132 mph (213 km/h);
0-60 mph (97 km/h) in 6.6 secs
YOU SHOULD KNOW:
The Ferrari Mondial could only do
0-60 mph (97 km/h) in 7.0 secs. It
remains a mystery why Austin-Rover
didn't trumpet the comparison – but
Austin-Rover's 'Three Ms' (Metro,
Montego and Maestro) have always
been seen as unloved outsiders.
Branding psychologists (as arcane as
any tuning specialist) say it's because
the names feature 'soft' consonants.

Always rare, the MG Maestro Turbo remains largely unknown even among MG owners. Unveiled without fuss at the 1988 Birmingham Motor Show, it was Austin-Rover's superficially dignified response (they could afford dignity – they knew what they had created) to doubts that they could compete with the growing number of high-performance 16-valve hot hatches in the late 1980s. Production began in 1989 with the slogan 'Faster than a Ferrari'. It was, too, but the lack of fanfare accompanying the claim meant that only the cognoscenti could appreciate it; and more than two decades later, its spreading word-of-mouth reputation still has the glow of a legendary secret in the telling.

The MG Maestro Turbo was a limited edition of 505 including prototypes. Tickford, already collaborators on the suspension tuning and handling, performed the conversion. Stylistically, the visual balance was a big improvement on the conventional Maestro or even the Maestro EFi, the Turbo's nearest cousin. The bumpers were much deeper (the front looked especially bold), and with full-length side skirts and a new tailgate spoiler collectively incorporating improved aerodynamics, the Maestro Turbo looked solidly fit for purpose. It was a genuinely practical daily car, but its purpose was acceleration and speed. It pulled like a train and then kept going. It produced more torque than a Ferrari 246 Dino, but no sign of torque steer during hard acceleration, which must have been a first for a front-wheel drive, transferring both the steering and the full force of its 150 bhp to the road. And it was, indeed, faster than a Ferrari Mondial.

It could see off its obvious competitors (VW Golf GTi and Ford Escort versions) but reliability problems sank any rallying or racing ambitions. Even so, it was MG's fastest production car to date, and one of the hottest hatches ever built.

As you would expect, the mighty MG Maestro was faster than a Ferrari Mondial.

Nissan 300 ZX (Fairlady Z)

By the early 1980s Nissan had enjoyed huge success with their Z car series. It had begun in 1970 with the Fairlady Z, a name used only in Japan where it was already well-established by Nissan's earlier Fairlady roadsters. Everywhere else it was sold as the Datsun 240 Z, and in America especially, it sold like hot cakes. Throughout the 1970s, upgraded versions appeared, and 'X' was added to the designation to denote its increasing luxury; but a design rooted in the 1960s inevitably began to show its age.

The Nissan 300 ZX, announced in 1983 as the 1984 model, was the third generation Z, and it was radically different from its predecessors. Usually known as the Z31 from its chassis code, the first incarnation of the 300ZX was a vision of 1980's styling. Instead of rounded contours and scooped headlights, it had a wedge profile accentuated by sharp lines, and the headlights were semi-concealed by the 'Italianate' long, low nose. It looked clean and powerful, and more luxury GT than pure sports car. Nissan's US boss claimed with every justification that 'Its heart is Japan and its soul is America'. Surging sales proved it.

The Nissan 300ZX was the first Z car to get a V6 engine; and though it was heavier and more complex than earlier models, in its standard turbocharged form it was very fast, and very reliable. The Z31 was America's best-selling sports car in its day, and prompted several important editions like the pearl-white Shiro Special (designated 300 ZX SS), a total of 1,002 identical cars produced for the US in 1988, capable of 153 mph (246 km/h), and the fastest cars to come out of Japan. No wonder Nissan dropped the Datsun badge – who wouldn't want their own name on the 300 ZX?

COUNTRY OF ORIGIN:
Japan
FIRST MANUFACTURED:
1984 (until 1989, but NB that the world-beating Z32 chassis model continued to be sold as a Nissan 300 ZX until 1996)
ENGINE:
2,960 cc V6 Turbo
PERFORMANCE:
(Z31)Top speed of 137 mph (221 km/h); 0-60 mph (97 km/h) in 8.8 secs
YOU SHOULD KNOW:
You'll see many references to the Nissan 300 ZX as 'One of the Top Ten Performance Cars' (*Motor Trend*, *Automobile* magazine and *Road & Track*), including seven consecutive years on *Car and Driver*'s 'Ten Best' list. In fact they refer to the Z32 chassis model. But the Z31 won many showroom stock races too. The actor Paul Newman raced a Trans-Am 300 ZX for Bob Sharp Racing in the 1985 and 1986 SCCA GTI championship.

It was good enough for Paul Newman – and everyone else!

The racy Manta exuded the menace of a much bigger car.

Opel Manta B GT/E

The Opel Manta both created its own wave and rode it successfully without interruption from 1970 to 1988. The enormity of that achievement in an overcrowded and competitive market is obscured by the reality that when most people think of the Manta, in fact they think of the facelifted 1980s Manta B GT/E that was the top of the range model from 1982 to the Manta series' demise in 1988. The GT/E represented the refinement of the technical and stylistic credibility that had made the marque so popular for so long. Crucially, it also had the extra glamour of genuine sporty performance that set it above close relatives like the Cavalier or the Ascona. For a standard production car, its price and performance equation made it a worthy King of the Hill.

It is sometimes called the 'face-lift' Manta B. The Manta A of 1970 gave way to Manta B in 1975; and thanks to various tuned versions, including the terrific Manta 400 limited edition, it was still very highly regarded when the GT/E was introduced in 1982. The GT/E made new sense of the Manta's familiar, low, sleek lines. The two bars of the grille became four, improving the cooling intake. Recaro seats offered better support to the driver, consistent with the uprated suspension with its stiffer springs and gas dampers. The addition of an integral deep front spoiler and a rear spoiler altered the classic Manta profile just enough to make it look like the grown-up version: it was noticed that the GT/E looked 'more menacing' in your rear-view mirror!

One other thing: all the chrome had gone. Not only was the Manta B GT/E enormous fun to drive, it had The Look. It was, of course, an archetypal Eighties Car, and all its triumphs recall Eighties Triumphs. Proust would have loved it.

COUNTRY OF ORIGIN:
Germany
FIRST MANUFACTURED:
1982 (until 1988)
ENGINE:
1,979 cc OHV Straight Four
PERFORMANCE:
Top speed of 120 mph (193 km/h);
0-60 mph (97 km/h) in 8.5 secs
YOU SHOULD KNOW:
The 'Holy Grail of Manta Ownership' is considered by the Manta Owners Club to be the Opel Manta 400, the 'jewel in Opel's crown' during the 1980s. The Manta 400 was a rally car homologated into the FISA Group B race category, and in tuned rally mode its power could beat 400 bhp. The road-going version was widely regarded as the best normally aspirated rear-wheel drive of its generation.

Peugeot 205 GTi

The launch of the Peugeot 205 supermini in 1983 changed perception of the company and saved its fortunes; but it was the Peugeot 205 GTi version of 1984 that captured international hearts as the most popular hot hatch of its day. Small, perky but unassuming, four-square, with a wheel at each corner (squeezing extra space inside), the 205 GTi came in 1.6 litre and 1.9 litre versions. The combination of light weight, taut chassis, raw power and tight steering made it a byword for nimble flitting – with the proviso that with no electronic driver aids, you had to learn to contain its tendency to oversteer on high-speed cornering. Mastery of the 205 GTi's 'personality' became a point of honour among its many devotees (eventually, the car became difficult to insure because it was targeted by joy riders out to win their spurs).

The 205 GTi's lightweight character came at the expense of safety features. It was a crumple zone. As safety issues became laws, the car's weight increased, and its top dog status was ended completely by the catalytic converter. Even so, its enormous success during its production led to many special editions and specialist versions like the stripped-down GTi Rallye; and many survive to demonstrate how exhilarating it is to be truly in control of a well-made mini-rocket.

There are, obviously, much more powerful hot hatches now, but few have ever matched the sensation of becoming one with the vehicle, that has been the defining judgement on the 205 GTi. It's why so many owners report having fallen in love with their car; and why there is still a strong market for them. The Peugeot 205 GTi is the definitive hot hatch of the pre-computer age – the best of the real thing.

COUNTRY OF ORIGIN:
France
FIRST MANUFACTURED:
1984 (until 1994)
ENGINE:
1,580 cc or 1,905 cc Straight Four
PERFORMANCE:
Top speed of 121 mph (195 km/h); 0-60 mph (97 km/h) in 8.9 secs
YOU SHOULD KNOW:
The most bizarre special edition was the Peugeot 205 GTi 1 FM series of just 25 cars, made in 1992 for the 25th birthday of BBC Radio 1 in the UK. Each car had every extra available, and was individually numbered with a brass plaque. They were all black, with dark grey wheels, black leather interior, and a special acoustic rear shelf designed for the car by Clarion. Radio 1 ran an on-air competition to win one.

Boy-racers of the world united to praise this hot hatchback.

Pontiac Fiero

COUNTRY OF ORIGIN:
USA
FIRST MANUFACTURED:
1984 (until 1988)
ENGINE:
2.8 l (173 cid) OHV V6
PERFORMANCE:
Top speed of 125 mph (201 km/h);
0-60 mph (97 km/h) in 8.7 secs
YOU SHOULD KNOW:
The prototype for the never-produced 1989/1990 Pontiac Fiero, with more than a hint of Ferrari in its fire-breathing look, has been displayed at shows including Fierorama 2005 and the 25th Anniversary Show 2008 in Pontiac, Michigan. The Fiero's continuing popularity owes much to the versatility of its engine bay – capable of holding almost anything including a V8.

The Pontiac Fiero was typical of John DeLorean. American manufacturers had watched for over a decade as Europeans like Fiat, Ferrari and Lamborghini had produced exotic, mid-engined sports cars. DeLorean was the first to believe that America could match that success, and do it more cheaply. The Pontiac Fiero (the name means 'proud') was the first, and as it turns out the only, mid-engined sports car designed and built in America. It was an immediate success, selling on the technical innovation of its space-frame construction and impact-resistant plastic body, and the kind of futuristic styling that looked more expensive than it was. It was cool enough to be chosen as Indy 500 pace car in its 1984 launch year.

DeLorean's savvy marketing raised expectations. The Fiero's performance and handling dashed them. It took four years of continuous redesign before the Fiero became the car it had always promised to be. Ironically, the 1988 Fiero was, technically, exactly as its engineers had originally designed it, and been prevented from implementing by a 1984 budgetary necessity to borrow suspension and brake components from downmarket 'mall machines' like the Chevette and Citation. The 1988 Fiero's suspension was both new and made-to-measure, along with nearly everything of importance. Finally, it had the balance and handling to make sense of its mid-

The mid-engined Fiero was not the easiest of drives.

engined sports potential, and a sleeker, snappier profile as aerodynamically improved as it was prettier.

The 1988 Pontiac Fiero was still not a great car of itself. Rather, it is a testament to what US car makers were missing out on. Corporate timidity killed it off just when the car incorporated the lessons engineers had learned from the racing programme, and from unhappy parts-sharing schemes. General Motors conjured a threat from the 1988 Pontiac Fiero's opportunity, and blitzed it.

Porsche 959

The Porsche 959 was designed for 'Group B' racing, a new category for factory-built experimental cars, and the racing prototype was unveiled at the 1983 Frankfurt Auto Show. Porsche had only just initiated the homologation production when the class was abandoned. By then, the company was gripped by a different ambition. The new twin-turbo, all-wheel drive machine, based on the heartstopping 911, was to be the ultimate road car, representing the acme of Porsche's 40 years of achievement in technology and design. On its first appearance, critics stopped just short of genuflecting. *Motor Trend*, reduced to humble simplicity, pronounced it 'the fastest, most technologically advanced sports car in history'.

The 959's impressive looks owe nothing to aesthetic choice. Its shape was determined by the need for zero lift. Every curve, duct and vent was subordinate to performance, including hollow-spoke wheels and the extra-wide tail with the loop spoiler. Drivers, used to correcting the 911's lethal tendencies on corners, were flabbergasted at the 959's apparently effortless self-correction, even at very high speed. The twin blowers delivered a smooth and relentless torrent of power, and the miraculous complexities of the 959's engineering ensured that the explosive thrust transferred to the road with no roll and no lift. Yet in town, it behaved like a choir boy, singing sweetly and quietly.

Mere money couldn't buy you one. You had to be an existing Porsche owner, promise not to sell your 959 for at least six months, and (irrespective of wealth, power or position) come to Stuttgart in person to collect it. Production was restricted to around 230 cars, all pre-sold at the 1987 price of US$225,000. Each car in fact cost Porsche around $530,000 to build. Best of all, everyone felt they had gained by the transaction – and that alone makes the Porsche 959 an extraordinary car.

COUNTRY OF ORIGIN:
Germany
FIRST MANUFACTURED:
1987 (until 1988)
ENGINE:
2,847 cc Boxer Flat Six
PERFORMANCE:
Top speed of 197 mph (317 km/h); 0-60 mph (97 km/h) in 3.6 seconds
YOU SHOULD KNOW:
The 'chosen few' whose applications to own the Porsche 959 were successful included Danny Sullivan, the winner of the Indianapolis 500; Herbert von Karajan, the conductor; the actor Don Johnson and Martina Navratilova. Another tennis champion, Boris Becker, was rejected, in Porsche's words, as 'too young and inexperienced'.

Porsche 964 Carrera 4

The philosophy of 'if it ain't broke, don't fix it' underscores the history of the Porsche 911. For more than twenty five years, Porsche colluded with 911 buffs by labeling every improvement and styling tweak as an 'edition' or 'version' of the globally-beloved original. The Porsche 964 Carrera 4 changed that perception. The Owner's Manual might say 'Porsche 911 Carrera 4', but the 964 (the factory model code) was a total revision, the first since 1963. Over 80% of its components were new or completely redesigned – but Porsche still managed to stay true to both the spirit and instantly recognizable profile of the old 911. The 964 Carrera 4 was as much a triumph of marketing tact as it was of engineering and elegant styling.

For the new car, Porsche looked to the technology of the Porsche 959, proven on the race track, at Le Mans, and in city centres. The 964 Carrera 4 of 1989 was a four-wheel drive with refined aerodynamics that integrated the front and rear bumpers into the body shape, greatly improving the drag coefficient and (with the flat undertrays as a seal) virtually eliminating lift at high speed. Instead of a fixed wing, the rear spoiler raised automatically at 50 mph (80 km/h); otherwise it cunningly recessed into the engine lid and acted as ventilation for the engine. Unseen, new brakes and new (Macpherson strut) suspension worked in effective and highly responsive symbiosis with the 3.6 litre engine – itself so crammed with 'modifications' it got a new name, the M64 series. Its advanced Motronic programme and high compression ratio dealt playfully with the 964's increased weight and strict emissions controls: performance went far beyond compensation.

The Porsche 964 Carrera 4 was a revolution, not an evolution. The 911 needed radical fixing – call it anything you like.

COUNTRY OF ORIGIN:
Germany
FIRST MANUFACTURED:
1989 (until 1993)
ENGINE:
3,602 cc Flat Six
PERFORMANCE:
Top speed of 163 mph (262 km/h);
0-60 mph (97 km/h) in 5.2 secs
YOU SHOULD KNOW:
The 964 Carrera 4's combination of performance and practicality beats out all the turbo, GT and RS editions of the Porsche 911. *European Car* stated emphatically: 'At its worst, this is the best Porsche ever. At its best, it is one of the most thoroughly competent road-going cars in the world – comfortable, easy to drive and practical enough to undertake even the most mundane motoring tasks.'

Renault 5 GT Turbo

When the 'Supercinq' ('Superfive') launched the second generation of the Renault 5 supermini in 1985, it brought with it a GT Turbo version which urban fashionistas dubbed not only 'cute' but 'Le Car, on Steroids'. Boy racers had their noses put out of joint. The Renault 5 GT Turbo was a proper ('serieux') sports car, designed for the World Rally Championship, the Monte Carlo Rally, and the most difficult road events like the Tour de Corse. It was also Renault's irritated response to the kudos of Peugeot's 205 GTi. On both counts, it was a worthy challenger – and a legion of admirers sprang up to refute any similarity with 'Le Car' at all, pointing out that the two cars had only a roof, glass and the doors in common.

Renault had to look backwards to go forwards: the 5 GT Turbo's engine was a 1.4 litre pushrod unit developed with racing specialists Alpine years earlier, and used in the spectacularly quick, and bigger, Renault 9 and 11 Turbos. With an air-to-air intercooler and Garrett T2 turbocharger, the power unit made the featherweight 5 GT Turbo a scorchingly hot hatch. Of course, you needed to control it, and learn to anticipate the turbo lag. It only took a few minutes to realize that the 5 GT Turbo's key characteristic wasn't acceleration or even top line speed, but its leech-like grip and one-touch sensitive response on the road, at speed. In the right hands, and on a suitable road, it could generate sustained G-forces normally unobtainable outside a jet fighter.

It was fun while it lasted. The specially developed sport suspension, dropped ride height and re-engineered chassis lost their point when emission controls deprived the engine of its competitive edge. Thank heaven there are still boy racers to be keepers of the 5 GT Turbo's flame.

COUNTRY OF ORIGIN:
France
FIRST MANUFACTURED:
1985 (until 1991)
ENGINE:
1,397 cc OHV Straight Four Turbo
PERFORMANCE:
Top speed of 115 mph (185 km/h);
0-60 mph (97 km/h) in 7.1 secs
YOU SHOULD KNOW:
Affection for the Renault 5 GT Turbo's wild, youthful joys runs deep and contrary. The car plays a big role in the film *Ali G In Da House* – but perhaps a better memorial is its elegiac appearance in *Les Randonneurs* or, tearfully, in *Nuovo Cinema Paradiso*.

Leech-like on the road, the GT Turbo punched above its weight.

Sinclair C5

COUNTRY OF ORIGIN:
UK
FIRST MANUFACTURED:
1985 (until October 1985)
ENGINE:
12 volt DC Philips Electric (250W)
PERFORMANCE:
Top speed of 15 mph (24 km/h)
YOU SHOULD KNOW:
1. The C5's greatest success is (allegedly) as a deck runaround for sailors on giant supertankers. 2. The C5's fans included Sir Elton John, who bought two to whizz round his garden, and Princes William and Harry, who used to race each other.

The mistake was to call it a car in the first place. The Sinclair C5 was a genuine attempt to create an environmentally-friendly, personal urban transport. It was a revolutionary idea, planned as the first in a series of experiments which would see an electrically-powered vehicle grow from a tiny three-wheeler for one, into a two- and then four-passenger, four-wheeler capable of holding its own against the performance of petrol or diesel cars. Unfortunately Sinclair allowed the pre-launch publicity to suggest that a proper eco-car was just around the corner, and the C5 was its harbinger. Disappointment intensified into anger at what was felt to be a deception.

The C5 was a glorified pedal tricycle. Designed for a maximum speed of 15 mph (24 km/h) (any more and the 'engine' incurred taxes) in practice it was slower and required frantic pedalling on any incline. The handlebars were set at hip level: you had to sit on your hands to steer. The driver had no protection at all either from the weather (and the C5 was launched in a British January!) or from traffic. It was so dangerous that even in the Netherlands, with its network of cycle paths, it was banned outright. On British roads its low stance made driving feel like suicidal lunacy.

Dreadful marketing made the C5 an object of derision. The 12 volt DC engine was manufactured by Polymotor, a Philips subsidiary that made washing machine motors. Nobody wanted to 'drive a washing machine', but think how different it might have been if they could claim to 'drive a torpedo' – which Polymotor

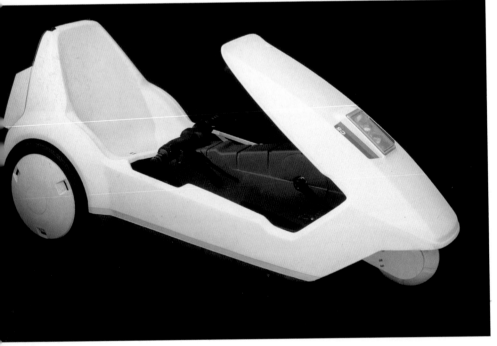

The C5 – another forgotten car that didn't change the world.

also made! Castigated as 'a dangerous joke' the C5's innovative technology was ignored, and it became a toy for the rich and for collectors. But let's not be sentimental – it was a ridiculous vehicle.

Suzuki Samurai (SJ Series)

The Suzuki Samurai had more aliases than Mr Nice. The early star of the SJ series began in 1982 as the Suzuki Jimny (SJ-30), a 'kei car' of restricted dimensions and power that exempted a domestic vehicle from various swingeing Japanese road taxes. For export, the Jimny became longer, wider and more powerful, but less easily identifiable as versions of the same car under a plethora of names including Sierra, Potohar, Caribbean, Santana, Sidekick, Holden Drover (Australia) and Maruti Gypsy (India). There were two principal models: the 1 litre SJ410 (short and long wheelbase), and the 1.3 litre SJ413, introduced in 1984 as a five-speed manual with a wider axle, power brakes, a revamped body and new interior with redesigned dashboard and seats. With unofficial imports rising to the USA, Suzuki incorporated every feature they could think of, and in 1985 unveiled the Suzuki Samurai as their 1986 offering to the US.

The Samurai felt like the ultimate off-road 4WD, and in the 1980s, it was. Whatever combination of engine, body style or equipment you wanted was readily available, cheap and easy to modify. In 1988 it was even re-tuned for better on-road performance, as urban fans sought to improve its all-round practicality for school and mall runs. It could look macho (take the doors off for the 'riding shotgun in attack helicopter' pose) or feminine or surfer cool; jounce across the dunes; pick its way up a ravine; or just flit quickly through the back streets to work. Among pro-active off-roaders it was a byword for manoeuvrability, traction (especially towing), acceleration, handling, fuel economy and above all reliability.

In 2007, a heavily modified Suzuki Samurai (SJ413) with a supercharged engine set a new World Record for the highest altitude attained by a four-wheeled vehicle, of 6,688 metres (21,942 ft). That's off-roading.

COUNTRY OF ORIGIN:
Japan
FIRST MANUFACTURED:
1986 (until 1995 in the USA)
ENGINE:
1,324 cc Straight Four
PERFORMANCE:
Top speed of 81 mph (130 km/h)
YOU SHOULD KNOW:
A damaging report by the Consumers' Union in 1988 appeared to imply that the Suzuki Samurai was liable to 'unacceptable' amounts of rollover (a charge also levelled at the AMC Jeep CV-5 and the CJ-7). Suzuki sued for 'fraudulent testing', but by the time the CU had agreed that their choice of wording was unfortunate and actually meant something different (the case was eventually settled out of court in 2004) US sales of the Samurai had plummeted.

This able warrior had fantastic off-road capability and was also great fun to drive.

Toyota MR2

The legendary influence of Lotus, especially strong throughout the 1970s, spread to some unlikely places. Toyota produced cars a world apart from Lotus' philosophy of sports car design. Only their research team had the freedom to explore the possibility of a practical, above all economical, car that was also fun to drive. Toyota's MR2 began not as a Lotus wannabe, nor even a sports car. It began with a purely Toyota brainwave, to base a design on a transversely-placed engine sited near the middle of the car. The obvious engine to use was the 4AG series developed in close consultancy with Lotus engineering; and that decision segued into the design of the MR2's suspension and handling under the supervision of Lotus engineer Roger Becker. At that point, Toyota realized they were building a sports car.

The Toyota MR2 had European and American manufacturers gnashing their teeth at being challenged on price and performance. Fiat, ahead of the economy game with the XI/9, winced at the MR2's highly affordable package. The MR2 had the soul of a sports car, its light weight and mechanicals distributed to devastating effect within a really stylish and visually balanced body. It was rigorously tested on real race tracks; tweaked, and tested again. Shown at the 1983 Tokyo Motor Show as the SV-3 concept car, it attracted an avalanche of publicity. By the time it went on sale, it had effectively created a new market outside Toyota's self-imposed remit of the purely practical and economic, and redefined it for everyone else. It was Japan's first mass-produced, mid-engined car: noting the MR2's 'unfailing reliability' and 'ability to thrill with superb handling', *Auto Trader* proclaimed it 'an absolute blast to drive', and it was on the Ten Best Cars lists of both *Road & Track* and *Car And Driver*.

The European manufacturers couldn't believe that the MR2 had such a low price ticket.

COUNTRY OF ORIGIN:
Japan
FIRST MANUFACTURED:
1984 (until 1989)
ENGINE:
1,587 cc DOHC Straight Four
PERFORMANCE:
Top speed of 130 mph (209 km/h);
0-60 mph (97 km/h) in 7.9secs
YOU SHOULD KNOW:
'MR2' was variously defined as 'Mid-engine Rear-drive 2 seater', 'Midships Runabout 2 seater' and 'Midships Recreational 2 seater'. In France it was called 'Coupe MR', because in French, saying 'MR2' sounded like *est merdeux* ('it's shitty'). But generally the world refers to the first generation of the MR2 by its factory code of 'AW 11'.

378

Toyota Supra Turbo Mark III

Like a child growing up and setting out on a life of adventure, in 1986 the Mark III was the Toyota Supra that stepped out of the Celica's shadow, dropping both its Celica prefix and its overtly derivative styling. The new, 2+2 Supra kept its rear-wheel drive (the Celica changed to front-wheel drive), but got its own engine platform. To begin with, its improved 3 litre engine (still a descendant of the Toyota 2000GT's M engine) was naturally aspirated. With dual overhead cams and four valves per cylinder, it was the flagship of Toyota power. Then in 1987, the addition of a CT 26 turbocharger created the 7M-GTE, the first Toyota engine without a distributor, and the Supra Turbo Mark III initiated one of the longest, uninterrupted, barely modified and successful production runs in Toyota history.

The Supra Turbo Mark III was a powerhouse of new technology devoted to high speed, sharp manoeuvres and clean braking. Standard options included four-channel ABS, TEMS (Toyota Electronically Modulated Suspension), ACIS (Acoustic Controlled Induction System) and R154 manual transmission (automatic was available, but why would anyone want to be a wet blanket?). Eventually there would be new tail lights, front bumper and other minor changes, but there was only one basic trim. The car was a roaring success as it stood – so much so, that in 1987 Toyota created a Supra Turbo-A special edition of 500, homologated to challenge for the 1988 World Touring Car Championships. All 500 came in black, with leather interiors and a hard top: they were too heavy to win a lot of races, but it was worth going to Japan just to test drive one.

Big, heavy, and powerful, the Supra Turbo Mark III catapulted Toyota into the elite of production sports car manufacturers.

Toyota's Mk III was highly manoeuvrable and very quick.

COUNTRY OF ORIGIN:
Japan
FIRST MANUFACTURED:
1986 (until 1992)
ENGINE:
2,954 cc DOHC Straight Six Turbo
PERFORMANCE:
Top speed of 140 mph (225 km/h);
0-60 mph (97 km/h) in 6.5 secs
YOU SHOULD KNOW:
Subsequent generations of the Toyota Supra Turbo built on the Mark III's status as the fastest road car (of its day) in Japan, acquiring a quasi-religious reverence for the model expressed by its appearance in the video game smash-hits *Gran Turismo* and *Need For Speed*.

TVR Tasmin 280i

COUNTRY OF ORIGIN:
UK
FIRST MANUFACTURED:
1981 (until 1988)
ENGINE:
2,792 cc OHV V6
PERFORMANCE:
Top speed of 130 mph (209 km/h);
0-60 mph (97 km/h) in 8.0 secs
YOU SHOULD KNOW:
Should you be privileged to drive a
TVR Tasmin 280i series II (produced
in the late mid-80s), be warned that
this model is widely feared as one
of the 'scariest cars ever in the wet'.
Of course, you might feel that
only makes the experience more
thrilling . . .

Every TVR sports car has been greater than the sum of its parts, and the Tasmin was no exception. Introduced as a replacement for TVR's M series Taimar, the Tasmin pillaged parts from a variety of other cars (mainly Fords) and reconfigured them with typical TVR chutzpah into a pocket rocket of real, if quirky, distinction. The Tasmin was almost a wedge car. For the first time ever, TVR appeared to be influenced by fashion: the Tasmin's profile and contours shared the '*origami*' (paper-folding) characteristics made popular by design specialist Giugiaro. It was almost pretty – a departure for TVR that brought its own problems.

The Tasmin's wheelbase was short, but longer than the Taimar; and the chassis still came as the same space-frame built of small diameter, round and square-sectioned tubes. The hood was long for the 'front mid-engine' siting, and tapered into a droopy 'anteater' nose which contrasted oddly with the cut-off rear. The effect would have been sleek, but for the stumpy, fat B-pillar of the coupe's roof. The convertible got round that effect with a folding, Targa-style hoop which became standard for all TVR's convertibles thereafter. At least the convertible didn't pretend to be more than a two-seater –

Many different engines were used in the Tasmin.

the rear seats of the 2+2 coupe were an optimistic joke.

But the car wasn't. The Tasmin was fast. TVR tried a variety of engines in the Tasmin's production lifetime, and the only failure was the 2 litre Pinto engine, introduced to offer a less expensive Tasmin experience, but depriving the car of its most desirable attribute. The Tasmin's good reputation rests on the standard 280i , a Ford V6 that made the most of the snappy styling. Later production versions were said to be able to 'outdrag a Porsche Turbo'. Alas, price prevented most people from finding out.

Vector W8

Automotive gamblers could easily lose their shirts on this one. Only 19 Vector W8s were built, hardly anyone has ever seen one – and anyone who did spot a W8 for the first time would bet anything that this low-slung, jet-age flying wedge was of Italian origin. Pay up!

For California-based Vector Aeromotive was American through and through; the W2 prototype and W8 production model were designed by Gerald Wiegert (also American through and through), both using the USA's most advanced aerospace materials. The hand-built two-door car had an aluminium honeycomb semi-monocoque chassis, and bodywork was fabricated in carbon fibre, kevlar and epoxy resin glass matrix.

The Vector W8 was assembled using thousands of aircraft-style rivets. The engine was a Chevy Rodeck V8 racing special with twin turbochargers, belting out a modest 625 bhp. The power was put down by a three-speed modified B&M transmission with a ratchet shifter. Power-assisted rack-and-pinion steering, a racing suspension set-up and large ventilated disc brakes dealt with handling matters. A steel roll cage protected the occupants from high-speed disaster and there was a removable sunroof for those who liked a gentle breeze ruffling their hair.

In a speed test at the famous Bonneville Salt Flats, a W8 with high-downforce wing left 200 mph (322 km/h) far behind. Aerodynamic efficiency was further enhanced with changes like a lower front fascia and air splitter, plus a revised rear spoiler that increased downforce without the need to use the massive rear wing inherited from the W2. There were minor changes to the body during the production run, so no two Vector W8s were exactly the same. Sadly for this bold venture, buyers were thin on the ground and the company folded in 1992 before the truly sensational WX-3 coupe and roadster prototypes could go into production.

COUNTRY OF ORIGIN:
USA
FIRST MANUFACTURED:
1989 (until 1992)
ENGINE:
6.0 l (365 cid) V8 Twin Turbo
PERFORMANCE:
Top speed of 242 mph (389 km/h);
0-60 mph (97 km/h) in 4.2 secs
YOU SHOULD KNOW:
After Vector Aeromotive ceased trading the newly formed Vectors Motors Corporation moved to Florida and put the Vector M12 into production – it was an unqualified disaster with just 14 cars built. Meanwhile, rumour suggests designer Gerald Wiegert is now quietly working on a new supercar.

1990s

The Ecosse was a handsome beast with power aplenty.

Ascari Ecosse

The brainchild of Dutch racing driver and self-confessed petrolhead Klaas Zwart, Ascari was named after the great Alberto Ascari, the first Formula 1 double champion. It all began in the mid-1990s when the company produced the FGT concept car that appeared at various motor shows and generated considerable interest. Designed by Lee Noble, this mid-engined masterpiece featured a big fuel-injected Chevy V8 and raced with some success in the British GT Championships between 1995 and 1997. Suitably encouraged, Ascari re-christened the FGT as the Ecosse, switched to a BMW V8 engine and decided to undertake a production run that delivered on Ascari's mission to produce road-legal racing cars.

Okay, so in the end it wasn't much of a production run – just 17 of these stunning two-door speedsters were built in the late 1990s and less than a dozen survive. But their performance is legendary and they are so much more interesting (and exclusive) than any old Ferrari. The comparison is valid: the Ecosse has a long, low body with a classically Italian look that wouldn't look out of place if it came out of Maranello, and shares those essential racing genes.

The fibreglass body sits atop a spaceframe chassis with independent wishbone suspension. The cabin is set well forward, with the pedal box placed between the front wheels. The wheels themselves are located at the car's extremities for super-adhesive roadholding and precise handling. The engine ultimately chosen for the road car was a 4.7 litre BMW V8, tuned by German specialist Hartge to deliver awesome power output.

Although so few examples of the Ecosse were built, they neatly encapsulate the aspiration that lay behind the company's enduring supercar philosophy – 'If we have the courage to pursue our dreams and transform our vision into reality, we invite magic into our lives'.

COUNTRY OF ORIGIN:
UK
FIRST MANUFACTURED:
1998 (until 1999)
ENGINE:
4,722 cc V8
PERFORMANCE:
Top speed of 200 mph (322 km/h);
0-60 mph (97 km/h) in 4.1 secs
YOU SHOULD KNOW:
Andalucia in Southern Spain is home to the Ascari Racing Club – a private circuit owned by Ascari boss Klaas Zwart where lovers of performance cars can drive their own supercars to the limit, or sample the delights of others chosen from Ascari's comprehensive fleet of speedsters.

Aston Martin DB7

The words 'entry level' and 'Aston Martin' don't seem instantly compatible, but all things are relative. Following Ford's takeover, the DB7 represented the company's first real effort to produce a model that would confer Aston Martin status on a wider buying public. This ambitious policy was a success, with around 7,000 DB7s sold over the production run, a number far in excess of anything achieved by any previous Aston Martin.

Styled by Ian Callum and Keith Helfet, the DB7 is a timeless British classic in its own right, despite beginning life as an evolution of the Jaguar XJ-S platform and the aborted Jaguar F Type. It initially featured a straight six engine to differentiate the new model from the hand-built V8 Virage, and came as a stylish two-door coupe or two-door convertible. A new factory was acquired to produce the DB7 family – which were the only Astons ever to have a steel body, using monocoque construction borrowed from Jaguar. Though hardly necessary, a Driving Dynamics package offered beefed-up handling and performance. With or without such enhancement, the DB7 remains one of the best-mannered 1990s grand tourers it's possible to find and it is real a pleasure to drive.

In 1999, the powerful DB7 V12 Vantage made its debut at the Geneva Motor Show, complete with six-speed manual or five-speed automatic gearbox. This flying machine had a top speed of 185 mph (298 km/h) with the manual box, and this superior manifestation of the DB7 soon saw off the straight six version, which ceased production. In 2002, the DB7 was tweaked yet again, with the introduction of the V12 GT (manual) and GTA (automatic) models. These would be the last of the DB7s, for the sensational DB9 was waiting in the wings to pitch for fame and fortune.

COUNTRY OF ORIGIN:
UK
FIRST MANUFACTURED:
1994 (until 2003)
ENGINE:
3,239 cc Straight Six; 5,935 cc V12
PERFORMANCE:
With 3.2 l engine – top speed of 157 mph (253 km/h); 0-60 mph (97 km/h) in 5.8 secs
YOU SHOULD KNOW:
For those who lust after the exclusive, Aston Martin sold just 99 examples of the DB7 Zagato after introducing this stylish special edition at the 2002 Paris Motor Show – the shortened DB7 chassis was built in the UK and shipped out to Zagato in Milan for a custom hand-built aluminium body to be fitted.

The DB7 was created as Ford's hot prospect to double or even treble Aston Martin sales.

Audi RS2 Avant

COUNTRY OF ORIGIN:
Germany
FIRST MANUFACTURED:
1994 (until 1996)
ENGINE:
2,226 cc Straight Five Turbo
PERFORMANCE:
Top speed of 163 mph (262 km/h);
0-60 mph (97 km/h) in 4.8 secs
YOU SHOULD KNOW:
The reason that there was no coupe version of the RS2 Avant was that co-producer Porsche considered it would be a direct (and formidable) competitor for Porsche's own sports car range.

Q-ships were innocent-looking merchantmen used to trap enemy submarines in two world wars. Their harmless appearance caused predatory subs to surface with a view to sinking defenceless quarry without wasting a precious torpedo, at which point the Q-ship's hidden armament was revealed and the biter was bitten. The principle was pretty much the same when it came to the Audi RS2 Avant. Any boy racer who pulled alongside this solid estate car and decided to make it look silly when the lights went green would have been in for an awful surprise – the RS2 Avant could hit 30 mph (48 km/h) from a standing start faster than a contemporary Formula 1 Grand Prix car.

The RS2 Avant was the first Audi to bear the company's limited-edition RS performance badge, and was a cooperative venture with Porsche using the 80 Avant as a platform. The engine was a turbocharged 2.2 litre Audi, which kicked out so much power that output had to be electronically limited by the time Porsche had finished modifying the motor. Porsche assembled the cars, though Audi supplied the running gear. Porsche also designed braking and suspension systems that were capable of handling the Audi's quattro four-wheel drive system, rapid acceleration and high top speed.

The Avant may have looked like an everyday estate car but when the hammer went down it could spring a big surprise.

Indeed, whilst the RS2 looked like any old Audi estate car (apart from the RS2 badge with its inbuilt PORSCHE inscription that might have alerted those in the know), it had the performance of a high-end sports car with the interior of a luxurious estate car – and was actually capable of outperforming many a contemporary supercar. The initial production run for the Audi RS2 Avant was pencilled in at 2,200, but demand was so keen that around 2,900 of these wolves in sheep's clothing were built.

Audi TT

When Audi unveiled the TT coupe as a concept car in 1995, public reaction was so ecstatic that a production run was ordered, though in the event this was delayed by tooling problems. By the time the neatly rounded Audi TT 2+2 fastback coupe appeared in late 1998 – soon joined by an equally pleasing two-seater roadster – there was a long waiting list of eager buyers.

The cars were named after the famous Tourist Trophy motorcycle races on the Isle of Man, where Audi predecessor NSU had excelled over the years. When they finally arrived, the TT cars were based on the Volkswagen A4 platform used by the New Beetle, Golf and Skoda Octavia (amongst others). There was a choice of two transversely mounted, turbocharged 1.8 litre engines with different power output (a 3.2 litre Volkswagen VR6 was added in 2003). The less powerful 1.8 came with Audi's famous quattro all-wheel drive system or standard front-wheel drive, with the meatier engine having the quattro option only. The gearbox was five- or six-speed manual, with automatic and fast DSG (Direct-Shift Gearbox) as later options.

The delight of early buyers who finally got their Audi TTs to play with turned to dismay when they discovered the car could become dangerously skittish at high speed – a fault requiring the company to issue a recall so the cars could be modified with a rear spoiler and ESP (Electronic Stability Programme) to improved handling.

The second generation TTs were introduced in 2007, with a rear spoiler that deploys automatically at speed and a choice of fuel-injection engines, plus options like Audi Magnetic Ride active suspension. There's even a diesel-engined TT available for green speedsters. For the money, the Audi TT has always been a machine that offers a great driving experience, with crisp handling and impressive performance.

COUNTRY OF ORIGIN:
Germany (built in Hungary)
FIRST MANUFACTURED:
1998
ENGINE:
1,781 cc Straight Four Turbo;
3,189 cc Staggered Six
PERFORMANCE:
Varied according to engine –
minimum top speed of 137 mph
(220 km/h); 0-60 mph (97 km/h)
in 8.1 secs
YOU SHOULD KNOW:
A limited-edition performance model
was released by Audi in 2005 – the
TT Quattro Sport (in the UK, Club
Sport in Europe) had a super-tuned
version of the 1.8 engine, uprated
suspension and brakes plus a special
two-tone paint job. These are both
scarce and desirable.

*The Continental R was a superb
but thirsty two-door luxury car.*

Bentley Continental R

Finally, in 1991, Rolls-Royce Motors got around to creating a Bentley that
owed nothing to a Rolls-Royce sibling, apart from the engine. The
Continental R cashed in on popularity the resurgent Bentley marque had
been enjoying since the early 1980s, and also plugged the gap left in the
corporate range by the demise of the Rolls-Royce Camargue back in 1986.

This sleek two-door car with its raked windscreen was styled with
more than a passing nod to aerodynamic efficiency, but was also a very
handsome beast – spontaneous applause broke out when it was
dramatically unveiled at the Geneva Motor Show. The interior finish and
seating plan were similar to that of the well-proven Bentley Turbo R,
though there were minor changes to the instruments and control panels,
with a centre console that extended into the rear compartment.

The electric gear-selector was mounted on the console – the first time
it had featured anywhere but on the steering column for an automatic
Bentley – and controlled a new four-speed automatic transmission that
delivered effortless cruising and improved fuel consumption (though that
old cliché 'if you have to ask how many miles it does to the gallon you
can't afford to run it' definitely applies). Another new feature of the
Continental R was ETBC (Electronic Transient Boost Control). This
could override the turbo when extra grunt was needed – for example
during a hairy overtaking manoeuvre – by providing a further temporary
boost when the turbo was already operating at maximum power.

In 2004 the new Continental GT superseded previous Continental
models but the Continental R remains a grand tourer *par excellence* –
and the beauty of these quality cars is that they retain their class and
style long after they have sunk into the almost-affordable price bracket.

COUNTRY OF ORIGIN:
UK
FIRST MANUFACTURED:
1991 (until 2003)
ENGINE:
6,750 cc V8 Turbo
PERFORMANCE:
Top speed of 145 mph (233 km/h);
0-60 mph (97 km/h) in 6.9 secs
YOU SHOULD KNOW:
The high-performance Continental
R Mulliner model was introduced in
1999 and ran until 2003 – boasting a
top speed of 170 mph (274 km/h).
A limited number of Continental R
Le Mans cars were produced in 2001.

Bentley Azure

The success of the Bentley Continental R made the debut of a convertible version inevitable – and the Azure duly made a grand entrance at the Geneva Motor Show in 1995. This magnificent open-top touring car was based on the Continental R, but fully justified Bentley's decision to classify it a separate model with a name and style all its own.

Inevitably, the designer was Pininfarina. Undoubtedly a – perhaps the – world leader in convertible design, the Cambiano studio produced a sinuous modern body with twin headlights and colour-matched bumpers. The Azure was the first entirely new Bentley convertible to come out of Crewe since the 1960s. This two-door beauty could accommodate four adults in extreme comfort and the powered top closed smoothly at the touch of a button.

The Azure was a large grand tourer, but the ever-reliable 6.75 litre engine with its intercooled Garrett turbocharger pumped out 400 bhp and massive torque, giving this heavy car performance figures that would make the average sports car blink. The transmission was a four-speed automatic sourced from General Motors. From 1999 the Azure was available with the Mulliner package, a trim option that allowed the customer to choose bespoke trim and have the car customized to meet personal requirements. As a result, no two Mulliner Azures are the same.

Although Volkswagen purchased Bentley in 1998, the German company took its time in updating the Azure, which therefore remained in production until 2003. An engine upgrade took place in 2001, introducing a twin turbocharger, and this was coupled with a new six-speed automatic box for optimum performance. The new Azure finally appeared in 2006, but the original remains a splendid motorcar that provides a fitting tribute to the Bentley marque's final years in British ownership.

COUNTRY OF ORIGIN:
UK
FIRST MANUFACTURED:
1995 (until 2003)
ENGINE:
6,761 cc V8 Turbo
PERFORMANCE:
Top speed of 150 mph (231 km/h);
0-60 mph (97 km/h) in 6.3 secs
YOU SHOULD KNOW:
The Azure was very expensive – partly because the sophisticated power-driven convertible top was not only designed by Pininfarina, but also built in Italy and shipped to Crewe for final assembly.

Bespoke coachbuilding meant no two Azures were the same.

BMW E53 X5

COUNTRY OF ORIGIN:
Germany (manufactured in the USA)
FIRST MANUFACTURED:
1999 (until 2006)
ENGINE:
2,979 cc Straight Six; 2,993 cc
Straight Six Diesel; 4,398 cc, 4,619 cc
or 4,799 cc V8
PERFORMANCE:
With 4.4 l engine – top speed of
129 mph (207 km/h); 0-60 mph
(97 km/h) in 7.3 secs
YOU SHOULD KNOW:
The first-generation E53 X5 had a
considerable facelift in 2004, with
external styling changes, a revised
four-wheel-drive system, towing
stability pack and more powerful
engine options.

What's the difference between SAV and SUV? Obvious! The Sports Activity Vehicle is a big passenger car that can go off road with some authority when necessary, whilst a Sports Utility Vehicle is a big passenger car that can go off road with some authority when necessary. The reason BMW was so keen to claim that its new X5 SAV was not really a SUV was bound up with its takeover of Rover.

That gave BMW access to Land Rover's world-leading off-road technology and made development of the first generation E53 X5 model much easier, but also ensured that BMW had to differentiate between its own-brand SUV and the Range Rovers that were genuine off-road superstars. The X5 was an early example of the crossover trend that would develop rapidly in the new century, whereby SUVs started switching from rugged body-on-chassis vehicles to luxury saloon-based road cars that rode high and could tackle uneven ground and slippery conditions if required to do so.

The E53 X5 was really a jacked-up 5 Series saloon with four-wheel drive, and even then most of the power was routed to the rear wheels to give smoother on-road performance and a comforting 'tall car' feel. The first X5 lacked any sort of serious off-road features like low-range and locking differentials, again helping to explain why BMW was so keen on the SAV tag. Various engines and manual or automatic transmission were offered during the E53 X5's life.

The second generation BMW X5 was the E70, which replaced the E53 at the end of 2006. It is wider and longer than the original with a completely new interior. For the first time, a third-row seat was offered, addressing the criticism that the E53 wasn't quite big enough for the X5's holy grail – those shared multi-kid school runs.

This refined SUV was really an elevated BMW 5 Series saloon.

Bugatti EB110

The EB110 was a pretty good car but it still drove Bugatti straight into an unyielding wall.

Entrepreneur Romano Artioli acquired Bugatti rights in 1987 and set about resurrecting the iconic French marque by building expensive supercars that paid homage to the most famous of motoring names. An architect-designed factory arose near Modena, in an area already populated by the likes of Ferrari, Maserati and De Tomaso, and the great adventure was soon up and running.

Those talented designers Stanzani and Gandini (creators of the Lamborghini Miura and Countach) were hired, and in 1989 they presented plans for (according to Bugatti boasts) the world's most technically advanced sports car. With suitably symbolic drama, the Bugatti EB110 was introduced in Paris and Versailles on 15 September 1991, 110 years to the day after Ettore Bugatti's birth.

This mid-engined coupe had a 60-valve V12 with four turbos, coupled with a six-speed gearbox and four-wheel-drive to deliver sensational performance. The lightweight body was fabricated in carbon fibre and suspension was double-wishbone. The EB110 was long and low, having an aircraft-style cockpit with rounded glass front accessed by a pair of Gandini's famous upward-opening doors. A nice touch was provided by a glass engine-cover that provided a view of the impressive power plant. Another neat idea was the electronic rear wing that could be raised and retracted at will.

The following year the Bugatti EB110 SS appeared. This was even lighter and faster than the base model, with the ability to go from sitting on the tarmac quietly growling to a howling 60 mph (97 km/h) in a tad over three neck-snapping seconds. But Romano Artioli was about to learn the harsh lesson that producing the ultimate supercar is like trying to fill a bottomless money-pit. The new Bugatti company went bust in 1995 after producing around 140 EB110s (including SS models).

COUNTRY OF ORIGIN:
Italy
FIRST MANUFACTURED:
1991 (until 1995)
ENGINE:
3,499 cc V12 Quad-turbo
PERFORMANCE:
Top speed of 213 mph (343 km/h);
0-60 mph (97 km/h) in 4.5 secs
YOU SHOULD KNOW:
Always blame the tools! When in 1995 the world's greatest-ever racing driver crashed his banana-yellow Bugatti EB110 SS into a truck, Michael Schumacher was quick to point an imperious finger at . . . the Bugatti's inadequate brakes.

Cadillac Escalade

American car makers can get hustled into precipitate action, and so it was with the Cadillac Escalade. This appeared in 1999 as a hastily conceived and poorly implemented response to numerous luxury SUVs from marques like BMW, Toyota and Mercedes that were appearing like a rash on roads everywhere. In particular, the boys at General Motors felt the need to tackle the Lincoln Navigator from arch rival Ford.

Unfortunately, Cadillac was caught on the hop, and the first generation Escalade was little more than a badge-engineered version of the lesser GMC Yukon Denali. The five-seater was smaller than the rival Navigator and underpowered, with a stodgy 5.7 litre Vortec 5700 V8 engine that impressed nobody. It was, in short, a dog – but people seemed to like it nonetheless and Cadillac pluckily kept the Escalade going unchanged through 2000.

This allowed the company to play catch-up, improving the 2002 Escalade to create a genuine contender and launching this handsome bruiser in January 2001. It came with rear-wheel drive as standard, along with an improved 5.3 litre Vortec V8 engine. Four-wheel drive was optional, as was a 6 litre V8. The new model was an eight-seater and was available as a four-door SUV or upmarket four-door EXT (extended cab) pickup truck. An ESC wagon followed in 2003, completing the second generation line-up. These powerful cars were laden with standard features and built to thrill, offering an exciting driving experience for anyone wealthy enough to buy one (and keep filling the tank).

After a shaky start, Cadillac had a hit on their hands, with sophisticated yet rugged Escalades accounting for 40 percent of Caddy's annual sales. The line was rewarded with a full third generation redesign in 2007 to reinforce the Escalade's unexpected youth appeal, which had seen an ugly duckling turn into a lucrative swan.

COUNTRY OF ORIGIN:
USA
FIRST MANUFACTURED:
1999
ENGINE:
5.7 l (348 cid), 5.3 l (323 cid),
6.0 l (366 cid) or 6.2 l (378 cid) V8
PERFORMANCE:
With 6.0 l engine – speed-limited top speed of 108 mph (174 km/h);
0-60 mph (97 km/h) in 8.7 secs
YOU SHOULD KNOW:
The Escalade is big enough to need handling with care, especially around the parking lot; to help out when reversing, the third-generation cars have a rear-facing camera that shows what lies behind on the sat-nav screen during backing-up manoeuvres.

Campagna T-Rex

Is it a boat? Is it a plane? Is it a starfighter? No, it's a motorbike. Or a three-wheeled sports car. Whatever, the futuristic Campagna T-Rex is definitely unlike any other form of wheeled thrillster devised by man. Actually, it's officially a motorcycle, though it does indeed have three wheels (two front, one back). The T-Rex is made in Quebec, Canada and had been around to delight those who've been aware of its exhilarating secrets since the mid-1990s, though the first street-legal examples were not imported into the USA until 2001.

The T-Rex was (and remains) an affordable alternative to supercars costing many times the price, with sensational performance, great roadholding and the sheer sense of speed that comes from scorching along close to the road with the wind in your face. The original concept was developed by Formula Ford racing driver and F1 mechanic Daniel Campagna, with space-age styling by Paul Deutschman.

With a lightweight reinforced fibreglass body on a multi-tubular steel chassis and frame, the T-Rex has two adjustable seats, side by side, with carbon-fibre headrests. The T-Rex has three-point seat belts and a foot-pedal box. The wind deflector is also fabricated in carbon fibre. The wheels are aluminium and there is a six-speed gearbox (with reverse). Engines have evolved over time. The first power plant was a 1.1 litre straight four, followed by a slightly smaller engine, then a 1.7 litre cc V-Twin, succeeded by two more straight fours at 1.2 litres and 1.4 litres respectively. The latest version received a substantial facelift prior to a worldwide export drive.

The T-Rex was a long time in development, but well worth waiting for. Acceleration is electric and top speed is quite frightening. The vehicle may be a mere supertrike, but it drives like a sensational miniature sports car.

COUNTRY OF ORIGIN:
Canada
FIRST MANUFACTURED:
1996 (until the present)
ENGINE:
1,074 cc, 1,052 cc, 1,164 cc or
1,352 cc Straight Four;
1,735 cc V-Twin
PERFORMANCE:
With 1.2 l engine – top speed of
140 mph (225 km/h); 0-60 mph
(97 km/h) in 4.1 secs
YOU SHOULD KNOW:
One mightily impressed motoring
writer enjoyed an eye-watering test
drive in this unique cross between
a racing car and a superbike and
promptly announced: 'Like its
Jurassic namesake the T-Rex is
a carnivore – one that eats cars
for lunch'.

The original T-Rex was a fast and dangerous predator, but the Campagna is merely fast.

*Although right up there
with the big boys, the Cizeta
couldn't survive when the
going got tough.*

Cizeta-Moroder V16T

Short of going looking for a lost one-off masterpiece, there could
scarcely be a rarer supercar for the would-be owner-driver to pursue
– for just eight examples of the Cizeta-Moroder V16T were built by
Cizeta Automobili in the 1990s and two of those are owned by the
Sultan of Brunei. The cars arose from a partnership between Ferrari
dealer Claudio Zampolli and record producer Giorgio Moroder.

They built a prototype designed by Marcello Gandini in the late
1980s. It was similar to Gandini's Lamborghini Diablo, as General
Motors had modified his design for the Diablo, leaving him free to
offer the original to Cizeta. In fact, the prototype was the only car to
carry a Cizeta-Moroder badge, as Giorgio Moroder pulled out before
the first production car was built. And what a car it was.

The engine was a transversely mounted V16 that consisted of
two coupled V8s sharing a single block, with gearing between them
providing output from the centre of the engine to longitudinal
transmission. The engine was mounted forward of the rear axle,
tight behind the seats, and carried on a honeycomb aluminium
chassis. Transmission was five-speed manual. The wide, two-door
coupe styling was typically Italian, as was performance – the V16T
could outrun just about anything else that was street-legal.

This was supposed to be the key to success, but the timing was
bad. Recession loomed and the dwindling band of buyers with
$400,000 to spend on a supercar were not inclined to go for an
unknown name, however good the performance. The V16T was
competing both with established makers like Ferrari and newcomers
like McLaren, at a time when speculators suddenly stopped buying
high-performance cars for investment purposes. It was too much for
Cizeta to bear, and the company went bust in 1995.

COUNTRY OF ORIGIN:
Italy
FIRST MANUFACTURED:
1991 (until 1995)
ENGINE:
5,995 cc V16
(Two DOHC flat-plane V8s)
PERFORMANCE:
Top speed of 204 mph (328 km/h);
0-60 mph (97 km/h) in 4 secs
YOU SHOULD KNOW:
Claudio Zampolli moved to America
after Cizeta Automobili went bust,
and continued to offer the Cizeta
V16T on a custom-built basis from
Fountain Valley, California.

Dodge Viper SR

Only in America! The Dodge Viper is a quintessentially American sports car, with a massive engine, aggressive retro styling and muscular performance. The Viper harked back to great cars like the Shelby Cobra, and indeed Carroll Shelby himself was involved in the development process. It all began in the late 1980s at Chrysler's Advanced Design Studios, where the Copperhead concept car was created – named for its broad, snakehead appearance. This received such an enthusiastic reception when the public clapped eyes on it that production was sanctioned by Chrysler boss Lee Iacocca, and in 1991 Carroll Shelby piloted the first re-named Viper pre-production model as the pace car in the Indianapolis 500 race.

The first generation appeared in 1992. The Viper SR was a two-door roadster with rounded contours, an 8 litre V10 truck engine (suitably modified and recast in aluminium by Chrysler subsidiary Lamborghini). The robust body consisted of a tubular steel frame clad in moulded fibreglass panels. There were no frills to dilute the macho appeal of the first Viper – no traction control, no anti-lock brakes, basic interior, no side windows or roof. This was a true driver's car, with fearsome performance and bad road manners that required firm hands on the wheel and a heavy foot on the brake pedal, but get-up-and-goers just loved it.

Second generation Viper SRs hit the road in 1996 and saw this great sports car through to the 21st century. Although it didn't look so very different from its predecessor, quite a few changes took place beneath the familiar skin. The engine was reworked to be lighter and more powerful, adding another 8 mph (13 km/h) to top speed and boosting acceleration. The chassis was stiffened and the suspension improved. The Viper line also acquired a sleek GTS coupe to complement the roadster.

COUNTRY OF ORIGIN:
USA
FIRST MANUFACTURED:
1992 (until 2002)
ENGINE:
8.0 l (490 cid) V10
PERFORMANCE:
First generation – top speed of 180 mph (290 km/h); 0-60 mph (97 km/h) in 4.5 secs
YOU SHOULD KNOW:
The third generation Viper ZB was launched in 2003 after a major revamp of the SR, initially as a roadster but with a coupe added in 2005. The fourth generation Viper ZBs arrived in 2008, completing the transformation from brutal sports car to sophisticated supercar.

Initially it was a brutal drive, but the Viper's 1996 second generation was almost refined.

Dodge Ram

COUNTRY OF ORIGIN:
USA
FIRST MANUFACTURED:
1994 (until 2001)
ENGINE:
Various, including a 3.9 l (239 cid) V6,
5.9 l (360 cid) V8, 5.9 l (359 cid)
Straight Six Diesel and
8.0 l (488 cid) V10.
PERFORMANCE:
With 8.0 l engine – top speed of
128 mph (206 km/h); 0-60 mph
(97 km/h) in 9.8 secs
YOU SHOULD KNOW:
In 1995 Dodge dipped a tentative toe
into ecowaters by offering a 'green'
natural gas engine, but it was not
popular and soon vanished – though
Dodge continued to promote
improved Cummings Turbo Diesels
that were belatedly challenging
American antipathy to anything that
didn't run on petrol.

The Dodge Ram pickup had been around since the early 1980s, and this full-size truck from the Chrysler stable had built up quite a reputation as the backwoodsman's best friend. But all good things come to the end, and every automaker's dream is to replace a best seller with an even more successful model that cashes in on the name and reputation of its predecessor.

That was certainly Dodge's gameplan when the squarish first generation pickups were replaced by the well-rounded second generation BR/BE Rams from 1994. The front end was deliberately styled to echo the appearance of a big lorry rig, with the intention of appealing to the open-road trucking instincts of would-be buyers of these large pickups. Even so, size was relative. The choice of engine capacity ranged from 3.9 litres all the way up to 8 litres, via a 5.9 litre diesel, with four-speed automatic or four- and five-speed manual transmission. The Ram itself could be had in 1500 half ton, 2500 three-quarter ton or 3500 one ton versions. Beyond that, it was possible to choose between the Ram's basic two-door configuration, a three-door extended cab or the four-door extended cab option.

Inside, considerable attention was paid to improving the first generation's somewhat spartan trim. This involved introducing ample storage space and a more user-friendly instrument cluster. Dodge's cunning plan was a triumph. Ram sales doubled in the first year that the BR/BE series pickups were available, with 1994 seeing sales more than double to 240,000 units. In 1996 the figure was 400,000 units, making the second generation Ram an outstanding success.

As soon as sales started to decline, Dodge repeated the relaunch trick. Second generation Rams didn't last as long as the first, being superseded by the massive third generation DR/DH trucks in 2002 after a major reworking that completely changed the Ram's appearance.

Good ol' boys loved this pickup.

Ferrari 456 GT/GTA

It may have looked decidedly blue – but the 456 was still a Ferrari through and through.

When the Ferrari 456 GT made its debut at the Paris Motor Show in 1992, everyone noticed – and not just because the show car was painted in a pleasing shade of metallic blue rather than traditional Ferrari rosso. No, it was instantly apparent that this was one of Pininfarina's best-ever designs for Maranello. The premium 456's smooth front end with pop-up headlights flowed gracefully into the raked windscreen, down over the coupe cabin and on to the compact boot. The resultant fastback profile was simple but stunning, complemented by five-spoke alloy wheels and a jutting front end.

This generous 2+2 coupe could accommodate four people comfortably within a luxurious leather interior, and the front-engined 456 GT had sensational performance for a four-seater – it was Ferrari's most powerful road car to date. The oomph was generated by a 5.5 litre V12 motor developed from the Dino-inspired V6 engine, coupled with a six-speed manual gearbox and Bosch engine management. The model name came from the capacity of each cylinder – 456 ccs. The tubular steel subframe carried a composite bonnet and aluminium body.

In 1996 the 456 GT was joined by the 456 GTA. This wasn't so very different, the only point of departure being the latter's four-speed automatic transmission as signified by the 'A'. This was unusual for Ferrari, which hadn't often offered an automatic. In 1998 the 456 M was introduced, and this was different. Aerodynamics, handling and cooling were improved, there were various styling changes and a new engine management system wrung over 440 bhp out of the ever-willing V12. It seemed impossible that the fabulous 456 GT could be improved, but that's precisely what Ferrari achieved with the 456 M. When your fairy godmother offers you the previously-owned Ferrari of your choice, ask for this one.

COUNTRY OF ORIGIN:
Italy
FIRST MANUFACTURED:
1992 (until 2003)
ENGINE:
5,474 cc V12
PERFORMANCE:
456 GT – top speed of 188 mph (302 km/h); 0-60 mph (97 km/h) in 5.1 secs
YOU SHOULD KNOW:
The car-mad Sultan of Brunei had some very special 456s custom-built by Pininfarina – these include a couple of saloon cars and two convertible Spyders – whilst the Sultan's brother (not to be outdone) ordered six special estate car versions named the 456 GT Venice.

The F50 was actually a thinly disguised F1 car.

Ferrari F50

How long does it take to celebrate a 50th Anniversary? In the case of Ferrari, the run-up to the big day in 1997 took two years, which is the time it took to produce and sell the 349 cars in the limited F50 series, which was created to celebrate the company's first half century of making road cars (though of course Ferrari had been producing racing cars since 1928).

The two-seater F50 was a mid-engined masterpiece designed by Pininfarina, which was a worthy successor to the legendary F40 – the last car from Maranello to bear Enzo Ferrari's personal stamp. The F50 was roadster with removable hardtop that incorporated many of the advanced technological features pioneered by Ferrari on the world's Formula 1 racetracks, including the 60-valve 4.7 litre race-derived V12 engine.

This was located behind the passenger compartment and drove the rear wheels through a six-speed manual gearbox. The body was a carbon-fibre monocoque with a wedge-shaped front, open cockpit with twin roll bars and an aggressively uptilted back end. The F50's low ground clearance and slippery shape created an aerodynamic package that delivered the tenacious roadholding required to control this supercar's unbridled power. The magnesium-alloy wheels had titanium hubs and the suspension was electronically controlled.

This was effectively a street-legal Grand Prix racer with covered wheels that represented an almost perfect marriage of racing car and ultimate grand tourer. Indeed, Ferrari did develop a prototype fixed-head F50 GT for sports car racing, complete with revised nose and large rear wing – testing it with considerable success – before abandoning the project to concentrate on GP racing. Although it was a tad slower that the competing McLaren F1 (at twice the price), the F50 gave its fortunate pilots the nearest thing to Formula 1 experience money could buy.

COUNTRY OF ORIGIN:
Italy
FIRST MANUFACTURED:
1995 (until 1997)
ENGINE:
4,698 cc V12
PERFORMANCE:
Top speed of 202 mph (325 km/h);
0-60 mph (97 km/h) in 3.9 secs
YOU SHOULD KNOW:
Why were precisely 349 F50s made and sold? It was said to reflect Ferrari's philosophy that they would always maintain exclusivity by 'producing one car fewer than the number we think we can sell', so clearly there was one disappointed punter who had to invest his $500,000 in alternative wheels.

Ferrari 550 Maranello

It may be too soon to mention immortality but if ever a Ferrari can be expected to become an enduring classic, it's the fabulous 550 Maranello. Why? Because this was the supercar that returned to its roots. Forget the mid-engined stuff that always made old Enzo Ferrari so nervous – the 550 Maranello was a top-of-the-line two-door V12 front-engined coupe of the kind not seen since the Daytona was discontinued back in the 1970s. No doubt Il Commendatore would have been thrilled to see the return of the configuration he loved – and delighted by the fact it bore the Maranello name to symbolize its connection with all his company's traditional virtues.

The styling of the 550 Maranello steered a skilful course between tradition and modernity, and was overseen personally by Sergio Pininfarina. The long bonnet had a pleasingly rounded front with a businesslike air scoop set between the angled glass headlight covers. The fastback passenger cabin had a roomy leather interior of the highest quality, set well back behind its sharply raked windscreen. The short flanks with air vents had an accentuated dihedral line. The boot was tall and wide and offered adequate space for a set of golf clubs.

The 550 Maranello's restrained look was based on the appearance of classic Ferraris from times past, but the aerodynamics were superb and this vehicle was one of the most technologically advanced cars ever to wear the Prancing Horse badge with pride. It had underpinnings in common with the Ferrari 456 GT, but had a shorter tubular chassis. It shared the 465 GT's double-wishbone independent suspension and coil springs, electronically controlled shock absorbers and antiroll bars, but in addition the 550 Maranello boasted a sensational three-phase traction control system (normal, sport and off). All this, coupled with the splendidly responsive engine, made the 550 Maranello a splendiferous car to drive.

COUNTRY OF ORIGIN:
Italy
FIRST MANUFACTURED:
1996 (until 2001)
ENGINE:
5,474 cc V12
PERFORMANCE:
Top speed of 199 mph (320 km/h);
0-60 mph (97 km/h) in 4.2 secs
YOU SHOULD KNOW:
An open-top Barchetta version of the 550 Maranello was introduced in 2000. The original production run was to be 444 cars (one less than the 445 Ferrari thought it could sell) – but when it was pointed out that 444 was an unlucky number in the important Japanese market the run was upped to 448 . . . which all sold anyway!

As a front-engined car, the 550 Maranello was a return to Ferrari's traditional roots.

Fiat Cinquecento

COUNTRY OF ORIGIN:
Italy (built in Poland)
FIRST MANUFACTURED:
1991 (until 1998)
ENGINE:
704 cc, 903/899 cc or 1,108 cc
Straight Four
PERFORMANCE:
Sporting – top speed of 93 mph
(150 km/h); 0-60 mph (97 km/h)
in 13.5 secs
YOU SHOULD KNOW:
Giorgetto Giugiaro was the
Cinquecento's original designer, and
he subsequently came up with a
completely new version of the little
car. Waste not, want not – when Fiat
decided not to pick up Giorgetto's
concept he promptly sold it to
Daewoo of South Korea as the basis
for their neat little 1998 Matiz
minicar.

*The Cinquecento was a neat
city car with an unusual choice
of engine configurations.*

Ital Design's Fiat Cinquecento was the replacement for the Fiat 126 and the name was a patent con – despite suggesting the engine was a modest 500 ccs, the truth of the matter was that the smallest engine offered in the new Cinquecento scoped out at an impressive 704 ccs. Naughty!

This little city car had one body style – an angular three-door hatchback with a deep wraparound front bumper. Despite its square looks, the Cinquecentro was aerodynamically efficient and had some advanced features for a budget car. These included independent suspension all round, front disc brakes, side impact bars and crumple zones. It even had better rustproofing than Fiats of earlier generations, offering hope that the driver's foot wouldn't go through the floorpan after a few years of wet running. There were optional extras available, such as electric windows, central locking and a sunroof (the Soleil version actually came with a retractable canvas roof).

There were alternative engines, too. The basic 704 cc motor was reserved for the Cinquecento's home market (it was manufactured at the FSM plant in Poland), whilst everyone else got the long-established Fiat 903 cc engine (reduced to 899 cc in 1993 for fiscal reasons). The interesting point here was that the smaller power plant was mounted longitudinally, but the larger one was arranged transversely.

Both configurations were produced simultaneously, which was a most unusual arrangement. The Cinquecento, unlike its predecessor, was a front-wheel drive car.

The Cinquecento Sporting was introduced in 1994, boasting the 1.1 litre FIRE engine from the contemporary Fiat Punto. This model boasted a close-ratio gearbox, lower ride height, roll bars and colour-coded bumpers and side mirrors. Inside there were sports seats, leather steering wheel and gear knob and a tachometer to underline Sporting credentials. This is definitely the one to zip around in!

Fiat Barchetta

For once Pininfarina was not the port of call for an Italian car company that wanted to create a stylish roadster. Instead, Fiat's own central design studio handled the development of the Tipo B Spider 176 project. This tidy little sports car with its rounded contours and coupe-like soft-top was based on the Fiat Punto Mk 1 platform. The Barchetta had Fiat's venerable 1.8 litre petrol engine, which wasn't the quietest motor in the car park – even though it was tuned and featured variable valve timing for the first time in a Fiat production car.

Fiat designed this snappy little sports tourer in-house.

Still, it was a pretty roadster with a nicely finished interior that went down rather well with junior boy (and girl) racers. It was a lightweight car that delivered good performance but what really sold it was the delightful appearance. The name (meaning 'small boat') was a generic Italian term used to describe a two-seater roadster that Fiat appropriated as its own, endowing the Barchetta with rounded front and rear bumpers, stylish headlamps beneath sloping glass on the front wings, elegant rear lamps and distinctive six-spoke steel wheels.

Although designed in-house, the delightful Barchetta was fabricated by outside coachbuilder Maggiora. After taking a break in 2003 (when Maggiora went bust), a revamped version was relaunched from Fiat's Mirafiori factory in 2004. But this snappy sports car's time had come and gone, for the Barchetta was discontinued in 2005. It was a sad demise for those interested in buying a classic open-top roadster, though plenty of enthusiastic drivers will continue to enjoy the Barchetta experience for years to come (there are dedicated owners' clubs in many countries that hold annual meetings). Better still, good used examples are inexpensive, so it's possible to join the Barchetta party for a very reasonable entry fee.

COUNTRY OF ORIGIN:
Italy
FIRST MANUFACTURED:
1995 (until 2002)
ENGINE:
1,747 cc Straight Four
PERFORMANCE:
Top speed of 118 mph (190 km/h);
0-60 mph (97 km/h) in 8.7 secs
YOU SHOULD KNOW:
Unfortunately it isn't possible to get hold of a right-hand drive example of the Barchetta – Fiat never commissioned this option, even though the car was exported to the important British and Japanese sports car markets.

The Puma – a car that failed to live up to Ford's high hopes.

Ford Puma

The Ford Motor Company in Europe was rather pleased with the impact of its New Edge design strategy in the late 1990s, first fruit of which was the highly individual Ford Ka. People either loved or hated this controversial small car, but Ford definitely liked the waves made by their daring style initiative and decided to return to the well with the revised Mondeo (1996), the German-built Puma (1997) and Focus (1998).

The Puma was not the most extreme example of New Edge design, though it still didn't please everyone. This three-door hatchback crouched in a somewhat feline manner, as though poised to spring forward suddenly from rest. The Puma was a 2+2 coupe based on the Ford Fiesta and came with front discs and rear drums, with an ABS system as an option. The Puma was a front-engined, front-wheel drive performance car that had four different engines over the production run, all 16-valve Sigmas branded as the Zetec-S. The various versions came in at 1.4 litres, 1.6 litres and two at 1.7 litres with different power output.

The Racing Puma was a bold enterprise that flopped. Originally one thousand high-performance specials were envisaged, but fewer than half were sold to the public. Each had a tuned 1.7 litre engine belting out 155 bhp, modified body shell, disc brakes all round and bucket seats. This model was painted in an exclusive shade of blue and sold only in the UK market as a right-hand-drive car. The Racing Pumas were created by the Ford Rally team at Boreham and modified by Tickford in Daventry.

When the Puma was discontinued in 2002 its replacement was not like for like, but instead the Ford StreetKa – a two-seater Fiesta-based convertible that at least used the Puma's transmission and suspension.

COUNTRY OF ORIGIN:
Germany
FIRST MANUFACTURED:
1997 (until 2002)
ENGINE:
1,388 cc, 1,596 cc or 1,679 cc
Straight Four
PERFORMANCE:
Racing Puma – top speed of 126 mph
(202 km/h); 0-60 mph (97 km/h) in
7.9 secs
YOU SHOULD KNOW:
The Puma's memorable launch campaign featured a born-again Steve McQueen in San Francisco together with a newborn Puma, thanks to clips from the iconic movie *Bullitt* and the latest digital wizardry.

Ford Escort RS Cosworth

It was the most illustrious – and exclusive – Ford Escort of all. Just over 7,000 Escort RS Cosworths were built in five years, and they remain the most desirable of performance Escorts. They replaced the Escort RS Turbo in the prestigious Ford Rallye Sport series.

A powerful Cosworth YBT 2 litre turbocharged engine beat at the heart of this ultra-fast Escort, punching out around 225 bhp in road mode but capable of producing four times that output when highly tuned. This motor had previously featured in the Sierra Cosworth, another legend in its own lifetime that contributed a chassis and mechanicals to the RS Cosworth. There was a five-speed manual gearbox and the car had a permanent four-wheel drive system. The first 2,500 were built to secure homologation for the World Rally Championship and were instantly identifiable by the 'whale tail' rear spoiler that rose above the cabin roof. These 'Cossies' occasionally bore a Motorsport badge.

The second generation appeared in 1994 and the prominent spoiler became optional, those most buyers opted on an 'if you've got it, flaunt it' basis. The Garrett turbocharger was more efficient, reducing turbo lag and making the engine altogether more responsive to hard driving.

As always with Ford performance cars, it was a question of which came first – chicken or egg? To put it another way, did Ford produce stunning rally cars to make a handsome profit by selling road-going versions to adoring petrolheads, or was the grand plan to sell road-going versions of stunning rally cars to adoring petrolheads to achieve homologation and subsidize racing costs? The answer may well be chicken and egg. Either way, the RS Cosworth was a multiple rally winner in the 1990s, acquiring legendary status and shifting every road car made in the process. A true win-win situation!

COUNTRY OF ORIGIN:
UK
FIRST MANUFACTURED:
1992 (until 1996)
ENGINE:
1,993 cc Straight Four Turbo
PERFORMANCE:
Top speed of 137 mph (220 km/h);
0-60 mph (97 km/h) in 6.2 secs
YOU SHOULD KNOW:
Ford only discontinued sale of the Escort RS Cosworth ahead of new 1996 European Union vehicle noise regulations, on the grounds that compliance would have been too costly – though the RS Cosworth continued to operate as the company's winning rally car until 1998.

The RS Cosworth was a big winner for Ford on every level.

Honda NSX

COUNTRY OF ORIGIN:
Japan
FIRST MANUFACTURED:
1990 (until 2005)
ENGINE:
2,977 cc or 3,179 cc DOHC V6
PERFORMANCE:
With 3.2 l engine – top speed of
170 mph (274 km/h); 0-60 mph
(97 km/h) in 5.7 secs
YOU SHOULD KNOW:
The Honda NSX's passenger
compartment was finalized after
studying the American F-16 jet
fighter's cockpit. Pre-production
models were extensively tested by
Formula 1 drivers Ayrton Senna and
Satoru Nakajima and subsequently
modified to reflect their
recommendations.

Don't go looking for one of these super sports cars in Hong Kong or North America, where the moniker of choice was the Acura NSX. But everywhere else an enquiry for a Honda NSX will be met by the sharp intake of breath that acknowledges that something rather special has been mentioned.

This mid-engined, rear-wheel drive coupe had supercar looks and performance to match, propelled by Honda's aluminium V6 engine – initially a 3 litre and subsequently a 3.2 version (from 1997). Anyone looking at the low, wide NSX would assume that it was styled in Italy . . . and would be right. The ubiquitous Pininfarina studio designed the HP-X prototype that became the NSX.

The NSX reflected Honda's all-conquering presence on the world's Grand Prix circuits. This beautifully styled, low-slung performance car was the first all-aluminium production car and was renowned for excellent manners, with great ride quality, precise handling, rugged reliability and meticulous build quality . . . not to mention an A+ in the street cred stakes. Honda had produced an everyday supercar that could justifiably claim to be the equal of the rival Ferrari 348 – no mean feat.

But while Ferrari moved on to the 355, 360 and 430 models, Honda merely produced evolutionary versions of the NSX – beyond the point where it was a technological marvel of the 1990s and became a reminder of past glories in the 21st century. That's not to say that versions like the NSX-R track racer, NSX-T targa top, NSX-S performance special or NSX-R GT were in any way inferior – far from it, especially as the NSX received a major facelift in 1997 and further tweaking in 2002. But by the time it was discontinued in 2005 only a few hundred NSXs were being sold annually. Its time was up.

Honda's very own entry in the prestigious supercar stakes.

Hummer H1

In the battle of the genuine off-road giants there really could be only one winner.

Oh what a lovely war – at least that must have been the thought at AM General in Mishawaka, Indiana, because Operation Desert Storm in the early 1990s created a civilian market for the company's HMMWV (High Mobility Multipurpose Wheeled Vehicle). As that's not an acronym that rolls kindly off the tongue, this heavyweight replacement for the military Jeep is generally known as the Humvee.

With enthusiastic support from action men like Arnold Schwarzenegger, AM General produced a civilian version of the Humvee. The Hummer H1 struck a suitably patriotic note and was soon strutting its stuff on the streets of America, making the average SUV look like a child's pedal car. The Hummer had amazing off-road capability, with enormous stability and high ground clearance negating the roughest terrain. It comfortably climbed tall steps, forded deep water and addressed the steepest of slopes. Though macho civilians rarely pushed their Hummers to the limit, the kick in owning one of these behemoths was knowing that you could if you wanted to – and everyone else knew it too.

The Hummer H1 came in three regular variants – soft-top, pickup truck and wagon. Various alternatives like a two-door pickup and four-door fastback were produced in small numbers. There was a selection of engines, mainly V8 diesels, though there was one inadequate petrol option. The choice of engine determined transmission, with three-, four- and five-speed boxes teamed with the various engines.

Soldiers bumping around in their spartan Humvees would certainly have been impressed by the creature comforts built into the Hummer – indeed, the US Army actually purchased civilian Hummers for the use of top brass and visiting politicians who were making field trips. But the Gulf War Humvee factor didn't last long – the beast was discontinued in 1996, though the name would subsequently return.

COUNTRY OF ORIGIN:
USA
FIRST MANUFACTURED:
1992 (until 1996)
ENGINE:
6.2 l (378 cid), 6.5 l (396 cid)
or 6.6 l (402 cid) Diesel V8;
5.7 l (348 cid) V8
PERFORMANCE:
Varied according to engine – typically
a top speed of around 80 mph
(129 km/h)
YOU SHOULD KNOW:
Inflation ruled – the price of a
Hummer H1 wagon with full spec
upon launch in 1992 was around
$55,000, but the equivalent wagon
made in the last model year of 1996
cost over $140,000, albeit with
considerable uprating from the
original version.

The XJ220 sadly proved to be an expensive miscalculation.

Jaguar XJ220

In the late 1980s supercar fever was reaching is height, with established classics appreciating rapidly as speculators drove up prices and various manufacturers scrambled to take advantage by custom building awesome performance cars that were billed as the classics of the future (with a price tag to match the hype).

Jaguar leapt aboard the gravy train in some style – coming up with the world's fastest production car, which ruled supreme in the speed stakes until the McLaren F1 shot past. But that's not to say that the XJ220 was an unqualified success story. It was initially conceived by Jaguar employees who came up with the idea of creating the ultimate road car and the mid-engined prototype certainly looked the part when it appeared in 1988.

The reaction was so positive that Jaguar announced that the XJ220 would go into production, as a strictly limited edition, with would-be buyers required to put down a substantial deposit to go on the waiting list. Dotted lines were signed upon and Jaguar set about turning their concept car into reality with the help of constructor Tom Walkinshaw Racing. The design by Keith Helfet was stunning, with flowing lines, a low cockpit and businesslike air scoops behind scissor-style doors. Sadly, by the time it was ready in 1992 the price had increased substantially, the supercar bubble had burst and many customers tried to wriggle out of their contracts. This controversy spoiled the debut of an excellent if expensive machine.

Despite the fact that Jaguar did not finally sell the last of 281 XJ220s until 1997, after drastically cutting the price, the XJ220 has become a sought-after collectors' car. But this stylish supercar did not prove to be a great investment, changing hands today at roughly a quarter of the original cost.

COUNTRY OF ORIGIN:
UK
FIRST MANUFACTURED:
1992 (until 1994)
ENGINE:
3,498 V6 Twin Turbo
PERFORMANCE:
Top speed of 220 mph (354 km/h);
0-60 mph (97 km/h) in 4 secs
YOU SHOULD KNOW:
If you ever come across a parked XJ220, take a peek through the curved rear window and admire the V6 engine with its twin Garrett turbochargers that can be seen lurking within.

Jaguar XK8/XKR

Despite having the best-selling sports car of all time in the stable, Jaguar decided to replace the XJ-S and unveiled a worthy successor at the 1996 Geneva Motor Show. The handsome XK8 bore Jaguar's classic styling signature, with the streamlined shape evoking past greats like the XK120, XK150, C-, D- and E-Types . . . even the XJ220 supercar.

The new XKs were available as convertibles and coupes. Although it was impossible to tell, they shared a platform with the Aston Martin DB7 as synergies generated by Ford's ownership of both classic marques started to filter into the model ranges. The XK8 had a normally aspirated 4 litre V8 engine giving 290 bhp whilst the identical XKR had a turbocharged version of Jaguar's new motor that delivered an impressive 370 bhp. Interiors were luxurious, with the mix of leather and burr walnut that turned these powerful sports cars into prestigious grand tourers.

The XK8/XKR series remained in production for a decade, with no more than a few modest styling changes. A number of special edition XKRs were introduced along the way. The XKR Silverstone, limited to 600 cars, was intended to celebrate Jaguar's return to Formula 1 racing in 2001. It was a standard car with a silver paint finish, improved running gear, larger wheels and a custom interior. The XKR 100 was also produced in 2001 to mark the centenary of Jaguar founder Sir William Lyons' birth – 500 coupes and 500 convertibles were built. The XKR Portfolio convertible of 2004 was for America only, with 200 cars in blue and 200 in red. The last XK based on the original design was the XKR 4.2 S, a debutant in 2005 that featured an enlarged 4.2 litre V8 engine. The XK8 and XKR were discontinued in 2006.

COUNTRY OF ORIGIN:
UK
FIRST MANUFACTURED:
1996 (until 2006)
ENGINE:
3,996 cc V8
PERFORMANCE:
The XK8 had an electronically limited top speed of 155 mph (249 km/h); 0-60 mph (97 km/h) in 6.4 secs
YOU SHOULD KNOW:
The XK series continued from 2007 with all-new Jaguar XK, XK 4.2 and XKR models – visual kinship with the contemporary Aston Martin DB7 and Vanquish coupes is explained by the fact they were all designed by Ian Callum, though interestingly the XKs were first created as convertibles from which the coupes derived rather than vice versa.

The new Jaguar XKs actually shared a platform with contemporary Aston Martins.

Jeep TJ Wrangler

COUNTRY OF ORIGIN:
USA
FIRST MANUFACTURED:
1996 (until 2006)
ENGINE:
2.4 l (148 cid) or 2.5 l (150 cid)
Straight Four; 4.0 l (241 cid)
Straight Six
PERFORMANCE:
With 4.0 l engine – top speed of 108
mph (175 km/h); 0-60 mph (97 km/h)
in 9.9 secs
YOU SHOULD KNOW:
A right-hand drive version of the
TJ Wrangler was produced for export
to left-side drive countries, and was
also sold to the US Post Office so
rural mail carriers could reach out
to mailboxes without leaving
the vehicle.

The modern successor of that famous Willys wartime Jeep
swaggered onto the scene in the form of the first generation
YJ Wrangler, a robust off-roader introduced by Chrysler with a Jeep
badge in 1987. Wranglers were initially built in Canada where –
ironically – the Wrangler name couldn't be used because Chevrolet
had already bagged it for a pickup. So Wranglers became the Jeep
YJ in home territory. Production switched to the USA in 1992, but
when the revamped second generation Wrangler arrived in 1996 the
same restriction applied, with Canadian exports bearing the Jeep TJ
name. To cut a confusing story short, the rest of the world now
refers to the YJ Wrangler and the TJ Wrangler to differentiate
between the two models.

The TJ Wrangler was much improved. It featured coil-spring
suspension borrowed from the larger Jeep Grand Cherokee. The
entry level TJ had a 2.5 litre four-cylinder motor (2.4 litre from
2003), but most opted for the big 4 litre straight six shared with the
Cherokee and Grand Cherokee. There was a choice of transmissions
over the production run, with three- and four-speed automatics or
five- and six-speed manuals on offer. Stylistically, the TJ had more
rounded contours than its predecessor, but this sturdy SUV
remained a no-frills two-door soft top.

*The TJ was an improvement on
its rather basic predecessor.*

There were various options within the range, such as the Sport (with the larger engine) and Sahara (a premium model with all the bells and whistles). Along the trail came the X (to replace the Sport from 2002), the Rubicon (another premium model with beefed-up off-road capability introduced in 2003) and the slightly larger Unlimited that offered more interior space and came in standard or Rubicon trim. The Jeep JK Wrangler displaced the TJ in 2007, carrying this no-nonsense SUV line into a third successful decade of production.

Koenig C62

What did a million dollars buy the supercar enthusiast in 1991? The most exclusive answer to that question was undoubtedly the Koenig C62. Customizer Willy Koenig's speciality was tuning other people's supercars and the German outfit produced some outrageous machines – like a thousand-horsepower Ferrari Testarossa – to delight those with bottomless pockets who wanted to go faster than anyone else on road or racetrack.

The C62 started life as a Porsche 962 C1 chassis, but the end result was so different from the legendary racer that it became the only Koenig production that actually bore the company name. This extraordinary mid-engined masterpiece had an entirely new carbon-fibre body with an aircraft-style domed cockpit set well forward, ground clearance that was just sufficient to allow regulation headlights to be fitted, flared wheel arches, flat flanks and an extraordinary raised back end terminating in prominent triangular wings and fat twin exhaust pipes beneath a businesslike spoiler. Access was via small transparent gullwings that formed part of the cockpit glass and an unusual lifting box section of bodywork. Rearward vision was provided by side mirrors attached to the top of the cockpit, whilst the engine was accessed through a sloping oval panel.

This was an out-and-out racing car that was street-legal and it was one of the fastest road cars the world had even seen. This rear-wheel drive missile could rocket past 125 mph (km/h) from a standing start in under 10 seconds and blast past 220 mph well before the pedal hit the metal. This was achieved with the willing cooperation of a highly tuned 3.4 litre twin-turbocharged engine that belted out 588 bhp, coupled to a five-speed manual gearbox. Not many people have even seen a C62, let alone driven one – it's the rarest of supercars.

COUNTRY OF ORIGIN:
Germany
FIRST MANUFACTURED:
1991
ENGINE:
3,368 cc Flat Six Twin Turbo
PERFORMANCE:
Top speed of 235 mph (378 km/h); 0-60 mph (97 km/h) in 3.3 secs
YOU SHOULD KNOW:
Racing driver Willy Koenig was joined in the family customizing business by son Walter and they're still busily modifying performance cars for discerning enthusiasts today. The real thing may cost megabucks, but mere mortals can get illustrated brochures from Koenig-Specials to drool over for a few euros apiece.

The Diablo continued to evolve throughout its lifetime.

Lamborghini Diablo

Despite being a devil in disguise (well, in Spanish then) it wasn't necessary to sell one's soul to get a Lambo Diablo – just greeting the model launch in 1990 with a briefcase containing around $250,000 would do the trick. This wide, low-slung wedge with its characteristic grooved skirt and rounded air scoops in front of the back wheels was Lamborghini's long-awaited replacement for the Countach.

The mid-engined Diablo had been under development since 1995, and was worth waiting for. This was no poseur's car, but an out-and-out performance model with a 48-valve 5.7 litre Lamborghini V12 with dual overhead cams and computer-controlled fuel injection. The brutish 492 bhp thus generated fed the rear wheels.

There was initially no choice of body style, as all Diablos were two-door coupes.

But interesting advances were afoot. After three years of tweaking the basic model a VT (for Viscous Traction) Diablo coupe appeared in 1993, followed by an open targa-topped version in 1995. Power was fed through a manual gearbox and four-wheel drive system to massive road wheels and fat tyres at each corner, making for adhesive roadholding, rapid acceleration and breathtaking top speed. The VT was uprated to a Version 2 in 1997, but when new owner Audi took over in 1998 the Diablo was given a 6 litre engine and major facelift even as a successor, the Murciélago, was developed.

There were various special editions in the Diablo's lifetime. The Diablo SE (1994-95 Special Edition) celebrated the company's 30th birthday. This hard-edged speedster could be further upgraded with the Jota package. The Diablo SV (Sport Veloce) lacked all-wheel drive. The Diablo SVR was a racing version created for a single-car pro-am series known as the Diablo Supertrophy. A few of these cars were subsequently modified for road use, reminding everyone of the Diablo's performance pedigree.

COUNTRY OF ORIGIN:
Italy
FIRST MANUFACTURED:
1990 (until 2001)
ENGINE:
5,707 cc or 5,992 cc V12
PERFORMANCE:
With 5.7 l engine – top speed of 203 mph (326 km/h); 0-60 mph (97 km/h) in 3.9 secs
YOU SHOULD KNOW:
Diablos were very much driver's cars, not noted for an excessively luxurious interior finish, but those who always liked to keep track of time as they sped along the highway were able to order an optional dashboard clock by prestigious Swiss maker Breguet – that'll be another $10,500 please.

Lexus SC 400

Toyota's plan to conquer the automobile world required a luxury brand, especially in the vital American market. Toyota wasn't the first Japanese carmaker to travel this road, as Honda had been offering luxury cars with an Acura badge since the mid-1980s. But Toyota wasn't that far behind, and the Lexus LS 400 saloon appeared in 1989 as the flagship of the new prestige marque. But Toyota also wanted to produce a personal luxury coupe to compete with the likes of Mercedes Benz, so the Lexus SC 400 made its debut in the summer of 1991.

Japanese styling for this superior segment of the market wasn't up to speed, and Toyota shrewdly handed the design job to Californian outfit Calty Design Research. It was an inspired decision. Starting from the LS 400 platform Calty produced a rounded two-door coupe with no straight edges that proved to be a trendsetter, pointing in a direction that other manufacturers would follow. The design may have been American, but the cars were built at Toyota's Motomachi plant in Japan and shipped to the States.

The SC 400 featured the super-smooth new 4 litre 1UZ-FE V8 engine. This was teamed with a four-speed automatic gearbox to deliver sports-car performance. The luxurious interior was finished in leather and this sporty coupe was an instant hit with American buyers, not least because it was half the price of a comparable Merc. It is a testament to the SC 400's advanced character that virtually no modifications were required during the nine-year production run, though the engine was upgraded in 1996.

Few British drivers have experienced the refined pleasure of schmoozing along in a Lexus SC 400. These luxury cars were never officially sold in the United Kingdom, though a few personal imports filtered in over time.

COUNTRY OF ORIGIN:
Japan
FIRST MANUFACTURED:
1991 (until 2000)
ENGINE:
3,969 cc V8
PERFORMANCE:
Top speed of 150 mph (241 km/h);
0-60 mph (97 km/h) in 6.9 secs
YOU SHOULD KNOW:
A junior version of the Lexus SC 400 was launched in North America in 1992, featuring a 3 litre straight six engine and an optional manual gearbox – visually the SC 300 was virtually identical to its big brother, and the two would run in parallel until second generation cars appeared in 2002.

Toyota boldly went for a share of the luxury car market by introducing the Lexus brand.

Lotus Carlton

COUNTRY OF ORIGIN:
UK
FIRST MANUFACTURED:
1990 (until 1992)
ENGINE:
3,615 cc Straight Six Twin Turbo
PERFORMANCE:
Top speed of 176 mph (283 km/h);
0-60 mph (97 km/h) in 5 secs
YOU SHOULD KNOW:
Very few contemporary cars could
outrun the Lotus Carlton (or Type
104, as Lotus designated this
extraordinary machine) – for it had
all-round performance figures that
outgunned most V12 supercars,
though it did reluctantly have to give
way to the Lamborghini Diablo.

Four years after the Vauxhall Carlton made its debut, the fearsome Lotus Carlton derivative smoked onto the scene. To the untutored eye, this looked pretty much like any other four-door Carlton saloon. But keener observers noted air intakes on the bonnet, a rear spoiler and wide wheel arches . . . plus discreet Lotus badging. Lotus Carltons came in Imperial Green only, a dark colour that looked almost black in most lights.

The innovative Lotus engineering outfit based at the former Hethel airfield outside Norwich certainly knew how to produce flying machines. Vauxhall's standard 24-valve 3 litre straight six engine was unceremoniously bored out to 3.6 litres. Twin Garrett T24 turbochargers were added, giving an impressive 382 bhp. A six-speed manual ZF gearbox was borrowed from the Chevy Corvette to feed all that power to the rear wheels. Ventilated disc brakes with racing calipers, a Bosch anti-lock system and tweaked suspension with self-levelling dampers ensured that this potent performer wouldn't get out of hand.

Parent General Motors marketed the Lotus Carlton in the UK and on the Continent, where it was known as the Lotus Omega. The original plan called for an exclusive run of just 1,100 cars, with UK models costing nearly £50,000. But recession bit hard in the early 1990s and even that modest target proved impossible to hit. Fewer than a thousand were actually built, and two-thirds of those were Omegas distributed in Europe by Opel (to at least seven countries).

This means that few drivers have ever experienced the staggering performance that Lotus squeezed out of the world's fastest-ever production saloon car – and those who want to experience it today will find the task nearly impossible. Lotus Carlton/Omegas rarely come up for sale, and when they do the price reflects their rarity (and desirability).

Vauxhall's answer to the Ford Cosworth proved to be even faster than its speedy rival.

Lotus Elise

The Lotus philosophy is simple – build 'em light, fit a small but powerful engine, design a striking but efficient body, add an advanced suspension and braking package… then put it all together, sit back and watch sporting drivers having fun. And that, ladies and gentlemen of the road, is the case for the Lotus Elise.

A low profile made the Elise seem even faster than it was.

It was a convincing case, too, for this splendid roadster with echoes of Italian supercar styling was an instant hit when it appeared in 1996. The Hethel-based outfit had been developing the Elise Series 1 convertible for a couple of years, taking a bonded aluminium chassis and adding a fibreglass body shell. Coupled with the 16 valve 1.8 litre fuel-injected K series engine, this ensured that the Elise's performance matched that of sports cars that cost more. But the real joy of the Elise is the all-round driving experience, as both handling and roadholding are exceptional.

But – although plenty of standard Series 1 cars were made and sold – performance was the name of the game, and numerous special editions of the Elise were built before Series 2 came along in 2001. Some were simply clever marketing ploys – like the green-and-gold Lotus 50th anniversary edition or the John Player Special black-and-gold Type 72. The Exige of 2000 was actually a hardtop Elise.

But others like the 1998 Elise 190 VHPD (Very High Performance Derivative) with its race seats and harnesses, roll cage, adjustable suspension and 187 bhp were for the driver who liked competitive weekend track outings. This market was also served by the Elise Sprint (later the 111S) of 1999, soon to be joined by the Sport 135. The final evolutions were the Elise Sport 160 and 190 in 2000. Special editions and performance models are the most highly sought-after Series 1 Elises.

COUNTRY OF ORIGIN:
UK
FIRST MANUFACTURED:
1996
ENGINE:
1,796 cc Straight Four
PERFORMANCE:
Top speed of 124 mph (200 km/h); 0-60 mph (97 km/h) in 5.6 secs
YOU SHOULD KNOW:
The ultimate development of the Elise Series 1 was the Lotus 340R (just 340 built) – this eye-catching open-top special with roll bars, external wheels and scooped bonnet was issued in 2000 as a performance special intended for track and road use.

413

*This awesome machine is
one of the most desirable –
and expensive – road cars
ever produced.*

McLaren F1

There have been many pretenders to the title of 'ultimate road car', but few have actually managed to grab the crown for long, as a new monarch invariably awaits just around the corner with more horsepower and a higher top speed. But the McLaren F1 delivered in spades, and remained unchallenged king of the road for longer than most.

McLaren Automotive's chief engineer Gordon Murray sketched out the concept on the way home from the 1988 Italian Grand Prix. McLaren boss Ron Dennis liked the audacious three-seater sports car and – yes – they did indeed decide to build it as the ultimate road car. After Murray shopped around for an engine without success, BMW offered to build a 6.1 litre aluminium-alloy power plant. This big 48-valve engine with quad overhead camshafts was fuel injected.

The engine was teamed with a light chassis and body fabricated with modern materials like kevlar and titanium. The F1 was constructed using a carbon-fibre monocoque derived from McLaren's racing expertise. The XP1 prototype was almost unchanged for the production run, and was one of the most visually attractive supercars ever produced. The driver sat in the middle with the two passenger seats slightly further back on either side. Entry was via two butterfly doors – effectively each side of the cockpit down to floor level lifted to allow easy access. The interior featured air conditioning, custom Kenwood stereo, auto defrosting, electric windows and remote central locking. This and numerous other useful features helped justify that 'ultimate road car' tag.

Fewer than 70 F1 road cars were built from 1992, though five F1 LMs were made to celebrate the 1995 Le Mans win, plus two evolution F1 GTs and 21 GTR racing models. Numbered amongst the most desirable supercars ever made, they have all appreciated considerably in price.

COUNTRY OF ORIGIN:
UK
FIRST MANUFACTURED:
1992 (until 1998)
ENGINE:
6,064 cc V12
PERFORMANCE:
Top speed (with rev limiter) of
231 mph (372 km/h);
0-60 mph (97 km/h) in 3.2 secs
YOU SHOULD KNOW:
The McLaren F1 was the world's
fastest-ever production car
(achieving a phenomenal 240.1
mph/386.7 km/h) until the Bugatti
Veyron came along in 2005 – an
enduring record that is all the more
impressive because the F1 had a
normally aspirated rather than a
turbocharged engine.

Mercedes-Benz SLK R170

Mercedes wasn't prepared to let the snazzy BMW Z3 and Porsche Boxster have the sporting arena all to themselves, and launched the SLK R170 compact roadster in 1997 to grab a slice of the action. This plainly styled but pleasing sports car followed the lead of Mitsubishi's 3000GT Spyder, featuring a retractable hardtop that changed a coupe into a convertible – a template that other manufacturers would copy.

The SLK designation comes from the Mercedes mission statement for these cars – *Sportlich, Leicht, Kurz* (sporty, light and short). The R170 platform was new for 1997, and lasted until the R171 arrived in 2005. During the relatively short life of the R170 there were a number of models, differentiated by engine size and power output. Three different transmissions were offered during the run – five-speed automatic and five- and six-speed manual.

The basic 2 litre 200 version was produced throughout. The 2 litre 200K was also offered from 1997 to 2004, with an engine change in 2001. The 230K appeared in 1998 with a 2.3 litre engine, upgraded in 2001 – the 'K' stood for Kompressor (supercharger). The 320 with its 3.2 litre V6 engine did not hit the road until 2001, which year also saw the introduction of the high-powered 32 AMG model. Chassis production for all models was by Karmann in Germany, though some 320s were built in other countries as Mercedes vehicle production went global.

The most potent SLK R170 was the 32 AMG. This rare tyre-smoker scorched from rest to 60 mph (97 km/h) in 4.5 secs, with a top speed of 193 mph (311 km/h). Around 4,300 were built. A thousand stayed in Germany, two thousand went to the States and a few hundred to the United Kingdom. It's worth trying to catch one if you can for the ultimate SLK R170 driving experience.

COUNTRY OF ORIGIN:
Germany (also built in South Africa and Mexico)
FIRST MANUFACTURED:
1997 (until 2004)
ENGINE:
1,998 cc or 2,295 cc Straight Four; 3,199 cc V6
PERFORMANCE:
With 3.2 l engine – top speed of 152 mph (245 km/h); 0-60 mph (97 km/h) in 6.5 secs
YOU SHOULD KNOW:
Hand-built engines for the 32 AMG were supplied by performance specialist AMG – the independent company founded in 1967 with a history of upping the power output of Mercedes engines that was taken over by DaimlerChrysler shortly before the 32 AMG was launched.

The SLK R170 was launched to compete with the BMW Z3 and Porsche's successful Boxster.

Mercedes-Benz A-Class W168

COUNTRY OF ORIGIN:
Germany
FIRST MANUFACTURED:
1997 (until 2004)
ENGINE:
1,397 cc, 1,598 cc, 1,898 cc or
1,998 cc Straight Four; 1,698 cc
Straight Four Diesel
PERFORMANCE:
With 1.9 l engine – top speed of
120 mph (193 km/h); 0-60 mph
(97 km/h) in 9.8 secs
YOU SHOULD KNOW:
The first A-Class W168 may have
failed the moose test, but the Baby
Benz did have a patented 'Sandwich'
front-impact protection system that
allowed the engine and transmission
to slide beneath the floor in the
event of a violent head-on collision,
rather than entering the passenger
compartment.

It was new and very different from anything Mercedes-Benz had produced previously – and the A Class W168 involved the company in a steep learning curve. This compact car was designed as a mass-market entry-level model that would spread the prestige of driving a Merc to a wider customer base than ever before. It was swiftly nicknamed 'The Baby Benz'.

Mercedes hadn't produced a front-wheel drive car before and the project didn't get off to an auspicious start. Although the debut of the A-Class created a frisson of excitement, this innovative little five-door car with its sloping front and square hatchback was soon in trouble as the wheels flew off – happily not literally. The whistleblower was a Swedish motoring publication, which road tested the new car and discovered that it flipped over during the soon-to-be-infamous 'moose test'. This involved swerving to avoid an imaginary moose at speed . . . at which point the A-Class turned turtle.

Shock-horror and knee-jerk denial in Stuttgart were swiftly followed by a recall of the few thousand cars that had already been sold, which

were fitted with electronic stability control and modified suspension. This was the first stability control system fitted to a small car and helped the A-Class survive its shaky start. There was a choice of models within the range, with various engine options. The four petrol engines were 1.4 litres, 1.6 litres, 1.9 litres and 2 litres. The diesel engine was a 1.7 litre unit. The vehicle did justify the initial optimism of the Mercedes marketing department, going on to become a high-volume seller.

Modifications following the failed moose test gave the original A-Class W168s a stiff ride quality on rough road surfaces, and would-be owner-drivers are advised to look for one of the later, improved A-Class W169 models that arrived in 2004.

Thanks to that wretched moose the new 'Baby Benz' got off to a more-than-uncertain start

MG RV8

This was an overdue revival, for the last MGBs had been built in 1980. But when the Rover Group noted the growing popularity of small roadsters in the early 1990s – following the lead set by the Mazda MX-5 – the company created an updated version of the MGB roadster, fitted the big 4 litre Rover V8 engine, added a limited-slip differential and designated the old-new model as the MG RV8.

This was a very special sports car in the traditional British style, which had a dual objective – to revive the hallowed MG name and remind the buying public that the MGB had been the best-selling sports car of all time. The body was a curvaceous and exceptionally attractive reworking of the MGB body (described at the time as resembling an MGB on steroids). The engine was fuel-injected and teamed with a five-speed manual gearbox, whilst suspension and handling were updated (though not to the most modern of standards).

The handcrafted interior of this expensive two-seater was superb, featuring burr-elm dashboard, door cappings and centre console. This exclusive look was complemented by the finest Connolly leather and thick pile carpeting, with the overall effect being one of refined luxury. The woven hood may easily be raised and lowered by one person and folds neatly behind the seats. If this super sports car does have a fault, it's the fact that it fails the golf bag test – the boot is small and mainly occupied by the large spare wheel.

Despite being written off as old-fashioned by many motoring writers, the MG RV8 enjoyed considerable popularity among well-heeled MG enthusiasts, and won the time Rover needed to develop and launch the successful MGF. With demand for RV8s exceeding limited supply, these modern-day classics are ultra-desirable and still offer an exhilarating drive.

COUNTRY OF ORIGIN:
UK
FIRST MANUFACTURED:
1993 (until 1995)
ENGINE:
3,947 cc V8
PERFORMANCE:
Top speed of 135 mph (217 km/h); 0-60 mph (97 km/h) in 5.9 secs
YOU SHOULD KNOW:
Ironically, as the MG RV8 had been inspired by the Mazda MX-5's success, a large proportion of the 2,000 RV8s built over the three-year production run were exported to Japan, then in the middle of a love affair with British luxury goods.

The RV8 proved to be popular with trendy Japanese buyers.

417

MGF

The first new MG since the MGB in 1962 arrived in 1995 as
something altogether different – a mid-engined, rear-wheel drive
roadster that was launched by the Rover Group following BMW's
takeover. There were two variations of the Mk I, each with a
16-valve 1.8 litre K-series engine. The base version put out 118 bhp
whilst the more powerful VVC (Variable Valve Control) option
delivered 145 bhp. One unique feature was Hydragas suspension,
which provided excellent ride quality and precise handling
characteristics.

　　Despite the fact that this was clearly not a traditional design, MG
enthusiasts old and new loved the newcomer and it shot straight to
the top of the affordable UK sports-car chart. But after four years of
brisk sales the MGF Mk II was introduced. This involved a face-lifted
interior, minor styling changes and new alloy wheels. A new base
model with a 1.6 litre engine also appeared in 1999, as did a high-

*MG Rover failed dismally,
but China knew a good
thing when it saw one.*

performance version badged as the Trophy 160 which had a tuned engine producing – surprise – 160 bhp that could deliver a superior 0-60 mph (97 km/h) time of 6.9 secs. However, relatively few examples of the Trophy 160 were built. The Mk II range also featured an automatic model with continuous-variable Steptronic transmission.

Once more, sales of the Mk II were brisk despite BMW's disposal of the Rover and MG marques to the Phoenix Consortium for £10 in 2000. The new company rebadged the car as the MG TF in 2002, reverting to a name from MG's illustrious past. This was actually an MGF Mk III by another name, though it had new coil-spring suspension, a tweaked engine and stiffened body shell. There were also various cosmetic style changes. The TF sold brilliantly too, but in 2005 MG Rover collapsed and production ceased.

COUNTRY OF ORIGIN:
UK
FIRST MANUFACTURED:
1995 (until 2002)
ENGINE:
1,598 cc or 1,796 cc Straight Four
PERFORMANCE:
With 1.8 l VVC – top speed of
123 mph (198 km/h);
0-60 mph (97 km/h) in 8.7 secs
YOU SHOULD KNOW:
China's state-owned Nanjing Automobile Group purchased the goodwill and plant of the collapsed MG Rover company and immediately set about building a production line in the eastern city of Nanjing, using machinery from Longbridge – and the first Chinese-built MG TF rolled off the line in 2007.

Mitsubishi Lancer Evolution

COUNTRY OF ORIGIN:
Japan
FIRST MANUFACTURED:
1992
ENGINE:
1,998 cc Straight Four Turbo
PERFORMANCE:
Evo V GSR – top speed of 147 mph
(237 km/h); 0-60 mph (97 km/h)
in 4.7 secs
YOU SHOULD KNOW:
Just as Rolls-Royce never gave brake-
horsepower figures for its cars, so
Mitsubishi went coy about the Evo's
power output with the Evo IV's debut
– it wasn't the done thing in Japan to
advertise that any car put out more
than 275 bhp, so Evos have
comfortably exceeded the officially
published bhp figures for years.

The Mitsubishi Lancer Evolution's nicknames began with Lancer Evo, became LanEvo and finished up as plain Evo. This contraction to a memorable three-letter sobriquet is a tribute to the formidable reputation this legendary car has acquired since its launch in 1992. In that time the Evo has lived up to its name and evolved through ten generations, each marked by a sequential Roman numeral.

The Evo I set the tone. This unremarkable four-door saloon was a devil in disguise, created to compete in the World Rally Championship. It had a 2 litre turbocharged engine and an all-wheel drive system, sharing a body with the Mitsubishi Lancer to satisfy homologation rules. There was a road version and a stripped-down club racer. The similar Evo II ran from 1994 to 1995. These early cars were available in Japan only.

In 1995 Evo III saw styling changes, like a new front end that made the car look altogether more businesslike, and in 1996 the Lancer was completely restyled, taking the Evo IV with it. The RS competition car was devoid of frills, whilst the GSR was a seriously powerful road car – both notable for huge round fog lamps. In 1997 the Evo V was modified to reflect a change in World Rally Championship rules.

The Evo VI (1999-2001) saw restyling and an RS2 model added to the RS and GSR cars. There were also special editions like the RS Sprint and the Tommi Mäkinen edition that celebrated his four WRC Drivers' Championships. The Evo VII was based on the Lancer Cedia platform, whilst the Evo VIII of 2003 was a supremely sophisticated performance car. By the time the Evo IX (2005) and X (2007) arrived, the rallying heritage was a distant memory leaving a legacy of awesome performance road cars that are infinitely rewarding to drive.

This was the first of a new generation of 'boy racer' performance specials.

Nissan Figaro

This curiosity was never meant to stray beyond the shores of Japan. The small, two-door Figaro convertible with its retro styling was a one-year wonder, being built only in 1991. It was styled by Shoji Takahashi and first shown at the 1989 Tokyo Motor Show, after which Nissan's special projects Pike Factory group brought it to market. The brief was to produce something looking like a 1960s classic but with all the performance and comfort of a modern car. The quirky Figaro definitely delivered.

Indeed, would-be Japanese buyers liked the concept so much that the original production run of 8,000 cars had to be more than doubled and still there weren't enough to go around, so a ballot was held. The Figaro was based on the Nissan Micra platform and had a 1 litre engine boosted by a turbocharger that provided plenty of zip, though in truth the Figaro was a triumph of style over performance. The engine was loud, the three-speed automatic gearbox laborious, steering skittish and wind noise intrusive. But who cared about any of that?

The Figaro came in four colours – topaz mist, emerald green, pale aqua and lapis grey – each representing a season of the year. The foldaway soft top in off-white was easy to erect and collapse, whilst there was a retractable glass rear screen.

Capacious front seats were trimmed in white leather and the CD radio that took pride of place on the dashboard had a satisfying Bakelite look to it, complemented by various chrome switches and knobs. Air-con, electric windows and power steering came as standard.

This was one of the most unusual cars to appear in the 1990s, and those attention-seekers who drive a Figaro today just love watching heads turning everywhere as this special little car buzzes by.

The quirky little Figaro was certainly a head-turner.

COUNTRY OF ORIGIN:
Japan
FIRST MANUFACTURED:
1991
ENGINE:
987 cc Straight Four Turbo
PERFORMANCE:
Top speed of 100 mph (161 km/h); 0-60 mph (97 km/h) in 13.5 secs
YOU SHOULD KNOW:
The fact that both the Japanese and Brits drive on the left encouraged a brisk trade in grey imports from Japan to the UK, and the Figaro became a popular choice with British buyers (especially celebrities) who wanted to be seen driving something rather eccentric.

Oldsmobile Aurora

The mid-sized Aurora was introduced by Oldsmobile in 1995. General Motors had been trying to freshen the brand for a while, and hoped the Aurora would provide a shot in the arm for sagging sales of Oldsmobiles. The first generation cars had a somewhat racy coupe profile with a distinctive rounded front end, frameless windows, wraparound rear window and full-width tail light array.

The Aurora's accent was on quality, and with the demise of the Olds Ninety-Eight in 1996 it became Oldsmobile's top-of-the-range flagship with lesser models taking their style cues from the Aurora. Build quality was excellent and the car had a refined 4 litre V8 engine that delivered the smoothest of rides. The interior was luxurious, with leather-trimmed seats, burr-walnut accents, power-adjustable front seats and a trip computer as standard. The Aurora initially sold well, but the ticket price was high and sales started dropping off, despite the addition of gizmos like an electronic compass and a nearside mirror that automatically tilted down to aid backing up when the car was put into reverse.

Although total first generation sales topped 130,000, there was no upgraded model in the 2000 model year, ahead of the introduction of a second generation Aurora. This was a substantially re-engineered car, as it had actually been planned as the lesser Antares model, which would have allowed the new Aurora to go still further upmarket. But changes elsewhere in the GM range meant that the Aurora returned as a slightly smaller and rather less exclusive car. The V8 engine was retained, but the Aurora's slide was reflected by the offer of a smaller V6 power plant. Although it remained a worthwhile luxury saloon car with much to recommend it, the Aurora's major facelift failed to capture sufficient sales and it was discontinued in 2003.

COUNTRY OF ORIGIN:
USA
FIRST MANUFACTURED:
1994 (until 2003)
ENGINE:
4.0 l (244 cid) V8; 3.5 l (212 cid) V6
PERFORMANCE:
First generation – top speed of
135 mph (217 km/h);
0-60 mph (97 km/h) in 8.6 secs
YOU SHOULD KNOW:
Oldsmobile (founded 1897) was the oldest-surviving marque in the USA and the historic badge had appeared on more than 35 million cars – but GM's brave attempt to revive the ailing brand with the new-look Aurora failed and the Oldsmobile division of General Motors was folded in 2004.

Panther Solo

Panther Westwinds was a bankruptcy waiting to happen, and it is a tribute to founder Robert Jankel that the company he established in 1972 lasted as long as it did. Surrey-based Panther actually enjoyed initial success, producing retro-styled sports cars and luxury sedans using components largely sourced from other manufacturers. Offerings ranged from the deliciously luxurious J2 roadster to the Panther de Ville, a shameless Bugatti Royale lookalike. But the inevitable collapse occurred in 1980 and Panther was taken over by Korean entrepreneur Young Kim.

He constructed a new factory in Essex, continuing Panther Lima production for a couple of years until the racy aluminium-bodied Kallista roadster appeared in 1982. But plans were soon afoot to replace the Kallista with the sensational new mid-engined Panther Solo 1 coupe with its lightweight glassfibre body, which would be powered by a Ford 1.6 litre high-performance engine. But the Toyota MR2 appeared at just the wrong time for the Solo 1, so a swift rethink was in order – Panther could not hope to compete against the Japanese giant.

The outcome was the slightly larger 2+2 Solo 2 of 1990, with wedge-shaped styling and a distinctive rear spoiler. The composite body consisted of aluminium honeycomb covered with carbon fibre, and was sufficiently distinctive to avoid being compared to the dreaded MR2. The Solo 2 had a punchy Ford Cosworth 2 litre engine and boasted a revised version of the FF (Ferguson Formula) four-wheel drive system made famous by Jensen Motors – the result being a rather impressive performance car. But few would get to be impressed. No sooner had production got under way than it became apparent that every car made was losing money and Panther folded yet again, leaving the Solo 2 as an interesting footnote in the performance-car bible.

COUNTRY OF ORIGIN:
UK
FIRST MANUFACTURED:
1990
ENGINE:
1,993 cc Straight Four
PERFORMANCE:
Solo 2 – top speed of 144 mph (232 km/h); 0-60 mph (97 km/h) in 6.8 secs
YOU SHOULD KNOW:
Trying to find a Panther Solo to admire is hard, and actually driving one nigh on impossible – it is thought that as few as 15 examples may still exist, and the whereabouts of even that number is unknown – though former Panther Westwinds owner Y C Kim is said to retain a fine red-painted Solo 2.

The Solo was an impressive car, but Panther was eaten alive by the larger cats.

Peugeot 406

COUNTRY OF ORIGIN:
France (also built in the UK, Italy and Egypt)
FIRST MANUFACTURED:
1995 (until 2004)
ENGINE:
Various including: 1,761 cc to 2,230 cc Straight Four; 2,946 cc V6; 1,905 cc to 2,179 cc Straight Four Diesel
PERFORMANCE:
With 1.8 l engine – top speed of 117 mph (188 km/h); 0-60 mph (97 km/h) in 11.5 secs
YOU SHOULD KNOW:
The Peugeot 406 competed in the British Touring Car Championship in 1996, winning a couple of races (one each for Tim Harvey and Patrick Watts) – a feat that helped to establish the 406 as a major player in the competitive UK car market.

As big family cars go, the Peugeot 406 with its smooth lines was pretty impressive. The most popular version was a four-door saloon that shared a platform with the Citroen Xantia, but this was complemented by a five-door estate car and a sporty two-door coupe designed and built near Turin by Italian performance specialist Pininfarina. There was a choice of engines – initially a 1.8 litre or 2 litre petrol engine, with a 1.9 litre turbodiesel option. But over time there would also be a 2.2 litre and 3 litre V6 lining up beside the petrol pump, with a 2 litre, 2.1 litre and 2.2 litre queuing for diesel. Two of the latter engines had the Hdi (High-pressure Diesel Injection) system.

The front-engined, front-wheel drive 406 superseded the ageing Peugeot 405 in 1995 and continued to sell well for nearly a decade, proving to be a great success for the French manufacturer. The key to the 406's commercial appeal was the fact that it offered efficient and sophisticated diesel engines at a time when there was a general switch (especially in Continental Europe) to the alternative fuel for reasons of economy and reduction in air pollution.

The 406 enjoyed a major facelift in 1999, with an external redesign that brought in a pleasing new ribbed look and style accents like a new honeycomb grille and smooth glass headlamp arrays. The interior got a serious makeover, too, with the emphasis on additional space. But the most significant changes were invisible – more powerful and fuel-efficient engine choices, improved transmission, better suspension and brakes. Thus fortified, the 406 continued to be a popular choice with European car buyers until it was finally discontinued in 2004. Egyptian production of the 406 carried on regardless after the Peugeot 407 took over elsewhere.

The 406 was a steady seller for the French company.

Plymouth Prowler

The extraordinary Plymouth Prowler retro-rocket appeared in 1997, though this two-door roadster was actually unlike anything anyone had seen before. The Prowler had a tapering bonnet ending in a triangular grille, open front wheels with motorcycle mudguards, a crouching cabin and high, rounded rear that had unmistakable hot-rod echoes. This fanciful confection was enhanced by zingy paint finishes that boasted names like Purple Metallic, Candy Red, High-Voltage Blue, Inca Gold, Prowler Orange or Black Tie . . . you get the picture.

This retro street fighter came with plenty of modern engineering beneath the skin.

The power train was a 3.6 litre V6 delivering 214 bhp (tuned to belt out 253 bhp from 1999), with four-speed automatic transmission located at the back end to facilitate even weight distribution. The layout was a front-engined, rear-wheel drive configuration – making the Prowler Plymouth's first car since the 1989 Gran Fury not to employ front-wheel propulsion. The aluminium body was built using the latest bonding techniques, with a little help from plastic for rear body panels and front mudguards, and the Prowler was assembled by hand.

Retro it may have been, but the trimmings were modern – disc brakes, run-flat tyres (there was no room for a spare), Autostick transmission that permitted manual gear changes, adjustable steering wheel, cruise control, electric windows, central locking, air conditioning and CD player. However, the Prowler did have an old-fashioned instrument pod with a full complement of gauges and a tachometer on the steering column.

Nearly 12,000 Prowlers were built, and they still have an avid following amongst besotted owners who like to drive on the wild side. There might have been more on the street, but the Plymouth marque vanished in 2001, so the last of the Prowlers bore a Chrysler badge – and the model was discontinued because Chrysler had the Crossfire ready and waiting to fill the specialist performance niche.

COUNTRY OF ORIGIN:
USA
FIRST MANUFACTURED:
1997 (until 2002)
ENGINE:
3.5 l (215 cid) V6
PERFORMANCE:
Top speed of 125 mph (201 km/h);
0-60 mph (97 km/h) in 7.7 secs
YOU SHOULD KNOW:
In 1998 a brand new Prowler was entombed within a time capsule in Tulsa's Centennial Park, sealed inside a plastic container – the mausoleum will be opened in 2048 and the car will be returned to Chrysler (if Chrysler still exists).

The superb Boxster may have been a cheaper Porsche, but finish and performance were in no way compromised.

Porsche Boxster

If looks could kill, everyone who glanced at the Porsche Boxster would be struck dead, for this is one handsome roadster. Designer Harm Lagaay was helped by the fact that he was able create a stunning soft-top from scratch as the company's first 'clean sheet' design since the Porsche 928 back in the 1970s. (Previous Porsche convertibles were, effectively, topless coupes.)

The mid-engined Boxster burst onto the sports-car scene in 1996, powered by a water-cooled Porsche 2.5 litre flat six that came with manual or automatic transmission. It may have been a cut-price alternative to the enduring 911, but there was no skimping on build quality, technical innovation or performance. This was bold, as Porsche had been experiencing hard times in the early 1990s and was strapped for cash.

With the help of a massive internal reorganization at Zuffenhausen, the gamble paid off. Despite accusations that the Boxster was no more than a knee-jerk reaction to the success of retro sports cars like the BMW Z3 or Mercedes SLK, the Boxster was technically more interesting, came with a very affordable price tag for all that automobile and – best of all – had a Porsche badge on the front. The motoring press and performance-buying public loved it and this stylish two-seater became the company's best-ever seller until the Cayenne SUV eventually overtook a long way down the road.

Supply could not keep up with demand and waiting lists proliferated, whilst a plethora of tempting extras ensured that few paid only the basic price. The next step was an enhanced base model (with a 2.7 litre engine) and the eagerly awaited 3.2 litre 'S' high-performance model in 1999. After various tweaks, the Boxster and Boxster S were completely reworked in 2005 to sustain a phenomenon that had already racked up 160,000 sales.

COUNTRY OF ORIGIN:
Germany (also built in Finland)
FIRST MANUFACTURED:
1996
ENGINE:
2,480 cc, 2,687 cc
or 3,179 cc Flat Six
PERFORMANCE:
With 2.5 l engine – top speed of
146 mph (235 km/h);
0-60 mph (97 km/h) in 6.7 secs
YOU SHOULD KNOW:
The Boxster name was a composite formed from the 'box' in boxer (the horizontally opposed flat engine) and the 'ster' of roadster, as the Boxster was Porsche's first stand-alone convertible.

Renault Alpine A610

Alpine was a French manufacturer of sports cars and racing cars that used Renault engines. The driving force was Jean Rédélé, who had enjoyed postwar success tuning and racing Renault 4CVs. His outfit constructed performance specials in the 1950s and 1960s, always working closely with Renault, and in addition to producing Alpine cars for sale the company was entrusted with Renault's competition budget.

This ushered in a period of rally domination, but Alpine's own manufacturing efforts were undermined by the oil crisis of 1973 and falling sales led to a Renault takeover. Thereafter, Renault Sport was formed by merging Alpine and tuning specialist Gordini. This division built successful rally cars (World Rally Championship winners) and GT racers (Le Mans 24 hour win in 1978), continuing to use the Alpine name on cars.

The first all-new road car to be produced after the takeover was the Renault Alpine GTA in 1986. This 2+2 sports coupe was effectively an update of its predecessor, the Alpine A310, but it wasn't a commercial success despite the production of assorted models with different engines. So in 1991 the Alpine A610 arrived. It didn't look so very different from the GTA, but was a completely different animal beneath the skin. It was built at Alpine's Dieppe factory and retained the company's essential design signature –
steel backbone chassis and Renault engine mounted behind the rear wheels, this time a powerful 3 litre V6 equipped with a Garrett turbocharger.

The motoring press loved this fiery coupe, but despite the glamour of the Alpine name – and special editions like the Albertville and Magny-Cours – the A610 was a miss, with less than a thousand produced over a production run that unsurprisingly ended in 1995. Thereafter the Alpine factory was used to produce the Renault Sport Spider.

COUNTRY OF ORIGIN:
France
FIRST MANUFACTURED:
1991 (until 1995)
ENGINE:
2,975 cc V6 Turbo
PERFORMANCE:
Top speed of 165 mph (266 km/h);
0-60 mph (97 km/h) in 5.9 secs
YOU SHOULD KNOW:
Although now generally known as the Renault Alpine A610, the car was originally marketed simply as the Alpine A610, in an attempt to maintain the prestige associated with the multiple track and rally successes of Alpine cars.

It was indeed an impressive car – but the A610 didn't generate enough sales to support a continued production run.

Renault Sport Spider

COUNTRY OF ORIGIN:
France
FIRST MANUFACTURED:
1996 (until 1999)
ENGINE:
1,998 cc Straight Four
PERFORMANCE:
Top speed of 131 mph (211 km/h);
0-60 mph (97 km/h) in 5.8 secs
YOU SHOULD KNOW:
The Spider racing series organized by
Renault took place in the UK
between 1995 and 1999, supporting
the British Touring Car Championship.
Far from creating a level playing field,
the Spider Trophy's final season saw
Andy Priaulx win all 13 races from
13 pole positions.

After the demise of the Alpine A610 – a sadly underrated sports coupe – Renault's Alpine factory in Dieppe turned to building the Renault Sport Spider, a dashing open-top roadster that made its debut in 1996. The Alpine A610 had been an attempt to consolidate Renault's reviving fortunes with a halo performance car – and the Spider was intended to fulfill the same objective.

The concept was to produce a small racing car to be used in a single-model competition series, where driving skill alone would be the deciding factor. The commercial advantages would be to put Renault's name back up in sporting lights, with consequent marketing benefits for the whole range and the ability to sell a road-going version of the racer.

A concept car was presented at the Geneva Motor Show in 1995. This memorably lacked a windscreen and had butterfly doors, though these had vanished and a windscreen had been added by the time the production version went on sale. The mid-engined rear-wheel drive car was a handsome open-top roadster complete with roll bar to underline its racing pedigree. Indeed, the first cars built at Alpine's Dieppe factory were special Spider Trophy racing versions with a top speed of 156 mph (251 km/h).

This ensured that the road-going Sport Spider would satisfy the most demanding of sporting drivers. The lightweight aluminium chassis was fitted with GRP bodywork. In a technical masterstroke, engine and gearbox were a single transversely fixed unit using an oscillating hinge that effectively eradicated engine shake at speed. That engine was a 2 litre F7R borrowed from the limited-edition Renault Clio Williams hot hatch created by Renault Sport in 1992 for homologation purposes.

The Sport Spider's production was short, and these stylish but rare roadsters have become desirable amongst collectors betting on future classic status.

The Sport Spider just might become a desirable classic.

Renault Megane Scenic

Every carmaker's dream is to think up a car that creates a lucrative new market segment. And that's precisely what Renault achieved with the Megane Scenic, which proved there was much demand for a smaller version of the increasingly popular MPV (Multi-Purpose Vehicle). Following its launch in 1996, the Megane Scenic was an instant hit with the buying public, creating a popular new compact MPV category that would swiftly be imitated by other manufacturers.

The Scenic was clever enough to create a new market sector.

The Scenic was based on the Megane hatchback (the two models were mechanically identical), so the clever part lay in the creation of a five-door body shape and roomy internal layout for the new car. Renault had already helped to pioneer the full-sized MPV concept with the well-received Espace, and the Scenic cashed in on that established reputation. It appealed to those who didn't need (or couldn't afford) the larger vehicle and its favourable reception took Renault by surprise – they expected the Scenic to be a niche product and started building under 500 per day at their Douai factory, but buoyant demand soon saw that number increase dramatically.

Buyers had a choice of economical engines. There were three petrol engines, at 1.4, 1.6 and 2 litres respectively, and one 1.9 litre diesel – also from the Megane hatchback range. The Scenic's engine was up front, driving the front wheels. The first evolution was in 1999, when these engines were uprated and the Scenic was significantly restyled.

After the 1999 facelift the model name was officially changed to a stand-alone Scenic, though a small Megane badge on the rear door reminded everyone of its illustrious ancestry. An all-new Scenic was launched in 2003, along with a seven-seater Grand Scenic, both cars being packed with the latest user-friendly technology. There was a further upgrade in 2006.

COUNTRY OF ORIGIN:
France (also built in Brazil)
FIRST MANUFACTURED:
1996
ENGINE:
1,390, 1,598 cc or 1,998 cc I Straight Four; 1,870 cc Straight Four Diesel
PERFORMANCE:
With 2 l engine – top speed of 114 mph (183 km/h); 0-60 mph (97 km/h) in 10.7 secs
YOU SHOULD KNOW:
Renault tried to repeat the trick of inventing a popular new type of car by launching a four-wheel drive version of the Scenic called the RX4, hoping the public would take to the idea of a compact SUV – but this time the venture was unsuccessful and the RX4 was soon discontinued.

Rover 75

Although the Rover 75 was intended to be an updated version of the Rover 600, BMW's takeover changed all that. The German company – following its promise to treat the Rover marque as the embodiment of traditional British automobile engineering – promptly decreed that the planned 75 would be an entirely new luxury saloon car. By coincidence, the Rover 75 was launched at the 1998 Birmingham Motor Show, which also saw the first appearance of the new S-Type Jaguar. The two cars had similar retro styling, and the consensus was that the Rover stood up well against its Ford-owned rival.

However, relations between Rover's new owner and the British government became strained as the enormity of the task BMW had taken on struck home and no subsidies were forthcoming to modernize the Longbridge plant, intended home of the 75. So the first 75s were built at Cowley, appearing in 1999, though production was soon switched to Longbridge after BMW retained the Cowley facility to build Minis and transferred everything else to the embryonic MG Rover company in 2000.

After a slow start, the Rover 75 sold well, for this was a refined luxury car with a beautiful interior, classic looks, precise handling and great ride quality. There was a choice of engines over time – two 1.8 litre options (one turbocharged), two 2 litre straight fours, two V6s and finally an impressive 4.6 litre V8 liberated from the Ford Mustang. Following the exit of BMW a five-door estate car (developed but never authorized by the Germans) was added to amplify choice. In 2004 the Rover 75 was facelifted, with more contemporary styling, whilst a powerful V8 model and a stretched Rover 75 Vanden Plas limo were introduced. It was a gallant but futile effort – MG Rover folded in 2005.

COUNTRY OF ORIGIN:
UK
FIRST MANUFACTURED:
1999 (until 2005)
ENGINE:
1,795 cc or 1,950 cc Straight Four;
1,991 cc or 2,497 cc V6; 4,601 cc V8
PERFORMANCE:
With 2.5 l engine – top speed of
137 mph (220 km/h); 0-60 mph
(97 km/h) in 8.8 secs
YOU SHOULD KNOW:
The 75 went east after MG Rover's collapse in 2005, with two carmakers owned by the Chinese government picking up the pieces. The Rover 75 design was purchased by SAIC (the Shanghai Automotive Industry Corporation) whilst its tooling went to NAC (the Nanjing Automobile Corporation).

Skoda Octavia

Those universal Skoda jokes were just starting to fade from the collective consciousness of petrolheads when the Octavia appeared in 1996, as it became apparent how quickly the Czech company had adopted Volkswagen quality control standards. To ram home the point these 'Volkswagens by another name' were sold at extremely tempting prices for the high specification and level of finish offered, with the intention of swiftly re-establishing the Skoda marque as a born-again player on the international scene.

The first generation Octavia came as a five-door estate and also a strange hybrid saloon/hatchback combo that had a saloon-like back end and lifting tailgate. The styling was pleasant but unremarkable. The Octavia shared a platform with the Golf, Audi A3 and Seat Leon Cupra. The most distinctive Skoda option was four-wheel drive capability, available on both models, and these cars had a slightly higher ride height and a larger fuel tank. There was also a high-performance Octavia vRS. As with any model line having a German connection, there was a wide assortment of engines, all shared by other cars within the Volkswagen Group. There were five diesel variants, all at 1.9 litres, and twice that number of petrol engines, ranging in size from 1.4 litres to 2 litres.

The first generation was given a facelift in 2000, giving independent rear suspension and enhanced interior trim, and this remained on sale in some markets (as the Octavia Tour) after the second generation appeared in 2004. Again, many engine variants were offered (nine petrol and six diesel). There were changes to increase internal space and the new Octavia had a higher ride height to eliminate previous difficulties with tall curbs and ramps. The off-road Octavia Scout was announced in 2006, which is a reworked estate car featuring the Haldex Traction four-wheel drive system.

COUNTRY OF ORIGIN:
Czech Republic
FIRST MANUFACTURED:
1996
ENGINE:
Various, from 1,298 cc to 1,984 cc
Straight Four; 1,896 cc or 1,968
Straight Four Diesel
PERFORMANCE:
With 2.0 l engine – top speed
of 139 mph (224 km/h);
0-60 mph (97 km/h) in 8.6 secs
YOU SHOULD KNOW:
The Octavia arrived in the UK during 1998 and was soon a staple of the taxi and hire car business, with its excellent build quality, roomy interior and competitive price.

The Octavia helped to bury Skoda's reputation for poor build quality and unreliability.

COUNTRY OF ORIGIN:
USA
FIRST MANUFACTURED:
1998 (until 2002)
ENGINE:
4.0 l (244 cid) DOHC V8
PERFORMANCE:
Top speed of 185 mph (298 km/h);
0-60 mph (97 km/h) in 4.1 secs
YOU SHOULD KNOW:
When new regulations required the
car to be recertified, this would have
been prohibitively expensive – so
Carroll Shelby decided to offer the
remaining 251 Series 1s as
'component cars' without engines,
which could then be retro-fitted with
a supercharged Olds engine capable
of hitting 60 mph (97 km/h) from a
standing start in 3.3 seconds.

Shelby American Series 1

Carroll Shelby just couldn't help himself – the former racing driver
never lost his enthusiasm for high speed and every so often just had to
create another awesome performance roadster. He chose to do just
that to celebrate his 75th birthday in 1998. This time the beast in
question was the Series 1, a more-than-worthy successor to previous
greats that included the Shelby Cobra GT350 and GT500. The
extended development of the Series 1 (from 1994) had plunged the
Shelby American company into financial difficulty, but body supplier
Venture Industries rode to the rescue by investing heavily in Shelby.

After endless glitches and problems the first Series 1 cars were
produced at Shelby's Las Vegas factory – the first model engineered
from the ground up by Shelby American. The production run was to be
500 cars. The chosen engine was a highly tuned 4 litre Aurora V8 from
Oldsmobile. The chassis consisted of extruded aluminium members

and the body was made from feather-light carbon fibre. There were two roll bars and independent suspension all round, complemented by large disc brakes borrowed from the contemporary Corvette. The Corvette also provided the six-speed manual gearbox that was located in the rear to help achieve ideal 50-50 weight distribution.

With all that going for it, the Series 1 provided classic Shelby thrills for anyone lucky enough to drive one. And they could even experience the joys of piloting this muscular sports car in some comfort. The Series 1 sported air conditioning, electric windows, a leather-trimmed cabin and loud sound system. But it remained a pure driver's car, with Carroll Shelby refusing to fit an antilock braking system. Unfortunately for posterity, few indeed were privileged to slide behind the wheel of a Series 1. Just 249 cars were built before production was suspended in 2002.

The Shelby was terrific to drive, but relatively few of these great cars made it to the starting line.

433

Smart City Coupe

COUNTRY OF ORIGIN:
Switzerland/Germany/France
FIRST MANUFACTURED:
1998
ENGINE:
799 cc Straight Three
PERFORMANCE:
Electronically limited top speed of
84 mph (135 km/h);
0-60 mph (97 km/h) in 15 secs
YOU SHOULD KNOW:
There's nothing clever about the
Smart name – it was a combination
of the 'S' from Swatch, 'm' from
Mercedes and 'art' for it's avant-
garde design. The use of smart with
a small 's' for marketing purposes
was intended to underline the car's
miniscule size.

This was definitely the smart choice for city driving.

Officially it's smart with a small 's', which looks so strange that everyone else calls it a Smart car. The venture started with the boss of Swiss fashion watchmaker Swatch suggesting a tiny eco-car that would offer fun motoring to the young (or young at heart) whilst offering a helping hand to the choking planet. Nicolas Hayek's first prospective partner was Volkswagen, but that venture came to nothing. He then jumped into bed with Daimler-Benz and a joint venture was formed using the MCC (Micro Compact Car) name.

The development phase at MCC's new French factory produced a car that Hayek wasn't happy with – it had a conventional engine rather than the electric or hybrid power plant he'd hoped for. Swatch pulled out, leaving Daimler-Benz to carry on alone. The first model was the City Coupe – a cube on wheels with a sloping front that made its debut in 1998. Initial sales were slow, but buyers soon began to appreciate the advantages.

Three tiny Smarts could park side by side, noses to the curb, in one conventional parking space. Fuel economy was excellent, as was safety – the Smart's Tridion steel safety shell proved to be remarkably tough in impact tests. This also gave the City Coupe and accompanying City Cabrio cabriolet their distinctive look, as this rigid cage shows through the outside of the cars. It was infilled with panels that were easily changed, allowing owners to alter the colour of their Smart on a whim.

In 2002 only the open-topped Smart Crossblade appeared. The Smart Roadster of 2003–2005 had a completely different design, whilst the Smart Forfour was clearly a stretched version of the Smart Fortwo (as the City Coupe and Cabrio were renamed in 2004, becoming the only Smarts in production from 2007).

Subaru Impreza Turbo

The Impreza Turbo – tough as old boots and fast as the wind.

The compact Subaru Impreza was introduced in 1993 and has been motoring ever since. It challenged the likes of the Honda Civic and Toyota Corolla, but one of the Impreza's unique selling points was that it offered all-wheel drive. This worked well with the traditional Subaru flat boxer engine, minimizing body roll and providing first-class handling and roadholding.

There were three models in the new range – a two-door coupe, four-door saloon and five-door estate. Trim levels were LX, GL and Sport, though widespread distribution saw different names used in different markets. Likewise there was considerable variety in the engines used for the Impreza over time. The most powerful, though not the largest, was the 2.0 litre turbocharged and intercooled motor – marketed variously as the Impreza 2.0 WRX, Turbo 2000, 2.0 Turbo, 2.0 GT or 2.0 GT Turbo. The Turbo had wider tyres, bigger brakes and firmer suspension than the base model.

This was the innocent-looking four-wheel drive saloon or station wagon that inspired a generation of petrolheads after taking the world by storm in the mid-1990s. Despite the fairly basic interior finish of dull grey plastic and uninspiring seating trims, the Impreza Turbo's performance caused all that to be forgotten in the few seconds it took to blast past 60 mph (97 km/h). Endless variants (about 15) were produced before the chassis was uprated in 2001, since when another 25+ (and counting) have been offered, depending on the market.

There couldn't be a better budget performance car for the aspiring boy racer to go looking for. It has become a cult car for good reason, being reliable, tough as old boots and fast as the wind. An Impreza isn't cheap to run, but the earlier models offer more boom for the buck than anything else in the same price bracket.

COUNTRY OF ORIGIN:
Japan
FIRST MANUFACTURED:
1993
ENGINE:
1,994 cc Flat Four Turbo
PERFORMANCE:
Depended on variant – typically a top speed of 137 mph (220 km/h); 0-60 mph (97 km/h) in 5.8 secs
YOU SHOULD KNOW:
There have been numerous special editions of the Impreza Turbo, many attracting a good premium for their rarity value and superior internal finish. UK examples to look for include the RB5, Series McRae, Terzo, Catalunya and Prodrive WR Sport.

This was a clever three-in-one car – with open roadster, soft top and targa top options.

Suzuki Cappuccino

The Japanese have an honourable tradition of building sports cars with tiny engines, and showed they hadn't forgotten how with the splendid little front mid-engined Suzuki Cappuccino that made an appearance in 1992. This met Kei-car specifications (allowing it to exploit Japan's favourable tax and insurance regime for small cars). Weighing in at a featherweight 1543 lb (700 kg), the Cappuccino had an alloy three-cylinder engine that was just 3 ccs beneath the ungenerous 660 cc Kei-car limit (albeit turbocharged). This was later uprated to a lighter, more powerful unit.

The Cappuccino was a clever triple-whammy car. Three roof panels turned it into a trim coupe. With those removed (and stored away in the boot) it became a targa-top. Finally, retracting the rear window and rollbar created an open-top roadster. It is apparent from the (relatively) long bonnet and short back end that front-back weight distribution is equal, giving great handling qualities. The Cappuccino sported disc brakes all round, power steering and aluminium double-wishbone suspension. There was an upgrade in 1995, offering optional automatic transmission, ABS, limited-slip differential and driver airbag.

Just 1,200 of these clever little sports cars were imported to the UK, with new emission control regulations in 1995 ending the flow. These individualistic machines are both highly regarded and hard to find, as anyone lucky enough to have one tends to be reluctant to part with that hot Cappuccino. Not only are they a joy to drive, with fantastic roadholding and an enhanced sense of speed caused by racing along close to the tarmac, but also the performance is extraordinary considering the minute size of the engine. Two words of warning – the gearbox can be sticky when cold, and don't even think of buying a Cappuccino unless you like everyone gawping at you as you drive.

COUNTRY OF ORIGIN:
Japan
FIRST MANUFACTURED:
1991 (until 1997)
ENGINE:
657 cc DOHC Straight Three Turbo
PERFORMANCE:
Top speed of 93 mph (150 km/h);
0-60 mph (97 km/h) in 8.5 secs
YOU SHOULD KNOW:
There were 28,000 Cappuccinos built, most of which were sold into the Japanese home market. But as international interest has increased, many of those have departed from home as personal imports to distant shores – notably Australia and Europe.

Toyota RAV4

The 1990s saw an explosion in the popularity of full-size crossover SUVs – luxury cars re-engineered to have all-wheel drive and tall ride height. The decade also saw a huge surge in the popularity of compact crossover SUVs. The principle was the same, but the smaller versions were targeted at those who didn't have to pack in loads of kids or gear, couldn't afford a full-sized SUV even if they wanted one but still liked the superior ride height and trendy character of the new four-wheel drive vehicles.

From 1994, Toyota's RAV4 blazed a trail other manufacturers would soon follow. RAV4 stood for Recreational Active Vehicle with 4WD, though some editions actually had two-wheel drive. The RAV4 was built on the Toyota Corolla platform and came in two-door and four-door form. From 1998 a two-door convertible briefly joined the range. All had five-speed manual or four-speed automatic transmission teamed with a 2 litre engine that was not particularly economical. No matter, the ladies in particular loved it.

A second generation appeared in 2001. The RAV4 underwent a serious upgrade and was offered as a base or luxury model with a wide choice of trim levels. Extras like ABS, air conditioning, electric windows and cruise control were offered on certain models. There was also a sport pack that actually consisted of no more than superior trim. The second generation RAV4 again came in two-door or four-door form, whilst an uprated 2 litre petrol engine was joined by a 2 litre diesel.

There was a further evolution in 2003, with the introduction of a 2.4 litre petrol engine into some markets. This was followed by a complete redesign for 2006, when the third generation RAV4 appeared. It had new engines and was a larger four-door SUV which carried on the good sales work of its successful predecessors.

COUNTRY OF ORIGIN:
Japan (also built in Canada)
FIRST MANUFACTURED:
1994
ENGINE:
1,998 cc or 2,362 cc Straight Four; 1,995 cc Straight Four Diesel (first and second generations)
PERFORMANCE:
First generation – top speed of 106 mph (170 km/h); 0-50 mph (80 km/h) in 7.8 secs
YOU SHOULD KNOW:
In the 1990s a small number of RAV4 EV models were produced for sale in California – with zero-emission electric motors and long-life guaranteed batteries, they have become very collectable with the rise of interest in eco-friendly motoring.

The RAV4 went through many an upgrade as time went by.

TVR Griffith

COUNTRY OF ORIGIN:
UK
FIRST MANUFACTURED:
1991 (until 2002)
ENGINE:
3,947 cc, 4,280 cc, 4,495 cc or
4,997 cc V8
PERFORMANCE:
With 4.3 l engine – top speed of
161 mph (259 km/h);
0-60 mph (97 km/h) in 4.7 secs
YOU SHOULD KNOW:
When the TVR Griffith prototype was
unveiled at the Birmingham Motor
Show in 1990 it proved to be a real
show stopper and a large number of
orders were taken there and then,
ensuring that a production run could
be safely undertaken.

This curvaceous high-performance sports car was built by Blackpool constructor TVR from 1991, until the Griffith was finally discontinued in 2002. In the final incarnation, with a 5 litre engine, it was known as the Griffith 500. This sparky two-seater convertible succeeded earlier Griffith 200 and 400 models and, like them, was powered by a V8 engine – a power plant that grew and grew during the course of the production run, and was always loud.

Beneath its smoothly rounded skin, the Griffith shared mechanicals with its speedy younger sibling, the Chimaera. But though the Griffith was the so-called 'First of the Big-League TVRs' it was produced in smaller numbers than the Chimaera (which appeared two years later) and is therefore rarer and more desirable as a classic in waiting. The first Griffiths had a 4 litre or 4.3 litre V8 engine. A few of the latter carried the BV badge that indicated a big valve conversion for even greater oomph. A 4.5 litre option was added, and in 1993 the Griffith 500 arrived.

There was then a hiatus for UK buyers as TVR concentrated on export sales, but minor development continued with a bullet-proof BorgWarner gearbox replacing the original Rover SDI box, and in 1997 the Griffith 500's engine was detuned to give more comfortable idling and better engine control at low speeds. In 2001 one hundred Special Edition Griffith 500s were built to end the production run in style. They had minor detail changes from previous cars and each came with a numbered plaque in the glove box and a Special Edition badge on its rounded rear. And the verdict on this super British sports car? In *Autocar* magazine's 1992 road test the conclusion was 'so close to being a world beater it hurts'.

For a while right-hand-drive versions of the mighty Griffith were quite difficult to come by.

TVR Chimaera

This pretty convertible arrived a year after the TVR Griffith, sharing a chassis and the same Rover-derived engine options, but visually the Chimaera was more of a traditional sports car than the racy Griffith. The Chimaera also had a fibreglass body but was rather longer than the Griffith, with softer suspension, more interior space and a larger boot, for it was intended as the GT-style TVR for those who wanted to tour in comfort rather than burn rubber at a track meet. The Chimaera had disc brakes and independent suspension all round.

The Chimaera was no sluggard – capable of zooming past 150 mph (241 km/h) even with the smallest 4 litre engine – but those who liked their home comforts were able to opt for goodies like button-opening doors, heated leather seats, wood trim, power-assisted steering, air conditioning, six-CD player with four speakers, wood-and-chrome steering wheel and deep-pile carpeting. Very civilized!

As with the TVR Griffith, a BorgWarner gearbox was installed from 1994, and the Chimaera 500 appeared the same year with the punchy 5 litre engine. There was a minor facelift in 1996, with the Chimaera's front end being changed to look like that of the TVR Cerbera. The mesh grille was lost and a horizontal split created across the grille space and indicator. In 1998 the rear lights were changed, but that was the extent of modifications before the last Chimaera was built.

Around 6,000 Chimaeras were sold during the decade-long production run, but only some 600 of those were ultra-desirable Chimaera 500s, which may be identified by Griffith-style wheels and a purple rocker cover. Those are the ones serious collectors go for, but any Chimaera is a modern classic that will give enormous driving pleasure and see off almost anything the driver cares to challenge.

The Chimaera was pretty – and also a splendid driver's car.

COUNTRY OF ORIGIN:
UK
FIRST MANUFACTURED:
1992 (until 2003)
ENGINE:
3,947 cc, 4,280 cc, 4,495 cc or 4,988 cc V8
PERFORMANCE:
With 5.0 l engine – top speed of 160 mph (257 km/h); 0-60 mph (97 km/h) in 4.4 secs
YOU SHOULD KNOW:
Anyone for Chimaera? The name is an alternative spelling of 'Chimera', that monstrous fire-breathing creature in Greek mythology with the head of a lion, body of a goat and tail of a serpent. Another meaning is a grotesque product of the imagination – just TVR's little joke.

TVR Cerbera

Under new owner Peter Wheeler, the Blackpool based TVR company
enjoyed a good decade in the 1990s. It produced both the butch
Griffith and well-received Chimaera convertible, and hit an impressive
hat trick by launching the Cerbera two-door coupe in 1996. This time,
the newcomer did not have one of the tuned Rover engines used in
the earlier cars, but a TVR-developed 'Speed Eight' the company
hoped would not only power the Cerbera, but also sell to other
manufacturers for use in racers or high-performance sports cars. Not
content with the considerable challenge that developing a serious
engine from scratch presented to a small manufacturer, TVR also
produced an own-brand 4 litre straight six and bored out the new V8
to 4.5 litres. All three engines were offered in the Cerbera.

The speedy Cerbera broke new ground for other reasons, too – it
was TVR's first hardtop and first 2+2 grand tourer. The new model
had a slinky outline with a rounded front, long bonnet, aerodynamic
cabin set well back, rearward sloping doors and a short back end. The
prototype attracted favourable attention at the Birmingham Motor
Show in 1994, but it would be two years before the first eager buyers
were able to slip behind the wheel. TVR actually described the car as
a 3+1 rather than 2+2, as the front passenger seat slid well forward to
provide an adequate third seat behind.

A truly astonishing concept Cerbera Speed 12 supercar – intended
to be the fastest production road car ever – was created in 1997. It
had a 7.7 litre V12 engine, went from 0-60 mph (97 km/h) in
2.9 seconds and had a top speed of 240 mph (390 km/h). Perhaps
other road users were lucky that it never went into production,
though a few racing versions were built.

COUNTRY OF ORIGIN:
UK
FIRST MANUFACTURED:
1996 (until 2003)
ENGINE:
3,996 cc Straight Six; 4,185 cc or
4,475 cc V8
PERFORMANCE:
With 4.5 l engine – top speed of
180 mph (290 km/h);
0-60 mph (97 km/h) in 4.1 secs
YOU SHOULD KNOW:
TVR returned to Greek mythology to
find a name for its spiffy new
coupe, this time opting for a variation
on Cerberus. This was the terrible
three-headed beast that guarded the
entrance to Hell, which also
happened to be a dog – another of
TVR's little jokes.

Venturi Atlantique

French sports car manufacturer Venturi was established in the early 1980s with the modest ambition of becoming a Gallic competitor to the likes of Ferrari and Porsche, by producing GT cars that would prove their worth on the racing circuits of Europe.

The mid-engined Venturi Atlantique 260 (named in unashamed tribute to the iconic French Bugatti Type 57 SC Atlantique from the late 1930s) made its first appearance in 1991. This fabulous-looking coupe had a Venturi-tuned development of the turbocharged 2.8 litre PRV V6 engine developed as a joint venture by Citroen, Peugeot and Volvo. When built into the lightweight Atlantique 260 with its fibreglass body the result was performance that justified those ambitious hopes of becoming the French Ferrari.

Soon, however, that would become the Scottish Ferrari – because although it was actually still French in concept and construction, Scotsman Hubert O'Neill purchased Venturi in 1994. He speedily caused a Venturi 400GT to be produced with a view to participating in sports car races, in which sphere the company enjoyed considerable success. The ambitious boss also sanctioned a new Atlantique 300 with a 3 litre engine. But the Scottish regime was brief – sales were lamentable, Venturi went bust and was bought by Thai firm Nakarin Benz, which in turn folded in 2000, taking the Atlantique with it.

Unlike many a specialist constructor of custom sports cars, Venturi has managed to remain in business – though it never did get to topple Ferrari or Porsche from atop the heap. Indeed, the company produced under a thousand cars and now concentrates on eco-friendly electric power, though the leopard hasn't entirely changed its spots – the futuristic Venturi Fétish concept car is a two-seater roadster that is said to accelerate from standstill to 60 mph (97 km/h) in around five seconds.

COUNTRY OF ORIGIN:
France
FIRST MANUFACTURED:
1991 (until 2000)
ENGINE:
2,849 cc or 2,975 cc V6
PERFORMANCE:
Atlantique 300 – top speed of
171 mph (275 km/h);
0-60 mph (97 km/h) in 4.9 secs
YOU SHOULD KNOW:
Straight-talking motoring guru
Jeremy Clarkson of the BBC's *Top Gear* show was certainly a huge fan of the Venturi Atlantique, describing the experience of driving this exciting sports car as 'like having your own personal jet fighter . . .
I love it to death'.

There weren't many of these about, but those that did roll earned the grand title of 'The French Ferraris'.

Volvo C70

COUNTRY OF ORIGIN:
Sweden
FIRST MANUFACTURED:
1997
ENGINE:
1,984 cc, 2,319 cc or 2,435 cc
Straight Five Turbo
PERFORMANCE:
With 2.3 l engine – top speed of
155 mph (249 km/h);
0-60 mph (97 km/h) in 6.3 secs
YOU SHOULD KNOW:
The launch of the C70 saw metallic
saffron-orange cars introduced to the
press, whilst Volvo's marketing
department cleverly placed a C70 in
the 1997 film *The Saint* – harking
nostalgically back to the 1960s TV
series where Roger Moore as Simon
Templar drove a Volvo P1800.

The first generation Volvo C70 was rolled out at the 1996 Paris Motor Show, with buyers able to choose between a handsome two-door coupe or a pretty four-seater cabriolet when the model line went on sale in 1997. The C70 saw Volvo daringly abandon several generations of boxy cars for something altogether more rounded and sexy . . . and also create the first Volvo soft-top of modern times.

The C70 had been some time in the making, with a little help from British specialist Tom Walkinshaw Racing. Volvo design boss Peter Horbury was determined to create a stylish performance car that offered a faultless ride and perfect roadholding . . . and nearly succeeded. The C70 came with a choice of three engines, all turbocharged straight fives. There was an entry-level 2 litre, a high-pressure 2.3 litre and low-pressure 2.4 litre. Transmission was four- or five-speed automatic or five-speed manual.

It was apparent from Day One that the convertible was the star of

the show, and the coupe was discontinued in 2002 whilst the convertible lived on. The latter had a natty powered top that opened and closed at the touch of a dashboard button, stowing neatly under a rigid tonneau cover when in open-top mode. This ultra-safe car featured a horseshoe-shaped safety cage, front and side airbags and boron-reinforced A-pillars. But despite Volvo's declared intentions, the C70 convertible wasn't actually an incomparable drive – suffering from that endemic convertible fault whereby the less-rigid open-top body causes vibration and shuddering when the chassis flexes at speed.

The second generation C70 arrived in 2006 as something completely different – a clever two-door hardtop coupe, built in a joint venture with Pininfarina, that becomes a convertible in less than 30 seconds as a retractable three-piece hardtop vanishes when the moment is right for blue-sky motoring.

It didn't take long to open the C70's top when the sun came out.

2000s

Ariel Atom

COUNTRY OF ORIGIN:
UK (also built in the USA)
FIRST MANUFACTURED:
2000
ENGINE:
1,998 cc Straight Four
PERFORMANCE:
Supercharged Atom 2 – top speed
of 150 mph (241 km/h);
0-60 mph (97 km/h) in 2.7 secs
YOU SHOULD KNOW:
For those who wish to enjoy the eye-
watering pleasure of experiencing
just what the tearaway Ariel Atom
can do without shelling out £40,000,
companies are springing up in the UK
that offer the opportunity to do just
that on special track outings, either
as a passenger or driver.

An excited newspaper motoring correspondent asked 'Is this the most amazing car of the century?' It was a rhetorical question, for the answer is clearly 'Obviously!' The Aerial Atom is unlike any other performance car ever made. This incredible machine has no doors, roof, windscreen, heater, sound system, carpeting or any creature comforts at all. So what exactly has the Atom got?

A striking external steel-tube chassis with a silver finish and stainless steel rocker posts. Two seats. A fuel-injected 2 litre Honda i-VTEC engine with an aluminium-alloy block. A close-ratio six-speed gearbox. Cast-alloy wheels. Rack-and-pinion steering. Sophisticated adjustable suspension. Ventilated front disc brakes and solid rear discs, all with twin-piston calipers. For those who want to cut a dash (literally) on the way to work (or better still the track), there is a road pack that makes the machine street-legal.

The Atom may look like a piece of modern art, but its entire rationale is delivering unbeatable performance on a budget. That becomes apparent when the Atom blasts through the 60 mph (97 km/h) mark from a standing start in less than three seconds, hurtles past the 100 mph (161 km/h) barrier in under seven seconds – and returns to rest inside a further four seconds. It is blistering acceleration combined with racecar handling and roadholding rather than high top-speed that makes the Atom so special – it's the ultimate thrill-seeking driver's car.

At Ariel's Somerset factory a handful of skilled engineers turn out fewer than one hundred cars a year. Atoms are built under licence in the USA, where they are fitted with GM Ecotec engines. Thus far the Ariel Atom has gone through three evolutionary generations – Atoms 1, 2 and 3 – and plans are now afoot to create an explosive Atom 500 with a 500 bhp 2.4 litre engine.

Yes, this really is the most amazing car of the century.

446

Alfa Romeo Brera

The gorgeous Brera concept car was shown at the 2002 Geneva Motor Show, powered by a Maserati V8 engine and sporting unusual doors that opened upwards. The reception it received was positive enough to encourage Alfa to plan a production run. The first cars appeared in 2005 and, although the Brera looked exactly like the original, it had actually shrunk from the full-sized GT concept coupe into a mid-sized two-door coupe.

Some drivers thought the speedy Brera was too powerful for its – and their – own good.

Pininfarina manufactured the Brera for Alfa, using the premium platform shared with the Alfa Romeo 159. Three engines were offered. The smaller petrol unit was a 2.2 litre straight four and the bigger power plant was a 3.2 litre V6. There was also a 2.4 litre JTD turbodiesel option (updated in 2007). Transmission choices were six-speed manual or automatic. All versions of the Brera were high-performance cars with even the slowest model capable of hitting nearly 140 mph (225 km/h) . . . and V6s were considerably faster.

Breras were front-engined cars with different drive systems, depending on the engine. The 2.2 litre petrol and the turbodiesel were both front-wheel drive, whilst the 3.2 litre V6 came only with a Torsen four-wheel drive system. From the 2008 model year a front-wheel drive version of the V6 Brera was offered, whilst all models acquired an electronic limited-slip differential and improved interior trim.

A Brera S special edition was offered in the UK from 2008. A limited run was planned, with British performance specialist Prodrive working with Alfa to enhance suspension and handling. This reflects some criticism of the standard car from those who tried to drive it to the limit, suggesting that the Brera was too powerful for its own (and owners') good. In 2009 a new turbocharged 1.7 litre TBi engine was introduced, with direct fuel injection and variable valve timing.

COUNTRY OF ORIGIN:
Italy
FIRST MANUFACTURED:
2005
ENGINE:
1,742 cc or 2,198 cc Straight Four;
3,195 cc V6; 2,387 cc
Straight Five Diesel
PERFORMANCE:
With 3.2 l engine – top speed of
155 mph (250 km/h);
0-60 mph (97 km/h) in 7 secs
YOU SHOULD KNOW:
A convertible two-seater Spider cabriolet version of the Brera was launched in 2006 to general acclaim. It replaced the Spider 916, which was only a year old, thus becoming the sixth generation. Although based on the Brera it was not badged as such, being described simply as the Alfa Spider.

Alfa Romeo 8C Competizione

COUNTRY OF ORIGIN:
Italy
FIRST MANUFACTURED:
2007 (until 2009)
ENGINE:
4,691 cc V8
PERFORMANCE:
Top speed of 182 mph (293 km/h);
0-60 mph (97 km/h) in 4 secs
YOU SHOULD KNOW:
Don't bother to rush down to the
nearest Alfa dealer with a flapping
cheque book – the 8C Competizione
came in a strictly limited edition of
500 cars which were all presold. But
wait! There might be a chance to bag
an 8C Spider convertible (another
limited run of 500, starting in 2010) –
for a mere 200,000 euros.

The Frankfurt Motor Show in 2003 saw the first appearance of an ab-fab Alfa Romeo two-seater coupe. Although its rounded body and streamlined profile were thoroughly modern, the prototype 8C Competizione had styling cues that harked back to great Alfas of the 1930s and 1940s and the name was a direct reference to the 6C Competizione that ran so well in Mille Miglia races and won the 1950 Targo Florio.

Naturally, those with deep pockets and an enduring affection for beautiful Italian sports cars had to have one and told Alfa so . . . loudly. These heavy hints were taken and a production version was duly sanctioned in 2006. Construction began the following year, with a traditional steel chassis elegantly clothed in carbon-fibre bodywork finished in black, yellow, and Italian competition red or 8C red. Beneath the rear-hinged bonnet (more or less the only change from the prototype) a 4.7 litre Maserati V8 engine could be found. As Ferrari were assembling, this it boded well for the Competizione's performance – which was indeed so spectacular that the officially announced top speed is thought to be a politic underestimate.

The sporty driver will have great fun playing the gear-change game. The car features a six-speed transaxle gearbox with

The 8C is a rare and desirable modern classic in the making.

computerized selection. Using levers which are mounted behind the steering wheel, the driver chooses between the five modes – manual-normal, manual-sport, automatic-normal, automatic-sport and ice conditions. In sport mode, it can take as long as a microsecond to change gear.

The 8C Competizione is assembled by Maserati at the Modena factory, with the chassis and bodies coming from different external suppliers. There seems little doubt that a racing version will be developed once homologation of the Competizione is achieved, with GT races like Le Mans and Daytona as the likely target.

Ascari KZ1

The story so far – in 1998 speed-loving Klaas Zwart purchased Ascari Cars, maker of the impressive Ascari Ecosse mid-engined sports car, built a new factory at Banbury to create custom performance cars and started developing a racing club in Southern Spain that came with its own racing circuit and a stable of supercars for members to enjoy. Now read on . . .

Klaas Zwart named the company's next high-performance car after himself (as the Ascari KZ1 and then KZ1R) and made it one of the most exclusive supercars in the world. This special edition beauty was limited to just 50 cars, each built by hand over eight months. Would-be owners can try before they buy at the Ascari Race Resort, which is billed as the world's ultimate drivers' club and luxury retreat.

The mid-engined KZ1 was created as a replacement for the Ecosse. Klass Zwart styled the body, building it around a carbon-fibre chassis and tuned BMW 4.9 litre V8 engine that delivered majestic performance figures. The car has a distinctly 21st century appearance, crouching low on the road with its sloping bonnet between rounded front wings, punctuated with stylish slanting headlight arrays. The flanks have deeply scalloped air intakes and the cockpit has raked front and rear glass. A discreetly curved rear wing completes the picture. Detailing is superb and the comfortable cockpit is beautifully designed and appointed.

Next out of the Ascari box was an A10 race prototype that used the KZ1's chassis and the same BMW engine. Then the KZ1R was unveiled at the 2008 Goodwood Festival of Speed. This has a leather interior, air conditioning, electric windows and central locking, but still manages to hit 60 mph (97 km/h) from rest in around three seconds and go on to 200 mph (322 km/h).

COUNTRY OF ORIGIN:
UK
FIRST MANUFACTURED:
2003
ENGINE:
4,941 cc V8
PERFORMANCE:
Top speed of 199 mph (320 km/h); 0-60 mph (97 km/h) in 3.9 secs
YOU SHOULD KNOW:
'Never rest on those laurels' must be a Team Ascari motto, as the awesomely fast KZ1R was further developed as the KZ1R-GT to race in the EuroBOSS series, where Klaas Zwart (wearing his racing-driver helmet) has enjoyed considerable success.

Ascari's formula for success: Big engine plus ultralight carbon-fibre body equals awesome performance.

Aston Martin Vanquish

COUNTRY OF ORIGIN:
UK
FIRST MANUFACTURED:
2001 (until 2007)
ENGINE:
5,935 cc V12
PERFORMANCE:
Top speed of 196 mph (315 km/h);
0-60 mph (97 km/h) in 4.4 secs
YOU SHOULD KNOW:
The paddle-shift gearbox on the
Vanquish was so temperamental that
(rather too late in the day) a manual
six-speed gearbox complete with
old-fashioned but efficient clutch
pedal appeared in 2007 (which could
be retro-fitted to earlier models for a
modest £13,250).

The Vanquish was the grandest of grand tourers when it went on
sale, after first appearing as the Project Vantage GT concept car at
the North American International Auto Show in 1998. This super-
refined machine designed by Ian Callum sat proudly at the top of
the Aston Martin totem pole from 2001 and remained there for six
good years, helped by an appearance as 007's wheels in the
twentieth Bond film, *Die Another Day*, in 2002.

The Vanquish had classic streamlined coupe lines and a
traditional front-engine, rear-wheel drive configuration. The engine
was a 5.9 litre V12 teamed with a six-speed clutchless manual
transmission and fly by wire throttle. Critics complained that the
engine consisted of two Ford Duratec 30 V6 engines bolted together
but in fact – though it shared components – the Aston engine was a
unique power plant designed by Ford in America.

From 2004 Aston Martin offered an optional Sports Dynamic Pack for the Vanquish, which delivered enhanced suspension, upgraded brakes and more precise steering. These improvements were incorporated as standard in the Vanquish S that appeared in 2005. In addition, there were minor style tweaks, new wheels and a more powerful engine. There was talk of a Vanquish convertible to challenge the Ferrarri 550 Barchetta, but nothing ever came of it. Two concept cars based on the Vanquish were shown at Geneva in 2004 – the Zagato roadster and Bertone Jet-2 estate car – but they, too, were stillborn.

To mark the end of the production run in 2007, the limited Vanquish Ultimate Edition was created. Just 40 cars were built, all painted black, with personalized sill plaques and a plush interior. The last Vanquish Ultimate was the final car to emerge from the historic Newport Pagnell works, before new management relocated production to Gaydon in Warwickshire.

The Vanquish was the last Aston Martin to be produced at the company's historic Newport Pagnell factory.

Aston Martin DBS V12

COUNTRY OF ORIGIN:
UK
FIRST MANUFACTURED:
2008
ENGINE:
5,935 cc V12
PERFORMANCE:
Top speed of 188 mph (302 km/h);
0-60 mph (97 km/h) in 4.1 secs
YOU SHOULD KNOW:
The James Bond connection was firmly maintained by the DBS V12. An original DBS featured in the 1969 film *On Her Majesty's Secret Service*, a pre-production DBS V12 greeted actor Daniel Craig's first appearance as 007 in *Casino Royale* (2006) and the car appeared again in the sequel, *Quantum of Solace* (2008).

Following the demise of the Vanquish S, Aston Martin's new leader of the pack was the DBS V12. Proudly reviving the iconic DBS designation of earlier years, this superb machine made a show-stopping inaugural appearance at the Pebble Beach Concours D'Elegance in 2007. The DBS V12 prototype was certainly an eye-catcher, shaped by the aerodynamic requirements of stable high-speed driving, flaunting impressive 10-spoke alloy wheels and finished in the striking new Casino Ice colour (graphite with a hint of blue). The interior was hand-crafted using the finest materials.

The first cars were delivered in 2008. They sported a potent V12 engine borrowed from the DBR9 racecar, coupled with six-speed manual or six-speed Touchtronic automatic transmission. The DBS was clearly based on the 2+2 DB9's design and platform but was an unashamed two-seater, with a lightweight bonded-aluminium chassis giving outstanding strength and rigidity. Ultra-light carbon-fibre body panels further reduced weight, as did a state-of-the-art braking system using vented carbon-ceramic discs front and back. Double-wishbone suspension featured adaptive damper control for instant adjustment of handling and ride characteristics.

No expense was spared in creating the ultimate touring car and the DBS V12 transferred the DBR9's race pedigree to Aston's flagship road car. The front mid-mounted engine was teamed with a rear mid-mounted transaxle to ensure near perfect weight distribution for stability, agility and an exhilarating driving experience. If the DB9 is a true grand tourer, the DBS V12 is an out-and-out sports car. It is better to drive than its GT sibling with more power and impressive cornering ability.

To Aston Martin's chagrin, in 2008 an Australian motoring website blew the whistle on what turned out to be the company worst-kept secret – the existence of a simply fabulous open-top DBS V12 Volante that was officially announced in 2009.

Make no mistake – the DBS V12 is the ultimate grand tourer.

Audi R8

Every ambitious car manufacturer in the heady pre-credit-crunch opening years of the 21st century aimed to put a supercar on the road, and Audi was no exception. By 2006 the German company had perfected its pitch to acquisitive city traders. The R8 was a mid-engined two-door sports coupe, which was based on the Le Mans quattro concept car presented in 2003. The new speedster was allowed to assume the hallowed name of Audi's R8 racing car.

The R8's styling was fairly typical of many a mid-sized sporting coupe, but no less pleasing for that. It was hand-built on the Audi Space Frame for lightness and the initial engine offering was an advanced FSI (Fuel-Stratified Injection) 4.2 litre V8 that developed 414 bhp. The manual six-speed transmission version had a Ferrari-style metal gate for gear shifting, while the alternative R-tronic gearbox was a semi-automatic sequential manual system.

The car employed the company's famous Quattro all-wheel drive system to deliver impressive performance, ride quality and handling precision that had many motoring writers and self-appointed experts declaring that the R8 was superior to the class-leading Porsche 997 – an accolade that doubtless delighted Audi. But this wasn't enough. The company couldn't resist a quick return to the well, and an FSI 5.2 litre V10 version of the R8 was offered from the end of 2008. This upped the R8's power output to 518 bhp with a corresponding increase in performance, whilst styling was tweaked to give the R8 a more aggressive look.

A 6 litre turbodiesel R8 TDI Le Mans concept car was presented at motoring shows in 2008, and that was also the year when one of those persistent auto paparazzi the manufacturers love to hate snapped a badly disguised convertible version of the R8 undergoing a road test – watch this space.

COUNTRY OF ORIGIN:
Germany
FIRST MANUFACTURED:
2006
ENGINE:
4,163 cc V8; 5,204 cc V10
PERFORMANCE:
With 5.2 l engine – top speed of 196 mph (316 km/h);
0-60 mph (97 km/h) in 3.9 secs
YOU SHOULD KNOW:
Serious students of the sports car will note that the Audi R8 shares a fifth of its DNA with Audi-owned Lamborghini's Gallardo, for the R8 is built on a Gallardo platform and the two dashing sports cars have several features, such as transmission, in common.

The Audi R8 was the German company's impressive entry in the great supercar stakes.

The fabulous Bentley tradition is alive and well – albeit with a little help from Germany.

Bentley Continental GT

Folk were puzzled when Volkswagen bought Rolls-Royce Motors . . . without the right to use the name. The Rolls-Royce trademark had been sold to BMW in a cut-throat side deal. VW saved face by insisting that it only really wanted the sporty Bentley marque (not true!) and has proceeded to prove the point by producing a series of beautifully designed and appointed cars that are seriously fast.

The Continental GT replaced Rolls-Royce Motors' Continental R and T models. This two-door 2+2 grand touring coupe was built on the same platform as the Volkswagen Phaeton, sharing many components with the upmarket luxury saloon, but the GT is a superb modern realization of Bentley tradition, showing that Volkswagen understands and appreciates the traditional character that made the marque great.

The GT has a 6 litre W12 engine with twin turbochargers. This innovative motor has four banks of three cylinders arranged in a double-V shape, driving a common crankshaft. It's a seriously powerful unit well capable of delivering the high top speed required of a Bentley. The average owner may be more interested in rapid acceleration and silky-smooth cruising, but still likes to know that his Bentley is as fast as pretty much anything but the most exotic supercar.

The Continental GT was the founding father for quite a dynasty. The Continental Flying Spur four-door saloon car, developed from the GT, appeared in 2005, as did the drop-dead gorgeous GTC convertible with a powered hood produced by Karmann in Germany. The GT Speed model hit the scene in 2007 – the first production Bentley capable of exceeding 200 mph (322 km/h). A Continental GTZ rebodied by Italian style master Zagato was shown at the Geneva Motor Show in 2008. A CTC Speed convertible followed in 2009, along with a Flying Spur Speed. Take your pick!

COUNTRY OF ORIGIN:
UK
FIRST MANUFACTURED:
2003
ENGINE:
5,998 cc W12 Twin Turbo
PERFORMANCE:
Top speed of 198 mph (318 km/h);
0-60 mph (97 km/h) in 4.6 secs
YOU SHOULD KNOW:
The new Continental Supersports is the first Bentley with pioneering FlexFuel technology that allows the car to run on petrol and/or biofuel (ethanol) – and it's the fastest road-going Bentley ever.

Bentley Brooklands Coupe

Out went the Mulsanne and Bentley Eight, in came the Brooklands as Bentley's top model. This full-sized luxury saloon was very much a product of the time when Rollers and Bentleys were identical, apart from the minor styling differences needed to differentiate one from the other. That was back in 1992, and when Volkswagen took over in 1998, the Bentley Arnage had been launched to replace the Brooklands – the last Bentley to share a common platform with a Rolls-Royce twin, in this case the Silver Seraph.

Volkswagen allowed the flagship Arnage to sail on (with tweaks and upgrades) and concentrated on developing the sporty Continental GT series. But the Brooklands name hadn't been forgotten and in 2008 it was resurrected. What a difference from its somewhat angular predecessor! The new Brooklands Coupe is a magnificent two-door grand tourer with flowing lines. At rest it looks both sleek and muscular, with a low roofline and dramatically raked glass fore and aft. In motion, it is immediately apparent that this is a serious performance car that can't wait to bite the bitumen.

The Brooklands Coupe is hand-built at Crewe using traditional coachbuilding expertise and the finest skilled craftsmen working in leather and wood. This enables each customer to personally configure their car, choosing colour, interior trim and desired accessories (most at least opting for the retractable Flying B bonnet mascot). But every Brooklands will have the 6.75 litre V8 engine that slams out 530 bhp – in the nicest possible way! Transmission is a ZF six-speed automatic gearbox with Tiptronic feature.

Bentley states that just 550 of these superb touring cars will be manufactured so, if this is the one you'd love to be seen driving, start buying lottery tickets now. This is one car guaranteed to become a serious collectors' classic.

COUNTRY OF ORIGIN:
UK
FIRST MANUFACTURED:
2008
ENGINE:
6,761 cc V8 Twin Turbo
PERFORMANCE:
Top speed of 184 mph (296 km/h);
0-60 mph (97 km/h) in 5 secs
YOU SHOULD KNOW:
The Brooklands Coupe is inspired by the exploits of the famously daring Bentley Boys on Surrey's steeply banked Brooklands racing circuit in the 1920s and pays them – as well as the legendary prewar track – a fitting tribute.

The Brooklands name returned in 2008 on this most refined of hand-built Bentleys from Crewe.

BMW E60 M5

COUNTRY OF ORIGIN:
Germany
FIRST MANUFACTURED:
2005
ENGINE:
4,999 cc DOHC V10
PERFORMANCE:
Electronically limited top speed of
155 mph (250 km/h);
0-60 mph (97 km/h) in 4.1 secs
YOU SHOULD KNOW:
An E61 M5 Touring estate car was
introduced in 2007 – only the second
M5 to be offered in this body style
after the E34 and intended to go
head-to-head with the Mercedes E63
AMG Estate and the Audi RS6.

Pick a letter – say M – and put it together with a number – say 5 – and what have you got? Lovers of performance cars know the answer, for the BMW M5 has been burning rubber since it was introduced in 1985. This souped-up special is made by BMW Motorsport and has shadowed the 5 series over time, the first version being the hand-built E28 that started as the M5 meant to go on – as the world's fastest production saloon.

Further evolutions kept up the speedy work as the E34 and E39 M5s were licensed to thrill, and the latest dazzler is the E60 M5, with us since 2005. This businesslike four-door saloon has a pleasant shape but little that hints at its performance potential. This is realized with the help of a BMW S85 V10 engine that socks out 500 bhp and redlines at 8,250 revs.

The ability to handle this massive power output is secured by a stiffened aluminium chassis and seven-speed SMG III electrohydraulic automatic transmission. Critics in the USA found this advanced system was perfect for track use but jerky in everyday road use, so BMW also offered a six-speed manual option. This, however, denies drivers the pleasure of using the SMG III's launch control to make spectacular standing starts. That's not all they lose, for SMG offers dynamic stability control and the Drivelogic system that gives no fewer than 11 programmes controlled from paddles on the steering wheel and a console shifter. Clever stuff!

If all the electronic gizmology can get rather confusing (it can), the M5's true *raison d'être* remains plain. It's a rather ordinary looking BMW saloon car that unexpectedly accelerates like a ballistic missile and would easily top the double-ton if some Teutonic killjoy hadn't decided to fit a limiter.

This ordinary looking BMW saloon car is a fearsome wild boar in sheep's clothing.

BMW 1-Series Coupe/ Convertible

As entry-level motoring goes, the BMW 1-Series isn't the least bit shabby – *au contraire*, it's rather dashing. It replaced the 3-Series in the aspirational 'become-a-BMW-driver-you-lucky-person' role back in 2004, allowing that popular line to ascend one rung up BMW's lengthy model ladder. The first offering was the E87, a five-door hatchback on its own platform. After becoming an instant bestseller, this was facelifted and joined by a sporty E81 three-door hot hatch, in 2007. At the same time, the stars of the 1-Series show swaggered onto the stage.

The 1-Series E82 Coupe and its E88 Convertible twin were, in truth, fairly impressive as entry-level models go, though it seems cavalier to describe such refined and powerful cars thus. The E82/88 offered a range of 2 to 3 litre petrol and diesel engines and enjoyed the benefit of 1-Series upgrades introduced in 2007 – including an innovative stop-start system, electric power steering, brake energy regeneration and various drivetrain modifications designed to increase performance, improve fuel economy and reduce emissions.

BMW called this package EfficientDynamics and planned to roll it out across the entire range. At its heart is the stop-start system – pioneering mild-hybrid technology that is nothing to do with an extra electric motor, but a clever system that automatically turns off the engine when the car is coasting, braking or stationary, instantly restarting when power is needed again. This has a very positive effect on both emissions and fuel consumption.

But however technically advanced they may be (very!), both the 1-Series Coupe and Convertible are a joy to drive, with punchy acceleration, immaculate roadholding and a more-than-satisfactory top speed. As a nice bonus, both cars are also rather pleasing to look at, offering a satisfying blend of performance, economy and style.

This is the natty two-door coupe version – but there's also a very attractive convertible model.

COUNTRY OF ORIGIN:
Germany
FIRST MANUFACTURED:
2007
ENGINE:
1,995 cc Straight Four; 1,995 cc Straight Four Diesel/Turbodiesel; 2,996 cc Straight Six; 2,979 cc Straight Six Turbo
PERFORMANCE:
With the most powerful 135i engine – electronically limited top speed of 155 mph (250 km/h); 0-60 mph (97 km/h) in 5.3 secs
YOU SHOULD KNOW:
German carmakers are masters at turning one model into several hundred (or maybe it just seems like that) . . . and no sooner had the 1-Series Coupe and Convertible been announced than variations on the theme started appearing, mainly with assorted levels of power output.

The Blenheim is thoroughly modern but still majors on good old-fashioned gentility.

Bristol Blenheim 3S

Is it a World War II British light bomber or is it a car? Trick question – it's both. The Bristol Blenheim bomber was made by the Bristol Aeroplane Company, which helped co-found Bristol Cars. That company made the Blenheim grand touring car through the 1990s, with the revised Blenheim 3 appearing in 1999 and remaining in production today. But the most exciting evolution of this refined machine did not happen until the 21st century, which makes this splendid coupe with echoes of American pony-car styling from an earlier generation a fascinating anachronism.

The Bristol Blenheim 3S was announced in 2001 with the not-inconsiderable price tag of £175,000 (built strictly to order at the Filton, Bristol factory). The 3S is an enhanced performance version of the Blenheim 3 – an old-fashioned touring car in the 'Best of British' tradition, with a steel chassis, live rear axle and aluminium bodywork. Despite its undoubted True Brit credentials, the Blenheim 3S has a dark secret – beneath the long bonnet is a Chrysler V8 engine with automatic transmission. The 3S has increased power output, better brakes, stiffened suspension, large five-spoke alloy wheels and an even more sumptuous interior finish. Though discreet luxury is fine, the 3S is not above emitting a satisfying boom from its four tail-pipes when the accelerator is floored.

Luckily for Bristol Cars, a certain class of well-heeled Brit wouldn't be seen dead in a fiery Ferrari or mincing Merc, and these gentleman motorists take almost perverse pleasure in being out and about in a Bristol, driving Britain's most exclusive luxury car and exchanging knowing nods with fellow travellers as the picnic comes out on the greensward during the Royal Ascot race meeting. For them, unobtrusive traditional values are infinitely more appealing than in-your-face glitz 'n' glam and a 23rd century computerized engine management system.

COUNTRY OF ORIGIN:
UK
FIRST MANUFACTURED:
2001
ENGINE:
5,900 cc V8
PERFORMANCE:
Top speed of 155 mph (250 km/h); 0-60 mph (97 km/h) in 5.4 secs
YOU SHOULD KNOW:
The ethos of Bristol Cars – makers of exclusive automobiles for over 60 years – is neatly captured in the company slogan . . . 'Hand-built cars for individuals'. Oh, it's also the last luxury car manufacturer in the UK that remains under British control.

Bristol Fighter 10

It was shaped by a Formula 1 designer. It's exclusive. It's original. It's hyper-fast. It's a Great British supercar. It's the Bristol 10. Following in the tradition of naming cars after aircraft, the Bristol Fighter 10's inspiration was a sturdy World War I biplane. Ironically, the car is capable of cruising at a higher speed than many modern light aircraft.

This majestic performance coupe owed nothing to any previous Bristol and was created from scratch as a supreme marriage of form and function. The Bristol Fighter 10 is one of the most aerodynamically efficient sports cars ever made, with a teardrop-shaped cabin and extensive curved glass screens front and back for excellent all-round vision. Gullwing doors provide easy access and once inside comfort has not been sacrificed on the altar of performance. The interior is beautifully finished, has leather sports seats and offers ample room for even the largest pair of occupants.

An all-aluminium 8 litre V10 engine sits up front. It's based on the one in the Dodge Viper, extensively modified to suit the Fighter 10's specific requirements. This cleverly gains power at high speed thanks to an aerodynamically induced supercharging effect. A six-speed manual box gets the Fighter 10 to 60 mph (97 km/h) in first gear, and no time at all. A strong chassis and roll cage provide protection even in the event of severe impact. Handling is agile and a low centre of gravity ensures limpet-like roadholding, whilst sophisticated independent suspension smooths out the bumps.

In 2004 the Bristol Fighter 10S became available with a super-tuned normally aspirated V10 engine, whilst from 2006 the Bristol Fighter 10T with turbochargers offered the best power output yet. If it hadn't been electronically limited, the Fighter 10T's top speed would be around 270 mph (425 km/h). Some car!

COUNTRY OF ORIGIN:
UK
FIRST MANUFACTURED:
2002
ENGINE:
7,994 cc V10 Twin Turbo
PERFORMANCE:
Bristol Fighter 10T – top speed of 225 mph (362 km/h); 0-60 mph (97 km/h) in 3.5 secs
YOU SHOULD KNOW:
Bugatti eat your heart out – the twin-turbocharged V10 engine in the Bristol Fighter 10T puts out more horsepower than the fearsome Bugatti Veyron (1,012 bhp against 1,001 bhp) . . . but relax you Bugatti fans, the Veyron is still the faster car (by far) thanks to the 109T's electronic limiter.

Few speedsters can beat the Bristol Fighter 10 when it comes to aerodynamic efficiency.

Bugatti Veyron EB 16.4

COUNTRY OF ORIGIN:
France
FIRST MANUFACTURED:
2005
ENGINE:
7,993 cc W16 Quad Turbo
PERFORMANCE:
With roof in place – top speed of
253 mph (407 km/h);
0-60 mph (97 km/h) in 2.5 secs
YOU SHOULD KNOW:
When testing a Veyron for the *Top
Gear* TV programme, after hitting top
speed presenter James May dryly
observed 'the tyres will only last
fifteen minutes . . . but that's okay
because the fuel runs out in twelve
minutes'. Would-be Veyron drivers
listen and learn!

You know what they say – it's a tough job, but someone has to do it. When it comes to hanging tough as the world's fastest production car the Bugatti Veyron EB 16.4 happily volunteers, knowing it will be rewarded by being one of the world's most expensive cars. As with Bentley, Volkswagen has provided sensitive stewardship for an iconic marque, imaginatively reinvented for the 21st century.

The new Bugatti is built near the original factory at Molsheim in Eastern France, and has been carefully crafted to respect illustrious forebears. Although the Veyron (named after winning prewar Bugatti racing driver Pierre Veyron) is a stunning example of contemporary automobile styling that puts it in the modern design icon bracket, it also pays homage to Bugattis of old. The horseshoe grille is there, as is the classic two-tone colour scheme with contrasting ellipsis and the signature crest line from bonnet to roof. Coupled with the racy design, the overall result is a stunning combination of sleek elegance and the very latest technology.

The Veyron's power plant is an 8 litre, 16-cylinder W16 masterpiece with four turbochargers that delivers an unbelievable (but true) 1,001 bhp. Transmission is a computer-controlled dual-clutch manual DSG (Direct-Shift Gearbox) with seven gears, that can be used in full-auto mode. It has permanent four-wheel drive and requires 10 different radiators to keep everything cool.

What's this flying machine like to drive? Activate launch control, engage gear, grab the steering wheel, stamp on the brake, floor the throttle with the other foot, release the brake . . . and the amazing Veyron will accelerate like a Formula 1 car and scoot past the 250 mph (402 km/h) mark inside a minute. But sadly that's a privilege accorded only to those with 1.4 million euros to spend (plus optional extras).

The Veyron has a simple claim to fame – it's the fastest of the fast.

Cadillac CTS-V

Caddys have a traditional image as luxurious barges that roll gracefully round the corners and then glide along the straightaway with an imperious smoothness. Yes? Actually no, because that stereotype has been blown clean away by the Cadillac CTS-V, the superstar in Cadillac's V-Series high-performance line that made its debut in 2004.

Your average Caddy is a bit of a barge – but not this one.

Admittedly the first generation got off to a somewhat sticky start with owners experiencing tiresome problems with a whining rear differential caused by inadequate half-shafts. Nothing was officially admitted by General Motors or Cadillac, but the upgraded diff unit fitted from 2006 was proof enough for most. But those teething troubles were just the learning curve needed to produce the extraordinary second generation CTS-V that was introduced in 2008.

This is a spectacular performance car that shares a 6.2 litre V8 with the Corvette ZR1, no slouch itself. Around 550 bhp is more than enough to deliver bitumen-blasting acceleration and searing speed that puts the CTS-V right alongside – or even in front of – German class-leaders like the BMW M5, Mercedes SLK32 AMG or Mercedes E63 AMG. The Caddy comes with six-speed manual or automatic transmission, the latter paddle-operated, and has ride and handling qualities that match the powerful engine. MagnaRide technology features dampers that adjust automatically (and instantly) to the road surface. The comfort of driver and passengers hasn't been overlooked, either, with a refined interior that features hand-stitched leather and performance Recaro seats that adjust every whichway. The unfussy styling of the CTS-V is restrained, with an almost European look.

The second generation CTS-V is a pleasure to drive and to prove the performance point a CTS-V went round Germany's famous Nürburgring in under eight minutes, smashing the record for a four-door production saloon car . . . and that was achieved by the slow old automatic version.

COUNTRY OF ORIGIN:
USA
FIRST MANUFACTURED:
2008
ENGINE:
6.2 l (376 cid) V8
PERFORMANCE:
Top speed of 191 mph (307 km/h);
0-60 mph (97 km/h) in 3.9 secs
YOU SHOULD KNOW:
Unfortunately, the credit crunch and tsunami-like recession that followed hit Cadillac parent General Motors hard, and the HPVO (High-Performance Vehicle Operations) team responsible for creating the CTS-V was disbanded, with no plans for reformation in the foreseeable future.

Cadillac One

COUNTRY OF ORIGIN:
USA
FIRST MANUFACTURED:
2009
ENGINE:
GM spokesperson: 'One of the
specifications is that we don't talk
about specifications' (true)
PERFORMANCE:
GM spokesperson: 'If I told you the
facts, I'd have to kill you' (false, but
the figures are a closely guarded
secret)
YOU SHOULD KNOW:
Don't think anyone will get to snoop
around Cadillac One when it is
decommissioned, after working
down the political pecking order over
time. The car won't finish up in the
Henry Ford Museum alongside other
Presidential limos, but will be
destroyed on the orders of the
Secret Service to preserve its
secrets.

*President Obama's 'Stagecoach'
needs rather more than four
horses to haul its massive bulk.*

Okay, so you'll never get to drive it, or ride in it, or maybe even see it (except on television). Shoot at it with a high-powered rifle and the bullet will bounce off. Let fly with a rocket-launcher before the Secret Service take you out and Cadillac One will barely be dented. But it can't be ignored.

Unlike some previous US Presidents who made do with hand-me-downs, Barack Obama got a new limo built by Cadillac – marque of first choice since Congress funded a White House car pool a century ago. President Wilson paraded in a Caddy to mark the end of World War I. Convertibles nicknamed Queen Elizabeth and Queen Mary after famous ocean liners loyally served Presidents Roosevelt, Truman and Eisenhower. Ronald Reagan used a Fleetwood, Bill Clinton preferred a newer Fleetwood Brougham and George W Bush had a Cadillac DTS.

Since the awful events of 9/11, security mania has swept the States and the new Presidential ride – codenamed 'Stagecoach' – reflects that. With sophisticated communications it's the earthbound equivalent of Air Force One and has been described by the Secret Service as 'the most technologically advanced protection vehicle in the world'. Exactly what that entails is a matter of speculation.

This handsome black 'armoured personnel carrier with tinted windows' is said to be completely bulletproof, capable of

withstanding an explosive blast and have an in-built oxygen supply to repel chemical attack. It looks not unlike an over-stretched Cadillac DTS but is built on a General Motors truck chassis with a large diesel engine to haul the weight, allegedly about 8 tons. The armour plating is up to 20 cm (8 in) thick, whilst the anti-ballistic glass is 13 cm (5 in) thick. Oh, one vital secret has leaked out – Cadillac One has a 10-disc CD player.

Callaway C16

There's nothing much wrong with the Chevy Corvette C6 – except it's not a Callaway C16. This is the customized C6 that was designed to compete with the Lambo Murciélago, Porsche 911 GT3 . . . not to mention Ferrari F430s and 599 GTBs. Not much to beat there, then. But the expensive Callaway C16 actually puts a buyer's money where its mouth is, living up to the corporate slogan (Powerfully Engineered Automobiles) and delivering a truly monumental performance car that looks very different from the Corvette C6 from whence it sprang – only the roof, rear hatch and mirrors are retained from the original.

When the C16 was unveiled, company founder Reeves Callaway proudly announced: 'The C16 says exactly what we want to say about the capabilities at Callaway Cars – it's gorgeous, it has class-leading performance and it's a true daily driver based on one the best sports-car platforms ever made.'

In practice this means a supercharged 6.2 litre V8 fuel-injected engine generating 650 bhp. Sophisticated Callaway/Eibach Multi-Pro coil-over suspension. Speed-sensitive, magnetic power-assisted rack-and-pinion steering. Forged magnesium wheels with carbon-fibre rims, fitted with special tyres. Six-piston (front) and four-piston (rear) caliper brakes with an optional carbon-ceramic alternative. Personal comfort hasn't been overlooked, either, with a leather interior and fanatical attention to detail that extends to colour-coordinated seat belts.

There are three versions of the Callaway C16 – the standard coupe, a seductive open-top Cabrio and an awesome topless Speedster, a raging (and outrageous) roadster that draws admiring crowds everywhere it goes. Best drive this one wearing the colour-coded crash helmet that's supplied, just in case – this is a viciously quick car with an open cockpit and miniscule wind deflectors. There are no mirrors on the Speedster, just tiny rear-facing cameras that feed images to the satnav screen.

COUNTRY OF ORIGIN:
USA
FIRST MANUFACTURED:
2007
ENGINE:
6.2 l (378 cid) V8
PERFORMANCE:
Manual transmission – top speed of 216 mph (410 km/h); 0-60 mph (97 km/h) in 3.3 secs
YOU SHOULD KNOW:
Getting hold of a C16 isn't a matter of nipping down to the nearest showroom armed with (at least) $180,000 . . . each car is custom built to order with the buyer deciding on the exact specification from a range of enticing possibilities, which soon crank up the price – the fitted luggage set is $8,800.

Caterham Seven CSR

COUNTRY OF ORIGIN:
UK
FIRST MANUFACTURED:
2005
ENGINE:
2,261 cc DOHC Straight Four
PERFORMANCE:
CSR Superlight – top speed of
155 mph (250 km/h);
0-60 mph (97 km/h) in 3.1 secs
YOU SHOULD KNOW:
The Caterham CSR's sporting
credentials were underlined by the
Caterham Cosworth Masters series
in 2006, sponsored by the engine
manufacturer. This was a semi-
endurance formula for the CSR,
featuring six double-header events
for one- and two-driver teams at
some of Europe's finest circuits.

The cheapish'n'cheerful, no-frills, max-thrills Lotus Seven has come a
long was since Caterham took on production back in 1972. Modern
manifestations may not share a single component with the original Lotus
but the principle remains the same – delivering the purest driving
experience possible with the best possible performance for the money.

The CSR made its debut in 2005, incorporating everything Caterham
learned in over three decades of manufacturing this unique sports car.
Three variants were offered – the CSR 200 (200 bhp), the CSR 260 (260
bhp) and the CSR Superlight (also 260 bhp). The difference between
models is power output, though the flagship Superlight not only has the
most powerful engine but special suspension that adds further precision
to handling and cornering ability.

The engine is the new Cosworth-developed 2.3 litre Ford Duratec, an
all-alloy twin-cam unit. Gearboxes are five-speed (CSR 200) or six-speed
manual (260 and Superlight). The Seven's tubular spaceframe was
revised and stiffened for the CSR generation, whilst aerodynamics were
improved with a larger nose cone and reprofiled cycle wings. The car has
aluminium wheels and fat tyres that were engineered by Avon for
Formula 3 racing. Although it was never a priority, the interior of the
cockpit has been improved with touches like silver dials, fresh-air vents,
storage space and a bespoke steering wheel.

This never has been, and never will be a speedster for those looking
for a comfortable ride. You only have to look at a Caterham CSR to know
that it has lost none of its feisty character, as it sits close to the tarmac
just waiting to be driven, with its streamlined body, open top, exposed
exhaust pipe and sturdy roll bar. Buy one from the factory or build it at
home, then burn some seriously entertaining rubber.

*If you love the smell of smokin'
rubber on a Sunday morning
the Caterham is the one for you.*

Chevrolet Corvette C6 ZR1

Many afficionados regard the C6 ZR1 as the finest Corvette of them all – some compliment!

Obviously the Chevy Corvette – top speed 198 mph (317 km/h) – wasn't enough for lovers of macho American supercars, for the Corvette ZR1 appeared in 2009. Coyly described as 'the performance version of the Corvette' and nicknamed 'The Blue Devil' during development, this fabulous flying machine has a supercharged LS9 6.2 litre small-block V8 engine delivering 638 bhp – the most powerful ever to sit in a Chevrolet.

The two-door ZR1 coupe with its sculpted cabin and unfussy styling sits up on large rear wheels, giving this streamlined star a menacing appearance even at rest, as though it just can't wait to start chewing tarmac. Chevrolet spent years perfecting the model that represents its serious entry in the world supercar stakes. The chassis is made of aluminium and the bodywork has many carbon-fibre panels to cut weight, including the bonnet, wings, rocker extensions and splitter.

The ZR1 has a six-speed manual gearbox, limited-slip differential and an advanced MSRC (Magnetic Selective Ride Control) system that automatically adjusts the suspension during rapid starts and irons out bumps along the way. There is ABS and the huge brakes share their carbon-ceramic design with Ferrari racing cars. Corvette models over the years have been brutishly fast and often great to look at, but never by the wildest stretch of imagination have they ever been described as good all-round cars to drive.

All that changes with the ZR1. This is a great driver's car. The engine is both docile and savage, the beast dawdles happily around town turning heads, has frightening acceleration and straight-line speed, sticks to the road like a rash when it corners and slams the occupants against their safety belts when the brakes are applied at speed. It may be the most expensive Corvette yet, but it's the best by far.

COUNTRY OF ORIGIN:
USA
FIRST MANUFACTURED:
2009
ENGINE:
6.2 l (378 cid) V8
PERFORMANCE:
Top speed of 205 mph (331 km/h);
0-60 mph (97 km/h) in 3.1 secs
YOU SHOULD KNOW:
It never hurts to be ambitious – at the ZR1's razzmatazz launch an enthusiastic Chevrolet employee boldly announced 'We can't wait to take on any Porsche and we're going to be right there with Ferrari and Lamborghini'. Time will tell!

465

*This technologically advanced
Chrysler with Mercedes
influence proved to be a great
commercial success – though
that was not enough to stave off
the company's bankruptcy.*

Chrysler 300C

The Chrysler 300 name has been around since medieval times –
well, the 1950s then – reappearing periodically on different
Chryslers ever since. The latest 300 hit the streets as a full-sized
luxury saloon in 2004, after impressing the previous year's New York
Auto Show as a concept car. The concept was for a sporty rear-wheel
drive performance car built on the LX platform that derived from
the discontinued Mercedes E-Class.

Styling was distinctive, with a prominent chrome grille and
square headlamp units, chromed alloy wheels, curved windscreen
with a steep rake, high waistline, low cabin with the look of a
stretched coupe and short rear end. There were assorted variations
in different markets around the world, with the 300 built in three
different countries and featuring several alternative engines. Ever
keen to be crystal clear, Chrysler tagged the base model as the 300
on home turf and the 300C in some overseas markets, while the real
300C was the top-of-the-range high-performance job fitted with a
state-of-the-art 5.7 litre HEMI V8 engine, though for wimps there
was a 3.6 litre V6 and a 3 litre V6 diesel. The 300C Touring estate
car was introduced in 2006 with the same engine choices.

The 300C has a five-speed automatic gearbox and the HEMI V8
is a particularly intelligent engine capable of running on only four
cylinders to conserve fuel when cruising at the speed limit. As the
model years unfolded the well-finished interior acquired delights like
Chrysler's MyGIG Infotainment System, a satellite radio and a
television to keep back-seat drivers quiet. If all that sounds a bit,
well, soft it should be noted that the 300C was no slouch when it
was firing on all cylinders, with rather hot performance . . . and it
has sold like those proverbial hot cakes.

COUNTRY OF ORIGIN:
USA (but built in Canada, China
and Austria)
FIRST MANUFACTURED:
2005
ENGINE:
3.5 l (212 cid) V6; 5.7 l (345 cid) V8;
3.0 l (184 cid) V6 Diesel
PERFORMANCE:
With 5.7 l engine – top speed of
155 mph (250 km/h);
0-60 mph (97 km/h) in 6.2 secs
YOU SHOULD KNOW:
Although it's officially top dog in the
Chrysler 300 line, the 'ordinary'
300C has to share the limelight
with the ultra-quick 300C SRT-8
special edition armed with the
grunty 6.1 l V8.

466

Citroen C3 Pluriel

The iconic all-purpose Citroen 2CV had a roll-back roof that was ideal when its owner wanted to take a sheep to market, and the 2CV's modern great-grandchild has inherited the feature – though it's unlikely that much livestock will be transported in the three-door Pluriel. This is a chic, cheap and cheerful way to experience open-top motoring. The roof can be a sunroof, retracted fully to create a convertible, or removed altogether (along with supporting bars) to make a true roadster.

There are three engines – two petrol versions at 1.4 and 1.6 litres, plus a 1.4 litre diesel. The small petrol engine is the choice for town driving, the diesel is ideal for long runs or general cruising and the larger petrol engine is for those who like a little oomph. The latter comes with a SensoDrive semi-automatic gearbox controlled by paddles behind the steering wheel.

In truth, the Pluriel is best suited to urban work where a high driving position, responsive power steering and small size make light of city traffic, whilst parking is a breeze and ABS is on hand to help when that rogue taxi cuts in. There's little boot space, but enough for a pile of supermarket shopping if the top's up. Kids fit the back seats perfectly, though adults find them a squeeze. Things aren't quite so good on the open road where there's body flex with the top down, plus intrusive wind noise.

No modern manufacturer can resist the temptation to boost sales by introducing different models and special editions. So it is with the Pluriel. The base model is joined by the Exclusive (two- or three-door, including the 1.6 litre performance model), Cote D'Azur (two- or three-door, also including the 1.6 litre option) and special editions like the Latte, Kiwi, Code and Charleston.

COUNTRY OF ORIGIN:
France
FIRST MANUFACTURED:
2003
ENGINE:
1,360 cc or 1,587 cc Straight Four;
1,398 cc Straight Four Diesel
PERFORMANCE:
With 1.6 l engine – top speed of
117 mph (188 km/h);
0-60 mph (97 km/h) in 12.2 secs
YOU SHOULD KNOW:
If the sun is shining and you can't resist the temptation to turn the Pluriel into a roadster to feel the wind in your hair, be warned – there's nowhere to stow the roof, so if a sudden shower looks like developing look for a bridge to park under.

A chic, cheerful opportunity to enjoy open-top motoring.

Daihatsu Terios

COUNTRY OF ORIGIN:
Japan
FIRST MANUFACTURED:
2006
ENGINE:
1,495 cc Straight Four
PERFORMANCE:
Top speed of 99 mph (159 km/h);
0-60 mph (97 km/h) in 12 secs
YOU SHOULD KNOW:
The Terios – like the rival Grand
Vitara and RAV4 whose original
shoes it filled – soon started along
the well-trodden path of sizing up,
with a seven-seater version added to
the compact original.

The second generation Terios is small but perfectly formed – though larger than its dwarfish first generation predecessor. This attractive compact SUV is one of the smallest off-roaders on the market, with four-wheel drive capability that's well up to modest mud-larking (helped by a locking centre differential function). It can accommodate four adults in reasonable comfort and drives well on the road, too, but lacks the power to cruise comfortably at high speed or tow a horsebox. In truth, it's designed to appeal to those who would once have opted for a Suzuki Grand Vitara or Toyota RAV4 before they started getting bigger and more expensive – ladies of the road take note.

The free-revving 1.5 litre petrol engine can be teamed with a five-speed manual gearbox or four-speed automatic transmission. The motor seems to be a tad small for the job in hand and has to be worked hard, which can cause it to complain noisily. The wheels are right at the corners and are all driven all the time, giving stability on- and off-road, with little roll on corners. The suspension is firm, giving a bouncy ride on rough roads, especially at speed. There are front disc brakes, anti-lock braking and independent suspension all round.

The five-door Terios has the high driving position that makes off-roaders so appealing to some, and the cabin has a solid feel with well laid-out controls. The back seats can be split or folded forwards to give good load space, accessed by a rear door that is side-hinged to carry the spare tyre. There are four versions to choose from – the S, SX, SE Auto and Kiri Limited Edition, all representing outstanding value for money at a price that makes the Terios a viable alternative to an average hatchback.

The splashy Terios started life small, but then like Topsy it just seemed to grow and grow.

Dodge Viper Gen IV

The Viper evolved into a seriously impressive piece of kit.

This is the archetypal muscular American sports car, first manufactured by the Chrysler Corporation as a halo car to showcase its ability to create monumental attention-grabbing automobiles. The first Dodge Viper struck venomously in 1992, surviving the DaimlerChrysler merger and Chrysler's return to American ownership. The fourth generation Viper was launched after the German retreat.

This new Viper had the mandatory V10 engine, this time a modest 8.4 litre job delivering 600 bhp with a little help from British engineering expertise – Formula 1 winners McLaren Automotive and Ricardo Consulting Engineers. The engine was promoted as the main advance from the third generation Viper ZB, for the streamlined appearance of the two-door SRT-10 line introduced in 2003 was little altered. Buyers could still choose between the racy roadster and a crouching coupe with its 'double-bubble' roof shape.

However, there were significant changes beneath the Viper's slinky skin that justified classification as a new generation SRT-10, aka Gen IV. Electrics and the fuel feed system were revised. There was a revamped six-speed manual gearbox. The rear axle acquired a new limited-slip differential that improved tyre adhesion under acceleration. Suspension was tweaked to enhance cornering capability. Ever mindful of image, Dodge even changed the exhaust system to give the Viper ZB a more masterful engine note.

This must surely be the last Viper to occupy a Chrysler stable, as the credit-crunched carmaker fights to survive and perforce lets its halo slip in the process. But at least Chrysler has saved the best for last, for this is a truly great Dodge Viper, with all those fourth generation improvements creating an awesome performance car, especially in race-prepped SR-10 ACR form. Traditional Viper straight-line speed is coupled with cornering ability that leaves German and Italian supercars trailing in its wake on track days . . . and petrolheads drooling.

COUNTRY OF ORIGIN:
USA
FIRST MANUFACTURED:
2008
ENGINE:
8.4 l (510 cid) V10
PERFORMANCE:
Top speed of 202 mph (325 km/h); 0-60 mph (97 km/h) in 3.5 secs
YOU SHOULD KNOW:
Automotive engineering group Prodrive handles the importation of Dodge Vipers to the UK and modifies the cars to meet European regulations. They are rebadged as Dodge SRT-10s because the Viper name is already spoken for in the UK.

469

Ferrari Enzo

The incomparable Enzo is a worthy bearer of Il Commendatore's names.

Strictly speaking, the correct model name is the Enzo Ferrari but, as this leads to confusion with the founding father, most refer to the magnificent machine as the Ferrari Enzo, or simply the Enzo. This Pininfarina-designed supercar was built to celebrate the company's first Formula 1 World Championship of the new millennium, but named as a tribute to the autocratic one, who had died back in 1988. The Enzo did his memory proud, featuring high on motoring-magazine lists like Top Sports Cars of the Decade or Best-Ever Ferraris.

Ironically, the Enzo featured the mid-engined layout that Il Commendatore had banned from road cars for many years before reluctantly relenting. However, he would have been delighted that it was one of the most powerful naturally aspirated cars in the world, with a new generation V12 engine producing 650 bhp. It also looked the part, with a thrustful front end complete with gaping intakes to cool the radiators, an aircraft-style cockpit and greedy air scoops in flowing flanks.

The Enzo deployed F1 technology to good effect. Its chassis consisted of carbon fibre and aluminium honeycomb panels complemented by lightweight bodywork in carbon fibre. The sequential-shift, semi-automatic transmission controlled by paddles had an LED display that told the driver when to change gear for optimum performance. The brakes were ceramic composite discs and the car had traction control (subsequently banned in F1) and active aerodynamics in the form of a rear wing that was computer-activated at high speed to maintain downforce (never allowed in F1).

The performance of this ultimate dream car is (almost) as good as it gets and anyone lucky enough to take one for a toe-curling spin will enjoy a memorable experience, not least because they're in the only 0.0000000000001 percent of the world's population ever to have driven an Enzo.

COUNTRY OF ORIGIN:
Italy
FIRST MANUFACTURED:
2003 (until 2004)
ENGINE:
5,998 cc 2xDOHC V12
PERFORMANCE:
Top speed of 227 mph (365 km/h); 0-60 mph (97 km/h) in 3.4 secs
YOU SHOULD KNOW:
Take a million dollars and don't expect change when you pop down to the used-car lot to pick up that Enzo that's been tempting you on the way to work each morning . . . in fact ongoing credit crunch notwithstanding that might not be enough to clinch the deal if it's a particularly fine example. After all, there are only 399 out there.

Ferrari 575M Superamerica

COUNTRY OF ORIGIN:
Italy
FIRST MANUFACTURED:
2005 (until 2006)
ENGINE:
5,748 cc V12
PERFORMANCE:
Top speed of 199 mph (320 km/h);
0-60 mph (97 km/h) in 4 secs
YOU SHOULD KNOW:
Even though the Superamerica was
itself a performance-enhanced
version of the 575M Maranello, it
could be further boosted with the
GTC package that added a retuned
exhaust, carbon-fibre brakes, firmer
springs and a larger roll bar.

Sorry – no prizes for naming the fastest convertible on the planet.

If ever a supercar deserved to be bought for its name alone the choice would surely be the Ferrari 575M Superamerica, a moniker resurrected from an earlier Ferrari glory era. This was an evolution of the Ferrari 575M Maranello that first appeared back in 2002. A total of 599 Superamericas were produced from 2005, the number dictated by Enzo Ferrari's enduring 'make one less than we can sell' mantra. Sell they did, for this stylish convertible benefitted from Ferrari's return to the classic front-engined configuration, was technologically advanced, had too-good-to-be-true-but-I'd-die-for-one looks and just happened to be the fastest convertible on the planet.

The Superamerica wasn't any old convertible, either, for it had Ferrari's innovative electrochromic glass panel roof that allowed the driver to determine the amount of light that entered the luxuriously appointed cockpit, with five tint levels available that changed from dark to light at the twirl of a dial. This unique roof could also be turned through 180° to lay flat over the boot when the moment to go topless arrived, using a patented mechanism that transformed the car from coupe to convertible in under 10 seconds. Meanwhile, the rear window remained in place to act as an effective wind deflector.

Exclusivity was further enhanced because the Maranello's 5.7 litre V12 engine was tuned to deliver an impressive 540 bhp, which was transferred to the quaking tarmac with the help of an F1-style paddle-change or conventional gate-change six-speed gearbox. Handling is laser-sharp, acceleration rapid, roadholding tenacious and top speed . . . well, you may never get there.

When that lottery win comes along, don't buy a Superamerica for the name alone, beguiling though it might be, but because this is one of the finest Ferraris ever to appeal to a devil-may-care millionaire.

Ferrari F430 Spider

Come in to my parlour, said the Spider . . . and the rich sporting driver duly obliged, tempted by one of the most delectable of Ferrari's 21 road-going convertibles. The Spider is derived from the mid-engined F430 coupe, which in turn is a fairly obvious evolution of the F360. No matter, the F430 Spider is very special in its own right.

One impressive feature – which has been described as 'a stunning 20-second mechanical symphony' – sees the automatic top vanish into a storage bay between the seats and engine. Another intriguing dimension is the transparent hatch that allows the engine to be seen in all its potency. The slanting front end has two elliptical air intakes joined by a spoiler, harking back to sharknose Ferrari racing cars from the early 1960s. There are large air intakes on the sides and the rear valance includes a diffuser honed by competition experience.

The Spider's new 4.3 litre V8 was the first departure from that long line of V8s derived from the Dino competition engine of the 1950s. The car has the full range of electronic wizardry, including launch control (not available in the USA), computer-controlled E-Diff limited slip differential and the *manettino* control knob on the steering wheel. This allows the driver to select one of five settings for the electronic stability-control system.

Needless to say the Spider is a breathtaking drive, with the usual caveat that its ideal habitat is uncluttered country roads rather than bustling city streets. The F430 is third only to the Enzo and 599 GTB in performance terms, and whilst the coupe is marginally faster than the Spider, the latter still has more power than most people will ever need or use – but is so tractable that it sticks tenaciously to the road however hard it may be driven.

COUNTRY OF ORIGIN:
Italy
FIRST MANUFACTURED:
2005
ENGINE:
4,308 cc V8
PERFORMANCE:
Top speed of 193 mph (310 km/h);
0-60 mph (97 km/h) in 4 secs
YOU SHOULD KNOW:
The Spider was a beneficiary of Ferrari's Formula 1 expertise, with a sinuous body shape that was refined with the help of the ultra-sophisticated computer simulations used to fine-tune the Scuderia's winning Grand Prix cars.

The Spider's powered top vanishes in a 'stunning 20-second mechanical symphony'.

Ferrari 599 GTB Fiorano

The endless quest for perfection ensured that a Ferrari model rarely lingered longer that it took to sell the modest production run. And so it was with the splendid 575M Maranello and its glamorous derivative, the 575M Superamerica. Four years was all it took (just two for the Superamerica) before high-powered wheels turned and delivered a new Ferrari flagship to the Geneva Motor Show in 2006. Enter the 599 GTB Fiorano.

Needless to say, this dashing two-seater berlinetta coupe was styled by Pininfarina, with a little help from Ferrari's Frank Stephenson, and the new model was lengthily named for its 5.99 litre V12 engine, Gran Turismo Berlinetta form and Ferrari's Fiorano test track where sporting pedigree was first proven. When wheels turn the world moves onward and hopefully upward and the 599 GTB was definitely in the upwardly mobile category, being the most powerful Ferrari production model ever to prance in the supercar jungle.

Many felt the 599 GTB had a slightly menacing air, despite its sleek curves and beautiful exterior, but this was no mindless brute. A new F1-Trac traction control system made its debut whilst MagnaRide suspension ensured comfort with no loss of handling or cornering prowess. There was a choice between FD1 paddle-change and a six-speed manual gearbox, with any serious driver choosing the latter – the sequential thing zips through the cogs with neck-jerking intensity.

That wasn't all the reviewers found to carp about: this big car isn't an ideal ride in traffic. But all are agreed that on the open road (or better still at your friendly neighbourhood circuit's track day) the 599 GTB's fabulous engineering and race-bred performance make such cares fall away and allow the magic to rule. After all, who ever bought a Ferrari to commute to work through rush-hour streets?

The Fiorano was named after the test track where it proved its road-going potential.

COUNTRY OF ORIGIN:
Italy
FIRST MANUFACTURED:
2006
ENGINE:
5,999 cc DOHC V12
PERFORMANCE:
Top speed of 205 mph (330 km/h);
0-60 mph (97 km/h) in 3.7 secs
YOU SHOULD KNOW:
That favourite unveiling location just over the Alps from Northern Italy – the Geneva Motor Show – saw another spectacular new arrival from Maranello in 2009 in the elegant shape of the Ferrari 599XX, a lightweight racing version of the 599 GTB.

Ford
F-150

It's said that some things improve with age, and whilst this might not be true of individual cars it tends to be the case with model lines that have been around for ever, evolving with every generation as wrinkles are ironed out and technological innovation marches on. A case in point is the Ford F-Series, which been rolling since 1948 – much longer than the vast majority of the world's population has been alive.

As the 21st century built up speed, Ford was busy redesigning a refined F-150, that popular half-ton pickup that first appeared as a sixth generation debutant in 1973. The eleventh generation F-Series was launched in 2004 consisting of the F-150, F-250 and F-350. The latter pair were Ford Super Duties that technically fell into a different category, leaving the F-150 as the only light pickup truck, whereas in some previous generations there had been numerous F numbers to choose from.

But time had wrought its magic and one eleventh generation F-150 was enough to satisfy everyone's needs – though of course in the weird and wonderful world of auto-think 'one' never actually equates with 'no choice'. Far from it. There were variations on the F-150 theme with three engine options, two-door and four-door models, four-speed automatic or five-speed manual transmission, two-wheel or four-wheel drive and four wheelbases. The latter went with (in ascending order) the regular cab with short box, SuperCab STX/FDX4/XLT, Crew Cab, SuperCab XL/Lariat.

Whilst many Europeans covet the hot-hatch versions of model ranges, their American counterparts tend to prefer hot pickups. Ford duly obliged with an FX2 Sport package and the iconic Harley Davidson edition, but the real flyers were customized after-market F-150s from the likes of Saleen (badged as the Saleen S331) and a Foose makeover of the FX2 that smacks out 450 bhp.

Tough as tough can be – the rugged F-Series has been up to any backwoods' challenge since way back in the 1940s.

COUNTRY OF ORIGIN:
USA (also built in Mexico, Brazil and Venezuela)
FIRST MANUFACTURED:
2004 (until 2008)
ENGINE:
4.2 l (256 cid) OHV V6; 4.6 l (281 cid) or 5.4 l (330 cid) V8
PERFORMANCE:
Varies according to engine and model – typically top speed of around 95 mph (153 km/h)
YOU SHOULD KNOW:
According to the US Consumer Union's monthly Consumer Reports the F-150 with a V6 engine was the most reliable American pickup truck ever built, scoring a never-before equalled 'excellent' for five straight years. The F-150 also got the maximum five-star safety rating in frontal collision tests – feel very sorry for the tree.

Ford Focus Mk 2 ST

Every carmaker loves a massive best-seller, and Ford has been basking in the warm glow of worldwide Focus sales figures since the model launch back in 1998, and the successful debut of the all-new Mk 2 cars in 2004. One hallmark of a successful series is

This was a hot, hot, hot hatch version of the best-selling Focus.

the ability to offer buyers almost infinite choice within the range, to cater for every taste. When it comes to hatchback cars, there must be at least one variety that falls into the 'hot' category to satisfy boy racers young and old.

The traditional RS (Rallye Sport) badge is used on Ford's high-performance variants, and – though produced in relatively low numbers – the Focus RS Mk 1 was a great success. Whilst a new RS was not immediately available when the Mk 2 models appeared in 2004, a stunning concept car was shown in 2008 at the British International Motor Show. In the meantime, the Focus hot-hatch slot has been filled by the Mk 2 ST, which delivers the required combination of performance and price.

Developed by Ford's UK-based TeamRS racing and performance arm and unveiled in 2005, the Focus Mk 2 ST used the 2.5 litre T5 alloy engine from Ford-owned Volvo's S40 and V50 models, turbocharged to produce 225 bhp. Suspension and brakes have been upgraded to handle the power. A deeper body kit gives the ST a road-hugging look, with a front apron borrowed from the Fiesta ST, some brushed-aluminium trim and aggressive twin exhaust pipes. The brightly colour-coded interior sports leather bucket seats, an extra instrument pod (colour-coded dials!), drilled alloy pedals and a leather steering wheel with alloy spokes.

Has it been a worthy replacement for the Focus Mk 1 RS? You bet – it scorched around the demanding Nürburgring track a full 10 seconds faster than the no-slouch RS!

COUNTRY OF ORIGIN:
UK
FIRST MANUFACTURED:
2005
ENGINE:
2,521 cc Straight Five Turbo
PERFORMANCE:
Top speed of 150 mph (241 km/h);
0-60 mph (97 km/h) in 6.5 secs
YOU SHOULD KNOW:
In the automobile business it's not enough to reinvent the wheel, for as soon as that's been achieved it has to be re-reinvented. And so it came to pass in 2008 that Ford offered a go-faster power upgrade for the S2 in conjunction with Mountune Performance.

Holden HSV E Series Maloo R8

Which is longer – an Australian novel or the name of the Holden HSV E Series Maloo R8? Don't answer that – simply sit back and admire the classiest ute (pickup truck to you) ever built. As the official name is a mouthful, it shall hereinafter be referred to simply as the Maloo R8.

HSV (Holden Special Vehicles) is the performance arm of GM-owned Holden. It was formed in 1987 as a partnership between Holden and Scottish guru Tom Walkinshaw, with a brief to customize standard Holdens to improve performance, styling and interiors. One of the first products was a souped-up utility vehicle. The VG Maloo appeared in 1990 and evolved through the decade shadowing Holden's mainstream VP, VR and VS utes. There was a revamp in 2001 when the VU Maloo was updated in line with the newly launched Holden Ute. There was a facelift the following year when the Y Series Maloo with its businesslike rear spoiler appeared, swiftly followed by the Z Series in 2004, the first to feature a 6 litre engine.

But the daddy of them all growled onto the scene in 2006. The fun-to-drive E Series is offered as the Maloo R8, retaining the 6 litre V8 engine fitted to its predecessor – though tuned for greater power output and fitted with electronic stability control. It has a six-speed manual gearbox, an advanced braking system and independent suspension.

The Maloo R8 looks stunning, with its racy coupe-style front and cab, alloy wheels, narrow rear window and load bed with lift-up metal tonneau. It has been described as 'a serious machine wrapped in full-throttle styling'. Whatever, this Australian masterpiece must be the most attractive pickup truck never to be seen bumping around the Outback with battered bodywork and a few sheep on board.

COUNTRY OF ORIGIN:
Australia
FIRST MANUFACTURED:
2007
ENGINE:
5,967 cc OHV V8
PERFORMANCE:
Top speed of 169 mph (271 km/h); 0-60 mph (97 km/h) in 5.5 secs
YOU SHOULD KNOW:
The Maloo was officially accredited by The Guinness Book of World Records as the globe's fastest standard production pickup truck when a Z-series model scorched past the incumbent Dodge RAM SRT-10 8.3 l V10's paltry 155 mph (249 km/h), outdoing the bumptious big American by a comfortable 14 mph (23 km/h).

As pick-up trucks go, the Maloo R8 is a bit different from your average Outback ute.

Jaguar XK60

COUNTRY OF ORIGIN:
UK
FIRST MANUFACTURED:
2008
ENGINE:
4,196 cc DOHC V8
PERFORMANCE:
Electronically limited top speed
of 155 mph (250 km/h);
0-60 mph (97 km/h) in 5.9 secs
YOU SHOULD KNOW:
Perhaps the XK60, Jaguar's heartfelt
tribute to the XK120, has been
marginally devalued by the fact that
the company managed to think up
reasons for creating no fewer than
four special editions of the XKR
between 2001 and 2005, and the
new XK series is already on its third
limited edition.

The first XK Jaguar – the 120 – was born in 1948 and its 60th birthday naturally couldn't be allowed to pass without a serious celebration – after all, how many other pensioners are capable of going from 0 to 60 in seven seconds? Jaguar's idea of a suitable tribute to the iconic XK-engined convertible that wrote Chapter One of the company's postwar success story was to create the XK60, a limited 'diamond' edition of the new XK model that coincided with the 2008 anniversary of the great roadster.

The current Jaguar XK series made a spectacular appearance at the Frankfurt Motor Show in 2006, going on sale the following year. The slinky coupe and fabulous convertible were soon complemented by the XKR and XKR-S variants. The XK was a worthy successor to the Jaguar tradition of performance with style, and the XK60 brought its own attributes to the party – a naturally aspirated AJ-V8 engine with continuous variable valve timing, sequential shift six-speed automatic transmission and a pile of extras (at no extra cost) that further enhanced the basic XK's already impressive specification.

XK60 goodies included big alloy wheels, a brushed-metal gear knob, revised front spoiler and rear valance panel, chrome side vents, bright-metal upper- and lower-grille mesh, custom tailpipes and special appliqués. The XK60's slippery shape is more than pleasing to the contemporary eye, but the true joy of this beautiful machine is tremendous performance that pays a fitting tribute to the illustrious predecessor it commemorates.

This is a driver's car *par excellence*, with all-aluminium construction making it the strongest and lightest car in its class. The outstanding V8 engine bristles with the latest technology, and computer-controlled active suspension management ensures that the XK60 not only offers refined luxury within, but also speed, agility and perfect control. It's magnificent!

Luxury, style, power – what more could you ask for?

Jeep Wrangler JK Rubicon

If you've got a good 'un, make the most of it. That's certainly been Chrysler's philosophy when it comes to the super-successful Jeep Wrangler, which first appeared in 1987 and had been delighting supporters of serious SUVs ever since. Their interest in off-roading was duly reflected in the 2003 launch of the TJ Wrangler Rubicon, named not for the Italian river that represents the point of no return, but the rugged Rubicon Trail in the Sierra Nevada Mountains beloved by serious four-wheel drivers.

The TJ Rubicon went down (and up) so well that when an all-new Jeep Wrangler JK series was launched in 2007 the Rubicon variant was a nailed-on survivor. The JK is longer and wider than its predecessor, though short- and long-wheelbase versions are offered. The two-door short-wheelbase Wrangler comes in X, Sahara and Rubicon trim, as does the long-wheelbase four-door Unlimited model.

A powerful 3.8 litre V6 provides the JK's grunt, though a 2.8 litre turbodiesel is also offered outside the USA. Six-speed manual transmission is standard, with an optional four-speed automatic. Stability control is a new feature, as is anti-lock braking and traction control with an electronic limited-slip differential. Although it is still possible to remove the doors for rough-country work, the new Wrangler has remote central locking and electric windows. The Sundowner convertible top is standard issue, with a three-piece hardtop as an option.

The JK Rubicon's dedicated package is the official off-road performance choice. It comes with the Rock-Trac 4:1 transfer case, front and rear 32-spline Dana 44 axles with special gearing, front and rear electronic diff-lock, rock rails and electronic sway-bar disconnect. It even has special seats and a seven-speaker sound system to entertain the wildlife when the JK Rubicon arrives in remote parts that other off-roaders can't reach.

The Rubicon has established quite a reputation in the Wild West.

COUNTRY OF ORIGIN:
USA
FIRST MANUFACTURED:
2007
ENGINE:
3.8 l (230.5 cid) OHV V6
PERFORMANCE:
Top speed of 109 mph (175 km/h);
0-60 mph (97 km/h) in 10.3 secs
YOU SHOULD KNOW:
Yup – Chrysler certainly knows a good thing when it sees one. The Wrangler JK was introduced at the 2006 North American International Auto show by being driven up steps and straight through a plate-glass window . . . replicating the Jeep Grand Cherokee's dramatic entrance to the event back in 1992.

Koenigsegg CCX

*The CCX was deliberately created
to be the best-ever supercar –
and certainly looks the part.*

Swedish company Koenigsegg Automotive was established in 1994 to fulfill the long-time dream of founder Christian von Koenigsegg – to create a world-class supercar. It took time to get up to speed, but the mid-engined CC8S appeared at the Paris Motor Show in 2000. This handsome roadster certainly passed the supercar test, briefly becoming the fastest road car in production. Next up was the CCR in 2004, a stubby coupe with an unusual cockpit design produced from 2004 to 2006. This had the first engine developed by Koenigsegg – a 4.7 litre aluminium V8.

It wasn't long before Koenigsegg's *pièce de résistance* was presented to the waiting world. The CCX of 2006 has a distinctive flowing design representing optimum aerodynamic efficiency, with a wedge-shaped front between wide mudguards that contain slanting headlight units. An aircraft-style cockpit has scissor doors that fold forwards and outwards. There are big air scoops in the flanks and a flat back end with a transparent viewport that reveals the impressive engine. It's a targa sports car with a top that lifts off and stores up front for open-top exhilaration. Uniquely, it's street legal in every country in the world.

But what's truly special about this sports car is its performance, which can only be described as supercalifragilistic. Koenigsegg's V8 puts out a staggering 806 bhp giving a top speed approaching 250 mph (402 km/h) with acceleration and braking to match. But this is no crude speedster, as it has incomparable ride quality and holds the road brilliantly. Anyone lucky enough to drive a CCX will find it hard to switch off the throaty engine and may have to be surgically removed – it really is that good.

Koenigsegg Automotive also builds the CCGT Le Mans racing model and the special CCXR edition, which has genuine claims to being the best-ever supercar.

COUNTRY OF ORIGIN:
Sweden
FIRST MANUFACTURED:
2006
ENGINE:
4,719 cc DOHC V8
PERFORMANCE:
Top speed of 245 mph (394 km/h);
0-60 mph (97 km/h) in 3 secs
YOU SHOULD KNOW:
Is it true? Legend has it that a Koenigsegg holds the record for the fastest speeding ticket in the USA, having been clocked at 242 mph (389 km/h) during the Gumball Rally from San Francisco to Miami. That must have been some radar gun.

Lamborghini Murciélago

Menacing and meticulous, raucous and refined, brutish and brilliant – the Lambo Murciélago has dominated the supercar decade in the minds of dedicated enthusiasts, for all that dozens of contenders have been clamouring for top honours. This wide, low teardrop coupe has extraordinary styling, with the cabin completely integrated into a flowing shape that forms a continuous arc from front to back – an aerodynamic statement of performance intent that's amply justified. Two doors scissor forwards and upwards to provide easy access to bucket seats.

The Murciélago was introduced in 2001 as the ultimate driving machine, not long after Audi's takeover rescued the struggling Italian marque. It featured a 6.2 litre power plant coupled with a six-speed manual gearbox or optional paddle-shift version. The Murciélago's awesome performance was supported by clever engineering, like intakes that self-adjusted for optimum airflow and a spoiler that deployed automatically according to speed.

A special 2003 edition celebrated Lamborghini's 40th anniversary. In 2006 the upgraded Murciélago LP640 coupe further advanced the performance cause, with a 6.5 litre engine and body tweaks to improve aerodynamic efficiency, plus an enhanced exhaust and suspension. The Thrust launch-control system was also introduced. The LP640 Roadster followed that same year, with shrewdly staggered launches that doubled the publicity impact.

Even as Lamborghini prepared a replacement for the Murciélago, the company devised a classic 'final edition' and 'final final edition' exit strategy. A limited-edition LP640 Versace, finished in black and white, appeared in 2008. The last, spectacular flourish came in 2009 with the Murciélago LP650-4 SuperVeloce, soon followed by the Murciélago LP650-4 Roadster, a sensational style statement in graphite with orange highlights that's sure to keep Lambo's name on the lips of chattering petrolheads as they await the next instalment of the thrilling Lamborghini adventure.

COUNTRY OF ORIGIN:
Italy
FIRST MANUFACTURED:
2001
ENGINE:
6,192 cc or 6,494 cc 2xDOHC V12
PERFORMANCE:
With 6.5 l engine – top speed of 211 mph (340 km/h); 0-60 mph (97 km/h) in 3.4 secs
YOU SHOULD KNOW:
The expression 'go like a bat out of hell' may be appropriate for the Murciélago ('bat' in Spanish) but in fact the car continues a tradition of using names associated with bullfighting – Murciélago being a famous 19th-century bull with legendary courage and spirit that was spared by the matador . . . a rare honour.

The Murciélago resisted every effort to dethrone it as the uncrowned king of the supercars.

Lamborghini Gallardo

COUNTRY OF ORIGIN:
Italy
FIRST MANUFACTURED:
2003
ENGINE:
4,961 cc or 5,204 cc 2xDOHC V10
PERFORMANCE:
LP560-4 – top speed of
202 mph (325 km/h);
0-60 mph (97 km/h) in 3.6 secs
YOU SHOULD KNOW:
Who'd be an Italian traffic cop? In
2008 Lamborghini presented a
Gallardo LP560-4 Polizia that was
intended to get Italy's State Police up
to speed. This replaced an earlier
first generation Gallardo police car
that had dawdled along Lazio's
highways, crime fighting at a mere
192 mph (309 km/h).

Lambo's 'Junior Murciélago' – the Gallardo coupe – was as sporty as mid-engined, mid-sized supercars come. Named after a renowned breed of fighting bull, the Gallardo (Spanish for 'gallant') first appeared as a rival to the Ferrari 360 in 2003 and went on to become Lamborghini's all-time bestseller.

This reflects the company's success in retaining driver and passenger comfort without compromising raw performance. The latter was achieved with the help of a 5 litre V10 putting out 500 bhp, coupled with a six-speed manual gearbox (or optional mechanized sequential shift) and Lambo's Viscous (no, not vicious) Traction all-wheel drive system. The Gallardo has double-wishbone suspension and a sophisticated aerodynamics package, including an electronically controlled rear spoiler. Unlike the Murciélago, the Gallardo didn't have scissor doors.

Lamborghini doesn't stand still for long and the Gallardo was soon a beneficiary of technological advance. A convertible Spyder came along in 2005, followed by two special editions – the SE (2005) and all-black Nera (2006-2008). Next out was the mighty Gallardo Superleggera, a star of the Geneva Motor Show in 2007. As the result of a disciplined slimming regime, the Superleggera improved on the Gallardo's already-impressive performance figures. But even this spectacular speedster failed to survive an upgrade in 2008, when all previous models were superseded.

The new Gallardo LP560-4 had a bigger fuel-injected engine (at 5.2 litres) than its predecessors and set new standards for super sports cars. The all-wheel drive system was upgraded, along with the suspension, and the Gallardo's slippery shape was further refined to improve aerodynamic efficiency. More power, traction and high-speed stability all contribute to increase driving pleasure – whether on a long-distance run or enjoying a track day. An LP560-4 Spyder appeared in 2009, as did the Super Trofeo destined for a one-make racing series.

As cop cars go, this one leaves little to be desired.

Lamborghini Reventón

Look hard and try to spot the Reventón – it's probably the one with its wheels on the ground.

It's much rarer than one in a million – just 20 Lamborghini Reventóns were scheduled following the sensational revelation of Lambo's most expensive road car to date at Frankfurt in 2007. Owners of this million-euro machine drive a car named after the fast fighting bull that killed ill-fated young torero Félix Guzmán in the 1940s.

The Reventón is also rather swift. Mechanically, this extreme supercar is derived from the Murciélago LP640, although the 6.5 litre engine has been further tuned to give the Reventón more horses than its fellow bull. In practice this means little – the limited edition has a similar top speed and identical 0-60 mph (97 km/h) acceleration. The engineering was tried and tested in Lambo's range-topper, but that wasn't the Reventón's rationale.

Its glory is an entirely new exterior that is a brilliant exercise in automotive geometry. The eye-catching bodywork has been artfully fabricated in a carbon-fibre composite material under the watchful eye of Lamborghini's Style Centre, which fine-tuned every detail – the happiest marriage of form and function, with an extraordinary combination of flowing curves and hard-edged straight lines.

The front comes to a dramatic arrow-point above an asymmetrical spoiler, between two rectangular air intakes that cool the carbon disc brakes. Headlight arrays are long triangles on each side of a sharply etched pentagonal bonnet. Further back, the crouching cabin justifies the manufacturer's claim that it is reminiscent of a fighter aircraft's cockpit. Twin doors open upwards in classic Lamborghini style to reveal the finest of interior finishes and space-age liquid-crystal instrumentation. The extended rear end maintains the angular design theme, sloping gently to further extraordinary geometric juxtapositions by way of a transparent engine hatch and zigzag patterning.

Is this the most striking supercar ever? You can't buy it, so believe it!

COUNTRY OF ORIGIN:
Italy
FIRST MANUFACTURED:
2008
ENGINE:
6,496 cc 2xDOHC V12
PERFORMANCE:
Top speed of 211 mph (340 km/h);
0-60 mph (97 km/h) in 3.4 secs
YOU SHOULD KNOW:
The very special new toy that Reventón owners were the first to enjoy was a G-Force Meter that showed a three-dimensional display of dynamic drive forces as the car went through its paces. This innovative in-car technology was borrowed from Grand Prix racing.

Advanced electronics and technological magic are hallmarks of the 600h L.

Lexus LS 600h L

The most expensive Japanese luxury car ever produced is a Lexus – but not just any old Lexus. For this is the long-wheelbase LS 600h L, the world's first fully hybrid V8-powered car. Needless to say, this mould-breaking machine was designed with the newly eco-conscious American market in mind, and made its debut at the New York International Auto Show in 2006.

The flagship Lexus LS is a huge four-door sedan that competes with Germans like the Audi A8 and BMW 7 Series. The usual 4.6 litre V8 is replaced by a 5 litre engine in the hybrid, which doesn't quite succeed in propelling the heavy LS 600h L as rapidly as the standard model when it comes to acceleration, though the electronically limited top speed is not affected.

Electronic wizardry and advanced safety features characterize every Lexus, but this one has the highest level of decadent comfort and most advanced technological features ever offered. Overall styling is typically bland, but build quality is robust and the interior finish is plush, though the instrumentation and controls do lack a certain *je ne sais quoi* for a car in this rarefied price bracket.

The Lexus Hybrid Drive system delivers 438 bhp, mating the powerful V8 with a high-output electric motor with a nickel-hydride battery pack. It has two-speed continuously variable transmission, a limited-slip differential and adaptive air suspension. At town-driving speeds the four-wheel drive LS 600h L ghosts silently along on its electric motor, but if the tempo increases or a sudden burst of speed is needed the engine cuts in instantly.

Unfortunately, the need to accommodate the large battery pack means that the LS 600h L's boot space is anything but generous, though no doubt that's a small price to pay for helping to save the planet.

COUNTRY OF ORIGIN:
Japan
FIRST MANUFACTURED:
2007
ENGINE:
5,000 cc V8 + Electric HDS
PERFORMANCE:
Top speed of 155 mph (249 km/h);
0-60 mph (97 km/h) in 6.1 secs
YOU SHOULD KNOW:
The LS 600h L offers a relaxation pack that allows the rear seat on the passenger side to recline fully . . . and deliver a soothing massage.

Lotus Exige S

The Exige – a chunky in-your-face coupe version of the successful Elise roadster – made its first appearance in 2000. This mid-engined sports car was powered by a tuned 1.8 litre Rover engine, replaced by a Toyota power plant when the Exige Series 2 came along in 2004. Development continued apace after the Exige was introduced to North America at the Los Angeles Auto Show in 2006.

Lotus soon announced that an Exige S (for 'Supercharged') model would be offered, with a stonking 240 bhp, allowing this lightweight to offer a potent mix of pace and sure-footed handling unmatched by anything in the price range. Rapid acceleration, superb roadholding and the ability to top 150 mph (241 km/h) make this the ideal choice for the sporting driver who likes to combine track days with scorching open-road performance – though it should be noted that this is not a docile beast that will happily plod through city traffic on a daily commute but, rather, a high-spirited thoroughbred that's born to run.

The Exige falls smack-bang in the 'sporty driver's car' category. The S's slick six-speed gearbox is teamed with an engine that just gets better as the revs rocket, with variable valve timing kicking in around 6,000 rpm to boost power. Sharp steering and adhesive cornering – even in wet conditions – are outstanding. This isn't an uncomfortable car, though small and low to the ground, but it requires a certain eel-like ability to get in through fairly narrow doors. Once there, ProBax seats are supportive and there's a pretty good level of trim – including aluminium knobs and passenger footrest, Blaupunkt CD player, remote central locking and an immobilizer cum alarm.

The Exige S has come in various editions – British GT, Touring, Performance and Performance Sports. They all go like the wind!

COUNTRY OF ORIGIN:
UK
FIRST MANUFACTURED:
2006
ENGINE:
1,796 cc DOHC Straight Four
PERFORMANCE:
S Performance models – top speed of 155 mph (249 km/h); 0-60 mph (97 km/h) in 4.1 secs
YOU SHOULD KNOW:
No manufacturer likes buyers marching off with the base model, so the Exige can be upgraded with an alluring Touring Pack (electric windows, full leather, carpeting) or Super Touring Pack (plus airbags, leather gearshift knob, trinket tray, cup holder). The Sport and Super Sport Packs add performance enhancements like traction control and improved suspension.

The Exige S – every version will go like a bat out of hell!

Maserati Gran Turismo

COUNTRY OF ORIGIN:
Italy
FIRST MANUFACTURED:
2007
ENGINE:
4,244 cc or 4,691 cc 2xDOHC V8
PERFORMANCE:
With 4.7 l engine – top speed of
183 mph (295 km/h);
0-60 mph (97 km/h) in 4.7 secs
YOU SHOULD KNOW:
In many a 2+2 the second '2'
doesn't equate with 'two rear-seat
passengers travelling in comfort over
long distances'. In the Gran Turismo
it does, and their convenience is
assisted by electric front seats that
automatically slide forward to aid
rear access or egress when the
backs are tilted.

This 2+2 fixed-head coupe launched in 2007 shows Pininfarina's design expertise at its most refined and elegant. The masterful Maserati Gran Turismo has a prominent front grille above a downforce spoiler that hints at the car's outstanding performance, combined with classical flowing lines that are both aerodynamically efficient and a delight to those discriminating eyes that note a certain similarity to the Gran Turismo's Ferrari 599 GTB Fiorano stablemate. The name also resonates, representing a reminder of Maserati's decisive decision to put a racing-car engine in a road car more than 60 years ago.

Today's opulent Gran Turismo simply oozes class, with that brilliant styling and an opulent interior, plus an exhilarating driving experience and performance to match anything in its class. The powerful V8 with its throaty roar can frighten even the most experienced driver, though happily this obliging car – helped by the latest electronic systems – sticks tenaciously to the road whatever the speed and corners as though it were on rails. For those daring souls who want to squeeze the last drop of performance out of their Gran Turismo, pressing the 'sport' button speeds up gear changes.

A new Gran Turismo S version appeared to dazzle visitors to the 2008 Geneva Motor Show. It boasted a larger 4.7 litre engine, new transaxle fast-shift gearbox and optional Skyhook adaptive suspension. The Gran Turismo S MC Sports Line was introduced the same year, and a Gran Turismo Automatic followed in 2009.

Rumours of a convertible in waiting are rife, but one thing remains the same – a price tag to deter all but the super-rich, though happily for lovers of automobile excellence (and owner Fiat) plenty of those who don't mind their expensive car halving in value over three years have joined the queue for a Gran Turismo.

There's only one drawback with the Gran Turismo – ownership is restricted to the super-rich.

Maybach 57/62

The auction of the prestigious Rolls-Royce/Bentley brands by Vickers in 1998 developed into a three-way scrap between German giants. Volkswagen got Bentley and the Crewe factory, BMW the right to produce Rolls-Royce cars, whilst Daimler got . . . nothing. The words 'sour' and 'grapes' spring to mind, but it may be merely coincidence that luxury saloon cars from Daimler's revived Maybach luxury marque appeared in 2002. The Maybach 57 and Maybach 62 were direct descendants of the Mercedes-Benz Maybach concept car that was shown at the Tokyo Motor Show in 1997.

The supremely refined Maybach was designed to compete with the luxury German-owned Rolls-Royce and Bentley marques.

The base model (if such a term can be applied to a palace on wheels) was the 57, with its 5.5 litre V12 engine. The list of features covers several pages and includes goodies like heated cupholders and massaging seats. Other essentials were voice recognition satnav, remote engine start, a premium sound system controlled from the heated wood, and leather-wrapped steering wheel, powered seats with lumbar adjustment, heated or cooled front seats, leather upholstery throughout, power sunroof, rear-facing camera . . . you get the picture. The Maybach 57 S (for 'Special") features a 6 litre engine and lower ride height.

The Maybach 62 and 62S make the 57 look, well, rather sparsely equipped. The 62's goodies require a full chapter – and that's before getting to optional extras like a retractable glass screen between driver and passengers, a two-way communications system that lets occupants talk to people outside the car without opening a window and the GUARD high-protection package that ensures no head of state will be seen dead in a Maybach.

Evolution versions are the 62 Landaulet (reviving a popular prewar luxury car form), and 57/62 Zeppelin models offering (yes, truly) a more luxurious interior. There is also a highly tuned aftermarket Brabus Maybach.

COUNTRY OF ORIGIN:
Germany
FIRST MANUFACTURED:
2003
ENGINE:
5,513 cc or 5,980 cc V12 Twin Turbo
PERFORMANCE:
With 6.0 l engine – top speed of
155 mph (249 km/h);
0-60 mph (97 km/h) in 5 secs
YOU SHOULD KNOW:
In a burst of PR extravagance, a Maybach 62 enclosed in a glass case was shipped from Southampton to New York on the liner Queen Elizabeth 2 (with pampered media and company reps for company). Once there, it was lifted ashore by helicopter and driven to the official US launch at a Wall Street hotel.

Mazda RX-8

Despite its not inconsiderable advantages, the Wankel engine never really caught on – except in the hearts and minds of Mazda's management. Mazda took the rotary concept and developed it brilliantly, ironing out snags and creating an innovative engine. The company started selling rotary-engined cars in the early 1970s and the company's RX series culminated in the RX-7, a high-performance sports coupe that went through several generations between 1978 and the mid-1990s, after which modest sales caused Mazda to pull the car from export markets.

But salvation was nigh in the form of resurgent interest in performance cars, and Mazda developed the RX-01 concept car from 1995 into the resurgent RX-8, launched in 2003. To address earlier concerns, Mazda's new twin-turbocharged 13-B MSP (Multi Side Port) Renesis engine overcame problems like poor fuel consumption and high emissions and re-opened the door to the lucrative US market. At just 1.3 litres, this ultra-smooth power plant punches way above its modest size, delivering 192 or 231 bhp according to tune, giving a top speed approaching 150 mph (241 km/h).

The RX-8 has a modest but attractive aerodynamic body shape with distinctive flared front wings. There's plenty of room for four in the cabin, accessed for passenger convenience by rear-hinged doors of the kind referred to during the Great Depression as 'suicide doors'. The RX-8 drives brilliantly, helped by perfect 50-50 weight distribution, responsive steering, sure-footed cornering and stickability in the wet.

After a succession of special editions were produced, the 2008 Detroit Motor Show saw the introduction of an evolutionary RX-8 that had been given a significant facelift for model year 2009 with a stronger chassis, improved suspension and front-end styling changes. At the same time an R3 performance package was announced, offering more aggressive styling, tuned sporting suspension and a smoother ride.

COUNTRY OF ORIGIN:
Japan
FIRST MANUFACTURED:
2003
ENGINE:
1,308 cc Twin-chamber Turbo Rotary
PERFORMANCE:
Top speed of 146 mph (235 km/h);
0-60 mph (97 km/h) in 6.4 secs
YOU SHOULD KNOW:
Although the latest Mazda rotary engine delivers greatly improved fuel economy, that doesn't mean much as it started from such a low reference point. Anyone who drives the Mazda hard (and who could resist?) will end up visiting the pumps rather frequently.

Mercedes-Benz SLR McLaren

The combination of German engine technology and advanced British racing-car design capability has seen the McLaren Mercedes team achieve success at the world's Grand Prix circuits. They have also teamed up to produce one of the world's most impressive sports cars, the Mercedes SLR McLaren, assembled at McLaren's ultra-modern Woking HQ. This was available as a two-door coupe (2003–2007) or roadster (2007–2009) and it was clearly competitive with contemporary GT cars from the likes of Ferrari and Aston Martin.

The design can only be described as stunning, inspired by the very special 300 SLR of 1955. The SLR McLaren has a classic coupe shape with a long bonnet, low cabin and short rear end. The front has an extraordinary jutting arrow shape with a large inset Mercedes motif, between and above gaping shark's-mouth air intakes. Scissor-opening doors fold upwards and forwards. Unlike many modern high-performance cars, this is a front mid-engined machine. The hand-built, supercharged 5.4 litre V8 from Mercedes performance unit AMG, together with McLaren's state-of-the-art motorsport technology, puts the SLR McLaren right up there with the great supercars of the early 21st century.

The two partners combined incomparable experience in the production of powerful cars to create an ultra-modern sports car that boasted one of the lightest bodies and best safety packages ever to take to the road. The cutting-edge Mercedes SLR McLaren also contained some of the most advanced features ever seen in a road car, such as fibre-reinforced carbon-ceramic brakes teamed with an automatic spoiler for increased rear downforce.

A special 722 edition, designed to compete on the racetrack, was produced in 2006 to commemorate the victory of the great Stirling Moss and Denis Jenkinson in the 1955 Mille Miglia race, driving car number 722, a Mercedes-Benz 300 SLR.

COUNTRY OF ORIGIN:
UK
FIRST MANUFACTURED:
2003 (until 2009)
ENGINE:
5,439 cc V8
PERFORMANCE:
Top speed of 208 mph (334 km/h);
0-60 mph (97 km/h) in 3.6 secs
YOU SHOULD KNOW:
Mercedes has stated that the SLR McLaren is a limited edition, with just 3,500 cars built – good news indeed for well-heeled buyers who will own an exclusive machine that will surely become one of the most sought-after classics in years to come.

Mark this special one down as a certain future classic.

Mini E

COUNTRY OF ORIGIN:
UK
FIRST MANUFACTURED:
2008
ENGINE:
150 Kw Asynchronous Electric Motor
PERFORMANCE:
Limited top speed of
95 mph (153 km/h);
0-60 mph (97 km/h) in 8 secs
YOU SHOULD KNOW:
With a special 50-amp socket the
Mini E is fully recharged and ready to
go again in just over two hours,
though using a conventional
American 110v supply extends that
time to 28 hours. The maximum
range per charge is around 160 mi
(257 km) though a safer limit is
120 mi (193 km) to allow for
wasteful driving.

California's battle with pollution-induced smog and increasing paranoia about the destructive consequences of global warming have made the West Coast state a hotbed of alternative automotive technology, with Hollywood stars (well able to afford a public conscience) invariably seen parading along the Strip aboard the latest eco-wheels.

BMW latched on to this trend by developing an all-electric Mini, building 500 examples and launching at the 2008 Los Angeles Motor Show. It was not for sale but, after journalists had tried it to their hearts' content, the handsome two-door prototype was leased to chosen individuals (250 in LA, 200 in New York and 50 in Germany) who would pay handsomely (and willingly) for the privilege of being the first to drive the innovative Mini E – and incidentally conduct a prolonged road test of the unproven car.

Space normally occupied by a standard Mini's rear seats contains over 5,000 AC propulsion lithium-ion cells, which extend into the boot and restrict storage space. The engine compartment bristles with electro-drive technology – the motor itself, an inverter that turns DC into AC (and vice versa) plus power-control electronics. Open the bonnet at your peril – not because of the risk of getting fried alive, but because the auto cut-out will save you . . . and require a BMW engineer to re-set it.

Performance is astonishing, with both acceleration and top speed limited well below their potential top-end figures. There is no transmission, simply an automatic-style lever that engages Drive. Then it's just a matter of hitting the accelerator and being startled by the alacrity with which the Mini E leaps away . . . and stands on its nose when the startled first-time driver lifts off as the motor regenerates power. Will this car of the future go into production? Switched-on opinion says 'yes'!

Plug in then potter off – though actually this concept Mini E has potentially electric performance figures, currently restricted.

Mitsubishi Colt CZC

The name Colt threads through Mitsubishi's model history, tweaking the noses of US carmakers who let the archetypal American weapon of choice slip away into Japanese hands. Slip it did, back in the 1960s when the tiny Colt 600 set about building Mitsubishi's fortunes. Various models in America and Australia used the Colt name in the 1980s and 1990s before Colt returned to its roots in 2003 with the launch of a slick supermini. The new Mitsubishi Colt came with a choice of engines ranging from 1.1 to 1.5 litres and in three- or five-door hatchback form.

In 2006 an eagerly awaited convertible version went on sale, after first showing its pretty face at the previous year's Geneva Motor Show. In truth, this clever little car actually belongs to the emerging hybrid hardtop-convertible class. Following the lead of many open-topped supercars, Mitsubishi's 2+2 Colt CZC brings a retractable hardtop to the masses. Perhaps that advance is easy to understand – Mitsubishi developed the CZC with Italian design firm (and convertible specialist) Pininfarina.

The base 1.5 litre engine is offered with a zestful turbocharged version that gives this sexy little convertible added zip. It's great fun to drive, being equally at home in city traffic or on winding country lanes, with crisp handling and great roadholding despite a little of the body shake that's inevitable in small convertibles when the going gets rough. With the top down, the CZC's sloping bonnet and raked windscreen cunningly deflect onrushing air to the point where civilized conversation is possible and hair remains surprisingly unmussed. The 2+2 description is somewhat misleading – even little people struggle and a better description would be 2+somewhere-to-dump-the-shopping. It hardly matters – the Mitsubishi CZC is about having some frivolous driving fun, not ferrying the family.

The dinky Colt's rear seat is really designed for the shopping.

COUNTRY OF ORIGIN:
Japan (built in the Netherlands, finished in Italy)
FIRST MANUFACTURED:
2006
ENGINE:
1,468 cc Straight Four
PERFORMANCE:
Turbo version – top speed of 126 mph (203 km/h); 0-60 mph (97 km/h) in 8.1 secs
YOU SHOULD KNOW:
The Colt was closely related to the short-lived Smart Forfour (2004 to 2006) – which was the only conventional car Smart ever produced, with the Franco-German company cutting costs to the bone by working with Mitsubishi to share a platform and numerous components with the new Colt.

Morgan Aero 8

This is the car that combined the stylish elegance of a bygone automotive era with the latest technology to create a handsome roadster that respects and enhances that great British habit of producing special hand-built sports cars. As Morgan's first all-new design since the 1940s, the Aero 8 advanced the old-fashioned marque into the 21st century upon its debut in 2001.

Morgan didn't entirely abandon tradition, however, for there was still some seasoned wood used to frame the body, but the thoroughly modern chassis is made of bonded aluminum. Out too went the trusty old Rover engine and in came a muscular BMW 4.4 litre V8. This powered quite a few performance cars, but none went better than the lightweight Aero 8. The Morgan Roadster offers a four-seater version, but not the Aero. This is strictly for two, with a low seating position within a narrow cabin – though sports seats provide ample support and a reasonably comfortable ride.

This is a robust machine but, despite its modern credentials, Morgan has been careful not to load the car with gizmology. Along with wooden frames, the company believes that its cars should provide an old-fashioned hands-on driving experience where the pilot makes the decisions and the car mostly does what it's told. And so it does, being quick off the mark with crisp handling and impressive roadholding. It also happens to be rather speedy.

There was a revamp in 2005 that did away with headlights that had been characterized as 'cross-eyed', and a 4.8 litre BMW V8 was fitted. This was partly to facilitate US sales because the new engine – though larger – was less powerful than its predecessor. Performance remained unchanged, but it did allow Morgan to produce a special Aero America that satisfied tough American regulations.

COUNTRY OF ORIGIN:
UK
FIRST MANUFACTURED:
2001
ENGINE:
4,398 cc or 4,799 cc V8
PERFORMANCE:
Top speed of 160 mph (257 km/h);
0-60 mph (97 km/h) in 4.4 secs
YOU SHOULD KNOW:
The one collectors of the future will all want is the Morgan AeroMax, a superb coupe variation of the Aero 8 with production limited to 100 cars. This is a modern classic that unashamedly evokes the golden prewar era of the Bugatti Atlantic – at a price.

Nissan Murano

Despite selling well in North America from 2003, the Nissan Murano's first generation wasn't sufficiently refined for European taste. However, by the time it came across the Atlantic in 2005 an extensive upgrade had taken place, with modifications in the areas of safety, comfort and handling. These were designed to fulfil Nissan's aspiration for the Murano – which was going head-to-head with the likes of Mercedes, BMW and Volvo in the booming luxury crossover market sector (combined 4x4 plus plush car) competing on quality and especially cost. The Murano did indeed represent great value for money with a host of standard features, many of which others only supplied as extras.

Nissan only offered a 3.5 litre petrol engine with the Murano, despite the fact that most of the competition boasted a turbodiesel option. No matter, the Murano with its high spec, clean styling and flowing lines was undoubtedly an attractive SUV – becoming more so with the introduction of a second generation in 2008. This reflected lessons learned from the first, offering a more powerful engine, improved interior trim and an altogether better driving experience.

The new Murano has a distinct family resemblance to the compact Nissan Rogue, though the larger model has a more aggressive front end. There are three trim levels – a base Murano S, mid-range SL and top-line LE. This big SUV makes little pretence at serious off-road capability, which means on-road performance has to be exemplary. By and large it is. The automatic gearbox pulls smoothly and this solid machine is pretty nimble around country roads and city streets alike. Roadholding is good and there is very little roll when cornering. The well-planned cabin is beautifully appointed and accommodates five adults comfortably. Nissan has promised a diesel version and has also announced a convertible model for some time in 2011.

COUNTRY OF ORIGIN:
Japan
FIRST MANUFACTURED:
2003
ENGINE:
3,498 cc DOHC V6
PERFORMANCE:
Second generation – top speed of 130 mph (209 km/h); 0-60 mph (97 km/h) in 7.8 secs
YOU SHOULD KNOW:
The Murano is one of those modern cars that can heal itself (within reason) – a special paint coating repairs light surface scratches, which vanish within hours (or days, depending on ambient temperature) The hotter it is, the faster blemishes vanish). Clever stuff.

This luxury SUV is mounting a serious challenge to up-market European competitors.

Nissan GT-R

COUNTRY OF ORIGIN:
Japan
FIRST MANUFACTURED:
2007
ENGINE:
3,799 cc V6 Twin Turbo
PERFORMANCE:
Top speed of 195 mph (314 km/h);
0-60 mph (97 km/h) in 3.2 secs (with
launch control) or 3.9 secs (without)
YOU SHOULD KNOW:
The motorsport arm of Nissan,
Nismo, produced a much-modified
version of the GT-R to race in the
Japanese Super GT Series. The GT500
racecar has a bigger engine with a
six-speed sequential gearbox and a
rear-wheel-drive layout inherited
from its predecessor, the 350Z.

This one squeaked into 2007, being released in Japan just in time to be giftwrapped for Christmas. It arrived in the USA in mid-summer the following year, with the rest of the world forced to wait on tenterhooks until 2009 for a test drive. The Nissan GT-R has real presence, with a chunky front end, bulging bonnet and square lines inspired by the ever-popular Gundam giant robots, giving the car a uniquely Japanese character.

The GT-R's slow rollout was caused by the limited number that can be produced, as both engine and dual-clutch gearbox are painstakingly built by hand. The 3.8 litre engine has twin turbochargers that squeeze out a not unimpressive 480 bhp, with acceleration and top speed to match. This impressive Japanese supercar has a clever all-wheel drive system, sophisticated semi-automatic transmission and Nissan's VDC (Vehicle Dynamics Control) system that includes launch control, also assisting handling and ensuring rock-steady stability at speed.

Perhaps a system like this – which makes key decisions – can take away the sheer pleasure of driving this car hard and fast, but it does make the GT-R a docile beast around town – and a car that a skilled driver can easily control at racing-car speeds on a hot track outing. In keeping with its dual role, the interior of the car is supremely comfortable, although the rear seats are rather more suited to shopping or the kids than to adults.

To the annoyance of many a would-be buyer, the first GT-Rs were only available in Japan.

The special edition trail soon began in Japan during 2009 with a GT-R SpecV model. This had body tweaks like a new carbon-fibre rear spoiler, revised brake ducts, altered grille and a fancy black paint job. The interior was lifted by oodles of carbon-fibre trimmings, whilst mechanical enhancements include a titanium-coated exhaust, carbon-ceramic brakes and reworked suspension. Unfortunately, it's not for the export market – at least not yet.

Noble M12/M400

There must be something to be said for a car that munches Porsche 911 turbos for lunch and can come close to showing a Lamborghini a clean pair of exhausts – and the 'something' is this . . . the Noble M12 is magnificent. Maker Lee Noble is a master at setting up a winning chassis and specializes in racecars and high-performance road cars with no pretensions to luxurious GT status.

The M12 was an uncompromising two-door, two-seater coupe that went through four evolutions in its short life – the GTO3, GTO 3R, GTO 3R(6) and M400. A 3 litre turbocharged Ford Duratec V6 was mounted on a steel chassis with full roll cage and a GRP (glass-reinforced plastic) body. This was styled along classic coupe lines, with a plunging front end between sculpted wings, terminating in air scoops and a spoiler, a low cabin with a large curved windscreen, side air scoops and a blunt rear end with a sexy upcurve and raised spoiler.

M12s offered few creature comforts and no storage space. This serious driving machine put performance above posing, with no traction control or ABS to rescue a novice from a tight spot – though the roll cage and race harness might save the day. Bucket seats are supportive and there is ample cabin space. The finish is leather and there's adequate soundproofing, but this is not a car for everyday use. Transmission is a crisp five-speed manual box and the ride quality is firm but not uncomfortable, even at track speeds.

The M400 is a racing evolution of the M12 with a more powerful Ford V6, enhanced shocks, stiffer springs, front roll bar and special Pirelli tyres. This may be an outstanding racer, but it's also street-legal and perfectly amenable to a little sure-footed roadwork.

They may have been Noble by name, but the M12/M400 cars were definitely streetfighters when the chips were down.

COUNTRY OF ORIGIN:
UK
FIRST MANUFACTURED:
2003 (until 2007)
ENGINE:
2,967 cc V6 Twin Turbo
PERFORMANCE:
M400 – top speed of
185 mph (298 km/h);
0-60 mph (97 km/h) in 2.97 secs
YOU SHOULD KNOW:
Even as Noble Automotive develops the new M15 and its racing equivalent, the M600, the M12/M400 line lives on, manufacturing rights having been sold to American outfit IG Racing/Rossion Automotive, who produce their own luxury version of the M400, the Rossion Q1.

Pagani Zonda Cinque

COUNTRY OF ORIGIN:
Italy
FIRST MANUFACTURED:
2008
ENGINE:
7,291 cc DOHC V12
PERFORMANCE:
Top speed of 218 mph (350 km/h);
0-60 (97 kmh) in less than 3.4 secs
YOU SHOULD KNOW:
Zonda is the name of an Argentinian
pampas wind. Although of Italian
origin, Pagani was born in Argentina;
he originally called his supercar the
Fangio F1 in honour of the legendary
Argentinian racing champion but
when Fangio died in 1995, Pagani felt
it was disrespectful to commercialize
his memory.

Technologist Horacio Pagani has devoted his life to dreaming up exotic cars, and his Zonda supercars are among the most exclusive on the planet. Inspired by fighter-plane materials technology, Pagani envisioned building a supercar out of carbon-fibre composite. In 1992, he established his own company and set about realizing his ambition. It took him seven years and a lot of hard work – he finally offered up his first painstaking labour of love, the Zonda C12 coupe in 1999. Powered by a 6 litre Mercedes-Benz M120 V12 engine, the C12 could reach 210 mph (340 km/h) with acceleration from 0-60 mph (97 km/h) in 4.2 secs. Pagani has continued to develop his Zonda and by 2008 he had produced 95 roadsters and coupes.

Pagani's latest offering is the Zonda Cinque (pronounced chin-kwae). Based on the Zonda R track car of 2007, the Cinque is a limited edition of only five (as its name suggests) road-legal racing cars, built to order for a select Hong Kong dealer and pre-sold for $1,600,000 each. This sensational silver, black and red coupe is made from carbon-titanium fibre, a new material Pagani has developed.

The Cinque has six-speed sequential transmission, with a paddle on the steering wheel for changing gear in under 100 millisecs, carbon-ceramic brakes and a fuel-injected Mercedes-AMG aluminium mid-engine. This is a whopping great 7.3 litre V12 producing 678 bhp, first used in the Zonda C12S model of 2002 and now produced by AMG exclusively for Pagani. The luxurious interior is the ultimate in sporty chic with an impeccable finish, down to the last nut and bolt. Literally. Every single one bears the imprint of the Pagani logo! The Cinque is Pagani's most mind-blowing Zonda yet – not just the last word in status symbols but a consummate work of art.

Only five Cinques were ever made – to exclusive order.

Panoz Esperante

Danny Panoz is the embodiment of the American Dream – for he is an independent small-volume manufacturer who has succeeded in playing the giants of the motor industry at their own game. He founded the Panoz Auto Development Company in 1989 with nothing but a chassis design and raw ambition; today the Esperante is the coolest supercar in America and Panoz has surely secured his place in automotive history.

A car nut from childhood, Panoz got his lucky break when, by pure chance, he managed to obtain the rights to a chassis designed by Frank Costin, renowned pioneer of monocoque technology. Panoz rented a workshop in Atlanta, Georgia and, using the Costin design and innovative materials technology, built an all-American high-performance car, comparable to European imports in quality but at a competitive price.

The Panoz Roadster was the world's first production car made from SPF (superplastically-formed) aluminium. It was enough of a hit to keep Panoz afloat (he sold 44) and in 1996 he created another first: an aluminium intensive vehicle – 70% aluminium – which he marketed as the Panoz AIV Roadster. In the same year, to raise his profile, he entered the world of motor sport and has since become one of the biggest players on the US racetracks.

The Esperante is the spin-off from a Panoz racer, replacing the AIV Roadster as the company's only production road car – a handmade luxury two-seater built on an aluminium frame with a superplastic aluminium body (stronger than steel yet only 40% of the weight) powered by a Ford Mustang four-cam V8 front mid-engine. The Esperante doesn't come cheap, but $115,000 buys quality, reliability, exclusivity (fewer than 400 have been built) and, above all, soul. Get behind the steering wheel of one of these and you just can't help brimming with joy.

Okay, this beauty is undoubedly America's coolest – and most exclusive – supercar.

COUNTRY OF ORIGIN:
USA
FIRST MANUFACTURED:
2000
ENGINE:
4.6 l (280 cid) 2xDOHC V8
PERFORMANCE:
Top speed of 155 mph (250 km/h); 0-60 mph (97 km/h) in 5.1 secs
YOU SHOULD KNOW:
Panoz's success is partly due to his service – every Esperante owner is made to feel special and cars are individually tailored to meet personal requirements. The Esperante comes either as a coupe or a convertible in three versions – a basic supercar, a slightly more powerful GT, and a road beast GTLM. There is also a GTS strictly for the race circuit.

The Carrera is the fastest and most expensive Porsche ever built – and is naturally a simply incredible car to drive.

Porsche Carrera GT

The Carrera GT is the most unusual car Porsche has ever produced, as well as the fastest and most expensive. Its debut at the Geneva Motor Show of 2003 caused a flurry of excitement. This was a supercar that looked as though it was meant for the track, not the road – and that was indeed more or less the case. Porsche's engineers had been working on designing a V10 engine intended as a prototype for a new Porsche racing car when their project was summarily scrapped on the grounds of overstretched resources and mounting costs. Instead, they were directed to channel their experimental design into a production sports car that could rival Ferrari's Enzo.

Like the Enzo, the Carrera GT was built using ultra-light materials at the cutting edge of technology: a carbon fibre monocoque and a silicon carbide (ceramic composite) clutch and brake system. The new V10 engine was mid-mounted for stability. The car was designed as an open-top but came with an easily attachable, lightweight roof, slickly designed in two sections that fitted into the boot. All this came at a price – $440,000. But the Carrera GT still managed to be some $200,000 cheaper than the Enzo whilst virtually its equal performance-wise.

The Carrera GT not only has dramatic looks but is also a phenomenal drive. Even the most experienced test drivers were shaken by its runaway nature and, if they didn't immediately stall, were aghast to find themselves literally careering down the road quicker than the brain could react. It takes iron nerve and immense concentration to trammel the wild power of this featherweight rocket, but therein lies the challenge; and the driver who has the knack of handling it is rewarded with a sensation verging on ecstasy.

COUNTRY OF ORIGIN:
Germany
FIRST MANUFACTURED:
2004 (until 2006)
ENGINE:
5,733 cc DOHC V10
PERFORMANCE:
Top speed of 205 mph (330 km/h);
0-60 mph (97km/h) in 3.5 secs
YOU SHOULD KNOW:
Porsche planned a production run of 1,500 Carrera GTs but called a halt in 2006 after only 1,270 had been built, citing new US airbag regulations as the reason. A new Carrera GT has been introduced for 2009. It comes as either coupe or cabriolet and is said to be capable of 208 mph (335 km/h).

Porsche Cayman S (987C)

With its satisfying guttural roar, the Cayman S is a beast of a car. Squeezed into a tiny corner of the market between the Boxster and the Carrera, it may be a rare sight on the road but it has become the benchmark for sports coupes, winning numerous plaudits in the motoring trade journals as 'Best Sports Car'.

A mid-engined two-seater with rear-wheel drive, it shares the same platform as the Boxster as well as many of the same parts. And that may be the essence of its image problem. The uninitiated might easily write it off as merely a more expensive, less attractive version of the Boxster; and lacking an open top and high tech interior gadgetry, it certainly doesn't immediately scream 'sports car of the year'. But cars are for driving and that's what the Cayman S does to perfection. It is absolute magic on the road. Once you're behind the wheel, the slightly offbeat styling – elements of which hark back to the classic mid 20th century 550 and 904 models – is neither here nor there. And at least nobody can deny that it's eye-catching.

The Cayman S is a superbly agile car, some would say the best of the Porsche range. Its 3.4 litre flat six leaps into instant response and it handles beautifully round bends with a stability that belies its lightness. Since 2007 a less powerful 2.7 litre Cayman (without the 'S') has been available for $10,000 less. The second generation 2009 version of this basic model has had its engine displacement increased to 2.9 litres. It too is a sublime drive, giving an outstanding performance that more than measures up to expectations and is hardly less thrilling than the S. Only a spectacularly power-hungry petrolhead could fail to feel sated.

COUNTRY OF ORIGIN:
Germany (but assembled in Finland)
FIRST MANUFACTURED:
2005
ENGINE:
3,436 cc Flat Six
PERFORMANCE:
Top speed of 171 mph (275 km/h); 0-60 mph (97km/h) in 5.1 secs
YOU SHOULD KNOW:
The latest generation of the Cayman S has had its Tiptronic six-speed gear system replaced by Porsche's tongue-twisting Porsche *DoppelKupplungsgetriebe* (PDK) double-clutch, seven-speed, sequential transmission, a state-of-the-art system imported from the world of motor racing, for even quicker acceleration and reduced fuel consumption. Porsche has also made a limited edition of 700 extra-powerful 'S Sport' versions.

The Cayman S is considered to be Porsche's most agile performer.

Porsche Cayenne Turbo S

COUNTRY OF ORIGIN:
Germany
FIRST MANUFACTURED:
2006
ENGINE:
4,511 cc V8
PERFORMANCE:
Top speed of 168 mph (270 km/h);
0-60 mph (97km/h) in 5.1 secs
YOU SHOULD KNOW:
No Turbo S versions of the Cayenne
were produced in 2007-8. It has been
brought back for 2009 (with an extra
30 hp) and the next generation in
2010 will have a 580 hp V10 engine.

The very idea of Porsche entering the SUV market caused an uneasy stir when the Cayenne first appeared in 2002. But Porsche was keen to tap the new wealth of countries like Russia and China, where multi-millionaire oligarchs were sprouting up everywhere but crumbling road surfaces ruled out high-status sports cars. Being Porsche, the company hasn't done things by halves: the introduction of the Cayenne has raised the SUV benchmark by several notches – albeit with a heavy emphasis on 'sports' and scarcely a trace of 'utility'.

The top-of-the-range Turbo S is twice the price of the basic model, which may seem exorbitant but, once you examine its spec, the reason becomes abundantly clear – the Cayenne Turbo S is simply the most powerful and luxurious SUV in the world. Its dexterity both on and off road belies its looks; despite its massive appearance, it is extraordinarily nippy – acceleration that matches Porsche's Cayman S! – and in difficult conditions its 521 bhp gives a performance that can only be described as awesome. It has a super-luxurious interior to match its price and advanced safety systems to appease even the most anxiety-prone neurotic.

The Cayenne could never be described as a 'fun' car; rather, it imposes itself on the road with a haughty efficiency. But if your aim is to be an imperious commander of the universe, safely cocooned from the rabble in your luxurious padded cell, then the Turbo S certainly goes all the way to realizing the fantasy. It just seems a pity that a vehicle superbly designed for crossing the Gobi desert should have its potential wasted on people-carrying in the posher parts of the home counties. The Cayenne is certainly powerful; only its street cred is a tad dubious.

The styling is not to everyone's taste, but this is one of the most capable off-roaders that money can buy.

Renault Clio Renaultsport 197

When it comes to hot hatches, few are much warmer than the super-spicy Clio 197.

Don't be fooled. This car is nothing like the girly 'Papa! – Nicole!' Clio of advert fame. The only thing it has in common is the 'Va Va Voom'. The Clio RS (Renault Sport) was first introduced in 1998 as a flagship version designed to give the Clio a more macho image. The Renault engineers have pulled out the stops for the third generation. They have used all the expertise of the marque's racing heritage and the latest Formula 1 aerodynamics technology to come up trumps with an exciting front-wheel drive, six-speed hot hatch that is seriously fast for such a small road car. Those plastic slats at the rear aren't just for show – they're air diffusers to prevent Clio from lifting off.

The 197 tag refers to the Clio's horsepower. Being French it is given in PS but that still translates to 194 bhp – an impressive figure for a car this size. It is a really exhilirating drive, with a genuinely racy zappiness and a satisfyingly throaty engine thrum; at the same time it feels extremely safe with tenacious grip and barely perceptible body roll. It is a car that gives its best at high revs, better suited to winding country roads than long, dull stretches of motorway. But the 197 is not just designed for thrills on the open road; its agility, manouevrability and practical interior make it a really pleasurable children-and-chores city car.

A few critics have argued that, despite the 197's greater power, it lacks some of the character of the second generation Renaultsport 182, but for others, the 197 is the jewel in the Clio crown. Certainly, it is widely regarded as the best performing and most attractive affordable small hot hatch around today.

COUNTRY OF ORIGIN:
France
FIRST MANUFACTURED:
2006 (Third generation)
ENGINE:
1,998 cc Straight Four
PERFORMANCE:
Top speed of 134 mph (216 km/h);
0-60 mph (97km/h) in 6.8 secs
YOU SHOULD KNOW:
The Clio Renaultsport 197 has won
the *Track & Race Cars Magazine*
'Hot Hatch Car of the Year' award for
two years in succession.

No modern manufacturer dares be without a pretty off-roader – so enter the Renault Koleos.

Renault Koleos

Despite the world stampeding towards SUVs from the 1990s and into the 21st century, Renault has stubbornly refused to join the many manufacturers around the globe who were equally swift in meeting demand. Indeed, despite showing a concept off-roader as early as 2000, their first entry in the four-wheel drive stakes didn't arrive until 2008, when credit crunch and world recession were about to puncture car sales and burst the SUV bubble in the process.

If there was a silver lining to be found, it was that Renault hadn't opted for some massive machine. The new Koleos turned out to be a rather neat 4x4 developed in conjunction with Nissan, based on the latter's X-Trail. True, the styling is rather bland, being reminiscent of a typical hatchback that happens to be rather elevated. But the Koleos fills a gap in the Renault offering, one up from the smaller hatches and one down from Renault's impressive range of family cars and (especially) people carriers.

The combination of Renault engines and Nissan's four-wheel drive system works particularly well and the Koleos cleverly doesn't pretend to be something it isn't. Whilst it is perfectly happy dealing with the occasional muddy field or unmade track, it has no pretensions towards being a world-class offroader. Neither does it aspire to the sporty performance claimed by some smaller 4WDs that claim sports car handling. Instead, the five-door Koleos simply provides refined and comfortable on-road transport with that all-important elevated driving position. To emphasize the point, the Koleos is available with front-wheel only drive.

The 2 litre turbodiesel comes with two levels of tune, teamed as standard with a six-speed manual gearbox, though automatic transmission is offered. Buyers have considerable choice, with Dynamique, Dynamique S and Privilege models accompanied by a range of optional extras.

COUNTRY OF ORIGIN:
France (built in Korea)
FIRST MANUFACTURED:
2008
ENGINE:
1,998 cc Straight Four Diesel
PERFORMANCE:
Varies according to model –
maximum top speed of
112 mph (180 km/h);
0-60 mph (97 km/h) in 9.7 secs
YOU SHOULD KNOW:
Renault may have made a super-comfortable four-wheel drive vehicle that's mainly designed for effortless road use, but it still likes to stress the off-road potential of the Koleos by offering a hill-descent control option. Perhaps it's a case of satisfying 'I-don't-actually-go-off-road-much-but-could-cross-the-Sahara-if-I-wanted-to' syndrome.

Rolls-Royce Phantom Saloon

Rolls Royce is now a wholly owned subsidiary of BMW but the cars that come out of its new Goodwood factory are as inimitable as they always have been. The Phantom saloon is the ultimate in sophistication, a classic RR design melded to BMW cutting-edge engineering. Built around a hand-welded aluminium space frame with a BMW 6.75 litre aluminium-alloy engine, it is still unmistakably a Roller, its massive but graceful proportions, dramatic long bonnet and opulent interior echoing Phantoms of the past.

The attention to detail is remarkable – everything has been thought of. Even the Spirit of Ecstasy mascot perched on top of the streamlined stainless-steel grille has an auto-retract mechanism to protect it from itchy vandals' fingers; and the RR logo on the centre of each wheel is self-correcting so that it always stays the right way up whether or not the wheels are revolving. Rear-hinged coach doors not only make it easier to strike a camera-friendly pose without the door frame getting in the way but also give increased protection from a side-impact hit; and they can be closed from inside the car at the touch of a button if the paparazzi start to become a bore.

The V12 engine is virtually silent: it's impossible to tell whether it's actually running. And once you do pull away, the six-speed automatic transmission and air-sprung suspension give a ride so smooth you hardly realize you're moving. As for the inside – passengers are cossetted in a fantasy palace of polished wood and pile carpet, completely detached from external reality, while the driver is enthroned at a majestic height all the better to command the road. A ride in a Phantom is a positively regal experience – luxury motoring at its absolute peak.

COUNTRY OF ORIGIN:
UK
FIRST MANUFACTURED:
2003
ENGINE:
6,749 cc V12
PERFORMANCE:
Top speed of 149mph (240 km/h);
0-60 mph (97km/h) in 5.7 secs
YOU SHOULD KNOW:
Around 5,000 Phantom saloons have been sold. Several limited editions have been produced, including a run of 25 Phantom Blacks. An extended wheelbase version was introduced in 2005, and in 2007 and 2008 drophead coupe and coupe models were added to the Phantom range.

The sound of silence – there is no longer a ticking clock so the ride is truly peaceful.

Rolls-Royce Hyperion Pininfarina Drophead Coupe

COUNTRY OF ORIGIN:
UK/Italy
FIRST MANUFACTURED:
2008
ENGINE:
6,749 cc V12
PERFORMANCE:
Top speed of 155 mph (250 km/h);
0-60 mph (97km/h) in 5.6 secs
YOU SHOULD KNOW:
Among the many extra-special
touches in the Hyperion are two
stowing compartments in front of
the windscreen, one of which has
been designed to fit a pair of hunting
rifles, and a white-gold watch
designed specifically for Pininfarina
by Girard-Perregaux, which can be
removed from the dash and attached
to a wrist bracelet

The Hyperion was unveiled in a sombre atmosphere on August 16, 2008. Andrea Pininfarina, grandson of the legendary Batista 'Pinin' Farina, had been tragically killed in a car accident just a few days before he was due to wow the crowds with his latest custom car at Pebble Beach Concours d'Elegance, the prestigious US annual show. His 'romantic and noble' Hyperion, named after one of the Titans of Greek mythology, was dedicated to his memory.

Built at the request of a wealthy private collector who wanted a bespoke version of a Phantom drophead coupe, the Hyperion is a consummate variation of the production model. It is the archetypal Rolls Royce of post-modern dreams: a retro art-deco roadster engineered from cutting-edge materials incorporating every conceivable nod to high-tech luxury.

Money was no object and Pininfarina's design team was given free rein to express itself. Inspired by marine architecture, Pininfarina revamped the Phantom drophead coupe to produce a car that evokes the heyday of French Riviera style. The rear seats have been removed and the windscreen moved back by 40 cm (15.7 in) to exaggerate the bonnet length, the soft roof has been redesigned, the sides sculpted, the rear shortened and the radiator grille inclined, all of which combine to give the car a more boat-like, 'surging' look than the production model. Instead of aluminium, the Hyperion has carbon-fibre coachwork with handcrafted doors of solid wood.

The Hyperion has been inspired by the legacy of previous Pininfarina Rolls-Royces, particularly the 1951 Silver Dawn saloon and Camargue coupe of 1975.The result is a magnificent work of art that reflects all that is best in both the Pininfarina and Rolls-Royce names. It is a fitting tribute to Andrea Pinifarina's life's work.

Saleen S7

Professional racing driver Steve Saleen is a pioneer of 'lifestyle performance autos', that is: all-American celebrity supercars designed to appeal to the Hollywood social set. Saleen became well-known on the race circuit for his skill at tweaking Ford Mustangs, a talent he invested in by setting up his own company as a manufacturer of limited edition, high-performance cars and parts in 1984. He has made Saleen versions of several existing production cars and has produced more than 8000 modified Mustangs for both road and track.

The S7 was the first Saleen to be designed from scratch rather

than being built on the platform of another badge, the intention behind it being to 'combine the performance of a track-only race car with the driving pleasure of a road car'. When it was unveiled in 2000, the S7 was the fastest production car in America and the only street-legal car with more than 500 bhp and more than 500 lb ft of torque.

In terms of style, the S7 is as glamorous as it gets: a rear mid-engine supercar with butterfly doors and an interior that oozes luxury as well as functionality. It was digitally designed and handbuilt from carbon fibre on a lightweight reinforced steel and aluminium space frame. Saleen boasted that it had the best aerodynamics of any car in the world: numerous vents and grilles control the airflow over, under and through it, and travelling at 160 mph (257 km/h) it creates its own weight in downforce.

In 2005, the S7 was replaced by a virtually identical but more powerful version with an all-aluminium twin-turbo engine and top speed of 248 mph. The S7 Twin Turbo produces 750 bhp (123 bhp more than the McLaren F1) and advertised itself as the fastest production car in the world.

The S7 – a new contender for the coveted 'fastest car' crown.

COUNTRY OF ORIGIN:
USA
FIRST MANUFACTURED:
2000 (until 2006)
ENGINE:
7.0 l (427.6 cid) OHV V8
PERFORMANCE:
Top speed of 200 mph (322 km/h) or (Twin Turbo) 248 mph (399 km/h); 0-60 mph (97km/h) in 3.9 secs or (Twin Turbo) 2.4 secs
YOU SHOULD KNOW:
Steve Saleen started to dissociate himself from Saleen Inc in 2007, finally leaving in 2008 and taking the rights to the S7 with him. He is now trading under the name SMS. Soon after he left, Saleen Inc was dissolved, leaving some disgruntled customers when it turned out that their car warranties were no longer being honoured.

Fast, sexy and affordable – fine qualities that somehow still failed to save the Sky Red Line.

Saturn Sky Red Line

The Saturn marque is a subsidiary of General Motors, set up in the 1980s in response to the flood of German and Japanese small car imports to the USA eating into GM's market share. The first Saturn, a small saloon, came off the assembly line in 1990 accompanied by advertising which depicted Saturn as a 'Different Kind of Car Company' that put 'People First', slogans that soon established it as a reliable marque providing value-for-money compact family cars.

In 2003, the company gave itself a sporty makeover by introducing Red Line – beefed-up versions of existing cars in the Saturn range – and for 2007, it produced its first proper sports car, the two-seater Saturn Sky. The Sky comes both as a basic (177 bhp) roadster and, for an extra $4,200, a Red Line (260 bhp) model with a posher interior, better suspension, dual exhaust and the most powerful of GM's turbocharged and direct-injected Ecotec engines.

The Sky is built on the same front-engine, rear-wheel drive platform as GM's Pontiac Solstice and Opel GT models but has cuter looks than either. In fact, it's one of the most eye-catching autos on the road, let alone to have emerged from the GM stable. Its phenomenal success can be put down more to the allure of its styling than its handling, which is no more than mediocre. It also has some irritating flaws – a removable soft top that is frustratingly awkward to manage, hardly any trunk space and disappointing quality in the overall finish.

But when eye-candy is as enticing as this, who really cares if it's not the most agile car on the road? The Sky goes fast and has undeniable sex appeal; moreover it's at an affordable price. Only the most pernickety petrolhead is going to moan about this adorable-looking little roadster.

COUNTRY OF ORIGIN:
USA
FIRST MANUFACTURED:
2007
ENGINE:
2.0 l (122 cid) DOHC Straight Four
PERFORMANCE:
Top speed of 141 mph (227 km/h);
0-60 mph (97km/h) in 5.8 secs
YOU SHOULD KNOW:
In February 2009 General Motors announced that no new Saturn models would be produced and that the marque would be phased out by 2011 as part of GM's restructuring plan to cut costs and make the company eligible for government assistance to prop it up during the global recession.

Spyker C8 Aileron

The name Spyker has the same resonance for the Dutch as Rolls-Royce has for the British – synonymous with the pursuit of quality before profit. The Spyker coachbuilding company, founded in 1880, built the 1898 Golden Coach that is still used by the Dutch Royal Family on State occasions. In the same year, it pioneered Benz-engined automobiles and later branched out into aircraft manufacture. Spyker finally went bankrupt in 1926, leaving as its legacy some of the most beautiful cars of the early 20th century.

The company was resuscitated in 2000 by Maarten de Bruijn, an enterprising young designer who built his own sports car and then had the sense to obtain the rights to the defunct Spyker name and propeller logo. Armed with these, he had no problem finding financial backing to put his car into production as the Spyker C8, a name that harked back to the C4, the most famous Spyker car of the past.

The Aileron is the second generation of the C8 limited-production series. Like the earlier Laviolette and Spyder C8, it is built of aluminium panels on an aluminium space frame but to a longer-wheelbase design that succeeds in giving much greater rigidity with no extra weight. It is powered by the same Audi 4.2 litre V8 mid-engine and has a six-speed transaxle, offered either as a manual or as an automatic with manual override and steering wheel controls.

When this quirky scissor-doored coupe was unveiled at Geneva in 2008, the press release stressed Spyker's (dubious) aircraft heritage and gave a tenuous explanation of the new C8's name: 'ailerons' are the hinged flaps on aeroplane wings that control turning manoeuvres, and it is the company's hope that the Aileron will be the car that at last turns Spyker into a profit-making concern.

COUNTRY OF ORIGIN:
The Netherlands
(partly built in the UK)
FIRST MANUFACTURED:
2009
ENGINE:
4,163 cc V8
PERFORMANCE:
Top speed of 187 mph (300 km/h);
0-60 mph (97km/h) in less than
4.5 secs
YOU SHOULD KNOW:
The Spyker Company motto is the Latin *Nulla tenaci invia est via* which translates as: 'No road is blocked for those who persevere'. In 1907, a Spyker car was one of only four to complete the Peking to Paris Rally and a Spyker co-starred in the classic 1953 film *Genevieve* about the London to Brighton Veteran Car Run.

Could the Spyker be the start of a Dutch supercar industry?

SSC Ultimate Aero

COUNTRY OF ORIGIN:
USA
FIRST MANUFACTURED:
2006
ENGINE:
6.35 l (387 cid) V8
PERFORMANCE:
Top speed of 256 mph (412 km/h);
0-60 mph (97km/h) in 2.78 secs
YOU SHOULD KNOW:
Shelby is working on the production
of an Ultimate Aero EV (Electric
Vehicle) to tap into the green market.

There is nothing remotely subtle or sophisticated about the Ultimate Aero. It is simply the fastest production road car in the world – yes, really! An all-American supercar that will appeal to testosterone-fuelled speed freaks everywhere.

SSC stands for Shelby SuperCars, a company founded in 1999 by Jerod Shelby, who sounds as though he should be connected to renowned racing driver and entrepreneur Carroll Shelby but is in fact no relation. But Jerod, like Carroll, is one of that fanatical breed of maverick designers who, starting with little but a fixation on cars and endless self-belief, succeed in pipping the big corporate manufacturers to the post in pursuit of their ambition.

The prototype of the Aero was unveiled in 2004 and the first cars went into production in 2006. Built of carbon fibre and titanium for lightness with scissor doors and a supercharged V8 mid-engine, the Aero was manufactured in two versions – a basic model that went pretty fast and a more powerful Ultimate that went even faster. The following year the basic model was phased out while the Ultimate Aero was given a twin-turbo engine that produced an incredible 1,183 bhp and 1,094 ft lbs of torque making it the most powerful production car in the world. The first one off the production line was auctioned on eBay, selling for $431,100.

Guinness World Records gave the SSC Ultimate Aero the title of the world's fastest production car in August 2007. Jerod hasn't looked back. For 2008 he gave his Ultimate Aero an all-aluminium engine block and even more power. He claims that the new 2009 model has yet another 15% added to bhp and is theoretically capable of speeds above 284 mph (457 km/h). He seems intent on hanging on to his record.

Toyota Prius NHW20

The urgent search for environmentally responsible cars and the economics of fuel efficiency are between them the harbingers of a real automotive revolution. In addition to questioning the very nature of a car and what makes it work, it's essential for drivers to become accustomed to new mechanics of driving. The Toyota Prius NHW20 is a landmark development in both subjects. Its very name is Latin for 'before' with all the implications of 'the way forward', and it's an attitude that has been gratefully seized on and shared by roughly a million people worldwide who have bought a Prius.

Ten years of research produced the Prius NHW20 in 2004, a midsized five-door hatchback with its mechanicals reconfigured to

give rear passengers significantly more room than in much bigger cars. Take the all-round increase in luxury passenger comforts as read, and ponder how Toyota did it. The NHW20 operates on Toyota's Hybrid Synergy Drive, an advanced version of the electric motor and petrol engine combination tested in earlier models. Its statistics are mind-boggling (90% fewer smog-contributory emissions than a conventional internal combustion engine!) and lengthy. For a single example, it is the first car to offer (as standard) air-conditioning that operates independently of the engine, guaranteeing comfort even when the car is running on its electric motor. Every one of its extraordinary range of systems is both improved, and self-adjusting to work in non-competitive harmony with, or actually to assist, the others.

The Prius changes the business of driving. Whatever your driving priority, it either anticipates or makes easier. Drivers are consistently freed to concentrate on the road with ergonomically brilliant push-button, computerized controls. You feel you're sitting in a cockpit – and with the traditional gear stick lever replaced by a small, dashboard-mounted joystick, you feel the car might even sprout wings. One day it will.

The Prius could be the future of motoring – available today!

COUNTRY OF ORIGIN:
Japan
FIRST MANUFACTURED:
2004 (until 2009)
ENGINE:
THS (Toyota Hybrid System) II
(Petrol: 1.5 l DOHC Straight Four;
Electric: 500 V AT-PZEV)
PERFORMANCE:
Top speed of 105 mph (169 km/h)
(combined electric/petrol motors),
and 42 mph (68 km/h)
(electric motor only);
0-60 mph (97 km/h) in 10.1 secs
YOU SHOULD KNOW:
The Toyota Prius NHW20 has
received many plaudits, including
'Car of the Year' (*Motor Trend*), 'Ten
Best Cars' (*Car & Driver*), and 'Ten
Best Engines' (*Ward's Auto World*).

TVR Tuscan S Mk II

COUNTRY OF ORIGIN:
UK
FIRST MANUFACTURED:
2005
ENGINE:
3,996 cc Straight Six
PERFORMANCE:
Top speed of
195 mph (314 km/h);
0-60 mph (97 km/h) in 3.8 secs
YOU SHOULD KNOW:
When journalists were invited by TVR
to road test the Mark Two Tuscan S,
the TVR test car was (allegedly) fitted
with one of the most sophisticated
Gatso (police highway speed camera)
detection units then available. TVR
rightly feared that journalists would
be swept away by reckless
enthusiasm for the car, and risk
losing their licences by speeding.

It took TVR six years to perfect the Tuscan two-seater sports coupe. The fifth attempt was the Mark Two, a 'refreshed' version of the already spectacular TVR Tuscan S. At its launch, enthusiasts noted their particular pleasure in the determination with which TVR had sought to perfect the marriage of form and function that the Tuscan was always intended to be. Other car manufacturers responded to declining sales with a new model, rushed from the ether on a whim. TVR preferred to make their existing star better.

Nothing was extraneous in the revised Tuscan S; and everything was thought through. The swooping lines of the bonnet functioned as low pressure exits for the hot air from the radiator. Long hours in the windtunnel suggested small styling changes that produced downforce over both axles. With the front headlights faired-in for better aerodynamic flow, the car was a diminutive vision of pure elegance. The interior remained as original, minimalist and striking as ever. Autocar described it as 'like a showcar that has gone straight from plinth to high street without meeting an accountant on the way . . . Everywhere you look there are details which will one day feature in the Sexiest Car Components of All Time lists'.

The Tuscan is pocket dynamite, capable of blowing away many another supercar.

The TVR Tuscan S was, of course, pocket dynamite, a sports car driver's unhealthily happy dream. It could embarrass Ferrari, Porsche or most other expensive supercars. It could even stop on a (gut-lurching) dime. Superquick and responsive, it could overtake in a hairsbreadth. The deep, spitting rumble of the exhaust is exhilarating enough to urge any driver's pedal to the metal. It was specially 'tuned' by TVR to parallel the power psychology of the Tuscan S. This car tells you it's playing 'Our Song' while effortlessly pulling 100 mph (161 km/h) in second gear.

Vauxhall VX220

It's not often you can accuse a car of being too good. When Vauxhall finally decided to create a small sports car, it approached the project with a gusto belying the timidity of the brand image. The VX220 took all its cues from the Lotus Elise, already established as a highly successful racer, and improved on them. Take it as a compliment to Lotus.

On its first appearance, the VX220 made do with a 145 bhp 2.2 litre Vauxhall engine, chosen because it produced more torque at lower speeds than any Elise power unit. It was consistent with Vauxhall's crafty intention to create a car that any driver worth his salt could justify to the family, without sacrificing the high performance that makes driving really exciting. The VX220 was marginally less raw than sitting on a drum of rocket fuel and lighting a match – but it was still a Lotus Elise in exceptionally fine clothes (the two cars shared 141 parts). But Vauxhall learned very quickly.

The VX220 got a turbocharged 2 litre engine. Now it boasted 200 bhp (against the fastest Elise 111's 156 bhp), accelerated like a Ferrari and, with its low weight, could dance and dart on the road with the finesse of a kingfisher. Everything fell into place. The VX220 was more refined than the Lotus (with which it now shared many fewer parts), quieter but still capable of a satisfying crescendo. It retained its impressive torque, but stayed smooth as it gripped the road with balletic response. It was very fast, very reliable, and brilliant fun to drive.

The only trouble was that not many people believed that Vauxhall could produce such a fabulous, driver-friendly, extreme sports car – and certainly not at the price. The Vauxhall VX220 should be much more famous.

COUNTRY OF ORIGIN:
UK
FIRST MANUFACTURED:
2000 (until 2005)
ENGINE:
1,998 cc Straight Four Turbo
PERFORMANCE:
Top speed of 151 mph (243 km/h);
0-60 mph (97 km/h) in 4.7 secs
YOU SHOULD KNOW:
Exerting the kind of marketing of which only a major manufacturer is capable, Vauxhall (along with the three year warranty and 'zero percent finance' offers you might get with a Corsa or Astra) initially offered VX220 buyers a free day of driver training under ex-Formula One supervision. Buy Fun, Get Fun Free.

The VX220 turned out to be a rather better car than most critics initially assumed.

Vauxhall (Holden) Monaro VXR500

This is the car with enough muscle to be elected Governor of, say, California. It's the limited edition of the Australian Holden Monaro VXR, with its 6 litre V8 engine supercharged by a snarling Harrap blower, and put together under the supervision of the specialist tuner Wortec and the loving hand of Greens of Kent. It seems desperately unfair that the apotheosis of their own VXR is not to be sold in Australia, especially because the VXR500 clamours for the wide open road. Its straight line speed and acceleration is breathtaking – a combination of exceptional torque and raw power that in any gear defies the normal laws of physics.

To the credit of its creators, the VXR500 looks and behaves much better than a mere rocket sled. It's a genuine, four-seat coupe, with pretensions to comfort but not luxury. You expect a hard ride to match the obvious machismo of the power unit. It will cost you extra for the six-piston AP Racing brakes to keep the VXR500's muscle on a tight leash, and yet more for the Wortec sports suspension package. Especially on European roads, these add-ons make for a reasonably civilized ride and handling characteristics. You still feel a bit like Mad Max – even ensconced in the superb seats and surrounded by at least the semblance of expensive driving, the swelling bellow of the supercharger is a regular reminder of the VXR500's true potency.

It's generous for such a mighty car. When there's not enough road to let it loose, it creates the noise or some other illusion of speed. It demands total respect and unfaltering concentration, and in return offers scintillating entertainment at half the cost of anything remotely comparable. The VXR500 redefines supercharged muscle; and though it's not a factory development, it redefines the idea of 'Vauxhall' as well.

COUNTRY OF ORIGIN:
UK
FIRST MANUFACTURED:
2006
ENGINE:
5,967 cc V8
PERFORMANCE:
Top speed of 185 mph (298 km/h);
0-60 mph (97 km/h) in 4.8 secs

YOU SHOULD KNOW:
The Vauxhall Monaro VXR500 has been described as the last word in 'anti-cool', because it's 'not very sophisticated' and offers its drivers too much uncomplicated, 'riotous fun'. That's a roundabout way of saying the traction control isn't wonderful in the wet; and pushing that power on icy roads is positively self-destructive. You have been warned!

The VXR500 is best driven with a modicum of care, especially as the double ton approaches.

CONCEPT CARS

Buick Y-Job

COUNTRY OF ORIGIN:
USA
FIRST MANUFACTURED:
1938
ENGINE:
5.2 l (320 cid) Straight Eight
PERFORMANCE:
N/A
YOU SHOULD KNOW:
Harley Earl supposedly called his car Y-Job because experimental cars were habitually designated with an X; he simply went to the next letter of the alphabet.

From the earliest years of the car industry, manufacturers had been producing elegant custom coachwork designs for wealthy patrons, but mass-market autos were an entirely different matter – functional, unimaginative wagon bodies were cobbled on to whatever chassis happened to be rolling off the production line and aesthetic appeal was low on the agenda. The Buick Y-Job broke the mould. It was the first-ever concept car – that is, a prototype designed specifically for the purpose of gauging consumer reaction.

Alfred Sloan, the far-sighted head of GM, realizing that style and mass-market production were not mutually exclusive, set up the Art and Color Section of GM (later to morph into the Styling Department) with Harley J Earl at its helm. Earl was the son of a wagon builder who had branched out into custom-built car bodies for the Hollywood film industry. He had made a name for himself by designing the hugely successful La Salle for Cadillac in 1927. Having been invited to join the GM team as designer-in-chief, he went on to become a vice-president of the company.

The Y-Job was Earl's first design for GM. Based on a stretched version of a standard Buick chassis, it was a streamlined two-seater sports car with numerous trend-setting features: electric windows, power-operated hidden headlamps and recessed tail lights; power-operated soft top; wraparound bumpers, flush door handles and seamless hood and fenders; the horizontal grille that was to become such a distinctive feature of Buick autos. After the Y-Job had been shown around America to widespread acclaim, Earl used it as his own daily car and could regularly be seen driving it through the streets of Detroit.

The Buick Y-Job is a truly iconic 20th century American design. It is on display at GM's Design Centre in Warren, Michigan as part of the GM heritage collection.

The first-ever concept car is as handsome today as it was back in the late 1930s.

Alfa Romeo BAT Series

By the early 1950s the frenetic developments in rocketry and aeronautical engineering were beginning to be absorbed by the front runners in motor sport and car design. Alfa Romeo teamed up with the specialist Italian design house of Bertone with the single aim of exploring the lowest possible drag coefficient for a functioning car. Their mind-meld produced a series of studies in innovative aerodynamics, presented each year from 1953 to 1955 at the Turin Motor Show, and called BAT (for 'Berlinetta Aerodinamica Tecnica') 5, BAT 7 and BAT 9. 'Unique' is too small a word for them. The BAT series sprang from fevered imaginations freed (from the seriousness of the war years and the grim resurrection of peace) to mix comic book juvenilia with the wonders of pure, technical curiosity.

BAT 5 came first, broke every rule of car design and caused the biggest sensation. From the frontal torpedos grouped to minimize disruptive airflow, the super-lightweight shell integrated the passenger compartment in a single, streamlined sweep – the side windows were angled at 45 degrees to the body – forming a large teardrop-shape ending in a rear windscreen set lengthwise and divided by a slim raised pillar, and enclosed by two fins that tapered both inwards and upwards with a slight curl. Everyone loved that the 'BAT' looked like a bat with folded wings.

It worked (so did BAT 7 & 9). With spats over the wheels, the design created few air vortices: though completely enclosing its Alfa 1900 chassis, BAT 5 sped up to 115 mph (185 km/h) on its standard, 100 horsepower engine. BAT 7 had fancier wings, looked part submarine and aircraft as well as car, and went faster. The BAT series was a triumphant vindication of the aesthetic of elegance as a valuable technical tool and an engineering inspiration.

The BAT was not your normal supercool Italian design number.

COUNTRY OF ORIGIN:
Italy
FIRST MANUFACTURED:
1953
ENGINE:
1,975 cc Cast-iron Straight Four w/ Light Alloy Head
PERFORMANCE:
Top speed of 115 mph (185 km/h)
YOU SHOULD KNOW:
The original three BAT cars appear regularly at Motor Shows. In 2008, a new model called 'BAT 11' was shown in Geneva. It is based on the Alfa Romeo 8C Competizione; but though styled – unmistakably – in a thoroughly modern take on the classic 1950s BAT cars, 'BAT 11' is a statement of retro aesthetics more than a demonstration of technical enquiry.

Oldsmobile Golden Rocket

COUNTRY OF ORIGIN:
USA
FIRST MANUFACTURED:
1956
ENGINE:
5.3 l (324 cid) V8
PERFORMANCE:
N/A
YOU SHOULD KNOW:
The Golden Rocket Concept car
starred in several Motorama
travelling shows. Its 'wow!' factor
tempted General Motors into naming
a 1957 production series the Golden
Rocket 88, but these cars, though a
close relative, looked nothing like the
concept original. The only surviving
concept model changed hands for
$3.24 million.

General Motors was more circumspect with its concept cars than its 1950s competitors. It had evolved an annual show called the General Motors Motorama which travelled from city to city giving potential customers a close look at the company's latest models. Each year, the star of the show was a one-off machine that incorporated the most extreme thinking of the designers, stylists and engineers who created the production models that people actually bought and drove. The difference was that all GM's concept cars, up there on the platform amid the 'ooohs' and 'aaahs' and the glitzy lighting, were equally driveable. Behind the glamorous presentation and the 'shocking' extremity of design was a carefully graded marketing exercise which might, as the Corvette had already proved, take fire in the public imagination, and create a whole new production success.

The Oldsmobile Golden Rocket Concept car of 1956 typified General Motors' ability to dramatize stylistic and technical innovation. It looked like an aggressive shark flanked by the fuselages of two fighter planes, with their chrome propeller cones as bumpers (pretty but ineffective, since the 'shark' nose protruded by several inches in the middle). With its wraparound front and split rear windows tapering into a teardrop, and arrow-flight fins curling slightly outwards above the slimmed sweep of the cigar-tube rear profile, the all-golden car really did suggest a rocket. It embodied the future. Open a door, and a roof panel raised automatically, the seat rose three inches and swivelled outwards, and the steering wheel tilted for better access. The Golden Rocket was full of ergonomic and technical innovations which influenced whole generations of production vehicles. It was everything a concept car should be – sacrificing safety considerations (the car would never be made in this form) for a glimpse of attainable desire. A beautiful and clever car.

The Golden Rocket from Olds was a heady combination of brains and good looks.

Ford Nucleon

The Big Three of 1950s Detroit car makers all had elite design teams charged with transforming half-baked dreams into roadgoing realities. Ford's Nucleon seized the high ground of the Atomic Age by suggesting a brave new world in which the internal combustion engine was replaced by a small nuclear reactor!

The power plant was suspended between heavy load-bearing booms, very slightly forward from the rear axle; and to compensate for its weight, the passenger compartment was cantilevered far ahead of the front axle. Visually, the Nucleon resembled a pick-up truck with shark fins; and with an otherwise fairly conventional, but entire family car, somehow growing out of the front where only the driver's cab should be. No amount of futuristically smooth styling could integrate the Nucleon's hybrid components.

Ford's designers envisaged a genuine scientific pedigree for the Nucleon and its claim to travel 5,000 miles on a single charge, but unwittingly acknowledged their own economy with the truth by stressing how the Nucleon was designed to keep passengers as far from anything radioactive as possible. In fact they had no real notion of how nuclear energy could be harnessed in any way applicable to a car, and the Nucleon remained a scale model of a theory about an idea.

As the New York Times much later remarked, it was one of a number of concept cars that 'each deserves credit for charging full-throttle down an amusing blind alley'. The Nucleon never got any throttle at all. It was actually one of the great conceptual 'rollers' – so called because they had to be rolled onto the stage, lacking any means of self-propulsion. Half a century later, you still wonder 'what if?'.

Yes, really – Ford thought it might be possible to produce a car driven by a nuclear reactor.

COUNTRY OF ORIGIN:
USA
FIRST MANUFACTURED:
1958
ENGINE:
Power capsule with radioactive core (different 'sizes' were 'designed' to be interchangeable according to varying demands of performance or distance to be travelled)
PERFORMANCE:
N/A
YOU SHOULD KNOW:
In 1958, nuclear power was pregnant with possibility. There was every reason to think the Nucleon might presage an automotive revolution; and every reason to fear that possibility. At least the Nucleon contributed to the design of the DeLorean-based time machine featured in the film *Back To The Future*.

Chevrolet Corvair Monza GT

COUNTRY OF ORIGIN:
USA
FIRST MANUFACTURED:
1962
ENGINE:
2.4 l (145 cid) Flat-Six
(with 'two carburettor lay-out',
a unique feature)
PERFORMANCE:
Top speed of 115 mph (185 km/h);
0-60 mph (97 km/h) in 10.8 secs
YOU SHOULD KNOW:
The Corvair Monza GT appeared at
many motor shows during 1963 with
its fellow concept cars, the
convertibles Monza SS (Sebring
Spyder) of 1961, and Monza SS
(Super Spyder) of 1962. Neither
convertible was anything like so
gorgeous or as technically advanced
as the Monza GT, which rather lost
out by the association.

By 1962 General Motors had refined its notion of a concept car. Far from encouraging designs rooted in whimsy or science fiction, it restricted imaginative research to the realms of practical possibility. Cars could still be bizarre or weird or even fabulous, so long as every gizmo, attachment, style feature or technical surprise had a point.

Chevrolet's Corvair Monza GT was certainly extraordinary, and as dramatic as it was beautiful. It was also the most advanced Corvair ever made. By 1962, the Corvair was already a successful production model, a compact sports coupe of thrilling power but tricky handling, thanks to its rear-mounted engine. It provided GM with the perfect raw material with which to persuade Larry Shinoda, the designer revered for creating the Sting Ray Corvette, to demonstrate his lateral thinking and flair for styling.

Shinoda came up with a pocket-sized thunderclap. He shortened the standard Corvair wheelbase, and rotated the Monza GT's rear engine through 180 degrees to sit just forward of the rear axle. The weight redistribution transformed the handling problems of the standard Corvair –

and that in turn enabled Shinoda to take full advantage of the Monza GT's aerodynamic potential. The headlights were hidden behind 'clam shell' lids in the sleek, low-slung, bumperless silver bullet; and the effortless billow of the streamlining that integrated the wheel arches and canopy into a single line was undisturbed by conventional interruptions like doors. For access, the entire canopy swept up and forward on front hinges, and the engine cover did the same from rear hinges.

Even the Corvair Monza GT's brochure managed to look pretty exciting.

The Corvair Monza GT was mean and lean enough to make its debut (at Elkhart Lake) in an actual race. It sprang into life fully-formed, beautiful and successful. The mystery is that it remained just a wonderful concept.

Holden Hurricane

The sharp-pointed Hurricane was a revolutionary shape from the land of kangeroos and koalas.

Typically forthright, the Australian Holden car company announced the Holden Hurricane of 1969 as 'Tomorrow's Holden'. It was the new Research and Development team's first creation, and it was conceived to show off and demonstrate the 'design trends, propulsion systems and other long range developments' of which Australia itself was capable. In 1969, the car was a catalogue of yesterday's wish-list made manifest so you could (just) imagine today what you might be driving tomorrow. Holden's timing was perfect, and the Holden Hurricane had a lot to say.

It was an aerodynamic wedge of pure speed, powered by the first fully-Australian designed and built V8 engine. Directly as a result of this first appearance, the 4.1 litre Holden V8 went into production and sold a million cars in five years. The Hurricane had no doors: the entire, wraparound glass canopy lifted up and forwards, the steering wheel tilted, and the twin 'astronaut' seats rose up and pivoted for easy access, all at the touch of a single button. Once inside, the driver and passenger were lowered to a semi-reclining position, and the car wouldn't even start until the canopy was locked down and the seat-belts fastened. Safety innovations included foam-padded interior trim and foam-lined fuel tank, integral headrests, pedals adjustable to the driver's height, and a fire warning system. Other features were pure science fiction, like the automatic station-seeking radio, the 'Pathfinder' automatic steering indicator, the 'Comfortron' automatic temperature control and air conditioning, and wide-angle, rearward-looking camera connected to a dashboard console (instead of a rear mirror). The dashboard itself was crowded with electronic digital displays to monitor the gizmos – most people had never seen one before, let alone in a car.

The Holden Hurricane teased its awestruck admirers in 1969 – but it really was a glimpse of the future.

COUNTRY OF ORIGIN:
Australia
FIRST MANUFACTURED:
1969
ENGINE:
4,147 cc V8
PERFORMANCE:
N/A
YOU SHOULD KNOW:
Among professional designers, the Holden Hurricane's super-low slung, wedge shape was its most revolutionary feature – and you can see it echoed in the Bertone Stratos Concept car of 1970, Ferrari's 1970 512S Berlinetta Speciale, and the 1972 Maserati Boomerang.

*A car from the future,
for the future, in the past.*

Ferrari Modulo Pininfarina

COUNTRY OF ORIGIN:
Italy
FIRST MANUFACTURED:
1970
ENGINE:
4,994 cc V12
PERFORMANCE:
Top speed estimated at 224 mph
(360 km/h)
YOU SHOULD KNOW:
Having conceived the Modulo as a
'white' car, Paolo Martin was
(allegedly) very upset to discover that
the prototype shown at Geneva was
painted black. It was repainted in
white for both Turin and Osaka in
1970, by which time it was the star
of every show at which it appeared,
and had overcome Pininfarina's
strongly expressed fear of being
considered 'controversial'.

Two elements of advanced car design seldom reach the official
histories – the bush telegraph that enables designers to share their
thinking, and the strong human emotions that so often fuel the
greatest inspiration. Paolo Martin was working on the Rolls-Royce
Camargue (the only Rolls-Royce to be designed in Italy) in 1968
when he got his 'Eureka' moment for a modular racing design more
futuristic and extreme than anything ever produced, even by his
employer the legendary Pininfarina. Neither his sketches nor his
crudely-sawn polystyrene model gained credence until early 1970,
when news spread of a fantastic Australian prototype that appeared
to be based on similar principles. Early in 1970, Ferrari had sought
homologation for its 512S race car. Out of the blue, Martin was
asked to adapt his modular ideas to the Ferrari 512S mechanicals,
using one of the spare chassis. Pininfarina sanctioned it with
misgivings, and it was unveiled at the Geneva Motor Show.

The Ferrari Modulo Pininfarina worked, but was never intended
to function on the road. Its geometry had the unholy beauty of

potential function raised to abstract art form. From every angle it defied convention, like a belated, three-dimensional chapter in the development of Italian Futurism. The front canopy slid up and forward for access to a cabin in which the sunken seats occupied the centre, and either side a black sphere contained all the control buttons driver or passenger needed (Paolo Martin smuggled two bowling balls into the Pininfarina studio to work out the details). The cutaway panels in the demi-monocoque shell showed how the chassis and wheels were completely enclosed: powered up, it could drive only in a straight line.

It might as well have flown. As a conceptual prototype, it was a glorious success, an earthbound spacecraft that won 22 International Design awards.

Lancia Megagamma

Minivans or MPVs erupted onto the scene in the 1980s. But where did the idea come from? And which was the first? The Nissan Prairie? Renault's Espace? The Chrysler Voyager?

The answer is: none of the above. It was the Lancia Megagamma, unveiled at the Turin Motor Show in 1978 and made by Italdesign under legendary master Giorgetto Giugiaro. As usual, Giugiaro created a trend-setting design that combined outstanding elegance with utter practicality – the Megagamma is a delight to the eye. On first seeing it, Fiat's boss Umberto Agnelli commented: 'Nice car. All that's required is the courage to produce it'. But, to Giugiaro's chagrin, the courage was lacking and Fiat let a great commercial opportunity slip from its grasp; the Megagamma was never put into production.

At a time when cars were being judged by their length, Giugiaro's design for a family vehicle was a breath of fresh air. It was based on the same platform as the Lancia Gamma, a flagship executive car introduced in 1976 (which, although not particularly successful at the time, has since become a collector's piece). To create extra room, Giugiaro stretched the car upwards instead of longways, enabling the occupants to engage in one-upmanship through superior height rather than by hogging extra road space – thus contributing to improved traffic flow.

Although the Megagamma doesn't look at all unusual now, at the time it was revolutionary – and hugely influential, sparking off a trend for space vehicles that continues to this day. And, although Giugiaro was disappointed, he was undeterred: he knew his idea was a good one, and he went on to design many more space-saving multi-use vehicles – not least the Maserati Buran, a concept MPV of 2000.

COUNTRY OF ORIGIN:
Italy
FIRST MANUFACTURED:
1978
ENGINE:
2,484 cc Flat Four
PERFORMANCE:
N/A
YOU SHOULD KNOW:
Giorgetto Giugiaro won an award as 'Car Designer of the Century' in 1999. His cars include the BMW M1, Lotus Esprit, VW Scirocco, Maserati Bora, Lancia Delta, De Tomaso Mangusta and Alfa Romeo Brera, to name but a few.

Aston Martin Bulldog

COUNTRY OF ORIGIN:
UK
FIRST MANUFACTURED:
1980
ENGINE:
5,341 cc Twin-Turbo DOHC V8
PERFORMANCE:
Top speed of 191 mph (307 km/h);
0-60mph (97 km/h) in 5.2 secs
YOU SHOULD KNOW:
Within the Aston Martin factory,
the Bulldog was known by the
code name K-9, after Dr Who's
robotic dog.

When the Bulldog was unveiled in early 1980, it was intended as the first of a limited-edition run of 25, but it turned out to be so far-fetched that it never made it into production. Styled by William Towns, of Lagonda fame, the Bulldog takes the concept of wedge-shaped design onto a whole new plane.

The Bulldog was designed to symbolize Aston Martin's intentions for the future, technically as well as aesthetically. On its test drive, it reached 191 mph (307 km/h), a remarkable feat at the time. Even more remarkably, it was theoretically capable of 237 mph (381 km/h), its twin-turbo V8 engine delivering around 650 bhp. The split-rim alloy wheels had blades around the edges which, though they may have looked as if they were intended for fending off bad guys in James Bond-style car chases, in fact fulfilled the function of directing cool air to the brakes in order to ensure reliability even at stratospheric speeds. The Bulldog also included the same innovative LED technology used in the Lagonda, and a rear view delivered via a TV monitor. It remains Aston Martin's only mid-engine car to date.

At the time, it was rumoured that the Bulldog project had been underwritten by a middle-eastern sheikh who then backed out of buying it. The car ended up in auction and was sold to a wealthy business tycoon from the Emirates. Eventually, it turned up in the USA but now resides back in the UK. The Bulldog is unlikely ever to be surpassed as Aston Martin's most bizarre creation. With its stunted height of just 110 cm (43 in), disproportionate width, massive power-operated gullwing doors and strange submerged headlights, it stands in the annals of automotive history as a madcap masterpiece from another dimension.

Unfortunately this particular British Bulldog never quite made it off the leash.

Briggs & Stratton Hybrid

Give a sharp lawn-mower manufacturer a grant to come up with alternative ideas . . . and what do you get?

The concept of a hybrid car emerged from an unexpected source, not a car manufacturer at all but a 100 year-old company called Briggs & Stratton that makes air-cooled engines for outdoor power equipment – everything from lawn mowers to go karts.

In the mid-1970s, concerned by the fuel crisis as well as ever-increasing pollution, the US government began to allocate generous grants for research into alternative forms of power. With its eye on the main chance, Briggs & Stratton was only too happy to oblige; it had a low-power twin-cylinder engine it wanted to market, and if it could become a mass-supplier to the car industry it was onto a winner.

Briggs & Stratton came up with an idea for a car with two power sources – its new little 18 hp twin-cylinder engine, which could be fuelled by either gasoline or ethanol, combined with an 8 hp battery-powered electric motor in what is now known as a 'parallel hybrid' configuration. Sounds almost old-hat today. And in fact, it was then too. The idea harks back to the early days of motoring at the beginning of the 20th century, but there had been no incentive to develop it in an era of apparently inexhaustible oil supply.

The Hybrid was designed to be a non-polluting, cheap-to-run town car. It was surprisingly stylish considering its bizarre platform – a three-axle (six-wheel) chassis borrowed from an electric van. Two sets of rear wheels were needed to support the weight of a pack of twelve batteries mounted over the rear axle – a weight that was compensated for by a lightweight fibreglass body.

But there were other practical problems that remained unresolved: the batteries took all night to recharge and could only power the electric motor for about 30 miles before going flat. And 30 years later . . .

COUNTRY OF ORIGIN:
USA
FIRST MANUFACTURED:
1980
ENGINE:
Air-cooled 2 cylinder + battery-powered electric motor
PERFORMANCE:
Single engine mode – top speed of 50 mph (80 km/h)
Dual engine mode – top speed of 68 mph (109 km/h)
YOU SHOULD KNOW:
Briggs & Stratton made their first foray into the car business in 1920, producing the cheapest auto ever: the Briggs & Stratton Flyer, costing under $50 (presently on sale for $23,500). The 1980 Briggs & Stratton Hybrid, described by *Car and Driver* magazine as 'what you get when you mate a garden tractor with a golf cart', can be seen in the company museum in Milwaukee, Wisconsin.

Italdesign Aztec

COUNTRY OF ORIGIN:
Italy
FIRST MANUFACTURED:
1988
ENGINE:
2,226 cc Straight Five
PERFORMANCE:
Top speed of 150 mph (241 km/h)
YOU SHOULD KNOW:
The Aztec wasn't Italdesign's only
sensational concept car at the 1988
Turin Motor Show – the company had
also created the Aspid, a coupe
version of the Aztec, and the
futuristic Asgard people carrier.

Sometimes a concept car is left as just that – a stunning example of what can be achieved by the best creative minds in the automobile industry and a headline-grabber for its creator. At other times, the concept car is a teaser ahead of a planned production run, allowing excitement to build and giving the manufacturer time to refine raw promise into a polished road car.

The two-door Italdesign Aztec supercar was both, and neither. For it first appeared at the Turin Motor Show in 1988 as the perfect concept car, showcasing the design excellence of the great Giorgetto Giugiaro, with the intention that selected features might be incorporated into future road cars. But a Japanese company liked the car so much that it commissioned a short production run. This was undertaken by building a bodied chassis in Italy, after which a tuned Audi 2.2 litre engine was transversely mounted behind the cabin by German performance specialist MTM, driving an all-wheel drive system based on Lancia Delta components.

The unexpected feature of the Aztec was that there were two cockpits that required the driver and passenger to sit separately and communicate via headsets. The interiors were well appointed with a set of instruments and controls for each occupant. The car had an unusual wedge-shaped design – though clearly efficient aerodynamically, it had a smooth, unadorned front, straight sides with external control panels and a squarish back end complete with an unusual raised spoiler. Access to cockpits was by side doors with glass panels and fold-up hatches, removable for open-top motoring.

It is easy to see why this bold and daring concept car appealed to the Japanese, who love anything that pushes the boundaries of technology, design and imagination. The Italdesign Aztec certainly did all of that . . . and more.

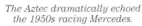
The Aztec dramatically echoed the 1950s racing Mercedes.

Ford GT90

Every manufacturer of state-of-the-art sports cars hopes people might think it of their latest flyer – but in 1995 Ford actually said it about theirs. Yes, according to the proud producer the Ford GT90 was 'the world's mightiest supercar'. No question. Mind you, nobody was able to test that bold claim, because this was a concept car never intended for Main Street. Admittedly, the geometric two-seater unveiled at the Detroit Motor Show looked the part. It had to, jumping aboard a wagon that all manufacturers suddenly wanted to ride – stardom in burgeoning electronic road-racer games like *Gran Turismo* and *Need for Speed*.

This sensational car was all glass and angles, looking like a hexagon in profile – albeit with just a hint of curvature to the cabin top and long engine cover. This was the ultimate expression of Ford's 'New Edge' design style, and the GT90's rationale was at least in part to publicize a design philosophy that would soon be rolled out in assorted road cars built in Ford's key markets.

Although very different, the GT90 built on the proud heritage of the 1960s GT40, though that was both a successful racing car and fearsome road car. There's no doubt that the GT90 could have followed a similar path if Ford had so decided. It had a 6 litre V12 created from two Lincoln V8s by chopping a pair of cylinders off each one before welding the result together. Four Garrett turbochargers boosted output past the 700 bhp mark. This growling power plant went into a honeycomb-section aluminium monocoque structure clad in carbon-fibre panels. The five-speed manual gearbox and independent double-wishbone suspension came from the Jaguar XJ220, then a Ford stablemate.

Was this special concept car indeed 'the world's mightiest supercar'? Perhaps not, but it was an impressive contender.

COUNTRY OF ORIGIN:
USA
FIRST MANUFACTURED:
1995
ENGINE:
5.9 l (362 cid) V12 Quad Turbo
PERFORMANCE:
Top speed of 235 mph (378 km/h);
0-60 mph (97 km/h) in 3.1 secs
YOU SHOULD KNOW:
The GT90's exhausts ran so hot that the bodywork had to be protected from heat damage by ceramic tiles similar to those used in insulating the Space Shuttle during fiery re-entry.

Ford's New Edge concept was intended for New Age motorists.

Mercedes F 300 Life-Jet

COUNTRY OF ORIGIN:
Germany
FIRST MANUFACTURED:
1997
ENGINE:
1,598 cc Straight Four
PERFORMANCE:
Top speed of 131 mph (211 km/h);
0-60 mph (97 km/h) in 7.5 secs
YOU SHOULD KNOW:
The F 300 Life-Jet's added stability
enabled it to corner at speeds
normally attainable only by the most
experienced motorcyclists, with the
centrifugal force that glues riders to
bikes ensuring that occupants of the
Life-Jet did not have to cling on when
cornering fast, but were moulded
into the car.

Sadly, the Life-Jet never took off.

One of the most interesting, provocative and exciting concept cars ever
built was a Mercedes – but not some awesome supercar that could
outrun a bullet and hurtle towards the speed of sound in second gear.
No indeed. For the F 300 Life-Jet was one of the best fun drives ever,
combining the thrilling cornering dynamics of a high-powered motorcycle
with the safety, weather protection and zip of a small sports car.

Shown at the Frankfurt Motor Show in 1997, this mould-breaking
three-wheel concept car was the fruit of a research project into active-tilt
systems (as used by the fastest modern trains). The front wheels of this
sporty in-line two-seater leaned into corners, tilting the cabin to a
maximum angle of 30°. The amount of tilt was determined by an
electronic control system that calculated optimum lean and passed
command information to a hydraulic cylinder that pushed the
appropriate spring-loaded strut outwards to achieve the desired result.
At night, a headlamp unit turned with the car to provide brilliant
illumination.

The streamlined silver aluminium body of the Life-Jet was unlike anything seen before. The cabin had a scissor door that folded forwards for the driver and rear-hinged passenger door on the opposite side. The removable roof could be stored in the back. Performance was more than impressive, with a compact 1.6 litre engine borrowed from the Mercedes-Benz A-class situated behind the passenger seat, delivering sports-car performance and miserly fuel consumption.

Had it gone into production, this fabulous driving machine would surely have sold well around the world. Sadly, Mercedes ignored many requests to turn concept into reality, though perhaps increasing interest in hybrid technology and electric locomotion may yet see a dramatic return for the F 300 Life-Jet, that looks as good today as it did back in 1997.

Bentley Hunaudières

No sooner had Volkswagen acquired Bentley than the German company made it clear that its new prize had a glamorous future in store. The 1999 Geneva Motor Show was chosen for the first appearance of a new Bentley concept car, the Hunaudières. This impressive two-door mid-engined coupe was named after the famous straight that forms part of France's Circuit de la Sarthe, which hosts the Le Mans 24 endurance race. The Ligne Droite de Hunaudières is generally known as the Mulsanne Straight in English, and it was here that prewar 'Bentley Boys' achieved lasting sporting glory.

The astonishing Hunaudières was quite unlike any Bentley seen before (or since) but after seeing it the automobile world certainly woke up swiftly to the fact that nothing would ever be the same again for the iconic British marque. About all that anyone familiar with Bentleys of old recognized about the Hunaudières was the famous grille. Otherwise it looked more like an Italian supercar than a traditional grand tourer – but perhaps that was precisely the point Volkswagen wanted to make with this mighty machine. The marker was down – as of then, Bentley was set to return to its stylish high-performance roots, suitably modernized for the 21st century.

The Hunaudières had a 64 valve W16 engine and there were rumours that VW harboured Le Mans ambitions that this new-look Bentley racer could pursue, though in the event nothing came of it. A few months after the debut of the Hunaudières the Bugatti Veyron concept car was rolled out in Tokyo . . . and knowledgeable observers quickly noted the similarities between the two concept cars. It wasn't hard – both speedsters shared a mighty similar profile, as both had been influenced by VW design guru Hartmut Warkuss.

COUNTRY OF ORIGIN:
UK
FIRST MANUFACTURED:
1999
ENGINE:
8,007 cc W16
PERFORMANCE:
Top speed of 220 mph (354 km/h); 0-60 mph (97 km/h) in 4 secs
YOU SHOULD KNOW:
Was it a coin toss? The Hunaudières made a big splash but was never produced. The Veyron made a big splash and was produced, hitting the headlines as the world's fastest road car. But at least the Hunaudières made a contribution in the form of the Veyron's W16 engine and internal design.

This big and bold Cadillac nearly made it from concept to street – but not quite.

Cadillac Sixteen

It almost (but didn't quite) make it to the street. The Cadillac Sixteen was a prototype that test-bedded General Motors' vast new 32-valve V16 engine, which was very clever. It measured up at a massive 13.6 litres, but could cruise happily on four cylinders, overtake briskly on eight and only unleash the awesome power of all 16 when the pedal was jabbed to the metal (or hand-woven silk carpet, in the case of the Sixteen). This ingenious arrangement allowed the big concept car to return respectable fuel consumption figures, with the help of four-speed electronically controlled transmission.

The four-door Sixteen had a wonderfully clean profile. The long bonnet gave the car a slightly racy look without diminishing its gravitas. This had centre-hinged panels that enabled the engine to be accessed from either side. Gently flared arches were designed to display big 'n' beautiful polished aluminium wheels. The low cabin was without pillars and had a transparent roof. The back end was short and neat, with both the trunk and grille sharing a shallow triangle design note.

COUNTRY OF ORIGIN:
USA
FIRST MANUFACTURED:
2003
ENGINE:
13.6 l (830 cid) V16
PERFORMANCE:
N/A
YOU SHOULD KNOW:
Although the Sixteen never made it to the production line, elements from this stylish prototype were used in subsequent models, notably the second-generation Cadillac CTS that appeared in 2008, and a scaled-down version of the Sixteen with a V8 or V12 is rumoured to be in the pipeline.

Cadillac's design team really went to town on the interior, determined to create a plush evocation of the luxurious trim that characterized the coachbuilt Fleetwoods of the 1930s. The two-tone interior contrasted hand-stitched Tuscan leather upholstery with burr-walnut fascia, cappings and centre console, whilst the driver had a backless seat and two rear-seat passengers each had a super-comfortable chair, one of which extended as a full-length recliner on demand, filling space that would have been occupied by a front passenger seat. No detail had been overlooked and the interior finish couldn't have been bettered.

Would there have been enough wealthy customers with discerning taste to make this opulent super-sedan a commercial success? For better or worse, we'll never know.

Rinspeed Splash

If you've got it, flash it – that's the philosophy of Swiss automotive group Rinspeed, noted for customizing modern high-performance cars and restoring classics of an older vintage. Every year, Rinspeed aims to design a concept car for the Geneva Motor Show to showcase considerable design and engineering talents.

One such was the Rinspeed Splash, the eye-catching effort in 2004. This was a true one-off concept vehicle. At first glance it appeared to be an attractive topless blue two-seater roadster (albeit with a quirky rear spoiler and strange front aerofoils) that would be perfect for a summer spin along country roads. But wait . . . as the name suggests, the Rinspeed Splash was also a boat.

As soon as it hit the water a rear panel flipped up to reveal a marine Z-drive fitted with a three-bladed propeller in the horizontal rest position. As the Splash reached a depth of around a metre, the driver could switch power from rear wheels to propeller, creating a very effective speedboat that was quite capable of towing a water skier, or simply tearing about allowing the Splash's occupants to enjoy the wind in their hair and spray in their faces. But wait . . . it was also a plane.

Well, not actually a plane, though to be fair the Splash could definitely fly. A sophisticated hydrofoil system allowed the cabin to lift off the water, with that quirky rear spoiler rotating through 180° and two V-shaped hydrofoils unfolding from the Splash's sides. Thus equipped, this unique vehicle lifted its wheels clear of the water and sped along at high speed.

The Splash was powered by a turbocharged 750 cc two-cylinder motor powered by natural gas, maintaining Rinspeed's interest in the latest eco-friendly technology.

COUNTRY OF ORIGIN:
Switzerland
FIRST MANUFACTURED:
2004
ENGINE:
750 cc Twin Cylinder
PERFORMANCE:
Top speed of 120 mph (193 km/h) on land, 45 knots on water; 0-60 mph (97 km/h) in 5.7 secs (on land)
YOU SHOULD KNOW:
Also on the land/water theme, Rinspeed's 2008 sQuba was an amazing tribute to the famous Lotus Esprit in *The Spy Who Loved Me*, that conveyed James Bond and his beautiful companion to safety after turning into a submersible. The sQuba, too, could 'fly' underwater – based on a Lotus Elise, it did require the occupants to wear aqualungs.

Volvo YCC

COUNTRY OF ORIGIN:
Sweden
FIRST MANUFACTURED:
2004
ENGINE:
5-cylinder PZE (Partial Zero
Emissions)
PERFORMANCE:
N/A
YOU SHOULD KNOW:
When the YCC was unveiled at
Geneva in 2004, the media went
wild. Write-ups filled more than
1.4 column miles (2.3 column km).
The YCC and its design team went
on to win numerous awards.

What sort of car would a woman design? This was not just a matter of passing curiosity to Volvo – more than half its US buyers are women and in Europe female sales have also been growing steadily. In order to find out, Volvo let loose not just one woman but an entire design team of them to see what they would come up with. And, surprise surprise! It turns out that women are after exactly the same things as men – performance, prestige and style. And then some extra: storage space, easy parking, excellent visibility, easy to get in and out.

Your Concept Car is a distinctly unfeminine four-seater hybrid-engined coupe with muscular styling, massive alloy wheels and sweeping, glass fastback roof. And even the advanced ergonomics and plethora of high-tech extras are gender neutral. It is the roomy interior which shows the female influence – more of an airy living-room than a cockpit, with interchangeable seat covers and carpets in a variety of fabrics, notched head rests to accommodate back hair-dos and clever flip-up theatre-style rear seats for extra space.

The YCC is a great car . . . and yet, there is something not quite right about it. It takes a while to realize – there's no bonnet! Who needs one? The combined forces of computer technology and your Volvo service station will provide. Once a year, trained mechanics will lift up the entire front section of the car to perform a service and oil change.

For any petrolhead worth his or her salt, the thought of being denied access to their car's innards is too abhorrent even to contemplate. Fortunately, Volvo have no intention of producing the YCC. Rather, it was simply a project for generating new ideas, many of which are likely to be incorporated into production models in the future.

Some folk used to think Scandanavians didn't do concept cars, but now . . .

Peugeot Moovie

It was nothing to do with Hollywood films, or cows, or films featuring cows. No, the Moovie was the winner of the Peugeot Design Competition in 2005 and appeared out of left field like some renegade escape pod from a passing spaceship. Created by Portuguese designer André Costa, this was slick personal city transport unlike anything that had previously been seen outside the pages of a science fiction comic.

No engine or wheels, so the Moovie remained fairly static.

Sitting on concealed wheels and appearing to hug the ground, the Moovie looked like a large polycarbonate-glazed comma, with a sweeping curved front framed in chrome. Inside was a pair of simple moulded seats behind a control console with a stylish single-spoke steering wheel and two instrument pods, all atop a central pillar. Beside each seat was a large circular viewport framed in blue, with a proud Peugeot lion affixed in the centre. The Moovie's circular sides doubled as access doors, hinging forwards. The interior was finished in two contrasting shades of yellow.

Peugeot's objective was never to find a workable car, but rather to see what the imagination of the world's most creative wannabe (and established) automotive designers might produce when asked to create the Peugeot of the future they would most like to drive, with the shackles of practicality thrown off. But that's not to say that the winning concept remained unrealized, for the grand prize was a full-scale model lovingly overseen by the Peugeot Style Centre and built over a three-month period to the exacting standards used to create the company's concepts cars.

And indeed it was at the Frankfurt Motor Show that the Moovie was shown to general admiration, whilst Peugeot gleaned maximum publicity from their design comp's winning entry by sanctioning a full production run . . . of 1/43 scale models.

COUNTRY OF ORIGIN:
France
FIRST MANUFACTURED:
2005
ENGINE:
N/A
PERFORMANCE:
N/A
YOU SHOULD KNOW:
The Moovie had to be pretty special, after coming out on top in a design competition that attracted 3,800 entries from no fewer than 107 countries, with 2,600 designers testing their skills against the strong international field.

Holden EFIJY

Since swaggering onto the scene at the Australian International
Motor Show in 2005, muscles rippling, the Holden EFIJY concept
car has travelled the world attracting admirers eveywhere. This
wildly exaggerated tribute to the 1953 Holden FJ – and American
bathtub styling of the same era – is a spectacular beauty and no
doubt the occasional tear has trickled because this fabulous
machine will never go into production.

The radical EFIJY two-seater pillarless coupe was the long-term
dream of Holden chief designer Richard Ferlazzo. Starting from
modified Chevy Corvette underpinnings from parent General
Motors, a great body was added. This curvaceous Aussie creation
begins with a thrusting brightwork front end and proceeds
rearwards via a bulging bonnet between pontoon wings. The car's
smooth lines then flow over a low cabin with teardrop windows,
swooping down to a dramatic point between twin exhausts. The
bodywork was constructed in reinforced fibreglass after a full-sized
model of the EFIJY had been built.

The retro two-tone interior in leather and wood is sumptuously
fitted, but has touch-screen LCD instrumentation and delightful
details like machined-aluminum pedals. The car sits low to the
ground until the air suspension is activated with a touch of a finger,
at which point the EFIJY rises to normal ride height. The
supercharged 6 litre GM V8 punches out an insane amount of
power, harnessed by four-speed electronically controlled automatic
transmission. When the engine is fired up – and propelling the
EFIJY at speed – the tuned exhausts emit a really great sound. So,
too, does the high-output stereo system housed in the boot.

The EFIJY is everything a concept car should be, showcasing
the creative skills of a talented automotive design team at the top of
its game and making hugely positive waves for the supportive
parent company that let it happen.

COUNTRY OF ORIGIN:
Australia
FIRST MANUFACTURED:
2005
ENGINE:
5,967 CC V8
PERFORMANCE:
N/A
YOU SHOULD KNOW:
Talk about attention to detail – the
ultra-bright LED headlamps are so
powerful that each unit requires a
mini-fan to cool it down . . . even
though the car never has and never
is likely to make an extended
after-dark trip. But that's the point,
for the EFIJY showcases Holden's
meticulous attention to detail.

Saab Aero X

All the best concept cars show themselves at the prestigious Geneva Motor Show, and so it was when Saab presented their brilliant Aero X in 2006. This streamlined coupe was a scene stealer, attracting admiring crowds to the chagrin of Ferrari, whose 599GTB on an adjacent stand had been expected to grab the limelight.

The front-engined Saab Aero X was certainly worthy of attention. It had a stunning supercar shape with an endless bonnet and wraparound windscreen. The assertive nose featured air scoops and complex headlight units with intricate floating layers and bright LEDs. Large, polished-alloy wheels resembled turbofans in jet engines, a theme repeated in the space-age cabin, accessed via a fighter-aircraft-style rear-hinged lifting canopy.

This was an extraordinary engineering feat. First, small side doors popped outwards, then the whole windscreen and roof lifted to provide access to the two-seater cabin. Once in, the outlook was sensational, with nothing to obstruct all-round visibility. Instrumentation in the cleanly designed interior came in the form of data displayed as three-dimensional graphics on acrylic 'clear zones'.

In an equally innovative move, the 2.8 litre 24 valve V6 engine had been modified to run on pure bio-ethanol, though still managing to output 400 bhp. This meant the Aero X was not responsible for any carbon dioxide emissions. The car had all-wheel drive and a manual seven-gear automated sequential transmission controlled by steering-wheel paddles. The unique chassis had inverted springs and dampers at the front, allowing the bonnet to ride as low as possible for maximum aerodynamic efficiency. Power-assisted rack-and-pinion steering and Saab's Active Chassis damping control ensured the smoothest of rides.

There has been talk of Saab producing a scaled-down version of the Aero X, but nothing has yet materialized. However, the car has already contributed style points to new road-going Saabs.

COUNTRY OF ORIGIN:
Sweden
FIRST MANUFACTURED:
2006
ENGINE:
2,792 cc V6
PERFORMANCE:
Top speed of 155 mph (250 km/h); 0-60 mph (97 km/h) in 4.7 secs
YOU SHOULD KNOW:
Management-speak is alive and well and living in Sweden. Said a Saab spokesperson of the possibility of an Aero X or derivative going into production: 'As we move forward with new Saab product we will remain focused on carefully cultivating this brand equity in the context of Scandinavian design values.'

The Aero X's driver had heads-up instrumentation, just like a modern fighter pilot.

Trident Iceni

COUNTRY OF ORIGIN:
UK
FIRST MANUFACTURED:
2006
ENGINE:
6,559 cc V8 Turbodiesel
PERFORMANCE:
Top speed of 200+ mph (322+ km/h);
0-60 mph (97 km/h) in 3.9 secs
YOU SHOULD KNOW:
A racing version of the Trident Iceni
has been campaigned, often painted
green and bearing a BIO-DIESEL
slogan to underline its eco-friendly
credentials (by normal supercar
standards, that is!).

The indomitable spirit of pioneering British automotive excellence is alive and well and living in East Anglia. But all those who nod sagely and say 'ah yes, Lotus' haven't quite got it right, for perhaps the name of Trident may yet be automatically added to that short sentence. The new Trident company, formed in 1999, revived an earlier name from the region, for Trident Cars operated in Suffolk during the 1960s and 1970s.

The new outfit based itself in Norfolk and set about developing an unusual supercar – the Trident Iceni, named for the warlike tribe led by Boudicca that gave the occupying Romans a bloody nose (no symbolism there, then). This two-seater sports car may have had a conventional front mid-engined, rear-wheel drive set-up, but in other respects was quite unlike your average super-sporter.

The Iceni's stainless steel chassis lasts for ever and provides a rigid safety cell. The 6.6 litre Duramax V8 turbodiesel was sourced from General Motors and, like the chassis, could last more or less indefinitely – at least 250,000 miles. The tremendous torque generated by this engine is fully utilized with the help of an innovative eight-speed automatic gearbox located at the rear of the car, controlled by a paddle shift. The Iceni can make one boast that will surely never be topped by another supercar – thanks to Trident technology fuel consumption is a meagre 69 mpg (25 km/l) at a constant 70 mph (113 km/h).

The Iceni looks striking, with the long bonnet, low cabin and short back end typical of modern high-performance coupes. But there are unmistakable hints of traditional British sports-car styling and a quite extraordinary – and attractive – oculight cabin roof. It's a word the Iceni puts in the automotive dictionary with those two transparent blister pods that give the car a unique appearance.

The Iceni – superb looks, innovative engineering and better fuel consumpion than the average small city car.

Chevrolet Volt

This is the Chevy concept car that invites people to guess what its power source might be.

If you had to think up a slogan for a new electric-powered car, what might it be? Chevrolet's answer when promoting the upcoming Chevy Volt was *The Future Is Electrifying*, which is undoubtedly better than What a Shocker!. To be fair, the interesting Volt is not quite at the production stage, so it's too early to know if this one will be a triumph or a tragedy.

What was clearly apparent from the innovative prototype shown at the 2007 North American International Auto Show in Detroit is that General Motors has taken the need to develop eco-friendly personal transport very seriously indeed. Starting from the pioneering work done with the short-run EV1 electric car of the late 1990s, Chevy developed the Volt concept car, a stylish four-door coupe with a curved windscreen, transparent roof and lifting tailgate. Nothing unusual there – just a handsome little car.

The magic was under the skin, where GM's E-Flec (subsequently Voltec) drivetrain is a clever combo system, whereby an electric motor with a plug-in lithium-iron battery pack is supplemented by a generation source. This means the Volt is not a hybrid (which requires two sources of propulsion) but a pure electric vehicle. However, if it strays outside its one-charge comfort zone of 40 mi (64 km), the generator kicks in, supplying electricity direct to the primary motor and recharging the batteries. Regenerative braking also helps with battery-charging duties when the car is being driven. Once home, the Volt can be fully recharged overnight from a household supply. In keeping with green objectives, the generator can run on biodiesel, part-ethanol or pure ethanol.

Chevrolet updated the Volt concept by creating a pre-production version that has more rounded lines. The Volt (Ampera in Europe) was scheduled for launch in late 2010.

COUNTRY OF ORIGIN:
USA
FIRST MANUFACTURED:
2007
ENGINE:
Electric Motor
PERFORMANCE:
Top speed of 120 mph (193 km/h);
0-60 mph (97 km/h) in 8 secs
YOU SHOULD KNOW:
Don't be surprised if the production Volt doesn't glide onto the streets of America quite as soon as planned. The credit crunch makes it look rather expensive even for buyers with an eco-conscience, whilst there is still some doubt as to whether sufficiently efficient lithium-ion batteries are yet available.

This concept sports car powered by hydrogen didn't actually go like a bomb – or go at all.

Honda FC Sport

By definition concept cars are meant to be impressive examples of cutting-edge automobile design that challenge established boundaries in the quest to discover the next step forward. As such, they often grab centre stage at motor shows – none more so than the bizarre Honda FC Sport that became an instant star of the 2008 Los Angeles Auto Show.

This fascinating study in contrasting black and white was more of a design concept than a concept car, as it was not a fully finished driveable vehicle. However, it definitely met the requirement to challenge boundaries, because the FC Sport demonstrated what the first Honda green sports car powered by a hydrogen fuel cell might look like. Thus it was styled around the drivetrain of the Honda FCX Clarity, Honda's fuel-cell saloon car prototype that went on limited trial in 2008.

The funky FC Sport looked like a car of the future, and was deliberately styled to show the possibilities created by the flexible alternative propulsion unit. It had a slanting front end occupied by twin air-scoop apertures that doubled as a front spoiler. Between and above them was a dramatic black shape that resembled nothing so much as a bull's head with elongated horns. The black-tinted cabin glass stretched from front to back, with the rear section revealing a tantalizing glimpse of a fuel-cell stack, electric motor and battery pack occupying the space normally reserved for a powerful petrol engine in the typical mid-engined supercar.

Inside, the cabin was laid out using the McLaren F1's three-seater configuration, with one passenger seat set back on each side of a central driver's station. In an increasingly used system, the whole cockpit canopy hinges upwards from the rear to permit access. Will there ever be a Ferrari like the Honda FC Sport? Probably not.

COUNTRY OF ORIGIN:
Japan
FIRST MANUFACTURED:
2008
ENGINE:
None (dummy electric motor with fuel cell and batteries)
PERFORMANCE:
N/A
YOU SHOULD KNOW:
The Honda FC Sport was actually designed at the company's Advanced Design Studio in Pasadena, California – helping to cement Honda's commitment to and leadership in developing eco-friendly automotive technologies of the future.

Lamborghini Estoque

Everyone blinked twice and looked again and – yes – it really was a Lamborghini. But of course this racy four-door sports saloon concept car was indeed most unlike any previous Lambo. It wowed the Paris Salon d'Automobiles in 2008, showing that the Audi-owned company was definitely thinking outside its traditional box . . . and was on the competitive ball, being aware that both Porsche and Aston Martin were working on high-performance saloons.

However different, there was unmistakable Lamborghini DNA in the long, lean Estoque with its compelling presence, rapacious front end, firm low profile, crouching stance, sharp styling and clean lines. This front-mid-engined car demonstrated the design flair contained within the Centro Stile at Sant'Agata Bolognese. Although the designers put the emphasis on performance, they ensured that the car looked great and could carry four in comfort on a long run, along with their luggage. The luxurious interior with four individual seats was inspired by the limited-edition Lamborghini Reventón with its aircraft-style instrument display.

The Estoque concept car shown in Paris was refined but powerful. It had been fitted with a 5.2 litre V10 from the Gallardo LP560-4, tuned to deliver more torque and less horsepower than the Gallardo. Power was transferred to the tarmac via Lambo's all-wheel drive system linked to a seven-speed, double-clutch sequential gearbox controlled by paddles.

Will the Estoque morph into the third Lamborghini model line, alongside the Murciélago and Gallardo? The general feeling amongst informed petrolheads was affirmative, because the Estoque looked like a seriously good car and rival manufacturers were on the same track. But that was before the credit crunch, evaporation of many a mighty bonus and unwillingness of those who still had piles of cash to be seen spending it extravagantly. Maybe in a year or two?

COUNTRY OF ORIGIN:
Italy
FIRST MANUFACTURED:
2008
ENGINE:
5,204 cc V10
PERFORMANCE:
Top speed of 202 mph (325 km/h); 0-60 mph (97 km/h) in 4.5 secs (both estimated)
YOU SHOULD KNOW:
Inevitably, the Estoque's name is derived from the *corrida de toros* – this time borrowing the Spanish word for the short, sharp sword that is used by the bullfighter to deliver the final, fatal blow to his tormented adversary.

Lamborghini's glimpse of what might be – if the wealthy customers required to justify a production run can be found.

Car jargon can be confusing. Below are some of the more common abbreviations and terms.

Some Common Abbreviations:

ABS	antilock braking system
ATV	all terrain vehicle
AWD/4WD	all-wheel drive (four-wheel drive)
DOHC	*See* OHC
ESC	electronic stability control
EXT	extended cab (four doors on a pickup truck)
FMR	front mid-engine rear wheel drive
FWD	front-wheel drive
GRP	glass-reinforced plastic
GT	gran turismo *(grand tourer: high-performance luxury auto for long-distance driving)*
GTi	gran turismo-injection *(grand tourer with fuel injection engine)*
GTO	gran turismo omologato *(GT car homologated for racing)*
LWB	long wheelbase
MPV	multi-purpose vehicle
NASCAR	National Association for Stock Car Auto Racing
OHC	overhead cam (DOHC = dual OHC *or* twin cam; SOHC = single OHC)
OHV	overhead valve
PZEV	partial zero-emissions vehicle
RMR	rear mid-engine rear-wheel drive
RS	Rally Sport
RWD	rear-wheel drive
SAV	sports activity vehicle *(alternative to SUV, see below)*
SOHC	*See* OHC
SUV	sports utility vehicle *(minivan/truck, usually AWD for on- and off-road driving)*
SWB	short wheelbase

Note on Horsepower

The power that an engine produces is measured in units of horsepower (or 'horses'). Some power is used up by the drivetrain so the actual horsepower available for propulsion is less than the gross power that the engine produces. This net power is known as **b**rake **h**orse**p**ower **(bhp)** although it is often referred to simply as horsepower or hp.

In Europe and Japan, power is measured in **P**ferde**S**tärke ('horse strength' in German) which is also known as metric horsepower or DIN *1 PS/DIN = 0.986 hp.* So *PS/DIN* and *bhp* are nearly equivalent to each other, but not quite.

Note on Engine Displacement (Capacity)

In Europe and Japan, manufacturers normally give displacement data in **c**ubic **c**entimetres **(cc)**. In the USA, it is conventionally given in *litres* or *cubic inches*. Throughout this book the data is given in cc except for cars manufactured in the USA for which it is given in *litres* **(l)** with the equivalent **c**ubic **i**nch **d**isplacement **(cid)** in brackets. *1 cu in =16.387 cc.*

Car Terms:

cabriolet	car with a removable/retractable soft top; convertible; drophead coupe
coupe	two-door car with hard top
crossover	vehicle built on a car platform with characteristics of van or SUV
drivetrain	*See* powertrain
drophead	*See* cabriolet
doors:	
butterfly	slide upwards and move outwards (similar to scissor)
gullwing	hinged at the top to lift upwards
scissor	slide upwards from single fixed hinge at end of windscreen
suicide	hinged at the rear rather than the front (also known as coach doors)
estate car	station wagon; shooting brake
flathead	*See* sidevalve
hardtop	a car design that has no central roof struts (B-pillars)
homologated	certified (or approved) as meeting the standard requirements for a particular class of car when taking part in racing
inline	*See* straight
monocoque	a way of manufacturing a car as an integrated piece (unibody) instead of a body mounted onto a separately built chassis
muscle car	large, fast gas-guzzler with supercharged V8 engine
pickup	truck-like vehicle (either two- or four-door) with open load bed at back
pillars	the struts that hold up the car roof.
A-pillars	struts at either side of front windscreen
B-pillars	centre struts behind the front doors
C-pillars	struts at either side of rear window
pony car	compact performance car of the late 1950s to 1970, inspired by Ford Mustang design
pushrod	an engine with an overhead valve (OHV) design
powertrain	parts of the car that deliver power to the road – engine, transmission, differential, driveshafts, drive wheels; drivetrain
roadster	two-seater convertible sports car
running gear	1. suspension, shock absorbers and steering *or* 2. transmission, driveshaft and wheels
saloon	four-door (family) hardtop car; sedan
sedan	*See* saloon
sidevalve	engine design in which valves are positioned at the side of the combustion chamber instead of at the cylinderhead – hence also known as 'flathead'
straight *or* inline	arrangement of cylinders in an engine. Cylinders are either in a line or a V (with variations such as staggered or W)
supercar	car with high horsepower engine for high speed and fast acceleration
woodie	estate car with a wooden body
ute	Australian utility vehicle *See* pickup

Alamy/Rodolfo Arpia 27; /Bruce Benedict/Transtock Inc. 382-383 main, 405, 505; /Paul Broadbent 56, 149; /Buzz Pictures 178; /Chuck Eckert 86; /Greg Balfour Evans 389; /eVox/Drive Images 392, 493; /Achim Hartmann/MPI/culture-images 491; /Jeremy Hoare 98; /INTERFOTO 6 picture 6, 37, 167; /Darrin Jenkins 421; /Uli Jooss/MPI/culture-images 320; /John Lamm/Transtock Inc. 279; /LH Images 109; /Simon Margetson Travel 114; /John Marian/Transtock Inc. 49, 67 inset 1, 101; /Roland Mühlanger/Imagebroker 47; /Hardy Mutschler/MPI/culture-images 319; /Glenn Paulina/Transtock Inc. 177; /Performance Image 190; /Stan Rohrer 66 inset 3, 76, 187; /Al Satterwhite/Transtock Inc. 257; /Mark Scheuern 53; /Dean Siracusa/Transtock Inc. 138, 422; /Guy Spangenberg/transtock Inc. 497; /Phil Talbot 38, 134, 197, 295, 343, 349, 416; /Jonathan Tennant 111 inset 1, 112; /E. John Thawley III/Transtock Inc. 247; /Trinity Mirror/Mirrorpix 402; /Tom Wood 212, 219, 266 inset 2, 309

Briggs & Stratton Corporation 514 inset 3, 525

Ron Callow 150 bottom left, 150 bottom right, 151 left, 151 right, 217 inset

Corbis/Car Culture 6 picture 2, 152

LAT Photographic 2 left, 2-3 centre, 3 centre, 3 right, 5 picture 1, 5 picture 2, 5 picture 4, 5 picture 5, 5 picture 6, 7, picture 3, 7 picture 5, 7 picture 6, 8-9 main, 8 inset 1, 8 inset 2, 9 inset 1, 9 inset 2, 10, 12, 14, 15, 17, 19, 20, 22, 23, 24, 25, 31, 32, 33, 34, 35, 36, 40, 41, 42, 43, 44, 45, 46, 48, 52, 58, 60, 61, 62, 63, 64, 65, 66 inset 1, 66 inset 2, 67 inset 2, 68, 69, 70, 71, 77, 78, 79, 80, 81, 83, 84, 85, 87, 88, 89, 90, 91, 92, 93, 94, 95, 97, 99, 100, 104, 106, 108, 110 inset 2, 110 inset 3, 113, 115, 118-119, 121, 122, 124, 125, 126, 129, 130, 140, 141, 144, 150, 153, 155, 156, 157, 160, 161, 162, 163, 164, 168, 170 inset 2, 171 inset 1, 172, 173, 174, 175, 176, 179, 181, 182, 184, 188, 189, 191, 192, 193, 195, 196, 206, 208, 210, 213, 214, 215, 216-217, 218, 220, 224, 225, 226, 227, 228, 229, 232, 233, 236, 237, 242, 243, 245, 246, 248, 249, 250, 253, 254, 255, 256, 258, 259, 260, 262, 264, 266 inset 3, 267 inset 1, 267 inset 2, 268, 272, 273, 274, 276, 278, 285, 286-287, 288, 291, 292, 293, 298, 300, 301, 305, 308, 310, 311, 312, 313, 314, 315, 317, 321, 323, 325, 326-327, 328, 329, 330, 331, 333, 334, 335, 336, 337, 338, 339, 340 inset 1, 340 inset 2, 341 inset 1, 342, 344, 347, 350, 351, 352, 353, 354, 356, 359, 360, 361, 363, 364, 365, 366, 367, 368, 369, 371, 372, 374, 375, 377, 378, 379, 380, 382 inset 1, 382 inset 2, 383 inset 1, 384, 385, 386, 387, 390, 393, 394, 396, 397, 398, 400, 401, 404, 407, 408, 410, 411, 414, 417, 418-419, 420, 423, 424, 425, 426, 427, 429, 430, 432-433, 434, 436, 437, 439, 441, 442-443, 444-445 main, 444 inset 1, 444 inset 2, 445 inset 1, 445 inset 2, 446, 448, 449, 450-451, 452, 453, 454, 455, 456, 457, 458, 459, 460, 461, 462, 464, 465, 467, 468, 469, 470-471, 472, 473, 474, 475, 476, 477, 478, 479, 480, 482, 483, 484, 485, 486, 487, 490, 492, 494, 495, 498, 499, 500, 502, 506, 507, 509, 510, 511, 512, 514-515 main, 514 inset 2, 515 inset 1, 515 inset 2, 516, 518, 519, 520, 521, 522, 524, 526, 527,528, 530, 532, 533, 534, 535, 537, 538, 539

National Motor Museum 2 centre, 5 picture 3, 6 picture 1, 6 picture 4, 6 picture 5, 7 picture 1, 7 picture 2, 7 picture 4, 11, 13, 18, 21, 26, 28, 29, 39, 54, 55, 57, 66-67 main, 72, 73, 75, 96, 102, 103, 134-135 main, 110 inset 1, 111 inset 2, 116, 123, 128, 132-133, 135, 137, 139, 142, 143, 146, 147, 148, 169, 170-171 main, 170 inset 1, 170 inset 3, 171 inset 2, 180, 183, 185, 186, 194, 198, 200, 201, 202, 203, 204, 207, 209, 211, 221, 222, 234, 235, 238, 239, 241, 244, 251, 252, 261, 263, 265, 266-267 main, 266 inset 1, 269, 270, 271, 275, 277, 281, 282, 284, 289, 294, 296, 297, 299, 302, 303, 304, 307, 322, 324, 340-341 main, 345, 348, 355, 358, 370, 376, 382 inset 1, 382 inset 3, 383 inset 2, 388, 391, 395, 399, 403, 406, 412, 413, 415, 428, 431, 435, 438. 440, 444 inset 3, 447, 466, 481, 488, 489, 501, 503, 514 inset 1; /Nick Georgano 59, 105, 332; /Nicky Wright 16, 30, 51, 107, 117, 120, 127, 131, 145, 154, 158-159, 223, 240, 283, 290, 316, 318, 357, 517

PA Photos/Barratts/S&G Barratts/EMPICS Archive 6 picture 3, 136

Pagani Automobili 496

Rex Features/Elliot Gilbert/Vistalux 280

Trident Performance 536

Wikipedia/Arpingstone 166; /Jagvar 230